Criminal Law

LESLIE W. ABRAMSON
Frost Brown Todd Professor of Law Emeritus
Louis D. Brandeis School of Law at University of Louisville

Twenty-First Edition

WEST ACADEMIC

860 Blue Gentian Road, Suite 350
Eagan, MN 55121
1-877-888-1330

Published in the United States of America

ISBN: 979-8-31770-145-1

For Ren, Rhys, Charlie, and Amelia, with love—LWA

Summary of Contents

Capsule Summary

I. INTRODUCTION

A. IN GENERAL

1. Crime Defined

A crime is an act or omission prohibited by law for the protection of the public, the violation of which is prosecuted by the state and punishable by fine, incarceration, and/or other restriction of liberty.

2. Sources of Criminal Law

The definition of the basic crimes and defenses are from the English common law. Statutes now largely govern criminal matters, but the interpretation of statutes often refers to the common law cases.

B. CLASSIFICATIONS OF CRIMES

1. Felonies and Misdemeanors

Except for treason, crimes traditionally are classified as felonies or misdemeanors. At common law, felonies are those offenses punishable by forfeiture of property. Statutory felonies are generally those offenses punishable by ***death or incarceration in a prison for more than one year***. Misdemeanors are those offenses that are not classified as felonies.

2. Malum In Se and Malum Prohibitum

Malum in se crimes are ***inherently*** dangerous, bad, or immoral (*e.g.*, the common law felonies). Malum prohibitum offenses are prohibited out of ***necessity*** to regulate the general welfare (*e.g.*, prohibition against driving on the wrong side of the road).

C. BURDEN OF PROOF AND RELATED MATTERS

1. Proof Beyond a Reasonable Doubt

Due Process and the defendant's Sixth Amendment right to a jury trial require that the prosecution prove ***each element beyond a reasonable doubt*** before a jury. A court cannot withdraw an element from jury consideration and decide that element as a matter of law.

2. Defensive Matters

Due Process permits placing the burden to prove most defenses on the defendant.

3. Presumptions and Inferences Modifying Burden of Proof

Presumptions and permissive inferences may interfere with the prosecution's burden of proof and violate Due Process. Presumptions regarding elements of crime, such as intent, may improperly relieve the prosecution of its burden of proof.

a. Permissive Inferences

No violation of Due Process occurs if a trial judge instructs a jury that it may, but need not, infer one fact from another if the ultimate fact to be inferred more likely than not flows from the fact.

4. Homicide Prosecutions: Allocating Burdens Regarding Provocation

a. Burden of Proof on Provocation by Presuming Malice

If the jury in a murder prosecution is permitted to presume malice aforethought from the killing itself, thus requiring the defendant to prove a sudden provocation in order to reduce the crime to voluntary manslaughter, Due Process is violated. The presumption of malice relieves the prosecution of its burden of proving the mental state for murder.

b. Burden of Proof on Extreme Emotional Disturbance

When the prosecution must prove intent to kill, the defendant's Due Process rights are *not* violated by requiring him to prove that he acted under extreme emotional disturbance which would reduce the killing to manslaughter. If the prosecution must prove the mental state for murder, the defendant may be required to prove "defensive facts" such as provocation.

II. THE CRIMINALIZATION DECISION

A. JUSTIFICATIONS FOR PUNISHMENT

1. Specific Prevention

Punishment may prevent an offender from committing future crimes through *deterrence* (fear of penalty) or *incapacitation* (restraint) of the offender, and by affording her the opportunity for *treatment and possible rehabilitation*.

2. General Prevention

Penalizing offenders also may prevent others from committing crimes by *generally deterring* them through anticipation of similar punishment, by *educating* the public as to the *moral wrong* of crime, by *creating social solidarity*, and by *keeping others from taking the law into their own hands*.

3. Retribution

That the defendant committed a crime is *itself* reason to punish her.

B. COSTS VS. BENEFITS

The benefits from making conduct criminal depend on whether the social interests justifying criminalization will be furthered. But any benefits must be weighed against the direct costs of criminalization (*e.g.*, costs of law enforcement, imprisonment), the incidental costs (*e.g.*, improper searches and seizures), and the effect on society.

III. BASIC LEGAL LIMITS UPON CRIMINAL LAW

A. CONSTITUTIONAL RIGHT OF PRIVACY

Although the Constitution does not expressly mention a right of privacy, such a right is implied in several constitutional provisions. A person thus cannot be convicted for engaging in conduct falling within the scope of this federal right (*e.g.*, the use of contraceptives, the private possession of obscenity, and private and consensual homosexual activity).

B. DUE PROCESS PROHIBITION AGAINST VAGUENESS

1. General Rule: Criminal Statute Must Be Precise

The Due Process Clauses of the Fifth and Fourteenth Amendments require that criminal statutes must give *notice* about what conduct is criminal in order to *discourage arbitrary enforcement*.

2. Criteria for Evaluating Vagueness

A criminal statute is unconstitutionally vague if it fails to define the offense with sufficient definiteness so that ordinary people can understand what is prohibited, in order to discourage arbitrary and discriminatory enforcement of the statute.

3. Curing Vagueness by "Scienter"

A statute that is otherwise unconstitutionally vague may be upheld if it requires that the offense be committed with "scienter," that is, prior knowledge or intent.

C. CRUEL AND UNUSUAL PUNISHMENT

The Eighth Amendment prohibition against cruel and unusual punishment is binding on the states via the Fourteenth Amendment and imposes several limits on criminal law.

1. Inherently Impermissible Punishments

Inherently barbaric or degrading punishment is prohibited. Torture, death by painful or lingering methods, and forfeiture of citizenship are probably also prohibited.

2. Disproportionate Penalties

Penalties that are so *grossly and outrageously disproportionate* to the defendant's conduct are also prohibited.

3. Death Penalty

The death penalty is constitutionally permissible if it is imposed under a procedure that adequately assures evenhanded determinations about whether the penalty is appropriate in a particular case. The death penalty is unconstitutionally disproportionate for the rape of an adult woman, or the rape of a child (at least when the defendant did not intend to kill the victim). Murderers who are younger than 18 or mentally impaired generally cannot be executed.

D. MULTIPLE LIABILITY FOR IDENTICAL OR RELATED CRIMINAL ACTS

1. In General: Overlapping Criminal Liability

Overlapping liability may be appropriate when the *same act constitutes several crimes* (*e.g.*, murder and battery) and when acts constituting *different offenses are committed closely together* and for *related reasons* (*e.g.*, burglary as a means to commit a larceny). Such overlapping criminal liability is sometimes criticized as resulting in a disproportionately severe punishment.

2. Common Law Doctrine of Merger

At common law, if the same act was both a felony and a misdemeanor, the misdemeanor merged into the felony and *no conviction* for the misdemeanor could occur. The merger doctrine did *not* apply if the crimes were both misdemeanors or felonies. Today, there is no *common law* merger in the United States.

3. Unit of Prosecution Analysis

a. Legislative Intent

The unit of prosecution for a crime is the legislative standard to determine whether one or more commissions of the crime arise from a single course of conduct.

b. "Single Larceny" Rule

The taking of multiple items at or about the same time constitutes only one larceny.

c. **Assaultive Crimes: One Crime Per Victim**

Homicide and assault crimes generally permit one prosecution for each victim killed or injured.

4. **Fifth Amendment Prohibition Against Double Jeopardy**

The constitutional prohibition against double jeopardy primarily applies to repeated prosecutions for the same or perhaps related crimes, but also imposes some limit on conviction for several crimes in one prosecution.

a. **No Bar to Legislatively-Intended Multiple Convictions in One Proceeding**

If a legislature defines the same conduct as two crimes, a defendant *may* be convicted in *one proceeding* of both offenses as long as this was the *legislative intent*.

b. **Determining Legislative Intent: *Blockburger* Rule**

A legislature presumably intended to prohibit punishing a defendant for two crimes arising from the same conduct, unless *each crime* requires proof of an *additional fact* that the other crime does not.

(1) **Caveat**

The *Blockburger* rule is a means of determining legislative intent. If there is *direct* evidence that Congress did intend double punishment, *Blockburger* does not apply.

5. **State Double Jeopardy Prohibitions**

Many state constitutions contain prohibitions against double jeopardy that are comparable to federal constitutional double jeopardy provisions. State courts may construe these provisions more stringently, thus giving defendants broader protection than the federal provision. For example, state double jeopardy provisions may bar punishment for related crimes unless those crimes are designed to protect different social interests.

6. **Statutory Bars to Multiple Conviction or Punishment**

State statutes sometimes prohibit multiple convictions for a *single act*. Some courts have interpreted "single act" to include several crimes related in their commission and committed pursuant to a *single and primary objective*.

7. **Modern Merger of Offenses as Matter of Legislative Intent**

Courts sometimes hold that a defendant cannot be convicted of related crimes because one offense "merges" into another. However, this is *not* the application of the *common law* merger rule but rather a determination of legislative intent barring convictions for both crimes. Courts often apply the *Blockburger rule* (*supra*) as a guide to such intent.

IV. ELEMENTS OF CRIMES

A. IDENTIFYING, DISTINGUISHING, AND CATEGORIZING ELEMENTS OF CRIMES

All elements of a crime must be identified and distinguished. There are four categories of criminal elements:

(i) ***conduct, act, or omission*** (*e.g.,* burglary requires an act amounting to "entry"),

(ii) ***a result*** (*e.g.,* a homicide requires proof that the victim died as a result of the defendant's conduct),

(iii) ***circumstances*** (*e.g.,* burglary sometimes requires that the place entered be the dwelling of another), and

(iv) ***mens rea**, or **culpable mental state**.*

B. CRIMINAL ACTS: ACTUS REUS

An *affirmative act*, or occasionally an omission or *failure to act*, is necessary for the commission of a crime. Mere thoughts are not enough.

1. Constitutional Limitation

A *status* (*e.g.*, being an alcoholic) cannot be a criminal offense. However, there is no constitutional bar to making acts *related to a status* criminal (*e.g.*, public drunkenness).

2. "Acts" Sufficient for Criminal Liability: Affirmative vs. Negative "Acts"

Acts that support a conviction vary with the crime itself; an act may be an affirmative act or a failure to act. Some crimes specifically describe which acts are required. Other crimes (*e.g.*, homicide) do not specify the requisite acts, so that any act or omission that meets the general concepts of a criminal act is sufficient.

a. Affirmative Acts (Acts of Commission)

An affirmative act suffices for criminal liability that constitutes some *conscious* and *volitional movement*.

(1) Exceptions

Although criminal liability is not ordinarily based on unconscious movements, a defendant may be liable if she *causes her own unconsciousness* or *was aware of her pending unconsciousness*.

b. Negative Acts (Acts of Omission)

A defendant's failure to act may support criminal liability *if*:

(i) She had a *legal duty to act*,

(ii) She had the requisite *knowledge*, and

(iii) It was *possible* for her to act.

(1) Situations Giving Rise to Legal Duties

A legal duty to act may arise from: (i) a relationship between the parties (*e.g.*, parent-child); (ii) a particular statute; (iii) a contract; (iv) the voluntary undertaking of a task; or (v) creation of a situation of peril. Also, a defendant who has a duty to control the conduct of others (*e.g.*, as an employer) may have an obligation to act. Note that a *moral* obligation is *not* enough.

(2) Knowledge Required for Liability

In omission cases, a majority of courts hold that a defendant must *know about the facts* giving rise to a legal duty to act. Some jurisdictions require in addition that a defendant know about *the law* that creates that duty. In some circumstances, knowledge of this sort may be required by Due Process.

(3) Act Must Be Capable of Performance

For criminal liability to attach, it must have been *possible* for the defendant to have committed the act. There is no liability where the omission was because she lacked the means or ability to perform.

C. ATTENDANT CIRCUMSTANCES

In addition to the requisite elements, many crimes require proof that certain circumstances existed at the time of the act in question. Without a showing of these circumstances, the defendant's actions are not criminal.

D. CRIMINAL STATE OF MIND: MENS REA

1. General Requirement of Mens Rea

Crimes generally require "mens rea" or a *culpable mental state*. Unlike other kinds of legal liability, criminal law considers (and even emphasizes) what the defendant was actually thinking when she committed the crime. Thus, criminal liability is generally subjective in nature. "Mens rea" is distinguishable from motive, which refers to the *reason* for acting and *generally is not essential* for criminal liability. Thus, proof of a good motive does not prevent a conviction.

a. Modern Analysis Focusing on Elements

Modern analysis requires consideration of any required knowledge concerning each element of a crime.

b. Object and Quality Dimensions

Modern analysis requires separate consideration of what objects the culpable mental state must involve and then what quality or level of knowledge must be proved.

2. Constitutional Considerations

The Supreme Court has never clarified what, if any, culpable mental states are required for crimes as a matter of federal constitutional law. Some of the Court's decisions suggest that Due Process of law might require some minimal knowledge by the accused.

3. Mens Rea Analysis and Terminology

Traditional *mens rea* analysis often used a number of specialized terms—"general intent," "specific intent," "scienter," "malice," "willfulness," etc.—that were sometimes not carefully defined. These terms often have little use under modern statutory analysis.

a. "General" vs. "Specific" Intent

Traditional criminal law analysis sometimes distinguished "general intent" from "specific intent." The distinction was significant because traditionally, the application of certain defenses hinged on whether the crime was a "general" or "specific" intent crime (*e.g.,* voluntary intoxication was sometimes held available as a defense only to specific intent crimes).

(1) Focus on Conduct or Actus Reus

General intent, some courts explain, did not require specific proof but can be inferred from the fact that the defendant engaged in the conduct constituting the crime. On the other hand, *specific intent*, courts sometimes say, cannot be inferred from the defendant's commission of the *actus reus* of the crime and thus was more difficult to prove.

(2) Focus on Elements of the Crime

Courts often use the term *general intent* to refer to the culpable mental state(s) required to prove *the nonmental elements of a crime*—the conduct, any result, and any circumstances required. Courts defining general intent often use the term *specific intent* to refer to any culpable mental state that *concerns something that itself is not the conduct, result, or circumstance* that must be proved.

b. Criminal Negligence

Liability for certain crimes (*e.g.*, involuntary manslaughter, battery) may be based on a showing of criminal negligence. In such cases, the defendant acted with *gross lack of care*. But note that the negligence must involve a *higher probability of harm* and a *greater degree of unreasonableness* than is necessary for civil liability purposes.

c. **Malice**

Some crimes require malice, which is usually construed as requiring the commission of a voluntary act *without legal excuse or justification*. Ill will or hatred need *not* be shown.

(1) **But Note**

Malice may be given a different meaning in relation to certain crimes (*e.g.*, malice aforethought for murder).

d. **"Willfully," "Deliberately," "Feloniously"**

These terms, as used in criminal statutes, are often equated with general intent (*supra*).

e. **Knowledge of Law Sometimes Required**

Some crimes require that the defendant knows the law and that his conduct violated it (*e.g.*, federal tax crimes).

f. **Proof of Intent: Federal Constitutional Requirements**

When a crime requires proof of intent, the prosecution must prove that intent beyond a reasonable doubt. A presumption relieving the prosecution of this burden violates the defendant's right to Due Process.

4. **Strict Liability Crimes**

A few crimes entirely dispense with a *mens rea* requirement for some or all of the elements.

a. **Interpreting Federal Crimes**

The Supreme Court construes federal statutory crimes that contain no explicit culpable mental state requirement as demanding proof of only that culpable mental state necessary to separate wrongful conduct from "otherwise innocent conduct."

b. **Identifying Strict Liability Crimes**

Whether a crime imposes strict liability is a matter of *legislative intent*. That intent will most likely be found if (i) the crime is a *"new" statutory offense*; (ii) the crime does *not infringe* on another person's rights; (iii) the crime is part of a *regulatory scheme*; (iv) the crime imposes a relatively *light penalty*; and (v) it appears that requiring proof of *mens rea* would *impede implementation* of the legislative purpose.

c. **Application**

Based on the above guidelines, *public welfare offenses* are likely to be strict liability crimes. However, despite those guidelines, *bigamy* and *statutory rape* are common law crimes that have been traditionally regarded as serious strict liability crimes.

d. **Constitutional Limitations**

Due Process prohibits strict liability in some situations, particularly if a serious penalty is involved and the crime resembles a traditional common law offense for which *mens rea* has usually been required.

5. **Modern Classifications of State of Mind**

The modern trend is for statutes to adopt the Model Penal Code approach, which distinguishes four levels of culpable mental state.

a. **Different States of Mind**

(1) **"Purpose"**

A *desire* to engage in certain conduct or cause a certain result.

(2) **"Knowledge"**

An *awareness* that something will occur or does exist.

(3) **"Recklessness"**

An *awareness* of a *substantial and unjustifiable risk* that something will occur or does exist, but the defendant consciously disregards that risk.

(4) **"Negligence"**

A situation in which a person *should have been aware* of a substantial and unjustifiable risk that a certain result would occur or that a certain circumstance would exist, but the defendant fails to perceive that risk.

(a) **Distinguish: Recklessness**

Recklessness requires a *conscious awareness* of the risk involved and a conscious disregard of it. Negligence involves circumstances in which a *reasonable person would have been aware* of the risk and this defendant failed to perceive it.

b. **General Requirement: At Least Recklessness**

Under the Model Penal Code and many modern statutes, unless specifically provided otherwise, a showing of at least recklessness is required as to *all elements* of the offense.

6. **Interpreting Culpable Mental State Under Modern Statutory Crimes**

Modern statutory crimes sometimes pose difficult questions of interpretation regarding those nonmental elements of the crime to which the required culpable mental state applies. *Example:* A federal statute provides that "[a] person commits an offense if the person knowingly uses, without lawful authority, a means of identification of another person." The question becomes whether the courts will apply the explicitly required culpable mental state—"knowingly"—to only the conduct element following that term knowingly (*i.e.,* "uses [something]") or whether they will apply knowingly to some or all of the remaining nonmental elements.

a. **Relationship to Strict Liability Analysis**

If the culpable mental state required for an offense does not apply to all material nonmental elements of the crime, the crime imposes "limited" or "partial" strict liability. Factors suggesting strict liability, therefore, weigh in favor of construing such a culpable mental state as not applying to one or more nonmental elements of the offense.

b. **Elemental Approach**

The Model Penal Code assumes that the policies of criminal law suggest a required culpable mental state should ordinarily apply to all material nonmental elements of a crime. Thus, the required culpable mental state will apply to all those elements unless a contrary legislative intent "plainly appears."

c. **Ordinary English Usage Approach**

The United States Supreme Court has relied on what it described as ordinary English grammar and general usage. When a federal statutory crime contains a required culpable mental state (as when it specifies that the crime must be committed "knowingly"), that culpable mental state often and perhaps generally applies to all the subsequently listed elements of the crime. Several Justices, however, have cautioned against applying this approach if the context or policy considerations suggest that Congress intended a less demanding culpable mental state.

d. Elements Separating Wrongful from Innocent Conduct

Some courts, including the Supreme Court, have indicated that a crime is often construed as requiring a culpable mental state regarding only those elements that distinguish criminal conduct from conduct that is not criminal at all.

e. Penalty Elements

Courts are often unwilling to require a culpable mental state for an element of a crime that determines either the grade of the offense or the penalty imposable on conviction.

7. "Transferred Intent": Responsibility for Unintended Results

Ordinarily, for criminal liability to attach, a defendant must have *intended the actual harm done*. However, if the defendant intends to harm one person or item of property and does *very similar harm* to another person or item, he is treated as if he had, in fact, intended the result that occurred (*i.e.,* the intent is transferred) and criminal liability will attach.

E. CONCURRENCE OF ACTUS REUS AND MENS REA

The defendant's act and intent must concur; *i.e.*, the act or result must be *attributable* to the culpable state of mind.

1. Concurrence Between Mens Rea and Act

Generally, the defendant must have had the requisite intent *at the moment he performed* the act.

2. Concurrence Between Mens Rea and Result

If proof of a result is required, the occurrence of the result must be *attributable* to the *mens rea*. However, it is *not* essential that the intent and result concur in point of time.

3. Special Problem: Mistake of Death Cases

Special problems arise where the defendant mistakenly believes he has caused death and then, without intent to kill, takes other action which actually does cause death. Jurisdictions are split, with some refusing to find liability because there is no intent, and others finding liability because the defendant's behavior was all part of a single scheme.

F. CAUSATION

If a crime requires proof of a result, the defendant's conduct must have been the *legal cause* of that result. Two kinds of causation must exist: factual and proximate.

1. "Direct" and Intervening Event Causation

Causation may involve intervening factors between the defendant's act and the occurrence of the result. If no such intervening factors are involved, the causation can be said to be "direct."

2. Factual Causation: "But For" Test

The prosecution must show that *"but for"* the defendant's actions, the result would not have occurred *when and as it did*.

a. Substantial Factor Requirement

Some courts require, in addition, that the defendant's actions were a substantial factor in bringing about the result.

b. Speeding up Result

Where the defendant simply speeded up an *inevitable result*, most courts find factual causation.

c. Exception: Concurrent Sufficient Cause

An exception to the general "but for" requirement applies when two factors acting concurrently cause a result, and either alone would have been sufficient to cause that result. *Both* factors will be considered as factual causes.

3. Proximate Causation

In addition to factual causation, there must be proof that the defendant's action is the proximate cause of a result. Generally, proximate cause is present when the result occurs as a *natural and probable consequence* of the defendant's act *and* there is *no intervening factor* sufficient to break the chain of causation (*i.e.*, a superseding factor). To constitute a superseding factor, an intervening factor must meet four requirements.

a. Intervening Factor

An intervening factor can be superseding only if it is "intervening," that is, one set in motion *after* the defendant's act. Therefore, a preexisting condition will not break the chain of causation.

b. Unforeseeable

The intervening factor must have been *unforeseeable* by the defendant at the time of the act.

c. Sole Direct Cause

The intervening factor must be the *sole major cause* of the result.

d. Independent

The intervening factor must be *independent of the defendant's original act.*

V. SCOPE OF CRIMINAL LIABILITY

A. COMPLICITY IN THE CRIME

1. "Parties" to the Crime

Liability for a crime is not limited to the actual perpetrator of the criminal act, but it generally extends to anyone who has *encouraged* (incited) *or assisted* (abetted) the commission of the crime or, at common law, *hindered apprehension* of the perpetrator.

2. Common Law Classification of Participants: "Party" Rules

a. Parties to Felonies

Parties are classified according to their role in the perpetration of the crime and whether they were present at its commission.

(1) Principal in the First Degree

This person *actually perpetrates* the crime by his own acts, by the acts of an innocent person, or by means of an inanimate agency.

(2) **Principal in the Second Degree**

This person *incites or abets* the commission of a crime and is *actually or constructively present* at its commission (*e.g.*, a lookout).

(3) **Accessory Before the Fact**

This person *incites or abets* the principal, but is *not actually or constructively present* at the commission of the crime.

(4) **Accessory After the Fact**

This person receives or assists another, *knowing* that the other person has committed a felony, in order to *hinder* the arrest, prosecution, or conviction of the perpetrator. At common law, a *wife* could *not* be an accessory after the fact.

b. **Significance of Party Rules**

At common law, a person charged as an accessory could *not* be convicted as a principal, and *vice versa*. An accessory also could *not* be convicted *unless the principal was convicted*, nor could an accessory be convicted of a *higher offense* than the principal.

c. **Misdemeanors and Treason**

No distinction was made among parties to these offenses; *all parties* were liable as *principals*. *Note:* There was *no liability* for aiding a person after the commission of a *misdemeanor*.

3. **Classification of Participants Under Modern Statutes**

Modern statutes tend to abandon the categories of participants and simply make *all who aid and abet* the commission of a crime *guilty of that crime*.

a. **Inciters and Abettors**

Many statutes make inciters and abettors principals, and the Model Penal Code provides that a person is guilty as an *accomplice even if* she commits it herself *or* if she is *legally accountable* for the conduct of the accused.

b. **Accessory After the Fact**

One who would be an accessory after the fact at common law is generally now punished for the commission of a *separate and distinct offense*; no liability is incurred for the crime of the principal.

c. **Effect of Modern Changes**

Procedural limitations accompanying the common law party rules no longer exist under most statutory schemes. The procedural aspects of the law of complicity thus have been substantially simplified.

(1) **Conviction of Principal Not Necessary**

An aider and abettor can be convicted even if the principal has not been convicted and even if the principal has been tried and acquitted.

4. **Accomplice Liability**

Accomplice liability attaches to those who aid or encourage the commission of a crime.

a. **Requirements for Accomplice Liability**

The defendant must have incited or abetted the perpetration of the crime *with the requisite mens rea*, and the person incited or abetted must *actually have committed the offense*.

(1) **"Abetting"**

One abets commission of a crime if he provides assistance in *any significant way*.

(2) **"Inciting"**

One incites commission of a crime if he *encourages* (*i.e.*, provides any inducement to) another to commit it. But the *perpetrator must be aware* of the encouragement.

(3) **Mens Rea Requirement**

Authorities agree that an accomplice *must have the mens rea required for the crime*. However, courts are *divided* as to whether an accomplice must *intend* that his efforts effectively assist or encourage the successful commission of the crime *or* whether awareness that the offense will be committed by the person aided or encouraged will suffice. (The modern trend is to require that the accomplice act with *purpose*.)

(4) **Perpetrator Must Have Committed Crime**

The person encouraged or aided must have committed the offense (although unlike at common law conviction of the perpetrator is *not necessary*). Jurisdictions are *split* on whether an accomplice can assert the *perpetrator's defenses*.

b. **Scope of Liability**

The scope of accomplice liability is a controversial subject. The *traditional rule* holds accomplices liable for *all probable consequences* of their conduct, *i.e.*, all crimes incited or abetted *and* all crimes committed by the perpetrator that were *reasonably foreseeable results* of the contemplated crime. A *minority view* limits accomplice liability only to those crimes of the perpetrator that the accomplice actually *anticipated and intended.*

c. **Possible Defenses to Accomplice Liability**

(1) **Withdrawal**

One who incites or abets another can avoid accomplice liability by *effective and timely* withdrawal before the crime is committed. If the defendant is an *inciter*, he must *communicate a renunciation* to the perpetrator; however, if the defendant is an *abettor*, he must also deprive his aid of its *effectiveness* (*e.g.*, where accomplice lent his gun to the perpetrator, he must retrieve the gun).

d. **Situations Where Accomplice Liability Inapplicable**

If the participant is (i) within a special *class of persons intended to be protected* by the statute (*e.g.*, a prostitute in a Mann Act prosecution), (ii) a *victim* of an offense, or (iii) a person *inherently necessary* to commission of the crime (*e.g.*, buyer of cocaine), she is not liable as an accomplice.

(1) **Distinguish: Accomplice Unable to Commit Crime as Perpetrator**

The fact that an accomplice cannot commit a crime by his own actions does not preclude liability as an accomplice to that crime. Thus, a husband can incur liability as an accomplice to the traditional rape of his wife.

5. **Liability of Post-Crime Aiders (Accessories After the Fact)**

At common law, a defendant is liable as an accessory after the fact if she *knew* the person she assisted committed a *felony*, and aid was given for the purpose of *impeding enforcement* of the law. However, *modern statutes* either retain the category of accessory after the fact but make it a *separate offense* with a penalty unrelated to the perpetrator's penalty, or else establish an entirely *new offense* (*e.g.*, hindering prosecution).

B. VICARIOUS LIABILITY

1. Definition: Liability for Acts of Others

Vicarious liability exists when one person is held guilty of a crime committed by another simply *because of the relationship* between the two persons. No affirmative participation is required.

2. When Vicarious Liability Is Imposed: Legislative Intent

In practice, vicarious liability is usually limited to *employer-employee* relationships. However, in all cases, legislative intent determines whether to apply vicarious liability. Absent an expressed legislative intent, courts look for the existence of certain circumstances in the governing law (*e.g.*, a business activity, light penalties, no personal fault requirement).

a. Disregard of Instructions

There is a split of authority regarding the imposition of vicarious liability when a crime was committed in *disregard of the defendant's (usually employer's) instructions.* Some courts *compromise* by allowing the defendant to *prove lack of fault.*

3. Constitutional Limits on Vicarious Liability

Vicarious liability may violate either Fourteenth Amendment Due Process or the Eighth Amendment prohibition against cruel and unusual punishment if the defendant had *no ability to control* the actual perpetrator or if conviction would impose a *severe penalty* on the defendant.

C. CRIMINAL LIABILITY OF CORPORATIONS AND ASSOCIATIONS

1. Background

At *common law*, corporations and associations could *not* be convicted of a criminal offense. The *modern rule* is to impose *corporate liability*, although certain *policy considerations* continue to cause controversy.

2. Requirements for Corporate Liability

Liability is often imposed on corporations for the acts and omissions of corporate employees if consistent with the *legislative intent* and dependent on the *nature of the crime* involved (*i.e.*, severity of the crime). If the crime is *minor*, a corporation is usually held liable merely upon proof that the employee was acting in the *course of his employment*. If the crime is *serious*, some courts require only that the offense was committed by an *employee in the course of the employment*. Others adopt the Model Penal Code approach, which permits conviction only if the perpetration of the offense was *authorized*, *performed*, or at least *recklessly tolerated* by the board of directors or a high managerial agent. Other jurisdictions require proof that the corporation gave the actual perpetrator *enough authority to engage* in the specific activities related to the criminal conduct.

3. No Effect on Individual Liability

The presence or absence of corporate liability has *no* effect on the actual perpetrator's criminal responsibility.

4. Liability of Unincorporated Associations

Generally, partnerships and other unincorporated associations cannot be convicted of crimes of individual partners or employees. However, some jurisdictions recognize the *entity theory* of partnership under which partnerships can sue and be sued in their own name. This may lead to criminal prosecutions of such associations in the future.

VI. DEFENSES

A. GENERAL CONSIDERATIONS

1. "True" Defenses

A "true" defense differs from a defendant's ability to challenge the prosecution's proof of one or more elements of the offense, particularly the culpable mental state element.

2. Burden of Proof

The true defenses on which the defendant has the burden of proof are often called "affirmative" defenses.

B. INFANCY

1. Common Law

At common law, a child *under age seven* is *conclusively* presumed incapable of forming criminal intent and thus cannot be guilty of a crime. Between the *ages of seven and fourteen* a child is *rebuttably* presumed incapable of forming criminal intent. Children aged *fourteen and older* are treated as adults.

2. Modern Statutes

Under both common law and modern statutes, the defendant's *chronological age at the time of the crime controls*. However, modern statutes vary in their treatment of the infancy defense and may depart from the common law rules.

3. Juvenile Court Jurisdiction

All American jurisdictions have juvenile court legislation under which children are "adjudicated delinquent" (rather than "convicted") in a juvenile court proceeding. Under some statutes, however, children may under certain circumstances be tried as adults.

C. INSANITY

1. In General

A defendant is entitled to acquittal if he was *so impaired by mental illness or retardation at the time of the crime* as to be "insane" within the meaning of the law.

a. Distinguish: Incompetency to Stand Trial

Incompetency to stand trial concerns the defendant's state of mind *at the time of the trial* and is *not* a defense to the criminal charge; incompetency to stand trial may, however, postpone the proceedings.

b. Distinguish: Diminished Capacity

The diminished capacity rule allows proof of the defendant's mental illness or retardation to show that the defendant *lacked the required mens rea* for the crime.

2. Condition Giving Rise to Insanity

Although all insanity tests require the defendant to have some sort of mental impairment, not all impairments give rise to insanity.

a. **Mental Illness or "Disease"**

A traditional mental illness (*e.g.*, psychosis) can support an insanity defense.

(1) **"Psychopathic Personality"**

Some courts hold that the insanity defense does not extend to "psychopaths," *i.e.*, persons whose abnormality is manifested only by repeated criminal or other antisocial conduct.

b. **Developmental Disability**

Developmental disability, formerly called mental retardation, if it satisfies the applicable test, may render a defendant legally insane.

3. **Tests for Insanity**

The basic issue giving rise to different approaches to an insanity defense is whether the defense should be limited to cognitive impairments or should also include impairments of control.

a. ***M'Naghten* Rule: The Traditional Approach**

Under this test, a defendant may be acquitted if at the time of the crime and as a result of his mental impairment, he did *not know* (i) *the nature and quality of his act*, *or* (ii) that his *act was wrong*. Under a modified approach to the test, acquittal is required only if the defendant did not know his act was wrong.

(1) **"Nature and Quality of Act"**

Most courts hold that the defendant does not know the nature and quality of his act only if he does not understand its *physical* nature and consequences.

(2) **"Wrong"**

Most courts define "wrong" as meaning *legally* wrong; it is no defense that a defendant believed that his actions were morally right. Some courts permit the defense, however, if the defendant believed he received a direct command from God to commit the crime ("deific decree" rule).

(3) **Criticism of Test**

Because the *inability to control conduct is irrelevant* under the *M'Naghten* test, the test has been widely criticized as too narrow.

b. **Loss of Control Tests**

(1) **Irresistible Impulse Test**

A defendant is entitled to acquittal if his commission of the crime was caused by an "insane impulse" that *overcame his will.*

(2) **Model Penal Code Test**

Until the early 1980s, this test was widely adopted to permit acquittal where, because of a mental impairment, the defendant lacked *substantial capacity* to *conform his conduct* to the requirements of the law.

(3) **Criticism of Tests**

It is difficult to determine whether an impaired defendant could avoid his criminal acts; furthermore, the necessary expert testimony leads to jury confusion.

c. **Broader Tests**

(1) ***Durham* (or "Product") Rule**

Under this test, a defendant is entitled to acquittal if with proof that the crime was the *product of a mental impairment*. Only New Hampshire appears to follow this test, which is criticized for providing juries with insufficient guidance.

(2) **"Sense of Justice" Test**

Because of the difficulty or the impossibility of applying a precise formula, it is suggested that a defendant should be acquitted if at the time of the crime he was so impaired that he cannot be held responsible.

d. **"Mens Rea" Approach**

Several states have abolished the insanity defense and have substituted specific authorization for proof of mental impairment that indicates a lack of the requisite *mens rea*.

4. **Proposal to Abolish the Insanity Defense**

Some arguments for abolition or limitation of the insanity defense are: the difficulty of the courts in making determinations, the time involved with this defense, jury confusion, a bias in favor of wealthier defendants, and inadequate treatment programs. Arguments favoring the retention and broadening of the defense are: certain impaired persons are not ethically blameworthy, individual responsibility is reinforced, and the process could divert proper persons into the mental health system.

5. **Burden of Proof on Insanity**

Before the Hinckley acquittal in the early 1980s, most jurisdictions provided that after the defendant raised the defense, the prosecution had the burden of proving beyond a reasonable doubt that the defendant was sane. However, the post-Hinckley *trend* is to place *on the defendant* the burden of proving insanity.

6. **Jury Instructions on the Consequences of an Insanity Acquittal**

Most jurisdictions do not instruct the jury on the consequences of an insanity acquittal, although others consider such instructions to be necessary or at least permissible.

7. **Procedure Following Acquittal by Reason of Insanity**

All jurisdictions have commitment procedures for the possible hospitalization of defendants found not guilty by reason of insanity ("NGRI"). Typically, the defendant is automatically committed; then a prompt hearing is held to afford the defendant an opportunity to show that she is no longer dangerous. This procedure is constitutionally adequate, and there is *no* constitutional right to release from hospitalization on expiration of the maximum prison term the defendant could have received if convicted.

8. **Guilty but Mentally Ill**

Several states allow a verdict of guilty but mentally ill as an alternative to an insanity acquittal if the jury finds that when the defendant committed the offense, she was mentally ill but not legally insane. The defendant is sentenced under the regular sentencing provisions. If imprisonment is imposed, defendant must undergo treatment.

D. DIMINISHED CAPACITY

In some jurisdictions, evidence of mental illness that does not establish insanity may be introduced to prove that the defendant *did not have or could not have formed the requisite mens rea* for the crime charged. This is known as the *Wells-Gorshen or diminished capacity rule.*

1. Majority Approach: Diminished Capacity Rejected

A majority of courts *reject* the rule, reasoning that the insanity defense is the vehicle for relating mental illness to criminal liability and that it should not be circumvented by manipulation of the *mens rea* requirement.

2. Application: Limited to Specific Intent Crimes

Even where recognized, the rule is applied only to specific intent crimes.

3. Distinguish: English "Diminished Responsibility" Rule

Under the English diminished responsibility rule, a defendant charged with murder will be convicted only of manslaughter if mental illness "substantially impaired his mental responsibility" for the killing.

E. INTOXICATION

Involuntary intoxication may be a complete defense, but voluntary intoxication is not, although it sometimes negates *mens rea*. In addition to the ingestion of liquor, the rules apply to the effect of other intoxicating substances (*e.g.*, drugs and medicine).

1. Involuntary Intoxication

Involuntary intoxication is a complete defense only if it rendered the defendant insane within the meaning of the jurisdiction's insanity test.

a. "Involuntary" Defined

"Involuntary" means that the defendant either *did not know* the substance ingested was intoxicating or consumed it under *direct and immediate duress* even though she knew it was intoxicating.

b. Pathological Intoxication

The Model Penal Code regards intoxication as involuntary if the intoxication is grossly excessive in proportion to the amount of the substance consumed and the defendant did not know of her unusual susceptibility.

c. Permanent Insanity

A permanent (or "settled") impairment (*e.g.*, organic brain damage) caused by the defendant's long-term and voluntary use of intoxicants can, under the majority view, support an insanity defense.

2. Voluntary Intoxication

The general rule is that voluntary intoxication is a defense only if it shows that the defendant lacked a *specific intent* required for the crime charged.

a. Minority Views

A few jurisdictions *entirely disregard* evidence of voluntary intoxication even if the proof demonstrates lack of specific intent; conversely, a few states permit evidence of voluntary intoxication to be used to *negate any required mental state*, not just specific intent.

b. Application: Convincing Trier of Fact That Intoxication Negated Mens Rea

If a jurisdiction's rule permits evidence of voluntary intoxication to negate the culpable mental state, the defendant must show, at a minimum, that her intoxication raises a reasonable doubt that the prosecution has proved the required *mens rea*.

3. Distinguish: Crimes Requiring Proof of Intoxication

Where intoxication is an element of the crime charged (*e.g.*, public drunkenness), courts have not applied the above rules. Arguably, however, involuntary intoxication should be a defense.

F. IGNORANCE OR MISTAKE OF FACT

1. In General

Ignorance or mistake of *fact* will prevent criminal liability if it shows the defendant *lacked a mental state* essential to the crime charged.

a. Distinction Between "Fact" and "Law"

The Model Penal Code and some states do not distinguish between mistakes of fact and law, simply requiring acquittal if a mistake negates the requisite *mens rea.*

2. Burden of Proof

Because the prosecution has the burden of proving the defendant acted with the required culpable mental state and mistake of fact is part of this, the burden of proof cannot constitutionally be placed on the defendant.

3. Requirement of "Reasonableness"

Traditionally, the mistake must be *reasonable*, but many courts depart from this rule where the mistake is offered to disprove *specific intent.*

a. Constitutional Issues

The requirement of reasonableness may violate the defendant's *Due Process* right to have the prosecution prove all elements of the crime and also her *Sixth Amendment right* to have a jury determination of guilt or innocence.

4. Prosecutions for Strict Liability Offenses

Ignorance or mistake of fact is ordinarily *no defense* to a *strict liability crime*. However, some courts have implied an intent requirement where the defendant offers evidence of a reasonable mistake. Furthermore, other courts unwilling to find a *mens rea* requirement have still sustained a *defense of reasonable mistake*.

G. IGNORANCE OR MISTAKE OF LAW

Ignorance or mistake of *law* arises in two situations: (i) where the defendant *lacked the requisite mental state*, or (ii) where the defendant had the requisite mental state but *believed that his conduct was not prohibited* by law.

1. Ignorance or Mistake Showing Lack of Mens Rea

When a crime requires a particular belief concerning a legal matter, the defendant's mistake about that matter may show she lacked the requisite mental state. If this is the case, the defendant may rely on the mistake to negate the *mens rea* element of the crime.

a. Reasonableness Not Required

The ignorance or mistake need not be reasonable because such a requirement would raise serious doubts regarding the defendant's Sixth Amendment right to have a jury determine guilt or innocence.

2. Mistaken Belief That Criminal Law Does Not Prohibit Intended Conduct

Generally, it is *no defense* that the defendant was passively unaware her acts were prohibited by the criminal law or that she affirmatively but mistakenly believed the acts were not prohibited. However, in limited situations, the defendant may base a defense on an *affirmative decision*, after consideration of the matter, that the law did not make the conduct a crime.

a. **Constitutional Considerations**

Some courts reason that under certain limited circumstances, convictions based on mistaken beliefs that conduct is not criminal violates Due Process.

b. **Requirements for Defense**

Two requirements limit this defense: (i) the defendant's belief that her conduct is not prohibited by law *is objectively reasonable*, and (ii) the defendant formed her belief *based on certain grounds* that provide assurance that a mistake was made (*see* below).

(1) **Reliance on Statute or Case Later Held Unconstitutional**

If the defendant acted in good faith reliance on a statute making her conduct permissible, she can assert a defense even though the statute is later held invalid. A similar reliance on a reasonable *judicial decision* precludes a conviction.

(2) **Reliance on Official Interpretations**

In some jurisdictions, a defense is also established by reasonable reliance upon an interpretation of the law *by an official* with responsibility for interpreting that law. However, reliance upon *advice of private counsel* will *never* support a mistake of law defense.

H. NECESSITY OR JUSTIFICATION

Necessity is a defense when the defendant *reasonably believed* his actions were necessary to avoid a *greater harm* than would be caused by commission of the crime. A necessity defense can arise only from situations created by *physical force of nature*. (If caused by others, the defense of "duress" might apply, but "necessity" would *not* apply.)

1. **Requirements**

a. **Objectively Reasonable Belief**

The necessity defense requires that the defendant reasonably believe the threatened harm is greater than that resulting from the crime; some courts require that, *in actual fact*, the threatened harm be greater. In any case, the defense is unavailable if the *legislature* has determined that the harm is not greater than that involved in the crime.

b. **Other Requirements: Limits on Defense**

Some courts require that the defendant show that the threatened harm was *imminent*, to assure that the necessity defense applies only if there were *no less harmful alternatives* available.

2. **Economic Necessity Sufficient?**

Some decisions indicate that economic necessity alone does *not* justify the commission of a crime.

3. **Defense to Prison Escape?**

Courts are especially reluctant to accept the necessity defense when it is offered in a prosecution for escape from prison. To limit the defense in this situation, some courts require that the defendant surrender (or at least attempt to do so) as soon as the necessity has lost its coercive force.

I. DURESS

It is a defense to all but the most serious crimes (*i.e.*, intentional murder) that the defendant committed the crime under duress (*i.e.*, a threat by another *human being*).

1. Requirements

Traditionally, duress is sufficient only where the conduct of another causes the defendant to *reasonably believe* that unless he perpetrated the crime, the other person would cause *imminent death or serious bodily harm* to the defendant or another.

a. Submission Must Be Reasonable

The defendant's submission to the coercion and demand that he commit the crime must be reasonable, *i.e.*, there must be no opportunity to obtain assistance or to avoid the harm by noncriminal means.

2. Limitation: Not Applicable to Intentional Killings

Duress is not applicable to intentional murder. It is unclear whether it can be asserted in defense to *felony murder* (because it provides a defense to the underlying felony). In a prosecution for first degree premeditated murder, however, duress may show a *lack of premeditation* and thereby preclude conviction for that crime.

J. ENTRAPMENT

1. In General

An entrapment defense rests upon enticement by a law enforcement officer or one acting as an agent of an officer.

a. Not a Constitutional Rule

No specific formulation of the entrapment has a constitutional basis, *i.e.*, as a matter of Due Process.

2. Substantive Limitations

Entrapment is *limited to nonserious crimes*; it cannot be asserted as a defense to crimes involving serious injury (*e.g.*, rape, murder). Further, *only law enforcement officers and agents can entrap*; the defense is inapplicable to acts by purely private individuals.

3. Procedural Limitation: Defendant Cannot Deny Act

In some jurisdictions, a defendant cannot both deny commission of the act constituting the crime and claim entrapment. However, the Supreme Court has held that under *federal criminal law*, a defendant *can* deny guilt and alternatively claim entrapment.

4. Entrapment Criteria

There are several views concerning what must be shown to establish entrapment.

a. Traditional (Subjective) Standard

Entrapment exists only if a law enforcement officer (or agent) *creates the intent* to commit the crime in the mind of a person who is *not otherwise predisposed* to commit crimes of this sort.

(1) Predisposition

The accused's predisposition to commit the crime is the *crucial issue* and is decided by the jury. Under federal law, it must be shown that the defendant was *predisposed to commit the crimes prior to first being approached* by government agents.

(2) **Burden of Proof**

The traditional approach requires the defendant to establish that officers *induced* him to commit the crime. The prosecution bears the burden of proving beyond a reasonable doubt that the *defendant was predisposed.*

(3) **Procedural Disadvantages**

Because predisposition is at issue, the prosecution may introduce much evidence that would otherwise be inadmissible (*e.g.*, evidence of prior crimes and reputation).

b. **Modern (Objective) Standard**

Entrapment exists if the offense was committed *in response to law enforcement activity* that was reasonably likely to cause a *reasonable* (though not predisposed) *person* to commit a crime. The *focus is on the nature of the police activity* and its likelihood to induce commission of the crime; the *defendant's predisposition is irrelevant.*

(1) **Fewer Procedural Disadvantages**

Entrapment is a matter for the court to decide (rather than the jury), and evidence of predisposition is *not* admissible.

c. **Broader Objective Standards**

In a few jurisdictions, entrapment may be found if a law enforcement officer engages in activity offensive for other reasons, *e.g.*, if an officer *provides materials* for the commission of the offense or approaches a subject *without probable cause* (or at least a reasonable suspicion) to believe the suspect is predisposed to commit crimes of the sort involved. At least one court has found entrapment where the police conduct, for any reason, was so offensive as to shake public confidence in law enforcement.

K. CONSENT AND RELATED MATTERS

1. Consent

To qualify as a defense, the consent must be *legally effective* and either (i) negate an element of the crime, or (ii) be offered as a defense to a minor assault or battery.

a. **Consent as Negating Element of Crime**

Consent prevents liability for a crime that requires that it be committed without the victim's consent (*e.g.*, rape).

b. **Consent as Defense to Assault or Battery**

As to all other crimes, consent ordinarily does *not bar a conviction.* However, it may be a defense to minor assault or battery if *no serious bodily injury* is involved, if there is *widespread acceptance of the risk* (*e.g.*, football game), and if there is a *distinct beneficial effect* attending the defendant's conduct (*e.g.*, medical surgery).

2. Legal Effectiveness of Consent

In all cases, the consent must be legally effective, because it was: (i) *given voluntarily*; (ii) by a person with *legal capacity* to consent; and (iii) the consent was *free of fraud or mistake* concerning the very nature of the conduct at issue.

3. Distinguish: Condonation No Defense

Ordinarily, the victim's *forgiveness* after commission of a crime is *no defense* unless it is a statutorily **authorized compromise.**

4. Negligence or Criminality of Victim No Defense

The victim's negligence or criminal activity is not a defense because crimes involve wrongs against the public.

L. SELF-DEFENSE

A person is privileged to use force that *reasonably* appears necessary to defend herself against an apparent threat of *unlawful* and *immediate* violence from another.

1. General Requirements for Self-Defense

Whether or not deadly force is used, the defendant has a *reasonable belief* that she was *threatened with imminent and unlawful physical harm,* and that *force was necessary to prevent the harm.*

2. Additional Requirements Where Deadly Force Used

Deadly force may be used in self-defense *only* if the defendant *reasonably believed* the other person would inflict *death or great bodily harm* upon her, and the use of deadly force is *necessary* to prevent this. If the defendant is threatened with *nondeadly harm* that can be prevented only with deadly force in self-defense, the law expects the defendant to submit to the nondeadly injury.

a. Duty to Retreat Before Using Deadly Force?

Most jurisdictions *no longer require the defendant to retreat* before using deadly force, even if safe retreat is possible. And, in jurisdictions where the duty to retreat is the rule, there is *no obligation to retreat* when it is *unsafe* or when *the defendant is attacked in her own home*.

3. Special Problem: Battered Victim Claiming Self-Defense

Assertion of self-defense arising from a long history of abuse creates problems involving issues of *imminence and unreasonableness*. A wife whose husband has repeatedly beaten her will take his life without any immediate threat of repetition of the husband's conduct, although the wife knew that more severe beatings were in the offing, *i.e.*, due to "battered woman syndrome." The reasonableness of the defendant's conduct is based upon her physical and psychological characteristics, her specific experiences, and perhaps the disadvantaged position of women in society.

4. Limitation: Right of Aggressor to Self-Defense

A person who was the *initial aggressor cannot* use force in self-defense *unless* (i) the victim has responded with *excessive force*, or (ii) the *aggressor first withdraws* from the situation or at least notifies the adversary of his desire to withdraw.

5. Resisting Unlawful Arrest as Self-Defense

Traditionally, force is used to resist an *unlawful* arrest. However, the trend is away from this rule. Some jurisdictions reject it entirely, and others allow force to resist only when the unlawful arrest is *accomplished by excessive force*.

6. Distinguish: "Imperfect" Self-Defense

If *the defendant causes death* while acting in what he honestly but *unreasonably believes* to be self-defense, he cannot escape conviction. However, some jurisdictions will reduce the crime from murder to manslaughter (*see infra*).

M. DEFENSE OF OTHERS

Reasonable force may also be used to defend another person against unlawful harm.

1. Relationship with Party Defended

In some jurisdictions, the defendant uses the defense only if he stands in a familial or employment relationship to the person aided. The *modern view*, however, requires *no special relationship*, and reasonable force may be used to defend *any third person*.

2. Right of Party Defended to Act in Self-Defense

Some courts uphold the defendant's use of *reasonable* force in defense of another *only* if the person aided has a right to defend himself (*i.e.*, defendant stands in the place of the person assisted). However, the better rule sustains the defense only if the defendant *reasonably believed* the person assisted had the legal right to act in self-defense.

3. Distinguish: Force to Prevent Criminal Offense

The circumstances under which the defendant may act in defense of others may also support the defense of crime prevention (*see infra*).

N. PROTECTION OF PROPERTY

1. In General

The right to use force in protection of property is much *more limited* than the right to use force in protecting persons. Deadly force ordinarily can *never* be used merely to defend one's property. However, deadly force may be justified when the defendant's reasonable use of force in protection of property is met with an attack threatening imminent serious bodily harm or, in some cases, in defense of one's *dwelling*.

2. Reasonable Nondeadly Force

Nondeadly force *may be used* where it reasonably appears necessary to prevent or terminate an unlawful intrusion onto, or interference with, property in the defendant's possession. Usually, a *request to desist* is necessary *before* using any force unless it would be futile or dangerous.

3. Property in Possession of Another

Traditionally, the property defended is in the defender's *lawful possession*. However, the Model Penal Code permits the use of nondeadly force when the property is in the possession of the defendant or another for whose protection the defendant acts.

4. Use of Force to Regain or Reenter Property

Nondeadly force may be used to regain or reenter property if the action is taken *immediately after the wrongful intrusion* or in *hot pursuit* of the dispossessor.

5. "Spring Guns" and Similar Devices

Traditionally, injuries inflicted by mechanical devices are justifiable only if the person who set the device would have been justified in inflicting the *same harm had he been present*.

O. PROTECTION OF DWELLING

Jurisdictions differ greatly regarding a defendant's right to use force in defense of his dwelling.

1. Common Law View: Deadly Force in Defense of Dwelling

Early common law permitted use of deadly force if the defendant reasonably believed it was necessary to prevent a forcible entry of the dwelling, and a warning to desist had first been given to the intruder. There was *no duty to retreat*.

2. Modern View: Limited Right to Use Deadly Force

Modern courts *limit* the right to use deadly force to situations where the defendant reasonably believed the intruder intended to *commit a felony or harm someone* in the dwelling.

a. Intruder Already Inside Dwelling

Courts are split regarding use of deadly force when the intruder has already entered. Some courts rationalize that once an intruder has gained entry, the defense of dwelling right no longer is applicable; use of force then is governed by other rules such as self-defense.

b. Statutory Provisions

Several jurisdictions have legislated provisions permitting use of force to defend one's dwelling (*e.g.*, Colorado's "Make My Day" statute authorizing *any degree of force* if certain minimal requirements are met). Several jurisdictions also have expanded the right to defend against unlawful entry to vehicles.

P. USE OF FORCE TO EFFECTUATE ARREST

1. Right of Police Officers

A police officer may use whatever *nondeadly* force reasonably appears necessary to make an arrest for a felony *or* misdemeanor. The use of *deadly force* has *traditionally* been limited to situations where an officer suspects commission of a *felony*.

a. Modern View

Deadly force is limited to arrests of defendants *reasonably* believed to have committed a *dangerous felony*. The Model Penal Code also allows such force to arrest dangerous defendants.

(1) Fourth Amendment Requirement

An arrest is unconstitutionally unreasonable if the arresting officer used deadly force while not reasonably believing that the arrestee posed a significant threat of death or serious bodily injury. Such an arrest may give rise to a *civil claim* for damages.

b. Reasonable Appearance Controls

The defense is available as long as the officer reasonably believes that the suspect is guilty, even if the suspect is actually innocent.

c. Distinguish: Self-Defense

An officer who is met with resistance in attempting an arrest may have the right to use force (including deadly force). Note that this would be *self-defense*.

2. Right of Private Persons

A private person also has the right to use force to make an arrest, but unlike police officers, it is *not enough that he had a reasonable belief* that grounds for the use of force existed. If he causes *death*, a defense exists *only if a felony was in fact committed* and the *person killed in fact committed it*. The law is less clear where death is *not* caused.

a. Distinguish: Private Person Called to Assist Officer

Where a private person is called on to *assist a police officer* in making an arrest, he has the *same privilege* as the officer.

3. Use of Force to Prevent Escape from Custody

Force may be used to thwart an escape from custody *if* that force would have been allowed to effectuate the arrest in the first place.

Q. CRIME PREVENTION

Sometimes force may be used to *prevent* commission of a crime, but this must be distinguished from the use of force to effectuate an arrest.

1. Common Law Position

Reasonable, nondeadly force can be used to prevent or terminate the commission of a felony or a misdemeanor amounting to a breach of the peace. However, *deadly force* can be used only to prevent perpetration of a *felony*.

2. Modern View

Deadly force is limited to the termination of felonies that create a risk of *death or serious bodily harm* to others.

R. PUBLIC AUTHORITY

A public officer may use *reasonable force* to carry out duties pursuant to a valid statute or court order. Under the better view, it is only necessary that the official reasonably believe that her actions are valid.

S. DOMESTIC AUTHORITY AND SIMILAR SPECIAL RELATIONSHIPS

Parents and schoolteachers may use *reasonable nondeadly force* to control and discipline their *minor* charges. Similar authority is extended to wardens of institutions, captains of ships and aircraft, etc.

VII. PRELIMINARY OR INCHOATE CRIMES

A. SOLICITATION

1. Common Law

One who intentionally *counsels, incites, or induces another* commits the common law misdemeanor of solicitation. The crime is *complete* upon the act of counseling, inciting, or inducing, no matter what the response is of the person solicited.

2. Modern Statutes

The modern trend is to limit the crime of solicitation to the incitement of *serious* offenses (*e.g.*, murder, rape) and to provide a lesser penalty than that imposed for the crime itself.

3. Special Problems in Solicitation

a. Uncommunicated Solicitation

An uncommunicated solicitation (*e.g.*, an intermediary fails to deliver a message) is generally a crime, although some jurisdictions limit the charge to attempted solicitation.

b. Defense of Renunciation?

It is unclear whether a solicitor can escape liability by withdrawing before the solicited offense is committed.

4. Relationship to Other Crimes

a. Accomplice Liability Distinguished

If the person solicited commits the target crime, the solicitor is *liable as a party* to that crime.

b. Conspiracy Distinguished

Conspiracy may follow a solicitation; however, an agreement is *not* required for solicitation.

c. Attempt Distinguished

If the solicitor *goes beyond* mere incitement, or if the person solicited progresses toward the commission of the crime, the solicitor may incur liability for attempt.

d. "Merger" of Solicitation

Solicitation is a *lesser included offense* of attempt or conspiracy, and thus, a solicitor *cannot* be convicted of *both*.

B. CONSPIRACY

1. In General

a. Common Law

At common law, conspiracy (a misdemeanor) is an agreement between two or more persons to accomplish *an unlawful purpose* or a *lawful purpose by unlawful methods*.

b. Modern Statutes

Modern statutes often limit the offense to agreements to commit a *crime* or specify the proscribed unlawful objectives.

2. Requirements for Liability for Conspiracy

a. Mens Rea

The conspirators must *intend to agree* with each other, *and* each person must have the *intent to accomplish the objective*. Intent is often proved by the defendant's expectation of some benefit from a successful completion of the conspiracy—*i.e.*, a "stake in the venture." In some circumstances, the conspirators' awareness that the target offense will be committed is sufficient.

(1) Providing Goods or Services

If the objective is *not a serious crime*, the defendant probably must have affirmatively *desired the accomplishment* of an unlawful purpose; mere knowledge that goods provided, for example, would be used for an unlawful purpose is generally not enough. However, the *more serious the crime*, the more likely the law regards the defendant as a conspirator merely upon proof he was *aware* of an unlawful purpose.

(2) Requirement of a "Corrupt Motive"

Some courts hold that conspiracy requires proof of a "corrupt motive," *i.e.*, knowledge that the objective was illegal.

b. Actus Reus

The conspirators *actually enter into an agreement*. The agreement need not be express; it can be *implied* from the cooperative action of the parties.

(1) Connection to Agreement

If the existence of a conspiracy is clear, relatively slight evidence is sufficient to connect a party to it.

(2) Overt Act Requirement

The common law crime is complete when the agreement is reached. However, some modern statutes impose the additional requirement of an overt act, *i.e.*, *any* single act by *any* member of the conspiracy that *tends to further* the unlawful objective.

(3) Number and Characteristics of Agreements

Complex situations involving many parties and several schemes may result in one large agreement among all participants or several smaller agreements with some overlap of members.

(a) One Agreement with Multiple Unlawful Purposes

If many crimes are plotted in a single agreement, there is only *one* conspiracy.

(b) "Chain" Situation

If the parties to a series of transactions individually have a general interest in the success of the *overall series* of transactions, there is *one large conspiracy* involving all participants (*e.g.*, sale and resale of narcotics).

(c) "Wheel" and "Spoke" Situation

If one person enters into many different transactions with various other persons who are concerned only with their own transaction, there are *several different* conspiracies.

(4) "Unknown" Co-Conspirators

The conspiracy includes all persons *known by other members to be involved*, even if each member does not know the identity of all the others or how many are involved.

(5) Husband-Wife Conspiracies

At common law, husband-wife conspiracies could not be formed (spouses were regarded as "one"); however, modern courts reject this limit.

(6) Corporate Conspiracy

A corporation can be a party to a conspiracy, but there is *no* conspiracy where the only members are a corporation and one of its agents or two corporations and one person acting as agent for both, because only one human actor is involved.

c. Objective of Agreement

The common law did not require commission of a crime to be the objective. *Modern statutes*, however, differ. Some require an objective to *commit a crime* while others designate specific unlawful purposes (*e.g.*, to obstruct justice). As a result, some conspiracy statutes raise constitutional *vagueness* problems.

3. Punishment

Modern statutes also depart from the common law (which made conspiracy a misdemeanor) by imposing penalties related to, but less than, those for the crime the parties agreed to commit or by imposing the same punishment as that provided for the most serious offense the parties conspired to commit.

4. Conviction for Conspiracy and Completed Crime

Contrary to the common law rule, if the target crime was committed, the conspirators can be convicted of *both* the conspiracy and the crime. There is *no merger*.

5. Special Problems Applying Conspiracy Law

a. Traditional "Plurality" Requirement

The requirement that a conspiracy involve an agreement between *two or more persons* means that no conviction may be obtained if *all other members* of the alleged conspiracy (other than the defendant) are *acquitted* or are shown to have been *feigning involvement*. The Model Penal Code, on the other hand, does not follow the traditional "plurality" requirement, only requiring that an agreement "*by*" the defendant be made. Unlike the traditional requirement of a bilateral agreement, the Model Penal Code standard requires only a unilateral agreement by the defendant with one or more others who *e.g.*, may be in law enforcement or insane.

b. Wharton's Rule: No Conspiracy to Commit Concerted Action Crimes

Many courts refuse to find a criminal conspiracy when the agreement is to commit a crime that *necessarily involves two or more people.* This is known as "Wharton's Rule."

(1) Exceptions

Many courts do not apply this rule if the number of conspirators *exceeds* the essential number of participants. Furthermore, some courts apply the rule only where the parties have *achieved their objective*. Thus, the rule, in effect, only *bars* conviction for *both* conspiracy and the completed crime.

c. Defenses to Conspiracy

(1) Impossibility: Usually No Defense

Most courts take the view that impossibility is *no defense* to a conspiracy. However, a few decisions have suggested that "legal," but not "factual," impossibility may be a defense.

(2) Withdrawal

Generally, withdrawal is *no defense* to a charge of conspiracy. However, the Model Penal Code allows a co-conspirator to defend on the ground that he "thwarted the success of the conspiracy under circumstances *manifesting a complete and voluntary renunciation* of his criminal purpose."

(a) Distinguish: Defense to Crimes of Co-Conspirators

Withdrawal *may* be a defense to *crimes* committed by conspirators in furtherance of the conspiracy.

6. Liability for Crimes of Co-Conspirators

All conspirators are guilty of those crimes committed by their co-conspirators that were *reasonably foreseeable results* of the conspiracy and committed *in furtherance* of it. Note that this *differs from accomplice liability* in that coconspirators may be liable for crimes of others even though they would not be liable as accomplices.

a. Crimes Prior to Joining

Some opinions suggest that a conspirator joining an existing conspiracy can also be held liable for crimes committed by other members *prior to his joining* the conspiracy. However, this is probably not the case.

b. Withdrawal Preventing Liability

A defendant is *not* liable for crimes of other conspirators committed *after his effective withdrawal*. A withdrawal is effective if *communicated to all* other members (unless perhaps this is an unmanageable task) and according to some courts, is also *timely*. Most courts, however, do *not* require the defendant to prevent the former co-conspirators from completing their plans.

7. Duration of the Conspiracy

A determination about when a conspiracy ended affects liability for co-conspirators' crimes and procedural matters (*i.e.*, statute of limitations). A conspiracy ordinarily ends once *all objectives* of the agreement are successfully completed.

a. Efforts to Conceal the Offense

The Supreme Court requires *direct evidence* of a specific agreement to conceal the crime in order to find that such behavior extended the conspiracy beyond the completion of the crime.

8. Tactical Advantage for Prosecution

Charging a criminal conspiracy provides the prosecution with many tactical advantages (*e.g.*, broad choice of venue, use of hearsay, etc.) and therefore may materially increase the chances of a conviction.

C. ATTEMPT

1. Elements of Attempt

An attempt consists of a *specific intent* to commit a crime and an *act in furtherance* of that intent which *sufficiently approaches completion* of the crime.

a. Mens Rea

The *mens rea* of attempt has two components: (i) the intent to commit the acts or cause the results constituting the target crime; and (ii) the intent necessary for the target crime (*e.g.*, attempted murder requires intent to cause death). Note that intent may be a necessary element of *attempt* to commit a *strict liability* crime.

b. Actus Reus

The *actus reus* of attempt is an act that *progresses sufficiently towards commission* of the attempted offense. A number of criteria are used or suggested to determine whether the defendant's act is sufficient:

(1) *Act must go beyond mere "preparation"* and into the zone of "perpetration."

(2) *Defendant must have committed the last proximate act* before actual commission of the offense.

(3) *Defendant must have obtained control over all factors indispensable* to the commission of the crime, *i.e.*, nothing remains undone.

(4) *Defendant's conduct must be physically proximate* to the intended crime.

(5) *Defendant must have gone so far* that in the ordinary course of events (without interference) the crime would be completed (*probable desistance test*).

(6) *The act itself must unequivocally show that the defendant intended* to complete the crime (*"equivocality" or "res ipsa loquitur" test*).

(7) The Model Penal Code requires that the defendant's *conduct constitute a substantial step strongly corroborative of defendant's intent* to complete the crime. This approach is gaining increasing acceptance.

2. **Defenses to Attempt**

a. **Impossibility**

(1) **"True" Legal Impossibility**

"True" legal impossibility arises when a defendant sets out to do things that he *believes* would, if completed, constitute a crime, but those acts are *not* illegal (*i.e.,* his *only misunderstanding concerns "the law"*). "True" legal impossibility is a defense to a charge of attempt.

(2) **Factual Impossibility**

Factual impossibility arises when a defendant does things that *would,* if completed, constitute a crime if the circumstances were as the defendant believed them to be, but there is no chance that the defendant will complete the act *because of factors of which he is unaware*. Factual impossibility is universally rejected as a defense to a charge of attempt.

(3) **Mixed Legal and Factual Impossibility**

Mixed legal and factual impossibility arises when the defendant sets out to do things (or to cause results) while believing that this *would* be a crime, but *due to a misunderstanding of the surrounding circumstances*, his conduct, if completed, would not actually constitute a crime. The conduct would be a crime if the circumstances were as he believed them to be. The traditional rule is that this type of impossibility is a defense to a charge of attempt. However, under the modern view and the MPC, this type of impossibility defense is rejected.

(4) **Inherent or Obvious Impossibility**

In a few very unusual situations, it has been held that an attempt is not criminal if it is *blatantly obvious* that the defendant's chosen methods could not result in the completion of a crime.

b. **"Withdrawal" or Abandonment**

Traditionally, once an attempt is complete, the defendant cannot avoid liability by abandoning her plan. The Model Penal Code and modern statutes would establish a defense of *complete and fully voluntary* abandonment. Note that even if not a defense, evidence of abandonment may be used to show that the defendant *lacked the requisite intent.*

3. **Punishment**

Attempts are usually punishable by a *lesser* penalty than that for the completed crime. Because an attempt is a lesser included offense of the completed crime, *defendants cannot be convicted of both.*

a. **"Attempt-Like" Crimes**

Some authorities urge that attempts to commit "attempt-like" crimes (*e.g.*, burglary, assault) should not be punished. However, convictions of this type are upheld.

b. **Solicitation as Attempt**

Although there is conflicting authority, the better view is that *mere* solicitation, without more, is *not* an attempt.

VIII. HOMICIDE CRIMES

A. DEFINITION AND CLASSIFICATION

1. Definition

A homicide is the killing of one human being by another human being.

2 Common Law Classifications

At common law, homicides are categorized as: (i) *justifiable* (those authorized by law), (ii) *excusable* (those in which the killer is not necessarily without fault but circumstances do not justify infliction of normal punishment), or (iii) *criminal homicide* (murder or manslaughter). At common law, murder is not divided into degrees.

3. Classification Under Modern Law

Because excusable homicides are no longer punished, the justifiable-excusable distinction is unnecessary. Modern statutes, however, often divide murder into two degrees and sometimes also create a *negligent homicide* offense. Recently, many states have distinguished murder from "capital murder," a separate offense for which the death penalty may be imposed.

B. MURDER

1. Murder Defined

At common law, murder is the unlawful killing of another human being with *malice aforethought*.

2. "Malice Aforethought"

Malice aforethought refers to *any* of several different mental states (below) plus the *absence* of factors sufficient to reduce a killing to voluntary manslaughter. Bad feelings toward or hatred of the victim is unnecessary.

a. Sufficient Mental States

(1) Intent to Kill

If the defendant *intended to cause the death*, the killing is with malice aforethought. In most cases, intent may be *inferred* from the defendant's conduct, *e.g.*, where defendant intentionally uses a deadly weapon to kill another person (*deadly weapon doctrine*).

(2) Intent to Inflict Great Bodily Injury

Proof that the defendant *intended to inflict serious bodily injury*, even though there was no conscious desire to cause death, supports a murder conviction.

(3) Intent to Commit a Felony

If a death occurred while the defendant was in the *process of committing a felony (infra)*, malice aforethought is present.

(4) Intent to Resist Lawful Arrest

A killing caused while resisting a lawful arrest establishes malice aforethought under the older cases. However, today such a killing is murder only if it satisfies one of the other tests of malice aforethought (*e.g.*, felony murder).

(5) Awareness of a High Risk of Death: "Depraved Mind" or "Abandoned and Malignant Heart"

A defendant may be guilty of murder if she consciously disregards an *unusually high risk* that her conduct *will cause death or (perhaps) serious bodily* injury.

Traditionally, this was called the "abandoned and malignant heart" test. The better view requires that the defendant is *subjectively* aware of the risk involved.

b. Proof of Malice Aforethought

Malice aforethought can be proved by circumstantial evidence and is inferred from the act of killing itself.

3. Degrees of Murder

There are no degrees of murder under common law. Modern statutes often divide murder into first and second degree.

a. First Degree Murder

(1) Premeditated Killings

Premeditated killings are those in which the intent to kill is formed *with some reflection, deliberation, reasoning, or weighing,* rather than on sudden impulse. Courts disagree on the evidence required to show premeditation and deliberation. Some courts will defer to a jury's finding that the defendant acted with premeditation and deliberation when the defendant had the opportunity to do so. Other courts require direct proof that the defendant did premeditate and deliberate prior to the killing.

(2) Killing During Enumerated Felonies

First degree murder includes killings committed during the perpetration of *certain enumerated felonies* (*i.e.*, arson, rape, robbery, burglary, kidnapping, and sexual molestation of a child).

(3) Killing by Poison, Bomb, Lying in Wait, and Torture

Killings by poison or a bomb, or after lying in wait for the victim, are sometimes specifically categorized as first degree murder. Killing by torture also constitutes first degree murder.

b. Second-Degree Murder

Under statutes that divide murder into degrees, all killings committed *with malice aforethought* but are *not specifically raised to first-degree murder* are typically classified as second-degree murder.

4. Capital Murder

This is a *separate offense* from murder and usually requires proof of at least one *statutory aggravating factor or "special circumstance."* A conviction for capital murder subjects the defendant to the possibility of a death sentence.

C. FELONY MURDER

1. Felony Murder Rule

Even an accidental killing constitutes murder if it was caused *with the intent to commit a felony. All co-felons are liable* if one of them accidentally causes a death, even when a *co-felon is killed*, although courts many times will find an exception when a co-felon is the victim.

2. Limitations on Felony Murder

Several limitations have emerged, perhaps as a result of increasing discontent with the rule.

a. **Death of Another Must Be "Foreseeable"**

Some courts require that the death was a *foreseeable consequence of the felony* (although deaths usually are found foreseeable).

b. **Felony Must Be "Dangerous"**

A number of states limit application of the rule to *dangerous* felonies. Some states require the felony to be *inherently dangerous*; others require only that the felony *as committed* involved a special or significant risk to human life.

c. **Felony Must Be "Independent"**

Some courts require that the felony be *independent of the killing*. If the predicate felony was the means by which the victim's death was caused, the felony *"merges"* into the killing and no felony murder exists.

d. **One of the Felons Must "Directly" Cause Death**

The modern trend holds that the felony murder rule does *not* apply when a victim is killed by a resisting victim or pursuing police officer rather than by the defendant or one of the co-felons. However, the killing may *still* be murder under the *awareness of a high risk* rule.

e. **Death Must Be Caused in Perpetration of Felony**

The killing must be caused *during the perpetration* or attempted perpetration of the felony. However, in some states, a death caused *after* the technical completion of the felony may still be felony murder. The preferable position applies the felony murder rule to killings occurring during the commission of the felony or *in immediate flight* from the crimes (*i.e.*, stops upon reaching temporary safety).

3. **Future of Felony Murder**

Several courts have wholly or in part *abandoned* the felony murder rule. The effect of abandonment may be minimal because many situations also support murder charges under the "depraved mind" doctrine.

D. VOLUNTARY MANSLAUGHTER

1. **Voluntary Manslaughter Defined**

A killing that would *otherwise be murder* but was committed *in response to adequate provocation* is voluntary manslaughter.

2. **Elements of Provocation Reducing Murder to Manslaughter**

The common law requires *all* four of the following elements: (i) reasonable provocation; (ii) the defendant was actually provoked; (iii) absence of adequate cooling period; and (iv) no actual cooling off. Modern statutes also often require *all or most of these requirements*.

a. **Reasonable Provocation**

The provocation must have been *reasonable* as judged by an *objective* standard. Generally, it must have rendered ordinary persons of average disposition liable to act rashly, without deliberation, and from passion rather than judgment.

(1) **"Reasonable Person"**

In deciding whether particular provocation would provoke a reasonable person, courts differ over the extent to which the reasonable person should be attributed with the defendant's peculiar characteristics. Some do not consider any of the defendant's characteristics, while others consider some characteristics, but not a reduced capacity for self-control.

(2) Particular Situations

Verbal taunts by the victim traditionally are insufficient to constitute an adequate provocation. (A minority view accepts that at least sometimes mere words constitute reasonable provocation in some cases.) By contrast, violent and painful blows (unless the defendant was at fault), aggravated assault, and witnessing one's spouse commit adultery all constitute adequate provocation. Some courts will consider an illegal arrest to be adequate provocation. A killing caused during a fight in which both participants voluntarily entered is reduced from murder to manslaughter.

(3) Mistake Concerning Provocation

If the defendant was mistaken as to the existence of provocation, the better view reduces a killing to manslaughter as long as the defendant *reasonably believed* she was responding to adequate provocation.

(4) Provocation by Someone Other than Victim

If the defendant intended to kill the provoking party but killed someone else by accident, the killing is manslaughter. But if the defendant intended to kill someone he knew did not provoke him, the killing is *not* reduced to manslaughter.

(5) Injury to Persons Other than Defendant

The subject of the provocation generally must be the defendant or a close relative. Some courts indicate that if the subject is only a friend or distant relative, the provocation will not be adequate.

b. Actual Provocation

The provocation must *actually* cause the killing, *i.e.*, the provocation must have been such that a reasonable person would lose control *and* the defendant *in fact* acted due to passion rather than reason (a *subjective* test).

c. Absence of Reasonable Cooling Period

The majority of courts hold that homicide is not reduced to manslaughter if sufficient time elapsed between the provocation and the killing to permit the *passions of a reasonable person* to cool (an *objective* test).

(1) "Reinflaming" Occurrences

Under the better view, if an intervening event reminds the defendant of the provocation and "reinflames" the passion, the cooling period begins to run again.

d. No Actual Cooling off

The defendant's passion must *not in fact* have subsided during the interval (a *subjective* test).

3. Model Penal Code Position: "Extreme Mental or Emotional Disturbance"

The Code would reduce murder to manslaughter if the killing was committed "under the influence of *extreme mental or emotional disturbance* for which there is a *reasonable explanation or excuse*." This is somewhat similar to the adequate provocation standard but encourages submission of the case to the jury.

4. "Imperfect" Defense Situations as Voluntary Manslaughter

Some courts reduce a killing to lesser form of homicide if the evidence tends to establish a recognized defense like self-defense but falls short of doing so because the defendant's conduct was unreasonable (*e.g.*, he overreacted). The defendant is guilty of reckless homicide.

E. INVOLUNTARY MANSLAUGHTER

1. Involuntary Manslaughter Defined

An *unintended* killing is involuntary manslaughter if (i) it is the result of *criminal negligence* or (ii) it is caused during the commission of an *unlawful act not amounting to a felony* or that for some other reason is insufficient to trigger the felony murder rule.

2. Killing by Criminal Negligence

An unintentional killing caused by the commission of *any* act in a *criminally negligent manner* is involuntary manslaughter.

a. More than "Civil" Negligence Required

A greater degree of unreasonableness is required for criminal negligence than would otherwise suffice for imposition of civil liability. Also, it may be necessary that the defendant was *aware of the high and unreasonable risk* of death, but consciously disregarded that risk and killed the victim.

3. Killing by Commission of Unlawful Act: "Misdemeanor Manslaughter"

Unintentional killings caused during the commission of an unlawful act are involuntary manslaughter (unless the unlawful act supports application of the felony murder rule). The act must be *unlawful* but need not be criminal (*e.g.*, killing caused during a defendant's attempted suicide).

a. Limitations

Some states hold that the unlawful act must be *malum in se* (inherently wrong). Others require that the unlawful act be perpetrated in a criminally *negligent* manner. A number of courts require that *death be caused by the unlawful aspect* of the defendant's conduct.

F. MODERN STATUTORY DISTINCTIONS

1. Modern Penal Code Scheme

Modern statutes tend to redefine homicide offenses by grading them according to the different states of mind defined by the Model Penal Code.

a. Murder

The Model Penal Code defines murder as a killing committed *purposely, knowingly, or recklessly* under circumstances manifesting *extreme indifference* to the value of human life.

b. Manslaughter

The Code establishes a single manslaughter offense which is a killing committed *recklessly or* under the influence of *extreme mental or emotional disturbance* for which there is reasonable explanation or excuse.

c. Negligent Homicide

The Code creates a new homicide offense of negligent homicide, *i.e.*, a killing committed negligently.

2. Homicide Caused During Operation of a Motor Vehicle

Other modern statutes often contain a separate offense for death caused in the negligent operation of a motor vehicle or by operating a vehicle in an unlawful manner.

G. GENERAL PROBLEMS RELATING TO HOMICIDE LIABILITY

1. Causation

All homicide crimes require that the conduct of the defendant be proved to have caused the death of the victim. Consequently, problems of causation often arise in homicide cases.

2. Victim Must Be a Living Human Being: Killing of Fetus

A fetus is not a living human being until fully brought forth from the mother and having an independent circulation. Some states have broadened their homicide statutes to include a fetus, contrary to common law.

3. When Does Death Occur

Under the *traditional* rule, death does not occur until *heartbeat and respiration stop.* However, some courts now hold that death occurs when the *brain ceases to function.*

4. Death Must Occur Within a Year and a Day

Death must occur within a year and a day from the time the cause of death was administered. However, some jurisdictions have *abandoned* this time limitation, while others have *modified* the time and its effect on a criminal case.

5. Aiding or Causing Suicide

At common law, suicide is murder. The modern view holds that suicide is *not* an offense; thus, the aider cannot be guilty as a party. Some statutes, however, make aiding suicide a *separate offense*.

a. Distinguish: Actively Killing Another

Generally, one who actively takes the life of another, even if at the other person's specific request, is guilty of murder.

IX. OTHER CRIMES AGAINST THE PERSON

A. ASSAULT AND BATTERY

1. Battery

Battery is the unlawful application of force to the person of another.

a. Actus Reus

The mere application of force is sufficient under traditional law; *no injury* or marks on the victim are required. Modern statutes, however, often require either some injury or that the touching (application of force) be *offensive*. Under either approach, the application of force may be *indirect* (*e.g.*, administering poison).

b. Mens Rea

The application of force need not be intentional; *negligence* is usually *sufficient.* Some courts do not even require negligence where the defendant was engaged in *unlawful* behavior.

c. Effect of Consent

There is no battery if the victim *effectively* consented.

d. Punishment

At common law, battery is a misdemeanor, as is today's classification of simple battery. However, certain aggravated batteries are felonies.

2. Assault

Two different activities may constitute a criminal assault, but not all states punish both types.

a. Attempted Battery as Assault

An attempted battery is most often an assault.

(1) Mens Rea

Generally, the defendant *intended the application of force* to the victim. An intent to frighten is *not* sufficient for this type of assault.

(2) Actus Reus

The defendant *progressed sufficiently towards completing* the battery. Some statutes require that the defendant have had the *present ability to succeed.*

(3) Conditional Assault

Representations by the defendant that she will not commit a battery if the victim complies with certain demands do not preclude an assault conviction.

b. Intentional Placing in Fear as Assault

The second type of assault, recognized in a probable majority of the states, is intentionally placing another in fear of immediate bodily harm. With this kind of assault, the defendant *intends* to cause apprehension of harm, the victim is *in fact apprehensive* (*i.e.*, aware of assault), and the defendant's *conduct is sufficient to create reasonable apprehension. Mere words* are *not* enough.

c. Model Penal Code

The Model Penal Code's definition differs in that the victim need not have actual fear, and the attempt must be to put the victim in fear of *serious* bodily harm.

d. Punishment

Assault was a misdemeanor at common law, and "simple" assault remains so today. Modern statutes, however, make certain "aggravated" assaults felonies.

B. MAYHEM

Mayhem (a felony) consists of maliciously depriving another of the use of one of her arms or legs (*disablement*) or injuring the victim so as to permanently change her appearance (*disfigurement*).

1. Actus Reus

The defendant caused bodily injury to the victim that *permanently* disfigures or disables her.

2. Mens Rea

Generally, the defendant must have *intended to injure* the victim.

3. Punishment

Mayhem is a felony at common law, punishable by mutilation. Although the penalty is less drastic today, mayhem often remains a felony under modern statutes.

C. RAPE AND RELATED OFFENSES

Rape is unlawful sexual intercourse with a female without her consent. Modern statutes often designate the crime as sexual assault and classify it as a crime against the person.

1. Forcible (or Common Law) Rape

The defendant must have completed an act of sexual intercourse with a woman *other than his wife* and against her will. The slightest penetration of the female sexual organ is sufficient.

a. Husband Cannot Rape Wife

Traditionally, a husband cannot rape his wife, but he may be convicted as a *party* to the rape of his wife by someone else. *But note:* Modern statutes in many states now allow forcible rape convictions for a husband's forcible rape of his wife.

b. Against the Woman's Will: Without Consent

Intercourse is against the will of the victim in several types of situations, all of which involve the lack of *effective* consent by the victim.

(1) Intercourse Accomplished by Force

Intercourse accomplished by force is against the victim's will. However, no rape occurs if the victim resisted at first but consented before the actual act of intercourse.

(2) Intercourse Accomplished by Threats

Consent obtained by threats of serious and immediate bodily harm is *ineffective*.

(3) Incapacity to Give Effective Consent

Consent given by a victim lacking capacity due to intoxication, mental deficiency, or insanity is also invalid.

(4) Consent Obtained by Fraud

Consent obtained by deceiving the victim as to the *nature of the act* (*i.e.*, as to whether the act is intercourse) is invalid. Some courts also hold that consent is ineffective if obtained by deceiving the victim into *believing she is married* to the defendant. Other types of fraud do *not invalidate* consent.

c. Mens Rea

The *mens rea* requirement for rape is not clearly defined. It is unclear whether the defendant must actually know the victim is not consenting. Some courts hold that it is enough that the defendant *should* have been aware of the lack of consent. A few courts do not focus on the *mens rea* required but rather recognize a defense consisting of proof that the defendant *reasonably* believed that the victim consented.

d. Special Problems

(1) Corroboration of Victim's Testimony

In some jurisdictions, the rape victim's testimony must be corroborated.

(2) Requirement of Resistance

Some courts also require proof that the victim resisted to the utmost unless resistance would have been *futile* or was *prevented by the defendant's threats*. The trend is to abandon this requirement.

(3) **Effect of Victim's Promiscuity**

There is no formal requirement that the victim was previously chaste, although evidence of past sexual conduct is sometimes admitted on the issue of consent. However, the *modern trend limits* the use of such evidence.

e. **Special Age Defense**

Under the common law, a boy under the age of 14 is deemed physically incapable of intercourse and thus is also incapable of committing rape. Many jurisdictions have explicitly abolished a specific age rule. Other jurisdictions have modified the rule to a rebuttable presumption, and a boy under age 14 may be convicted of rape where the evidence proves beyond a reasonable doubt his ability to have intercourse.

2. **"Statutory" Rape**

In most jurisdictions, intercourse with a female who is too young to give legally effective consent is rape. The *age of consent* is set by statute.

a. **Awareness of Victim's Age Not Necessary**

Statutory rape is a *strict liability crime*. The defendant's awareness of the victim's age (or his reasonable mistaken belief that she was older) is irrelevant under the general rule. However, some states permit a defense on the basis that there was only a *small difference* between the *defendant's age and the age of the victim.*

3. **Equal Protection Issues Regarding Sex Offenses**

Because sex crime statutes penalize mostly males, it is argued that those statutes violate equal protection. However, such statutes are upheld if the distinction made realistically reflects a difference in the actual situation of the sexes (*e.g.*, statutory rape laws are aimed at preventing teenage pregnancies).

4. **Modern Trend: "Sex Neutral" Offense of Sexual Assault**

Some jurisdictions have replaced rape with a more sexually neutral offense (*e.g.*, crime of "sexual assault"). Under such statutes, sexually intrusive assaults other than vaginal penetration are punished, as are assaults on males.

5. **Deemphasis on Consent: Intercourse "By Forcible Compulsion"**

Several states have statutorily eliminated the concept of consent from the rape definition. These jurisdictions instead focus on the defendant's use of *force* in sexual intercourse.

D. FALSE IMPRISONMENT

False imprisonment is the *intentional unlawful confinement* of another person.

1. **Actus Reus: Confinement**

The victim is compelled by the defendant's use of *force or threats* to remain somewhere or go somewhere against his desire. There is *no* confinement where the victim is simply *prevented from proceeding* in a certain direction.

2. **Mens Rea**

Traditionally, the defendant must have *intended to confine* the victim. The Model Penal Code requires only that the restraint be *knowingly* accomplished.

3. **Unlawful Confinement**

The confinement is *without legal authority*.

4. Punishment

Generally, under both common law and modern statutes, false imprisonment is a *misdemeanor*.

E. KIDNAPPING

1. Common Law

At common law, kidnapping is the forcible abduction or stealing away of a person from his own country and sending him into another country.

2. Modern Statutes

Today, kidnapping is extended to a form of *aggravated false imprisonment*. Various statutes include the following conduct as kidnapping:

a. *Confinement and movement (asportation)* of the victim,

b. *Confinement* of the victim *in a secret place*,

c. *Confinement accomplished by deadly force*,

d. *Confinement for ransom or sexual abuse*.

3. Confinement: How Accomplished

Statutes vary regarding the methods of accomplishing confinement. Some prohibit use of *deception* as well as *force or threats*.

4. Mens Rea

Generally, *actual intent to confine or move* the victim is required.

5. Relationship of Kidnapping to Other Crimes

During a kidnapping, the defendant often confines or moves the victim during the commission of another crime such as rape or robbery. Most courts hold that a conviction for kidnapping requires that the confinement or movement of the victim *must not be merely incidental* to the other crime, *i.e.*, if it can be established that the confinement or movement a) went beyond what is necessary for the other crime, b) increased the risk to the victim, or c) helped the defendant escape or avoid detection. Some courts conclude that neither constitutional considerations nor the definition of kidnapping bar conviction for both kidnapping and the other crime as long as the evidence shows the confinement or movement required for kidnapping.

6. Punishment

Kidnapping is usually punished as a *felony*, although some statutes provide a more *severe penalty* for certain *aggravated kidnappings*, *e.g.*, the defendant sought money to release the victim. Other statutes authorize a *reduced penalty* where the defendant releases the victim in a *safe condition*.

X. CRIMES AGAINST THE HABITATION

A. BURGLARY

1. Common Law

Common law burglary is the breaking and entering of the dwelling house of another in the nighttime with the intent to commit a felony.

a. Entry

There must be *actual or constructive* entry. A "constructive" entry occurs when the defendant sends an *innocent* agent into the structure. The slightest intrusion by the defendant or the innocent agent suffices for an entry. The *insertion of an instrument* into the structure is an entry *only* if the instrument is intended for use in *committing the intended felony*.

b. Breaking

Entry must be accomplished by the use of *actual or constructive force to create an opening* of a structure by *trespass* (without the occupant's consent).

(1) Use of Force to Create Opening

Defendant must use at least a small amount of force to create an opening. "Force" also is satisfied by *fraud, threats, or collusion* with someone already inside (*e.g.*, a servant).

(2) Distinguish: Breaking to Leave

If the defendant uses force only to leave the structure, most courts hold a burglary did not occur.

(3) Trespass: Consent to Enter

Because the breaking must be *trespassory*, one who enters with consent is not a burglar. However, the defendant must have had authority to be in the *particular area* of the premises at *the relevant time*. If the defendant exceeds the scope of consent, there may be a trespass.

(4) Causal Relationship

The breaking must be the *means by which the entry is accomplished*.

c. Dwelling House

A dwelling is a place *regularly used to sleep*, even if it is *also* used for business or *other purposes*. Buildings within the *curtilage* (*e.g.*, barns, garages) are also included, as are structures from which the usual inhabitants are *temporarily absent* (*e.g.*, summer cottage).

d. Of Another

A person cannot burglarize her own dwelling. Because the right of *habitation*, rather than ownership, is determinative, a landlord can commit burglary in a tenant's apartment even though she owns the building.

e. In the Nighttime

Nighttime is the period when the countenance of a person cannot be discerned by natural sunlight. Although the breaking and entering must occur at night, the two acts can occur on *different nights*.

f. With the Intent to Commit a Felony

At the *time of entry*, the defendant must *intend to commit a felony* within the structure.

(1) Actual Commission of Felony Not Required

Burglary is complete at the time of entry with the requisite intent. Thus, *abandonment* of the plan once entry is accomplished does *not* preclude a burglary conviction.

(2) "Within" the Structure

Traditionally, the situs of the intended felony must be "in" the structure entered. However, a close connection between the place of entry and the situs of the felonious scheme may be enough.

2. Modern Statutes

Modern statutes have *significantly modified* common law burglary.

a. Structure Need Not Be a Dwelling

The structure entered need *not* be a dwelling. Some statutes include *any* building or a *motor vehicle.*

b. Breaking Not Required

Any entry, however accomplished, is often sufficient, but statutes generally require that the entry be "unlawful" or at least without consent.

c. Time of Entry Irrelevant

Entry in the nighttime is unnecessary, although nighttime burglary is often a more serious offense than daytime burglary.

d. Intent to Commit Misdemeanor Sufficient

The intent element is frequently broadened to include intent to commit a felony or *any theft.*

e. Punishment

Burglary is a felony, but many statutes divide the crime into *degrees*, penalizing certain *aggravated burglaries* (*i.e.*, burglary of an inhabited dwelling or with a deadly weapon) more severely.

(1) Conviction for Both Crimes

If the defendant successfully completes the intended crime, she can be convicted of both the burglary *and* the target crime.

3. Distinguish Home Invasion

New statutory crimes in some jurisdictions, called "home invasion," sometimes require forcible entry of residences for assaultive purposes.

B. ARSON

1. Common Law

Arson is the *malicious burning of the dwelling house of another*. The burglary definitions of "dwelling" and "of another" also apply to arson.

a. Distinguish: "House-Burning"

At common law, arson requires the burning of another person's dwelling. If someone intentionally burns his own dwelling, he commits the *misdemeanor* of house-burning if a risk of burning other houses exists.

b. Burning

Some part of the structure itself *must be physically damaged* by fire. Although the slightest damage (*charring*) will suffice, mere discoloration by heat (*scorching*) is *not* enough.

c. Mens Rea: Malice

The defendant must (i) *intend* the burning, (ii) *know* that it will occur, or (iii) intentionally and without justification or excuse create an *obvious fire hazard* to the structure. Simple *negligence* is *not* enough.

2. Modern Statutes

Arson's scope is commonly broader under modern laws than at common law.

a. **Act and Result Required**

The Model Penal Code basically defines arson as starting a fire with the purpose of destroying a statutorily defined structure. Some modern statutes take this approach, although some expand the crime to include starting a fire with intent to either destroy or merely damage a covered structure. The Model Penal Code also has a less serious offense, "reckless burning or exploding," consisting of starting a fire or causing an explosion and thereby recklessly placing a building or occupied structure of another in danger of destruction or damage. Some modern statutes follow a more traditional approach and require actual damage to the structure.

b. **Culpable Mental State**

Most modern statutes do not require traditional "malice." Those modern statutes defining the offense as starting a fire require a purpose to damage or destroy protected property, and starting the fire itself must be at least reckless. Statutes defining the offense as requiring actual damage to the protected property often require that the defendant had the purpose of causing damage or knowing that damage would occur.

c. **"Burning" Not Required**

Modern statutes based on the Model Penal Code do not require a "burning" in the technical sense of common law arson. Even modern statutes requiring damage to a structure do not require that the damage satisfy the common law definition of a burning. Modern statutes sometimes explicitly provide that arson is committed by fire or by explosion.

d. **Structures Other than Dwellings Protected**

Statutory arson expands the scope of the damaged or targeted building beyond a dwelling. Some modern arson statutes even expand the crime to include damaging motor vehicles and other personal property.

e. **Ownership and Occupancy**

Some modern arson statutes prohibit the burning of defined property, regardless of ownership or occupancy, at least under certain circumstances. Thus, a person commits the offense by burning a structure she owned and occupied.

f. **Arson with Intent to Defraud Insurer**

Modern arson statutes often include certain conduct that is accompanied by an intent to defraud an insurer. "Arson" under the Model Penal Code, for example, includes starting a fire or causing an explosion with the purpose of destroying or damaging any property, with the intent to collect insurance for the loss.

3. **Punishment**

Arson is a felony.

XI. CRIMES AGAINST PROPERTY: ACQUISITION OFFENSES

A. INTRODUCTION

The basic crimes against property involve a wrongful acquisition of property. At common law, these crimes have differing and detailed technical requirements, but the modern trend is to consolidate the common law crimes into a single crime of *theft*.

B. LARCENY

1. Elements

Larceny is a crime against another's *possessory* interest in property. It requires a *trespassory* (wrongful) *taking and asportation of the personal property of another* with the *intent to permanently deprive* the owner thereof.

2. Subject Matter of Larceny: Personal Property

Only *tangible personal property* is the subject of larceny. Realty, fixtures, pets and wild animals, services, and intangibles are generally outside the scope of larceny at common law. Domestic animals such as pigs, chickens, and horses are the subject of larceny.

a. But Note

Severed fixtures, crops, or minerals, and *wild* animals may be the subject of larceny *if* they remain on the victim's property long enough to come into his possession before they are taken by the defendant.

b. Modern Statutes

Today there is a trend to broaden the scope of property subject to larceny to include the wrongful appropriation of realty, intangible property, services, computer programs, etc.

3. Asportation

The property must be *carried away*. The *slightest movement* in a *carrying away motion* is enough. Modern statutes often require only a "taking" or "exercising of control" over property.

4. Taking

The defendant acquires *dominion and control* over the property, either by "taking" the property herself, or by use of an innocent agent. Modern statutes often define larceny-type crimes in terms of an "appropriation" or an "exercise of control," and thus likely apply the common law analysis of a "taking."

5. Requirement of a "Trespass"

The taking is wrongful, *i.e.*, *without effective consent* of the victim.

a. Larceny by Trick

Consent *induced by deception* is ineffective and the defendant may be guilty of larceny by trick. (However, if a defendant defrauds the victim into parting with *title* as well as possession, the crime is only false pretenses, *infra.*)

b. Modern Statutes

Modern statutes typically define "theft" as requiring that the defendant exercise unlawful control over property, with "unlawful" defined as lacking effective consent. Deception or a false promise is "theft" under modern statutes, and the distinctions between larceny, larceny by trick, and false pretenses are abolished.

6. "Of Another"

The property must be taken from the *possession* of someone who had a right to possession *superior* to the defendant's right.

a. "Possession" vs. "Custody"

If the defendant has *possession* at the time of misappropriation, she has *not* taken the property from *another's* possession. Thus, she is not guilty of larceny (*but see* embezzlement, *infra*). If the defendant has only *custody*, her misappropriation is from the possession of another and *may be larceny*.

(1) **Possession Requires Significant Authority**

The distinction between possession and custody generally turns on the *nature of control* vested in the defendant, *i.e.*, the more limited the defendant's authority, the more likely she has only custody. (*But see* the special rules for delivery of property to employees, *infra.*)

b. **Joint Owners**

Because joint owners each have a right to possession, one joint owner cannot commit larceny of the jointly owned property.

c. **Larceny from Spouse**

At common law, spouses are considered as "one," and thus cannot commit larceny of the other's property.

7. **Mens Rea: "Intent to Permanently Deprive"**

Generally, the defendant intends to *permanently deprive* the victim of the property. It is not necessary that the defendant permanently deprive the victim; the controlling factor is defendant's intent *at the time of taking*.

a. **Effect of Intent**

Intent *to keep* is sufficient for larceny; an intent to *borrow and return* the same item does *not* satisfy for larceny. However, if the defendant takes property with the intent of dealing with it in a manner that would create *a substantial risk of permanent loss to the owner*, larceny occurs.

b. **Intent to Sell to Owner**

An intent to sell property back to the owner or an intent to pledge the property will support a larceny conviction on the theory that the action involves a sufficient risk of permanent loss.

c. **Intent to Pay for Property**

A taking with the intent to pay the owner may be larceny *depending on the circumstances*, *e.g.*, whether property was for sale.

d. **Intent to Return Equivalent Property**

There is *no larceny* when the defendant acted with intent to return the *identical* property. However, if the defendant intended to return equivalent property, the result usually turns on the nature of the item (*e.g.*, is it an adequate substitute?).

e. **Intent to Collect Debt**

Cases are split when the defendant takes property in satisfaction of a debt, but knows the property was not specifically owed her under the terms of the debt. However, most courts hold there is *no* larceny when the defendant takes the *specific money* that she reasonably believed was owed her.

f. **Modern Statutes**

Theft statutes generally retain the common law requirement of intent to permanently deprive.

8. **Taking and Intent Must Coincide**

Generally, the defendant must have the requisite intent *at the time of the initial taking* of the property. An *exception* to this requirement applies where the defendant *wrongfully obtains* the property and *afterwards forms the intent* to steal it, *i.e.*, constituting a *continuing trespass* and thus larceny.

9. **Special Problem Areas**

a. **Property Acquired by Finding**

(1) **Abandoned Property**

Abandoned property is not the subject of larceny, because it is not the "property of another."

(2) **Lost or Mislaid Goods**

Lost or mislaid property *can* be the subject of larceny. The taking of such items is *larceny only if* a) the defendant has the intent to steal when first finding and taking possession of the property, and b) the defendant has some clue about the ownership.

b. **Misappropriations by Employee**

(1) **Delivery by Third Party**

An employee who takes delivery of goods for his employer receives *possession* and thus does *not* commit larceny by misappropriating those items, although the employee may be guilty of embezzlement. However, if the employee *first* deposits the goods in a *receptacle* designated by the employer for such goods, the employer has possession and the employee who takes the goods has committed larceny.

(2) **Delivery by Employer**

Ordinarily, an employee who is entrusted with property by her employer receives only *custody*, and thus misappropriation is from the employer's possession and is larceny. However, if the employee has been delegated *considerable discretionary responsibility*, she may have possession and there can be *no* larceny.

C. EMBEZZLEMENT

1. **Statutory Crime**

Generally, embezzlement involves the *fraudulent conversion* of the *property of another* by one who is *already in lawful possession*. Embezzlement is a crime against *ownership.*

2. **Elements of the Crime**

a. **Conversion**

Conversion requires a *serious act of interference* with the owner's rights. Mere movement is not enough.

b. **Property**

Property that is embezzled is often defined more broadly than in larceny statutes (*e.g.*, real property may be the subject of embezzlement).

c. **Of Another**

Regarding issues such as advance payments, commissions, or partnership property, the critical question often is whether the property was transferred to the defendant and thus was his property or whether it remained the property of the victim.

d. **Lawful Possession**

The primary distinguishing characteristic of embezzlement is that the *defendant must be in lawful possession* at the time of conversion.

e. **Fraudulent Intent**

The conversion must be accompanied by the defendant's intent to defraud the victim. Thus, conversion under *claim of right* or with the *intent to return* the *identical* property is *not* embezzlement.

3. **Demand for Return**

Although *not a formal element* of embezzlement, a demand for return of the property facilitates proof of conversion.

D. FALSE PRETENSES

1. **Statutory Crime**

In general, false pretenses is *obtaining title* to the property *by means of a material false representation with intent to defraud* the victim.

2. **Elements of the Crime**

a. **Obtaining Title**

The defendant must obtain *title* to the property by means of the misrepresentation. If only possession is obtained, the crime is not false pretenses, but it may be larceny by trick. Whether the defendant has acquired title or possession usually depends on what the victim intends to convey.

b. **Property**

Broader in scope than larceny, property subject to false pretenses includes title to real property, securities, and sometimes services, credit, etc.

c. **False Representation**

Several traditional restrictions regarding the false representation will suffice for this crime:

(1) **Nature of False Representation**

The misrepresentation is of a *past or existing fact*. Traditionally, a false *promise* (even if made with no intent to perform) is *not* sufficient, *nor* is the failure to correct a false impression harbored by the victim. However, false promises are sufficient under some modern statutes.

(2) **Materiality**

The misrepresentation concerns a *material fact*, *i.e.*, it must be a *controlling inducement* (although it need not be the sole inducing reason) for the victim's decision to part with the property. Additionally, the victim *must in fact have been deceived* and acted on that deceit.

d. **Mens Rea**

The *mens rea* element is twofold: The defendant must a) *know* the representation is false, and b) *intend to defraud* the victim.

3. Special Evidentiary Requirements

Some jurisdictions require additional evidentiary proof (*e.g.*, corroboration, witness to misrepresentation) to prevent conviction based solely on the victim's testimony.

E. ROBBERY

Robbery is *larceny* (*supra*) in which the property is *taken from the victim's person or presence* by means of *violence or intimidation.*

1. Taking from Victim's Person or Presence

Property is within the *presence* of the victim if it is close to him and *within his control* in the sense that he could have prevented its taking had it not been for the defendant's violence or threats.

2. Taking by Violence or Intimidation

a. Violence

If violence is used, *any force* applied to obtain the property or to overcome the victim's immediate resistance is sufficient. But a *pickpocket* does *not* commit robbery because no force is involved. Similarly, *snatching* property from a person's grasp is not robbery where the defendant acts so suddenly that the victim offers no resistance.

b. Intimidation

If *threats* are used, the subject of the threats may be the victim herself, a member of her family, or someone in her presence. Traditionally, the threatened harm must *actually* place the victim *in fear* of *immediate* death, bodily injury, or destruction of the dwelling house, and the fear must be *reasonable.*

(1) Model Penal Code

The Model Penal Code requires that the threat is of serious bodily injury.

c. Violence or Intimidation Used to Take Property

The force or intimidation must occur *before or during the taking* of the property.

3. Possible Defense: Claim of Right

Because robbery is aggravated larceny, if the facts show that the defendant *honestly believed* he is entitled to the property, he does not have the intent to permanently deprive another of property. However, courts do not always recognize this defense because self-help can produce violence.

4. Punishment

Robbery is a common law felony *regardless of the value* of the property taken. It is often classified as *aggravated robbery* if serious bodily harm results, and subjects the defendant to increased penalties.

F. EXTORTION (OR BLACKMAIL)

1. Common Law

Extortion is corrupt collection of an unlawful fee by a public officer under color of office. It is a misdemeanor.

2. Modern Statutes

Statutory revisions significantly broaden the crime of extortion, generally defining it either as *obtaining property* by means of certain *threats or* as the making of certain threats with the *intent to thereby obtain property.*

a. **Type of Threats Required**

The prohibited threats vary among jurisdictions, but typically include threats to injure a person or property, accuse a person of a crime, or expose a secret affecting another.

b. **Limitation: Causation Required**

Under statutes requiring that property is acquired, a showing of a *causal connection* between the threats and the surrender of property is necessary.

c. **Claim of Right Defense**

Some jurisdictions permit as a defense a good faith belief by a defendant that he was legally entitled to the money or property.

d. **Punishment**

Extortion is generally punished as a felony.

G. RECEIVING STOLEN PROPERTY

1. Historical Background

At early common law, there was no criminal liability for receiving stolen property.

2. Elements Under Modern Statutes

The statutory offense consists of *receiving stolen* property *knowing* it to be stolen *with the intent to deprive* the owner thereof.

a. **Stolen Property**

The property must be stolen at the time the defendant receives it. Property obtained by robbery or burglary suffices. However, some statutes do not cover property obtained by embezzlement or false pretenses.

(1) **Property Recovered**

If the owner (or police) recovers the property, it is *no longer "stolen,"* and the defendant thus is *not* guilty of receiving it. He may be liable for an *attempt* to receive stolen property, although some courts find that this involves legal impossibility.

b. **Receiving**

"Receiving" includes actual physical possession of the property, or *exercising control* over it without taking possession.

c. **Knowing Goods Are Stolen**

The defendant's knowledge can be inferred from circumstances (*e.g.*, a disproportionately low purchase price).

3. Conviction of Thief for Receiving Stolen Property

Although one who actually stole the property *cannot* be convicted of receiving it, other participants in the theft can be convicted of receiving the property *from the actual thief.* However, they may *not*, under the better view, be convicted of both offenses.

H. CONSOLIDATION OF ACQUISITION OFFENSES: THEFT

The modern trend is to consolidate many of the acquisition offenses into one crime of theft, consisting of *exercising control* over the *property of another unlawfully* with the *intent to permanently deprive* that person of property.

1. **Statutory Patterns**

Jurisdictions have various approaches toward the crime of theft. Some statutes consolidate the traditional offenses, particularly larceny, false pretenses, and embezzlement, into a *single crime*. Others create *multiple theft crimes* that correspond to the traditional common law crimes.

2. **Punishment**

Theft is typically divided into degrees: grand theft (a felony) and petty theft (a misdemeanor). Grand theft often includes theft of property (or services) above a given value, theft of certain enumerated items (*e.g.*, farm animals), and theft from the person of another.

XII. OFFENSES AGAINST GOVERNMENT

A. TREASON

1. **Ancient Definition**

Under early English law, treason was neither a felony nor misdemeanor, but a crime in a separate class by itself. There were two types: high treason (crimes against the king), and petit treason (*e.g.*, killing of spouse, clergyman, master).

2. **Modern Formulations of the Crime**

Under modern statutes, treason consists of levying war against the United States (or, under state codes, against the individual states), adhering to their enemies, or giving their enemies aid and comfort. Treason is the only crime prohibited by the U.S. Constitution.

3. **Requirements**

A defendant commits treason only if he owes *allegiance* to the prosecuting government, and acts with *intent to betray* that government. Disloyal thoughts alone are not enough; some *overt act* of aid is necessary.

a. **Special Evidentiary Requirement**

Conviction of treason requires either *two witnesses* or the defendant's *confession in open court*.

4. **Misprision of Treason**

This offense consists of the *concealment* of a known treason against another.

B. TREASON-LIKE CRIMES

1. **Rebellion**

It is a federal offense to incite or engage in any rebellion against the United States.

2. **Advocating Overthrow of Government**

It is a federal crime knowingly or willfully to advocate the overthrow or destruction of the government of the United States or any state.

XIII. OFFENSES AGAINST THE ADMINISTRATION OF JUSTICE

A. HINDERING APPREHENSION OR PROSECUTION OF FELON

Modern statutes often make it an *independent crime* to aid or warn another with the intent to hinder that person's apprehension, conviction, or punishment. This crime is sometimes called "accessory after the fact," but unlike the common law "parties' rule" of that name, it does not create liability for the crime committed by the person aided or warned.

B. MISPRISION OF FELONY

At common law, misprision of felony is the failure to report or prosecute one known to have committed a felony. Today, federal law requires some *affirmative act* to conceal a felon.

C. COMPOUNDING A CRIME

1. Common Law

One who agrees for consideration not to prosecute another person for a felony is guilty of the misdemeanor of compounding a crime.

2. Modern Statutes

Modern codes often extend the offense to agreements to forgo prosecution of *any* offense, felony or misdemeanor. There must be an *agreement* and *valuable consideration*.

3. "Settlement" of Crimes

It is unclear whether compounding is committed by a victim of a crime who agrees not to press charges in return for restitution from the offender.

D. PERJURY

1. Common Law

Perjury is the willful giving of a false statement under oath in a judicial proceeding.

2. Modern Statutes

Modern statutes may extend the crime of perjury to *any proceeding* in which the law authorizes the *administration of an oath*. Some statutes require that the false testimony be *material* to the proceeding, *i.e.*, likely to influence its outcome.

3. Special Evidentiary Requirements

Testimony of *two witnesses* is generally required for conviction.

4. Effect of Retraction

Many jurisdictions provide a defense where the defendant retracts false testimony in the same proceeding.

5. Subornation of Perjury

Subornation of perjury consists of intentionally causing another person to commit perjury. The crime is essentially the same under common law and modern statutes: The defendant must have *known* the testimony to be given by the witness is false *and* the perjured testimony must actually have been given.

Exam Strategies

The ultimate issue in a Criminal Law examination question is whether the defendant's conduct creates criminal liability. This involves consideration of three main issues: (i) whether the conduct, on its face, ***constitutes a crime***; (ii) if so, whether there are ***any defenses*** which may be asserted; and (iii) whether there are ***any constitutional bars*** to conviction and punishment. Sometimes a statute defining the crime will be presented in the question, and often there will be statutes relating to possible defenses. However, these statutes may explicitly or implicitly incorporate common law rules and therefore even these questions require you to have a thorough understanding of the common law crimes and defenses.

With this in mind, approach Criminal Law questions using the following basic analytical framework. And don't forget to review the more detailed approaches to specific topics in the Key Exam Issues sections at the beginning of each chapter and the Exam Tips found throughout the Summary.

A. Does Defendant's Conduct, on Its Face, Constitute a Crime?

If the defendant ***actually perpetrated*** the crime, ask:

1. Did his conduct constitute the requisite ***"act,"*** did it meet the general requirements for an "act", ***and*** did it satisfy the specific requirements of the statute creating or defining the crime? (Keep in mind that the criminal "act" may consist of a failure to act when under a legal duty to do so.
    a. If the defendant apparently intended to commit the act constituting the crime but did not actually succeed, consider possible liability for the inchoate crimes—*i.e.,* ***solicitation, attempt,*** and ***conspiracy***.
2. If the crime requires proof of ***certain circumstances*** that must have existed at the time of the defendant's act, can they be shown? (For example, if the defendant is charged with common law rape, it must be established that the victim was not his wife.)
3. Did the defendant, at the time of the act, have the ***mens rea*** or state of mind required by the crime? Ordinarily, at least ***"general intent"*** is required; however, certain crimes also require proof of ***"specific intent."***
    a. Consider the possibility that the crime imposes ***"strict liability"*** and thus does not even require full general intent.
4. Does the definition of the crime require a ***concurrence of the act and mens rea***, and if so, was there such a concurrence?
5. If the crime as defined requires proof of a result, did such result occur and was it ***"caused"*** by the defendant's act? Consider possible problems of ***factual causation***, ***proximate causation*** and any special causation requirements that may be imposed (as in the case of felony murder.

B. Is Defendant Liable for a Crime Committed by the Actions of Another Person?

If a crime was ***perpetrated by another person***, consider whether the defendant may incur liability therefor under one of the following theories:

1. Can the defendant be held liable because of his participation in the events ***before*** the commission of the crime?

a. Under the law of complicity, did the defendant render the sort of assistance or encouragement that would make him, in common law terms, a ***principal in the second degree*** or an ***accessory before the fact***?

b. Is he liable as a ***co-conspirator*** for the crime of another conspirator?

c. If the defendant's guilt is sought to be based on one of the above two theories, consider the possibility that he made a legally effective ***withdrawal*** before the crime was actually perpetrated.

2. Is there a basis for imposing ***vicarious liability***? (This is usually limited to employer-employee cases)

3. Can liability be imposed based on the defendant's participation in the events ***after*** the commission of the crime? Did he act to hinder a felon's apprehension or prosecution and thus qualify as an ***accessory after the fact***?

    a. In addition, consider whether the defendant's post-crime involvement with the actual perpetrator might render him liable for the separate crimes of ***misprision of felony*** or ***compounding a crime***.

C. If Defendant's Conduct Constitutes a Crime, Are There Any Defenses?

1. Do the facts show that the defendant ***lacked the mens rea*** required for the crime? Consider mistake of fact, mistake of law, intoxication, or a mental defect short of insanity that negates intent under the diminished capacity rule.

2. Do the facts show additional matters that prevent conviction? Consider problems of infancy, insanity, and other defenses such as self-defense, defense of others, entrapment, duress, necessity, etc.

D. Are There Any Constitutional Bars to Conviction?

Specifically, you should consider:

1. Does holding the defendant liable violate ***privacy rights***?

2. Is the statute creating the crime ***unconstitutionally vague***?

3. Is the penalty imposed so disproportionate to the conduct involved as to violate the Eighth Amendment ***prohibition against cruel and unusual punishment***?

4. Is there an applicable prohibition against convicting and punishing defendant for ***several crimes arising out of one act***?

Criminal Law

Twenty-First Edition

Chapter One

Introduction

CONTENTS	PAGE

Key Exam Issues

The ultimate issue in your Criminal Law examination question is whether the accused's conduct creates criminal liability. Criminal liability is to be distinguished from other forms of liability: It is liability arising from the commission of a "crime." Although at common law crimes were defined by case law, today criminal law is almost entirely a statutory matter. Your decision as to whether the accused's conduct creates criminal liability necessarily involves consideration of the ***definition of the crime*** according to a ***given statute and/or with reference to the common law***. The prosecution has the burden of proof on all elements of the crime as so defined, and to convict the accused the prosecution must prove those elements beyond a reasonable doubt.

A. In General

1. Crime Defined

A crime is an act or omission prohibited by law for the protection of the public, the violation of which is prosecuted by the state in its own name, and punishable by fine, incarceration, other restrictions upon liberty, or some combination of these. [Model Penal Code § 1.04(1)]

2. Sources of Criminal Law

a. English Common Law

The English common law is a major source of modern criminal law. Definitions of the basic crimes and defenses developed through the English court and became part of the common law adopted in early America. Even where criminal law matters are now statutory, courts often refer to common law cases to clarify the meaning of statutory language.

b. Statutory Codes

Statutes largely govern the current definitions and scope of substantive criminal law. Many jurisdictions use comprehensive criminal codes to define general principles of liability, specific crimes, and defenses. Even jurisdictions without comprehensive codes generally define criminal offenses by statute.

EXAM TIP

Although you may have spent a lot of time in your Criminal Law class discussing the common law elements of a crime, before you start answering a question on your exam according to the common law, be sure to check to see whether the facts of an essay question and the question presented also signal application of a statute. If so, read the statute carefully to see how it defines the crime, especially whether its definition differs from the common law crime. In answering the question, you ***must follow the statute***. Only if the statute does not fully define an element (*e.g.*, it describes the crime as a killing done with "malice aforethought," but doesn't define that term), or if there is no statute in the question at all, should you discuss common law elements.

c. Model Penal Code

The Model Penal Code is a proposed penal code developed and approved by the American Law Institute. Final approval to the Model Penal Code was given in 1962. The Code does not itself constitute "law," because the Institute has no authority to promulgate law. However, the Code has served as the basis for almost all post-1962 revision of state criminal statutory provisions.

B. Classifications of Crimes

1. Introduction

There are several methods of classifying crimes, which may be useful for different purposes.

2. Felonies and Misdemeanors

Traditionally, crimes divided into felonies and misdemeanors; treason was categorized separately. Modern statutes often retain this distinction between felonies and misdemeanors.

a. Common Law Distinction

At common law, misdemeanors were offenses not classified as felonies. Felonies are offenses punishable by total forfeiture of land, goods, or both. Common law felonies include murder, manslaughter, rape, sodomy, mayhem, robbery, arson, burglary, and larceny.

b. Statutory Distinctions

Under modern statutes, felonies are offenses for which a defendant may be sentenced to death or imprisonment for a certain period. [Model Penal Code § 1.04(2) (an offense punishable by imprisonment for more than one year is a felony)]

3. Malum In Se and Malum Prohibitum

Crimes may also be classified as "malum in se" or "malum prohibitum."

a. Malum In Se

Crimes that are ***inherently*** dangerous, bad, or immoral in themselves are regarded as malum in se. Common law felonies, for example, are all *malum in se* because they involve acts that are inherently immoral.

b. Malum Prohibitum

Other acts are made criminal not because they are inherently wrong, but because their prohibition is necessary to regulate the general welfare. For example, the prohibition against driving a motor vehicle on the left side of the road is not based upon the inherent wrongfulness of such conduct, but rather upon the practical need for persons to agree on which side of the road to use.

C. Burden of Proof and Related Matters

1. Prosecution Has Burden

The prosecution has the burden of proof in a criminal proceeding. As a general matter, the prosecution must prove ***all elements*** of a crime ***beyond a reasonable doubt***. This burden of proof has a number of implications, some of them constitutional in nature. [**Victor v. Nebraska,** 511 U.S. 1 (1994)]

2. Constitutional Considerations

a. Due Process Requirement: Proof Beyond a Reasonable Doubt

The prosecution's burden of proof is so important to reducing the risk that an innocent person will be convicted that it is incorporated into the principle of Due Process of law, *i.e.*, it is a federal constitutional requirement. [**In re Winship,** 397 U.S. 358 (1970) (criminal convictions require "proof beyond a reasonable doubt of every fact necessary to constitute the crime with which [defendant] is charged.")]

b. Right to Trial by Jury

The Due Process requirement of proof beyond a reasonable doubt is closely related to a criminal defendant's Sixth Amendment right to jury trial. Together, the two rights require the prosecution to prove to the satisfaction of the jury all elements of the crime beyond a reasonable doubt. [**Sullivan v. Louisiana,** 508 U.S. 275 (1993)]

3. Element of Crime Cannot Be Treated as "Matter of Law"

Treating an element of the crime as a matter of law and withdrawing it from jury consideration violates the defendant's rights to Due Process and to a jury trial. [**United States v. Gaudin,** 515 U.S. 506 (1995)]

e.g. **Example:** In a perjury trial requiring the prosecution to prove that a material false statement was made under oath, the trial judge told the jury that the materiality of the statement was a matter of law for decision by the court (not the jury) and that the statement at issue was material. The judge's statement violated the defendant's federal constitutional rights. [**United States v. Gaudin,** *supra*]

4. Federal Constitutional Right to Jury Determination of Facts

The Due Process Clause of the Sixth Amendment and the notice and jury trial guarantees of the Sixth Amendment give a defendant a right to have the jury unanimously determine facts that increase the maximum and minimum sentence which can be imposed upon conviction. [**Ramos v. Louisiana,** 590 U.S. 83 (2020); **Apprendi v. New Jersey,** 530 U.S. 466 (2000)]

e.g. **Example:** A federal crime prohibiting possession of a firearm is punishable by imprisonment for between 5 and 10 years. But it is punishable by imprisonment for between 10 and 20 years if the defendant acted with the purpose of intimidating another because of race or ethnicity. A defendant has the right to have the jury determine whether the prosecution has proved beyond a reasonable doubt that he acted with the purpose required to increase the maximum sentence. [**Apprendi v. New Jersey,** *supra*]

a. Distinguish: Prior Conviction Increasing Possible Sentence

An exception for prior convictions in *Apprendi* dicta permits a prior conviction to be treated as a sentencing factor that is not an element, even when proof of that prior conviction results in a much longer sentence. [**Almendarez-Torres v. United States,** 523 U.S. 224 (1998)] Several opinions in later cases have debated continuation of the exception. [*See* **Erlinger v. United States,** 602 U.S. 821 (2024)] To enhance a current sentence with multiple prior convictions, a jury can determine beyond a reasonable doubt whether a defendant's past offenses were committed on separate occasions. [**Erlinger v. United States**, *supra*]

b. Distinguish: Facts Affecting Judicial Discretion in Sentencing

A defendant has no right to have a jury decide facts that a judge considers when exercising discretion on the length of the sentence within the statutorily described minimum and maximum time periods. [**United States v. O'Brien,** 560 U.S. 218 (2010) (prohibiting use or carrying of firearm in relation to a crime of violence or drug trafficking crime, the fact that the firearm was a machine gun, bringing into play a higher mandatory minimum sentence, was an element of the offense, to be proved to the jury beyond a reasonable doubt, rather than a sentencing factor)]

5. Defensive Matters: Burdens May Be Imposed on Defendant

If a matter is not an element of the crime but relates instead to a defense, federal constitutional requirements are considerably more flexible.

a. Burden of Going Forward with Evidence

The burden of going forward with evidence on a defensive matter may be placed on the defendant. Using this approach, the defendant must produce evidence supporting the defense before the court instructs the jury on the defensive matter. [**Simopoulos v. Virginia,** 462 U.S. 506 (1983) (state is not required to disprove medical necessity defense on abortion charge until defendant invoked the defense; placing burden of going forward on defendant is permissible, because it did not negate element of the offense)]

b. Burden of Proof or Persuasion

With regard to some and perhaps all traditional defenses, Due Process permits placement of the burden of proving the defense on the defendant, even if that burden is quite high. [**Martin v. Ohio,** 480 U.S. 228 (1987) (in a murder prosecution, the defendant may have the burden of proof by a preponderance on self-defense); **Leland v. Oregon,** 343 U.S. 790 (1952) (the defendant may have the burden of proof beyond a reasonable doubt on insanity)]

6. Presumptions and Inferences Modifying Burden of Proof

Procedural devices such as presumptions and even permissive inferences may so interfere with the prosecution's burden of proof as to violate Due Process.

a. Presumptions: Shifting of Burden of Proof

A presumption concerning elements of the charged crime is likely to have the practical effect of relieving the prosecution of its burden of proof and thus violating Due Process. [**Sandstrom v. Montana,** 442 U.S. 510 (1979)]

e.g. **Example:** At D's trial for "deliberate homicide," the trial judge told the jury that "the law presumes that a person intends the ordinary consequences of his voluntary acts." This was likely understood by the jury as requiring the prosecution to prove only that D voluntarily committed the act that caused death as an ordinary consequence, thus relieving the prosecution of its burden of proving criminal intent. Because the judge's statement also shifts the burden to D to prove that he did not intend the death caused by his voluntary acts, a violation of Due Process occurred. [**Sandstrom v. Montana,** *supra*]

e.g. **Example:** At D's trial for theft by fraud, the judge told the jury that intent to commit theft by fraud is presumed if one who rents property fails to return it within 20 days after expiration of the rental contract and after demand for return by the owner. That statement violated the Due Process mandate that the prosecution prove the required intent to defraud. [**Carella v. California,** 491 U.S. 263 (1989)]

b. Permissive Inferences: Ultimate Fact Must "More Likely than Not" Flow from Proved Fact

A "permissive inference" rather than a presumption is used if a jury is told that it may, but need not, infer one fact from another. A permissive inference does not violate Due Process if the ultimate fact (the fact to be inferred) more likely than not flows from the fact that the prosecution proved. [**County Court of Ulster County v. Allen,** 442 U.S. 140 (1979)]

e.g. **Example:** At D's trial for possession of a firearm, the jury was told that it could—but need not—infer from the presence of the firearm in a car occupied by D that D possessed the firearm. While this was only a permissible inference rather than a presumption, it did not violate Due Process because the ultimate fact (D's possession of the firearm) was more likely than not to flow from the proved fact (the presence of the firearm in a car occupied by D). [**County Court of Ulster County v. Allen,** *supra*]

7. Homicide Prosecutions: Allocating Burdens Regarding Provocation or Its Equivalent

In two confusing cases, the Supreme Court has addressed constitutional limits on the characterization of and burdens of proof regarding provocation, which traditionally distinguishes voluntary manslaughter from murder.

a. Burden of Proof on Provocation if Malice Is "Presumed"

Due Process is denied in a murder prosecution if the judge tells the jury that the malice aforethought required for murder is "presumed" from the killing of the victim by the defendant, and that the defendant must prove that he acted in the heat of passion on sudden provocation in order to reduce the crime from murder to voluntary manslaughter. [**Mullaney v. Wilbur,** 421 U.S. 684 (1975) ("the Due Process Clause requires the prosecution to prove beyond a reasonable doubt the absence of the heat of passion on sudden provocation when the issue is properly in a homicide case.")]

b. Burden of Proof on "Extreme Emotional Disturbance" Under Modern Statutory Scheme

When murder requires the prosecution to prove intent to kill beyond a reasonable doubt, Due Process is ***not*** violated by placing on the defendant the burden of proving by a preponderance of the evidence that he killed under the influence of an extreme emotional disturbance for which there was a reasonable explanation or excuse, which would reduce the killing from murder to manslaughter. [**Patterson v. New York,** 432 U.S. 197 (1977)]

(1) Rationale

If murder requires proof of a meaningful *mens rea*, as in *Patterson*, additional facts such as heat of passion/provocation or extreme emotional disturbance (that distinguish murder from manslaughter) are "defensive facts" on which the burden of proof can be placed on the defendant. In *Mullaney*, however, the *mens rea* required for murder was "presumed," and the facts distinguishing manslaughter from murder were not really defensive because the prosecution was not required initially to make any meaningful showing.

Chapter Two

The Criminalization Decision

CONTENTS	PAGE

Key Exam Issues

Exam questions occasionally call for discussion of the policy considerations that make certain conduct criminal. Although you should have no problem justifying the criminalization of murder or robbery, the wisdom of criminalizing less serious crimes (*e.g.*, possession of marijuana) may not be as clear. In addressing general examination questions concerning the wisdom of criminalizing conduct, you should ask the following questions:

1. ***Does criminalization of the conduct further any social interests,*** and if so, how?
2. ***What "costs" of criminalizing conduct must be weighed against those benefits***, and what is the probable result of a ***balancing of those costs and benefits***?

A. Justifications for Punishment

1. Introduction

Clearly, when specific conduct constitutes a crime, criminal punishment can be imposed upon those who engage in the proscribed behavior. But what are the justifications for punishing those who violate the criminal law?

2. Specific Prevention

One theory often advanced is that of "specific" prevention, *i.e.,* punishment may prevent the offender from committing future crimes. Specific prevention may work in several ways:

a. "Specific" Deterrence

Imposing punishment may cause the offender to fear the penalty for future crimes and thus deter her from committing them.

b. Incapacitation

Punishment also may involve restraints on the offender's liberty, thus making it virtually impossible for her to engage in criminal behavior during the period of restraint.

c. Treatment

Punishment in the form of restraints also enables authorities to treat and perhaps rehabilitate the offender. (Treatment differs from specific deterrence because the purpose of the former is to alter the offender's basic motivations, rather than to frighten her into relinquishing the commission of crimes that she may still desire to commit.)

3. General Prevention

Penalizing offenders may also prevent the commission of crimes by others, *i.e.*, so-called "general" prevention. For instance:

a. "General" Deterrence

Punishing the offender may have a "general deterrent" effect, by indirectly warning others to anticipate similar punishment if they violate the criminal law.

b. "Moralizing" Effect

In addition, punishment may educate others that the violation of criminal statutes is morally wrong. Apart from the fear of punishment, such persons might abstain from criminal conduct because of their unwillingness to engage in morally reprehensible behavior.

c. "Social Solidarity" Effect

Some argue that social order requires a widespread consensus that criminal behavior is wrong and that subjecting offenders to punishment will maintain this consensus. Otherwise, the "social solidarity" encouraged by criminal punishment will dissolve and people will regard themselves as free to violate other criminal laws.

d. Channeling Resentment

Moreover, some feel so strongly that persons who violate criminal statutes should be punished that they will inflict punishment themselves if the law does not. Therefore, punishment pursuant to law is necessary to prevent others from committing additional criminal offenses by taking the law into their own hands.

4. Retribution

Punishing an offender is justified simply because she has committed a wrongful act. Thus, retribution indicates that the commission of an offense itself justifies punishment.

a. Distinguish: The "Social Solidarity" Effect

Unlike the social solidarity theory, which urges that punishment of what the community regards as morally wrong in order to maintain general order and thus prevent future criminal conduct, the retribution notion rests solely on the premise that what the offender did was "wrong."

A SUMMARY OF JUSTIFICATIONS FOR PUNISHMENT		
SPECIFIC PREVENTION	**GENERAL PREVENTION**	**RETRIBUTION**
Specific deterrence: offender's fear of punishment deters future criminal acts	***General deterrence:*** Fear of punishment deters others from committing criminal acts	***Punishment*** of the offender is justified because she has committed a wrongful act
Incapacitation: Offender cannot commit crimes while imprisoned	***Moralizing effect:*** People may refrain from committing a criminal act that is viewed as immoral	
Treatment: Rehabilitation of offender prevents future acts of misconduct	***Social solidarity effect:*** Social order requires a consensus that criminal behavior is wrong, and subjecting offenders to punishment maintains this consensus	
	Channeling resentment: Other members of society will not feel the need to "take the law into their own hands"	

B. Costs vs. Benefits

1. Benefits

The benefits from criminalizing conduct depend on the extent to which the social interests justifying criminalization will be furthered. As mentioned, the interests that might be furthered are prevention of crime and retribution.

a. Prevention

Whether criminalization prevents offenders and others from future criminal acts through general or specific prevention may depend on whether the conduct is of a type likely to be deterred or whether the offender herself is likely to be rehabilitated during imprisonment.

b. Retribution

Is the conduct sufficiently "wrong" that the retributive notion is significantly valuable?

2. Costs

Obviously, criminalization has direct costs (*e.g.,* costs of law enforcement, prosecution, imprisonment, etc.). Besides direct costs, criminalization costs affect those who commit the acts. For instance, criminalization may subject offenders to physical discomfort as well as stigmatize them in a way that produces a long-term disability.

a. Incidental Costs

Enforcement of criminal sanctions may also involve incidental costs, such as improper searches and seizures.

b. Impact on Society

Apart from the effect on the offenders themselves, criminalization of a widespread activity may tend to bring the law into disrespect among a significant portion of the population. In such cases, the crucial question becomes whether the benefits are worth the sacrifices.

Chapter Three

Basic Legal Limits upon Criminal Law

CONTENTS	PAGE

Key Exam Issues

On your exam you may encounter a defendant who appears to be guilty of a crime under the definition of the crime charged and who is without any specific defense available to him. Don't give up on the defendant just yet because there may be a basic prohibition against convicting or punishing him. Most of these prohibitions are ***constitutional rules***, and most bar any form of criminal conviction or punishment. Sometimes, however, only particular penalties are prohibited. The last doctrine discussed in *this* chapter considers a bar to conviction (or perhaps only punishment) for multiple offenses that may be based on statutes or case law.

On your exam, remember, before concluding that defendant can be convicted and a particular penalty imposed, always consider whether any of the following bars to conviction or punishment exist:

1. Would holding defendant criminally liable violate his constitutional ***right of privacy***?
2. Is the statute that creates the crime ***unconstitutionally vague*** and therefore in violation of Due Process?
3. Is the criminal penalty to be imposed inherently impermissible or so disproportionate to the conduct as to violate the Eighth Amendment prohibition against ***cruel and unusual punishment***?
4. If by an act or course of conduct the defendant may have committed what are technically several crimes, is ***conviction and punishment for several crimes*** permissible? Is there evidence of legislative intent to allow multiple liability for identical or related criminal acts? Are there statutory or constitutional bars to multiple liability?

A. Constitutional Right of Privacy

1. In General: Right of Privacy

No right of privacy is expressly mentioned in the United States Constitution, although some state constitutions provide such a right. Nevertheless, the Supreme Court has found in various provisions of the Constitution a federal right of privacy. Certain conduct is protected by the right of privacy, and a person may not be convicted of a crime for engaging in such protected conduct. [**Griswold v. Connecticut,** 381 U.S. 479 (1965); *see* detailed discussion in Constitutional Law Summary]

2. Application

The following examples illustrate the impact of the right of privacy on substantive criminal law:

a. Contraceptive Information

A state statute making it a criminal offense to use or assist others in using any drug or medical instrument to prevent conception violates married couples' right of privacy. [**Griswold v. Connecticut,** *supra*]

b. Private Possession of Obscenity

Although obscenity does not enjoy First Amendment protection, a person's right of privacy means that one cannot be convicted of a crime for possession of obscene materials in one's own home. [**Stanley v. Georgia,** 394 U.S. 557 (1969)]

c. Private Participation in Homosexual Activity

The constitutional right of privacy protects an adult person's consensual and private homosexual activity. Such activity cannot be made criminal. [**Lawrence v. Texas,** 539 U.S. 558 (2003)]

B. Due Process Prohibition Against Vagueness

1. General Rule: Criminal Statute Must Be Precise

The Due Process Clauses of the Fifth and Fourteenth Amendments prohibit enforcement of statutes defining crimes, if those statutes are impermissibly vague. [**Winters v. New York,** 333 U.S. 507 (1948)] "In our constitutional order, a vague law is no law at all." [**United States v. Davis,** 588 U.S. 445 (2019)]

a. Rationale

The Due Process rule serves in part to assure that persons can tell, by examining the statutes, whether the conduct anticipated will be criminal. Thus, it assures ***notice***, and also requires that statutes be sufficiently precise to ***discourage arbitrary enforcement.***

2. Criteria for Evaluating Vagueness

A criminal statute is unconstitutionally vague if it fails to define the offense with sufficient definiteness:

(i) So that ordinary people can understand what conduct is prohibited; or

(ii) So as to discourage arbitrary and discriminatory application.

[**Johnson v. United States,** 576 U.S. 591 (2015); **Kolender v. Lawson,** 461 U.S. 352 (1983)] Void-for-vagueness challenges occur in two instances: 1) when the challenge is to the statutory language "on the face" of the statute, even before the statute is applied to specific facts, and 2) when the challenge is from parties against whom the statute in question has been applied. [**Coates v. Cincinnati,** 402 U.S. 611 (1971); *see also* **United States v. Bell,** 755 F.Supp.3d 992 (E.D.Mich. 2024) (there is no authority "for the proposition that a *judicial ruling* pertaining to a statute can make the statute unconstitutionally vague")]

a. Application: No Notice

A statute provided that "any person not engaged in any lawful occupation, who is known to be a member of any gang consisting of two or more persons, is guilty of a crime." The statute is unenforceable because the meaning of "gang" is so unclear that it is virtually impossible to determine in advance which persons are within the scope of the statute. [**Lanzetta v. New Jersey,** 306 U.S. 451 (1939) (everyone is entitled to be informed about what the law requires or forbids)]

A public vagrancy statute is vague by failing "to give a person of ordinary intelligence fair notice that his conduct is forbidden by the statute" and because it "encourage[s] arbitrary and erratic enforcement." [**Papachristou v. City of Jacksonville,** 405 U.S. 156 (1972)] The Court invalidated the Armed Career Criminal Act ("ACCA"), which defined "violent felonies" or "crime of violence," because they failed both prongs set out by *Papachristou.* [**Sessions v. Dimaya,** 584 U.S. 148 (2018); **Johnson v. United States,** 576 U.S. 591 (2015)] The Court also rejected any defense of ACCA's language based on the existence of *some* crimes that clearly fall within its scope.

b. Application: Opportunity for Arbitrary and Discriminatory Enforcement

A local ordinance created an offense consisting of proof that: (i) the defendant did not promptly obey a police officer's order to disperse; (ii) the police officer observed the defendant and at least one other person loitering—*i.e.*, remaining in any one place with no apparent purpose—in a public place; (iii) the officer had reason to believe at least one of the persons was a criminal street gang member; and (iv) the officer ordered all of the persons to disperse and leave the area. The definition of loitering is so imprecise that it gives police officers absolute discretion to determine what activities constitute loitering and thus can serve as the basis for an order and prosecution. Consequently, the ordinance fails to provide constitutionally required minimal guidelines to govern law enforcement and is constitutionally vague. [**City of Chicago v. Morales,** 527 U.S. 41 (1999)]

3. Vagueness Evaluated "as Applied"

Generally, a defendant can challenge only whether a criminal statute is vague ***as applied to the facts of the defendant's case.*** This means the defendant must show that the statute failed to give him notice that the conduct for which he is being prosecuted was prohibited. Such a defendant cannot argue that the statute would deny notice to some other hypothetical defendant. However, if a criminal statute covers a considerable amount of constitutionally protected conduct (such as speech), the courts will evaluate its vagueness "***on its face***" rather than as applied to the defendant's situation. Furthermore, when a criminal statute infringes on constitutionally protected rights and its tendency to encourage arbitrary application by police "permeates [its] text," a defendant can attack it on its face. [**City of Chicago v. Morales,** *supra*]

e.g. **Example:** The Chicago Gang Congregation Ordinance (*see* above) infringes on others' constitutionally protected right of freedom of movement (and to remain in a public place of choice). Its vagueness permeates its text. Consequently, it was subject to ***facial attack*** on vagueness grounds by a defendant. The defendant did not have to show it was constitutionally deficient as applied to him. [**City of Chicago v. Morales,** *supra*]

4. Curing Vagueness by "Prior Knowledge or Intent"

If a statute requires that an act be committed "willfully" or "knowingly," it is probably sufficient that the defendant knew that he was committing the act, even if he did not know it was illegal. [**Bryan v. United States,** 524 U.S. 184 (1998)] In a case prosecuted under the Controlled Substance Analogue Enforcement Act of 1986, the prosecution must establish that a defendant knew he was dealing with a substance regulated under the Act.

Knowledge can be proved by showing he knew the substance was controlled (whether or not he knew its identity) or evidence that he knew which analogue he was distributing, even if he did not know it was controlled. [**McFadden v. United States,** 576 U.S. 186 (2015)] Any person denied actual notice by a statute's imprecision, *i.e.*, any person left uncertain about whether a statute applied to their situation, cannot be convicted and thus were not harmed by the statute's vagueness. [**Screws v. United States,** 325 U.S. 91 (1945)] In a close case, however, a prior intent or knowledge requirement may mitigate a statute's imprecision. [**Posters 'N Things, Ltd. v. United States,** 511 U.S. 513 (1994)] e.g. **Example:** It was not necessary that proprietors of a head shop intend that the drug paraphernalia sold be used in conjunction with illegal drugs, as long as they knew that it was likely that illegal drugs would be used. [**Posters 'N Things, Ltd. v. United States,** *supra*]

e.g. **Example:** A statute makes it a crime to "willfully" deprive a person of federal rights while acting under state law. The phrase "federal rights" may be vague, but the requirement of willfulness permits conviction only if the defendant understood that his conduct violated what he knew was a federal right of the victim. Any accused harmed by the vagueness (and thus uncertain as to whether the victim's federal rights were violated) could not be convicted. [**Screws v. United States,** *supra*]

C. Cruel and Unusual Punishment

1. In General

The Eighth Amendment prohibition against cruel and unusual punishment, binding on the states by virtue of the Fourteenth Amendment, imposes a number of different limits upon criminal law. Some of these limits are discussed below, *and see infra,* p. 25, considering whether a status can be made a crime.

2. Inherently Impermissible Punishments

The Eighth Amendment "draw[s] its meaning from the evolving standards of decency that mark the progress of a maturing society." Under this standard, some punishments are so ***inherently*** barbaric or degrading, *i.e.*, disproportionate to defendants' culpability, as to preclude them from ever being used. This doctrine likely bars the use of torture, death by painful and lingering methods, or expatriation (*i.e.,* forfeiture of citizenship). [**Wilkerson v. Utah,** 99 U.S. 130 (1878); **Trop v. Dulles,** 356 U.S. 86 (1958)]

3. Disproportionate Penalties

Some penalties are not inherently cruel and unusual but are nevertheless prohibited in particular cases or particular categories of cases, because they are so ***grossly and outrageously disproportionate*** to the defendant's conduct. [**Miller v. Alabama,** 567 U.S. 460 (2012); **Weems v. United States,** 217 U.S. 349 (1910)]

e.g. **Example:** D was convicted of falsifying entries in a public record. A sentence of 15 years' imprisonment at hard labor carrying chains as well as perpetual disqualification from political rights was so excessive that it violated the Eighth Amendment. [**Weems v. United States,** *supra*]

a. Disproportionately Long Prison Terms

In certain exceptional situations, the Court has held that a prison term is so excessive that it violates the prohibition against cruel and unusual punishment. [**Solem v. Helm,** 463 U.S. 277 (1983)] However, because of the absence of objective standards for judging excessiveness, an Eighth Amendment violation is seldom found. [**Rummel v. Estelle,** 445 U.S. 263 (1980)]

(1) Relevant Considerations

In deciding whether a penalty is unconstitutionally disproportionate, the courts consider: (i) the gravity of the offense committed and the harshness of the penalty imposed; (ii) sentences imposed on other offenders in the same jurisdiction; and (iii) sentences imposed upon others committing the same offense in other jurisdictions. [**Solem v. Helm,** *supra*] The latter two parts of the *Solem* test appear to fall outside the Court's current disproportionality decision-making. [**Harmelin v. Michigan,** 501 U.S. 957 (1991)]

e.g. **Example:** A sentence of life imprisonment without the possibility of parole imposed under a recidivist statute for several minor offenses violated the Eighth Amendment, because no such penalty could be imposed for the crime in 48 of the 50 states. [**Solem v. Helm,** *supra*]

cf. **Compare:** No violation occurred when a defendant convicted of theft of $120 worth of property was sentenced to life imprisonment because of his two prior convictions for similar offenses, though he was eligible for parole after serving 12 years. [**Rummel v. Estelle,** *supra*] No violation occurred when a defendant was sentenced to life imprisonment without parole after his conviction for possessing 672 grams of cocaine. [**Harmelin v. Michigan,** *supra*]

(2) Mandatory Life Without Parole for Juveniles

A statutory requirement of life imprisonment without the possibility of parole constitutes cruel and unusual punishment when applied to a defendant who committed a crime as a juvenile, *i.e.*, when he was under 18 years of age. [**Graham v. Florida,** 560 U.S. 48 (2010) (juvenile convicted of nonhomicide crime). **Miller v. Alabama**, *supra* went even further: a State may not impose a mandatory life-without-parole sentence on a murderer under 18, because a sentencer must have discretion to impose a lesser sentence on a juvenile after considering "the mitigating qualities of youth." Moreover, *Miller* applies retroactively to state cases on collateral review, because it announced a substantive rule of constitutional law. [**Montgomery v. Louisiana,** 577 U.S. 190 (2016)]

Caveat: A sentence of life without parole imposed on a defendant for a crime committed when the defendant was under 18 years of age may be permissible if it is not mandatory, *i.e.*, the trial judge uses her discretion regarding sentence to decide that the sentence is appropriate under the facts of the particular case.

4. Death Penalty

a. General Rule: Death Penalty Not Prohibited

The death penalty is not inherently excessive and therefore may, pursuant to a proper procedure, be imposed and carried out on a defendant. Death penalty procedures must assure evenhanded determinations about whether the penalty is appropriate in each case. [**Gregg v. Georgia,** 428 U.S. 153 (1976); **Tuilaepa v. California,** 512 U.S. 967 (1994)] The prosecution must prove beyond a reasonable doubt at least one statutory aggravating circumstance in order to limit the death penalty to the most serious homicides, *e.g.*, death of a law enforcement official. [**Romano v. Oklahoma,** 512 U.S. 1 (1994)] In the absence of at least one aggravating circumstance, a judge cannot impose a death sentence. Generally, a capital defendant has the right to present mitigation evidence. [**California v. Brown,** 479 U.S. 538 (1987)]

b. Death Penalty Sometimes Disproportionate

In non-homicide cases, the death penalty is so disproportionate to the offense that it violates the Eighth Amendment. [**Coker v. Georgia,** 433 U.S. 584 (1977); **Enmund v. Florida,** 458 U.S. 782 (1982)]

(1) Sexual Assaults

The death penalty is unconstitutionally disproportionate for the rape of an adult woman, even if serious physical harm was caused to the victim. [**Eberheart v. Georgia,** 433 U.S. 917 (1977)] Death is also unconstitutionally disproportionate for the rape of a child, at least when the defendant did not intend to kill the victim. [**Kennedy v. Louisiana,** 554 U.S. 945 (2008)]

(2) "Non-Shooter" in Murder

Under complicity rules and the co-conspirator rule, a person may be criminally responsible for a murder directly committed by someone else. However, the Eighth Amendment limits the imposition of the death penalty upon such "non-shooters" only if the person's participation in the offense was "major" and the person participated either with the intention to cause death or with "extreme indifference" to whether death would result from the conduct. [**Tison v. Arizona,** 481 U.S. 137 (1987)]

(3) Young Murderers

A murderer who was younger than 18 years of age at the time of the crime cannot be executed for that crime as a matter of Eighth Amendment law. [**Roper v. Simmons,** 543 U.S. 551 (2005)]

(4) Mentally Impaired Offenders

The death penalty is constitutionally excessive for an offender shown to have an intellectual disability when he committed the offense. [**Atkins v. Virginia,** 536 U.S. 304 (2002)] An intellectual disability diagnosis requires consideration of the defendant's intellectual-functioning deficits (*e.g.*, roughly an IQ below 70), the inability to learn basic skills and adjust behavior to changing circumstances, and these deficits began when the defendant was a juvenile. [**Hall v. Florida,** 572 U.S. 701 (2014)]

c. "Insane" Prisoner Cannot Be Executed

A defendant sentenced to death who is, at the time of the proposed execution, "insane" cannot under the Eighth Amendment be executed while he remains insane. In this context, a defendant is probably insane if the defendant does not realize the fact of an impending execution or the reason for it. [**Ford v. Wainwright,** 477 U.S. 399 (1986)]

d. Statutory Standards Must Not Be Vague

Statutory standards for determining which convicted defendants are eligible for the death penalty and who will be sentenced to death violate the Eighth Amendment if those standards are not sufficiently precise. [**Maynard v. Cartwright,** 486 U.S. 356 (1988)]

e.g. **Example:** A statute permitting the jury to consider whether murder was "especially heinous, atrocious, or cruel" was so vague as to violate the Eighth Amendment. [**Maynard v. Cartwright,** *supra*]

e. Challenging the Execution Method

Persona may challenge the method of execution. [**Baze v. Rees,** 553 U.S. 35 (2008)] and [**Glossip v. Gross,** 576 U.S. 863 (2015)] govern any Eighth Amendment facial or as-applied challenge to methods of execution. A successful claim must show that the method creates a risk of severe pain and that the risk is substantial compared to known and available alternatives. [**Baze v. Rees**, *supra* (upholding three-drug injection method)]

D. Multiple Liability for Identical or Related Criminal Acts

1. In General: Overlapping Criminal Liability

Criminal defendants may incur overlapping liability in several ways: (i) the same act may constitute several crimes (*e.g.,* a person commits a murder by activity that also constitutes a battery); (ii) different acts constituting different crimes may be committed closely together and for related reasons (*e.g.,* a person commits a burglary as a means of accomplishing a larceny or theft inside the entered premises, although the entry constituting the burglary is different from the act constituting the theft of the property); (iii) different acts committed closely together and perhaps for related reasons may be prosecuted as several commissions of the same crime (*e.g.,* a person takes a homeowner's TV from the house, puts it in that homeowner's pickup truck and drives away, so the act of taking and carrying the TV is different from the act of stealing the truck). Can the defendant in (i) be convicted of both murder and battery, the one in (ii) of both burglary and larceny, and the one in (iii) of two larcenies?

a. Policy Concerns with Overlapping Liability

Some object to convicting and punishing defendants for all offenses technically committed by arguing that this permits imposition of liability and punishment disproportionate to defendants' actual blameworthiness. A thief who steals after entering a dwelling to find the item, for example, may not be twice as blameworthy as another thief who steals a similar item he finds in a public place. Yet the first thief is subject to conviction for two crimes and to twice as long a prison term. Some courts, as a result of these concerns, have sought ways to limit criminal liability for one act or related acts.

2. Common Law Doctrine of Merger

At common law, if the same act constituted both a felony and a misdemeanor, the misdemeanor is regarded as "merging" into the felony and there can be no conviction for the misdemeanor. However, this doctrine does not apply if ***both*** crimes were felonies or misdemeanors. Nor does it apply if the two crimes were based upon ***different conduct*** or acts. [**Lovgren v. Byrne,** 787 F.2d 857 (3d Cir. 1986) (rejecting common law doctrine in this case)] The doctrine of merger as it was known and applied at common law is no longer applied in American jurisdictions.

3. Unit of Prosecution Analysis

In situations of the third sort distinguished above, the first question must be whether several convictions are permitted given the unit of prosecution of the charged crime. The unit of prosecution is the standard the legislature intended to be applied to determine whether one or more commissions of the crime arises from a single course of conduct.

a. Relevant Considerations

If the unit of prosecution is a matter of legislative intent, the words used to define the crime are important. [**Mason v. Commonwealth,** 636 S.E.2d 480 (Va.App. 2006) (where crime is defined as possession of "a picture" depicting child sexual activity, a unit of prosecution was each picture and the defendant could be convicted for each picture found in his possession)] Some courts apply a "rule of lenity" in construing criminal statutes, under which crimes will be construed as providing for a narrow unit of prosecution unless the legislature has unambiguously provided otherwise. [**Bell v. United States,** 349 U.S. 81 (1955) (federal Mann Act criminalizing transportation of any woman for immoral purposes did not permit conviction of one crime for each of several women transported together)]

b. Continuing Crimes: One Crime for Each Course of Conduct

Some crimes are construed as "continuing" crimes, *i.e.*, a course of conduct, even if it consists of distinguishable acts, constitutes commission of only one crime. For example, assume that a criminal suspect escapes from police custody. If the police give chase and apprehend the suspect several blocks away, might multiple charges be brought for the crime of "eluding a police officer?" [*Compare* **People v. McMinn,** 412 P.3d 551 (Colo.App. 2013) (permitting multiple charges of eluding a police officer, even from a single episode, if there were discrete acts of eluding with each constituting a new volitional departure in the defendant's course of conduct), *with* **Washington v. State,** 28 A.3d 164 (Md.App. 2011) (prohibiting eluding charges that were for same offense even though defendant tried to escape police officer in a vehicle and then on foot)]

c. "Single Larceny" Rule

Larceny is traditionally defined as only a single crime of taking multiple items of property at or about the same time from the same general location, *i.e.*, especially if the items are taken pursuant to a single impulse and in the execution of a single general criminal plan. [**Millard v. Commonwealth,** 539 S.E.2d 84 (Va.App. 2000)]

d. Homicide and Assaultive Crimes: One Crime for Each Victim

The homicide offenses, assault, battery and related crimes are generally construed as permitting one conviction for each victim killed, injured or threatened, even if this is the result of a single indivisible act of the accused. [**Albrecht v. State,** 658 A.2d 1122 (Md.App. 1995)] Thus, if a defendant fired only one shot which struck and killed two victims, the defendant can be convicted of two homicide crimes. [*Compare* **Hennemeyer v. Commonwealth,** 580 S.W.2d 211 (Ky. 1979) (six gunshots fired at police during a chase resulted in six different counts of reckless endangerment)]

4. Fifth Amendment Prohibition Against Double Jeopardy

The Fifth Amendment bar against double jeopardy applies primarily to repeated prosecutions for the same or possibly related crimes. Sometimes, therefore, double jeopardy may bar a second prosecution (and a conviction) for a crime where the defendant has already been tried and convicted of a related offense. [**Harris v. Oklahoma,** 433 U.S. 682 (1977); *and see* detailed discussion in the Criminal Procedure Summary] It also provides some, but limited, protection against overlapping criminal liability when the prosecution seeks multiple convictions in a single proceeding.

a. Possible Multiple Convictions and Cumulative Punishment in One Proceeding Based on Legislative Intent

Overlapping liability for several crimes in the three situations described above violates federal double jeopardy when the prosecution brings the charges in a single proceeding only if the legislature did not intend to permit liability for multiple crimes. [**Missouri v. Hunter,** 459 U.S. 359 (1983); **Whalen v. United States,** 445 U.S. 684 (1980)]

e.g. **Example:** D robbed V using a pistol. D was convicted of robbery and, in addition, of the separate crime of using a dangerous weapon in the commission of a crime. Consecutive prison terms were imposed for the crimes. Because the legislature intended to permit punishments for both crimes on the basis of the same conduct (using a gun to obtain property from another), no double jeopardy as prohibited by the federal Constitution occurred. [**Missouri v. Hunter,** *supra*]

(1) Rationale

Why does double jeopardy impose no more rigorous limits on multiple convictions? Partly, no objective standards exist for determining when multiple convictions result in constitutionally offensive disproportionality. Further, legislatures could circumvent any constitutional limits by manipulating penalty provisions, *e.g.*, by providing that robbery is punishable by X years but if a gun was used it is punishable by 2X years.

b. Determining Legislative Intent: *Blockburger* Rule

In the absence of a clearly expressed legislative intent to permit multiple punishments, the *Blockburger* rule applies. [**Blockburger v. United States,** 284 U.S. 299 (1932)]

(1) Overlapping Liability for Multiple Commissions of the Same Offense

If a defendant is prosecuted for committing multiple related commissions of the same crime and that crime is not a "continuing crime," conviction for all is permissible under the *Blockburger* rule if each commission is based on a distinguishable act. For example, if a defendant shoots and kills multiple victims at or about the same time, the defendant can be prosecuted and convicted of all the homicides because each homicide involved a different victim.

(2) Overlapping Liability for Multiple Crimes Committed by a Single Act

If a defendant is prosecuted for two crimes committed by the same act, the defendant may be convicted of both offenses under *Blockburger* as long as ***proof of each crime*** requires proof of an ***additional fact*** that the other does not.

e.g. **Example:** D made one sale of morphine. He was convicted of two crimes, one consisting of sale of morphine not in its original tax-stamped package and the other of sale of morphine not pursuant to a written order. This does not violate double jeopardy. Although the convictions were based on the same act, each crime required proof of at least one element that the other crime did not. [**Blockburger v. United States,** *supra*]

(3) Overlapping Liability for Multiple Crimes Related in Their Commission

If a defendant is prosecuted for two crimes committed at or about the same time, the legislature is presumed under *Blockburger* to have intended to prohibit punishing a defendant for two crimes ***unless each crime*** requires proof of an ***additional fact*** that the other does not.

Example: D was convicted in federal court of rape and felony murder on the basis of the victim's death that occurred during the rape. Consecutive sentences were imposed. Under the *Blockburger* test, when only one crime requires proof that the other crime does not, it is assumed that Congress intended no double punishment; *i.e.*, here the felony murder requires proof of the victim's death during commission of a rape, but proof of the rape does not require proof of any fact that the felony murder (consisting of rape and the causing of death in that rape) does not. In effect, the felony murder is the greater included offense, and the rape is the lesser included offense. In the absence of any evidence that Congress intended a different result, convictions for both felony murder and the predicate rape felony violated D's federal constitutional rights. [**Whalen v. United States,** *supra*]

(4) Caveat: Direct Evidence of Legislative Intent

The *Blockburger* rule is only a means of determining legislative intent. ***Direct evidence of legislative intent*** to permit conviction and punishment for multiple offenses is constitutionally permissible, even if each crime does not require proof of at least one fact that the other does not. [**Missouri v. Hunter**, *supra*]

5. State Double Jeopardy Prohibitions

Many state constitutions contain prohibitions against double jeopardy similar in terminology to the Fifth Amendment of the United States Constitution. The state provisions are sometimes construed by state courts as giving defendants broader protection against multiple prosecution than is afforded by the federal Constitution.

a. "Multiple Interests" Approach: Alaska Constitution

The Alaska constitutional prohibition against double jeopardy has been construed as barring multiple punishment for several crimes arising out of the same criminal event or episode unless the different crimes were designed to protect different social interests. [**Whitton v. State,** 479 P.2d 302 (Alaska 1970)]

Example: D pleaded no contest to sexual assault and official misconduct. Both crimes were designed to protect the "legislature's policy of not allowing police officers to engage in any sexual activity with a person who is in their custody." Per *Whitton*, punishing the defendant for violating both criminal statutes offended the Alaska Constitution's prohibition against double jeopardy. [**Fedolfi v. State,** 456 P.3d 999 (Alaska App. 2019)]

6. Statutory Bars to Multiple Conviction or Punishment

In some jurisdictions, statutes prohibit defendants from being convicted or punished for more than one crime arising out of a single act. For example, Cal. Penal Code § 654 states that when "[a]n act" is punishable by different provisions of the Penal Code, it may be punished only under one provision. Consideration of whether only a single act is involved has produced widely differing views.

a. Separable Actions Approach

Some courts find such statutes inapplicable if each crime consists of actions that can be mechanically distinguished.

Example: D, intending to steal V's wallet, enters V's house and takes the wallet. Under this approach, D can be convicted of both burglary and larceny, because the burglary is committed by the act of entering and the larceny occurs by the distinguishable act of taking and moving the wallet.

b. "Single Objective" Standard

Some courts have defined a "single act" to include crimes related in their commission that were committed pursuant to a single and primary objective. [**People v. Latimer** 858 P.2d 611 (Cal. 1993); **Webb v. State,** 971 A.2d 949 (Md.App. 2009)]

e.g. **Example:** D, intending to steal V's wallet, enters V's house and takes the wallet. Under the "single objective" approach, D cannot be convicted of both burglary and larceny, because both crimes were committed pursuant to the primary objective of the taking of the wallet.

7. Modern Merger of Offenses as Matter of Legislative Intent

Courts sometimes hold that defendants cannot be convicted of related crimes, because one offense "merges" into another. This is not, however, an application of the old common law merger rule (*see supra,* p. 22). Instead, it represents a construction of legislative intent that convictions for both crimes should not be permitted. [**State v. Burroughs,** 636 A.2d 1009 (Md. 1994); *see* **State v. Manion,** 112 A.3d 506 (Md.App. 2015) (consolidated theft statute expresses legislative intent for merger)]

a. *Blockburger* Rule as Guide to Intent

Courts often apply the *Blockburger* test as a guide to legislative intent. Legislatures are regarded as having intended to merge two crimes and to bar conviction for both unless each crime requires proof of facts that the other does not. When only one of the crimes requires proof of an added fact, the offenses *are* the same, and generally there can be no conviction for both crimes, *i.e.*, a greater offense and a lesser included one. [**Commonwealth v. Jones,** 416 N.E.2d 502 (Mass. 1981)]

e.g. **Example:** If one offense is included in the other (either inherently or as charged), the court must examine the facts underlying those offenses, as presented in the charging instrument and as adduced at trial. Based on these facts, if the defendant's actions were "so compressed in terms of time, place, singleness of purpose, and continuity of action as to constitute a single transaction," the prosecutor may charge the offenses as alternative sanctions only." [**Wadle v. State,** 151 N.E.3d 227 (Ind. 2020)]

Chapter Four

Elements of Crimes

CONTENTS	PAGE

Key Exam Issues

Most examination questions ask you to discuss the potential criminal liability of a defendant (or defendants) in a particular fact situation by questions such as "Can the defendant be charged with (or convicted of) the crime?" or "Is the defendant guilty of the crime?" In responding to such questions, it is important to address whether the prosecution can ***prove all elements of the crime*** charged. You first must identify the elements of the crime. If your exam provides you with a statute defining the crime under which the defendant is charged, you should focus on that statute in identifying the elements. For statutory or common law crimes, you can identify the elements by asking yourself:

1. ***What "acts"*** must the defendant have performed in order to be guilty? (This is the ***actus reus*** element.)
2. ***What attendant circumstances*** must have existed (usually at the time of the conduct) for the acts to constitute the crime?
3. ***What state of mind*** must the defendant have had to be guilty? (This is the ***mens rea*** element.)
4. ***Must there have been concurrence of the actus reus and the mens rea***? (Must the act have been attributable to the state of mind required?)
5. ***Is there any particular result*** that must be shown, *i.e.,* something that must have occurred as a result of the defendant's acts?

Not all crimes involve ***all*** five elements. All crimes, though, have an *actus reus* requirement, and most include a *mens rea* element.

In addition to the specific requirements imposed by the statute or other definition of the particular crime, you should consider certain general issues. For example, for acts constituting the *actus reus,* you must consider both the specific requirements of the crime (*i.e.,* an act constituting an "entry" in burglary) and the more general requirements of the *actus reus* element considered in this chapter (*e.g.,* whether the conduct constituting entry was "volitional").

A. Identifying, Distinguishing, and Categorizing Elements of Crimes

1. Introduction

Careful analysis of criminal law issues requires that all elements of that crime be identified and distinguished. This task is often facilitated by careful consideration as to which, if any, elements in each of several categories is required by a specific crime.

2. Categories of Elements

Four categories of elements of crimes are useful:

a. Conduct or "Act"

Crimes always require some ***conduct or "act" (or omission)*** on the part of the defendant. Sometimes the required conduct or act is specifically defined. Burglary, for example, requires an act amounting to an "entry." Some crimes impose no specific requirements at all. Murder, for example, can be committed by acts or omissions that meet the general requirements of the criminal law, as long as the act or omission is proved to have caused the death of the victim.

b. Results

Some crimes require proof that the defendant's conduct caused some ***result*** to occur. Murder and the other homicide offenses, for example, require proof that the victim died and that the defendant's conduct was a cause of that death (*see infra,* p. 201 *et seq.*).

c. Circumstances

Some crimes require proof that some ***circumstance*** existed at the time of the defendant's conduct. Unlike a result, the defendant does not have to cause a circumstance. Common law burglary, for example, requires that the place entered be the dwelling of another (*see infra,* p. 255). No proof is required that the defendant caused the place to be a dwelling.

d. Mens Rea or Culpable Mental States

Crimes usually require that the defendant ***consciously desired*** or at least ***was consciously aware*** of certain matters, *i.e.,* most crimes require a *mens rea* or one or more culpable mental states.

3. Terminology: Mens Rea and Actus Reus

Courts and commentators often say that crimes usually require both an *actus reus* and *mens rea. Mens rea* refers to one or more culpable mental states. Some courts use the term *actus reus* to refer only to the conduct elements. However, others use the term to refer to all nonmental elements of the crime, *i.e.,* elements that are not culpable mental states. Under this approach, *actus reus* includes the conduct, any result, and any circumstances required by the crime.

B. Criminal Acts: Actus Reus

1. Introduction

To be convicted of a crime, the defendant must have committed a criminal act; the law does not punish mere criminal thoughts (*see infra*). Generally, liability is based upon an ***affirmative physical act*** by the defendant; however, under some circumstances, liability can rest upon a ***complete failure to act***, *i.e.,* an omission. A crime's required act is commonly referred to as the "actus reus" of the crime.

2. Requirement of an Act

Whether the criminal conduct is an act or a failure to act, there is general agreement that basic principles of jurisprudence demand that crimes be defined in terms of acts. Indeed, the requirement of an act is to some extent embodied in the federal Constitution.

a. Rationale

If no act is required, punishment would be imposed on the basis of mere intent. However, thoughts are often not converted into action, and thus intent alone poses an insufficient danger to society to justify criminal liability. [*See, e.g.,* **State v. Eversole,** 371 P.3d 293 (Idaho 2017)] ("the plain language of the driving under the influence statute only requires that the defendant be in the driver's position of the motor vehicle with the motor running to show that the defendant was in 'actual physical control' of the vehicle.")]

b. Scope of Actus Reus

For most criminal offenses, a physical act that appears visible satisfies the *actus reus* requirement, *e.g.*, brandishing a weapon, or signing a worthless check. Other offenses meet the *actus reus* requirement by acts that are more difficult to observe, *e.g.*, perjury and solicitation both include vocal acts. Some offenses include unobserved acts, such as carrying a concealed weapon, and persons commit other offenses even though there is not a physical connection between the offense and the offender, *e.g.*, downloading child pornography, carrying a concealed weapon in a vehicle's glove box. An even more attenuated satisfaction of the *actus reus* requirement occurs with a failure to perform a legally required act, known as an omission, *e.g.*, a person's failure to file taxes, failure to report a child abuser.

c. Result Crimes vs. Conduct Crimes

With result crimes, the person's action produces an actual result or harm, as when one person stabs another person who suffers physical injuries or death. The purpose of criminalizing that conduct is to prevent or punish a harmful result. Conduct crimes do not require a specific result from the act, because it is the conduct itself that must be prevented or punished, *e.g.*, driving a vehicle while intoxicated.

d. Constitutional Limitation

Defining a crime as a ***"status,"*** rather than a particular activity, violates the Eighth Amendment prohibition against cruel and unusual punishment. [**Robinson v. California,** 370 U.S. 660 (1962)]

e.g. **Example:** Conviction of a person for a crime consisting of "being addicted to narcotics" violates the Eighth Amendment. [**Robinson v. California,** *supra*]

(1) Rationale

It does not necessarily follow from the fact that a person has a certain status that he will commit serious antisocial acts; hence, conviction for status alone would amount to punishing for "propensity" or "intent." The definition of a given "status" is often so vague that prospective defendants are denied adequate notice of the nature of the criminal offense (*e.g.,* what amounts to being an "addict" and how does one stop being an "addict"?). [**Powell v. Texas,** 392 U.S. 514 (1968)]

(2) Distinguish: Acts Related to Status

The rationale for prohibiting status crimes does not apply to crimes consisting of conduct merely related to the offender's status. Thus, a person can be convicted of a crime requiring a particular act, even if that act is closely related to the person's status.

e.g. **Example:** Local and state governments prohibit sleeping in public spaces like sidewalks and public parks, using a system of penalties to deter homeless persons with possible imprisonment for recidivists. Defendants challenged the criminal penalties as improperly directed at their status as poor persons who needed a place to live. A state cannot not enforce a law making the 'status' of narcotic addiction a criminal offense." [**Robinson v. California**, *supra*] Instead of relying on *Robinson*, the Court analogized the case to *Powell*. State and local governments retain their authority to secure a conviction, regardless of whether the defendant's act "in some sense" might be described as " 'involuntary' or 'occasioned by' " a particular status. [**City of Grants Pass, Oregon v. Johnson,** 603 U.S. 520 (2024)]

3. "Acts" Sufficient for Criminal Liability: Affirmative vs. Negative "Acts"

The act required to support conviction of a given crime varies with the crime itself; it may be one of commission (affirmatively doing something) or omission (failing to do something). Some crimes are specifically defined in terms of the acts the defendant has committed. With such crimes, proof of these acts is essential to a finding of guilt (*e.g.*, burglary requires a "breaking" and "entering," rape requires "intercourse," and embezzlement requires a "conversion"). However, other crimes such as the homicide offenses do not specify the requisite acts; a conviction must be based upon the general concepts of what constitutes a criminal "act." Regardless of the extent to which the requisite act is described in the crime itself, all "acts" for criminal law purposes must meet certain fundamental requirements.

a. Affirmative Acts (Acts of Commission)

Every criminal statute requires an act or omission to be a crime; a person is not guilty of an offense unless his conduct includes a voluntary act. Voluntary act requirements generally are required for a person to be guilty of a crime. Modern courts treat the voluntary act requirement as an important, though an implicit, element of criminal statutes, supported by common law origins. Broadly speaking, an "act" could include involuntary actions like bodily movements during sleep or unconsciousness. Narrowly, an "act" includes only voluntary bodily movement. When criminal liability is based upon the defendant's affirmative act (as is the usual case), that ***movement must be voluntary, or volitional***.

The Model Penal Code requires a voluntary act in Model Penal Code § 2.01: no one may be convicted of a crime unless his conduct "includes a voluntary act or the omission to perform an act of which he is physically capable." The MPC defines "voluntary" "partially and indirectly" by listing bodily movements that are involuntary, such as reflexes, seizures, convulsions, spasms, conduct during unconsciousness, sleep, or due to hypnosis. More generally, involuntary conduct "is not a product of the effort or determination of the actor, either conscious or habitual." [Model Penal Code § 2.01(2)(d)]

(1) Movement

Ordinarily, the "act" is a physical movement of the defendant's body, such as pulling the trigger of a gun or stabbing the victim with a knife. The consequences of that activity, *e.g.*, the firing of the gun, the killing of another, are deemed the "results" of the act rather than part of the "act."

(2) Act Must Be "Volitional"

The physical movement constituting the act must be conscious and ***volitional***. A defendant may be held criminally liable only if his conduct includes a voluntary act, which is a bodily movement performed consciously and as a result of effort and determination. [**State v. Almaguer,** 303 P.3d 84 (Ariz.App. 2013)] "An instruction that the state must prove the defendant committed a voluntary act is appropriate only if there is evidence to support a finding" that the defendant acted involuntarily. The voluntary act requirement serves an important normative function, *i.e.*, to render liable to criminal punishment only those who voluntarily do what the criminal law forbids.

By contrast, reflexes, convulsions, movements during sleep, and conduct during hypnosis or resulting from hypnosis are not sufficient "acts," because they are not volitional. Similarly, criminal liability cannot ordinarily be based on movements made while the defendant was ***unconscious.*** [Model Penal Code § 2.01(2)(b); *see* **Bradley v. State,** 277 S.W. 147 (Tex. 1925) (conviction reversed because the trial judge failed to give jury an instruction that presented the defense of somnambulism)]

e.g. **Example:** After police officer observed vehicle driven by defendant run a stop sign, he stopped the vehicle and noticed that her speech was slurred and her breath smelled of alcohol. Defendant claimed that she was unable to drive the vehicle voluntarily, because she was involuntarily intoxicated after being given a "date rape" drug that caused her impairment. The appellate court approved defendant's assertion of automatism as an affirmative defense. [**City of Missoula v. Paffhausen,** 289 P.3d 141 (Mont. 2012)]

e.g. **Example:** Police arrested a man at his home and took him to a highway where he acted like he was drunk by being loud and shouting obscenities. Because of his conduct on the highway, he was arrested for being drunk in a public place. On appeal, the man challenged his conviction because the public drunkenness statute requires that a defendant appears on the highway voluntarily. The appellate court held that the conviction was illegal, because the defendant was involuntarily taken to the highway. Even if a criminal statute does not appear to require a voluntary act, courts will read that requirement into the meaning and application of the statute. A defendant must voluntarily commit the act constituting a crime to be guilty of that crime. [**Martin v. State,** 17 So.2d 427 (Ala.App. 1944)]

e.g. **Example:** Defendant was guilty of DUI, even though her vehicle was stuck in the snow and immobilized, and incapable of being driven or moved. The appellate court held that she was in "actual physical control" of her vehicle, because she was found in the front seat with the engine running. The vehicle was only temporarily stuck in the snow and would be capable of movement once it was dug out. [**People v. McAndrew,** 251 N.E.3d 1026 (Ill.App. 2024)]

EXAM TIP

Questions that raise the issue of whether the act was "volitional" tend to present rather odd facts, and you may find them hard to believe (*e.g.*, how ***does*** someone shoot a person while unconscious?). But if presented with those odd facts, don't waste time thinking about how ridiculous they are—just analyze them to determine whether the person was ***conscious when he acted*** and whether the ***act itself was volitional***. If not, there is no criminal liability (except possibly if the person caused his own unconsciousness).

(a) Distinguish: Altered Consciousness Arising from Certain Causes

If the defendant's loss of consciousness is caused by a factor covered by a specific defense, its effect on liability is determined by that defense. Thus, if the defendant was mentally ill, criminal liability turns on the law of insanity (*see infra,* p. 106 *et seq.*). If he was too drunk to know what he was doing, *e.g.*, eluding police to avoid arrest, the law of intoxication controls (*see infra,* p. 118 *et seq.*). [**State v. Wilson,** 830 N.W.2d 849 (Minn. 2013)]

(b) Exception: Defendant Caused Unconsciousness

A state of unconsciousness will ***not*** preclude a finding of criminal liability if the defendant was at fault in causing his unconsciousness. In such a case, there is a sufficient "act." This exception equates the volitional conduct that *causes* unconsciousness with the act *committed* while unconscious. Arguably, such a person's criminal liability would most appropriately be limited to the initial wrongful act, *i.e.,* to the crime involved in starting the fight.

e.g. **Example:** After starting a fight with V, D was struck on the head and became unconscious. During the period of unconsciousness, D killed V. Because D was at fault in starting the fight and thus in causing his own unconsciousness, he committed an "act" for purposes of criminal homicide. [**Watkins v. People,** 408 P.2d 425 (Colo. 1965)]

e.g. **Example:** If D intentionally ingested drugs or alcohol and became unconscious, he induced his own **unconsciousness** and his act of ingestion was voluntary. [**Farmer v. State,** 411 S.W.3d 901 (Tex.App. 2013)]

(c) Exception: Knowledge of Pending Unconsciousness

A person may incur criminal liability by engaging in a course of conduct while ***aware*** that he will or might become unconscious and do harm.

e.g. **Example:** Aware that he is subject to "sleep driving" automatism that renders him unconscious, D nevertheless decides to drive his car. While driving, he experiences a "sleep driving" episode, and during the period of unconsciousness the car runs over and kills V. By placing himself in a position where his anticipated unconsciousness would cause harm, D may be held criminally responsible for the homicide. [**State v. Newman,** 302 P.3d 435 (Or. 2013) (liability is not imposed for the act committed while unconscious but rather for the earlier act committed while fully conscious, *i.e.*, driving with knowledge that "sleep driving" may occur)]

e.g. **Example:** On the other hand, D would have an automatism defense to driving under the influence charge "if (1) he took a prescription dose of zolpidem, (2) he was rendered unconscious by this drug and engaged in sleep driving, and (3) he neither knew nor had reason to anticipate that the drug would have this effect." [**Wagner v. State,** 390 P.3d 1179 (Alaska App. 2017)]

(3) Possessory Crimes

"Possession" constitutes an act if the possessor either knowingly obtained the object possessed or knew that she was in control of it "for a sufficient period to have been able to terminate . . . possession." [Model Penal Code § 2.01(4)] Although possession of controlled substances or possession of burglar's tools does not include a bodily movement, these crimes are upheld. Courts interpret the act of possession as being ***conscious possession***, *i.e.*, awareness of physically procuring, receiving, or controlling the item. Possession of items may be criminal, based on the nature of the item or knowledge that the item has a particular characteristic, such as being stolen. Possession of such items may be criminal even if the possessor does not use the item.

(a) Actual and Constructive Possession

Criminal possession may be actual or constructive. Constructive possession may be used to convict a person even without direct proof of actual physical control. Constructive possession suggests that the defendant had the ability to place the item under his control.

Example: A defendant's constructive possession in the age of computers produces varied decisions. Constructive possession is not established by dominion and control over the computer on which the images were found, because that approach "would make a computer owner strictly liable for anything that inadvertently lands on a computer;" however, the number of pornographic images found on the computer and evidence that D used multiple search terms associated with pornography" filled the gap. [**State v. Linson,** 896 N.W.2d 656 (S.D. 2017); *see, e.g.*, **United States v. Ramos,** 685 F.3d 120 (2d Cir. 2012) (defendant had constructive possession over images on his computer); **People v. Flick,** 790 N.W.2d 295 (Mich. 2010) (defendant constructively possessed images on his computer when he viewed them)]

Example: Regarding the possession-of-firearm-by-felon offense, courts rely on "constructive possession" concept to cover the instance in which defendant lacked "physical or personal custody" of the item, but yet "has the intent and culpability to maintain control and dominion over that thing." [**State v. Malachi,** 821 S.E.2d 407 (N.C. 2018)]

(b) Joint Possession

Possession does not have to be exclusive. Possession by multiple persons is recognized, especially when defendants have a possessory interest in the premises, showing they had the ability and intent to exercise dominion and control. Both slept there, and personal papers belonging to both were found and drugs and a gun were in areas of common use. The small size of the apartment and the location of the drugs in the hallway, bathroom and kitchen rendered them available to both defendants. Sufficient evidence permitted the jury to conclude that they exercised joint and constructive possession of cocaine. [**State v. Gutierrez,** 130 A.3d 985 (Md.App. 2016)]

(c) Relationship Between Possession and State of Mind

The defendant's state of mind may determine whether possession is criminal, *e.g.*, possession of stolen property includes the act of holding the property after becoming aware of physically controlling it.

b. Negative Acts (Acts of Omission)

Under certain circumstances, liability may be based upon a defendant's ***failure to act.*** This issue most typically arises in homicide cases where the defendant's conviction is sought on the ground that he failed to take steps to save the victim's life. However, regardless of his intent or motives, the defendant's omission will support a finding of criminal liability only where it is shown that:

(i) Defendant was under a ***legal duty*** to act;

(ii) Defendant had the necessary ***knowledge***; and

(iii) It would have been ***possible*** for defendant to act.

[**State v. Burris,** 544 P.3d 841 (Kan. 2024) (omission, or failure to act, may serve as *actus reus* only when a legal duty of care has been breached; wife's failure to provide food caused husband's death); **Davis v. Commonwealth,** 335 S.E.2d 375 (Va. 1985) daughter moved in to care for elderly mother who died due to gangrene and extreme neglect; daughter's involuntary manslaughter conviction affirmed because she undoubtedly had a duty to act after voluntarily assuming care of her mother, which "created criminal liability for the negligent performance of that duty"]

EXAM TIP

Although all three of the requirements above must be proven before a defendant can be held criminally liable for his omission to act, the most significant of these three requirements (and the one most likely to be tested in an exam question) is the first: Defendant must be under a ***legal duty to act.***

---

(1) Rationale for Legal Duty Requirement

Requiring that an actionable omission be traced to a legal duty to act is apparently based primarily on the need to set ***reasonable and discernible limits*** on liability for omissions. Otherwise, it is at least arguable that persons would not have sufficient advance notice of when they would have to act to avoid liability. [**People v. Heitzman,** 886 P.2d 1229 (Cal. 1994) (crime consisting of permitting infliction of pain on elderly person would deny notice to defendants unless construed as limited to those with a special relationship to the victim)]

(2) Alternative: "Common Decency" Approach

It has also been urged that, absent the legal duty limitation, liability could reasonably be imposed whenever "the failure to take action constitutes a substantial deviation from common decency." This would arguably be no more objectionable than imposing liability for negligent affirmative acts. Bystanders who act to assist others may lead courts to impose a legal duty on others whose duty at the time was ambiguous.

(3) Situations Giving Rise to Legal Duties

The legal duty that will suffice to make an omission an "act" may arise from a number of different sources.

(a) Duties Based upon Relationship of Parties

The common law imposes certain affirmative duties on persons standing in a particular relationship to others. For example, parents have a duty to prevent physical harm to their children. "The inherent dependency of a child upon his parent to obtain medical aid, *i.e.*, the incapacity of a child to evaluate his condition and summon aid by himself, supports imposition of such a duty upon the parent." [**Commonwealth v. Konz,** 450 A.2d 638 (Pa. 1982)] A mother owes a duty to protect her child from a fatal beating by her lover. [**People v. Rolon,** 160 Cal.App. 4th 1206 (2008)]

1) Common Law Duties

Courts are divided over whether to extend duties to rescue to people who have not expressly consented to assuming legal responsibility for a custodial role over the children. [*Compare* **State v. Miranda,** 878 A.2d 1118, 1131 (Conn. 2005) (overruling lower court's conclusion that a live-in boyfriend had a duty to rescue his girlfriend's child because it would be difficult to stop liability from extending to "other members of the extended family, to longtime caregivers who are not related to either the parent or victim, to regular babysitters, and to others with regular and extended relationships with the abusing parent and the abused victim") *with* **Leet v. State,** 595 So.2d 959 (Fla.App. 1991) (finding that the live-in boyfriend of a child's mother had a legal duty to the child to prevent the mother's abuse after establishing a "family-like relationship")]

(b) Statutory Duties

1) General Duties

In addition, a various duties to act are prescribed by a statute imposing a duty. [*See* Model Penal Code § 2.01(3)(a) (criminal liability impose a statutory obligation to file tax returns, or to stop after involvement in an automobile accident. If an injured victim dies due to a lack of assistance, the driver who fled the scene also may be criminally liable for the homicide. The duty to act to preserve life is part of a hit-and-run statute.]

Statutory failure to perform the duties of a driver to injured persons did not require a driver to return to the scene of the accident after learning that he was involved in an accident that resulted in injury or death to another person. The statute contains an implicit assumption that the driver would know that he had been in an accident at the time of the accident. [**State v. Garcia-Cisneros,** 397 P.3d 49 (Or. 2017)]

e.g. **Example:** A statute declaring that "[i]t is the duty of the operator of a vessel involved in an accident. . . to render aid to those affected by the accident" applied to the owner on board when the boat, operated by friend, hit and injured a swimmer. [**State v. Shepherd,** 357 P.3d 598 (Utah 2015)]

(c) Duties "Otherwise Imposed by Law"

At common law, other legal duties existed, independent of any criminal statute. [*See* Model Penal Code § 2.01(3)(b)]

1) Duties Based on Creation of Peril

A person who wrongfully places another in a position of danger has an affirmative duty to aid that person. Failure to render assistance will give rise to criminal liability.

e.g. **Example:** When D assaulted V and left him beaten and shirtless in the freezing desert, he was guilty of homicide. [**United States v. Hatatley,** 130 F.3d 1399 (10th Cir. 1997)]

a) Distinguish: Accidental Creation of Peril

The result is less clear, however, where the defendant has ***accidentally*** created the perilous situation—although some authorities would hold that a similar duty exists, *i.e.,* even those who innocently create the danger have a duty to act to prevent harm. [*See* **Commonwealth v. Cali,** 141 N.E. 510 (Mass. 1923) (D accidentally set fire to house but intentionally let it burn down to collect insurance; held guilty of arson)]

2) Duties Based on Relationships

Many common law duties evolved prior to enactment of statutes in the jurisdiction. (Some duties based upon the relationship of the parties, above, are now enacted in state statutes. *See, e.g.,* Cal. Penal Code § 270a (duty of one spouse to support and provide other spouse with necessary food, clothing, shelter, and medical care) There may be a duty for *un*married couples to protect each other, similar to duties for spouses. [*See, e.g.*, **State ex rel. Kuntz v. Thirteenth Judicial District,** 995 P.2d 951 (Mont. 2000)]

e.g. **Example:** D moved in with his girlfriend and her 5-month-old daughter, and regularly cared for the child; D had a legal duty, eventually imposed by statute on anyone with "actual custody" (as compared with "legal custody") is a sensible approach; the traditional household of two biological parents residing with their minor children [has] become less common." [**Staples v. Commonwealth,** 454 S.W.3d 803 (Ky. 2014)]

3) Duties Arising from Contract

Failure to perform a duty created by contract will, at least in some situations, be sufficient to create criminal liability. This will clearly be the case if the defendant was under a contractual duty to ***protect or care for others.*** [**State v. Bermisa**, 90 P.3d 1256 (Haw.App. 2004) (nurse's aide at nursing facility convicted of manslaughter for failure to treat bed sores)]

e.g. **Example:** A defendant who contracted to provide shelter and food to an elderly person who was an invalid but who failed to provide food as required by the contract could be convicted of murder, where the elderly person died from starvation. [**Commonwealth v. Pestinikas,** 617 A.2d 1339 (Pa. 1992)]

e.g. **Example:** A personal relationship with another person may create an affirmative duty to control the other's conduct in the interest of public safety, so that omission to control the other person's conduct may give rise to criminal liability. For example, a friend of the victim had a contractual duty to act as the victim's caretaker, which included a duty to prevent the victim from a drug overdose. [**Zemek v. Superior Court,** 257 Cal.Rptr.3d 729 (Cal.App. 2020)]

a) What if the Contract Is Unrelated to Safety?

Courts may be reluctant and perhaps completely unwilling to impose criminal liability for breach of a contractual duty if the contract has nothing to do with the safety of others.

4) Duties Arising from Voluntarily Undertaking a Task

A person who has no legal obligation to render aid to another (*e.g.,* because there is no preexisting familial or contractual relationship, *supra*) but who voluntarily undertakes to render such aid has a duty to use reasonable care. Indeed, refusal to continue a voluntary assumption of care may constitute a criminal "act," at least where abandoning one's efforts would leave the imperiled person in a worse condition.

Example: Grandmother who took care of her grandchild violated her duty of reasonable care when she was so drunk that the child smothered. Grandmother was guilty of manslaughter. [**Cornell v. State,** 32 So.2d 610 (Fla. 1947)]

Example: D was a visitor in an apartment where drug activity occurred. Although three children lived there, D never fed, baby sat, or otherwise cared for the children in any manner or had any authority over them. In fact, he was never alone with them. Thus, he is not liable for the crime of permitting children to enter or remain in a place of drug activity. [**People v. Berry,** 56 N.E.3d 207 (N.Y. 2016)]

5) Duties Arising from Voluntarily Acting, Thereby Causing Peril to Another

When a defendant voluntarily acts to assist another person, he may thereby cause victim to be "in danger" or "at risk," thereby making that person "worse off" than if the defendant had done nothing.

(a) Moral Duty Alone Is Not Always Enough

Despite the increased flexibility toward finding a legal duty, the law still does not impose criminal liability for an omission simply because the defendant has a *moral* obligation to act. [**State v. Sherman,** 266 S.W.3d 395 (Tenn. 2008); **People v. Beardsley,** 113 N.W. 1128 (Mich. 1907) (a married man had no duty to call a physician for a woman with whom he spent the weekend when she overdosed on morphine at his home)] Would a court in the 21st century refuse to recognize the defendant's duty to aid his paramour, because the woman was not the defendant's spouse?

Problems with recognizing moral duties begin with defining a moral duty in a specific context. A moral duty based on common decency arguably is no more general than the liability standard for negligent acts. Yet, a moral duty would broaden the circumstances when ordinary citizens are subjected to prosecution.

Example: Victim may be drowning in a lake. As Defendant swims toward Victim to save her, other Good Samaritans who had begun to aid Victim see the Defendant and resume what they were doing. At the last moment, Defendant decides not to help Victim, who then drowns. Defendant may be criminally responsible, because she volunteered to rescue Victim but increased the danger to Victim when the others gave up their efforts to help. Is Defendant's liability different if he was the only person available but never began to help her?

SUMMARY OF SITUATIONS GIVING RISE TO LEGAL DUTY TO ACT
A LEGAL DUTY TO ACT MAY ARISE WHEN:
☑ The victim and the accused ***stand in a special relationship*** (*e.g.*, child/parent, husband/wife),

- ☑ A ***statute*** prescribes the specific duty (*e.g.*, filing a tax return),
- ☑ A ***contract*** creates the duty to act (*e.g.*, contract to provide care for disabled person),
- ☑ The duty is ***voluntarily*** undertaken (*e.g.*, volunteer babysitter),
- ☑ The defendant ***created the peril*** (*e.g.*, defendant who renders victim unconscious must assist victim to avoid potential criminal liability for murder), or
- ☑ The defendant has ***a level of control*** over the actor such that a duty to prevent criminal conduct is created (*e.g.*, an employer may have a duty to prevent an employee from committing crimes while "on the job").

d) Trend Toward Creation of New Duties

The law has trended toward the recognition of new duties and the expansion of duties well settled under the criminal law. For instance, a landowner may have an affirmative duty to provide for the safety of persons invited onto his land. [**Commonwealth v. Welansky,** 55 N.E.2d 902 (Mass. 1944) (patrons of nightclub killed as result of owner's failure to supply proper fire escapes; owner held guilty of manslaughter)]

e) Constitutional Limitation

Recall the constitutional Due Process limitation that criminal statutes must be sufficiently specific and precise as to give fair warning of the required conduct. Imposing criminal liability for failing to perform a duty imposed by law may sometimes violate this Due Process requirement. [**State v. Lisa,** 919 A.2d 145 (N.J.App. 2007), aff'd 945 A.2d 690 (N.J. 2008)]

EXAM TIP

For questions involving an omission to act, remember that ***criminal liability will be imposed only if there is a legal duty to act.*** Don't be fooled by a question that sets up only a moral duty. The need of one person and the ability of another to help are ***not*** enough. Thus, if Adult is at a pool and sees Child floundering in the water, Adult has no legal duty to help—or even to call for help—and cannot be convicted of a crime if Child drowns. The fact that a "reasonable" person would help is irrelevant. You must view the situation objectively no matter how "bad" the defendant seems to be. On the other hand, be sure that Adult doesn't have a legal duty to do something, *e.g.*, if Adult is the parent or babysitter of Child, or is the pool's lifeguard, or he pushed Child into the deep end of the pool? If so, there is a legal duty for Adult to try to save Child.

(4) Knowledge Required for Liability

Omission cases raise two questions on the issue of knowledge: (i) whether the defendant must be aware of the facts giving rise to a legal duty; and (ii) whether she must have knowledge of the law creating the duty.

(a) Knowledge of Facts Creating Duty

While the courts split on the issue, the majority view is that, although one may be under a duty to act, an omission will render the defendant criminally liable only if she has knowledge of the facts creating the duty. The rationale is that a person does not have a fair opportunity to perform her duty unless she is at least aware of the circumstances prompting the duty. [**Dailey v. State,** 65 P.3d 891

(Alaska App. 2003)] While a parent has a legal duty to rescue his child from drowning, his failure to know that his child is in the water may relieve him of criminal liability for the child's death.

1) Distinguish: Duty to Know the Facts

However, in some situations the law may impose an ***obligation to know the facts*** creating a legal duty. In such cases, it need not be shown that the defendant was aware of the facts, *i.e.*, criminal liability may be imposed for failure to exercise reasonable care in learning the facts. [**Cornell v. State,** *supra*]

(b) Knowledge of Law Creating Duty

Courts seldom require that the defendant have knowledge that the law imposes the duty to act. The general rule is that "ignorance of the law is no excuse." However, if a statute requires a "willful" failure to act, courts may require knowledge of the law creating the duty on the theory that ignorance of the existence or scope of the duty negates the requisite mental state. [**United States v. Murdock,** 290 U.S. 389 (1933) (failure to file tax return not criminal unless defendant was aware of legal duty to file return)]

1) Constitutional Due Process Limitation

Imposing criminal liability for an omission, without proof that the defendant had knowledge of the law creating the duty to act, may violate Due Process, especially if the circumstances are that persons in the defendant's position are generally unlikely to be aware of the duty. [**Lambert v. California,** 355 U.S. 225 (1957) (Due Process is violated by conviction for failure to register with police as a sex offender, where knowledge of the duty was not an element of the offense and any circumstances motivating persons to inquire about a duty are lacking)]

(5) Possibility of Performing the Act

Regardless of the facts giving rise to a duty to act and the defendant's knowledge of the duty, the omission must have been one that the defendant could have avoided; *i.e.,* it must have been possible for her to have done what she failed to do. Thus, there is no criminal "act" where the defendant's omission was because she lacked the means or ability to perform. [*See, e.g.,* Model Penal Code § 2.01(1) (criminal liability imposed for "the omission to perform an act of which [a person] is physically capable"); **People v. Likine,** 823 N.W.2d 50 (Mich. 2012) (common law defense of impossibility is permitted to a non-support charge if D explored all reasonable methods of obtaining the money in order to comply)]

(a) Distinguish: Mere Inconvenience or Need to Solicit Assistance

Mere inconvenience does not excuse a failure to perform a duty. Also, a defendant even physically incapable of performing herself cannot escape criminal liability if it was reasonably possible to obtain the help of others. [**Stehr v. State,** 139 N.W. 676 (Neb. 1913) (failure to provide food and shelter for children would not be criminal if the parent is unable to obtain such necessaries, but the failure to seek help at available welfare agency would be a breach of duty; stepfather liable for manslaughter for death of sick stepchild for whom he failed to contact doctor in time)]

C. Attendant Circumstances

1. Introduction

In addition to the elements ordinarily common to most crimes (*actus reus*, *mens rea*, etc.), many crimes require proof of certain attendant circumstances that must exist at the time of the act in question. Absent proof that these circumstances exist, the conduct of the accused will not constitute a crime.

e.g. **Example:** A statute provides: "It is an offense to injure a federal officer while that officer is performing his duties." Thus, in addition to the element of an injury to a person caused by the defendant, two attendant circumstances are required: (i) that the victim was a federal officer, and (ii) that the officer was engaging in his official duties at the time of the injury. Both factors are crucial elements of the offense and, absent a showing of their existence when the defendant acted, the crime cannot be established.

2. Why Circumstances Differ from Results

Attendant circumstances differ from the result required by a crime in that circumstances need not have been caused by the defendant's conduct. (In the example above, the fact that the victim was a federal officer or was performing his official duties need not be attributable to an act of the defendant.)

3. Mens Rea Issues

Attendant circumstances elements often raise questions as to whether the defendant must have been ***aware*** of the existence of the circumstances. These issues involve application of the *mens rea* requirement, discussed below.

D. Criminal State of Mind: Mens Rea

1. General Requirement of Mens Rea

Crimes generally require "mens rea" or some culpable mental state. Unlike other kinds of legal liability, criminal law considers, and even emphasizes, what the defendant was thinking when she engaged in the conduct that might constitute a crime. Thus, to a considerable extent, criminal liability is subjective in nature. The definitions of most crimes include a *mens rea* or culpable mental state. Some do not, however. These crimes sometimes impose what is called "strict liability."

Broadly, *mens rea* means "guilty mind" and is characterized as culpability. Narrowly, *mens rea* refers to the mental state the defendant must have had with regard to the social harm elements set out in the definition of the offense. The terminology and scope of many *mens rea* terms are confused, ambiguous and often misused; the common meaning of the terms is not consistent with the attributed legal meaning.

a. Rationale

There are at least two basic reasons for the mental element, or *mens rea*, aspect of crimes:

(1) **Demonstrates Moral Culpability**

If a criminal conviction imposes a stigma of moral condemnation, it is important to define them to encompass only morally reprehensible behavior. Generally, however, only "intentional" conduct is regarded as morally wrong. Therefore, the requirement of *mens rea* tends to assure that only morally blameworthy persons are convicted of crimes.

(2) **Identifies Persons Dangerous to Society**

The *mens rea* requirement tends to identify persons most dangerous to society. Arguably, one who "*un*intentionally" engages in conduct or causes a result is less inclined to repeat dangerous conduct than one who "intentionally" does the same thing. Accordingly, a *mens rea* requirement focuses on those who pose a serious danger to others and helps to assure that society is protected from persons most likely to do it harm.

b. **No Single Mens Rea**

There is no single state of mind, or *mens rea*, that suffices for imposing criminal liability. Rather, the requisite state of mind is defined separately for each specific crime. [*See* **United States v. Garrett,** 984 F.2d 1402 (5th Cir. 1993) (when a crime is not measured by strict liability, a "minimum level" of culpability, *i.e.*, "the 'should have known' standard," is sufficient for liability)]

c. **Traditional vs. Modern Analysis of State of Mind**

Modern criminal statutes, usually based on the Model Penal Code, define culpable mental states more carefully and comprehensively than traditional criminal law. Often, therefore, it is necessary to separate and distinguish traditional *mens rea* analysis from the analysis necessary under modern criminal statutes.

d. **State of Mind Dimensions**

There are two dimensions to criminal state of mind requirements under modern statutory analysis:

(1) **Object Dimension**

On the one hand, the *mens rea* element embraces what state of mind is required. For example, a crime might require a particular state of mind concerning a possible consequence of conduct (such as the death of another person) or regarding certain attendant circumstances (such as the victim's lack of consent to the intercourse in rape).

(2) **Quality Dimension**

The *mens rea* element also concerns the ***quality*** of the state of mind required. For example, in the case of murder, the mental element might be satisfied only by a showing that the defendant desired the victim's death. Or, it might be satisfied by a showing that she was aware that a risk of death existed at the time that she acted. (*See infra,* p. 203 *et seq.*)

e. **Distinguish Motive from Mens Rea**

"Motive" refers to the defendant's ***reason*** for perpetrating the crime in question (*e.g.*, hatred, revenge, jealousy, etc.). Although a showing of motive may reliably prove that the defendant did in fact commit the crime, it is ***irrelevant*** to proving criminal liability, unlike proof that a defendant acted with a certain *mens rea.* Conversely, proof of a good motive does not *prevent* conviction.

e.g. **Example:** A son who killed his father to put him out of his misery from an incurable and painful disease may still be convicted of first degree murder. [**State v. Evans,** 956 N.W.2d 68 (S.D. 2021) (sufficient similarity between defendant's ex-wife and rape victim-former girlfriend and between the crimes committed against them to support admission of other act evidence to prove motive and a common plan)]

(1) Motive May Trigger a Defense

A defendant's motive may trigger a defense. If a person who kills another is motivated by a desire for self-preservation, that motive may trigger self-defense.

EXAM TIP

Exam questions sometimes play up the motive for a defendant's actions, as in the case of a "mercy killing" such as in ***State v. Forrest****, infra, Premeditated Murder.* Don't be thrown off by the defendant's motive (*e.g.,* he was trying to save his suffering father from more pain). Again, you must view the situation objectively, and not consider how "good" the defendant seems to be. What is important is whether he had the required *mens rea* (*e.g.,* did he intend to kill him?). If so, the defendant ***can be convicted despite his good motive.***

---

(2) Motive and Sentencing

The motive that prompts an act may be relevant when the judge sets the defendant's sentence. A judge may impose the minimum sentence, or perhaps no sentence at all, if the judge believes that the defendant was acting with good motives. Sentence enhancement statutes sometimes reflect the defendant's motives. [*See, e.g.,* **Wisconsin v. Mitchell,** 508 U.S. 476 (1993) (statutory sentence for aggravated battery was seven years instead of two years when the victim was selected on account of the victim's race)]

f. Awareness of Law Not Required

Mens rea generally requires awareness of ***factual matters,*** and does not usually require that the defendant is aware that the law makes his conduct grounds for criminal liability.

2. Constitutional Considerations

The United States Supreme Court has never clarified what, if any, culpable mental states are required for crimes as a matter of federal constitutional law. Some of the Court's decisions suggest the federal constitutional requirement of Due Process of law might require some minimal awareness by one accused of a crime. [**Lambert v. California,** 355 U.S. 225 (1957)] In other words, some of the Court's decisions suggest that a crime imposing complete or even "limited" or "partial" strict liability may be unconstitutional (*see infra,* p. 30).

3. Mens Rea Analysis and Terminology

Traditional *mens rea* analysis often used a number of specialized terms: "general intent," "specific intent," "scienter," "malice," "willfulness," etc. Even then, the terms were sometimes not carefully defined. These terms often have little use under modern statutory analysis.

a. "General" vs. "Specific" Intent

Criminal law analysis sometimes distinguished "general intent" from "specific intent." The significance of the distinction is that, traditionally, the application of certain defenses depended on the determination of whether the crime was a "general" or "specific" intent crime. Voluntary intoxication was sometimes held ***available as a defense only to crimes that required specific intent.*** A mistake of fact was sometimes held to be effective as a defense only if it was reasonable, unless the charged offense required a specific intent.

(1) Focus on Conduct or Actus Reus

The act and the mental state are connected, but are also distinct from one another. *Mens rea* signifies a defendant's state of mind about the social harm of the offense, whereas the element of voluntariness applies to the act that caused the social harm. All elements of a crime must exist at the same time in order for a crime to have been committed, *i.e.*, the *actus reus* (the act) + the *mens rea* (culpable mental state) = the resulting harm.

(a) General Intent Can Be "Inferred" from the Conduct

Some courts explain that general intent does not require specific proof, but ***can be inferred (not presumed) from the fact that the defendant engaged in the conduct*** constituting the crime. A person who voluntarily engages in conduct is presumed to have the general intent necessary for that conduct to constitute a crime. [**State v. Thurman,** 730 N.W.2d 805 (Neb. 2007)]

e.g. **Example:** D swung a wine bottle at V's friend who ducked, but the bottle hit V's head, causing serious injuries. D was charged with and convicted of aggravated battery based on permanent disability and bodily harm. On appeal, D argued that he did not intend to inflict permanent disability to V. The appellate court found that, from D's words, weapon, and the force used, it could be inferred that he was consciously aware that the statutory harm was practically certain to be caused by D's conduct. [**People v. Conley,** 543 N.E.2d 138 (Ill.App. 1989)]

(b) Specific Intent More Difficult to Prove

On the other hand, "specific" proof of intent is required, although the proof may be circumstantial. Courts sometimes say that a specific intent is more difficult for the prosecution to prove, because it cannot be inferred from the commission of the *actus reus* of the crime. [**People v. Salcido,** 186 P.3d 437 (Cal. 2008)] Burglary may be the most familiar specific intent crime; the defendant completes the *actus reus* for criminal trespass when he unlawfully enters or remains in a structure that belongs to another person. For burglary, the prosecution further must prove that the defendant intended to commit a felony in that structure. Even if the prosecution cannot prove that the defendant actually committed a felony once inside, the offense of burglary is complete when he trespassed and meant to commit a serious crime.

(2) Focus on Elements of the Crime

(a) General Intent: Awareness of Nonmental Elements of the Crime

Courts often use the term "general" intent to refer to the culpable mental state(s) required concerning the nonmental elements of a crime, *i.e.*, the conduct, any result, and any circumstances required. With a general intent crime, the requisite culpability is present because the actor's mistake of fact was unreasonable, *i.e.*, negligent or reckless.

(b) Specific Intent Is the Intent to Do Something Further

Courts defining general intent as above often use the term "specific" intent to refer to any culpable mental state that is required above and beyond the mental state required for the *actus reus* of the crime (*i.e.*, not the conduct, result, or circumstances that must be proved). [**State v. Fleck,** 810 N.W.2d 303 (Minn. 2012)] With a specific intent crime, a mistake of fact is a "defense" when it negates the specific intent required in the definition of the offense. Whether the defendant was acting reasonably does not matter. For example, theft requires a taking with the intent to permanently deprive the victim of property. A defendant either has the intent to steal or the defendant does not. [*See* **People v. Hendrix,** 515 P.3d 22 (Cal. 2022) (mistake of fact is a defense that a particular factual error in the defendant's case disproves specific intent)]

(c) Illustration

Assume that a crime consists of recklessly causing injury to another person with the intent to humiliate the person. The nonmental elements of this offense are: (i) some conduct by the accused; and (ii) a result, *i.e.*, injury to another person caused by the defendant's conduct. The offense requires a culpable mental state of recklessness concerning those two elements. The prosecution must prove that a person charged with this offense was aware of a risk that he would engage in the conduct constituting the crime *and* that this risky conduct would cause the injury that actually resulted. These culpable mental states relate to "general" intent, because the conduct and the injury are nonmental elements of the crime.

This crime also requires proof that the defendant intended to humiliate the victim. The subject of this culpable mental state is the humiliation of the person. This humiliation need not, however, be proved to have actually occurred. The crime is complete even if the defendant did not cause actual humiliation of the victim. The subject of this culpable mental state, *i.e.*, humiliation of the victim, is not itself an element of the crime. For this reason, the intent to humiliate the victim is a "specific" intent.

b. Criminal Negligence

For some crimes, liability can be based on a showing of criminal negligence, *i.e.*, the defendant may be convicted for an act done without awareness of the facts but with a "gross" lack of care. The most frequent examples involve the crimes of common law involuntary manslaughter, battery, and criminal nuisance.

(1) Definition: Gross Deviation from Reasonable Care Standard

Both civil and criminal negligence involve a breach of the duty owed by a reasonable person under the circumstances. (*See* Torts Summary.) However, civil and criminal negligence differ in the degree of deviation from socially accepted conduct that is required. Criminal negligence is not established simply by the fact that the defendant failed to exercise due care; instead, the negligence must comprise a ***higher probability of harm*** and a ***gross deviation from the standard of reasonable care*** than exists for imposing civil liability. By statute or by court decision, many jurisdictions further describe criminal negligence when the defendant takes a ***substantial and unjustifiable risk of causing the harm*** that constitutes the crime. [*See, e.g.*, **State v. Lewis,** 290 P.3d 288 (Ore. 2012) (criminal negligence shown when defendant drove an unloaded tractor-trailer on a dangerous section of wet road at the maximum permitted speed was distracted and inattentive prior to accident)]

c. Malice

As indicated earlier, crimes are sometimes defined in case law or by statute as requiring "malice." Although there is no clear meaning for the term, it most commonly requires the commission of a volitional act ***without legal excuse or justification.*** Ill will toward or hatred of the victim need ***not*** be shown. [**State v. Lambert,** 178 So. 508 (La. 1938)]

e.g. **Example:** While D was trying to steal a gas meter, the attached gas pipes released gas that led to the nonfatal asphyxiation of V. D argued that he lacked the malice for the charged endangerment felony. The trial court construed statutory malice to mean "wicked" in the broad sense of the word, but the appellate court rejected that meaning and stated that foreseeability or recklessness is sufficient to prove malice, *i.e.*, the intent to steal is insufficient to show the intent to injure another person. However, it ordered a new trial because the jury instructions did not reflect the narrower definition of malice. [**Regina v. Cunningham**, 2 QB 396 (1957) (court applied elemental definition of malice, *i.e.*, although defendant acted with a morally blameworthy state of mind, he is not guilty unless the Crown proved that he intentionally or recklessly caused the social harm of the offense; malice is the shorthand term for the specific state of mind required by the statute)]

e.g. **Example:** Criminal libel is generally defined as the malicious publication of durable defamation of another. But the requirement of "malice" is satisfied by a showing of an ***intentional*** publication ***without justification or excuse.*** No ill will by the defendant directed toward the victim needs to be proved.

(1) Other Meanings of Malice

However, as will be seen, "malice" has a different meaning in relation to certain other crimes, such as murder (which requires "malice aforethought."

d. "Willfully," "Deliberately," "Feloniously"

Various criminal statutes may also use words such as willfully, deliberately, or feloniously to describe the requisite state of mind. Again, these terms have no generally agreed upon meaning but are often equated with general intent, *supra.* Sometimes, however, courts will construe the terms to require more than is usually required by general intent.

e. Knowledge of Law Sometimes Required

Courts will occasionally construe crimes as requiring that the defendant was aware of the law and aware that his conduct violated the law, *i.e.*, this pertains to crimes where the defendant's conduct is not always regarded as illegal and thus persons lacking actual knowledge of the illegality are likely to unwittingly commit the crime. Courts are especially likely to so interpret a crime if that crime by its terms requires that it be committed "willfully;" *i.e.,* the Government must prove that the defendant acted with knowledge that federal law prohibits his conduct. [**Ratzlaf v. United States,** 510 U.S. 135 (1994)] Soon after *Ratzlaf,* Congress enacted 31 U.S.C. § 5324 with its own criminal penalty, and deleted the requirement that a defendant act "willfully" in order to be convicted.

e.g. **Example:** Federal tax crimes prohibit willfully failing to pay taxes and require proof that the defendant voluntarily and intentionally knew of and understood his legal duty to pay the tax, but the Government is not required to prove that the defendant acted with a bad motive or purpose. [**United States v. Curtis,** 781 F.3d 904 (7th Cir. 2015)]

e.g. **Example:** A word such as "knowingly" modifies not only the words directly following it, but also those other statutory terms that "separate wrongful from innocent acts." For example, when an offense penalizes persons who "knowingly violate" a provision making it unlawful for persons to possess a firearm, the government must prove that the defendant knew he possessed a firearm *and* knew that he belonged to the relevant category of persons barred from possessing firearms. [**Rehaif v. United States,** 588 U.S. 225 (2019)]

e.g. **Example:** Defendant medical doctors were charged with a violation of law making it a federal crime, "except as authorized, for any person knowingly or intentionally . . .to manufacture, distribute, or dispense . . . a controlled substance." Defendants first have the burden of proving that their conduct was authorized. Once they produce evidence that they were authorized to dispense controlled substances, federal prosecutors must prove beyond a reasonable doubt that Defendants knew they were acting in an unauthorized manner. [**Ruan v. United States,** 597 U.S. 450 (2022)]

f. Proof of Intent: Federal Constitutional Requirements

When a crime requires proof of intent, the federal constitutional requirement that the prosecution has the burden of proving guilt beyond a reasonable doubt applies and requires that the prosecution's burden also apply to the element of intent. [**Sandstrom v. Montana,** *supra*]

(1) "Presumptions" of Intent Prohibited

A "presumption" that has the effect of relieving the prosecution of its burden of proving criminal intent violates the defendant's right to Due Process. [**Sandstrom v. Montana,** *supra*]

e.g. **Example:** D is tried for "deliberate homicide," which requires proof that D "purposely or knowingly" caused the death of the victim. The trial judge instructs the jury that "the law presumes that a person intends the ordinary consequences of his voluntary acts." This violates the D's right to have the prosecution prove intent beyond a reasonable doubt, because the jurors might construe the instruction as requiring that the prosecution prove that D voluntarily did an act that caused death as an "ordinary consequence." [**Sandstrom v. Montana,** *supra*]

(2) Distinguish: "Permissible Inference" of Intent

It remains possible, however, that the trial judge can constitutionally instruct the jury that if it finds that certain results are the natural and ordinary results of a defendant's conduct, it *may but need not* infer from the defendant's conduct that he intended those results. Such rebuttable or permissible inferences of intent are sometimes constitutionally permissible.

4. General Rule: Mens Rea or Culpable Mental State Required

Generally, *mens rea*, "criminal intent," or a culpable mental state is required for criminal liability.

a. Silent Statute Creating a Crime Nevertheless Requires Mens Rea

The policy favoring a culpable mental state for criminal liability is so strong that as a general rule where a statute creating and defining a crime does not explicitly require criminal intent, a court nevertheless will read such a *mens rea* requirement into the statutory crime on the basis that the legislature must have intended to require the *mens rea*.

b. The Presumption of Scienter

The United States Supreme Court, when construing *federal* statutes creating and defining crimes, applies a presumption in favor of scienter, *i.e.*, a defendant's knowledge that an act or conduct is wrongful and her intent to act despite this knowledge. When a federal statute is silent on the matter of criminal intent, the Court assumes that Congress nevertheless intended to require *mens rea*. The presumption is not applied, of course, if there *is* evidence of Congressional intent, express or implied, to not require *mens rea*. [Sandstrom v. Montana, *supra*, **Morissette v. United States,** 342 U.S. 246 (1952)]

5. Strict Liability Crimes

Criminal liability without a *mens rea* requirement (or with a limited *mens rea* requirement) is called "strict liability." It is an exceptional type of criminal liability, and constitutional considerations limit the extent to which it can be imposed. For a defendant, simply engaging in a voluntary act makes her guilty because the injury to the victim is the same regardless of the defendant's culpable mental state. No mistake of fact and mistake of law defenses may be proved, because strict liability carries no required knowledge or *mens rea*.

In **United States v. United States Gypsum Co.,** 438 U.S. 422 (1978), the Court warned that offenses that do not contain a *mens rea* element are "generally disfavored." "[A]t least with regard to crimes having their origin in the common law, ***an interpretive presumption [exists] that mens rea is required"*** in federal statutes. "[T]he failure of Congress explicitly and unambiguously to indicate whether *mens rea* is required does not signal a departure from this background assumption of our criminal law." [**Arthur Andersen LLP v. United States,** 544 U.S. 696 (2005) (with a statute making it a crime to "knowingly . . . corruptly persuad[e] another" with intent to cause that person to withhold documents from an official proceeding, it makes sense both linguistically and in the statutory scheme to conclude that "knowingly" modifies the term "corruptly persuades")]

e.g. **Example:** D was convicted of posting statements on Facebook that were interpreted as threats to his spouse, co-workers and an FBI agent; merely because a statute does not mention a criminal intent does not dispense with such a requirement; jury instruction requiring only negligence to support a criminal conviction was insufficient to convict the defendant of making "a communication containing any threat to injure the person of another." [**Elonis v. United States,** 575 U.S. 723 (2015); *see* **People v. Relerford,** 104 N.E.3d 341 (Ill. 2017) (appellate court's conclusion that Due Process does not permit criminal liability based on negligent conduct is unfounded; relying on *Elonis*)]

a. Types of Strict Liability

(1) "Complete" Strict Liability

A few offenses contain no requirement of a *mens rea* whatsoever; these offenses have traditionally been characterized as "strict liability" crimes. A guilty mind is "a necessary element in the indictment and proof of every crime." [**United States v. Balint,** 258 U.S. 250 (1922) (drug trafficking)] Thus, even when a statute contains no *mens rea* requirement, it is generally interpreted to include one. This does not mean that a defendant must know that his conduct is illegal, but a defendant must have knowledge of "the facts that make his conduct fit the definition of the offense." [**Staples v. United States,** 511 U.S. 600, 608, n. 3 (1994)]

(2) "Limited" or "Partial" Strict Liability

Other offenses include no requirement of awareness with regard to *one or more important aspects* of the offenses, although some *mens rea* must be proved. These offenses are sometimes also called strict liability crimes, although they are more accurately characterized as imposing "limited" strict liability as contrasted with "complete" strict liability.

e.g. **Example:** The National Firearms Act creates an offense consisting of: (i) possession of a weapon (ii) of certain specified types, such as a machine gun or a grenade (iii) that is not registered under the Act. The Supreme Court has considered separately whether the Act imposes strict liability with regard to the second and third elements (*see infra*). As in many modern cases, however, it was clear that some *mens rea* was required and the real issues were whether the Act imposed limited strict liability by dispensing with *mens rea* regarding *some* of the elements of the crime. [**Staples v. United States**, *supra*]

b. Identifying Strict Liability Crimes: Legislative Intent

Whether a crime imposes strict liability turns initially at least upon the legislature's intent. However, as is often the case, criminal statutes do not clearly indicate on their face what the legislative intent was, requiring courts to look at other factors.

(1) Burden of Establishing Strict Liability

The criminal law's tradition of requiring *mens rea* for liability and the likelihood that legislatures will follow this approach means that strict liability is disfavored. Thus, a party arguing for strict liability has the burden of establishing that the legislature intended to impose this kind of liability. [**Staples v. United States**, *supra*]

(2) Factors Regarding Legislative Intent for Strict Liability

Several considerations bear upon legislative intent to impose strict liability: (1) a statute's silence on a mental element is not dispositive of legislative intent, (2) the statute must be construed in light of the background rules of the common law, and its conventional *mens rea* element, (3) whether the crime can be characterized as a "public welfare offense" created by the Legislature, (4) the extent to which a strict liability reading of the statute would encompass seemingly entirely innocent conduct, and (5) and the harshness of the penalty, *i.e.*, the more severe the potential sanction the more likely *mens rea* is required. Other considerations include: (6) the seriousness of the harm to the public, (7) the ease or difficulty of the defendant ascertaining the true facts, (8) relieving the prosecution of difficult and time-consuming proof of fault where the Legislature thinks it important to stamp out harmful conduct at all costs, "even at the cost of convicting innocent-minded and blameless people", and (9) the number of prosecutions to be expected. [**Staples v. United States**, *supra*; *see* **State v. Yishmael,** 456 P.3d 1172 (Wash. 2020) (applying Staples' eight factors in determining that unlawful practice of law is a strict liability offense)]

(a) Arguments Favoring Strict Liability

Legislative intent to impose strict liability for the defendant's conduct is suggested by the characteristics in the chart, *infra.* Moreover, if most persons charged under the statute would in fact have the *mens rea* that might otherwise be required, this will encourage a court to find that *mens rea* need not be proven in each particular case. [**Morissette v. United States,** 342 U.S. 246 (1952)]

Morissette is an example of an offense using a *mens rea* requirement for some but not all elements of the offense. Possession of bomb casings was not criminal conduct, until Morissette knew that he had stolen another person's property. The statute became one of strict liability, because the prosecutor did not have to prove the knowledge which had changed otherwise innocent conduct into criminality.

(b) Arguments Disfavoring Strict Liability

On the other hand, courts are less likely to conclude that the legislature intended to eliminate *mens rea* as an essential ingredient for the factors listed in the chart, *infra.* Moreover, if strict liability would create a serious risk of convicting many entirely "innocent" persons, *i.e.*, persons neither aware nor alerted to the possibility that their conduct is criminal, courts are unlikely to find strict liability. [**Staples v. United States,** *supra*]

e.g. **Example:** The National Firearms Act prohibits possession of certain unregistered weapons, such as grenades and machine guns. It imposes limited strict liability because it requires no awareness that the weapons were in fact unregistered; *see supra.* Dispensing with a requirement that a defendant know the nature of a weapon (as, for example, that a rifle would fire automatically and therefore was a "machine gun") would create a significant risk that entirely innocent gun owners would incur criminal liability, and therefore the Act was not construed as imposing strict liability with regard to the nature of the weapon. [**Staples v. United States,** *supra*]

(3) Constitutional Considerations

If strict liability would clearly or likely be unconstitutional (*see infra*), the legislature probably did not intend it. Therefore, a showing that a serious constitutional issue would be presented by strict liability will encourage courts to construe legislative intent as requiring ordinary *mens rea.*

CHECKLIST OF STRICT LIABILITY FACTORS

THE FOLLOWING SUGGEST THAT A STRICT LIABILITY CRIME WAS INTENDED:	THE FOLLOWING SUGGEST THAT A STRICT LIABILITY CRIME WAS *NOT* INTENDED:
☑ The crime is a ***"new" statutory offense*** rather than one of the traditional common law offenses; ☑ It does not involve a ***direct and positive infringement on the rights of other persons;*** ☑ It is part of a ***broad regulatory scheme;*** ☑ It imposes a ***relatively light penalty*** upon conviction;	☑ The crime ***closely resembles*** a traditional common law crime; ☑ The act constituting the crime involves ***a direct and serious infringement on the rights of others;*** ☑ A ***severe penalty*** is imposed on conviction; and ☑ Strict liability would clearly or likely be ***unconstitutional.***

☑ Requiring proof of *mens rea* would ***impede implementation of the legislative purpose;*** and ☑ The "offense" is part of a ***regulatory scheme*** designed to further the ***general welfare,*** or it is a ***traffic offense.***	

(4) "Regulatory" or "Public Welfare" Offenses

Morissette v. United States, *supra,* described a type of criminal statute applicable to ***public welfare or regulatory offenses*** that do not innately involve harm to the State, persons, property, or public morals, but are characterized only by "neglect where the law requires care, or inaction where it imposes a duty." Examples include public health laws, building codes, or food and drug safety laws that do not require a mental state or awareness by the defendant. Since *Morissette*, courts often construe such crimes as imposing strict liability. These "regulatory" or "public welfare" offenses are especially likely to impose strict liability if they regulate items that are potentially harmful or injurious. [**Staples v. United States**, *supra*]

e.g. **Example:** Criminal violations of regulations governing taking protected birds is a strict liability offense; the penalty is small and there is no grave harm to the offender's reputation. [**United States v. Apollo Energies, Inc.,** 611 F.3d 679 (10th Cir. 2010)]

e.g. **Example:** Sale of opium under an early federal statute was held not to require proof that the defendant *knew* the item sold was opium. "Congress weighed the possible injustice of subjecting an innocent seller to a penalty against the evil of exposing innocent purchasers to danger from the drug, and concluded that the latter was the result preferably to be avoided." [**United States v. Balint,** *supra*]

e.g. **Example:** The strict liability approach to proving unlawful possession of drugs for unintentional, unknowing possession violated Due Process; insufficient relationship to the regulation of drugs. [**State v. Blake,** 481 P.3d 521 (Wash. 2021)]

(5) Traffic Offenses

Traffic offenses are often construed as imposing strict liability, because requiring proof of *mens rea* would impede the rapid and efficient enforcement that is necessary to make these crimes an effective incentive for citizens to comply with traffic laws.

e.g. **Example:** "Because driving under the influence presents a serious risk of death", the court concluded that "the legislature intended to impose strict liability for vehicular homicide while under the influence" [**State v. Burch,** 389 P.3d 685 (Wash. 2016)]

(6) Distinguish: Traditional Serious Strict Liability Crimes

Despite the general guidelines above, certain common law crimes involving more serious penalties have traditionally been regarded as strict liability offenses, *i.e.*, *non*-public welfare crimes.

e.g. **Example:** Bigamy consists of marrying someone while having another living spouse. Generally, conviction is permitted even if the defendant was unaware that her spouse was alive or that a purported divorce was invalid. Thus, the crime does not require any *mens rea* in regard to the requirement that a spouse still be living.

e.g. **Example:** Statutory rape has been held not to require an awareness of the female's age, *i.e.,* in regard to the victim's age, it is a strict liability offense.

c. Policy Considerations

Whether strict criminal liability is desirable as a matter of policy has been hotly debated. [*See* 69 Hastings L.J. 1609 (2018)]

(1) Considerations Favoring Strict Liability

- If the prosecution were required to prove *mens rea* in all cases, convictions would be so difficult to obtain that some crimes would not provide effective deterrents. In turn, important schemes of social regulation would be frustrated, and courts would be burdened with frequent and extensive litigation about whether the requisite *mens rea* was present.
- Regardless of the above considerations, dispensing with the mental element as to certain crimes does not create a risk of convicting many persons who are not morally blameworthy. Strict liability is generally imposed only in situations where those in danger of being charged are operating in a heavily regulated area (*e.g.,* sale of firearms).

(2) Considerations Against Strict Liability

- Strict liability opens the door for conviction of persons who, because of their ignorance, have not in fact done anything sufficiently "wrong" to justify criminal sanctions. The requisite *mens rea* is easily proved in most cases. Only in the few cases where there is some doubt about the accused's state of mind will there be extensive litigation. In these instances, defendants most need an opportunity to contest proof of their blameworthiness.
- Requiring proof of *mens rea* will not only remove the danger of unjustly convicting those who should not be subject to criminal punishment, but there would be minimal disruption to enforcement of regulatory schemes by criminal prosecution. [*See, e.g.,* **City of Cleveland v. Krebs,** 107 N.E.3d 774 (Ohio 2018) (strict liability inappropriate "to implement various principles of the Model Penal Code" where liability is limited to offenses with lesser punishment)]

d. Constitutional Limitations

Aside from the policy considerations affecting the issue of strict liability, there is also a question of whether the *mens rea* requirement can be *constitutionally* eliminated. As will be seen below, at least in some cases, strict liability crimes have been held to violate Due Process. [**Morissette v. United States,** *supra*; *see*, *e.g.*, **Hentzner v. State,** 613 P.2d 821 (Alaska 1980) (selling unregistered securities); **State v. Moser,** 884 N.W.2d 890 (Minn.App. 2016) (child solicitation statute barring mistake-of-age defense in Internet communications)]

(1) Rationale

The Due Process argument against strict liability offenses is twofold:

(a) No Notice

Persons subjected to conviction under strict liability statutes are arguably denied advance notice of their potential liability. Because they have violated the law before they have notice of those facts that would otherwise warn them to cease the proscribed conduct, they do not have a fair opportunity to avoid liability.

(b) Grossly Disproportionate Punishment

Those strict liability offenses that impose serious criminal penalties may be fundamentally unfair (and hence a Due Process violation) on the ground that the punishment is grossly disproportionate to the blameworthiness of the conduct involved.

e.g. **Example:** A statute made it a felony to fail to return a rented motor vehicle but did not require an intent to deprive the owner of the vehicle or to injure the owner in any way. This was held to violate Due Process, the court reasoning that to convict a person for a serious offense without requiring a "guilty mind" is "contrary to the general conditions of penal liability" that require a guilty mind in addition to the commission of a prohibited act. [**Speidel v. State,** 460 P.2d 77 (Alaska 1969)]

(2) Factors Affecting Constitutional Prohibition

Due Process does not always prohibit strict liability. Strict liability crimes are more likely to be held unconstitutional if they are serious and if they are one of the traditional common law crimes for which *mens rea* has been required (or if they resemble such crimes). Conversely, Due Process is less likely to bar strict liability if the crime is a "new" statutory offense and imposes only a minor penalty upon conviction.

e. Model Penal Code

The Model Penal Code in § 2.02 expressed disdain for the use of strict liability as a tool to convict. Except for violations that result in a fine, a voluntary act and some form of *mens rea* must support each element of every prosecution. [Model Penal Code § 2.05(1)] In other words, the MPC drafters had little use for almost any form of strict liability.

SUMMARY OF REQUISITE INTENT FOR MAJOR CRIMES

SPECIFIC INTENT	GENERAL INTENT	CRIMINAL NEGLIGENCE	MALICE	STRICT LIABILITY
1. Solicitation	1. Rape	1. Involuntary Manslaughter	1. Common Law Murder	1. Statutory Rape
2. Conspiracy	2. Mayhem	2. Battery	2. Common Law Arson	2. Bigamy
3. Attempt	3. False Imprisonment			

4. First Degree Premeditated Murder				
5. Assault				
6. Burglary				
7. Larceny, Robbery				
8. Embezzlement				
9. False Pretenses				

6. Modern (Model Penal Code) Classifications of State of Mind

Under modern law, the trend is away from the traditional classification analysis (above). In its place, contemporary criminal codes tend to adopt the Model Penal Code approach, which provides a more structured and carefully defined analysis. These codes distinguish among *purpose* (or intent), *knowledge, recklessness, and negligence,* reflecting varying quality dimensions (*see supra,* p. 42).

a. "Purpose": Conscious Desire

A person acts purposefully if her conscious desire is to engage in certain conduct or cause a certain result. [**State v. Granillo,** 384 P.3d 1121 (N.M. 2016)] She acts purposefully with regard to attendant circumstances if she hopes that they exist, or if she believes or is aware that they exist. [Model Penal Code § 2.02(2)(a)]

b. "Knowledge": Awareness of a Certainty

A person acts knowingly with respect to the nature of her conduct or attendant circumstances if she is aware that her conduct is of that nature or that the circumstances exist. She acts knowingly in regard to a result of her conduct if she is aware that it is "practically certain" that her conduct will cause the result. [Model Penal Code § 2.02(2)(b)] Knowledge of an important fact is an element of an offense, *e.g.*, when a defendant knowingly transports illegal drugs. A person knows about an important fact if she is aware of it or correctly believes that it exists. Jury instructions in a prosecution for being aware of a fact require the jurors to find beyond a reasonable doubt that the defendant knew, *i.e.*, was aware that she was transporting illegal drugs. [**State v. Ducker,** 27 S.W.3d 889 (Tenn. 2000) ("A result-of-conduct offense requires that the culpable mental state accompany the result as opposed to the nature of the conduct. The focus is on whether the actor possessed the required culpability to effectuate the result that the legislature has specified. Generally, an offense may be classified as a result-of-conduct offense when the conduct is the only element contained in the offense. . . . The 'nature of the conduct' that causes death or the manner in which one is killed is inconsequential under the second degree murder statute. The statute focuses purely on the result and punishes an actor who knowingly causes another's death.")]

(1) Distinguish: Purpose from Knowledge

Knowledge differs from purpose, because the latter requires a ***desire to cause a result,*** while knowledge simply requires that the actor be ***aware of a practical certainty*** that the result will occur.

e.g. **Example:** D places a bomb in an airplane, setting it to go off when the plane reaches 10,000 feet. Although her sole motive is to destroy the plane's cargo, D is aware that the explosion will kill the crew of the aircraft, and that in fact happens. Because D did not consciously desire to cause the death of the crew members, she has not acted purposely in regard to them. However, because she acted with awareness that their death was practically certain to follow from her conduct, she has acted ***knowingly.***

e.g. **Example:** "It is the difference between a utility that provides telephone service to a customer 'knowing it is used for bookmaking' and someone else who strings a telephone wire in order to set up the bookmaking operation; the difference between a "farm boy [who] clears the ground for setting up a still, knowing that the venture is illicit" but just looking for a paying day's work, and someone who clears the ground in order to work a still." [**United States v. Manatau,** 647 F.3d 1048 (10th Cir. 2011) citing Model Penal Code, § 2.06 cmt. 6(c)]

(2) Willful Blindness of Knowledge

A jury instruction may enable the factfinder to ***impute knowledge*** to the defendant about the illegal character of a substance she was transporting, by her ***"willful blindness" toward or "deliberate ignorance" of a circumstance.*** In other words, she willfully blinds herself to direct information of a fact, in order to avoid criminal liability. [**Global-Tech Appliances, Inc. v. SEB S.A.,** 563 U.S. 754 (2011)] "Willful blindness" would exist if the defendant believes that there is a high probability that a fact exists, *e.g.*, the illegal nature of drugs she is transporting, but she deliberately avoids learning the truth about the drug. [**United States v. Galecki,** 89 F.4th 713 (9th Cir. 2023); **United States v. Macias,** 786 F.3d 1060 (7th Cir. 2015)]

c. "Recklessness": Awareness of High Risk

A person acts recklessly if she consciously disregards ***a substantial and unjustifiable risk*** that a certain result will occur because of her conduct, that a certain circumstance exists, or that her conduct is of a particular nature. [Model Penal Code § 2.02(2)(c)]

e.g. **Example:** D was not shown to have acted with conscious disregard for the safety of human life in shining a laser at a helicopter. The prosecution produced no evidence in D's trial showing that the risk posed by lasers are matters of common knowledge; D claimed that his only purpose was to see how far the laser would go. [**United States v. Rodriguez,** 790 F.3d 951 (9th Cir. 2015)]

(1) Risk Required

The risk is that the actor's conduct "involves a gross deviation from the standard of conduct that a law-abiding person would observe." [Model Penal Code § 2.02(2)(c)]

(2) Distinguish: Knowledge

Recklessness differs from knowledge in that knowledge requires awareness of a practical ***certainty*** that a result will occur or that a circumstance will exist. Recklessness, however, simply requires awareness of something far less than certainty or even probability, *i.e.*, an awareness of a substantial and unjustifiable ***risk***.

e.g. **Example:** D places a bomb in an airplane, setting it to go off at 8:30 the next evening. Although she does not know whether the plane will be flying at that time or whether any persons will be in or near the airplane, she does know that the plane is used with some frequency and that a person in the vicinity of the explosion may be severely injured or killed. The bomb goes off when B is loading freight on the airplane and B is killed. D has not acted purposefully in regard to B's death, because it was not her conscious desire to cause the death. She also has not acted knowingly, because she was not aware (and it was not true) that B's death was practically certain to result. However, because the evidence suggests that D was aware of a substantial and unjustifiable *risk* that her conduct would result in the death of B or someone like B, D has acted ***recklessly.***

d. "Negligence": Existence of High Risk

A person acts negligently if she *should have been aware* of (or has failed to perceive) a substantial and unjustifiable risk that a certain result would occur, that a certain circumstance would exist, or that her conduct is of a particular nature. [Model Penal Code § 2.02(2)(d)]

(1) Risk Required

The risk must be of the same type required for recklessness (*supra*).

(2) Distinguish Recklessness

Negligence differs from recklessness in that recklessness requires a ***conscious awareness*** of the risk involved. Negligence, on the other hand, refers simply to circumstances in which a ***reasonable person would have been aware*** of the risk; the accused herself need not have had actual knowledge of the risk.

e.g. **Example:** D places a bomb in an airplane and sets it to go off at 8:30 the next evening, believing that no one will be near the plane at that time. However, the plane is used with such frequency that a reasonable person would have been aware that it might be in use at the time of the scheduled explosion. Moreover, a reasonable person would have been aware that anyone in the vicinity of the explosion might be killed or injured. The bomb goes off when B is loading freight onto the plane, and B is killed. Although there was a substantial and unjustifiable risk that B or someone like B would be killed by the explosion, D was not aware of that risk, and so did not act recklessly in regard to B's death. However, because a ***reasonable person*** would have been aware of the risk of B's death, D has acted ***negligently.***

SUMMARY OF CRIMINAL STATES OF MIND	
MENS REA	**STATE OF MIND REQUIRED**
COMMON LAW	
General Intent	Intent to voluntarily engage in conduct; or reference to nonmental aspects of crime
Specific Intent	Specific proof of intent; or intent to do something that is not an element of the crime
Malice	Commission of a volitional act without legal justification
Strict Liability	No requirement of *mens rea*

MPC FAULT STANDARDS	
Purposely	Conscious desire to engage in proscribed conduct, that a particular result will be caused, or that a circumstance exists
Knowingly	Awareness that conduct is of a particular nature, that certain circumstances exist, or that a result will occur (practical certainty)
Recklessly	Consciously aware of, but nonetheless acting in disregard of, a substantial and unjustifiable risk that conduct is of a particular nature, that a certain result will occur, or that her conduct is of a particular nature
Negligently	Failure to be aware of a substantial and unjustifiable risk that a certain result would occur, that a certain circumstance exists, or that her conduct is of a particular nature

7. Modern (Model Penal Code) General Requirement: At Least Recklessness Regarding All Elements

The Model Penal Code, and many modern statutes based on it, provides that unless a criminal statute provides to the contrary, such a statute will be interpreted to require that the defendant acted with ***at least recklessness in regard to each significant element.*** [Model Penal Code § 2.02(3)]

a. Compare Traditional Approach

This rule is similar to the ***general intent*** requirement of traditional analysis (*see supra,* p. 44). However, it is more carefully structured and makes clearer the state of mind required for particular crimes.

b. "Higher" State of Mind Suffices

Where recklessness is required, the prosecution can also prevail upon a showing that the defendant acted knowingly or purposefully. In other words, whenever a lower level of *mens rea* is required, a higher level will suffice.

c. Negligence May Be Sufficient

A statute may require only negligence regarding one or more elements, but because liability for negligence should be the exception rather than the rule, a crime will be so interpreted only where the legislative intent is clearly indicated in the language of the statute itself.

d. Higher State of Mind May Be Required

A crime may be defined as imposing a requirement of knowledge or purpose in regard to one or more elements.

e.g. **Example:** The federal crime of treason, which consists of giving aid and comfort to an enemy of the United States, requires that the accused act with the *conscious purpose* of aiding the enemy. The extremely serious nature of the crime and the penalty require a showing of purpose to assure that only persons with sufficient culpability commit the crime. [*See* **United States v. Bailey,** 444 U.S. 394 (1980)]

e.g. **Example:** The federal crime of escape, which consists of absenting oneself from federal custody without permission, does ***not*** require that the defendant acts with purpose, *i.e.,* with the conscious objective of leaving such custody and of doing so without permission. *Bailey* held that there was no basis for concluding that Congress intended this requirement. The Court declined to decide, however, whether the Government must prove knowledge, *i.e.*, that the defendant knew he was leaving custody and that he lacked permission, or whether instead either recklessness or negligence suffices. [**United States v. Bailey,** *supra*]

e. "Specific Intent" May Be Required

Under the Model Penal Code approach, crimes may require proof of a state of mind concerning something that is not an element of the offense. This requirement would be in addition to those imposed by this rule, and would be analogous to the "specific intent" sometimes required under traditional analysis (*see supra,* p. 45). Model Penal Code analysis, however, would not label such requirements as requiring "specific intent."

f. Analysis Under Modern Approach

Suppose a statute provides: "A person is guilty of arson if he causes an explosion with the purpose of destroying a building." To ascertain the state of mind that will support a conviction under modern codes, the following analysis is correct.

(1) What State of Mind Concerning the Nonmental Elements of the Crime Must Be Proved?

The nonmental elements of this crime are (i) that the defendant did some act (no specific act is designated) and (ii) that there was an explosion caused by the act. Thus, only the state of mind regarding those elements, *i.e.*, some "act" and the occurrence of an "explosion" as a result of the act, must be considered in this step of the analysis.

(a) Does the statute require a state of mind ***higher than recklessness?*** No.

(b) Does the statute provide that ***not even recklessness*** is required, *i.e.,* that negligence is sufficient? No.

(c) Therefore, ***recklessness is adequate.*** Accordingly, the prosecution must prove that at the time of his act, the defendant was aware of a substantial and unjustifiable risk that he was engaging in the act and that his conduct would cause an explosion. The prosecution is not required to show, however, that the defendant knew that an explosion would occur or that he desired it to occur.

(2) Does the Statute Require a State of Mind Regarding Something That Is Not an Element of the Offense?

Yes. The defendant must have acted "with the purpose of destroying a building." The prosecution need not prove that a building was destroyed; "destroying a building" is not an element of the offense. However, the prosecution must show that the defendant had a particular state of mind regarding this result. The requisite state of mind is *"purpose"; i.e.,* the defendant must have had the *conscious desire* to cause destruction of a building.

(3) Summary

In addition to establishing that the defendant acted and caused an explosion, the prosecution must prove:

(a) The defendant was ***aware of a substantial and unjustifiable risk*** that he was engaging in certain conduct and that ***an explosion would occur*** as the result of his conduct; and

(b) The defendant had a ***conscious desire to cause the destruction of a building.***

8. Culpable Mental State Analysis Under Modern Statutory Crimes That Prescribe a Culpable Mental State

Modern statutory crimes sometimes pose difficult questions of interpretation regarding the nonmental elements of the crime to which a specified required culpable mental state applies. Several approaches can be taken to this task.

a. Illustrative Problem

A federal crime exists when a person "knowingly transfers, possesses, or uses, without lawful authority, a means of identification of another person." [18 U.S.C. § 1028A(a)(1)] Clearly the crime requires proof that a defendant acted "knowingly," but with regard to what "objects" must he act knowingly? This crime contains several nonmental elements: (i) the person must "use" something; (ii) this must be done "without lawful authority"; (iii) the thing used must be "a means of identification"; and (iv) the means of identification used must be "of another person." "Knowingly" certainly applies to (i), so the prosecution's evidence must show she knew she was using something. But will the courts apply "knowingly" to the list of nonmental elements (ii), (iii) and (iv)? What standard should be used to decide how far down the line "knowingly" applies?

b. Relationship to Strict Liability Analysis

If the culpable mental state required for an offense does not apply to all material nonmental elements of the crime, the crime imposes "limited" or "partial" strict liability. (*See supra,* p. 43) Therefore, factors suggesting strict liability weigh in favor of construing such a culpable mental state as *not* applying to one or more nonmental elements of the offense.

c. Model Penal Code "Elemental" Approach

The Model Penal Code assumes that some culpable mental state should ordinarily apply to ***all material nonmental elements*** of a crime. If a crime, such as the federal crime above, prescribes a culpable mental state such as "knowingly" without distinguishing among the material elements of the offense, the culpable mental state applies to each and every material element unless a contrary legislative purpose "plainly appears." [Model Penal Code § 2.02(4)] One *mens rea* applies to all the elements of the crime.

e.g. **Example:** A person knowingly possesses child pornography when he knows of the nature or character of the material and of its presence and has dominion and control over it. [**State v. Mucia,** 871 N.W.2d 221 (Neb. 2015)] The prosecutor must prove that, at the time of committing the offense, the defendant knew that he (1) possessed pornography, and (2) received, procured, controlled that pornography. Directly or circumstantially, proof of the defendant's knowledge is necessary to prove each element of the offense.

e.g. **Example:** A statute provides: "It is a misdemeanor to knowingly sell liquor to a person less than 21 years of age." Does "knowingly" apply to the age element, *i.e.*, proof that defendant furnished liquor to a person who then was less than 21 years old? Arguably, the impracticality of requiring proof of knowledge suggests a "plainly" appearing legislative purpose to not apply knowingly to this element and instead to require only recklessness under a general rule that recklessness is to be required if a statute fails to specify the level of mental state required for an element. [*Compare* **Commonwealth v. Scolieri,** 813 A.2d 672 (Pa. 2002) (culpable mental state of "knowingly" applied to the age element)]

d. Ordinary English Usage Approach

The United States Supreme Court has relied on what it described as ordinary English grammar and general usage. When a federal statutory crime contains a required culpable mental state (as when it specifies that the crime must be committed "knowingly"), the culpable mental state often and perhaps generally applies to all the subsequently listed elements of the crime. [**Flores-Figueroa v. United States,** 556 U.S. 646 (2009)] Several Justices, however, cautioned against applying this approach if the context or policy considerations suggest that Congress intended a less demanding culpable mental state. [**Flores-Figueroa v. United States,** *supra* (Justice Scalia, joined by Justices Thomas and Alito, both concurring in part and concurring in the judgment)]

cf. **Compare:** At least one court has challenged this approach as a matter of proper grammar. It reasoned that an adverb ordinarily modifies only the verb or verb phrase with which it is associated. [**State v. Hunter,** 164 Wash.App. 1045 (2011)] Under this approach, the federal statute above would be construed as requiring only that the defendant act knowingly regarding the act of using something.

e. Elements Separating Wrongful Conduct from Otherwise Innocent Conduct

In some cases, the Supreme Court has indicated that a federal crime will ordinarily be construed as requiring a culpable mental state regarding those elements that distinguish wrongful conduct from innocent conduct. [**United States v. X-Citement Video, Inc.,** 513 U.S. 64 (1994)] Using this approach, courts should construe a required culpable mental state as applicable to (and only to) those material elements that distinguish the conduct prohibited by the statutory crime from conduct that is not criminal at all.

f. Illustrative Problem Revisited

If the Model Penal Code approach was applied to the federal statute summarized above, knowingly would be applied to all the elements. The same result is suggested by the approach described, *supra*, *i.e.*, if any of the four nonelements is lacking, the conduct constituting the crime is "innocent" and thus not criminal. All of the elements distinguish criminal from innocent conduct. Relying heavily upon its version of the ordinary English usage approach, the Supreme Court construed the statute's requirement of "knowingly" as applicable to all the elements and specifically to element (iv). [**Flores-Figueroa v. United States,** *supra*]

g. Compare: Culpable Mental State Analysis Under Modern Statutory Crimes Does Not Explicitly Prescribe a Culpable Mental State

If a modern statutory crime does not explicitly prescribe a culpable mental state but one is read into the crime under the general rule that crimes require *mens rea*, the courts must then address the nonmental elements to which that culpable mental state applies. The approaches described *above* may be used to resolve this. The Supreme Court, for example, has suggested that the presumption of scienter requires a court to read into a statutory crime only awareness regarding those elements that separate innocent from criminal conduct. [**Carter v. United States,** 530 U.S. 255 (2000)]

h. Culpable Mental States Concerning Penalty Elements

Courts have been reluctant to apply a required culpable mental state to an element that either distinguishes a crime from a less serious offense or concerns the penalty. [**Dean v. United States,** 556 U.S. 568 (2009) (not unusual for criminal law to punish persons for unintended consequences of their unlawful acts; for the crime of discharging a gun, it is not necessary that the "discharge be done knowingly or intentionally," an accomplice may be sentenced whenever such discharge is "a reasonably foreseeable result" of bringing the gun to the place where the underlying crime is to be committed.)]

(1) Example: Amount of Drugs

Sales of controlled substances are often covered by several increasingly serious crimes that differ only regarding the amount of drugs sold. Almost all courts applying such statutes do not require proof, for the more serious offenses, that the defendant was aware of the amount or weight of the drugs that brought the sale within the charged crime. [**Ex parte Washington,** 818 So.2d 424 (Ala. 2001) (in a prosecution for sale of 28 grams or more of cocaine, the prosecution did not need to prove that defendant knew that the cocaine sold weighed more than 28 grams)]

9. Mens Rea Requirements and "Defenses"

Some so-called defenses are not really defenses in the traditional sense but instead are ways by which defendants contest whether the prosecution has really proved the *mens rea* required by the crime charged. These "defenses," for example, mistake of fact, some aspects of mistake of law, voluntary intoxication, and "diminished capacity", are often described as means by which a defendant can "negate" the *mens rea* required. In reality, though, because the burden of proof is on the prosecution, a defendant is entitled to acquittal if the defense raises a reasonable doubt as to whether the prosecution has proved *mens rea.*

a. Constitutional Issues Related to Mens Rea Defenses

Due Process, the Sixth Amendment right to jury trial, or these rights in combination may entitle defendants to an unrestricted opportunity to rely on whatever evidence they choose to negate *mens rea.* Limitations on these *mens rea* "defenses" may thus be unconstitutional, and are addressed further in the discussions of those "defenses," *Chapter 6, infra.*

10. "Transferred Intent": Responsibility for Unintended Results

a. General Requirement: Contemplation of Harm Actually Caused

Ordinarily, criminal liability attaches only where the defendant is shown to have intended the actual harm resulting from his conduct. Thus, one who throws a stone at another with the intent to strike that person (*i.e.,* commit a battery), but misses and breaks a window instead, is not guilty of "maliciously causing harm to property." Because he did not contemplate the result required by the crime charged, destruction of the window, he lacked the *mens rea* required for the crime. It is irrelevant that his intent was to cause a different, albeit criminal harm. [**Regina v. Pembliton,** 12 Cox Crim. Cas. 607 (1874); **Regina v. Faulkner,** 13 Cox Crim. Cas. 550 (1877)]

(1) Rationale

Where the actual result differs from the one intended, there is insufficient indication of the defendant's ability and willingness to act successfully on his criminal intent to justify holding him liable for a crime. This is true even though the unintended result is harmful.

b. Exception: "Transferred Intent"

Where the contemplated result is criminal and there is *great similarity* between that harm and the result that actually occurs, courts indulge in a fiction: the defendant is treated as though he had in fact contemplated the result that occurred. This situation is often known as the doctrine of transferred intent. The defendant's intent will be "transferred" from the intended object or person to the object or person actually injured, and criminal liability will follow.

e.g. **Example:** A defendant who intends to kill a pregnant woman, but instead inflicts injuries on fetus that proved to be fatal only after the fetus is born alive is guilty of murder as a result of the transferred intent doctrine. [**State v. Courchesne,** 998 A.2d 1 (Conn. 2010)]

e.g. **Example:** The defendant fired gunshots into a residence occupied by intended and unintended victims, but no one was injured. Defendant is guilty of attempted murder of the intended and unintended persons inside the residence. [**State v. Williams,** 812 S.E.2d 917 (S.C. 2017)]

e.g. **Example:** As host and his three guests opened the door to leave his apartment, D immediately started shooting at them. The guests including V quickly returned to the apartment; when V then fled further into a bedroom, bedroom occupant S shot and killed V by mistaking him for an intruder; D was prosecuted for V's death because S shot him as "a reasonably foreseeable consequence of D's acts." [**State v. Wilson,** 421 P.3d 742 (Kan. 2018)]

(1) Rationale

When there is such similarity between the intended and actual results, the defendant is regarded as sufficiently "dangerous" in the eyes of the law to justify subjecting him to criminal sanctions.

(2) Similarity of Harm Required

Some courts do not require similarity between the harm intended and that accidentally caused. [**Birt v. State,** 645 S.E.2d 596 (Ga.App. 2007) (as with *Pembliton, supra,* transferred intent applies where D shot intending to injure police officer but accidentally struck and damaged property)]

(3) Exception: Intended Crime Committed

Some courts do not apply transferred intent when the defendant is guilty of the intended crime. In the example above if the stone thrown by D hit and injured B and then bounced into C injuring C, D is guilty of battery upon B. Some courts apply transferred intent only to avoid exonerating D from all criminal liability, so they would not apply the doctrine to hold D guilty of the additional crime of battery on C. [**Ford v. State,** 625 A.2d 984 (Md. 1993) (where "the means employed to commit the crime against a primary victim create a zone of harm around that victim, the factfinder can reasonably infer that the defendant intended that harm to all who are in the anticipated zone")]

c. Model Penal Code Position

The Model Penal Code would impose broader liability than described above, on a transferred intent theory where either of two requirements is met:

(i) The contemplated result and the actual result differ only in that a different person or property is involved or in that the contemplated harm would have been more serious or extended; or

(ii) The contemplated result and the actual result "involve the same kind of injury or harm" and the actual result was not "too remote or accidental. . . to have a [just] bearing" on the defendant's guilt.

[Model Penal Code § 2.03]

EXAM TIP

Note that a person found guilty of a crime on the basis of transferred intent has usually committed ***two crimes:*** the completed crime against the actual victim ***and attempt*** against the intended victim. Thus, if a question indicates that D intends to shoot and kill A, but instead shoots and kills B, discuss D's liability for the murder of B (under the transferred intent doctrine) *and* D's potential liability for the attempted murder of A.

E. Concurrence of Actus Reus and Mens Rea

1. In General

As indicated at the outset, there must be a concurrence between the *mens rea* and the act or result required by the crime at issue. This means that the act or result must be ***attributable*** to the culpable state of mind. This principle is sometimes expressed as the requirement of a "union" or "joint operation" between the act and intent. [**Thabo Meli v. Regina,** (1954) 1 All E.R. 373]

2. Concurrence Between Mens Rea and Act

The act constituting the crime must be the result of the intent that constitutes the *mens rea*. Generally, this means that the defendant must have had the requisite intent ***at the moment he performed the act.***

e.g. **Example:** The crime of receiving stolen property knowing it to be stolen is not committed when *A* receives from *B* property which he does not know to be stolen, though when *A* later learns it is stolen he decides to keep it. [**United States v. McDougald,** 990 F.2d 259 (6th Cir. 1993) (no showing D purchased a car with knowledge that the funds used were drug money, as D's false statements over a month later, after he knew authorities thought "he had done something wrong," do not show state of mind at time of purchase, and thus requisite concurrence not established)]

e.g. **Example:** Similarly, D could not be convicted of burglary if he entered B's home to seek shelter and ***while inside*** he formed the intent to steal B's jewels. Again, the intent to steal did not cause the entry; *i.e.,* there is no liability where the act was performed "innocently" and the *mens rea* was later formed. (Of course, if D took the jewels, he could be prosecuted for theft.)

e.g. **Example:** In the crime of knowingly failing to appear in court on a specified date, defendant's awareness that he is failing to appear must exist "at the time, date and court specified in the citation"; state's argument that defendant's knowledge "at some previous point" suffices conflicts with requirement of "a coincidence if mental state and action." [**State v. Servatius,** 395 P.3d 910 (Ore.App. 2017)]

3. Concurrence Between Mens Rea and Result

If the crime in question requires proof of a result, there must be concurrence between that result and the requisite intent, *i.e.*, the occurrence of the result must be ***attributable*** to the *mens rea.* Generally, a showing will suffice that the defendant had the necessary intent at the time he committed the act that caused the result. However, when the requisite intent follows the physical conduct, the mental state is not legally related to the prior acts or omissions of the defendant.

e.g. **Example:** D drives his car toward A, intending to injure A. At the final moment, D changes his mind and attempts to stop the vehicle but is unable to do so, and A is injured. Because the harm to A was caused by and is attributable to D's act of driving the car toward A, the requisite concurrence existed. It is irrelevant that at the exact moment of injury, D did not have the necessary intent; having had the prohibited intent at the time he perpetrated the act that caused the harm, D can be convicted of battery. [**People v. Claborn,** 224 Cal. App. 2d 38 (1964)]

a. Concurrence in Time Is Not Essential

As the above example makes clear, it is not essential that the intent and result concur in point of time. It need only be shown that the result was *attributable* to the intent. [**People v. Claborn,** *supra*]

4. Special Problem: Mistake of Death Cases

Special problems are posed where the defendant mistakenly believes he has caused death and then, without the intent to kill, performs an act that *actually does cause the death* of the victim. Some courts find no liability here, on the ground that the result is not attributable to the intent. Others, however, do find liability, often reasoning that the defendant's behavior was all part of a single scheme or constituted part of a single transaction with a single intention.

e.g. **Example:** D planned to kill V and then make the death look accidental. She gave V beer and then struck him over the head. Thinking that he is dead, D rolled him over a cliff and made the scene look like V had accidentally fallen. In fact, the blow to the head did not kill V, but merely rendered him unconscious. The cause of his death was exposure. Even though D did not intend to kill V when she rolled him over the cliff and left him there (having thought she had already accomplished her goal), many courts would find the necessary concurrence between the intent to kill and V's death, on the theory that D's action was all part of the original plan that caused the death. [**Commonwealth v. Cyr,** 744 N.E.2d 1082 (Mass. 2001); **Thabo Meli v. Regina,** *supra*]

F. Causation

1. In General

If a crime requires proof of a result, the prosecution must prove that the defendant's conduct was the ***legal cause*** of that result. Problems of causation arise most often in connection with homicide crimes, where the prosecution must show a causal relationship between the defendant's act and the victim's death. However, the issue can also be encountered in the context of other crimes. The necessary causation is of two types: ***"factual"*** causation (also known as but-for causation or "cause in fact") and ***"proximate"*** causation (also known as "legal causation"). Both must be proved before liability is imposed. Causation, whether it is factual or proximate, may be "direct" or it may instead cause the particular result by means of other "intervening" causes.

While causation issues focus on whether the defendant's conduct produced a result, a defendant may cause that result, *e.g.*, bodily injury, by an omission as well as by action. [**Delligatti v. United States,** 604 U.S. 423 (2025) ("an individual may knowingly or intentionally cause bodily injury or death by" not taking action)] *See* Criminal Acts: Actus Reus, *supra.*

a. Direct Causation

Causation is direct if the defendant's act causes the result without the involvement of any intervening factor or cause.

b. Causation Through Intervening Causes

Causation may exist even if other factors, such as the actions of other people, intervene and thus contribute to the result. The fact that causation involves such intervening causes does not necessarily mean that the defendant's act was not the legal cause of the result. Where intervening causes contribute to the result, however, a defendant has a stronger argument that, under the analyses discussed below, proximate and perhaps even factual causation do not exist.

e.g. **Example:** D pointed a gun at A with the intent to kill A. Before D could shoot him, A grabbed D's gun that was pointed at him, causing the weapon to discharge and kill V. D is guilty of V's murder. [**Rogers v. State,** 232 P.3d 1226 (Alaska App. 2010)]

APPROACH TO CAUSATION (TRADITIONAL VIEW)

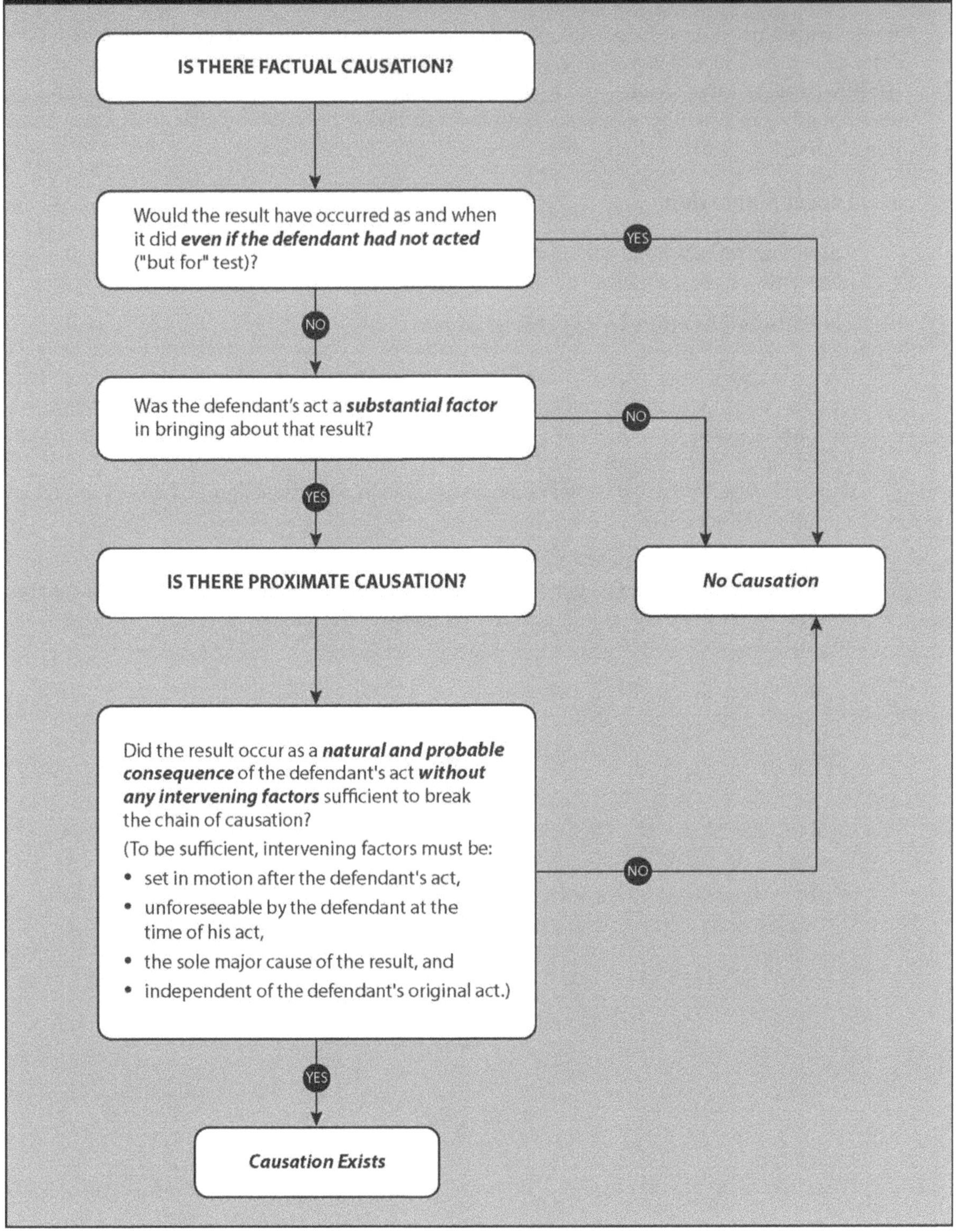

2. Factual Causation: "But For" Test

The prosecution must first establish that the defendant's acts were the ***"factual cause"*** of the result, *i.e.*, ***"but for" the defendant's acts, would the prohibited result have happened as and when it did?*** Sometimes a situation arises where two or more causes, each alone sufficient to bring about a harmful result, together also cause a harmful result. For example, A shoots and kills B, and C at the same time stabs and kills B, who dies from the combined effect of two wounds. The test for causation-in-fact may be more accurately worded, not in terms of but-for cause, but as whether A's or C's conduct a substantial or contributing factor in the result. For each defendant, if the result would not have occurred but for his conduct, his conduct is a substantial or contributing factor in bringing about the result.

Either a "substantial factor" or "contributing cause" test may determine cause-in-fact. Each concept is broader than "but-for" causation, *e.g.*, a pathologist testified that gunshot wounds from two different weapons were the cause of the victim's death, but the pathologist could *not* say which of the wounds caused the death, stating that either of the two wounds could have killed the victim. The defendant's acts alone did not have to have caused the result; causation exists even if other actions and circumstances contributed to the result as long as it would not have happened as and when it did "but for" the defendant's acts.

a. Substantial Factor Requirement

As mentioned, the substantial factor approach is used when there are multiple "but-for" causes of the result, although no one is the but-for cause. It is then said that factual causation requires that the defendant's act is a ***"substantial factor" in bringing about the result.*** [**Rivers v. State,** 768 S.E.2d 486 (Ga. 2015) (proximate cause "played a substantial part" in bringing about results)] If the defendant's act did affect the situation sufficiently to be a literal "but for" cause of the result but its impact was ***de minimis,*** a court may well find that factual causation was lacking.

e.g. **Example:** Defendant's eight-month old daughter died from a skull fracture. During one afternoon, defendant left the two young children with her husband while she ran errands. The daughter appeared normal when she left. Defendant returned four hours later at 7 p.m., and the husband said the daughter was asleep in her crib. An hour later, the daughter was unresponsive. When Defendant contacted a nearby hospital, she was told to bring the daughter to the Emergency Room. When they arrived about 11:00 p.m., the daughter's body was cold. A physician diagnosed a hematoma on the left side of the daughter's head. At 1:30 a.m. a CT scan indicated a skull fracture and other signs of brain injury. More tests revealed brain death. An autopsy revealed that the daughter had died from a skull fracture and accompanying brain swelling.

Defendant was charged with felony child abuse resulting in death. At trial, the doctor testified that the daughter "might have survived" if treatment was sought earlier during the four hours between Defendant's arrival at her home and the trip to the hospital. The court convicted her, finding that (1) she knowingly and intentionally failed to provide necessary care during the four hours before she took the daughter to the hospital, (2) the daughter's condition worsened as a result, and (3) her worsening condition led to her death. The appellate court reversed the conviction because of insufficient proof that the daughter would have survived with earlier treatment. The prosecution did not prove that Defendant knowingly and intentionally deprived the daughter of necessary care. The State proved only the *possibility* of survival with earlier treatment. [**State v. Muro,** 695 N.W.2d 425 (Neb. 2005)]

e.g. **Example:** D struck V, causing a slight cut. X then shot V, causing a serious wound that bled severely. V lost several drops of blood from the wound inflicted by D and quarts of blood from the wound inflicted by X and died from loss of blood. Although it could be argued that D's actions were a "but for" cause of V dying from blood loss, those actions were not a "substantial factor" in bringing about the result and therefore may be held not to have factually "caused" it.

(1) Distinguishing "Substantial Factor" from Traditional Cause-in-Fact?

In **Burrage v. United States,** 571 U.S. 204 (2014), the issue was whether a defendant who unlawfully distributes drugs is subject to the mandatory minimum sentence applicable when "death or serious bodily injury results from the use of such substance." The Court held that the statutory "results from" language imposed a requirement of but-for causation, rather than similar statutes that require only that the drug "contribute to" the death or injury. The "contribute to" approach is the minority view if the drug was a substantial or a contributing factor. of causation generally. *Burrage* is heavily criticized. *See*, *e.g*., 68 Fla.L.Rev. 1727 (2016).

b. Speeding up Result

On appeal, a defendant cannot escape criminal liability by arguing that victim was going to die anyway. Applying the "but for" rule, factual causation will be present even though the defendant's acts simply speeded up the result. [**State v. Phillips**, 656 N.E.2d 643 (Ohio 1995)]

e.g. **Example:** Although V would have ultimately died from previously being shot by another, when D shot V in the head and that hastened death, D was the cause of death. [**State v. McDonald,** 953 P.2d 470 (Wash. 1998)]

(1) But Not Substantial Factor

A few courts would disagree, however, and find the required substantial causation lacking where the result would otherwise have occurred within a short period of time.

c. Negligence of Victim or Third Party

The fact that the victim (*e.g.,* in a homicide case) or a third person was negligent, and this negligence contributed to causing the result, does not establish the lack of factual causation. However, in specific cases, such negligence might constitute a ***superseding factor*** (*see infra,* p. 61), and thus establish the lack of proximate causation. [**Commonwealth v. Root,** 170 A.2d 310 (Pa. 1961)]

d. Exception: Concurrent Sufficient Causes

The general requirement of a showing of "but for" causation does not apply where the result is brought about by two factors operating concurrently, either of which would have been sufficient itself to cause the result. In such cases, ***both*** factors will be regarded as "but for" causes, even though the result would have occurred as and when it did if either one of the factors had not come into operation. [**Cox v. State,** 808 S.W.2d 306 (Ark. 1991), **Wilson v. State,** 24 S.W. 409 (Tex. 1893)]

e.g. **Example:** A and B both shoot C, killing him instantly. Medical testimony establishes that C would have died when and as he did from either wound alone. Nevertheless, both A's and B's acts are the factual cause of C's death, because they are concurrent sufficient causes. [**Wilson v. State,** *supra*; *cf.* **State v. Tyler,** 873 N.W.2d 741 (Iowa 2016) (D struck V with nonfatal blows, knocking V to the ground, after which others present "immediately jumped and stomped on" V, causing his death, D is guilty of murder as a principal, as his "punch was a but-for cause" of V's death; if D had not hit V "and put him in a position of relative helplessness, he would not have died that night from the stomping and kicking that immediately followed")]

e. Exception: Effect of Action Comes to Rest in Position of Safety

If the direct effect of the defendant's acts comes to rest in a position of apparent safety, matters that occur later as a result of the defendant's act will not be regarded as having been caused by the defendant's act.

e.g. **Example:** D rolls a boulder down a hill. The boulder wedges against a tree and stops. A week later, the tree breaks and the boulder rolled down the hill, striking and killing V. Although "but for" D's initial actions, V would not have died as and when he did, D's act did not "cause" V's death because the direct effect of that act came to rest in a position of apparent safety when the boulder wedged against the tree.

3. Proximate Causation

The existence of factual causation does not alone support criminal liability. In addition, there must be proof of ***"proximate"*** causation. Proximate causation is a flexible analysis involving a variety of policy considerations, which ultimately ask whether as a matter of policy the defendant should be held responsible for a particular result. [**People v. Acosta,** 284 Cal. Rptr. 117 (1991)]

e.g. After the defendant hit the victim on the back of the head with a gun, the victim fell to the pavement and died; the medical examiner concluded that the victim died from either the blow or the fall; The court ruled that the defendant's acts were the proximate cause of the victim's death, from either event. The fall was reasonably foreseeable. [**Chaney v. State,** 640 S.E.2d 37 (Ga. 2007)]

a. Usual Problem: Result Occurs in Unexpected Manner

Proximate causation problems arise primarily when an ***expected result*** occurs in a ***manner not contemplated*** by the defendant. The issue is whether the difference between the anticipated sequence of events and what actually transpired is enough to break the chain of proximate causation.

APPROACH TO SUPERSEDING FACTORS AND CAUSATION

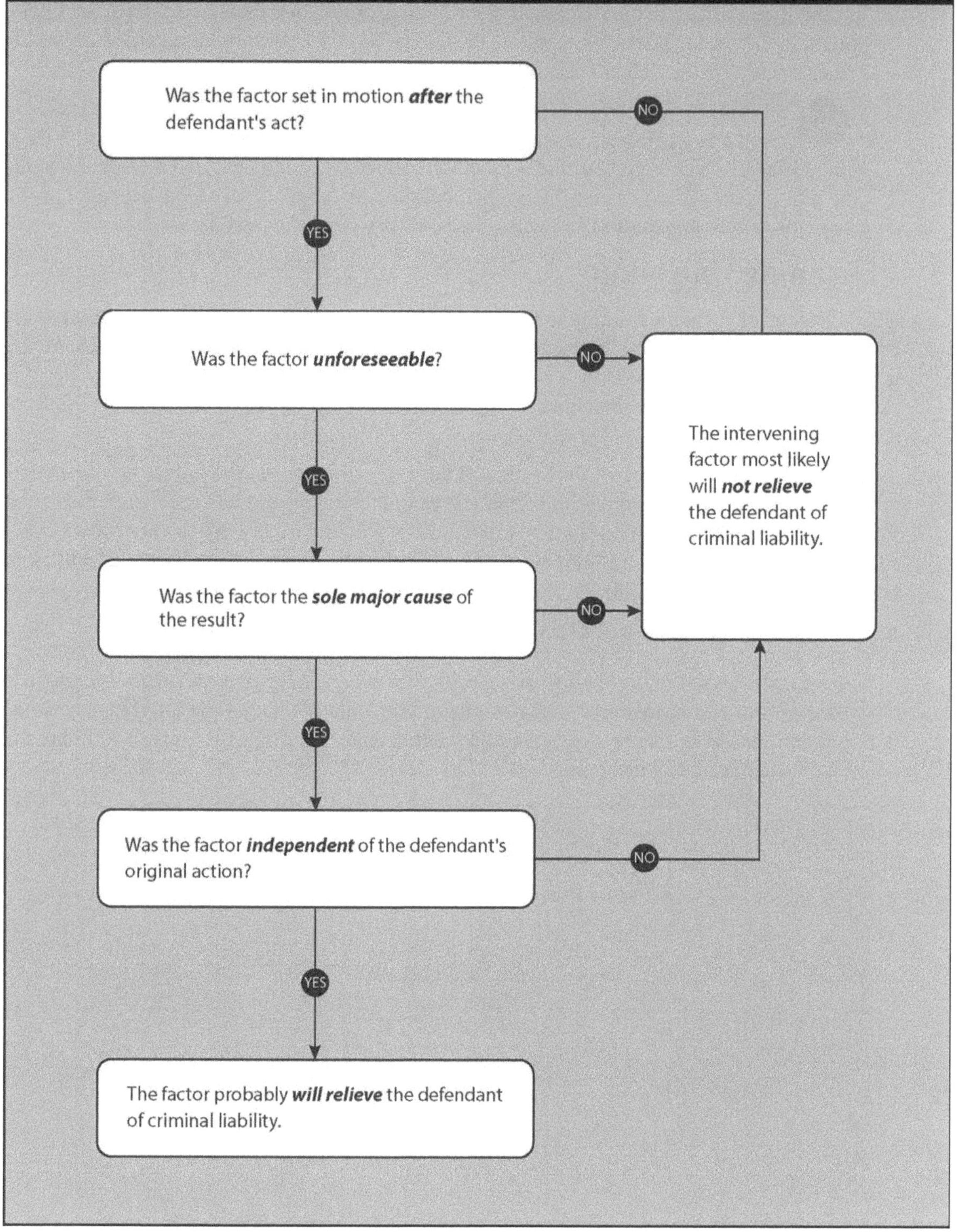

(1) Unintended Victim

If the only difference between the expected result and the actual result is that the actual result involved a ***different victim*** than was contemplated by the defendant, the issue is not one of proximate causation but rather one of transferred intent (*see supra,* p. 62 *et seq.*).

(2) "Substantial Factor" Test Not Met

If a defendant's acts were not a sufficiently substantial factor in causing a result (*see supra,* p. 67), the lack of liability may be explained in terms of no proximate causation rather than no factual causation.

b. General Rule: "All Natural and Probable Consequences" and No Superseding Factor

As a general rule, the defendant is regarded as the "proximate cause" if the result occurred ***as a "natural and probable consequence"*** (also known as a foreseeable consequence) of his act ***and no intervening factor*** sufficient to break the chain of causation (a "superseding" factor) affected the events. Whether a particular result is a "natural and probable consequence" of a particular act may require nothing more than that the result occurred as a factual consequence of the defendant's act without the interjection of a superseding factor. Note that even if the result occurred in a manner different from what the defendant expected, a court will regard the defendant as the proximate cause. [**People v. Geiger,** 159 N.W.2d 383 (Mich. 1968)] In other words, the defendant will not be relieved of liability simply because the result that he intended materialized by an unanticipated sequence of events.

e.g. **Example:** D struck V, aware of a high risk that V might die from the blow. In fact, V was only rendered unconscious. However, while unconscious, V vomited and choked to death. D did not anticipate causing V's death ***in this manner*** (by choking). Nevertheless, V's death was the "natural and probable consequence" of D's action and there were no intervening factors; therefore, D's conduct (striking V) was the proximate cause of V's death. [**People v. Geiger,** *supra*]

c. Superseding Factors: Breaking the Chain of Causation

Proximate causation does not exist if the causal chain between the defendant's act and the result was affected by a ***"superseding factor"***, *i.e.,* an additional act or occurrence that will supersede the defendant's act as the legally significant causal factor. Whether an additional act or occurrence constitutes a superseding cause depends on several considerations.

(1) Must Be "Intervening"

An act or occurrence is a superseding factor only if it is an ***intervening*** one, *i.e.,* one act set in motion ***after*** the defendant's act. Therefore, a preexisting condition cannot be a superseding factor and will not break the chain of proximate causation.

e.g. **Example:** D shot V three times in the head; bullet fragments embedded in V's sinus cavity. The medical negligence in treating the gunshot wounds was not "a new and independent force" that broke the causal connection; "[o]nly medical care that is shown to be the sole cause of death will operate to break the chain of causation." [**State v. Surbauch,** 786 S.E.2d 601 (W.Va. 2016)]

e.g. **Example:** D sold regular-strength Sterno, containing methanol, to alcoholics on skid row in Philadelphia, knowing that the skid-row alcoholics who bought Sterno from him "would extract the alcohol for drinking purposes." While a prior version of Sterno contained 3.75% methanol, Sterno began selling an industrial strength version containing 57% methanol in an almost identical can. While affirming the thirty-one manslaughter convictions, the state Supreme Court did not impose a duty on D to determine how the customers would use the product. However, it did rule that "if a seller of Sterno is aware that the purchaser is an alcoholic and will use Sterno as a source of alcohol, then the seller is grossly negligent and wantonly reckless selling Sterno to him." The voluntary acts of the victims were not deemed independent supervening causes of the deaths. [**Commonwealth v. Feinberg,** 253 A.2d 636 (Pa. 1969)]

(2) Must Be Unforeseeable

The intervening factor must also be ***unforeseeable*** (*i.e.*, not foreseen) by the defendant at the time of his action. [**People v. Brady,** 129 Cal. App. 4th 1314 (2005)] Some intervening factors include:

(a) Improper Medical Treatment

D shoots V. Although the wound is not fatal, surgical treatment is required. The surgery is performed, but V dies because of inadequate blood transfusions. Because the risks of surgery are foreseeable, the ineffectively administered transfusion is ***not*** a superseding factor. Therefore, D's shot is the proximate cause of V's death.

1) Distinguish: Grossly Negligent Treatment

Some courts hold that deficient medical care is unforeseeable, and thus may break the chain of causation, if it is ***grossly*** negligent or so poorly administered that it constitutes medical malpractice. [**Neal v. State,** 722 S.E.2d 765 (Ga. 2012) (severance of victim's jugular vein by emergency medical personnel during intubation constituted gross mistreatment and thus an intervening cause)]

(b) Acts of the Victim

A defendant's criminal conduct may lead a victim to engage in dangerous, impulsive and perhaps lethal acts in order to avoid further harm by the defendant. The victim's response is a foreseeable consequence of the defendant's actions, and the defendant is the proximate cause of the V's death or injury. [*See, e.g.*, **Rogers v. State,** 232 P.3d 1226 (Alaska App. 2010) (V's defensive action in grabbing a firearm D pointed at him with intent to kill caused weapon to fire and kill; D is guilty of murder)]

e.g. **Example:** After an accident caused by D's drunk driving, V consented to a blood thinning medication and insertion of a stent to save his leg. However, V died during the treatment. V's consent was not regarded as a superseding cause of death. [**Levenson v. Commonwealth,** 808 S.E.2d 196 (Va. 2017)]

(c) Intervening Disease

D shoots V and injures her. V is taken to a hospital, where lung damage from the shooting made V more susceptible to contracting a lung infection. The infection led to V's death from pneumonia. If a court characterizes the infection as a coincidence and unforeseeable, and thus a superseding factor, the defendant would not be criminally responsible. [*Compare* **State v. Harris,** 398 P.3d 1229 (Wash.App. 2017)] When a wound, though not itself fatal, brings on a fatal disease, *e.g.*, pneumonia, D may be responsible for V's death. [**People v. Love,** 373 N.E.2d 1312 (Ill. 1978)]

(3) Must Be Sole Major Cause of Result

An intervening factor will be a superseding one only if it is the ***sole major cause*** of the result. If it simply combines with the effects of the defendant's conduct, both are concurrent proximate causes and the chain of proximate causation will not be broken. [**People v. Lewis,** 124 Cal. 551 (1899)]

e.g. **Example:** A stabs B and leaves him dying on the ground. C then comes along and also stabs B. B dies from loss of blood caused by both wounds. Although C's act intervened, it is not a superseding factor because it did not become the sole direct cause of B's death. It merely combined with the results of A's act to become a concurrent cause of death. Hence, A (as well as C) is subject to liability for the homicide. [**People v. Lewis,** *supra*]

e.g. **Example:** After D shot V, his wound required surgery which brought on a pulmonary embolism from which V died. D was adjudged the cause of death. [**Anderson v. State,** 385 S.W.3d 214 (Ark. 2011)]

(4) Generally Must Be "Independent" of the Defendant's Action

An intervening factor is more likely to break the chain of proximate causation the more ***independent it is of the defendant's original action.*** On the other hand, if the intervening act was committed in response to the defendant's original actions, it is not independent and is less likely to constitute a superseding factor breaking proximate causation.

e.g. **Example:** Where the victim of perverted sexual acts by the defendant took her own life (*see* above), her suicidal actions were in response to the defendant's actions and thus were not independent. This further suggests that they would not break the chain of causation. [**Stephenson v. State,** 179 N.E. 633 (Ind. 1932)]

EXAM TIP

Remember that in analyzing a criminal law question concerning causation you must consider ***both types*** of causation. Whether there is factual causation is usually fairly easy to determine; you would use the ***"but for" test.*** Then consider proximate causation, which requires an analysis of considerations closely related to judgments about whether the defendant ***should*** be held liable in situations of the sort involved. (*See* Approach to Causation (Traditional View) chart, *supra,* for details.)

---

d. Special Problems—Felony Murder

Felony murder and misdemeanor manslaughter pose special problems of causation because they do not require any *mens rea* in regard to the death of the victim. (*See infra,* p. 223 *et seq.*)

4. Alternative Approaches to Causation

The complexity, technicality, and uncertain nature of traditional causation analysis has led some to suggest that parts of it, especially proximate causation, should be abandoned in favor of alternative approaches. The Model Penal Code, like the traditional approach, has no difficulty in establishing causation-in-fact of the harm. where the result or harm happens to the intended victim in the manner contemplated by the defendant. Likewise, no problem of causation occurs with an unintended killing where the death as it occurred was precisely the risk which makes the defendant's conduct culpable.

a. Model Penal Code Approach: Not Too Remote or Accidental

If the defendant's conduct was the cause-in-fact, the second question is whether the defendant can be properly regarded as criminally responsible for the result? In situations such as those already discussed where a result occurs in an unanticipated manner, the Model Penal Code provides that the defendant is treated as causing the result unless the manner in which it occurred is ***too remote or accidental to have a just bearing on the defendant's liability.*** [Model Penal Code § 2.03(2)(b) and (3)(b)]

e.g. **Example:** H is tried for reckless manslaughter, based on evidence that he was aware that his wife, W, was failing to feed their child and there was a considerable risk the child would die from starvation. Before that happened, W threw the child to the floor, and the fall killed the child. H could be convicted only if the jury found the prosecution had proved the actual harm, death by throwing to the floor, was not too remote or accidental as compared to the anticipated harm, death by starvation. [**Johnson v. State,** 224 P.3d 105 (Alaska 2010)]

e.g. **Example:** Fight between two teenage girls in bathroom of their school resulted in death of one of the girls. While the trial court noted that the defendant should have realized that her attack might have deadly results on a hard tile floor, the appellate court emphasize that the victim's death was not the result of such risks but instead was from a rare heart conditions that she did not know about. [**Cannon v. State,** 181 A.3d 615 (Del. 2018) (state statute followed Model Penal Code § 2.03(3)(b))]

e.g. **Example:** When the defendant consciously disregarded a risk that he might shoot and hit B, but in fact he shot and killed the victim, a type of transferred recklessness may apply. [**Phillips v. Commonwealth,** 17 S.W.3d 870 (Ky. 2000)]

b. Result Not "Highly Extraordinary" in Light of the Circumstances

One court has suggested that in these situations, the defendant should be regarded as having caused the result unless the unanticipated way in which the result occurred was ***"highly extraordinary in light of the circumstances."*** [**People v. Acosta,** *supra*]

e.g. **Example:** D drives a stolen car and leads officers on a 50-mile high speed chase which creates a high risk that someone will be killed in a vehicle accident. Two police helicopters follow the chase, and during a maneuver to exchange positions one pilot is negligent, the helicopters collide, and the occupants of one are killed. Did D cause the death of the helicopter occupants? The court urged that rather than ask whether the pilot's actions were a superseding cause, it should inquire whether, in the context of a high speed chase dangerous because of the risk of a vehicle accident, the result that actually occurred (the aircraft accident) was so highly extraordinary that D should be regarded as not having caused it. A majority concluded that the helicopter accident was not so highly extraordinary and therefore D did cause it. [**People v. Acosta,** *supra*]

Chapter Five

Scope of Criminal Liability

CONTENTS	PAGE

Key Exam Issues

A person may be subject to criminal conviction because, by her own actions, she has engaged in conduct that amounts to a crime. A person's criminal liability can be based on the commission of a crime ***by someone else*** in several ways. In any examination question, be certain to consider whether a person whose liability is at issue is subject to conviction for conduct actually committed by another. The following questions focus attention on the main possibilities:

1. Was the defendant involved in the offense in such a way as to be liable under the ***law of parties*** (*e.g.,* principal in the second degree) or under a more ***modern form of liability for offenses committed by others***?
2. Is the situation one giving rise to ***vicarious liability*** for offenses committed by others?
3. Was the offense committed by a person who was a member of a ***criminal conspiracy*** and the defendant was also a member? (If so, consider the co-conspirator rule discussed in Chapter 7, *infra,* p. 182 *et seq.*)

In addition, a corporation or unincorporated association may be criminally liable, even though this liability is based on crimes actually committed by agents of the corporation or association. When this occurs, the financial penalty imposed on the corporation or association falls indirectly upon the shareholders or other members, who in a sense are penalized for offenses actually committed by the corporation or association's agents.

A. Complicity in the Crime

1. "Parties" to the Crime

Liability for a crime is not limited to the person who actually commits the prohibited act. Liability extends to anyone who has ***encouraged*** (incited) or ***assisted*** (abetted) the perpetration of the crime, or (at common law) who has ***hindered apprehension*** of the perpetrator after commission of the offense. [*See* **Standefer v. United States,** 447 U.S. 10 (1980)] All such persons are regarded as "parties" to the crime and can be convicted as if *they* themselves had committed the criminal act.

2. Common Law Classification of Participants: "Party" Rules

Under the common law, the parties to a crime are carefully classified. Traditionally, these distinctions were primarily important for procedural purposes. Once the procedural limitations were overcome, all parties were subjected to the same penalty.

a. Parties to Felonies

The parties to a felony are classified by their role in perpetrating the crime and whether they were present at its commission.

(1) Principal in the First Degree

Principals in the first degree are those who ***actually perpetrated*** the crime by their own acts, by the acts of ***innocent*** human beings, or by means of an inanimate agency.

e.g. **Example:** Adult causes his two minor children to have sex with one another. Child, because of his immaturity, cannot be held liable for his act. [**State v. Bobenhouse,** 214 P.3d 907 (Wash. 2009)]

(2) Principal in the Second Degree

Principals in the second degree are those who either ***incite or abet*** the commission of the crime ***and*** who are actually or constructively ***present*** at the time of its commission. [**State v. Foster,** 656 S.E.2d 74 (W.Va. 2007)]

(a) "Constructive" Presence

A person is "constructively" present when he assists the principal in the first degree at the very time the offense is committed but from such a distance that he is not actually present.

e.g. **Example:** While V's uncle engaged in intercourse with his niece, her aunt was in the next room. The aunt was constructively present because her "malevolent, intimidating influence on her niece was present and continued unabated." [**Sutton v. Commonwealth,** 324 S.E.2d 665 (Va. 1985)]

(3) Accessory Before the Fact

Those who ***incite or abet*** the commission of a felony by another but are ***not actually or constructively present*** at the commission of the offense are accessories before the fact. This form of liability covers those who provide ***pre-crime*** assistance or encouragement to the actual perpetrators.

e.g. **Example:** A assisted B in encouraging C to come to a place where B raped C. Because A was not present at the time of the rape but did render pre-crime aid, he is an accessory before the fact to the crime of rape. [**State v. Spillman,** 468 P.2d 376 (Ariz. 1970)]

(a) Distinguish: Crime of Solicitation

One who incites or counsels another to perpetrate a crime commits the misdemeanor of solicitation. However, if the person solicited *commits* the target offense, the inciter is liable for that crime as a party.

(4) Accessory After the Fact

Accessories after the fact are those who receive, comfort, or assist another, ***knowing*** that the other has committed a felony, in order to ***hinder*** the perpetrator's arrest, prosecution, or conviction. [**State v. Brown,** 930 A.2d 410 (N.H. 2007)]

e.g. **Example:** A person can be an accessory through words alone spoken to the police during an interview, but only where she aids and assists the principal by providing the police with a false alibi or comparable information that would exculpate the principal, a false narrative of the crime that would give the principal a defense, or false information to assist in the principal's escape. [**Commonwealth v. Rivera,** 121 N.E.3d 1121 (Mass. 2019)]

(a) Exception: Wife Excluded

Under the common law, a wife could not be an accessory after the fact to a crime committed by her husband, because she was considered to be under her husband's control and thus presumed to have acted under his coercion. [**State v. Kelly,** 38 N.W. 503 (Iowa 1888)] Many states broadened the exception to others like husbands, parents, children, ascendants, descendants and even servants, because it was improbable to expect such persons to be deterred from giving aid. [*See, e.g.*, **State v. Williams,** 451 A.2d 1142 (Vt. 1982)]

b. Significance of Party Rules

The law of parties has considerable procedural significance at common law.

(1) Variance Between Pleading and Proof

Whenever there was variance between the pleading and the proof, a party to the crime could potentially escape liability altogether. Under the common law rules of pleading, a person charged as an accessory could not be convicted upon proof that he was a principal. Similarly, one charged as a principal could not be convicted as an accessory. [**Shelton v. Commonwealth,** 86 S.W.2d 1054 (Ky. 1935)]

(2) Conviction of Principal Necessary

At common law, an accessory could not be convicted unless the principal was convicted, although both could be convicted at the same trial if the principal's guilt was determined first. [**State v. Ward,** 396 A.2d 1041 (Md. 1978)]

(3) Conviction of Higher Offense than Principal

Also at common law, an accessory could not be convicted of a higher offense than the crime for which the principal was convicted. [**State v. Ward**, *supra*]

(4) Not Applicable to Principals

The common law rules do not apply to the two degrees of principals. Therefore, one charged as a principal in the second degree can be convicted despite the acquittal of the principal in the first degree, and even if the proof at trial showed him to be a principal in the first degree.

c. Misdemeanors: No Distinction Among Parties

Those who aid or incite the commission of a misdemeanor are, of course, liable for the resulting crime at common law. However, no distinction is made between principals and accessories or between the degrees of principals. [**Snead v. State,** 8 S.E.2d 735 (Ga. 1940)] Moreover, there is no common law liability at all for aiding a misdemeanant ***after*** the commission of the offense (*see infra,* p. 90).

d. Treason: No Distinction Among Parties

Similarly, distinctions among parties do not apply to treason; all participants are liable as principals.

3. Classification of Participants Under Modern Statutes

Under modern statutes, most of those who would be "parties" to crimes under the common law are still made guilty of the crimes, but the technical distinctions have largely been abolished.

a. Inciters and Abettors Guilty as Principals

Under many modern statutory schemes, those who aid, abet, counsel, command, induce or procure commission of an offense (*i.e.,* those who under the common law would be principals or accessories before the fact) are deemed "principals" and are guilty of the crime. [*See, e.g.,* 18 U.S.C. § 2; Cal. Penal Code § 31]

b. Model Penal Code Position: Inciters and Abettors Guilty as "Accomplices"

Similarly, the Model Penal Code provides that a person is guilty of an offense if she commits it by her own conduct ***or*** if it is committed by another for whose conduct she is ***legally accountable.*** One is "legally accountable" for the conduct of another if she ***causes*** an innocent person to engage in conduct constituting a crime or if she is an ***accomplice*** to the conduct of the other person. An "accomplice" is one who, with the purpose of promoting or facilitating the offense: (i) solicits another to commit it; (ii) aids, agrees to aid, or attempts to aid in planning or committing it; or (iii) having a duty to prevent the offense, fails to make proper efforts to do so. [Model Penal Code § 2.06(1)–(3)] This is the same effect as the modern statutes discussed above, but different terminology is used.

c. Accessory After the Fact Not Participant

Persons who provide assistance ***after*** the crime (*i.e.,* common law accessories after the fact) are no longer made guilty of the crime committed by the perpetrator. Instead, those persons are usually guilty of a ***separate offense*** that usually carries a lower penalty than the offense committed by the perpetrator (*see infra,* pp. 91, 312).

d. Effect of Modern Changes

The above changes made by modern statutes substantially simplify procedural aspects of the law of complicity.

(1) Fewer Pleading and Proof Problems

For instance, it is no longer necessary to specify in the charge whether the defendant is guilty as an accessory or as a principal, *i.e.*, there are no problems of variance between the pleading and the proof. [**Castillo v. State,** 974 N.E.2d 458 (Ind. 2012)]

(2) Conviction of Principal Is Unnecessary

Many jurisdictions have abolished the requirement that a principal be convicted before an accessory may be convicted. Thus, one who otherwise would have been an accessory before the fact at common law may be convicted even if the actual perpetrator (the principal in the first degree) is acquitted. [**State v. Spillman,** 468 P.2d 376 (Ariz. 1970)]

(a) No Constitutional Bar

Neither the prohibition against double jeopardy nor the requirement of Due Process prohibits trial and conviction of an aider and abettor after acquittal of the principal. [**Sandefer v. United States,** 447 U.S. 10 (1980)]

4. Accomplice Liability

The liability of those who commit crimes by their own actions (*i.e.,* those who would be principals in the first degree under common law terminology) is the subject of this whole Summary. But the liability of those who may be responsible for crimes perpetrated by another because of their involvement in that offense presents special problems. This section considers the issues presented by the liability of those participants in a crime who, at common law, would be principals in the second degree or accessories before the fact. For simplicity, these participants are often collectively called "accomplices."

a. Requirements for Accomplice Liability

Basically, accomplice liability requires proof that the defendant committed the requisite acts (*i.e.,* incited or abetted), that he had the requisite *mens rea*, and that the person incited or abetted actually committed the offense. Complicity *mens rea* is established either by direct evidence, or by the factfinder drawing an inference based on the accomplice's presence, companionship, and conduct. [**Sauder v. State,** 901 S.E.2d 124 (Ga. 2024)]

The federal aiding and abetting statute [18 U.S.C. § 2] derives from common-law standards for accomplice liability, with two components: an affirmative act in furtherance of the underlying offense and the intent to facilitate that offense's commission. [**Rosemond v. United States,** 572 U.S. 65 (2014) ("a person may be responsible for a crime he has not personally carried out if he helps another to complete its commission.")]

(1) Requisite Acts: "Abetting" or "Inciting"

The defendant must have directly or indirectly ***encouraged or facilitated*** the commission of the offense. [**People v. Wright,** 26 Cal. App. 2d 197 (1938) (encouragement may be communicated to the principal through an intermediary)] For example, in **Rosemond v. United States**, *supra*, the Court held that a defendant aided and abetted a federal drug violation by proving that the defendant actively participated in the underlying drug trafficking or violent crime with advance knowledge that a confederate would use or carry a gun during the crime's commission.

(a) "Abetting": Any Significant Assistance

It need not be shown that, without such aid, the perpetrator would have been unable to complete the crime. [**State ex rel. Attorney General v. Tally,** 15 So. 722 (Ala. 1894)]

e.g. **Example:** D was one of three people trying to sell a pound of marijuana to buyers who absconded with the drugs. As they ran off, D and the others fired at them with a semiautomatic handgun. D was prosecuted for being either the shooter or the other shooter's accomplice. As to the act portion, it is *not* necessary that the accomplice's aid facilitate each of the elements of the crime that's promoted. The Court unanimously held that the prosecution had proved the act component, *i.e.*, showing "facilitat[ion of] any part—even though not every part—of a criminal venture." [**Rosemond v. United States,** *supra*]

e.g. **Example:** At a murder trial, one defendant allegedly participated in a drive-by shooting as a passenger in the vehicle from which the shots were fired. The evidence identified him only as a back seat passenger. There was no evidence that he fired shots or was aware when he entered the vehicle that the shooters intended to commit a drive-by murder. That he did not attempt to leave the group after the shooting did not mean beyond a reasonable doubt that he encouraged or assisted the shooting. [**Buchanan v. State,** 316 So.3d 619 (Miss. 2021)]

1) Perpetrator Need Not Be Aware of Aid

No communication between the participants is necessary, and the actual perpetrator does not have to be aware that he is benefiting from the accessory's assistance. [**State v. Lord,** 84 P.2d 80 (N.M. 1938)]

2) Effect on Actual Perpetrator Is Necessary

Courts sometimes say that the accomplice's actions must contribute to the commission of the crime, suggesting that some discernible impact upon the actual perpetrator is necessary. [**Commonwealth v. Rodriguez,** 931 N.E.2d 20 (Mass. 2010) (insufficient evidence to support defendant's conviction as accessory before the fact to murder)] However, courts almost always hold that the prosecution has proved a sufficient actual effect upon the actual perpetrator to establish accomplice liability.

e.g. **Example:** There was sufficient evidence that the defendant aided and abetted the codefendant in the stabbing murders where he helped restrained the victims while the codefendant attacked and killed them. There was evidence that it would have been very difficult for one person to have committed the murders. [**Felts v. State,** 858 S.E.2d 708 (Ga. 2021)]

a) Distinguish: Model Penal Code View

Under the Model Penal Code, liability can be based upon an ***attempt to aid*** another in committing a crime. Under this approach, it is not necessary that the defendant successfully provide any actually effective assistance. [Model Penal Code § 2.06(3)(a)(ii)]

3) Omission as Abetting

Generally, the mere failure to prevent the commission of an offense does not constitute abetting. If a person has a legal duty to intervene, however, the failure to do so becomes an "act" (*see supra,* p. 29), and the person may be liable as an abettor for his failure to make the proper effort to prevent the offense. [Model Penal Code § 2.06(3)(a)(iii)] Some courts, on the other hand, are reluctant to expand accomplice liability. [*See* **Commonwealth v. Raposo,** *supra* (accomplice liability statute requires more than an omission to act)]

SUMMARY OF PARTIES TO FELONY

PARTIES	AT COMMON LAW: DEFINITION	AT COMMON LAW: LIABLE FOR PRINCIPAL CRIME?	UNDER MODERN STATUTES: LABEL	UNDER MODERN STATUTES: LIABLE FOR PRINCIPAL CRIME?
PRINCIPAL IN FIRST DEGREE	Actually perpetrates felony	Yes	"Principal" (perpetrates felony)	Yes
PRINCIPAL IN SECOND DEGREE	Incites or abets and is present (actually or constructively) at time of crime	Yes	"Accomplice" (incites or abets with requisite intent)	Yes
ACCESSORY BEFORE THE FACT	Incites or abets but not present at time of crime (pre-crime aid or encouragement)	Yes	"Accomplice" (incites or abets with requisite intent)	Yes
ACCESSORY AFTER THE FACT	Aids in hindering arrest, prosecution, or conviction of person she knows committed felony	Yes	Not a party to felony	No (but may be liable for separate offense)

(b) "Inciting": Any Inducement

Quite apart from abetting the commission of an offense, the accomplice must have intended to give aid or encouragement, even if not accompanied by any physical aid. [**State v. Tyler,** 873 N.W.2d 741 (Iowa 2016)]

1) Limitation: Perpetrator Must Be Aware of Encouragement

However, encouragement, by definition, cannot exist unless the person who is encouraged is ***aware*** of the efforts. Therefore, one who merely attempts to encourage the commission of a crime is not an inciter if the perpetrator had no knowledge thereof. [**State v. Tyler,** *supra*]

2) Presence in Readiness to Assist

Presence at the scene of the crime, without more, does not constitute incitement. However, if by ***prior agreement*** one is present for the purpose of rendering aid to the perpetrator if aid becomes necessary, this ***is***

sufficient encouragement and is enough to create accomplice liability. Often, the major issue is one of proof, *i.e.,* whether presence and other circumstantial evidence sufficiently demonstrate the existence of a prior agreement between the perpetrator and the accused accomplice so that the accomplice's presence is sufficient for liability. [**Evans v. State,** 643 So. 2d 1204 (Fla. 1994)]

(2) Mens Rea Requirement

Much confusion exists as to the mental state required for accomplice liability. Basically, the issue is twofold: (i) whether the accomplice must have the ***mens rea required for the crime,*** *and* (ii) whether he must *also* have ***intended that his actions have the effect of assisting or encouraging*** the successful completion of the crime. [**State v. Segura,** 2 N.W.3d 142 (Minn. 2024) (mental element for accomplice liability requires that the defendants "intentionally aid," *i.e.*, the defendant had knowledge that perpetrators were going to commit crime *and* defendants "intended" that their presence or actions further the commission of that crime)]

(a) Mens Rea for Crime Required

e.g. **Example:** For a federal drug trafficking offense involving a firearm, D must intend to facilitate "the specific and entire crime charged." The aider and abettor must have knowledge of the full scope of the crime, that is, "that the plan calls not just for a drug sale, but for an armed one." The knowledge has to be "advance knowledge," meaning "knowledge at a time the accomplice can do something with it—most notably, opt to walk away." [**Rosemond v. United States,** *supra*]

e.g. **Example:** D is charged with aiding and abetting production of child pornography involving depiction of a minor child. If D is unaware that the victim was underage, he cannot "wish. . . to bring about" such criminal conduct and "seek . to make it succeed." Therefore, an aider and abettor of such an offense must have known the victim was a minor when it was still possible to decline to participate in the conduct. [**United States v. Encarnacion-Ruiz,** 787 F.3d 581 (1st Cir. 2015)]

(b) Mens Rea Regarding Assistance or Encouragement

There is considerable uncertainty as to the *mens rea* required as to the effect of the accomplice's action, *i.e.,* the assistance or encouragement. All courts agree that one who had no contemplation that his acts would encourage or assist the perpetrator cannot be convicted as an accomplice. [**State v. Tyler,** *supra*] In addition, though, must the accomplice **intend** that his conduct have the effect of encouraging or assisting, or is it enough that he acted with **knowledge** that his conduct would promote or facilitate a crime? Moreover, will an awareness of a substantial risk that his actions would have this effect (*i.e.,* recklessness) suffice?

e.g. **Example:** A provides B and C with a small amount of his blood. B and C later pour the blood over selective service records, and A is charged as an abettor to the offense of mutilating public records. To convict A, must it be shown that he desired that his blood be used to facilitate the commission of the crime? Is it enough if the prosecution proves that A was aware that his blood would be put to such use? Or, will a showing that A was aware of a high risk or likelihood (but not a certainty) that his blood would be so used suffice?

[**United States v. Eberhardt,** 417 F.2d 1009 (4th Cir. 1969) (supplying blood with knowledge it would be used for unlawful purpose held sufficient for accomplice liability)]

1) Modern Position: Purpose Required

The modern trend, adopted in many states and embodied in the Model Penal Code, requires that an aider and abettor act with ***purpose,*** *i.e.,* with an affirmative desire that his acts have an encouraging or assisting effect. [*See* **State v. Tyler,** *supra* (aider or abettor must have intent or purpose of encouraging or facilitating commission of the crime; Model Penal Code § 2.06(3)(a))]

a) Rationale

Because accomplice liability permits conviction even though the accused did not actually commit the crime himself, special assurance is necessary that the accused is in fact both dangerous and blameworthy enough to justify conviction. This assurance requires an exceptionally stringent *mens rea, i.e.,* a showing of purpose. Those who assist another in committing a crime with an affirmative desire that their actions have an encouraging or assisting effect are sufficiently dangerous and blameworthy to justify criminal conviction.

b) Distinguish: Liability for "Facilitating" Crime

Jurisdictions that require purpose for accomplice liability sometimes provide a separate offense for the liability of ***knowingly*** assisting another in committing a crime. This is often done by creating the crime of "criminal facilitation," defined as ***knowingly providing assistance*** to another in committing a crime. [*See*, *e.g.*, Ky.Rev.Stat. § 506.080(1)]

2) Contrary View: Knowledge or Even Recklessness Sufficient

Some courts disagree and hold that an accomplice is guilty so long as he ***knew*** that his acts would encourage or assist the commission of an offense. [**United States v. Rebolledo-Delgadillo,** 820 F.3d 870 (7th Cir. 2016) (despite language in decisions purporting to require purpose, courts in actual practice require only that an accomplice be shown to have known that his actions would assist the perpetrator)] Furthermore, a few decisions regard recklessness or negligence as sufficient. [*See, e.g.,* **Peacher v. Commonwealth,** 391 S.W.3d 821 (Ky. 2013) (evidence supported conviction for complicity to reckless murder)]

a) Rationale

Those who act knowing that their conduct will assist in the perpetration of a crime (and those who are aware of a substantial risk that such will occur) have demonstrated that they are dangerous to society and ethically blameworthy. Consequently, criminal penalties are justified.

3) Compromise: Nature of Crime Determinative

One court has suggested a compromise between the two views, which would require that purpose be shown unless the crime involved is a ***serious*** one, in which case proof of knowledge alone will suffice. [**People v. Lauria,** 251 Cal. App. 2d 471 (1967)]

a) Rationale

Where the crime is serious (*e.g.,* criminal homicide or burglary), the social need to intervene is significant; a participant should be liable simply upon proof that he knew his conduct would facilitate perpetration of the offense. But when the crime is less serious (*e.g.,* gambling, unlawful sale of liquor) there is less need for social intervention and liability should be limited to those peripheral participants who are most dangerous and blameworthy. [*See* **People v. Lauria,** *supra*]

(3) Perpetrator Must Have Committed Crime

Generally, a person can be convicted as an accomplice only if the crime at issue was actually committed. In other words, the person who was "incited" or "abetted" must be guilty of the offense. [**People v. Chirchirillo,** 913 N.E.2d 635 (Ill. 2009) (in a burglary in which a firearm was taken, defendant-accomplice was not guilty on accomplice theory of crime of possession of weapon by convicted felon, as defendant was convicted felon but principal was not)] However, an accomplice is not relieved of liability just because the reasonably foreseeable result occurred in an unexpected manner. [**State v. McAllister,** 862 N.W.2d 49 (Minn. 2015)]

(a) Conviction of Perpetrator Unnecessary

Under modern statutes, it is not necessary that the actual perpetrator be convicted. However, the prosecution must ***always prove the perpetrator's guilt*** as part of its case in chief at the trial of the accomplice. [**People v. Vaughn,** 465 N.W.2d 365 (Mich.App. 1990)] It is unnecessary to prove the identity of the principal. [**United States v. Mullins,** 613 F.3d 1273 (10th Cir. 2010) ("it follows that the jury didn't have to agree unanimously on that person's identity")]

EXAM TIP

Note this change from the common law. At common law, the accomplice (accessory) could not be convicted unless the perpetrator (principal) had already been convicted (or could be convicted at the same trial) (*see supra,* p. 71). Under modern statutes, the accomplice can be convicted even though the actual perpetrator has not been convicted, but the perpetrator's guilt ***must be proven as part of the case against the accomplice.***

(b) Availability of Perpetrator's Defenses to Accomplice

Can an accomplice rely on a defense such as justification that would be available to the perpetrator? [*See, e.g.,* **People v. Rajput,** 949 N.W.2d 32 (Mich. 2020) ("an aider and abettor is relieved of liability if the principal acted in self-defense")] By contrast, if a jury in an accomplice's trial concludes that the principal was excused, may the jury still convict the accomplice? [*See, e.g.,*

Taylor v. Commonwealth, 521 S.E.2d 293 (Va.App. 1999) ("Because excuses relate to a condition that is peculiar to the actor, such defenses are generally considered to be non-delegable and, thus, unavailable to an accomplice.")] May a person charged as an accomplice defend on the theory that the perpetrator was insane or had been entrapped into committing the crime? If a conviction of the principal is not a prerequisite to conviction of the accomplice, perhaps there is no reason to permit the accomplice to assert defenses available to the perpetrator. But if the purpose of the defense is to discourage improper police conduct (as is arguably true in regard to entrapment, *see infra,* p. 136 *et seq.*), perhaps it would be sound policy to allow the accomplice as well as the perpetrator to rely on it. [*But see* **United States v. Azadian,** 436 F.2d 81 (9th Cir. 1971) (accomplice could not defend on basis of entrapment of perpetrator)]

(c) Distinguish: Other Theories of Liability

If the crime at issue was not completed, so that neither the perpetrator nor the accomplice can be convicted, there may be other offenses for which the aider or inciter may be liable.

1) Attempt

If the perpetrator progressed far enough toward the commission of the crime to be guilty of attempt (***see infra,*** p. 186 *et seq.*), the accomplice's actions may make him an accomplice to that attempt. [**Gilbert v. Commonwealth,** 838 S.W.2d 376 (Ky. 1991)]

2) Conspiracy

If there was a ***preliminary agreement*** between the participants, all may be guilty of conspiracy. (*See* discussion ***infra,*** p. 170 *et seq.*)

ACCOMPLICE LIABILITY CHECKLIST
FOR A PERSON TO BE GUILTY AS AN ACCOMPLICE, THERE MUST BE PROOF THAT:
☑ The accomplice ***aided*** the commission of the crime ***in a significant way*** or ***incited*** its commission;
☑ The accomplice ***had the intent required for the crime,*** and, under the modern view, the ***desire to assist or encourage***; and
☑ The ***perpetrator actually committed*** the crime or a criminal ***attempt*** thereof.

b. Scope of Accomplice Liability

There is some question as to the actual scope of liability of an accomplice and a substantially greater question as to what the scope of liability should be.

(1) Traditional Rule: Accomplice Liable for All Probable Consequences

Traditionally, an accomplice is held liable for all probable (*i.e.,* foreseeable) consequences of his conduct. Thus, liability may be imposed not only for the offense incited or abetted but also for ***all other crimes*** committed by the perpetrator that were a ***reasonably foreseeable result*** of the contemplated crime. In effect, the accomplice is liable for those crimes that, in the exercise of reasonable care, he should have foreseen; this is something akin to a negligence theory. [**State v. Sellers,**

898 S.E.2d 116 (S.C. 2024) (when two people join together to commit a crime, and during the commission of that crime one of the two commits another crime, both may be criminally liable for the unplanned crime if it was a natural and probable consequence of their common plan to commit the initial crime)]

e.g. **Example:** When a carjacking V is taken hostage, the crime continues at least while D maintains control over the V and his car. D was an accomplice to the carjacking because of aid given at some time after the seizure of the car, because V and his car were still in control of the carjackers. [**United States v. Figueroa-Cartagena,** 612 F.3d 69 (1st Cir. 2010)]

cf. **Compare:** D goes with sister P to kill L and trash L's car. After D shoots L, P impulsively fired several shots into a car and killed W. D was not an accomplice in W's murder, because it was not reasonably foreseeable to D. [**United States v. Andrews,** 75 F.3d 552 (9th Cir. 1996)]

(2) Minority Rule: Liability Limited to Contemplated Crimes

Some courts and commentators have argued that the traditional rule is unjust and inconsistent with well-accepted notions of criminal liability, *i.e.*, A's guilt as an accomplice to one crime should not *per se* be a basis for holding A accountable for a related crime merely because the latter offense was carried out by A's principal. This would result in A's guilt of a crime as to which he did not have the requisite mental state. Some courts have recognized this point that an accomplice is liable only for those crimes of the perpetrator that he ***actually anticipated*** and that he therefore intentionally incited or abetted. [Model Penal Code § 2.06; *see* **Commonwealth v. Knox,** 105 A.3d 1194 (Pa. 2014) (the "natural and foreseeable consequences" approach was "expressly rejected" when the legislature adopted the MPC accomplice liability approach)]

e.g. **Example:** Defendant was convicted of aiding theft from interstate shipment, but he cannot be convicted of aiding interstate transportation of the stolen goods as a "foreseeable consequence of their theft," *i.e.*, that would base criminal liability upon negligence rather than criminal intent.[**United States v. Greer,** 467 F.2d 1064 (7th Cir. 1972); *see* **People v. Weiss,** 256 A.D. 162, *aff'd,* 280 N.Y. 718 (1939)]

c. Possible Defenses to Accomplice Liability

There are several possible defenses that might apply when accomplice liability is at issue.

(1) Withdrawal

One who has encouraged or assisted the commission of a crime may escape liability as an accomplice by making an ***effective and timely withdrawal.*** The requirements for a legally effective withdrawal differ somewhat with the nature of the accomplice's initial action. The burden of proof is on the defendant who is trying to escape liability by manifesting her voluntary withdrawal. [**United States v. Burks,** 678 F.3d 1190 (10th Cir. 2012)]

(a) Withdrawal Must Be Timely and Voluntary

In all cases, the withdrawal must be communicated "at such time as will give the others a reasonable opportunity to withdraw," *i.e.*, it must take place before the chain of events leading to the crime has progressed so far as to become unstoppable. [**Commonwealth v. Chhim,** 851 N.E.2d 422 (Mass. 2006)] The withdrawal must be motivated by a change of heart, rather than for a concern about being caught for his misdeeds. [**O'Shaughnessy v. People,** 269 P.3d 1233 (Colo. 2012)]

(b) Communication of Renunciation by the Inciter Is Sufficient

If the initial action consisted only of ***inciting*** (*i.e.,* encouraging or soliciting commission of the offense), a legally effective withdrawal may be accomplished by ***communicating a renunciation*** of the crime to the perpetrator. [**Commonwealth v. Chhim,** *supra*]

(c) Abettor Must Countermand His Prior Aid

If the initial action consisted of ***abetting*** (*i.e.,* physically assisting commission of the crime), renunciation alone is not enough; the abettor must act to render whatever assistance he has given ***ineffective.*** [**Commonwealth v. Huber,** 15 Pa. D.&C.2d 726 (1958)]

e.g. **Example:** A gave his gun to P for use in a robbery. When P asked A to come along on the robbery, A responded that he did not wish to get involved. P committed the robbery and A was held liable as an accessory. Having provided P with the gun, A became an abettor. Therefore, A could not effectively withdraw by renouncing the robbery; rather, to withdraw A had to retrieve the gun from P prior to perpetration of the offense. [**Commonwealth v. Huber,** *supra*]

EXAM TIP

Remember that at common law, the requirements for effective withdrawal differ depending on whether the accomplice was initially an inciter or an abettor. One way to remember the difference is through this rough summary: ***A "talker" can talk his way out, but an "actor" must act to withdraw.*** In other words, an inciter, who encouraged or solicited ("talked"), must communicate his renunciation to the perpetrator, while the abettor, who physically assists the commission of a crime ("acted"), must act to render his assistance ineffective. Also remember that for both inciters and abettors, the withdrawal must also be ***at a time when the crime could be stopped.***

(d) Model Penal Code Provisions

Under the Model Penal Code, an accomplice may withdraw and thus avoid liability for the crime by any of the following methods:

(i) ***Wholly depriving*** his prior assistance of its ***effectiveness,***

(ii) ***Providing timely warning*** of the perpetrator's plan to law enforcement authorities, or

(iii) Making proper ***effort to prevent commission*** of the offense by the perpetrator.

[Model Penal Code § 2.06(6)(c)]

(2) Situations When Accomplice Liability Is Inapplicable

Generally, accomplice liability applies regardless of the offense involved. There are several exceptional situations, however, in which liability for participation as an accomplice is not available.

(a) Members of Protected Class

If a crime is ***defined to protect persons in a particular category***, persons within that category are not guilty of the crime despite their participation. [**Gebardi v. United States,** 287 U.S. 112 (1932) (violation of Mann Act)]

1) Rationale

Because the legislature enacted the statute to protect persons like the inciter or abettor, it must not have intended to subject such persons to the severity of a criminal conviction in the event the statute failed to prevent the crime. [**Regina v. Tyrell,** 17 Cox Crim. Cas. 716 (1893)]

e.g. **Example:** A prostitute who willingly joins a scheme to transport her across state lines cannot be held liable as an accomplice to a violation of the Mann Act (which prohibits transporting a woman over state lines for an immoral purpose). The statute was intended to protect women; thus, it would be contrary to the legislative purpose to impose accomplice liability on the "victim" (*i.e.,* the woman transported). [**Gebardi v. United States,** *supra*]

(b) Victims of Offense

Similarly, the ***victim of an offense*** is not liable even if the victim participated in it. Again, this is because the legislature could not have intended to criminalize both victimizing such persons and being victimized. [**United States v. Southard,** 700 F.2d 1 (1st Cir. 1983)]

e.g. **Example:** By paying D's blackmail demand, V obviously assists D in completing the crime of extortion. Nevertheless, V is not guilty of extortion as an accomplice to D's commission of the offense.

(c) Participants Necessary to Commission of Offense

If a crime ***inherently and necessarily involves several types of participants*** but explicitly ***provides for the guilt of only one*** type of participant, the other types of participants are not liable for participation of a sort that would usually create accomplice liability. This is because the legislature obviously knew that such persons would be involved in the crimes and by failing to provide for their liability evinced an intention to exclude them from liability. [**United States v. Southard,** *supra* (a gambler-accomplice of those violating statute covering persons "engaged in the business of betting or wagering" was neither a victim nor a person for whose protection the statute was passed, and thus did not come within this exception)]

e.g. **Example:** D sells cocaine to X, who participated in the crime of ***sale*** of narcotics. That crime inherently involves ***both*** sellers and buyers. Because the legislature knew that buyers would be involved and made no provision for their liability, it must have intended that buyers be immune from prosecution despite their involvement.

(d) Accomplice Liability Inconsistent with Legislative Purpose

In some situations, accomplice liability may be inconsistent with the legislative purpose in creating the crime, and thus, such liability does not exist because the legislature must have so intended. [**United States v. Hill,** 55 F.3d 1197 (6th Cir. 1995)]

Example: The federal "drug kingpin" statute provides for liability of certain drug offenders with five or more employees. An employee of a "kingpin" cannot be prosecuted as an accomplice to his employer's crime, because this would be inconsistent with Congress's intention to limit liability to those in a controlling position of such organizations. [**United States v. Hill,** *supra*]

(e) Distinguish: Accomplice Unable to Commit Crime as Perpetrator

Some crimes require that the actual perpetrator have certain characteristics, and thus limit those persons who can commit the crimes as actual perpetrators. However, such limitations do not apply to those who simply encourage or abet commission of the offense. Hence, one who lacks the requisite traits, although he would not be liable had he been the actual perpetrator, ***can*** be convicted as an accomplice. [**People v. Fraize,** 36 Cal. App. 4th 1722 (1995)]

Example: H, who is married to W, encourages P to force W to submit to sexual intercourse with P. If by definition, a husband cannot commit rape upon his wife, *i.e.,* he cannot incur liability as a principal in the first degree, by inciting P to commit the offense, H can be punished as an accomplice to P's rape of W. [**Rozell v. State,** 502 S.W.2d 16 (Tex.App. 1973)]

5. Liability of Post-Crime Aiders (Accessories After the Fact)

At common law, an accessory after the fact is a party to the crime of the person assisted (*see supra,* p. 77). Modern criminal codes, however, have significantly changed the potential liability of those who assist one who is known to have already committed an offense.

a. Common Law Requirements for Liability

Under the common law, there are three prerequisites to the conviction of a person as an accessory after the fact:

(1) Commission of Completed Felony

The person assisted must have actually committed, *i.e.,* ***completed***, a felony offense. Those who render post-crime assistance to known misdemeanants are not subject to criminal prosecution; therefore, a ***felony*** must in fact have been committed. The defendant's mistaken belief that a felony had been perpetrated is not enough. [**People v. Hardin,** 207 Cal. App. 2d 336 (1962)]

(2) Knowledge of Felony

The defendant must have ***known*** that the person assisted did commit the felony. [**State v. Hanna,** 341 P.3d 629 (Mont. 2014) (defendant's act of driving robber away from the scene of the crime, executed after defendant knew what had occurred, was aiding and abetting the commission of the crime; "ensuing flight is considered part and parcel of robbery")]

(3) Prohibited Aid to Felon

Some assistance must have been given *directly* to the felon for the *purpose of impeding enforcement of the law.*

b. Liability Under Modern Criminal Codes

Modern statutes vary in their treatment of those who assist the perpetrator after commission of a crime.

(1) Retention of Common Law Classification

Some jurisdictions have retained the category of accessory after the fact, although it is usually made a separate offense and assigned a penalty unrelated to the penalty provided for the person assisted. [*See* Cal. Penal Code §§ 32, 33 (providing for accessory after the fact but assigning uniform penalty of up to $5,000 fine and/or one year imprisonment)]

(2) Model Penal Code: "Hindering Prosecution"

Many modern criminal codes create distinct offenses consisting of providing aid to others who may have committed an offense. These offenses are sometimes called "hindering prosecution." [*See* Model Penal Code § 242.3; **Montoya v. People,** 394 P.3d 676 (Colo. 2017) (defendant "rendered assistance to his cousin intended to prevent his apprehension")] Some typical provisions include the following:

(a) Person Aided Need Not Have Committed Offense

Under these modern statutes, the prosecution often need not prove that the person whom the defendant sought to aid actually committed a criminal offense. It is enough that the defendant provided aid to another with the purpose of hindering the other's apprehension, prosecution, conviction, or punishment. [Model Penal Code § 242.3]

(b) Person Providing Prohibited Aid to Felon

The types of prohibited aid generally are (i) harboring or concealing the criminal, (ii) providing him with certain means (*e.g.*, a weapon, transportation, a disguise) of avoiding apprehension, (iii) concealing, destroying or tampering with evidence, (iv) warning the criminal of his impending discovery or apprehension, and using force, deception or intimidation to prevent or obstruct the criminal's discovery or apprehension.

e.g. **Example:** After several men stole a gun safe, they contacted D and told him they needed a place to take it and help break it open. They then met D at his campsite where he helped open the safe and advised the others where to dispose of it; D "willingly aided the other thieves in their continued efforts to carry away the safe and the guns" [**State v. Tourville,** 876 N.W.2d 735 (Wis. 2016)]

e.g. **Example:** D does not violate the accessory after the fact "statute when he or she merely 'abandons' physical evidence of a street crime while running from police or fleeing the scene of the crime." [**State v. Hawkins,** 406 S.W.3d 121 (Tenn. 2013)]

(c) Exception for Family Members

Modern statutes often contain exceptions providing that no crime is committed by aiding a spouse or a close relative, such as a child, parent, or sibling. [*See* N.M. Stat. Ann. § 30–22–4]

B. Vicarious Liability

1. Introduction

Criminal liability usually must be based upon the defendant's own acts (or sometimes failure to act) that show some participation in the offense. The major exception to this rule covers limited situations in which vicarious liability may be imposed.

2. Definition: Liability for Acts of Others

"Vicarious liability" is liability for the crimes committed by another person imposed simply ***because of the relationship*** between the defendant and the perpetrator. In such situations, the prosecution need not show that the defendant acted in any way or participated in the offense; it need only establish that the crime was committed by another, and that the defendant stood in the required relationship to that person.

a. Distinguish: Accomplice Liability

Accomplice liability is not vicarious. An accomplice's liability is based upon ***her affirmative participation*** in the offense rather than upon her relationship to the perpetrator (*see supra,* p. 76).

b. Distinguish: Strict Liability

Strict liability and vicarious liability are both forms of liability without "fault." However, they dispense with the fault requirement in entirely different ways and therefore are two distinct concepts. Strict liability consists of eliminating (or reducing) the ***mens rea*** requirement; vicarious liability consists of eliminating the requirement of an ***act.*** Accordingly, even though vicarious liability crimes may often impose strict liability, the two issues should be distinguished and analyzed separately. [**State v. Beaudry,** 365 N.W.2d 593 (Wis. 1985)] Unfortunately, courts sometimes fail to make this distinction and confuse the two issues.

e.g. **Example:** The president of a company was charged with violating the Food, Drug and Cosmetic Act, prohibiting the shipment of misbranded or adulterated products in interstate commerce. The prosecution was based on shipment by the company's employees of a defective product in interstate commerce. Proper analysis would require an examination of three issues: (i) whether the statute imposes vicarious liability upon the president for the acts of the company employees; (ii) whether the statute requires that the employees have known that the product shipped was defective (*i.e.,* is strict liability imposed as to this issue); and (iii) assuming that the president can be held vicariously liable for the employees' acts, whether the president must have known that defective products were being shipped (*i.e.,* is strict liability imposed as to this issue?). By failing to make a careful analysis, the Supreme Court found an intent to impose strict liability and then summarily concluded that this also meant vicarious liability was to be imposed. [**United States v. Dotterweich,** 320 U.S. 277 (1943); *see* **People v. Wilcox,** 269 N.W.2d 256 (Mich. 1978) (appellate court understands the distinction that a strict liability statute does not automatically impose vicarious liability)]

3. When Vicarious Liability Is Imposed: Legislative Intent

In all cases, whether a statute creating a crime imposes vicarious liability depends initially on the ***legislative intent.*** As a general rule, courts will assume that vicarious liability was ***not*** intended unless some indication to the contrary appears. In practice, evidence of legislative intent to impose vicarious liability will ordinarily be found only in ***employer-employee situations,*** *i.e.,* where an employer is prosecuted for the crimes of her employees.

a. Statutes Expressly Providing for Vicarious Liability

Some statutes expressly impose vicarious liability. For example, if it is made criminal to do an act "by oneself or by one's employee or agent," it is clear that the legislature intended to make the employer vicariously liable for the crimes of employees or agents. Courts split about upholding these criminal provisions, based on the police power. [*Compare* **Ex parte Marley,** 175 P.2d 832 (Cal. 1946) *with* **Lady J. Lingerie, Inc. v. City of Jacksonville,** 176 F.3d 1358 (11th Cir. 1999) (ordinance unconstitutional because it includes imprisonment)]

b. Statutes Lacking Express Provision for Vicarious Liability

Frequently, the legislature does not make its intent clear on the face of the statute. In such cases, courts are likely to interpret the statute as imposing vicarious liability only if vicarious liability seems so necessary to the statute's effectiveness that the legislature must have intended to provide for such liability. [**State v. Beaudry,** *supra*] This is most likely to be the case if:

(1) ***The activity*** covered by the statute ***is of the sort likely to be engaged in by employees*** of a business concern;

(2) ***Prosecution of only the employees*** who actually engage in the prohibited activity appears ***unlikely to accomplish the legislative purpose***;

(3) ***The statutory penalty is relatively light***; and

(4) ***There is no language in the statute suggesting that personal fault is required*** for its violation (*e.g.*, a requirement that the crime be committed "willfully" or "knowingly").

c. Crimes Committed by Employee Beyond Scope of Employment

When an employer is prosecuted for the crimes of her employees, some courts limit the employer's liability to crimes committed by employees ***within the scope*** of their employment. [**State v. Beaudry,** *supra*] Whether a particular act was beyond the particular employee's scope of employment sometimes poses a difficult issue.

e.g. **Example:** A corporation cannot be convicted because of employees' illegal sales to minors, because that conduct was not an omission to discharge a duty of affirmative performance imposed on the corporation. In addition, the conduct requested or tolerated by the corporate board of directors or a high managerial agent. In most of these jurisdictions this "superior agent" requirement is not applicable in misdemeanor cases. [**State v. Casey's General Stores, Inc.,** 587 N.W.2d 599 (Iowa 1998)]

(1) Crimes Committed in Disregard of Instructions

Courts have split as to whether vicarious liability can be imposed where the actual perpetrator committed the offense in disregard of the defendant's previous instructions, *e.g.*, factory owner instructs his manager not to employ children under 14, but the manager disregards the instruction and does so. [*Compare* **Commonwealth v. Morakis,** 220 A.2d 900 (Pa. 1966) (no liability) *with* **Granite Construction Co. v. Superior Court,** 149 Cal.App.3d 465 (Cal. 1983) (liability)]

e.g. **Example:** D, the designated agent of a corporation that owned a tavern, was charged with an after-hours sale of liquor by the bartender. D did not authorize the sale and was not present when it was made. The bartender had been instructed to serve no drinks after closing hour. Nevertheless, the court held that a jury could find that after-hour serving of drinks was "sufficiently similar" to the bartender's authorized activity that it was within the scope of his employment. Thus, vicarious liability could be imposed upon D. [**State v. Beaudry,** *supra*]

4. Compromise Position: "Defense" of Lack of Fault

Vicarious liability may lead to harsh results. These may be mitigated by construing the applicable statutes as providing a defense that the accused could not have prevented the offense or perhaps that she was for some other reason completely without fault for commission of the offense. [**United States v. Park,** 421 U.S. 658 (1975) (under Pure Food and Drug Act, a corporate agent charged with crimes committed by employees could come forward with evidence that he was powerless to prevent or correct violation and prosecution would then have to prove his power to prevent or correct violation); *see* **Ex parte Marley**, *supra* (reserving judgment on whether vicarious liability statute would permit employer to avoid liability by showing conspiracy between employee and others to incriminate employer)]

5. Policy Considerations

Whether vicarious liability should be imposed as a matter of policy has been vigorously disputed.

a. Arguments Favoring Vicarious Liability

Those who support vicarious liability argue that it is essential to the effective enforcement of a number of important regulatory schemes, such as pure food regulations and prohibitions against child labor. To encourage employers to prevent violations by their employees, and thus facilitate adherence to the law, employers must be held liable for violations. At the same time, however, employer involvement is for the most part difficult, if not impossible, to prove. Hence, only by imposing vicarious liability can the law deter violations. Moreover, prosecutors can be relied on to invoke vicarious liability statutes only where their application would not do injustice.

b. Arguments Against Vicarious Liability

It has also been stressed that vicarious liability is inconsistent with a basic principle of American criminal law that people should be held criminally liable only where they have demonstrated by their ***own*** actions that they are morally blameworthy. Indeed, imposing vicarious liability often allows for the conviction of those who are entirely innocent. Those supporting this position contend that requiring proof of the defendant's participation would not place that difficult a burden on the prosecution and would avoid injustice in many cases.

6. Constitutional Limits on Vicarious Liability

The constitutionality of vicarious liability statutes, or at least their application to particular cases, can reasonably be called into question. This is particularly so in light of the constitutional requirement of an "act" (*see supra,* pp. 57–61). Vicarious liability, then, may violate the Eighth Amendment prohibition against cruel and unusual punishment. Or, the lack of notice and an opportunity to avoid criminal liability that results from the lack of any requirement that the defendant herself participate in the crime may mean that vicarious liability violates the Fourteenth Amendment requirement of Due Process. Courts, however, have generally upheld vicarious liability statutes, subject to the following limitations. [**Ex parte Marley,** *supra*]

a. Defendant Must Have Had Control over Perpetrator

Due Process may well preclude the imposition of vicarious liability for the crimes of persons over whom the defendant had no control. Consequently, to avoid such constitutional difficulties, statutes imposing vicarious liability are likely to be interpreted as being limited to employer-employee and similar situations. [**United States v. Park,** *supra;* **Kougl v. Board of Liquor License Commissioners for Baltimore City,** 137 A.3d 1062 (Md.App. 2016)]

b. Penalties Must Not Be Serious

Case law has also restricted the nature of the penalty that can be imposed on those who are held only vicariously liable. Generally, serious penalties are not upheld, because while there is a social interest in imposing vicarious liability, it is not weighty enough to justify the imposition of serious criminal sanctions. [**Commonwealth v. Koczwara,** 155 A.2d 825 (Pa. 1959) (punishing tavern owner by imprisonment for bartender's violation of liquor code violated Due Process)] [*But see* **Ex parte Marley**, *supra* (short prison term upheld)]

c. There Must Be No Less Onerous Alternatives

One court has held that Due Process is violated by imposing vicarious liability on a store owner for illegal liquor sales by an employee, even if only a fine is imposed, where the important public interests involved could be served by less onerous noncriminal alternatives, such as revocation of a liquor license. [**Davis v. Peachtree City,** 304 S.E.2d 701 (Ga. 1983)]

C. Criminal Liability of Corporations and Associations

1. Background

Current law governing the criminal liability of organizations, such as corporations, reflects a major modification of traditional notions of criminal responsibility.

a. Common Law Rule: No Corporate Liability

At common law, corporations and associations could not be convicted of criminal offenses. This position was, in part, traceable to various conceptual problems in holding corporations liable. Basically, because a corporation is not a person, it cannot personally participate in a trial or be imprisoned if convicted. To some extent, however, it is likely that the common law rule was based on policy considerations militating against such liability.

b. Modern Rule: Corporations May Be Held Liable

The common law position now has only historical significance. The trend away from the rule of no liability began with the imposition of corporate liability for acts of nonfeasance, *i.e.,* failure to perform duties owed to the general public (such as keeping railroad bridges in repair). By 1909, the Supreme Court conceded that it was constitutionally permissible to hold a corporation criminally liable for affirmative acts of its employees while acting in the course of their duties. Today, corporate liability for both employee acts and omissions is widely recognized. [**New York Central & Hudson River Railroad v. United States,** 212 U.S. 481 (1909) (violation of revenue act by not having the proper tax stamps on shipping document; "the act of agent, while exercising the authority delegated to him . . . may be controlled, in the interest of public policy, by imputing his act to his employer and imposing penalties upon the corporation for which he is acting."); *see, e.g.,* **United States v. Ionia Management S.A.,** 555 F.3d 303 (2d Cir. 2009)]

2. Policy Considerations

Despite the general consensus that criminal liability should extend to corporations at least in certain situations, a number of policy considerations continue to be a subject of much debate.

a. Arguments Favoring Corporate Liability

The basis most often advanced in support of corporate liability rests on the deterrent effect of criminal fines. The threat of fines provides corporate managers with an incentive to take steps to avoid the commission of criminal offenses by corporate employees in the course of their employment. Moreover, corporate organizations wield such tremendous power in modern society that in many contexts social interests are most efficiently served by providing those organizations with a criminal incentive to minimize the commission of offenses by their agents and employees. In some contexts, this may be the only effective method of enforcing important regulatory schemes. [*See* Model Penal Code § 2.07 comment (Tent. Draft No. 4, 1955)]

b. Arguments Against Corporate Liability

The case against criminal liability of corporations rests on the proposition that liability results in ineffective punishment of nonblameworthy persons. A fine is the only penalty that can meaningfully be imposed upon a corporation, yet the burden of a conviction ultimately falls upon the corporation's shareholders, who will usually have no responsibility for commission of the offense. Moreover, the reality of organizational behavior is such that these shareholders are unlikely as a practical matter to be in a position to prevent future crimes of the same sort. In addition, prosecution of the corporation itself tends to detract attention from the corporate employees or managers directly responsible and who should more justly be subjected to criminal sanctions.

EXAM TIP

For your exam, remember that, before a ***specific*** corporation may be held criminally liable, there must be a general statute authorizing liability of corporations. (*See infra.*) The policy considerations above are to be used to determine whether such a statute should be enacted.

3. Requirements for Corporate Liability

The requirements for criminal liability depend in part upon an expression of legislative intent and in part upon the nature (and primarily the severity) of the crime involved.

a. Legislative Intent

Whether an organization can be convicted of a statutory crime depends on the legislative intent. If a statute creating a crime evidences a legislative intent to limit liability to ***natural persons,*** corporations cannot be convicted of the offense. However, if a crime provides for liability of "persons," this may suggest an intention to limit liability to natural persons but it is not determinative. Rather, the ultimate question is whether extending liability to corporations is consistent with the "spirit" of the legislation. [**Granite Construction Co. v. Superior Court,** *supra* (argument that defendant corporation could be liable only for property crimes "overlooks the substantial indirect economic benefit that may accrue to the corporation through crimes against the person. To get these economic benefits, corporate management may shortcut expensive safety precautions, respond forcibly to strikes, or engage in criminal anticompetitive behavior.")]

b. Nature of Crime

The standard for holding corporations responsible for crimes depends in part on the nature of the crime at issue.

(1) Minor Offenses: "Course of Employment"

Corporations are held liable for minor offenses (in particular, strict liability offenses) if the crime was committed by a corporate employee ***while acting in the course of employment.*** If the offense requires a showing of intent or knowledge, courts generally hold that the intent or knowledge of the *employee* suffices. [**Standard Oil Co. of Texas v. United States,** 307 F.2d 120 (5th Cir. 1962) (corporate agent's acts are not in behalf of the corporation if undertaken solely to advance the agent's own interests or interests of parties other than the corporate employer; "the taking in or paying out of money by a bank teller, while certainly one of his regular functions, would hardly cast the corporation for criminal liability if in such 'handling' the faithless employee was pocketing the funds as an embezzler or handing them over to a confederate under some ruse.")]

(2) Major Offenses

Where a corporation is charged with a serious offense (especially one involving a specific intent), there is disagreement concerning the requirements for liability. Several approaches have been recognized:

(a) "Respondeat Superior" Approach

Some courts apply the rule applicable to minor offenses (above), often called the "*respondeat superior*" approach. These courts simply require that the offense have been committed ***with the requisite intent*** by an employee ***in the course of employment*** and (perhaps) that the employee have had the intention of benefiting the corporation. This is the case even if commission of the crime is contrary to general corporate policy and/or the express instructions of the perpetrating employee's superiors. [**United States v. Hilton Hotel Corp.,** 467 F.2d 1000 (9th Cir. 1972)]

(b) Model Penal Code Approach: Authorization by High Managerial Agent

In contrast, the Model Penal Code and statutes based on it permit conviction for such an offense only if its perpetration was ***authorized, performed,*** or at least ***recklessly tolerated*** by the board of directors or "a high managerial agent acting on behalf of the corporation within the scope of his office or employment." The rationale for this approach is to effectively encourage corporate managers to avoid criminal offenses by limiting corporate responsibility to those situations in which persons with authority to prevent major offenses are at least aware of a substantial likelihood that such crimes will be committed. [Model Penal Code § 2.07(1)(c)]

(c) **Compromise Approach: Perpetrator with Authority for Particular Activity**

Some courts have adopted a middle position, requiring proof that the corporation gave the actual perpetrator "***enough authority and responsibility*** to act for the corporation in handling the particular corporate business, operation, or project in which he was engaged at the time he committed the criminal act." This approach does not require commission or approval by a person with overall managerial responsibilities, but instead focuses upon whether the corporation vested the perpetrator with broad responsibilities concerning the activities related to the criminal conduct. [**United States v. Wise,** 370 U.S. 405 (1962) (corporation may be criminally liable for actions or omissions of its agents in its behalf; corporate agent who engages in criminal conduct may also be personally liable)]

c. **"Defense" of Reasonable Effort to Avoid Offense**

Under the Model Penal Code, a corporation charged with a crime other than a strict liability offense may successfully defend by establishing that the high managerial agent having supervisory responsibility over the subject matter of the offense employed due diligence to prevent its commission. [Model Penal Code § 2.07(5)]

4. No Effect on Individual Liability

The imposition of corporate liability does ***not*** affect the criminal responsibility of the actual perpetrator. Hence, ***both*** the corporation and the guilty employee may be convicted of the offense. [Model Penal Code § 2.07(6)(a)]

5. Liability of Unincorporated Associations

In contrast to corporations, unincorporated associations are much less frequently subject to criminal prosecution, conviction, and punishment.

a. **General Rule: No Liability**

The law has been more reluctant to extend criminal liability to partnerships and other unincorporated associations. As a general rule, such associations are not subject to criminal conviction for the crimes of their individual partners or employees. Indeed, even if vicarious liability is imposed on several partners for the crime of one partner, the partnership ***as an entity*** cannot be convicted, because it is regarded as having no legal existence apart from the individual partners. [**Miller v. State,** 438 P.2d 87 (Kan. 1968)]

(1) **Exception: Duty Imposed by Law**

However, if a law clearly imposes a duty on the partnership (rather than upon the individual partners) and provides a penalty for failing to perform that duty, the partnership itself may be held liable. [**Brown v. State,** 111 So. 760 (Ala. 1927) (partnership could be fined for failure to obtain license for vehicle)]

(2) **Exception: Legislative Intent to Make Partnerships Liable**

In addition, a partnership may be prosecuted and convicted where the statute in question expressly or by reasonable interpretation shows an intent to make the entity liable for the crime. [**United States v. A. & P. Trucking Co.,** 358 U.S. 121 (1958) (partnership could be prosecuted under Motor Carrier Act, which is directed at "any person" but defines "person" to include any firm, partnership, or association)]

b. Distinguish: Implications of Entity Theory

Despite traditional adherence to the general rule of no liability, some jurisdictions recognize an "entity theory" of partnership, under which partnerships can sue and be sued in their own name. In turn, courts that follow this theory may arguably conclude that partnerships have sufficient legal standing to justify subjecting them to criminal liability under the same terms as corporations.

Chapter Six

Defenses

CONTENTS	PAGE

Key Exam Issues

If the facts in your exam question indicate that the prosecution can prove the elements of the crime charged, always consider whether there are defenses that may be available to the defendant. There are many recognized defenses to criminal liability, although the defenses available to a particular defendant depend somewhat on the crime charged.

The following is a "checklist" useful in considering what defenses may be available to your defendant. (The specific defenses are discussed in detail in the following chapter.)

1. Was the defendant young? (Consider ***infancy.***)
2. Was the defendant "abnormal" at the time of the conduct? (Consider ***intoxication, insanity,*** or ***diminished capacity.***)
3. Was the defendant mistaken or ignorant in a manner that might show lack of *mens rea*? (Consider ***mistake of fact*** or ***mistake of law.***)
4. Was the defendant subjected to pressures to commit the offense? (Consider ***necessity, duress,*** or ***entrapment.***)
5. If the crime is an assaultive one (*i.e.,* homicide, assault, battery, etc.), was the attack by the defendant motivated by any conduct of the victim or others that might give rise to a defense? (Consider ***self-defense, defense of others, consent of the victim, protection of property.***)
6. Did the defendant have any public authority or similar right to engage in the conduct? (Consider ***right to arrest, right to prevent commission of a crime, public authority,*** or ***domestic authority.***)

A. Defenses: General Considerations

Several aspects of "defenses" generally should be considered before attention is turned to specific defenses. For example, in some jurisdictions, a defendant is permitted to present alternative theories of defense, and even inconsistent alternative theory defenses, unless one defense "necessarily disproves the other." [**State v. Avidiya,** 563 P.3d 763 (Mont. 2025)]

1. "True" Defenses vs. Challenges to Proof of Mens Rea

Some defenses consist of challenges to the prosecution's proof of one of the elements of the charged offense, usually the *mens rea* required. These are sometimes described as providing defendants with an opportunity to "negate" the required *mens rea.* Mistake of fact is the most obvious example. Other defenses assume the prosecution can prove the elements of the charged offense but rely on additional facts as entitling the defendant to exculpation. These can usefully be regarded as "true" defenses. Most of the defenses in this chapter are true defenses.

2. Burden of Persuasion: Affirmative Defenses

Allocation of the burden of persuasion or proof differs among the defenses. If a defense is one permitting a defendant to negate the required culpable mental state, conceptually and perhaps constitutionally the burden of persuasion cannot be placed on the defendant. If a defense is a "true" defense, there is more flexibility and the burden of persuasion can be placed on a defendant. It may also, however, be placed on the prosecution, in which case if the defendant raises the defense, the prosecution must prove it does not apply. The term "affirmative defense" is defined in different ways in different jurisdictions. Most frequently, it is used to describe those "true" defenses on which the defendant has the burden of proof. [*See* **State v. Collins,** 320 A.3d 1094 (N.H. 2024) (when evidence of self-defense is admitted, conduct negating the defense becomes an element of the charged offense)]

3. Justification Defenses v. Excuse Defenses

America's criminal justice systems define various defenses against criminal charges; when successful, defenses absolve or mitigate liability. Distinguishing between justification and excuse is important because when seemingly wrongful conduct is deemed justified, the law is, in effect, condoning that action. Although this is not true for excused conduct, it may be troubling to exempt individuals from full or partial responsibility for wrongdoing even when they have some excuse, especially when the excuse seems contrived.

In justification, defendants deny that their conduct was wrong and claim that under the circumstances their conduct was correct and justified. An example of a justification is killing in defense of one's own life. That killing is not a violation of the law against murder but instead is a "justifiable homicide." A defendant admits to killing another person, often along with a concession that the taking of life is typically wrong. The law also covers other forms of justifiable killing, such as when defending another person, protecting property, or to prevent a crime.

When people offer excuses for misconduct, they admit that their actions were wrong but state that they are not fully to blame. With excuses, culpability is denied, as is full responsibility for the misconduct. By contrast, with justifications the individuals take responsibility for their conduct but insist that it was the proper way to act in that situation. Excuses commonly recognized in American law include duress, ignorance, mistake, and insanity, which are subject to careful definition and limitation.

4. "Cultural" Defenses

Occasionally a question arises as to the effect on a criminal defendant's liability of the defendant's cultural background and beliefs or attitudes attributable to that background.

a. No Cultural Defense

No doctrine of criminal law permits a defendant to avoid criminal liability upon the basis of her cultural background and beliefs or attitudes attributable to that background. Criminal liability is not affected, for example, by evidence that in the defendant's culture the conduct constituting the charged offense is accepted or even admired.

b. Cultural Background May Be Relevant to Issues Under General Doctrines

In unusual situations, evidence of a defendant's cultural background may be relevant to whether the prosecution has proven what it needs to prove or whether a defense applies. Such evidence may show that language used by the defendant was not intended as the particular threat it seemed to be. Or it may show a reasonable (for the defendant) belief in danger from the victim and thus be relevant to self-defense. [*Compare* **Douangpangna v. Knowles,** 2007 WL 1040967 (E.D.Cal. 2007) (in a murder case, trial judge should have instructed the jury that the defendant's Laotian culture and belief in black magic could be considered on mental state and self-defense) *with* **People v. Assad,** 189 Cal.App.4th 187 (2010) ("cultural variance" evidence constitutes an improper comment on the evidence)]

B. Infancy

1. Common Law

At common law, some children were regarded as incapable of committing a crime and thus could not be convicted. One of several different presumptions is applied regarding a child's capacity to commit a crime:

a. Under Age Seven

A child under age seven is ***conclusively*** presumed unable to form a criminal intent and therefore cannot be convicted of a crime.

b. Between Ages Seven and Fourteen

A child between seven and 14 years of age is likewise presumed incapable of forming criminal intent, but this presumption is ***rebuttable,*** and the prosecution can therefore obtain a conviction by introducing evidence sufficient to establish that the defendant knew what she was doing and knew that it was wrong. Attempts to conceal the commission of the crime, to bribe witnesses, and to accuse others are often relied on to rebut the presumption.

(1) Distinguish: Incapacity to Commit Rape

A male child under age 14 is ***conclusively*** presumed incapable of committing rape. (*See infra,* p. 242)

c. Age Fourteen and Older

At ages 14 and older, children are treated as adults, and there is ***no presumption*** of incapacity.

COMMON LAW INFANCY DEFENSE—A SUMMARY	
AGE AT TIME CRIME IS COMMITTED	PRESUMPTION
UNDER 7 YEARS	***Conclusive*** presumption that child is unable to form criminal intent.
7 TO 14	***Rebuttable*** presumption that child is unable to form criminal intent; evidence may be admitted showing child knew what she was doing and knew it was wrong.
14 AND OLDER	***No*** presumption of incompetency.

2. Modern Statutes

Modern statutes vary in their treatment of the infancy defense, some codifying the common law rules and others modifying them. Of those jurisdictions that depart from the common law, a few have raised the minimum age for criminal liability; others, however, have made the presumption of incapacity a rebuttable one regardless of the age of the child. [*See, e.g.,* Cal. Penal Code § 26 (children under age 14 are presumed incapable of committing crime, but the presumption is rebuttable by "clear proof" that the child knew the wrongfulness of her act)]

3. Determining Defendant's Age

a. Age at Time of Crime Controls

Under both the common law and modern statutes, it is the child's age ***at the time of commission*** of the crime, rather than at the time of trial, that controls. [**Triplett v. State,** 152 So. 881 (Miss. 1934)]

b. Chronological Age Controls

Similarly, the child's chronological age (rather than his "mental age") is determinative. [**State v. Dillon,** 471 P.2d 553 (Idaho 1970)]

4. Juvenile Court Jurisdiction

All American jurisdictions have legislation that confers upon juvenile courts jurisdiction over children of certain ages alleged to have committed a crime. In juvenile court proceedings, the child is not "convicted" but is "adjudicated delinquent." Statutes often permit the juvenile court to waive its jurisdiction over a specific child and allow the child to be tried as an adult. [*See, e.g.,* Model Penal Code § 4.10 (child under 16 to be processed in juvenile court; child 16 or 17 to be so processed unless juvenile court waives jurisdiction)]

C. Insanity

1. In General

A defendant is entitled to an acquittal (usually pursuant to a verdict of "not guilty by reason of insanity" or "NGRI") if, ***at the time of the crime,*** he was so impaired by mental illness or developmental disability (formerly retardation) as to be "insane" within the meaning of the law. Whether a defendant is not convictable because of insanity, however, does not depend solely upon the severity of the impairment or other medical conclusions. Rather, criminal responsibility turns upon whether as a result of impairment the defendant ***met the applicable legal standard.***

a. Distinguish: "Incompetency to Stand Trial"

Insanity concerns the defendant's state of mind ***at the time of the crime***. It must be distinguished from "incompetency to stand trial" which concerns the defendant's condition at the time of trial. Unlike insanity, incompetency to stand trial is ***not a defense,*** but it requires that the proceedings be postponed until such time as the defendant regains his competency. [**Dusky v. United States,** 362 U.S. 402 (1960) (defendant is incompetent to stand trial if he lacks sufficient present ability to consult with his lawyer with a reasonable degree of rational understanding or to have a rational as well as factual understanding of proceedings against him)]

b. Incompetency at Time of Execution in Capital Cases

The Eighth Amendment prohibits capital punishment for a prisoner who is either insane or intellectually disabled at the time set for execution. [**Atkins v. Virginia,** 536 U.S. 304 (2002)] In **Madison v. Alabama,** 586 U.S. 265 (2019), the Court held that execution may occur even if the prisoner cannot recall committing the crime, but she cannot be executed while suffering from dementia or other disorder rather than delusion. The standard focuses on whether a mental disorder has had a particular effect, not on the precise cause for the disorder. [**Panetti v. Quarterman,** 551 U.S. 930 (2007)]

c. Distinguish: "Diminished Capacity"

Insanity must also be distinguished from "diminished capacity" (*see infra,* p. 116 *et seq.*). The rule of diminished capacity permits a defendant to introduce evidence of mental impairment to show that he ***lacked the mens rea*** required for the crime. Under most approaches, however, insanity is not invoked to disprove *mens rea* but rather to prove that the defendant lacked the more basic capacity to engage in morally reprehensible behavior—*i.e.,* to understand what he was doing or (in some jurisdictions) to control his conduct. [**State v. Maas,** 744 P.2d 1222 (Kan. 1987) (diminished capacity is a rule of evidence, and can be argued to jury during defense closing argument, and may require an instruction on a lesser-included offense that does not require the questioned mental state)]

d. Approach to Insanity Defense Analysis

In considering whether a defendant is entitled to acquittal on insanity grounds, it is necessary to address two matters: (i) whether at the time of the crime the defendant had a ***sufficient impairment*** to constitute insanity; and (if so) (ii) whether that impairment ***so affected the defendant*** as to meet the legal standard.

EXAM TIP

Just as in other areas, don't be led astray by exam facts. No matter how "disturbed" a defendant might seem, if he doesn't meet the technical requirements of the jurisdiction's insanity defense, he is not ***legally*** "insane" and has no insanity defense.

2. Condition Giving Rise to Insanity

While the various formulations of the insanity test (*infra*) differ significantly, all require that the defendant have had some sort of ***mental impairment.*** However, not all impairments can give rise to insanity.

a. Mental Illness or "Disease"

A traditional mental abnormality, such as a psychosis, neurosis, or organic brain disorder, may be a basis for an insanity defense. "This result has been codified in modern statutory provisions providing for a defense based on a "mental disease." [*See* Model Penal Code § 4.01] Recent legislation in some jurisdictions, however, specifically requires that the mental condition be severe. [*See, e.g.,* 18 U.S.C. § 17(a) ("severe mental disease or defect" required)]

(1) "Psychopathic Personality"

Many jurisdictions follow the Model Penal Code and provide that the insanity defense ***cannot*** be based upon "an abnormality manifested only by repeated criminal or otherwise antisocial conduct." [Model Penal Code § 4.01(2)] This is intended to mean that so-called psychopaths or sociopaths are not eligible for the insanity defense. [*See* **Blocker v. United States,** 274 F.2d 572 (D.C.Cir. 1959)]

(2) Multiple Personality Disorder

Multiple personality disorder ***can*** serve as the basis for an insanity defense, but jurisdictions are divided on how to evaluate whether such a defendant was in fact insane. Courts use three approaches with MPD: (1) the majority view that looks at the culpability of the personality that allegedly committed the crime; (2) the rarely-applied unified approach, focusing on the person as a whole without regard to which personality was in control at the time of the offense; and (3) the host approach, which can support a finding of not guilty by reason of insanity because the host personality neither planned nor participated in the crime. [**United States v. Denny-Shaffer,** 2 F.3d 999 (10th Cir. 1993) (critical question is whether the "host" or "dominant" personality met the insanity standard)]

b. Developmental Disability

Even developmental disability (previously called mental retardation or even "feeblemindedness") can, if it satisfies the applicable test, render the defendant legally insane. [**State v. Johnson,** 290 N.W. 159 (Wis. 1940)] This is codified in many modern statutes as a defense based on a "mental defect." [*See* Model Penal Code § 4.01]

APPROACH TO INSANITY DEFENSE ANALYSIS

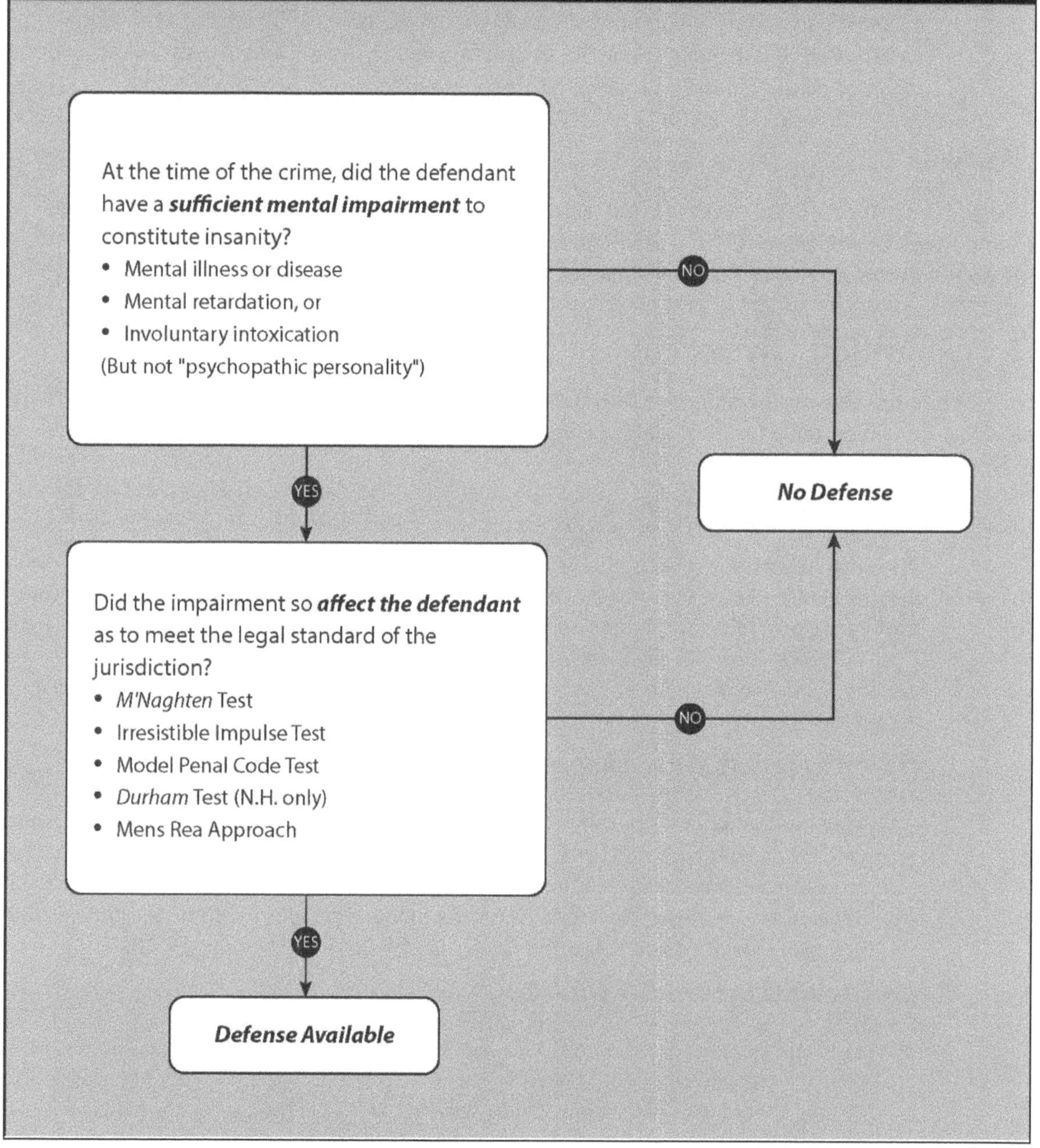

c. Intoxication

Involuntary intoxication can support an insanity defense if it produces the required effect on the defendant's mind. [**Burrows v. State,** 297 P. 1029 (Ariz. 1931) (driver picked up a hitchhiker, and threatened to evict the youngster if he did not drink an intoxicating substance; the youth drank so much that was no longer able to appreciate the consequences of his actions; he shot the driver to death; held that his intoxication was not the result of duress)] Similarly, a reasonably settled physical or psychological abnormality caused by repeated use of intoxicants supports the defense. [**People v. Griggs,** 110 P.2d 1031 (Cal. 1941) (chronic alcoholic killed another; insanity may occur from continuous intoxication)] Narcotics addiction raises no issue of mental disease or defect to support an insanity defense, but evidence that addiction has caused physiological damage to defendant's brain is admissible to show defendant lacked substantial capacity to conform his conduct to the requirements of law. [**Licklieter v. Commonwealth,** 142 S.W.3d 65 (Ky. 2004)]

(1) Distinguish: Voluntary Intoxication

Voluntary intoxication does not give rise to insanity, but it is the subject of a specific and different "defense" (*see infra,* p. 119 *et seq.*). [**State v. Williams,** 889 N.W.2d 99 (Neb. 2017)]

3. Tests for Insanity

All jurisdictions agree that a mental impairment alone does not constitute grounds for acquittal on insanity grounds. The impairment must have ***created a certain effect*** on the defendant's mental condition at the time of the crime.

a. Basic Analysis: "Cognitive" and "Volitional" Impairment

Insanity analysis assumes that impairments consist of two distinguishable types: (1) "Cognitive" impairments concern the person's intellectual processes and involve impaired ability to ***perceive reality*** and to ***reason*** about it, and (2) "Volitional" impairments, in contrast, concern the person's ability to *control his behavior* and involve impaired ability to avoid engaging in conduct that the person intellectually or cognitively recognizes is wrong.

b. Basic Issue: Should Loss of Control Constitute a Defense?

The basic issue that divides jurisdictions is whether the legal standard for insanity should be limited to the defendant's thinking or reasoning abilities (cognitive impairment), or whether the defense should also be permitted based on the defendant's loss of ability to control his conduct (volitional impairment; *see infra,* p. 111).

(1) Historical Developments

Insanity was originally limited to cognitive defects. Until the early 1980s, the trend was toward expansion of the defense, often by adoption of the Model Penal Code's formulation. However, after the acquittal of John Hinckley on charges arising from his attempt to assassinate President Ronald Reagan, many American jurisdictions returned to a restrictive cognitive standard.

c. *M'Naghten* Rule

The traditional standard for insanity, the *M'Naghten* rule, was formulated by the English House of Lords in 1843. What this standard means, however, depends on how critical phrases are defined.

(1) Statement of Rule

Under the *M'Naghten* rule, which is a cognitive test, a defendant is to be acquitted by reason of insanity only if, at the time of the crime and as a result of his mental impairment, he either (i) did not know the ***nature and quality of his act;*** or (ii) did not know that the act was ***wrong.*** [**M'Naghten's Case,** 8 Eng. Rep. 718 (1843)]

(2) Modified *M'Naghten* Rule Approach

Under a modified approach, acquittal is required only on proof the defendant did not know his act was wrong. The Supreme Court has held that federal constitutional requirements are not violated if a state adopts a modified *M'Naghten* rule approach that omits the provision for acquittal on proof that the defendant did not know the nature and quality of his act. [**Clark v. Arizona,** 548 U.S. 735 (2006) (the trial court refused defendant's attempt to introduce evidence of diminished capacity; but testimony was admissible from witnesses who observed what defendant did and who heard what he said," which "could include testimony that an expert witness might give about defendant's tendency to think in a certain way and his behavioral characteristics")]

(3) Definition of "Nature and Quality of Act"

Most jurisdictions hold that a defendant does not "know the nature and quality of his act" only if, as a result of his mental impairment, he did not **understand its** *physical nature and consequences* (*e.g.,* that holding a **flame** to a building will cause it to burn). A minority of courts, however, defines this as requiring a more basic and accurate understanding of the significance of the action. These courts hold that a defendant should be acquitted if, because of his impairment, he lacked ***"true insight" into the nature of his conduct*** *and that it was forbidden.* [*See, e.g.,* **State v. Esser,** 115 N.W.2d 505 (Wis. 1962)] [*Compare* **Kassa v. State,** 485 P.3d 750 (Nev. 2021) (sufficient evidence that defendant understood the nature and capacity of his act in setting fire to a home, and that knew that his act was wrongful)]

(4) Definition of "Wrong"

Authorities have long debated how "wrong" should be defined under *M'Naghten.*

(a) "Legal Wrong" Approach

English courts define "wrong" to mean that the defendant knew that his act was ***legally wrong.*** [**Regina v. Windle,** [1952] 2 Q.B. 826] American courts have differed, but most adopt this view although most courts give the issue to the jury without any explanation. [**State v. Crenshaw,** 659 P.2d 488 (Wash. 1983)] Thus, a defendant is to be convicted unless his impairment caused him to believe his action was legally permissible.

1) Distinguish: "Deific Decree" Rule

Some jurisdictions that define "wrong" as legally wrong nevertheless will acquit a defendant who believes his action was ordained by God as a result of a **direct command from God,** *i.e.,* a "deific decree" to commit the act. [**State v. Worlock,** 569 A.2d 1314 (N.J. 1990)]

e.g. **Example:** D, because of his severe schizophrenia, believes W, his wife, has been unfaithful. He also believes that God permits and in fact directs one spouse to kill the other if that other spouse has been unfaithful. Nevertheless, he recognizes that if he kills W he may be convicted of a crime. He kills W. *Analysis:* (i) D has a ***sufficient impairment*** to trigger insanity; (ii) D's impairment did not prevent him from knowing the ***nature and quality*** of killing W, as *M'Naghten* is usually interpreted; (iii) D's impairment did not prevent him from knowing that killing W was ***legally*** wrong; (iv) even if the jurisdiction recognizes the "deific decree" rule, D cannot bring himself within it because he has no evidence that he believed his moral view was stimulated by a relatively ***direct message to him from God.*** [**State v. Crenshaw,** *supra*]

(b) "Moral Wrong" Approach

Some argue that "wrong" should mean ***morally wrong.*** Thus, a defendant should be acquitted if, as a result of his impairment, he believed his action was morally acceptable, even if he also recognized that it was (and would be treated by authorities as) legally impermissible. Those few American jurisdictions that take this approach limit it by requiring that the defendant believe his action was morally acceptable according to general societal standards. Thus, acquittal is not required on a showing that the defendant believed his action morally right under his own subjective standards of right and wrong, if those standards are not accepted by society as a whole. [**State v. Wilson,** 700 A.2d 633 (Conn. 1997); *see* **State v. Romero,** 463 P.3d 225 (Ariz.App. 2020)]

(5) Loss of Control Irrelevant

Under most applications of the *M'Naghten* test, the defendant's ability or inability to control his conduct is not relevant. If the defendant could reason and think about his conduct, he is not entitled to acquittal on the ground that mental impairment deprived him of the ability to avoid committing a crime. [**Carnes v. State,** 275 S.W. 1002 (Tex. 1925)]

(6) Criticism of *M'Naghten* Test

The basic criticism of the *M'Naghten* test is that it is so limited that it permits conviction of some impaired persons who, because of their illnesses, could not have avoided committing crimes and thus are not morally blameworthy despite their actions. Some people experience severe impairments that impact only their ability to exercise control over their conduct, yet the *M'Naghten* test provides them with no defense on this ground. As a result, people who have not acted in a morally reprehensible manner are improperly convicted of criminal offenses.

"The science of psychiatry now recognizes that a man is an integrated personality and that reason, which is only one element in that personality, is not the sole determinant of his conduct. The right-wrong test, which considers knowledge or reason alone, is therefore an inadequate guide to mental responsibility for criminal behavior." [**Durham v. United States,** 214 F.2d 862 (D.C.Cir. 1954)] *M'Naghten* restricts expert testimony, thereby preventing the factfinder from learning relevant information about the defendant's mental condition that is important to their final judgment in the case. [**United States v. Freeman,** 357 F.2d 606 (2d Cir. 1966); **State v. Carpio,** 43 A.3d 1 (R.I. 2012)]

d. Loss of Control Tests

Some formulations of the insanity test permit acquittal if the defendant shows sufficient cognitive impairment (usually as required under *M'Naghten,* above) ***or*** sufficient volitional impairment—*i.e.,* loss of the ability to control behavior. For example, the Model Penal Code proposes that a defendant be acquitted if as a result of mental impairment he lacks substantial capacity ***either*** to (i) "appreciate the criminality [wrongfulness] of his conduct" (thus incorporating a modernly phrased cognitive test based on *M'Naghten*) ***or*** to (ii) "conform his conduct to the requirements of law" (thus incorporating a control test).

(1) Irresistible Impulse Test

Some jurisdictions have long provided that a defendant is entitled to acquittal on insanity grounds if his commission of the crime was caused by an "insane impulse" that ***overcame his will*** to avoid the crime. [**State v. Hartley,** 565 P.2d 658 (N.M. 1977)]

(2) Model Penal Code Test: Lack of "Substantial Capacity" to Control Oneself

As stated above, under the Model Penal Code, a defendant is entitled to acquittal if the evidence shows that, because of a mental impairment at the time of the crime, he "lacked substantial capacity to conform his conduct to the requirements of law." [Model Penal Code § 4.01(1)] Until the early 1980s, this formulation was widely adopted.

(3) Criticism of Control Tests

Critics of the loss of control tests argue that few if any persons really are rendered unable to refrain from engaging in conduct they know is criminal. Even if some persons are so affected, courts even with the help of expert psychiatric testimony simply cannot determine whether particular impaired defendants were rendered unable to avoid committing crimes. Furthermore, testimony on the matter is likely to confuse juries and to cause unjustified acquittals because of jury misunderstanding.

e. Broader Tests

Some argue for standards that go beyond the *M'Naghten* or control tests.

(1) *Durham* (or "Product") Rule

The *Durham* rule would require the factfinder to determine "whether the defendant had a mental disease or defect and whether the crime was a product of such disease or defect." [**State v. Cegelis,** 638 A.2d 783 (N.H. 1994)] *Durham* was supposed to enable psychiatrists to testify without the evidentiary restraints of the right-wrong and irresistible impulse tests. *Durham* was abandoned in 1972. [**United States v. Brawner,** 471 F.2d 969 (D.C. Cir. 1972) (adopting the Model Penal Code test)] Those who criticize *Durham*'s "product of an impairment" rule stress that it fails to give juries guidance in determining when a specific crime is the product of a defendant's impairment. Attempts to apply the *Durham* Rule led to the same disputes about nomenclature that characterized trials under *M'Naghten.*

(2) "Sense of Justice" Test

A leading federal judge suggested that the law should not attempt a precise formulation of when impaired defendants should be acquitted, because this is difficult or even impossible. Inevitably, the question is a complex ethical-social one. Therefore, jurors should be told simply to acquit a defendant if they determine that "at the time of his unlawful conduct his mental or emotional processes or behavior controls were impaired to such an extent that he cannot justly be held responsible for his act." [**United States v. Brawner,** *supra* (Bazelon, C.J., concurring)]

f. Revised Cognitive Tests

After the acquittal of John Hinckley, many American jurisdictions adopted somewhat "modernized" versions of the *M'Naghten* test (*see supra,* p. 109).

e.g. **Example:** Under a California statute adopted by initiative, a defendant is to be found insane only if he was incapable of knowing or understanding the nature and quality of his act ***and*** of distinguishing right from wrong at the time of the commission of the offense. [Cal. Penal Code § 25(b)]

e.g. **Example:** The broader terminology in the 1984 federal statute provides for acquittal if the defendant, as a result of severe mental disease or defect, "was unable to ***appreciate*** the nature and quality or the wrongfulness of his acts." [18 U.S.C. § 17(a)] By using the term "appreciate" rather than "know," Congress may have adopted a test broader than the old *M'Naghten* test; a defendant arguably can be less impaired than was required under the old test yet still unable to "appreciate" his situation.

g. "Mens Rea" Approach Alternative

Several jurisdictions have abolished any insanity defense as such (*see infra*) but have substituted an explicit authorization for defendants to use evidence of mental condition to show that they did not have the *mens rea* required by the crime charged. [*See, e.g.,* Idaho Stat. Ann. § 18–207; Utah Code Ann. § 76–2–305] One court has held that this approach denies defendants federal Due Process [**Finger v. State,** 27 P.3d 66 (Nev. 2001)], but others have upheld the *mens rea* approach [*see, e.g.,* **State v. Bethel,** 66 P.3d 840 (Kan. 2003)].

h. Constitutionality

The Fourteenth Amendment Due Process Clause does not require the states to provide an insanity defense that allows a defendant to be acquitted for being unable to distinguish right from wrong. [**Kansas v. Kahler,** 589 U.S. 271 (2020)]

4. Proposal to Abolish Insanity Defense

Some critics of the insanity defense have urged its total abolition in any form.

a. Arguments for Abolishing or Limiting Defense

The major arguments supporting abolition or limitation of the insanity defense are as follows:

SUMMARY OF INSANITY DEFENSES		
TEST	**DEFINITION**	**TYPE**
M'NAGHTEN	Because of mental impairment, defendant did not ***know*** (i) ***the nature and quality of act*** or (ii) that it was ***wrong***	Cognitive test
IRRESISTIBLE IMPULSE	Crime caused by insane impulse that ***overcame defendant's will***	Loss of control test
MODEL PENAL CODE	Because of mental impairment, defendant ***lacked substantial capacity*** to (i) ***appreciate criminality*** of conduct or (ii) ***conform it to the law***	Combination of cognitive and loss of control tests
DURHAM	Crime was a ***product of defendant's impairment***	Causation test
MENS REA	Because of mental impairment, defendant ***lacked mens rea*** required by crime	*Mens rea* or state of mind test

(1) Despite the help of expert testimony, ***courts cannot make the determinations*** necessary to apply insanity standards. Even applying more limited criteria, like the *M'Naghten* test (*supra*), is simply too difficult.

(2) Efforts to apply insanity standards are ***time consuming*** and too often so ***confuse juries*** that improper acquittals result.

(3) As applied, the insanity defense ***favors wealthier defendants,*** because they are better able to hire the expert witnesses necessary to make a successful defense.

(4) The defense is ***not a useful way of diverting those who need treatment*** into a more treatment-oriented system. Those acquitted are not suffering from the kind of impairments that are better treated in the mental health system than in correctional programs.

(5) Persons acquitted on insanity grounds often spend more time in mental hospitals than they would in prison if convicted; thus, the defense ***does not really benefit impaired offenders.***

b. Arguments for Retention of Defense and Broader Standards

Arguments in favor of retaining the insanity defense and of using a broader standard (such as the control tests, *see supra,* p. 105 *et seq.*) include:

(1) Criminal conviction implies that a person has engaged in ethically blameworthy behavior, and many persons suffering from impairments are ***not ethically blameworthy;*** it is therefore important to provide a method whereby certain impaired persons can ***avoid the stigma and harsh punishment*** imposed for criminal responsibility.

(2) ***Individual responsibility is reinforced*** by inquiries into whether certain defendants were so impaired as to be non-responsible; thus, the insanity defense tends to strengthen attitudes of general responsibility that keep people from violating the law.

(3) The process can be made into an ***effective way of diverting proper persons*** into the mental health system. Post-acquittal commitment can be reformed so that only acquitted defendants who are still dangerous are hospitalized, effective treatment not available in prisons is provided, and such persons are released when, but not before, they are no longer dangerous. [A. Goldstein, The Insanity Defense (1967)]

5. Burden of Proof on Insanity

There is a general ***presumption of sanity.*** Hence, the defendant has at least the initial burden of going forward with the evidence, *i.e.,* the insanity issue is not raised unless the ***defendant presents some evidence*** tending to show he was insane at the time of the offense. Prior to the post-Hinckley acquittal changes, most jurisdictions provided that once a defendant raised the issue of insanity, the ***prosecution*** was required to prove beyond a reasonable doubt that the defendant was ***sane.***

a. Recent Trend: Burden on Defendant

As part of the reform of insanity law following the Hinckley acquittal, a trend has developed placing on the ***defendant*** the burden of proving ***insanity.*** [18 U.S.C. § 17(b) (defendant must prove insanity by clear and convincing evidence); Ky.Rev.Stat. § 504.020 (defendant must prove insanity by preponderance of evidence)]

b. Constitutionality

A state may, consistent with Due Process, require a defendant to prove his insanity, even beyond a reasonable doubt. [**Leland v. Oregon,** 343 U.S. 790 (1954)]

6. Jury Instructions on Consequences of Insanity Acquittal

Jurisdictions are split on whether the trial jury should be told the procedural consequences of acquitting the defendant on insanity grounds. Defendants argue that such instructions are necessary to assure that the jury does not mistakenly believe that an acquitted defendant will be permitted to simply and immediately return to the community. Nevertheless, most jurisdictions do not instruct the jury on the matter. [**Shannon v. United States,** 512 U.S. 573 (1994) (absent some misstatement to the jury on the subject, a federal trial judge is not to instruct the jury on the consequences of a not guilty by reason of insanity verdict)]

7. Procedure Following Acquittal by Reason of Insanity

A defendant who is acquitted on insanity grounds may nevertheless pose a serious risk of further harm to others. As a result, all jurisdictions have special procedures for processing defendants found ***not guilty by reason of insanity*** ("NGRI").

a. Verdict of NGRI

Although verdicts in criminal cases are usually "general," an exception is made in insanity cases. Juries are instructed that if the defendant is entitled to an acquittal on insanity grounds, the verdict should specify that the defendant is found specifically "not guilty by reason of insanity." [18 U.S.C. § 4242(b)]

b. Post-Acquittal Commitment

In all jurisdictions, some provision is made for possible hospitalization of defendants found NGRI. Under the federal statute, which is typical of modern statutory schemes, an

NGRI defendant is ***automatically committed*** to a hospital for a limited period. This commitment is continued only if, at a hearing held within 40 days, the defendant fails to show that he is no longer dangerous. [18 U.S.C. § 4243]

c. Constitutionality

Although other mentally ill persons cannot be committed unless their dangerousness is affirmatively demonstrated, the Supreme Court has held that defendants found NGRI can constitutionally be committed on that basis. There is no federal constitutional right to be released from hospitalization on the expiration of the maximum time the defendant could have spent in prison had he been convicted. [**Jones v. United States,** 463 U.S. 354 (1983)]

8. Guilty but Mentally Ill Alternative

Some states give juries the option, when a defendant claims impairment at the time of the offense, of rejecting the defense of insanity but instead finding the defendant "guilty but mentally ill." This approach is modeled on a Michigan statute. [Mich.Comp. Laws § 768.36]

a. Requirements

A verdict of guilty but mentally ill is to be returned only if the jury finds that the defendant committed the offense, was ***not legally insane, but was mentally ill*** at the time of the crime.

b. Effect of Finding of "Guilty but Mentally Ill"

A defendant found guilty but mentally ill is sentenced under regular sentencing provisions. If sentenced to imprisonment, however, the defendant is to be given whatever treatment is indicated. If probation is imposed, treatment may be required as a condition of probation.

D. Diminished Capacity

1. In General

In some jurisdictions, evidence of mental illness that does not establish insanity is still admissible to prove that the defendant did not have, or could not have formed, the culpable mental state necessary for the crime charged. This position is sometimes referred to as the *"Wells-Gorshen"* rule, after two leading California Supreme Court decisions that adopted it. It is also often called the doctrine of "diminished capacity" because it permits the use of evidence (usually psychiatric testimony) to establish that the defendant's capacity was so ***diminished that she could not have formed the requisite mens rea.*** [**People v. Wells,** 202 P.2d 53 (Cal. 1949); **People v. Gorshen,** 336 P.2d 492 (Cal. 1959)]

a. Rationale

Courts accepting the *Wells-Gorshen* rule generally reason that if *mens rea* is essential to criminal liability, a defendant should have the right to prove that she lacked the requisite mental state by any evidence that is logically relevant to the issue. In addition, the rule is said to provide a reasonable compromise between the extremes of holding a mentally ill person fully liable and completely exonerating her by extending the insanity defense, *i.e.,* even where diminished capacity is established, the accused can ordinarily be found guilty of a less serious offense (*see infra*).

b. Federal Constitutional Considerations

The Supreme Court has made it clear that the federal constitutional requirement of Due Process of law does not require state adoption of a broad diminished capacity rule. However, the Court stopped short of holding that Due Process permits exclusion of all defensive evidence based on mental impairment except in support of an insanity defense. [**Clark v. Arizona,** *supra* (Arizona rule barring most such evidence, but permitting "observation testimony" as to a defendant's thinking and behavioral characteristics, did not violate Due Process)]

c. Legislative Modification of California Rule

After the *Wells* and *Gorshen* cases, California legislation modified the rule there. Under the legislation, diminished capacity is not a defense in a criminal case. Evidence of mental illness is not admissible to negate a defendant's ***capacity*** to form any mental state, but such evidence may be admitted on the issue of whether the defendant ***actually did form*** a mental state required by the crime charged. However, evidence that the defendant, because of mental illness, lacked the ***ability to control*** his conduct cannot be used to show that the defendant did not form a required mental state. [Cal. Penal Code §§ 28, 29.2; **People v. Saille,** 820 P.2d 588 (Cal. 1991) (legislative modification of the *Wells-Gorshen* rule does not violate Due Process)]

2. Majority Approach: Diminished Capacity Rejected

A majority of courts reject the *Wells-Gorshen* rule, reasoning that the insanity defense is the vehicle for relating mental illness to criminal liability and should not be circumvented by manipulation of the *mens rea* requirement. It is also contended that expert testimony to establish diminished capacity is unreliable, and juries are not equipped to understand or adequately evaluate it. [**State v. Provost,** 490 N.W.2d 93 (Minn. 1992)]

3. Application: Limited to Specific Intent Crimes

Even where recognized, the diminished capacity rule is usually applied only to specific intent crimes. Therefore, a defendant who successfully asserts it in defense to a major specific intent crime can generally be convicted of a lesser included offense that requires only a general *mens rea*. [**People v. Noah,** 487 P.2d 1009 (Cal. 1971)]

a. Distinguished: Model Penal Code Position

The Model Penal Code would admit evidence of mental illness whenever it is relevant to whether the defendant had the state of mind required for the offense. There is no limitation to specific intent offenses or any other category of crimes. [Model Penal Code § 4.02(1)]

4. Tactical Advantage: Advance Notice Not Required

Defendants in jurisdictions following the diminished capacity rule may have a tactical advantage in that, unlike the insanity defense, advance notice of intent to raise the issue may not be required. (Some pretrial notice provisions do cover diminished capacity, however. *See, e.g.,* Federal Rule of Criminal Procedure 12.2(b), requiring pretrial notice of intent to offer evidence that, because of mental illness, the defendant lacked the requisite intent.)

5. Distinguish: English "Diminished Responsibility" Rule

By statute in England, a defendant charged with murder is to be convicted only of manslaughter if he establishes that, at the time of the killing, mental illness "substantially impaired his mental responsibility" for the killing. This does not involve disproof of *mens rea*, but it permits a defendant to establish that although he was not so disturbed as to be insane, his "responsibility" as addressed by the insanity defense, although not totally lacking, was sufficiently impaired by mental illness to make a murder conviction inappropriate. [Homicide Act, 1957 (5 & 6 Eliz. II, ch. 11, § 2)] No American jurisdiction has adopted such legislation; there is no "diminished responsibility" rule in the United States.

E. Intoxication

1. In General

The effect of intoxication upon criminal liability depends upon whether the accused was voluntarily or involuntarily intoxicated. While involuntary intoxication may be a complete defense, voluntary intoxication is never a defense, although it may sometimes be used to prove lack of *mens rea* or capacity.

a. Source of Intoxication Is Irrelevant

Although the intoxication defense is most frequently based upon conditions arising from the ingestion of alcohol, the rules equally apply to the consumption of other intoxicating substances. such as drugs and medicine. [**People v. Penman,** 110 N.E. 894 (Ill. 1915) (involuntary intoxication analysis is used to determine the legal effect of ingesting cocaine tablets); *see* **Poitra v. State,** 275 P.3d 478 (Wyo. 2012) (involuntary intoxication renders defendant temporarily legally insane)]

2. Involuntary Intoxication

Involuntary intoxication is a ***complete defense*** if it so affected the defendant as to render her insane within the meaning of the insanity test adopted in the jurisdiction. [**People v. Scott,** 146 Cal.App.3d 823 (1983) (defendant was involuntarily intoxicated because, unknown to him, PCP was punch that he drank)]

a. "Involuntary" Defined

Intoxication is involuntary only if the defendant ***did not know*** the substance ingested was intoxicating, or if she consumed it knowing that it was intoxicating but under ***direct and immediate duress.*** Courts require strong evidence of duress to sustain a finding of involuntary intoxication. [**People v. Penman**, *supra*]

b. Pathological Intoxication

The Model Penal Code also regards intoxication as involuntary if it is "pathological," *i.e.,* if it is grossly excessive in proportion to the amount of the substance consumed and the defendant did not know that she was unusually susceptible to such intoxication. [Model Penal Code § 2.08(4), (5)(c)]

c. Medical Permission to Ingest Substance

Another example of involuntary intoxication occurs when a substance is taken pursuant to medical advice. [**State v. Leteve,** 354 P.3d 393 (Ariz. 2015) (a defendant who can prove that his use of prescription drugs was pursuant to a doctor's instructions should be able to plead involuntary intoxication as a defense); *cf.* **Commonwealth v. McDermott,** 864 N.E.2d 471 (Mass. 2007) (defendant was denied an involuntary intoxication instruction because his ingestion of an anti-depressant medication, because he increased his dose of the medication without the prescribing physician's permission or advice)]

d. Permanent Insanity from Use of Intoxicants

Under the majority view, a relatively permanent (or "settled") impairment, such as organic brain damage caused by the defendant's long-term use of intoxicants, can serve as the basis for an insanity defense despite its link to repeated and voluntary intoxication. Some courts, however, question the wisdom of this rule and find limited statutory intoxication defenses as rendering it unavailable. [**Bieber v. People,** 856 P.2d 811 (Colo. 1993) (comprehensive statute providing for limited voluntary intoxication defense is a legislative rejection of the "settled condition" rule); *compare* **Morgan v. Commonwealth,** 646 S.E.2d 899 (Va.App. 2007) ("defense of 'settled insanity' is not available to an accused unless he can make a prima facie showing that he suffers from a mental defect or disease, traceable to long-term, chronic, and habitual alcohol or drug abuse, that is permanent in duration.")]

3. Voluntary Intoxication

Voluntary intoxication is never a defense in the sense that it constitutes a defensive doctrine (like insanity) unrelated to the elements of the charged offense. At common law, voluntary intoxication apparently had no mitigating or defensive significance whatsoever. Under modern law in most jurisdictions, however, it may be used as evidence to ***"negate" some culpable mental states*** and thus may preclude conviction of some crimes. Most states, though, limit the culpable mental states that can be so negated.

a. General Rule: Voluntary Intoxication Can "Negate" a Required Specific Intent

Under the majority view, a defendant can rely on voluntary intoxication to negate only ***a specific intent*** if one is required by the crime charged. Thus, if the crime in question does not require a specific intent, the defendant's voluntary intoxication has no bearing on liability. [**People v. Atkins,** 18 P.3d 660 (Cal. 2001); **King v. Commonwealth,** 513 S.W.3d 919 (Ky. 2017) ("because third-degree arson requires only the general intent to start a fire. . . plus [MPC recklessness] as to the risks of doing so, voluntary intoxication is not a viable defense)] By contrast, a defendant is entitled to an intoxication instruction only if he was so intoxicated that he was unaware of what he was doing. [**Conyers v. Commonwealth,** 530 S.W.3d 413 (Ky. 2017)] [*See* **People v. Snelling,** 523 P.3d 477 (Colo.App. 2022) (reversible error for trial court to refuse to answer juror's question, "Can you be so inebriated that you are unable to form intent?")]

e.g. **Example:** During an arrest attempt, D strikes one officer with his fist and shoots at another with the officer's own gun. D is tried for assault with a deadly weapon and assault with intent to murder but introduces evidence that he was very intoxicated (voluntarily) at the time. Because assault with a deadly weapon is a ***general intent*** crime, D's intoxication has no relevance to his liability for that charge. Assault with intent to murder, however, requires proof of a ***specific intent*** (*i.e.,* the intent to kill). Therefore, if D's intoxication shows that he lacked specific intent, or if it simply raises a reasonable doubt about whether he acted with that intent, he cannot be convicted of that offense. [**People v. Hood,** *supra*]

(1) Rationale

The rationale for the majority rule is unclear. To some extent, it reflects a desire to minimize the exculpatory effect of intoxication on the grounds that those who commit crimes while intoxicated are undoubtedly dangerous and, to some extent at least, blameworthy by virtue of having become intoxicated. Beyond this, however, the limitation may reflect a perception that intoxication seldom, if ever, prevents persons from forming the relatively simple states of mind required for general intent crimes. Consequently, there is no need to consider voluntary intoxication in cases where only a general *mens rea* is required. [**People v. Hood,** *supra;* **Bieber v. State,** *supra*]

(2) Burden of Proof

Because voluntary intoxication tends to negate the *mens rea*, a matter on which the prosecution has the burden of proof beyond a reasonable doubt, a defendant should be acquitted if the evidence of intoxication simply raises a reasonable doubt as to whether the defendant had the required *mens rea*. Nevertheless, some jurisdictions treat voluntary intoxication as an affirmative defense, putting the burden on the defendant.

(3) Constitutional Issue

Defendants have argued that, because Due Process permits them to rely on any relevant evidence to challenge whether the prosecution has proved the *mens rea* required by the crime, any limitation upon defendants' ability to rely on voluntary intoxication to negate *mens rea* is unconstitutional. A few courts have accepted this. [*See, e.g.,* **Terry v. State,** 465 N.E.2d 1085 (Ind. 1984), overruled by **Sanchez v. State,** 749 N.E.2d 509 (Ind. 2001)]

However, the United States Supreme Court has narrowly held that federal constitutional requirements permit a state to prohibit a defendant from using voluntary intoxication to show he lacked the requisite *mens rea*. [**Montana v. Egelhoff,** 518 U.S. 37 (1996)] Charged with purposely or knowingly causing the death of another, D wanted to use evidence of his voluntary intoxication to show that he did not act purposely or knowingly.

(a) Rationale

A four-justice plurality in *Egelhoff* reasoned that the common law view banning voluntary intoxication as a defense has not been so completely rejected as to make it violative of Due Process, especially because that view is supported by reasonable modern policy considerations, *i.e.*, intoxication does not really "make" a person commit crimes and juries are too quick to accept misleading testimony that intoxication prevented defendants from forming *mens rea*. Justice Ginsburg, the fifth member of the majority, reasoned that the state was in effect defining the charged crime as requiring either that the defendant have killed knowingly or purposely or that he have killed under circumstances that would show he did so knowingly or purposely except for his voluntary intoxication. State legislatures' right to define the *mens rea* of state crimes as they wish means that this was a constitutional exercise of the Court's power to define crimes.

(b) But Note

State constitutional provisions may still require that defendants be permitted to rely on voluntary intoxication as negating *mens rea* in some or conceivably even all situations. [**Sanchez v. State,** *supra* (Sullivan, J., concurring in result)]

b. Minority Rule: Voluntary Intoxication Is Irrelevant to Liability

In a few jurisdictions, voluntary intoxication is irrelevant to criminal liability, even if it shows the lack of a specific intent required for guilt. [Texas Penal Code § 8.04 (voluntary intoxication cannot be considered as bearing upon guilt or innocence and may be considered in mitigation of penalty only if it reached the point of "temporary insanity")]

c. Another Minority Rule: Voluntary Intoxication Can Negate *Any* Required Mental State

A few jurisdictions, sometimes motivated by a perception that this is constitutionally required, permit a defendant to rely on evidence of voluntary intoxication to negate ***any*** culpable mental state required by the crime without regard to whether this might be characterized as a "specific intent." [**Terry v. State,** *supra*]

d. California Rule: Negates Mens Rea but Not "Capacity"

Under a California statute, evidence of voluntary intoxication cannot be used to show that the defendant lacked the ***capacity to form*** any mental state required by the crime. However, evidence that the defendant was voluntarily intoxicated at the time of the crime is admissible on whether the defendant ***actually did form*** a required mental state. [Cal. Penal Code § 29.4]

e. Model Penal Code Rule Negates Mental State Higher than Recklessness

The Model Penal Code defines intoxication as a "disturbance of mental or physical capacities resulting from the introduction of any substance into the body." [Model Penal Code § 2.08(5)(a)] This definition *does not distinguish ingestion of alcohol from other substances such as medications and illegal drugs.*

Under modern codes using the state of mind analysis established by the Model Penal Code, evidence of voluntary intoxication can be used to show the absence of the state of mind required for the crime, provided that state of mind requires proof of ***purpose or knowledge.*** If, however, recklessness is sufficient for liability and the defendant was unaware of the risk involved because of his voluntary intoxication, her unawareness is immaterial to guilt. [Model Penal Code § 2.08(2)] Some statutes are even more restrictive. [*See* Alaska Stat. § 11.81.630 (intoxication can be used only to show lack of intentionally causing a result)]

f. Convincing Trier of Fact That Intoxication Negated Mens Rea

If a jurisdiction's rule permits a defendant to rely on evidence of voluntary intoxication to negate the culpable mental state required by the charged crime, the defendant will be acquitted only if she can convince the trier of fact that her intoxication at a minimum raises a reasonable doubt that the prosecution has proved the required *mens rea.* That often is a very difficult task. If despite her intoxication the defendant was able to devise a plan and/or perform actions requiring some physical skill, a jury is likely to find that the intoxication does not negate the mental state required. [**Weaver v. State,** 643 N.E.2d 342 (Ind. 1994) (despite intoxication from LSD, jury properly found that defendant had intent to kill necessary for attempted murder)]

4. Distinguish: Crimes Requiring Proof of Intoxication

Where intoxication is an element of the crime charged (*e.g.,* public drunkenness), courts have assumed that the above rules do not apply, and consequently intoxication cannot prevent liability. [**Shelburne v. State,** 446 P.2d 56 (Okla. 1968) (driving under the influence of intoxicating substances)] It remains possible, however, that on an adequate showing that intoxication was truly *in*voluntary, a defendant might successfully defend against this type of charge.

SUMMARY OF DEFENSES NEGATING CRIMINAL CAPACITY		
DEFENSE	**ELEMENTS**	**APPLICABLE CRIMES**
INFANCY	Defendant under age 14 at common law	Under age seven, absolute defense to ***all*** crimes; under 14, rebuttable presumption of defense to all crimes
INSANITY	Meet applicable insanity test (*M'Naghten,* irresistible impulse, M.P.C., or *Durham*)	Defense to ***all*** crimes
INTOXICATION		
– INVOLUNTARY	Taking intoxicating substance without knowledge that it is intoxicating, or under direct and immediate duress	Treated as mental illness (*i.e.,* apply appropriate insanity test); may be a defense to ***all*** crimes
– VOLUNTARY	Voluntary intentional taking of a substance known to be intoxicating	Defense to ***specific intent*** crime if intoxication prevents formation of required intent

F. Ignorance or Mistake of Fact

1. In General

Ignorance or mistake as to a matter of ***fact*** is ordinarily not a defense in the sense that it invokes a defensive doctrine (like insanity) unrelated to the elements of the charged offense. It will, however, sometimes prevent liability if it shows that the defendant ***lacked a mental state*** essential to the crime charged, *e.g.*, defendant did not know that an aspirin was actually heroin, even though she knew about the controlled substance law against heroin. [Model Penal Code § 2.04(1); **State v. Pfeiffer,** 14 N.W.3d 636 (S.D. 2024) (mistake of fact is sometimes referred to as a "failure of proof" defense, because evidence suggests to factfinder that prosecution failed in its burden to establish that defendant acted with required mental state for the offense)]

a. Rationale

It is a basic principle of the criminal law that the defendant cannot be convicted where it is shown that he did not have the necessary mental state. Hence, simple ignorance (*i.e.,* defendant never thought about the matter) or affirmative mistake (*i.e.,* defendant thought about the matter but reached a wrong conclusion) that negates an essential mental state is a valid defense.

b. Distinction Between "Fact" and "Law"

Mistake or ignorance of "fact" is often treated differently than mistake or ignorance regarding "law." (*See infra,* p. 125 *et seq.*) This is somewhat misleading, because *any* ignorance or mistake that negates the required *mens rea* should require acquittal. Hence, the Model Penal Code and statutes based on it draw no such distinction and simply provide that ignorance or mistake "as to a matter of fact or law" requires acquittal if it negates the *mens rea* required by the crime charged. [Model Penal Code § 2.04(1)]

c. Burden of Proof

Because mistake of fact serves only to negate *mens rea*, which is an element of the crime on which the prosecution has the burden of proof, a defendant's **Due Process** right to have the prosecution prove all elements of the crime prohibits placement of the burden of proof on the defendant. If the evidence of mistake of fact raises a reasonable doubt as to whether the defendant had the necessary *mens rea*, the defendant must be acquitted. [**Wilson v. Tard,** 593 F.Supp. 1091 (D.N.J. 1984)]

d. Burden of Raising the Issue

The defendant may have the burden of going forward on the issue of mistake of fact. If so, the trial judge does not have to instruct the jury on mistake of fact, unless the defendant offers evidence suggesting that he was mistaken (or ignorant) in a manner raising a doubt as to whether he acted with the required *mens rea*. If the defendant produces such evidence, the trial judge instructs the jury on mistake.

EXAM TIP

For your exam, it is critical for you to remember that, although the defendant may have the burden of raising the issue of mistake, ***the burden of proof*** cannot be placed ***on the defendant.***

2. Requirement of "Reasonableness"

Traditionally, a mistake of fact must be ***reasonable,*** *i.e.*, a reasonable person would have made the same mistake under the circumstances. Many courts, however, have not required a showing of reasonableness where the mistake is offered to negate the existence of a ***specific intent*** required for guilt. [**United States v. Short,** 4 C.M.A. 437 (1954) (only a reasonable mistake about whether the victim consented would prevent liability for rape or assault with intent to commit rape; dissent argued that because assault with intent to commit rape requires proof of specific intent, reasonableness should not be required); **Commonwealth v. Blache,** 880 N.E.2d 736 (Mass. 2008) (defendant charged with rape of someone incapable of consent is entitled to mistake of fact instruction re whether he knew or reasonably should have known that victim was incapable of consent)]

a. Comment

Although an intoxicated defendant did not realize the risk to others involved in his conduct at the time he caused an injury, he nevertheless engaged in drinking at a time when he realized the risk to others of his getting drunk, *e.g.*, where he drinks just before he knows he will drive a car. Then, he has the required awareness of the risk. [*See, e.g.*, **People v. Decina,** 138 N.E.2d 799 (N.Y. 1956)]

b. Constitutional Issue

Requiring that a mistake be reasonable means that the prosecution may not have to satisfy the burden of proof because the defendant's mistake was unreasonable. The requirement of reasonableness may violate Due Process, in that the prosecution is not required to prove all elements of the crime. [**State v. Bougneit,** 294 N.W.2d 675 (Wis. 1980) (no mistake of fact as to victim's physical location at the time shot was fired; thus, trial court properly refused to instruct jury on mistake of fact] Additionally, the Supreme Court has indicated that a defendant's good-faith belief that the tax laws did not impose any duty on him did not have to be objectively reasonable in order to be considered by the jury. [**Cheek v. United States,** 498 U.S. 192 (1991)]

c. Model Penal Code Position

Under the Model Penal Code, the mistake of fact need not be reasonable as long as it negates the state of mind required for liability. [Model Penal Code § 2.04(1)(a)]

e.g. **Example:** D is charged with reckless manslaughter, which requires proof that he caused the death of the victim with recklessness, *i.e.,* awareness of a substantial and unjustifiable risk of death. D offers evidence that before pulling the trigger on the gun he removed the magazine and believed as a result that the gun would not fire and that pulling the trigger posed no risk of killing the victim. *Analysis:* (i) D's mistake, if he in fact made it, ***tends to negate the mens rea*** required, because if D believed the gun would not fire, he was not consciously aware of any risk that his actions would cause death; (ii) D's evidence ***raises the issue of mistake,*** and the jury should be instructed on it; (iii) the trial judge must instruct the jury that it must acquit D if, given the evidence of mistake, it has a ***reasonable doubt*** about whether D acted recklessly; and (iv) if the judge tells the jury to give weight to D's evidence of mistake only if it finds that the mistake was ***objectively reasonable,*** D's Due Process and jury trial rights might well be violated. [**Wilson v. Tard,** *supra*]

3. Requirement That Conduct Was Morally and Legally Permissible Had the Facts Been as Defendant Believed

Some decisions apparently require a showing that the defendant's conduct would have been legally permissible (*i.e.,* neither a crime nor a violation of civil duty) and (as suggested by some courts) morally defensible had the facts been as the defendant believed them to be. [**Regina v. Prince,** L.R. 2 Cr. Cas. Res. 154 (1875)]

e.g. **Example:** D was charged with abandonment of his pregnant wife. Proof that he was not aware of his wife's pregnancy was held to be no defense because even if the facts had been as he supposed them to be (*i.e.,* if his wife had not been pregnant), this abandonment would have been a violation of his civil duty to support her. Therefore, he acted "at his peril." [**White v. State,** 185 N.E. 64 (Ohio 1933)]

a. Criticism

This limitation is criticized as imposing strict liability for serious offenses, contrary to basic principles of criminal liability. Thus, it is doubtful whether the early decisions imposing this limitation would be followed today.

b. Model Penal Code Position

The Model Penal Code provides that the defense of ignorance or mistake is unavailable if the defendant would still have been guilty of a ***criminal offense*** had the facts been as he supposed them to be. In such cases, the defendant may be liable for an offense no more serious than he would have been guilty of had the facts been as he believed them to be. [Model Penal Code § 2.04(2)]

4. Prosecutions for Strict Liability Offenses

Because ignorance or mistake of fact is tied to the required *mens rea*, it applies differently if the crime charged imposes strict liability.

a. General Rule: Mistake Irrelevant if Offense Imposes Strict Liability

If an offense imposes strict liability, no mental state is negated and no mistake or ignorance of fact or law suffices to exonerate. [**State v. Fideler,** 992 N.W.2d 19 (S.D. 2023) (trespassing was strict liability offense permitting no mistake of fact defense)] If the offense imposed strict liability with regard to *some* elements, ignorance or mistake cannot be used to negate the *mens rea* for those elements. Thus, ignorance or mistake of fact is ordinarily ***no defense*** to complete strict liability crimes and may or may not be a defense to those crimes that impose limited strict liability. For example, in applying the transferred intent doctrine to the crime of sexual assault where the intended victim was an adult but the actual victim was under 13, no mistake of fact defense exists because "strict liability applies . . . to the complainant's age." [**State v. Austin,** 788 N.W.2d 788 (Minn.App. 2010)]

b. "Defense" of Reasonable Mistake in Strict Liability Situations

Some courts are unwilling to hold that *mens rea* is required for a particular crime, but nevertheless recognize a "defense" of reasonable mistake. [**People v. Vogel,** 299 P.2d 850 (Cal. 1956)]

e.g. **Example:** D was tried for bigamy (*see supra,* p. 45) under a statute that did not require proof of the defendant's knowledge that he had a spouse living when he remarried. In his defense, D offered evidence that he reasonably believed that he had obtained a valid divorce from his first wife before the second marriage. The trial court refused to read the element of conscious awareness into the bigamy statute, but it interpreted the statute as inapplicable to a person who marries under a reasonable mistake that he has no living spouse. [**People v. Vogel,** *supra*]

e.g. **Example:** When fornication is itself not criminal, it should not become criminal merely because the defendant has made a reasonable mistake about the age of the girl with whom he has intercourse. In other words, a defendant should be permitted to show as a defense that he acted under a reasonable, although mistaken, belief that the woman was over the age of consent. [**People v. Hernandez,** 393 P.2d 673 (Cal. 1964)] However, courts are nearly unanimous that a reasonable mistake of fact about a victim's age is not a defense to a charge of statutory rape. [*See, e.g.,* **People v. Olsen,** 685 P.2d 52 (Cal. 1984)]

G. Ignorance or Mistake of Law

1. In General

A defendant's mistake of law generally does not excuse her conduct, *e.g.*, "I thought the conduct was covered in the statute because . . . ." Ignorance or misunderstanding of the law rarely qualifies as a basis for claiming that a defendant lacked the necessary *mens rea* for an offense, *e.g.*, "I wasn't aware that prostitution is a crime." Because knowledge, recklessness, and negligence about whether conduct qualifies as an offense are not elements of that offense, no *mens rea* element in defining an offense is negated by the defendant's ignorance or mistake of law.

Issues concerning the defendant's ignorance or mistake of ***law*** arise in two entirely different contexts: (i) those in which, because of ignorance or mistake, the defendant ***lacked the mental state*** required for a conviction; and (ii) those in which the defendant had the requisite mental state but claims he was mistaken about the applicable law and consequently ***believed his conduct was not prohibited*** by the criminal law. It is important to distinguish between the two situations, because only rarely is the latter recognized as a defense.

a. Ignorance Compared to Mistake

Some aspects of this body of law distinguish between two types of claims by defendants: (i) some defendants claim they were simply and ***passively ignorant*** regarding certain matters of law; (ii) some defendants claim not passive ignorance but rather that they addressed the matter and reached an ***affirmative but mistaken conclusion.***

2. Ignorance or Mistake Showing Lack of Mens Rea

Sometimes, a defendant's ignorance or mistake concerning a matter of law tends to negate the *mens rea* of the crime charged. When this happens, the defendant may rely on that ignorance or mistake. If as a result the trier of fact has a reasonable doubt about whether the prosecution has proven the required *mens rea*, the defendant must be acquitted. [**Cheek v. United States,** *supra,* p. 123; Model Penal Code § 2.04(1)(a)]

e.g. **Example:** A travel agent retained a customer's passport, but it was not regarded as a theft if customer had "pledged the passport to the travel agent as security for [the agent] advancing her the money for the airline ticket." [**Guzell v. Hiller,** 223 F.3d 518 (7th Cir. 2000)]

a. Reasonableness Not Required

Under federal criminal law, a defendant's ignorance or mistake must be given its full logical significance, even if that ignorance or mistake was unreasonable, *i.e.,* even if a reasonable person in the defendant's situation would not have made it. [**Cheek v. United States,** *supra* (error in federal tax prosecution for the trial judge to tell jury to consider defendant's mistake as to the law defining income only if it finds the mistake was reasonable)]

(1) Constitutional Issue

The Supreme Court has indicated that limiting defendants to reasonable mistakes of law would raise a serious question about the defendant's Sixth Amendment right to have the jury determine guilt or innocence. [**Cheek v. United States,** *supra*]

b. Belief in Unconstitutionality Usually Not Relevant

Under this rule, a defendant's mistaken belief, that although the crime applies to his conduct it is unconstitutional and thus cannot be enforced, usually ***cannot be relied upon.*** This is probably because the *mens rea* of most (and perhaps all) crimes requires no understanding that the law defining the crime is constitutional. [**Cheek v. United States,** *supra*]

c. Preliminary Issue: Content of Required Mens Rea

In most cases, the major issue is whether the *mens rea* of the crime requires awareness of the law about which the defendant claims to have been ignorant or mistaken. Usually, if the crime does require such awareness, application of this rule is fairly obvious.

e.g. **Example:** Federal tax laws make it a crime to "willfully" fail to file a return as required by the tax law or to "willfully" evade a tax due under that law. "Willfully" in the statute requires that the defendant have known of and understood the legal duty to file the return or pay the tax and nevertheless have intentionally failed to do so (*see supra,* p. 42). D was prosecuted for failing to file returns and evading tax due on wages received. D testified that he believed that "income" as used in federal tax law did not include wages and that the entire federal tax system was unconstitutional and hence unenforceable. *Analysis:* (i) D's testimony that he believed the law defined "income" as excluding wages tends to negate the required awareness that tax was due on the wages, and that because he received wages he was required to file a return; (ii) the jury must be instructed that if D's testimony raises a reasonable doubt whether he acted "willfully," it must acquit D; (iii) the jury is not to be told that it may give effect to D's mistaken perception of the law defining income only if it finds that mistake objectively reasonable; and (iv) D's testimony that he believed the federal tax system unconstitutional is irrelevant to his guilt or innocence. [**Cheek v. United States,** *supra*]

3. Mistaken Belief That Criminal Law Does Not Prohibit Intended Conduct

In limited situations, a defendant who had the *mens rea* required by the crime charged can nevertheless establish a defense that a mistaken perception of the law caused her to believe her conduct would not constitute a crime. [*See* Model Penal Code § 2.04(3) (defense consisting of a belief that conduct does not legally constitute an offense); **Ostrosky v. State,** 704 P.2d 786 (Alaska 1985)]

a. Passive Ignorance Not Sufficient

This defense must ordinarily be based on more than passive unawareness that the law makes the conduct a crime. [*See, e.g.,* **State v. Ramos,** 305 P.3d 921 (N.M. 2013) (defendant's "failure to read the contents of the [protective] order is no defense" to a charge of violating the order)] The defense must be based on evidence that the defendant addressed the matter and ***affirmatively decided***, *i.e.,* mistakenly believed, that the law did not make the conduct a crime. Thus, "ignorance of the law is no excuse," even under this rule.

b. Distinguish: Negating Mens Rea

Criminal *mens rea* requires only that the defendant "intended" to do the prohibited act or had "knowledge" about the act or failure to act; it does not require that the defendant know the act was illegal and "intended" to violate the law. [**State v. Mikulak,** 903 N.W.2d 600 (Minn. 2017) ("ignorance of the law is a defense when the charged offense prohibits a knowing violation of a statutory provision, as here, knowing violation of sex offender registration statute; knowledge of the law is an element of the offense")]

c. Rationale for Limited Nature of Defense

The law is traditionally reluctant to permit defendants to escape conviction because of ignorance or mistake. While this approach is often defended on the theory that "everyone is presumed to know the law," such a presumption is not realistic. Perhaps the better justification is that permitting defendants to raise the defense would open courts to extensive and often meritless litigation. Some commentators argue that the rule encourages the public to be aware of legal requirements, thereby avoiding confusion and uncertainty about what conduct is criminal.

d. Constitutional Considerations

(1) In General

Some courts have reasoned that convicting a defendant, despite the mistaken belief that her conduct is not criminal, would be unfair and violate federal constitutional Due Process. Thus, at least a limited defense of mistake of law may be constitutionally mandated. [**Commonwealth v. Twitchell,** 617 N.E.2d 609 (Mass. 1993) (failure to seek medical care for a child could be grounds for involuntary manslaughter if the parents acted wantonly or recklessly, even when religious belief was involved)]

(2) Duty or Right to Violate the Law

In a prosecution for unlawful entry on public property, defendants' bona fide belief of the right to enter or remain as a defense does not exonerate persons who believe they have a right, or even a duty, to violate the law in order to effect a moral, social, or political purpose (regardless of the genuineness of the belief or the popularity of the purpose). Defendants' mistaken belief in a constitutional law defense does not support a bona fide defense theory. [**Larson-Olson v. United States,** 309 A.3d 1267 (D.C. 2024)]

(3) Misleading by Official

If someone in an official capacity misleads defendants into concluding that their conduct will not be criminal, Due Process bars their criminal conviction for this conduct. [**Cox v. Louisiana,** 379 U.S. 559 (1965) (police official incorrectly told demonstrators that picketing at a particular place would be permissible); **Raley v. Ohio,** 360 U.S. 423 (1959) (defendants relied upon assurances of government commission that they had a privilege to refuse to answer, although in fact they did not)]

e. Requirements for the Defense

This defense is limited by two categories of requirements:

(1) Belief Must Be Reasonable

The defendant's belief that the law does not prohibit her conduct must be ***objectively reasonable***, *i.e.,* a belief that a reasonable person would have formed under the circumstances. [Model Penal Code § 2.04(3)]

(2) Reliance Must Be Placed on Particular Matters

The defendant must have formed her belief on the basis of certain limited grounds (*see* below), thereby providing special assurance that the defendant's mistake was both actually made and objectively reasonable.

(a) Statute Later Held Unconstitutional

A defendant can successfully defend when he relied in good faith upon a statute making his conduct permissible, even though the statute was subsequently found to be unconstitutional. [**Fowler v. State,** 676 S.W.2d 725 (Ark. 1984) (reasonable reliance on statute relating to fishing nets, afterward determined to be invalid, would be valid affirmative defense; here though, defendant never relied on the statute and never raised it as an affirmative defense)]

(b) Judicial Decision

A defendant can escape conviction where she acted in reasonable reliance on a judicial decision holding that her conduct was not criminal. While some courts hold that the decision must be of the highest state court, no such limitation exists, although the court's authority is a factor in determining whether the defendant's reliance is reasonable. [**Ostrosky v. State,** *supra* (defendant must show by preponderance of the evidence a reasonable reliance upon a judicial decision; the reliance may even be on a trial court's decision that is under appeal)]

(c) Official Interpretation

There is a split of authority about whether reliance on a legal interpretation by a person or agency responsible for administering or enforcing that law will prevent liability.[**Northcraft v. Commonwealth,** 892 S.E.2d 351 (Va.App. 2023) (to assert the affirmative defense to criminal liability under due process principles, based on advice from a government official, a defendant must prove that 1) he was assured that his conduct resulting in the conviction was lawful, 2) the assurance was from a public officer or body charged by law with responsibility for defining permissible conduct regarding the offense at issue, and 3) based on totality of circumstances, reliance upon the advice was reasonable and in good faith)] Courts apply the defense very carefully, *i.e.*, a defendant may act in reasonable reliance on the statement of the law that exists in a statute later declared invalid, a judicial decision from a jurisdiction's highest court that is later declared to be erroneous, or an erroneous explanation of the law, obtained from a public official responsible for its interpretation. [Model Penal Code § 2.04(3)(b); **Commonwealth v. Twitchell,** *supra*]

e.g. **Example:** D's reliance on a state statute purporting to exempt any firearm possessed with the state from provisions of the National Firearms Act was no defense. The state legislature is not responsible for interpreting, administering or enforcing the NFA. [**United States v. Cox,** 906 F.3d 1170 (10th Cir. 2018)]

e.g. **Example:** D was prosecuted for violation of a sign ordinance and argued in defense that the local prosecutor had advised D that the sign would not violate legal requirements. The court rejected the defense, reasoning that otherwise the prosecutor's advice "would become paramount to the law." [**Hopkins v. State,** 69 A.2d 456 (Md. 1949)] Other courts, however, and perhaps the Model Penal Code would disagree. [Model Penal Code § 2.04(3)(b) (requiring an ***official*** interpretation); *see* **United States v. Hancock,** 231 F.3d 557 (9th Cir. 2000) ("The government cannot be estopped from prosecuting D on the ground that it expressly told him the law in 1982, but failed at that time to inform him of the possibility that he could be exposed to prosecution in 1998 under a 1996 law.")]

1) Comment

The Supreme Court has observed that permitting conviction of a person for conduct that state officials have stated is permissible "would be to sanction an indefensible sort of entrapment by the State." [**Cox v. Louisiana**, *supra*] Thus, demonstrators may not constitutionally be convicted of parading "near" a courthouse when they did so after the highest police officials of the city told them, in effect, that they could lawfully meet 101 feet from the courthouse steps.

2) Distinguish: Reliance on Advice of Private Counsel

Good faith reliance on the advice of privately consulted counsel is ***no defense.*** While it appears preferable for a person to seek legal advice, concerns relate to that person intentionally seeking advice from an unethical or incompetent attorney. The issue often then becomes a problem of whether the advice that is relied upon should come from a bona fide "expert" in the legal area or at least not from a newly minted attorney who just passed the bar exam.

e.g. **Example:** The defendant claimed lack of willfulness in violation of health care fraud and anti-kickback laws because of reliance on advice of counsel. The court found that the defense was properly rejected, because the defendant "did not fully disclose all material facts" to his lawyer and began his course of conduct "well before" consulting with counsel. [**United States v. Vernon,** 723 F.3d 1234 (11th Cir. 2013); *cf.* **Winstock v. Galasso,** 64 A.3d 1012 (N.J.App. 2013) (a defendant who has relied upon incorrect advice may seek damages for legal malpractice)]

e.g. **Example:** A court properly denies a D an advice-of-counsel instruction when the record shows that D did not make a "full and accurate report to [her] attorney of all material facts." [**State v. Flynn,** 127 A.3d 1239 (Me. 2015); *see* N.J. Stat.Ann. § 2C:2–4 ("The actor otherwise diligently pursues all means available to ascertain the meaning and application of the offense to his conduct and honestly and in good faith concludes his conduct is not an offense in circumstances in which a law abiding and prudent person would also so conclude.")]

(d) Personal Interpretation of the Law

Some versions of the defense, including the Model Penal Code, provide that the defense can be based on a statement or interpretation of the law contained in the statute defining the crime. Under this formulation, a defendant might argue that he is entitled to rely on his own personal interpretation of the statute, if he is able to convince the jury that this interpretation was objectively reasonable. However, the Model Penal Code would make this argument unavailable by its further provision that the official statement of the law in the statute be "afterwards determined to be invalid or erroneous." [Model Penal Code § 2.04(3)(b); *but see* **McFadden v. United States,** 576 U.S. 186 (2015) (regarding a statute for knowingly possessing or distributing a controlled substance, the knowledge requirement may be "met by showing that the defendant knew the identity of the substance he possessed" but did "not know [it] is listed on the schedule," as "ignorance of the law is typically no defense")]

e.g. **Example:** After his arrest for possession of a loaded pistol, in violation of a statute that requires a permit in order to carry a handgun, D, a prison guard, looked at the state statutes prohibiting the carrying of handguns. The statute exempted peace officers from liability by defining "peace officers" as a guard at "any state prison or of any penal correctional institution." D thus believed that he was exempt from the statute's coverage, also based on what a criminal law professor(!) and gun dealers had told him. Trial court granted D's motion to dismiss the charge because there was a reasonable misinterpretation of the words "peace officer" in the statute that implied that the defendant could carry a gun. On appeal, the dismissal was reversed based on legislative intent. A mistake of law defense was unavailable to defendant. Because the defense implicitly requires that an official interpretation relied upon was later adjudicated as wrong, D was unable to prove any such later adjudication. Although the defendant's claim was reasonable, it was based on her own reading of the law. [**People v. Marrero,** 507 N.E.2d 1068 (N.Y. 1987)]

H. Necessity or Justification

1. In General

The defense of "necessity" is available where the accused acted in the ***reasonable belief*** that perpetration of the offense would prevent the occurrence of a ***greater harm*** or evil. [**Regina v. Dudley & Stephens,** 14 Q.B.D. 273 (1884); **United States v. Holmes,** 26 F. Cas. 360 (C.C.E.D.Pa. 1842); Model Penal Code § 3.02 (calls defense "justification" rather than "necessity")] "Necessity" covers the few situations that are not included by any other justifications defenses because they are so rare.

e.g. **Example:** Sailors on a ship who refused to obey the captain's orders were held not guilty of mutiny where their purpose was to force the captain to return the ship to port for necessary repairs. [**United States v. Ashton,** 24 F. Cas. 873 (C.C.Mass. 1834)] The Model Penal Code suggests that the defense is also available where a pharmacist dispenses a drug without a prescription to alleviate suffering in an emergency. [Model Penal Code § 3.02, comment]

a. Distinguish Duress

Necessity is raised only when the pressure to commit the offense is created by the ***physical forces of nature.*** If pressure is exerted by other persons, the accused may have the defense of duress (*see infra,* p. 125), but he cannot escape liability on grounds of necessity.

2. Requirements

a. Objectively Reasonable Belief

As discussed below, several requirements constitute the defense. Authorities are not clear whether all requirements must exist or, rather, whether the defense requires only that the defendant believe, perhaps "reasonably," that they exist. On principle, a ***reasonable belief*** on the defendant's part should be sufficient. [**Nelson v. State,** 597 P.2d 977 (Alaska 1979)] With a reasonable belief, defendant may raise the necessity defense even if, unknown to him, the situation did not in fact call for the drastic action taken.

b. "Greater" Harm Threatened

The defendant must commit the crime to avoid foreseeable harm or evil to himself or someone else. In principle, all that should be required is that the defendant ***reasonably believes*** the threatened harm is greater than that involved in the crime. A few court courts, though, may require that ***in actual fact*** the threatened harm was greater.

e.g. **Example:** D was charged with criminal trespass and the unlawful obstruction of a train. He raised a necessity a defense. D was protesting coal and oil trains while advocating for combating climate change. It was for the jury to determine whether he did not bring about the threatened harm. [**State ex rel. v. Spokane County District Court,** 491 P.3d 119 (Wash. 2021)]

(1) Exception: Legislature Has Determined Greater Harm

The defense of necessity is unavailable if the legislature has determined that the harm sought to be avoided by the defendant is not greater than that involved in the crime.

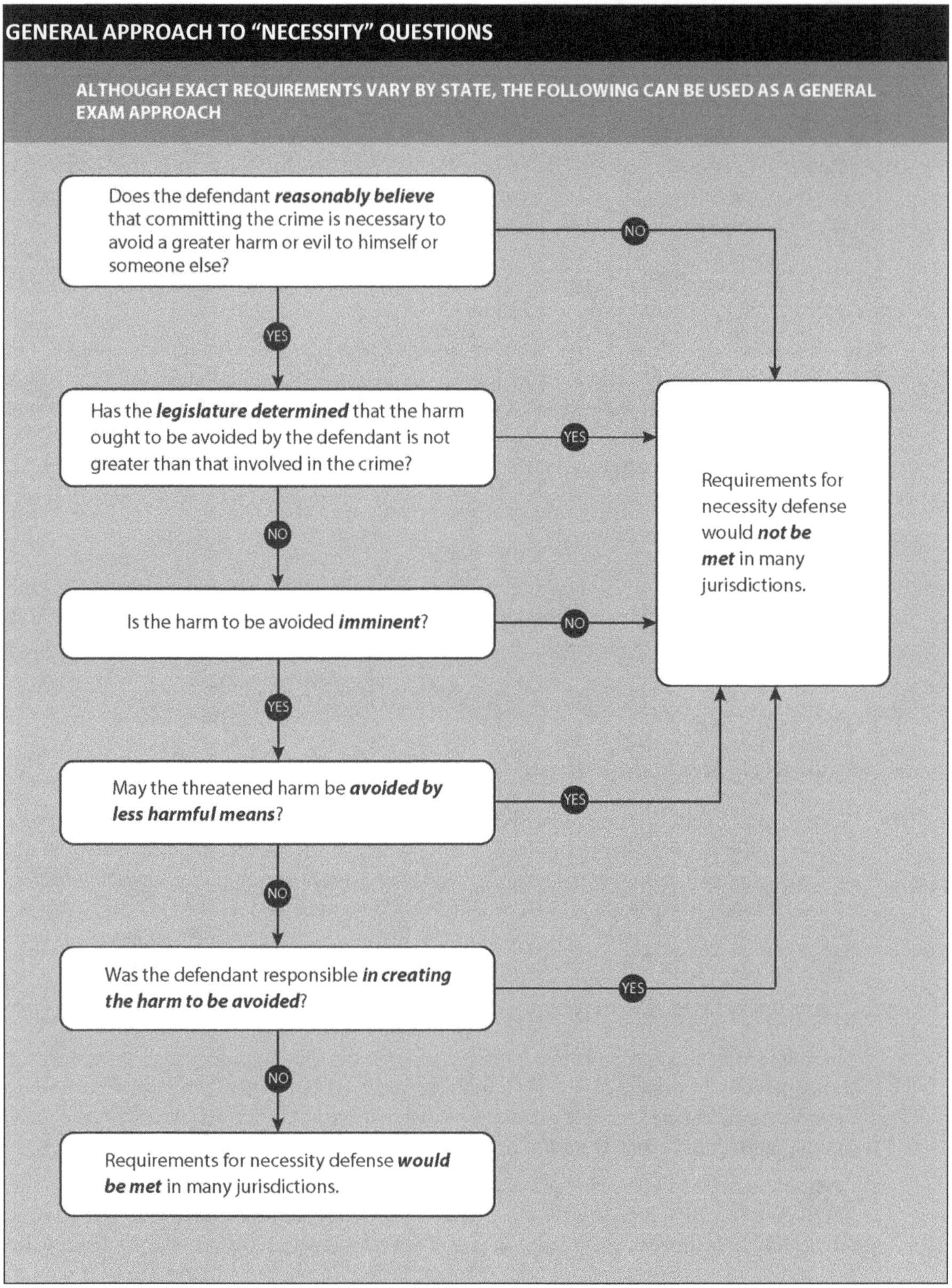

e.g. **Example:** The federal Controlled Substances Act makes the manufacture and distribution of certain drugs, including marijuana, a crime. This activity is not criminal if it occurs pursuant to limited government-approved research projects. Although some drugs may be prescribed and dispensed for medical use, no authorization for medical use applies to marijuana. Thus, the Act reflects Congress's decision that the benefits of marijuana use for medical reasons never outweigh the harm from such action. Therefore, a defendant charged with violating the Act has no defense of "medical necessity," based on proof that the defendant believed the alleviation of symptoms of illness by distribution of marijuana outweighed the harm from that conduct. [**United States v. Oakland Cannabis Buyers' Cooperative,** 532 U.S. 917 (2001)]

c. Threatened Harm by Aggressor Was "Imminent"

Some decisions require a showing that the harm sought to be avoided was imminent. Until the threatened harm becomes imminent, there ordinarily are options available to avoid the harm other than violating the criminal law. [*See, e.g.*, **State v. Daniels,** 682 P.2d 173 (Mont. 1984) ("imminent" refers to the aggressor's threatened conduct rather than the defender's response)] Thus, the defendant should wait until there is no longer the possibility of a less drastic alternative.

e.g. **Example:** For the charge of being a felon-in-possession-of-firearm, D did not act to prevent imminent harm. There was "no evidence that the children had already obtained possession of the gun or were about to do so" or even that they were "in close proximity to the firearm." [**United States v. Barnes,** 895 F.3d 1194 (9th Cir. 2018)]

d. No Less Harmful Alternatives Available

The necessity defense normally applies only if there was no less harmful way to avoid the threatened danger. [*See, e.g.*, **State v. Thayer,** 14 A.3d 231 (Vt. 2010) (no necessity defense for marijuana grower who needed marijuana to treat son's medical condition, because the state "had legalized medicinal use of marijuana under certain circumstances," but defendant made no effort to pursue lawful alternative)]

e. Model Penal Code: Defendant Not at Fault

Some versions of the defense require that the defendant was not at fault in creating the situation that made it necessary to choose between a crime and a more serious harm. Under the Model Penal Code, the defense may not be used by a defendant who was reckless or negligent in bringing about the situation if recklessness or negligence is sufficient for the crime charged. [Model Penal Code § 3.02(2)]

3. Economic Necessity Sufficient?

Some decisions indicate that "economic necessity" alone does ***not*** justify the commission of a criminal act. Thus, one who is unemployed and hungry (but not presently starving) may be convicted of larceny if he steals groceries. However, this result may be explained on the theory that the harm avoided by the crime has not yet become imminent. [**State v. Moe,** 24 P.2d 638 (Wash. 1933)]

4. Defense to Prison Escape?

Persons charged with prison escape have often argued that escape was necessary to avoid greater evils that awaited them in prison, such as sexual assault. Generally, these claims have been rejected on the ground that there were ***other, noncriminal options available,*** such as reporting the danger to authorities. [*See, e.g.*, **United States v. Capozzi,** 723 F.3d 720 (6th Cir. 2013) (no necessity for escape from federal custody to seek treatment for heart condition; defendant never pursued legal alternative of reporting medical needs to prison staff)] However, a few decisions have upheld the defense where the defendant establishes that efforts to secure assistance from prison authorities or the courts would have been impossible or ineffective.

a. Duty to Surrender

Many courts have indicated that necessity may apply to the crime of escape. In this context a successful defense would require a showing that, once the immediate threat of harm ceased, the defendant promptly reported to authorities. [**People v. Lovercamp,** 43 Cal. App. 3d 823 (1974)]

e.g. **Example:** Construing the federal law concerning necessity and duress as it applies in a prosecution for the federal crime of escape, the Supreme Court held that both defenses required a showing of a bona fide effort to surrender or return to custody as soon as the claimed duress or necessity lost its coercive force. Vague and "necessarily self-serving" claims of a future intent to surrender or "ambiguous conduct" are insufficient. The Court did not reach the question of what, if any, jail conditions would constitute a serious and immediate enough threat to raise either defense, if an effort to surrender or return after escape was shown. [**United States v. Bailey,** 444 U.S. 394 (1980)]

I. Duress

1. In General

It is sometimes a defense to a criminal charge that the defendant committed the criminal act under "duress" (or, as it is often called, "coercion" or "compulsion"). Duress is an imminent threat made ***by another human being*** to cause serious bodily injury to the defendant or another unless the defendant commits the offense. [Model Penal Code § 2.09]

2. Requirements

a. Objectively Reasonable Belief

Authorities are not clear on whether the defense requires only that the defendant reasonably believe that he has been sufficiently threatened to meet the following requirements. Many formulations of the defense require that the defendant have actually been "coerced," which suggests that a reasonable belief is not enough and that ***there must in actual fact have been a sufficient threat made.***

b. Threat Must Be of Sufficiently Serious Harm

The common law defense requires that the threat be of ***death or serious bodily injury.*** Some modern formulations impose no such limitation and thus permit the defense to be based on threats of lesser bodily harm. [*See* Model Penal Code § 2.09(1) (requiring only a threat to use unlawful force against the person)] Threats of economic reprisals, damage to property or reputation, or minor injuries are insufficient. [*See* **State v. Verrecchia,** 766 A.2d 377 (R.I. 2001)]

c. Subject of Threat

It is not necessary that the defendant himself be the subject of the threats. Threats to harm a member of the defendant's family, or even a stranger, are sufficient. [Model Penal Code § 2.09(1) (threats of force against the person of the defendant or the person of another)]

d. Threat Must Be of "Immediate" Harm

Many formulations of the defense require that the threat be of ***immediate*** harm. Threats to do harm in the future, no matter how serious, do not suffice. The Model Penal Code and statutes based on it impose no such requirement, but the immediacy of the threatened harm is clearly relevant to whether the defendant's submission was reasonable (*see* below). [**United States v. Mora-Carrillo,** 80 F.4th 712 (5th Cir. 2023) (defendant must be in serious danger at moment he commits offense; four days between his own abduction and offense provides no proof that defendant was in danger at moment of his offense of smuggling people across the border)]

e.g. **Example:** D was accused of passport fraud. He claimed that he was at risk in the Dominican Republic, because he was falsely accused of murder there. The duress instruction was properly refused, because the murder occurred six months before the fraudulent passport application which took place in a different country where D had been for three months. [**United States v. Lebreault-Feliz,** 807 F.3d 1 (1st Cir. 2015)]

e. Defendant's Submission Must Have Been "Reasonable"

The defendant's submission to the coercion and to commit the crime must always be ***reasonable.*** There must, for example, have been no opportunity to obtain assistance or avoid the harm by some other, noncriminal method, *i.e.*, the defendant lacked a reasonable opportunity to escape harm other than by engaging in the illegal activity.

e.g. **Example:** While participating in a kidnapping and robbery as an accomplice, D had a reasonable opportunity to escape from harm while the offenses were ongoing. D had possession of the murder weapon while sitting in the driver's seat of a vehicle as the co-defendant was out of sight down a hill engaged in disposing of V's body. [**United States v. Zayac,** 765 F.3d 112 (2d Cir. 2014)]

(1) Model Penal Code: Person of Reasonable Firmness Unable to Resist

The Model Code states that the situation must have been such that a person of reasonable firmness in the circumstances would have been unable to resist the demand to commit the crime. [Model Penal Code § 2.09(1)]

3. Limitations

a. Not Applicable to Some Criminal Homicides

Duress often is ***no defense*** to the ***intentional killing*** of another person. Similarly, it cannot be asserted in defense to a charge of ***attempted*** intentional killing. [**Watson v. State,** 55 So. 2d 441 (Miss. 1951)]

EXAM TIP

When a defendant in an exam question seems to have acted under duress, examine the facts carefully. The defense of duress will apply only if strict requirements are met. Thus, for example, if the threat is to the defendant's ***business,*** this would not be enough. The threat must be to the defendant or to another. Also, check to see that the threat is of harm that is ***imminent***, *e.g.*, "I'll kill you before the year is out" is probably not enough. And, in any case, remember that duress is ***never a defense to intentional murder.***

(1) Felony Murder

Courts are split on whether duress can constitute a defense to felony murder. In principle, it should be a defense; felony murders are not intentional killings. Further, if a felony murder defendant has a duress defense to the predicate felony, this will preclude conviction for felony murder because there is no felony on which to base felony murder. [**People v. Sims**, 869 N.E.2d 1115 (Ill. 2007)]

(2) Duress as Negating Premeditation

Even if duress is not a defense to a charge of first-degree premeditated murder, evidence of duress may be introduced to ***establish a lack of premeditation*** and thereby preclude a conviction for the charged crime. [**Rizzolo v. Commonwealth,** 17 A. 520 (Pa. 1889)]

(3) Statutory Reduction to Manslaughter

In at least one jurisdiction, a showing of duress in a homicide case reduces the severity of the offense of which the defendant is convicted. [*See, e.g.,* Wis. Stat. Ann. § 939.46; *but see* **United States v. LaFleur,** 971 F.2d 200 (9th Cir. 1991) (the "same rationale which dictates that duress is not a complete defense to murder demands that duress not be used to mitigate the intentional killing of an innocent third person" to manslaughter)]

b. Not Applicable if Defendant Subjected Himself to Duress

The defense is not available if the defendant intentionally or recklessly placed himself in a position in which he should have foreseen that he would be subject to duress. [**United States v. Hernandez,** 894 F.3d 496 (2d Cir. 2018); *see* Model Penal Code § 2.09(2) (duress unavailable if the accused "recklessly placed himself in a position in which it was probable that he would be subject to duress")]

4. Distinguish: Coercion of Wife by Husband

Claims by a wife that she was coerced by her husband into committing an offense traditionally posed special problems.

a. Common Law: Presumption of Coercion

At common law, a wife is not responsible for a crime committed by her under the coercion of her husband. Although a showing of marriage alone carries no evidentiary weight, proof that a wife perpetrated the crime in her husband's ***presence*** raises a ***rebuttable presumption*** that he coerced her. [**Rex v. Hughes,** 168 Eng. Rep. 1137 (1813)]

b. Modern Rule: No Presumption

Most courts or legislatures have abandoned the above presumption [**People v. Statley,** 206 P.2d 76 (Cal. 1949)], and the Model Penal Code expressly provides that a woman claiming coercion by her husband must prove duress under generally applicable standards [Model Penal Code § 2.09(3)].

(1) Rationale

The common law rule developed at a time when married women were often under their husbands' control. Today the position of women is quite different; women are so infrequently controlled by their husbands that the presumption no longer has sufficient basis in fact.

J. Entrapment

1. In General

It is a defense to most crimes that the defendant was "entrapped" into committing the act by a law enforcement officer or one acting as agent of a law enforcement officer.

a. Not a Constitutional Rule

Despite repeated attempts to elevate the entrapment defense to constitutional status, the Supreme Court has refused to require that the states adopt the modern objective formulation (or any other specific formulation) of the defense as a matter of Due Process of law. [**United States v. Russell,** 411 U.S. 423 (1973)]

b. Due Process Considerations

The Supreme Court has left open the possibility that law enforcement conduct related to the commission of an offense may be so outrageous "that Due Process principles would absolutely bar the government from invoking judicial processes to obtain a conviction." But such a case has never been brought before the Court, and it is clear that the police action would have to be extremely offensive before a Due Process violation would be found. [**United States v. Russell,** *supra*; *see* **United States v. Leal,** 32 F.4th 888 (10th Cir. 2022) (not outrageous for government to infiltrate ongoing criminal enterprise, induce a defendant to repeat or continue a crime, induce a defendant to expand or extend previous criminal activity, or suggest the illegal activity)]

2. Substantive Limitations

a. Applicable Only to Nonserious Crimes

It is generally agreed that entrapment ***cannot be claimed*** as a defense to crimes involving ***serious injury*** to others, such as rape or murder. In practice, the defense is most commonly raised in connection with the so-called victimless crimes (*e.g.,* solicitation, sale of drugs). [Model Penal Code § 2.13(3) (entrapment not available if crime consists of causing or threatening bodily injury to person other than person perpetrating entrapment)]

b. Only Law Enforcement Officers and Agents Can "Entrap"

A defense is available only where the entrapment was by a law enforcement officer or a person working ***in cooperation with law enforcement officers*** (*e.g.,* informers or "undercover agents" who are paid for their services but who are not formal employees of law enforcement agencies). Accordingly, the act of a purely private individual, although it may have induced another to commit a crime, will not support an entrapment claim. [**Henderson v. United States,** 237 F.2d 169 (5th Cir. 1956)]

EXAM TIP

Often on an exam it is not the police themselves who induce a person to commit a crime. If the inducement is not by a police officer, see whether the inducer was hired or ***encouraged by the police*** to act. If so, entrapment may be a viable defense. But if the inducer had no connection with the police and decided on her own to induce the defendant to commit a crime, there is no defense.

---

3. Procedural Limitation: Defendant Sometimes Cannot Deny Committing Crime

Defendants in entrapment cases are prohibited in some jurisdictions from taking inconsistent positions. Thus, a defendant cannot both deny committing the offense and claim entrapment. Some courts even require the defendant to affirmatively ***admit guilt of the crime*** in order to argue entrapment. [**State v. Nilsen,** 657 P.2d 419 (Ariz. 1983) (defendant must affirmatively admit offense, either by testifying, stipulating as to guilt, or in some similar way)]

a. Rationale

Prohibiting a defendant from taking inconsistent positions is based upon the desire to encourage defendants claiming entrapment to waive their right not to testify and thus make themselves available for cross-examination by the prosecution. In addition, the rule avoids sanctioning a defendant's perjurious denial that he committed the crime and means that juries will not be confronted with potentially confusing inconsistent positions. It also rests on the premise that absent the commission of a crime there can be no entrapment; thus, the accused should not be allowed to take the inconsistent positions that he did not commit the offense, but if he did, he was entrapped. This latter point has been criticized, however, because in other areas of criminal litigation there is no prohibition against a defendant adopting inconsistent positions. [**State v. Soule,** 811 P.2d 1071 (Ariz. 1991)]

b. Alternative Position: Defendant Can Rely on Inconsistent Positions

Some jurisdictions permit defendants relying on entrapment to take inconsistent positions. The Supreme Court has held that under federal criminal law a defendant ***can deny guilt*** of the crime and alternatively claim entrapment. ***Rationale:*** Generally, litigants are not barred from taking inconsistent positions, and there is no reason to deviate from that position in entrapment cases. Further, the awkwardness of this position will discourage most defendants from doing it. Thus, the practical risk that permitting inconsistent positions will encourage perjury by defendants is relatively low. [**Mathews v. United States,** 485 U.S. 58 (1988)]

4. Entrapment Criteria: "Subjective" vs. "Objective" Approaches

Jurisdictions are split on the criteria for determining whether particular facts show entrapment constituting a defense. This split reflects an underlying difference regarding the conceptual basis and rationale for the defense.

a. Traditional (Subjective) Standard

Under the traditional approach, entrapment occurs only if a law enforcement officer ***created the intent*** to commit the crime in the mind of a person who was ***not predisposed*** to commit crimes of the sort involved in the case. The test is subjective because a finding of entrapment depends on what subjectively stimulated the defendant to commit the crime—the defendant's predisposition or the officer's inducement. Federal courts apply this standard under a long line of Supreme Court decisions. [**Sorrells v. United States,** 287 U.S. 435 (1932); **Sherman v. United States,** 356 U.S. 369 (1958); **United States v. Russell,** *supra*]

(1) Rationale: Legislative Intent

The traditional entrapment defense is based on the assumption that the legislature did not intend to include within the crime those persons who were induced by the police into perpetrating the offense. Consequently, an entrapped person is not guilty of criminal conduct as that conduct was defined by the legislature. [**Sorrells v. United States,** *supra*]

(2) Analysis: Predisposition Is Crucial Issue

Under the traditional subjective standard, the critical question is often whether the accused was ***predisposed*** to commit crimes of the sort involved. If the jury finds that the defendant was predisposed, it must reject the entrapment defense regardless of the nature of police participation in the events. [*See* **Jackson v. State,** 699 S.E.2d 884 (Ga.App. 2010) (issue of the defendant's predisposition was for the jury to decide)]

(a) Showing "Predisposition"

Under the traditional view, it is not entrapment merely because a law enforcement officer afforded the defendant an opportunity to commit the crime (as where undercover agent poses as drug addict and purchases drugs from a dealer). Evidence that the defendant ***responded readily to the opportunity*** to commit the crime and had ***previously committed similar offenses*** indicates a predisposition to commit the crime and thus tends to negate the entrapment defense. [**Sherman v. United States,** *supra*] Conversely, evidence of repeated requests by the police that the crime be committed, and appeals by officers to the defendant's sympathy, tends to support the entrapment defense.

EXAM TIP

Most exam questions on entrapment are going to require you to consider the issue of the defendant's predisposition. Be sure to focus first on the ***defendant's past conduct*** and on his ***behavior in the transaction for which he was arrested.*** Look for things that tend to show he was predisposed to commit this type of crime. You may then want to examine the police activity involved for hints of a ***lack*** of predisposition, but don't lose sight of the fact that under this approach to entrapment, the focus is on the defendant's predisposition, not on the government's conduct.

(b) Predisposition Prior to First Approach

In applying the federal entrapment standard, courts are to require proof that the defendant was predisposed before first being approached by government agents. Therefore, if government agents had considerable contact with the suspect before actually providing him with an opportunity to commit the offense, and if the proof shows the suspect was at that time predisposed to commit the offense, the government must also show at trial that his predisposition was not caused by the earlier contact between the government agents and the suspect. [**Jacobson v. United States,** 503 U.S. 540 (1992)]

(3) Burden of Proof

Under the traditional approach, a ***defendant*** claiming entrapment has the burden of establishing that ***he was induced*** by officers to commit the charged crime. Upon proof of such inducement (which raises the entrapment issue), the ***prosecution*** has the burden of proving beyond a reasonable doubt that the ***defendant was predisposed*** in order to preclude entrapment. [**Jacobson v. United States,** *supra*]

(4) Procedural Disadvantages

The subjective entrapment criterion usually results in several procedural disadvantages for defendants who claim entrapment.

(a) **Issue Tried to Jury**

If the defense relates to the defendant's guilt or innocence, it must be decided by the jury. Juries may be less receptive to entrapment arguments than are trial judges. [**Sorrells v. United States,** *supra*]

(b) **Evidence Showing Predisposition Becomes Admissible**

Once a defendant raises the entrapment issue, his predisposition becomes relevant, and the prosecution can introduce otherwise-inadmissible evidence of prior crimes, reputation, and the like to show this predisposition. That evidence creates a danger that the jury will reject the entrapment defense and convict the defendant simply on the basis of his "bad character."

b. **Modern, Objective Standard**

Some courts apply an entrapment criterion that ignores the defendant's subjective motivation for committing the crime and instead focuses on the ***propriety of the officers' conduct*** judged by an objective standard. [*See* **People v. Watson,** 22 Cal.4th 220 (Cal. 2000); **People v. Barraza,** 591 P.2d 947 (Cal. 1979)]

(1) **Rationale: Need to Discourage Police Misconduct**

This formulation of the entrapment defense is not based on a perception of the entrapped defendant as "innocent" of the crime. Rather, the defense is based on the ***need to deter government officials*** from engaging in undesirable conduct. [**Sorrells v. United States,** *supra* (Roberts, J., concurring)]

(2) **Analysis: Tendency of Police Conduct to "Create" Crime**

Under the usual version of the objective standard, courts are to find entrapment whenever the offense was committed in response to law enforcement activity that was reasonably likely to cause a ***reasonable person*** (who was not predisposed to commit crimes of the sort at issue) to commit a crime. In contrast to the traditional approach, the test under this formulation is objective. Whether or not entrapment occurred depends ***solely on the conduct of the law enforcement officers;*** any effect the government's conduct had on the defendant is irrelevant.

(a) **Model Penal Code**

The Model Penal Code has adopted this view, and provides that entrapment exists if a law enforcement officer has induced or encouraged the commission of the crime by "employing persuasion or inducement which creates a substantial risk that the offense will be committed by persons other than those who are ready to commit it." [Model Penal Code § 2.13(1)(b)]

(b) **Focus on Police Conduct**

The determinative issue under this approach is whether a reasonable person would have responded to the officer's conduct by committing the crime. Hence, the focus is on the nature of the police activity, and especially the ***vigor*** with which officers urged that the crime be perpetrated and any ***inducements*** they offered the accused.

1) Limited Scope of Police Behavior

Under most entrapment standards of this sort, the only characteristics of law enforcement behavior relevant to entrapment are those bearing on the ***likelihood of the police behavior to induce commission of the crime.*** Evidence that the police conduct was offensive for other reasons (*e.g.*, unlawful invasion of the defendant's privacy) is not relevant to whether entrapment occurred.

(3) Burden of Proof

Jurisdictions adopting the objective approach generally place the burden of proof regarding entrapment on the ***defendant.***

(4) Procedural Advantages of Objective Approach

The procedural implications of the objective approach to entrapment often mean that the procedural disadvantages of the traditional rule are eliminated or reduced.

(a) Issue Tried to Court

Because the "defense" is a rule unrelated to guilt or innocence, the entrapment issue is determined by the judge rather than the jury. [Model Penal Code § 2.13(2)]

(b) Evidence of Predisposition Not Admissible

Because the defendant's predisposition is not in issue, evidence otherwise inadmissible which only tends to prove predisposition (*e.g.*, the defendant's prior criminal record) is not rendered admissible simply because entrapment has been claimed.

COMPARISON OF ENTRAPMENT APPROACHES

	TRADITIONAL (SUBJECTIVE) STANDARD	MODERN (OBJECTIVE) STANDARD
TEST	Did a police officer create the intent to commit the crime in the mind of a person who ***was not predisposed to commit it***?	Was the offense committed in response to police activity that was reasonably likely to cause a ***reasonable person*** (who was not predisposed to commit the crime) to commit the crime?
CRUCIAL ISSUE	Predisposition	Reasonableness of police activity
WHO DECIDES	Jury	Judge
EVIDENCE OF PREDISPOSITION	Admissible	Not Admissible
BURDEN OF PROOF	On Prosecution	On Defendant

c. Broader Objective Standards

A few jurisdictions have adopted ***very broad objective standards*** for entrapment that permit the defense to be based on police misconduct that would not satisfy the modern objective standard discussed above.

(1) Providing Materials for Offense

Some courts have upheld claims of entrapment based on showings that government agents provided the materials for commission of the offenses (such as the drug for an illicit drug sale). [**People v. Strong,** 172 N.E.2d 765 (Ill. 1961)] The Supreme Court has held, however, that the government's supplying the material for the commission of an offense, even if that material is contraband, is not entrapment under federal law and does not violate the defendant's constitutional rights. [**Hampton v. United States,** 425 U.S. 484 (1976)]

(2) Approach Suspect Without Adequate Justification

A few courts have suggested that entrapment would occur if a police officer approached a suspect and offered the opportunity to commit an offense without probable cause, or at least reasonable suspicion, to believe the person was predisposed to commit such offenses. [**Walker v. State,** 262 N.E.2d 641 (Ind. 1970) (probable cause required) *overruled by* **Hardin v. State,** 358 N.E.2d 134 (Ind. 1976); **Childs v. United States,** 267 F.2d 619 (D.C. Cir. 1958) (reasonable suspicion required)]

(3) General Prohibition Against Misconduct

A few courts have adopted broad rules permitting findings of entrapment on the basis of police conduct found offensive for general policy reasons. [**State v. Molnar,** 410 A.2d 37 (N.J. 1980) (entrapment occurs if police conduct is so egregious as to impugn the integrity of the court); **State v. Sainz,** 501 P.2d 1247 (N.M. 1972), *overruled by* **State v. Fiechter,** 547 P.2d 557 (N.M. 1976) (entrapment occurs whenever the police conduct, for any reason, is "such that if allowed to continue would shake the public's confidence in the fair and honorable administration of justice")]

K. Consent and Related Matters

1. Consent

Consent is a "defense" if it ***negates some element*** of the crime or if the charge is for a ***minor assault or battery.*** In either case, however, the consent must be ***legally effective.***

a. Consent as Negating Element of Crime

Some crimes are defined in terms of the victim's lack of consent. For example, traditional rape requires intercourse without the consent of the woman (*see infra*). Clearly then, if lack of consent is an essential element of the crime, proof of consent will be a bar to conviction.

b. Consent as True Defense, as to Assault or Battery

As to those crimes not requiring lack of the victim's consent, consent of the victim could only be a "true" defense. Ordinarily, it is not such a defense. The major exception arises in the case of certain assaults or batteries. Here, courts are more likely to recognize the defense of consent if: (i) the criminal act did ***not involve serious bodily injury*** or the risk of such injury; (ii) there is ***widespread acceptance of the risk*** (*e.g.,* in sporting events); and (iii) there is a ***distinct beneficial effect*** attending the defendant's conduct (as in the case of medical surgery). [**People v. Fitzsimmons,** 34 N.Y.S. 1102 (1895)]

e.g. **Example:** D was charged with aggravated assault by reason of his appearance in a sadomasochistic film in which he beat another person with a riding crop. Despite his testimony that the so-called victim had been paid and had acquiesced in the beating, D was convicted of the crime. Because of the severity of the injuries inflicted, consent was no defense. [**People v. Samuels,** 250 Cal. App. 2d 501 (1967) (rejects consent as a defense for serious injury if the victim was a masochist who derived pleasure from severe treatment)]

(1) Model Penal Code Position

The Model Penal Code adopts a similar approach, providing that consent is a defense to conduct causing or threatening to cause harm if:

(i) The harm involved is *not serious; or*

(ii) The defendant's conduct and the harm "are ***reasonably foreseeable hazards*** of joint participation in a ***lawful athletic contest or competitive sport*** or other concerted activity not forbidden by law."

[Model Penal Code § 2.11(2)]

2. Legal Effectiveness of Consent

Even when consent is recognized as an available defense, a particular consent will be a defense only if the consent is ***legally effective.*** For this to be the case, three requirements must be met:

a. Voluntarily Given

The consent must have been given ***voluntarily***, *i.e.,* by a party acting of her own free will without compulsion or duress.

b. Consenter Must Have Legal Capacity

Consent must have been given by a person ***legally capable of consenting***, *i.e.,* someone not disabled by youth, intoxication, or mental abnormality. [*See, e.g.*, **State v. Ortega-Martinez,** 881 P.2d 231 (Wash. 1994) (mental defect, even if victim understands "physical mechanics" but not "a wide range of particulars" regarding consequences of intercourse)]

c. Free of Fraud or Mistake

Consent given under fraud or mistake as to the very ***nature of the defendants conduct*** ("fraud in the factum") is ***ineffective.*** However, "fraud in the inducement," which involves deception as to some matter ***collateral*** to the nature of the defendant's conduct, will ***not*** vitiate an otherwise effective consent. [**People v. Cook,** 228 Cal. App. 2d 716 (1964)]

e.g. **Example:** D obtained possession of a motor vehicle in exchange for a bad check and was prosecuted for the statutory crime of taking an automobile without the consent of the owner. D was not guilty, although the owner's acquiescence was falsely induced. The fraud related only to a collateral matter (the consideration given for the consent) and thus did not render the consent legally ineffective. [**People v. Cook,** *supra*]

SUMMARY OF DEFENSES BASED ON EXCUSE		
DEFENSE	**APPLICABLE TO**	**WHEN AVAILABLE**
MISTAKE OF FACT	Crimes with a mental state element (*i.e.,* all crimes ***except*** strict liability)	For ***specific intent*** crimes, any mistake that negates intent; for other crimes, ***only reasonable mistakes***
MISTAKE OF LAW	Crimes with a mental state element and statutory crimes	*Two different contexts:* (i) Mistake negates *mens rea* of crime charged; ***or*** (ii) mistake is due to: reasonable reliance on statute or judicial interpretation, or (in some states) reasonable reliance on official advice
NECESSITY OR JUSTIFICATION	All crimes ***except*** intentional killing	Defendant reasonably believed crime was necessary to avoid greater harm to himself or others
DURESS	All crimes ***except*** intentional killing	Defendant reasonably believed that another would imminently harm him or a family member if he did not commit the crime
ENTRAPMENT	Most crimes but ***not*** to those involving serious injury	Criminal design originated with the police and the defendant was ***not predisposed*** to commit the crime before contact with police (traditional standard)
CONSENT	Crimes requiring lack of consent (*e.g.,* rape) and minor assaults and batteries	Applicable only if: consent is freely given, the party is capable of consenting, and no fraud was used to obtain consent

3. Condonation Ordinarily Is No Defense

The victim's ***forgiveness*** after the commission of a crime (*i.e.,* "condonation") is ordinarily ***no defense,*** even if that forgiveness follows full restitution by the defendant. [**People v. Haissig,** 976 N.E.2d 1121 (Ill. 2012) (while voluntary restitution is not a defense, in a theft case it may show lack of intent to deprive the owner permanently of his property, if the restitution constitutes a return of the property)]

a. Rationale

The principal injury from the commission of a crime is suffered by the public. The defendant's willingness to settle with the victim does not affect this and therefore should not bar prosecution. [**Commonwealth v. Rotonda,** 747 N.E.2d 1199 (Mass. 2001)]

b. Exception: Compromises Authorized by Statute

Some jurisdictions authorize victims of certain crimes (usually misdemeanors) and offenders to negotiate compromises. In such cases, if the victim acknowledges that she has received satisfaction, the court may dismiss the criminal prosecution. [Cal. Penal Code § 1377]

4. Negligence or Criminality of Victim No Defense

The fact that a specific victim was negligent or engaged in criminal activity at the time of the crime is not a defense to a crime against that victim. This is because crimes involve wrongs against the public and therefore the unworthiness of a particular victim is not a sufficient basis for barring conviction. [**Frazier v. Commonwealth,** 165 S.W.2d 33 (Ky. 1942)]

a. Effect on Causation

If the crime is one involving a required result, such as criminal homicide, the fact that the victim was negligent after the defendant's behavior may affect proximate causation and thus the defendant's liability for the result. (*See supra,* p. 69 *et seq.*)

L. Self-Defense

1. In General

As a justification defense, self-defense has both a subjective requirement, that defendant actually believed he was threatened with the imminent use of deadly physical force, and an objective requirement, that defendant's reactions were those of a reasonable man acting in self-defense. [**People v. Castillo,** 250 N.E.3d 650 (N.Y. 2024)] A defendant charged with an assaultive crime may assert in defense that she reasonably believed her actions were necessary to defend herself against an apparent threat of unlawful and immediate violence from another. A defendant must produce "some evidence" on the issue of self-defense to be entitled to a jury instruction. [**Jarvis v. State,** 321 A.3d 1 (Md. 2024) (circumstantial evidence and reasonable inferences therefrom also can satisfy the "some evidence" standard)] The requirements that apply to self-defense defense differ depending upon whether the crime charged involved the use of deadly force.

2. General Requirements for Self-Defense

In all cases where the defendant claims to have acted in self-defense, whether or not deadly force was involved, the defense contains several elements:

a. Reasonable Belief That Self-Defense Necessary

A defendant need not "present adequate evidence that every reasonable person would have believed he was in imminent danger and that deadly force was necessary." Instead, defendant's evidence must show that "a reasonable person, under the same circumstances and with the same subjective beliefs and faculties (as *this* defendant), would have believed that he was in imminent danger and that deadly force was necessary." [**State v. Palmer,** 238 N.E.3d 33 (Ohio 2024)] An honest and reasonable belief is enough; the defense is available even though it turns out that the belief was wrong and there was, in fact, no actual need to use force in self-defense. [**People v. Goetz,** 497 N.E.2d 41 (N.Y. 1986); *see* **State v. Esdel,** 317 A.3d 756 (R.I. 2024) (regarding reasonableness of defendant's fear, defendant may present relevant evidence of specific acts of violence perpetrated by the victim against third parties, if defendant was aware of such acts at time of the encounter with victim.)]

b. Threatened Harm

The defendant must have reasonably believed she was threatened with ***physical harm*** at the hands of another.

c. Imminent Threatened Harm

The defendant must have reasonably believed the threatened harm was ***imminent***, *i.e.*, that the harm ***would be inflicted immediately*** if she did not act in self-defense. [**Richardson v. United States,** 98 A.3d 178 (D.C. 2014) (it is the defendant's beliefs (not the victim's beliefs) about whether he was in imminent danger of serious bodily harm or death)] The court must consider whether the threatening person was actually present and, if so, whether that person appeared willing and able to injure the defendant. [*Compare* **People v. Williams,** 205 N.E.2d 749 (Ill. 1965) (gang member who was beating an old man in the street threw a brick at a taxi parked across the intersection, after which the taxi driver shot at the gang; danger to the taxi driver was imminent, because the gang was near him and was able to carry out threatened harm) *with* **Douglas v. State,** 540 S.W.3d 685 (Ark. 2018) (defendant not entitled to self-defense instruction, even though victim was initial aggressor, because the initial dispute had concluded and the victim had left the scene and returned to his home, where defendant later traveled with gun and shot the victim as he attempted to flee)]

d. Unlawfulness of Threatened Harm

The defendant must have reasonably believed the threatened harm would be ***unlawful.*** This may raise issues as to whether force is appropriate to resist an unlawful arrest and whether one who is the initial aggressor in an affray can claim the defense at all (*see infra*).

e. Force Used Was Necessary to Prevent Harm

The defendant must have reasonably believed that the threatened harm was such as to require the ***defensive force actually used.*** There is no defense available to the use of force beyond that which reasonably appeared necessary to prevent the threatened harm. [Model Penal Code § 3.04(1)]

f. Duty to Retreat Before Using Nondeadly Force

Although the amount of force used must be reasonable in relationship to the amount of force confronted with, there is no duty to retreat before using ***nondeadly*** force. The duty to retreat is an issue only when deadly force is used in self-defense.

3. Additional Requirements Where Deadly Force Used

Although there is no absolute prohibition against the use of deadly force in self-defense, there are some special limits on when it may be used. "Deadly force" is force used with the ***intent to cause death or serious bodily injury*** or which is ***known*** by its user ***to create a substantial risk*** of death or serious bodily injury. [Model Penal Code § 3.11(2)]

EXAM TIP

To determine whether the force or harm is "deadly," think about the likely result from the ***action or instrument used.*** Shooting a gun is clearly using deadly force. Even if the shooter doesn't intend to kill the person (*e.g.,* he intended only to "wing" victim), he knows that there is a substantial risk of death or serious bodily injury. But some instruments are not so obviously deadly. For example, hitting someone with a baseball bat is likely to cause serious bodily injury and so would be considered deadly force. By contrast, hitting someone with a ruler across the hands would not be. Swinging a machete would be deadly force; brandishing a small nail file probably would not. Consider whether the likely result of the force would be ***at least serious injury,*** if not death, to determine whether the force used is deadly.

a. Perceived Threat of Death or Serious Bodily Injury

All courts agree that deadly force may be used in self-defense ***only if*** the defendant ***reasonably believed*** that the other person was ***about to inflict death or serious bodily injury*** upon her. [*Compare* **Dorsey v. United States,** 935 A.2d 288 (D.C.App. 2007) (where a defendant was not in imminent peril of death or serious bodily harm from his attacker, defendant's lethal response not reasonable)]

EXAM TIP

Keep in mind that the law frowns on the use of deadly force and thus limits its use in self-defense. Generally the allowable force in self-defense must be ***roughly equal to the force threatened.*** Thus, ***deadly*** force can be used only when death or serious bodily injury is threatened (or the defendant reasonably believed that it was). If a defendant is threatened with ***nondeadly*** harm and she cannot prevent this by using nondeadly force in self-defense, the law expects the defendant to ***submit to the nondeadly injury*** rather than resort to the deadly force necessary to prevent that injury.

b. Deadly Force Necessary to Prevent Death or Serious Bodily Injury

The defendant will be allowed to use deadly force in self-defense if she ***reasonably*** believed that the deadly force used was ***necessary*** to prevent the death or serious bodily injury with which she was threatened. If she realized, or, in the exercise of reasonable care, would have realized that nondeadly force would suffice, she has ***no defense*** to a crime consisting of the use of deadly force.

c. Duty to Retreat Before Using Deadly Force?

A difficult problem is presented by the question whether a defendant should have a defense to the use of deadly force if she had an opportunity to retreat instead of using deadly force.

(1) Common Law and Minority Rule: Retreat Required

For a self-defense defense to a crime consisting of deadly force, the common law required the defendant to show that she had ***no opportunity to retreat*** or that she unsuccessfully sought to use an available opportunity. Some jurisdictions still follow this approach, which is based on the position that human life should not be jeopardized if reasonable alternatives are available and that retreat, despite its degrading impact, is a reasonable alternative.

(a) Exception: Safe Retreat Not Possible

Jurisdictions requiring retreat generally demand such retreat only where it appears available ***in complete safety.*** If the defendant reasonably believed that retreat would increase the risk of an attack by deadly force, she may use deadly force herself in self-defense without attempting retreat. [**State v. Anderson,** 631 A.2d 1149 (Conn. 1993)]

(b) "Castle Rule" Exception: Attack in the Home

Jurisdictions requiring retreat generally do ***not*** demand it if the defendant is attacked in her ***own home*** or "castle." Some do not require retreat if the attack occurs in the defendant's place of business. [**State v. Brooks,** 167 S.E.2d 307 (S.C. 1969)] ***Rationale:*** Persons in these locations are already in the places of safety to which attacked victims are usually encouraged to retreat; thus, to demand more of them would be unreasonable. However, if a person is engaging in illegal activity or is unlawfully present, the duty to retreat remains. [**State v. Johnson**, 7 N.W.3d 504 (Iowa 2024)]

e.g. **Example:** D had a duty to retreat from his apartment building's hallway before acting in self-defense, even though D's apartment was in a secured building. D did not exercise exclusive possession and control over the hallway, and the hallway was not D's safest place or sanctuary. [**State v. Devens,** 852 N.W.2d 255 (Minn. 2014)]

(c) Model Penal Code: Retreat Required

The Model Penal Code is similar to the minority rule, requiring the defendant to retreat, surrender possession of a thing demanded by another asserting a claim of right to it, or comply with a demand that she abstain from any action she has no duty to take, if the defendant knows this can be done with complete safety. [Model Penal Code § 3.04(2)(b)(ii)]

(2) Majority Modern Rule: Retreat Not Absolutely Required

Most American jurisdictions have abandoned the common law rule. Instead, a defendant who was not the original aggressor need not retreat (even though he can do so safely) before using deadly force against an assailant whom he reasonably believes will kill him or do serious bodily harm. [*See, e.g.*, **State v. Carridine,** 812 N.W.2d 130 (Minn. 2012) ("if a person begins or induces an assault that leads to the necessity of using force in that person's own defense, that person must attempt to retreat, regardless of whether the victim escalates the situation by using deadly force")]

(a) Opportunity to Retreat Is Relevant to Reasonableness

Under the modern view, any evidence that the defendant could have retreated, the safety of such retreat, and the places to which retreat might be made are relevant to whether the defendant decided that deadly force was ***reasonably necessary.*** [**Culverson v. State**, 797 P.2d 238 (Nev. 1990)]

(3) Expanded Castle Rule Exception: "Stand One's Ground" Statutes

Some American jurisdictions have adopted expanded versions of the Castle Rule, sometimes creating a legal presumption that a defender using force against an invader was acting out of a reasonable fear of death or great bodily harm, with no duty to retreat and the right to stand his ground "and use or threaten to use" nondeadly or deadly force, respectively, against another's "imminent use of unlawful force" or "prevent the imminent commission of a forcible felony." [Fla. Stat. § 776.013; *see* **Elder v. State,** 296 So.3d 440 (Fla.App. 2020) (unlike self-defense, the Castle Rule's legal presumption eliminates the need for the defendant to establish the reasonable fear of death or great bodily harm)] Florida has refined its statute to state that a defender engaged in illegal activity is not entitled to stand his ground. Fla. Stat. § 776.012]

(a) Immunity from Prosecution for the Defendant

The preceding Florida statute also grants immunity from prosecution, prohibiting criminal charges against a defendant who demonstrates at a pretrial hearing that the statute applies. Initially the petitioner must make a prima facie claim; the burden then shifts to the state to show by clear and convincing evidence that the statute does not apply. If the state fails in its burden, the court prohibits the state from charging the defendant.

SELF-DEFENSE REQUIREMENTS CHECKLIST
TO ESTABLISH SELF-DEFENSE, THE DEFENDANT MUST SHOW THAT SHE *REASONABLY BELIEVED* THAT:
☑ It was ***necessary*** to defend herself
☑ ***Physical harm*** was threatened
☑ Harm was ***imminent*** (about to be inflicted)
☑ Harm was ***unlawful*** (resisting arrest and initial aggressor issues)
☑ Harm required the ***defensive force actually used*** (use of only the amount of force reasonably necessary to prevent harm)
☑ And for ***deadly force:*** ○ Death or serious bodily injury was ***imminent*** and ○ Deadly force was ***necessary*** to prevent it.

4. Special Problem: Battered Victim Claiming Killing in Self-Defense

Assertion of self-defense arising from a long history of abuse creates problems involving the issues of *imminence and unreasonableness*. A wife whose husband has repeatedly beaten her will take his life when there was not any immediate threat of repetition of the husband's conduct, although the wife knew that more severe beatings were in the offing, *i.e.*, due to "battered woman syndrome." The reasonableness of the defendant's conduct is based upon her physical and psychological characteristics, her specific experiences, and perhaps the disadvantaged position of women" in society. [**State v. Smullen,** 844 A.2d 429 (Md. 2004) (recognizing that "battered child syndrome" and "battered spouse syndrome" may influence claims of self-defense)] Although not independently recognized in the federal and most state systems, the battered spouse syndrome can support a self-defense or duress affirmative defense. [*See* **United States v. Dixon,** 413 F.3d 520, 523 (5th Cir. 2005), *aff'd*, 548 U.S. 1 (2006) (court relies on Model Penal Code approach about whether "person of reasonable firmness in [the defendant's] situation would have been able to resist"; expert testimony was properly refused because it went to defendant's "subjective vulnerability to coercion")]

a. Major Problems with Defense

(1) Imminence of the Threatened Harm

In many cases, the defendant attacked the victim after a particular episode of abuse had ended. Consequently, any harm she may have feared from the victim arguably was not "imminent" as required by self-defense law. [**State v. Norman,** 378 S.E.2d

8 (N.C. 1989) (defendant shot abusive husband while he was asleep; evidence thus did not show she feared imminent harm from him; court found that defendant presented no issue of self-defense)] On the other hand, a battered woman's constant alertness (proven through expert testimony) can show the jury that a threat from the victim was imminent. [**United States v. Nwoye,** 824 F.3d 1129 (D.C. Cir. 2016)]

(2) Options to the Use of Force

In some cases, the absence of any physical barrier to the defendant leaving the relationship suggests that options were available that made her use of deadly force objectively unreasonable. The battered wife-defendant may believe she has only two alternatives: either wait for the spouse to return and kill her or striking at the spouse first. That argument had persuaded some that the imminency requirement should be applied less strictly.

b. Responses

(1) Expert Testimony on Battered Woman and Related Syndromes

Defendants often produce evidence of mistreatment of them by the victims and expert testimony about the effect of such "battering." It may also involve other types of situations. [**State v. Smullen**, *supra* (if proper evidentiary basis laid, murder defendant could introduce "battered child" evidence)]

(a) Relevance of Battering Evidence

Battered spouse or battered child testimony generally suggests that the effects of a battering relationship cause the battered person to conclude that further violence is inevitable, and that leaving the relationship or otherwise preventing further abuse is not a practical and available option. The defendant usually believed that the force used was actually necessary to protect her own safety, and showed that the defendant's belief was objectively reasonable. Other persons subject to battering would reach that conclusion. [**State v. Norman,** *supra*]

(2) Need to Consider Defendant's Position

At least one court held that the reasonableness of a battered spouse's actions must be evaluated in light of the spouse's ***physical and psychological characteristics,*** the spouse's ***specific experiences*** as a victim of battering, and perhaps the ***disadvantaged position*** that women have occupied in society. Juries may be so instructed. Under this approach, certain attacks upon battering spouses may be found, in light of these factors, to have been reasonable responses to the battering spouses' conduct. [**State v. Leidholm,** 334 N.W.2d 811 (N.D. 1983)]

(3) Elimination of Requirement of Imminent Harm

Some have urged that in these cases the law should no longer impose a requirement that the defendant have reasonably perceived the threatened deadly harm as imminent. Instead, the relevant policy concerns would be satisfied if the law required only that the defendant reasonably perceived the ***necessity*** for using deadly force in self-defense. [**State v. Norman,** *supra* (Martin, J., dissenting)]

5. Limitation: Right of Aggressor to Self-Defense

The ***initial aggressor cannot use force*** in self-defense unless (i) the victim has responded with *excessive force*, [**State v. Grott,** 458 P.3d 750 (Wash. 2020)] *or* (ii) the *aggressor first* *withdraws* from the affray or at least clearly notifies the adversary of his desire to withdraw [**Diggs v. State,** 168 So.3d 156 (Ala.App. 2014)]

a. Rationale

The victim, in defending herself against the aggressor, is ordinarily using lawful force, and (as discussed above) the defendant can only use self-defense in response to threats of ***unlawful*** harm.

b. "Arming Oneself" as Aggression

Merely because a defendant carried a gun to an encounter with the victim did not make the defendant the "aggressor," where it was the victim "who ended the discussion by suddenly, and without provocation pulled out his pistol and shot at [the defendant]. [**Diggs v. State**, *supra*] If the defendant armed herself and returned to the scene of a prior difficulty for the purpose of further conflict with the abuser, this is sufficient to render self-defense inapplicable. [**Howard v. United States,** 656 A.2d 1106 (D.C. 1995)]

c. Exceptions

There are two situations in which a person, although the initial aggressor, ***regains the right*** to act in self-defense:

(1) Nondeadly Aggressor Met with Deadly Force

If the victim responds to the aggressor's use of ***nondeadly*** force with ***deadly*** force, the aggressor can use whatever force appears reasonably necessary (including deadly force) to repel the attack. ***Rationale:*** Because nondeadly force cannot be met with deadly force (*supra*), the victim has threatened unlawful harm. [**State v. Grott,** 458 P.3d 750 (Wash. 2020)]

(2) Withdrawal by Aggressor

An aggressor regains the right to act in self-defense by ***withdrawing*** from the affray. Ordinarily for an effective withdrawal, the defendant must either physically remove herself from the fight or actually notify her adversary of the desire to desist, but some jurisdictions hold that even unsuccessful efforts to so notify her adversary, if reasonable, will suffice. [**Diggs v. State**, *supra* (withdrawing from encounter or clearly manifesting an intention to do so will restore right of self-defense)] However, if the aggressor retreats but then returns with deadly force that is disproportionate to the crime being committed, his claim of deadly force in self-defense is unreasonable. [**United States v. Peterson,** 483 F.2d 1222 (D.C.Cir. 1973)]

6. Resisting Unlawful Arrest as Self-Defense

Criminal charges based on force used to resist an ***unlawful*** arrest present a special problem of self-defense law.

a. Traditional View: Force Permitted to Resist Unlawful Arrest

Traditionally, courts held that a person subjected to an ***unlawful*** arrest, even by a person known to the defendant as a law enforcement officer, may act in self-defense and resist with reasonable force. [**Bad Elk v. United States,** 177 U.S. 529 (1900)] The threatened harm is the indignity and inconvenience of undergoing arrest and its accompanying detention.

b. Modern Rule: No Right to Resist Arrest by Officer

Many jurisdictions have rejected the traditional rule, and hold that force may ***not*** be used to resist even an unlawful arrest if the arrestee ***knows*** that the arresting person is a ***law enforcement officer. Rationale:*** The legality of an arrest is too complicated an issue to reliably be resolved "in the street." Modern weapons make the cost of so resolving disputes too high. Moreover, because legal processes are readily available for the release of persons unlawfully arrested, it is not burdensome to require safer and more rational legal methods of resolving the situation. [**State v. Crawley,** 901 A.2d 924 (N.J. 2006); Model Penal Code § 3.04(2)(a)(i)]

(1) Exception Under Modern Rule: Unlawful Arrest Using Excessive Force

Some jurisdictions prohibit the use of force against unlawful arrests, because they permit force to be used to ***resist excessive force*** being used to make an arrest. ***Rationale:*** Later resort to legal proceedings to challenge the officer's actions cannot effectively prevent undue physical harm caused by excessive force, and thus do not provide an adequate alternative to immediate self-defense. [**People v. Curtis,** 450 P.2d 33 (Cal. 1969) (defendant unsuccessfully argued that a statute forbidding the use of force to resist an unlawful arrest by a known police officer was unconstitutional, because it eliminated the remedy of self-help against arrests in violation of the Fourth Amendment)]

7. Distinguish: "Imperfect" Self-Defense in Homicide Prosecutions

Self-defense is usually a "perfect" or ***complete defense*** that, if successful, entitles the defendant to acquittal. [**Cook v. State,** 321 A.3d 765 (Md. 2024) (perfect self-defense requires a showing that the accused (1) had reasonable grounds to believe himself in apparent imminent or immediate danger of death or serious bodily harm from assailant, (2) believed himself in this danger, (3) was not the aggressor or did not provoke the conflict, and (4) used reasonable force that was not more force than the exigency demanded)]

In murder prosecutions, however, some jurisdictions provide an "imperfect" defense to those unable to prove a complete self-defense. Under this approach, a defendant who killed under the ***unreasonable belief*** that this was necessary to defend against an imminent attack or by the use of an ***unreasonable amount of force*** cannot escape conviction on grounds of self-defense, ***but*** may be guilty of lesser degree of homicide (*see infra,* p. 222). [**People v. Rangel,** 367 P.3d 649 (Cal. 2016); **State v. Jones,** 8 P.3d 1282 (Kan. 2000); **Ky.Rev.Stat.** § 503.120]

e.g. **Example:** V began striking D, who was larger and stronger than V. D responded by shooting and killing V. D says he really thought that the shooting was necessary to prevent V from causing serious bodily injury. Even though D had acted to save his own life, D could not claim a complete defense to murder because his belief that he was threatened with deadly force was objectively unreasonable. The "imperfect defense" doctrine treats the crime of which he was guilty as mitigated from murder to manslaughter.

M. Defense of Others

1. In General

A defendant charged with an assaultive crime may assert in defense that he reasonably believed his actions were necessary to defend ***another person*** against an apparent threat of unlawful and immediate violence from another. [**Regina v. Prince,** *supra*]

2. Relationship with Party Defended

There is some split of authority on whether the defense is available if the defendant acted in defense of a complete stranger.

a. Early View: Special Relationship Required

Early English case law suggested that force could be used in defense of others only if the defender stood in some special relationship to the person in need of protection (*e.g.,* husband-wife, parent-child, or master-servant), and some American statutes still impose such a limitation. [*See, e.g.,* Model Penal Code § 3.05, comment (Tent. Draft No. 8, 1958)]

b. Modern View: No Special Relationship Required

Under the modern (and preferable) approach, no prior relationship need be shown between the defendant and the person assisted; as a general rule, reasonable force may be used in defense of ***any third person,*** even a stranger. [**Williams v. State,** 27 S.E.2d 109 (Ga.App. 1943); Model Penal Code § 3.05(1)] ***Rationale:*** The only basis for requiring a special relationship, *i.e.*, that people will impulsively and hence unwisely and unnecessarily attack others under the mistaken impression that this is necessary to protect strangers, has no basis in fact.

3. Right of Party Defended to Act in Self-Defense

Courts differ on whether the defendant has a right to use force in defense of another if the person defended did not in fact have the right to use force in her own defense (as where she was the initial aggressor).

a. Objective (or "Alter Ego") Rule: Defense Turns on Right of Person Defended

Formerly, many courts followed the "alter ego" rule, which held that a defendant who comes to the aid of another ***stands in the place of the person assisted.*** Thus, one who intervened to protect others did so at his peril, and if the person assisted had no right to use force in self-defense (even if it reasonably appeared that such a right existed), the defendant had no privilege. [**Batson v. State,** 941 P.2d 478 (Nev. 1997)]

(1) Rationale

It has been argued that this rule is necessary to "orderly society," because it discourages persons from impulsively, and unnecessarily, attacking others under the mistaken belief that a third person is in danger. It does this by telling persons that they had better be certain that a third person is in danger before they come to the aid of that person because they cannot later rely on reasonable but mistaken beliefs that the person aided was in danger.

b. Subjective Rule: Reasonable Appearances Control

Today most jurisdictions and the Model Penal Code follow what is seemingly a more just rule, under which a defendant has the right to use force in defense of others as long as it ***reasonably appeared*** that the person assisted had the right to use force in self-defense. [**Commonwealth v. Young,** 959 N.E. 2d 943 (Mass. 2012) ("the circumstances must be viewed from the perspective of the intervening defendant, not of the third party"); *see* Model Penal Code § 3.05(1)(b)] e.g. **Example:** D assaulted naked man in apartment of D's friend when he found that man fighting with friend; reasonable belief instruction required even if, in fact, friend was not victim but rather the aggressor regarding man sleeping with his wife. [**State v. Beeley,** 653 A.2d 722 (R.I. 1995)]

(1) Rationale

Those supporting this position stress that there is no reason to impose criminal liability upon persons who conducted a reasonable investigation of the circumstances and acted reasonably on their conclusions. Moreover, a contrary rule might well discourage bystanders from rendering aid to those who legitimately and desperately need it. [**State v. Fair,** 211 A.2d 359 (N.J. 1965) (as matter of justice, a defendant should "not be convicted of a crime if he selflessly attempts to protect the victim of an apparently unjustified assault, but how else can we encourage bystanders to go to the aid of another who is being subject to assault?")]

4. Limitation: Force Used Must Be Reasonable

As with self-defense, the defendant must not have used more force than reasonably appeared necessary under the circumstances. Thus, the danger to the person assisted must appear ***immediate,*** and ***only that amount of force reasonably believed necessary*** to eliminate the risk may be exercised. [Model Penal Code § 3.05(1)]

5. No Duty to Retreat

A defendant does not have a duty to retreat before acting in defense of another. However, the person in peril's ability to retreat safely is important in measuring the reasonableness of defendant's actions, *i.e.*, the person in peril must not have had a reasonable possibility of safe retreat. Whether retreat existed is assessed from the perspective of the defendant, who must subjectively believe that the person in peril has no reasonable possibility of safe retreat, The defendant's belief also must be objectively reasonable based on the information available to the defendant at the time that force is used to defend the person in peril. [**State v. Valdez,** 12 N.W.3d 191 (Minn. 2024)]

EXAM TIP

Recall that the use of deadly force is to be discouraged, and its use in defense of others is limited only to cases where it is ***reasonably necessary*** to defend the other person ***against death or serious bodily injury.***

6. Distinguish: Force Used to Prevent Criminal Offense

The circumstances under which the defendant claims to have acted in defense of others may also support the defense of crime prevention. Thus, as will be seen *infra* (p. 161), if the defendant reasonably believes that the person assisted is the victim of a criminal offense, he may have a right to use force to prevent or terminate the commission of a crime.

N. Protection of Property

1. In General

A defendant charged with an assaultive crime may sometimes successfully assert that he reasonably believed his actions were necessary to defend property from wrongful interference.

The right to use force in protection of property, however, is ***much more limited*** than the right to use force in protection of persons, and therefore this defense is quite limited.

a. Deadly Force Not Allowed

A person ***cannot use deadly force*** simply to defend his property against unlawful interference even if there is no other way to prevent the threatened harm. This rule is based on the premise that the interest in security of property does not justify jeopardizing the lives of others (*i.e.,* society places a much higher premium on the preservation of human life than on the protection of property). [**Sydnor v. State,** 776 A.2d 669 (Md. 2001) (even if robbery is not completed until robber reaches place of temporary safety, deadly force during that time "to recover the stolen property" is "excessive")]

b. Distinguish: Other Privileged Use of Force

Deadly force may be justified where the facts also support ***another privileged use*** of force, as where the defendant's reasonable nondeadly force in protection of his property is met with an attack threatening ***imminent serious bodily harm to the defendant.***

EXAM TIP

This issue makes a tricky exam question. For example, the facts may present Escaped Convict, who is known to be armed and dangerous, in the process of breaking into and stealing Owner's valuable antique car. Owner has ***no right*** to defend his car with deadly force, even if it is irreplaceable and his most prized possession. He must call the police or possibly try some other method to prevent the crime, but he cannot pull out his shotgun and fire. On the other hand, if Owner is in the car and Convict threatens him with a large hunting knife, Owner would be justified in defending himself with deadly force. The difference here is that Owner is using deadly force to ***defend himself*** against death or serious bodily injury and is ***not defending his property.*** Defense of property alone generally does not justify use of deadly force. (*But see* "Defense of Dwelling," *infra,* p. 157 *et seq.*)

(1) Defense of Dwelling

The right to use force in defense of one's dwelling may sometimes permit the use of deadly force (*see infra,* p. 157 *et seq.*).

2. Reasonable Nondeadly Force Permissible

Nondeadly force may be used to protect real or personal property in one's lawful possession if the force used reasonably appears necessary to prevent or terminate an unlawful intrusion on or interference with that property.

a. Request to Desist

Some courts hold that force is not reasonable under this rule unless a ***prior request*** has been made for the other to desist from interfering with the property. It is likely, however, that even these courts would hold that no such request need be made where it reasonably appears that doing so would be ***useless,*** dangerous, or otherwise not a viable alternative (*e.g.,* where it would permit the other person to do substantial harm to the property before the request is made). [**Akinbi v. United States,** 321 A.3d 634 (D.C. 2024) (unreasonable for defendant to use any force if the intrusion can be remedied by simply requesting the intruder to desist or by seeking the assistance of police who are on the scene; there is a careful sliding scale of reasonableness to which parties must adhere prior to resorting to forceful means)] e.g. **Example:** Persons initially entered D's premises with D's consent. However, when those persons refused to leave after D told them to do so, the use of nondeadly force in defense of his property was available to D to end those persons' trespass. [**State v. Starke,** 800 N.W.2d 705 (N.D. 2011)]

Note: The Model Penal Code adopts this position. [Model Penal Code § 3.06(3)(a) (request to desist required unless exception applies)]

3. Property in Possession of Another

The traditional rule and many modern rules require that the property defended be in the ***lawful possession*** of the person using the force. Thus, there is generally no right to use force in defense of property in the possession of another (or at least the case law does not clearly establish such a right). [*See*, *e.g.*, Minn.Stat.Ann. § 609.06; **State v. Lilienthal,** 889 N.W.2d 780 (Minn. 2017) (defense of dwelling cannot be raised when "the defendant and the victim reside in the same dwelling")]

a. Distinguish: Model Penal Code Position

The Model Penal Code permits the use of nondeadly force to protect property in the defendant's possession or ***in the possession of another for whose protection the defendant acts.*** [Model Penal Code § 3.06(1)(a)]

4. Use of Force to Regain or Reenter Property

The right to use force to protect property must generally be used ***at or near the time of the initial wrongful intrusion*** upon the property. The common law rule is that one who is illegally dispossessed of property cannot use force to regain it or, in the case of real property, to reenter it.

a. Exception: Hot Pursuit

Nondeadly force can be used to regain property unlawfully taken if the action is taken immediately after the loss of the property or while in "hot pursuit" of the dispossessor. [**State v. Dooley,** 26 S.W. 558 (Mo. 1894)]

b. Model Penal Code Position

The Model Penal Code would expand the exception, permitting the use of force to retake property when the defendant is in ***"hot pursuit" or*** when he reasonably believes the dispossessor has ***no "claim of right" to the property.*** However, if real property is involved, the defendant must show that it would have been an "exceptional hardship" to postpone reentry until a court order was obtained. [Model Penal Code § 3.06(1)(b)(ii)]

5. "Spring Guns" and Similar Devices

Special problems are posed by the use of mechanical devices in the protection of property.

a. Traditional Rule

Traditionally, an injury or killing caused by means of a ***mechanical device*** is justifiable only if the person who set the device would have been justified in inflicting ***the same harm had he actually been present.*** Thus, where a trespasser is killed, the use of such devices is tied to the very restricted right to use deadly force in defense of a dwelling (*see* below). [**State v. Barr,** 39 P. 1080 (Wash. 1895) (spring gun, set to protect empty cabin, killed trespasser trying to enter but not to commit burglary; conviction of murder affirmed, but court intimates that spring gun might be proper to protect an occupied dwelling against burglary)]

EXAM TIP

In these cases, recall the general rule that deadly force is ***not justified*** to defend property, and for such force to be used there must be another privilege. Therefore, even under the traditional rule, either the jurisdiction must allow a defense of dwelling privilege (*see infra,* p. 157 *et seq.*) or there must be a threat to human life before deadly force by a mechanical means would be justified.

b. Model Penal Code Position: Mechanical Devices Never Permissible

The Model Penal Code provides that a mechanical device designed or known to cause death or serious bodily harm is ***never*** permissible. [Model Penal Code § 3.06(5)] Nondeadly mechanical devices, under the Model Penal Code, may justifiably be used to protect one's property, if three requirements are satisfied: 1) the device is not designed to cause or known to create a substantial risk of causing death or serious bodily harm; 2) use of the device is reasonable under the circumstances, as the actor believes them to be; and 3) the device is customarily used for this purpose or that reasonable care is taken to make its use known to probable intruders.

c. Compromise Position: Reasonableness

One court has rejected the traditional position but has also refused to regard spring guns and similar devices as totally impermissible. Apparently, the test is whether the device was reasonable under the circumstances considering, among other things, that if the defendant was personally present he might decide not to use deadly force even if such force was technically permissible under the law. [**People v. Ceballos,** 526 P.2d 241 (Cal. 1974)]

O. Protection of Dwelling

1. In General

When property defended is the defendant's own dwelling, many authorities recognize a somewhat greater right to use force in defense of that property. Although there is considerable dispute as to the scope of the right to use force in this situation, all formulations of this rule sometimes permit the use of even ***deadly force.***

2. Common Law View: Deadly Force in Defense of Dwelling

Under the early common law view, deadly force could be used in defense of one's dwelling if it reasonably appeared necessary to prevent a forcible entry of the dwelling, and a warning had first been given the intruder to desist and not enter. [**State v. Patterson,** 45 Vt. 308 (1873) (discussing English cases indicating that defense of the home that shelters life is as important as defense of life itself)] Modern statutes and court decisions do not contain such a broad rule.

a. No Duty to Retreat

If a jurisdiction requires retreat before the use of deadly force in self-defense or defense of others, this requirement may be inapplicable if the situation also gives rise to the right to use deadly force against one seeking to enter the habitation. [**State v. Carothers,** 594 N.W.2d 897 (Minn. 1999) ("duty to retreat is incompatible with the right to prevent the commission of a felony within one's home.")]

3. Modern Views: Limited Right to Use Deadly Force

Modern courts have limited the right to use deadly force in defense of a dwelling. Some hold that deadly force is permissible only if the defendant reasonably believed the intruder intended to ***commit a felony or to harm someone*** in the dwelling. Others adopt a narrower view, recognizing the use of deadly force only against an entry reasonably believed to be for the purpose of committing a felony. [**State v. Warren,** 794 A.2d 790 (N.H. 2002)]

a. Model Penal Code

The Model Penal Code would require that the defendant believe the intruder is attempting to commit a felony ***and*** either (i) that the intruder has ***used or threatened deadly force,*** or (ii) the use of nondeadly force would expose someone in the dwelling to ***substantial danger of bodily harm.*** [Model Penal Code § 3.06(3)(d)(ii)]

b. Intruder Already Inside Dwelling

Courts are split on whether the right to use deadly force in defense of the dwelling applies only to prevent an entry or whether it can also be used against an intruder who has already accomplished entry. [**State v. Brookshire,** 353 S.W.2d 681 (Mo. 1962) (once intruder had gained entry, rationale for defense of dwelling no longer applies and use of force is governed by other rules such as self-defense); La.Rev.Stat. § 14:20(4)]

c. Statutory Provisions for Protection of Dwellings

Several jurisdictions have enacted provisions that are meant to broaden the right to use force in connection with invasions of the dwelling.

e.g. **Example:** A California statute provides that a defendant is ***presumed*** to have had the reasonable fear of imminent death or serious bodily injury required to trigger self-defense if the defendant: (i) used deadly force within his residence against another not part of the household; (ii) the other unlawfully and forcibly entered the residence; and (iii) the defendant knew or had reason to believe that an unlawful and forcible entry occurred. [Cal. Penal Code § 198.5] Florida's "Stand Your Ground" law is very similar. [*See* Fla.Stat.Ann. § 776.013]

P. Use of Force to Effectuate Arrest

1. In General

Both private citizens and police officers have a right to use force in effecting an arrest and a defense against a criminal prosecution based on force used for this purpose. The scope of the defense may differ depending upon the status in which the defendant acted.

2. Right of Police Officers

Arrests by peace officers are favored over arrests by private parties and thus officers are given the broader defense. Nevertheless, increasing limits have been placed on officers' defense to the use of ***deadly*** force.

a. Traditional Rules

Under traditional rules an officer may use whatever ***nondeadly*** force reasonably appears necessary to make an arrest for a felony or misdemeanor. ***Deadly force*** may be used if the officer ***reasonably believes*** that the suspect committed a ***felony,*** but it is limited to those situations. [**Stinnett v. Virginia,** 55 F.2d 644 (4th Cir. 1932)] Thus, if the officer can apprehend a ***misdemeanor*** suspect only by using a gun (or other deadly instrument), the officer must forgo the arrest and let the suspect escape. [**People v. Klein,** 137 N.E. 145 (Ill. 1922)] Thus, an officer is not justified in shooting at a speeding driver who does not follow his signal to stop. If he aims at the driver, he is guilty of murder when he kills; if he aims at the tires, such criminally negligent conduct could make him guilty of manslaughter for the resulting death to a motorist.

b. Modern View: Deadly Force Limited to "Dangerous" Felonies

Some courts reject the traditional distinction between felonies and misdemeanors and hold that deadly force is only permissible if the officer has reason to believe that the suspect has committed a ***dangerous felony,*** *i.e.,* one involving a risk of physical harm to others, such as murder, manslaughter, kidnapping, rape, or burglary. [**Commonwealth v. Chermansky,** 242 A.2d 237 (Pa. 1968)]

(1) Rationale

There are far more felonies today than there were at common law and many modern felonies are not as "serious" as common law felonies, so the mere fact that a felony is implicated does not establish that the social interest in apprehending a suspect is sufficient to outweigh the potential for harm to innocent parties resulting from the use of deadly force.

(2) Model Penal Code Position

The Model Penal Code follows the modern view and would permit the use of deadly force only where the crime for which the arrest is made involved the use or threatened use of deadly force, or if there was a substantial risk that the subject would cause death or serious bodily injury if the arrest were delayed. [Model Penal Code § 3.07(2)(b)]

(3) Fourth Amendment Requirement

Under the Fourth Amendment, an arrest is constitutionally reasonable only if the arresting officer had "probable cause to believe that the suspect pose[d] a significant threat of death or serious physical injury to the officer or others, and reasonably believed that deadly force was necessary. Use of deadly force in violation of this rule often leads to a ***civil cause of action*** for damages. [**Tennessee v. Garner,** 471 U.S. 1 (1985)] This does not mean that such use of deadly force is a crime; states may absolve the police officer of criminal liability for the use of deadly force if the officer had reason to believe that the suspect committed a felony. Many states, though, have chosen to make it a crime for an officer to use force in violation of this Fourth Amendment rule. The Supreme Court has revisited the issue since *Garner.*

(4) Post-Garner Decisions

In 2007, the Court warned that any case alleging excessive force "must still slosh through the fact bound morass of 'reasonableness.' " [**Scott v. Harris,** 550 U.S. 372 (2007)] A court must balance the interests of the defendant against society's interest in making an arrest. In another case alleging excessive police force, a driver sped away in excess of 100 mph from a traffic violation, prompting police to fire more than a dozen shots to kill the driver and his passenger. The Court extended its reluctance to uphold such civil suits for damages, stating that the driver's "outrageously reckless driving" and the risk to innocent drivers justified the police action in using deadly force to halt the car. [**Plumhoff v. Rickard,** 572 U.S. 765 (2014)] The balancing of interest approach suggests that no bright-line rule exists to decide when deadly force becomes unconstitutionally excessive.

(5) Assessing the Reasonableness of Police Force

Judicial evaluation of force must be objectively reasonable from "the perspective of the reasonable officer at the scene." [**Graham v. Connor,** 490 U.S. 386 (1989)] To assess whether a reasonable officer was in danger immediately prior to a shooting, courts look at the "totality of the circumstances" inquiry, which has no time limit. A court considers earlier facts and circumstances that relate to how a reasonable officer understood and responded to later facts, *i.e.,* why a reasonable officer perceived otherwise ambiguous conduct as either threatening or as innocuous.

(a) How a Reasonable Officer Perceives Facts Before Using Force

A "moment-of-threat" rule is a judicial evaluation about whether a police officer was in danger when a threat resulted in a shooting. For example, this rule may show that a law enforcement officer reasonably believed he was in danger for two seconds prior to shooting a deceased. [**Barnes v. Felix,** 605 U.S. 73 (2025) (the "moment-of-threat" approach improperly narrows to a single moment the required totality-of-circumstances inquiry under Fourth Amendment)]

c. Reasonable Appearance Controls

A police officer is entitled to act on ***reasonable appearances*** in using force to effect an arrest. Thus, as long as the officer reasonably believes the force used is necessary for the arrest, the suspect is guilty of a felony, and if necessary that the felony was a dangerous one, the officer has a defense even if his belief turns out to be wrong. Reasonable appearances, not the ultimate truth, control. [**Bursack v. Davis,** 225 N.W. 738 (Wis. 1929)]

d. Distinguish: Use of Force in Self-Defense

An officer who ***is met with resistance*** in attempting an arrest may well have the right to use force (including deadly force) in his own defense. However, the issue here is one of self-defense and should be carefully distinguished from the right to use force to make an arrest.

3. Right of Private Persons

Arrests by private persons are less favored by the law. Hence the defense available for force used to make a "citizen's arrest" is ***more limited*** than what is available to a peace officer.

a. Reasonable Appearances Not Enough

A private person's defense, unlike that available to a peace officer, does not depend entirely upon the private person's reasonable belief that grounds for the use of force existed. Authorities are generally in agreement that if a private person causes ***death*** in the making of a "citizen's arrest," he has a defense only if a ***felony was in fact committed*** and the ***person killed in fact committed it.*** To some extent, a private person ordinarily acts at his peril in using deadly force to make an arrest. [**Commonwealth v. Chermansky,** *supra*]

(1) Distinguish: Commission of Felony Unnecessary

A defendant does not have to "prove that in fact a felony was committed; it is enough to establish facts from which a jury can find that the defendant had a good-faith, reasonable belief that a felony had been or was being committed" based on "facts and circumstances within the defendant's personal knowledge" [**State v. Johnson,** 930 P.2d 1148 (N.M. 1996)]

(2) Model Penal Code Position

The Model Penal Code takes a somewhat stricter approach regarding deadly force and would give a private citizen using such deadly force to make an arrest ***no defense*** unless the person believes he is assisting a police officer (*see* below). [Model Penal Code § 3.07(2)(b)(ii)]

(3) Distinguish: Where Death Not Caused

Where death is ***not*** caused, the law is less clear. Most likely, courts would protect the citizen (defendant) in his use of force if a felony was in fact committed, the defendant reasonably believed the arrested person committed it, ***and*** the defendant used no more force than reasonably appeared necessary to effect the arrest.

b. Distinguish: Private Person Called to Assist Officer

Where a private person is called upon by a police officer to ***assist*** the officer in making an arrest, the private person has the ***same privilege as the officer.*** This is so because those summoned to assist the police in effecting an arrest are required by law to comply. Accordingly, the private person is protected in such cases if it reasonably appeared that the arrest and force were justified; the suspect's actual innocence will not negate the defense. [**Commonwealth v. Fields,** 183 A. 78 (Pa. 1936)] Because the person summoned cannot delay to inquire into the officer's authority to make the arrest, the person's good faith assistance is justified even if it turns out that the officer exceeded his authority. Model Penal Code § 3.07(4)(a) states that a private person summoned by an officer is justified in using whatever force would be proper if the arrest were lawful, provided that "he does not believe the arrest is unlawful." Many modern codes likewise say it is sufficient the private person did not know or believe the arrest was unlawful.

4. Use of Force to Prevent Escape from Custody

Once a person has been taken into custody, force may be used to prevent his escape if the force could have been used to effectuate the arrest in the first place. [Model Penal Code § 3.07(3)]

Q. Crime Prevention

1. In General

A defendant charged with an assaultive crime may assert in defense that the force was used to prevent the commission of a crime. ***But note:*** Use of force to ***prevent*** the commission of an offense must be distinguished from the use of force to effectuate an arrest (*see supra*).

ALLOWABLE FORCE IN JUSTIFICATION DEFENSES		
DEFENSE	AMOUNT OF FORCE ALLOWED	
	NONDEADLY FORCE	DEADLY FORCE
SELF-DEFENSE	If reasonably necessary to protect self ***from immediate and unlawful harm***	Only if threatened with immediate death or serious bodily injury
DEFENSE OF OTHERS	If ***reasonably*** necessary to protect person	Only if threatened with death or serious bodily injury
DEFENSE OF DWELLING	If ***reasonably*** necessary to ***prevent or end*** unlawful entry	Only if person ***inside*** is threatened or to prevent felony ***inside*** (modern view); some states have expanded further
DEFENSE OF OTHER PROPERTY	If ***reasonably*** necessary to defend property in one's possession	Never
EFFECTUATE ARREST		
– POLICE	If ***reasonably*** necessary to arrest for felony or misdemeanor	Only if ***reasonably*** necessary to arrest felon who threatens human life (modern view)
– PRIVATE PERSON	If felony in fact committed, ***reasonable*** belief that this person committed it, and force limited to no more than ***reasonably*** needed	Only if felony ***actually*** committed and only against person who ***actually*** committed felony
CRIME PREVENTION	If ***reasonably*** necessary to prevent felony or serious breach of peace	Only to prevent or end felony ***risking human life*** (modern view)

2. Common Law Position

At common law, one who reasonably believes that a felony or a misdemeanor amounting to a breach of the peace is being committed or is about to be committed in his presence can use reasonable ***nondeadly force*** to terminate or prevent it. ***Deadly force*** can be used only to avert the perpetration of a ***felony***, not to prevent a misdemeanor.

3. Modern View: Deadly Force Limited to "Dangerous" Felonies

Modern authorities hold that the right to use ***deadly*** force is limited to those situations where the felony involved creates a substantial risk of ***death or serious bodily harm*** to others. *Rationale*: Deadly force is too dangerous to be justified in the prevention of certain felonies that pose no direct danger to others. [**Commonwealth v. Emmons,** 43 A.2d 568 (Pa. 1945) (murder, arson, burglary, rape, kidnapping, or sodomy are atrocious felonies or crimes committed by force)]

4. Model Penal Code Position

The Model Penal Code would authorize the use of ***nondeadly*** force to prevent crimes involving or threatening bodily harm, damage to or loss of property, or a breach of the peace. But ***deadly*** force would be permissible only if the defendant believed that the subject would cause death or serious bodily injury to another unless the crime were prevented, ***and*** the use of deadly force poses ***no substantial risk of injury to third persons.*** [Model Penal Code § 3.07(5)]

R. Public Authority

1. In General

A public officer is authorized to use force and sometimes to take or damage property in carrying out official duties pursuant to a valid statute or court order. If charged with a crime based upon such actions, the officer may assert as a defense that she acted pursuant to her public authority. But the force employed must be ***reasonable*** and may not exceed what is necessary for the proper performance of the duties. [Model Penal Code § 3.03]

e.g. **Example:** A soldier may kill an enemy during battle. But if a soldier intentionally kills a prisoner of war, this would be murder. The force used is unnecessary to the performance of the soldier's duty. [**State v. Gut,** 13 Minn. 341 (1868), *aff'd*, 76 U.S. 35 (1869) (during warfare between the United States and Sioux tribe, the defendant aided in killing a member of the Sioux tribe who was lodged in jail)]

2. Effect of Mistake as to Validity of Authority

While there is authority to the contrary, the better view is that a public officer is protected if she ***reasonably believed*** the statute or process under which she acted was valid. Thus, a showing that the statute or process was in fact invalid will not *per se* preclude reliance on the defense. [Model Penal Code § 3.03(3)]

S. Domestic Authority and Similar Special Relationships

1. In General

Persons with legally designated authority over others have the right to use ***reasonable nondeadly force*** in the performance of their duties. If they are charged with a crime based upon their use of force, they have a defense to liability. [Model Penal Code § 3.08]

2. Parents of Minor Child

Parents may inflict nondeadly force on their minor children for the purpose of achieving discipline and thereby promoting the children's welfare. This right also extends to those *in loco parentis*, such as stepparents, guardians, and even a person living with the child's parent out of matrimony. [*See* **Commonwealth v. Packer,** 39 N.E.3d 753 (Mass.App. 2015) (declining "to adopt a general presumption that stepparents act *in loco parentis*," but concluding such characterization proper here, as "defendant was the child's long-term stepparent who lived full time in the same household" and "there was no evidence that the daughter's biological mother played any ongoing role in her life"); *compare* **Commonwealth**

v. Rosa, 114 N.E.3d 111 (Mass. 2018) (parent's decision to kick minor child was wholly unrelated to purpose of safeguarding or promoting her welfare)]

3. Schoolteachers

Teachers have the right to use reasonable and not excessive nondeadly force to maintain school discipline and promote the child's education. This right is independent of the parents' right to discipline their children and can be exercised whether or not the parents approve. Moreover, the privilege applies to all pupil misconduct affecting school discipline, even if the behavior takes place off the school grounds. The modern view emphasizes the reasonableness of the punishment and its purpose and restricts the amount of force to the equivalent authorized for parents. [Model Penal Code § 3.08(2)]

4. Other Special Relationships

Similar rights belong to captains of vessels and aircraft, wardens and superintendents of institutions, and other persons with authority over others. [Model Penal Code § 3.08(5)–(6)]

Chapter Seven

Preliminary or Inchoate Crimes

CONTENTS	PAGE

Key Exam Issues

Inchoate crimes are favorite topics for examination questions because of the variety of issues posed. On your exam, be sure to consider solicitation whenever you see someone encouraging another to commit or join in the commission of a crime. When the person in question considers committing a crime but decides not to do so, or when the person makes some effort but fails to complete the crime, think of writing about an attempt. And, when there are several participants in a crime or in preparatory discussion or activity, always consider conspiracy issues, even if no other crime is committed.

In regard to these possible inchoate crimes, consider first whether the "elements" can be proved, and if so, second, whether the "defenses" unique to each of those crimes may apply.

When you see possible ***solicitation*** issues, consider:

1. Did the defendant ***sufficiently encourage*** another person to commit a crime of adequate seriousness?
2. If the defendant ***renounced his desire*** that the crime be committed, should this be a defense?

When you see possible ***attempt*** issues, consider:

1. Can the ***elements*** of attempt be proved?
   a. Did the defendant ***intend*** to commit the object crime ***and*** have the ***intent*** necessary for that crime?
   b. Did the defendant ***proceed*** far enough beyond preparation towards the commission of the crime?
2. Are there any ***defenses*** available?
   a. Is this a ***"legal impossibility"*** situation? "Factual impossibility"?
   b. In your jurisdiction, consider whether ***voluntary abandonment*** is a defense? (Usually not.)

In any situation where the facts involve more than one participant, there are almost certain to be ***conspiracy*** issues. Initially, it is very important to separate and discuss separately the persons' liability for the crime of conspiracy itself and, if raised by the facts, their liability under the co-conspirator rule for crimes committed by others.

To determine whether there is ***liability for the conspiracy itself*** ask yourself:

1. Can the ***elements*** be proved?
   a. Was there an ***agreement*** of which the defendant was a member?
   b. Was the ***object*** of the agreement sufficient to make the agreement criminal?
   c. Did the defendant ***intend*** to agree ***and*** to further the object crime?
   d. Is an ***overt act*** required, and, if so, was one committed by any party to the agreement?
2. Are there any ***defenses***?
   a. Has it been shown that the other members of the agreement failed to agree so that there is ***no real agreement***?
   b. Is the agreement one that is not a criminal conspiracy under ***Wharton's Rule*** (the crime necessarily involves two or more people)?
   c. If the object crime was ***impossible*** to attain, might this be a defense? (Usually not.)

d. Is this an unusual jurisdiction in which ***withdrawal*** is a defense? (Usually not.)

As to ***liability for the crimes of co-conspirators,*** discuss:

1. Can the ***elements*** of such liability be shown?
   a. Has another member of the conspiracy ***committed the crime*** at issue?
   b. Was the crime committed in ***furtherance of the objectives*** of the conspiracy?
   c. Was the crime a ***foreseeable result*** of the conspiracy?
2. Are there ***defenses*** to such liability?
   a. Had the conspiracy ***terminated*** before the crime was committed?
   b. Did the defendant ***effectively withdraw*** from the conspiracy before the crime was committed?

A. Solicitation

1. Common Law

At common law in both England and the United States, it is a misdemeanor to ***counsel, incite, or induce another to*** commit or to join in the commission of any offense, whether that offense is a felony or a misdemeanor. [**Rex v. Higgins,** 102 Eng. Rep. 269 (1801); **Denicolis v. State,** 837 A.2d 944 (Md. 2003)]

a. Mens Rea

The common law crime of solicitation apparently requires a showing that the defendant acted volitionally and with the intent or purpose of ***causing the person solicited to commit the crime.*** [**Rex v. Higgins,** *supra*; **People v. Miley,** 158 Cal.App.3d 25 (1984) (defendant's direction to intended killer to kill intended victim's daughters if they were at home when victim was murdered constituted solicitations of daughters' murder, notwithstanding the contingency); *Compare* **Porter v. State,** 166 A.3d 1044 (Md. 2017) (conviction of solicitation improper when the jury found that the defendant "feared imminent danger at the time she solicited" others and thus "cannot be deemed to have solicited them to kill with malice")]

b. Actus Reus

The only act required for the commission of the crime is the ***counseling, inciting, or inducing*** of another to commit the offense. Solicitation is complete upon the performance of this act; it is ***not necessary that the person solicited respond affirmatively.*** Nor need the incitement be directed at a specific person; thus, even a general solicitation addressed to an assembled crowd will suffice. [**Melina v. People,** 161 P.3d 635 (Colo. 2007) (conversations with multiple people about a solicitation may constitute one transaction of solicitation when the conversations provide corroborating evidence of the defendant's intent to persuade another to commit a felony)]

EXAM TIP

An important point to remember is that the crime of solicitation is complete when a person with intent ***counseled, incited, or induced*** another to commit an offense. To be guilty of solicitation, the solicitor does not have to be "successful," *i.e.,* the offense is complete when the defendant intentionally incites or induces; the defendant does not have to actually induce the other person to commit the crime or even form the intent to commit the crime.

2. Modern Statutes

Modern statutes tend to limit the crime to the counseling, incitement, etc., of ***serious*** offenses, *e.g.,* murder, rape, kidnapping, robbery, and to provide a lower penalty for the solicitation than is imposed for the commission of the crime itself, for an attempt to commit it, or perhaps even for a conspiracy to commit it. [*See, e.g.,* N.Y. Penal Law §§ 100.00 *et seq.* (New York's five degrees of solicitation)]

e.g. **Example:** A criminal statute prohibiting an offer to purchase any official ballot is not a "contemporary variant' of "common-law crime of solicitation," because the statute lacked "an element of intention that the solicited crime be accomplished." [**State v. Hirschman,** 379 P.3d 616 (Ore. 2016)]

a. Distinguish: Model Penal Code

The Model Penal Code, however, retains the broader common law formulation, making it a crime to solicit the commission of any offense. Moreover, the Code would make solicitation punishable to the same degree as is authorized for the offense solicited. [Model Penal Code §§ 5.02(1), 5.05(1)]

b. "Encouragement" as Solicitation

Model Penal Code § 5.02(1) also includes the word "encouragement." The Comment describes this term as the most expansive in the section, "and encompasses actors who bolster the fortitude of those who have already decided to commit crime, so long as the encouragement is done with the requisite criminal purpose." [Model Penal Code § 5.02(1), comment]

3. Special Problems in Solicitation

a. Uncommunicated Solicitation

A solicitation is still criminal even if the defendant fails to effectively communicate it to the intended subject (as where an intermediary fails to pass on the message). ***Rationale:*** By engaging in the proscribed act with the requisite intent, the solicitor has manifested his dangerousness and should not escape punishment because of a fortuitous event. [Model Penal Code § 5.02, comment (Tent. Draft No. 10, 1960)]

(1) Note

Some jurisdictions limit the charge in such cases to attempted solicitation. [**United States v. Desposito,** 704 F.3d 221 (2d Cir. 2013) (defendant's repeated efforts to solicit false evidence satisfied attempted solicitation)] However, the Model Penal Code specifically authorizes a conviction for the crime of solicitation itself. [Model Penal Code § 5.02(2)]

b. Defense of Renunciation

It is not clear whether a solicitor may escape liability by demonstrating that he later renounced his intention. The matter has not been definitively resolved by the courts, but many courts refuse to recognize renunciation as a defense to solicitation. [*See, e.g.,* **State v. Lynch,** 125 P.3d 1148 (Mont. 2005) (no renunciation defense available, in absence of legislative action); **State v. Boehm,** 379 N.W.2d 874 (Wis.App. 1985) (renunciation cannot undue what has been done; it has no effect on the elements of solicitation)]

(1) Model Penal Code

The Model Penal Code would recognize a defense of renunciation. It would require, however, the defendant to show that he persuaded the subject not to commit the crime under circumstances manifesting a "complete and voluntary" renunciation of the defendant's criminal purpose. [Model Penal Code § 5.02(3)]

4. Relationship to Other Crimes

a. Distinguish: Accomplice Liability

The solicitor is clearly an "inciter" and is therefore ***liable as a party*** for the crime or attempt if the person solicited actually commits or attempts to commit the crime. However, unlike conspiracy, under which a person may be vicariously liable for a co-conspirator's foreseeable crimes in furtherance of the conspiracy (*see infra,* p. 182 *et seq.*), criminal liability here flows from being deemed to be a party to the crime rather than from being guilty of the crime of solicitation. [*See* **State v. Thoman,** 955 N.W.2d 759 (S.D. 2021) (D asked friend to acquire a gun for him so he could kill the intended victim; solicitation was a preparatory offense while aiding and abetting occurs during the crime's completion)]

b. Distinguish: Conspiracy

Unlike conspiracy (*see infra,* p. 170 *et seq.*), solicitation does not require that any agreement be reached. Thus, although conspiracy may follow solicitation (*i.e.,* when the person solicited agrees to the criminal scheme), if the person solicited ***refuses to enter into a conspiracy or does not respond to the incitement,*** the solicitor is nevertheless liable for the crime of solicitation.

c. Distinguish: Attempt

Unlike solicitation, attempt requires that the defendant have progressed far enough in his criminal scheme to have gone beyond mere preparation (*see infra,* pp. 187–206). Generally, a person who does the bare minimum that suffices for solicitation will not have done enough to be guilty of attempt, but if a person does more than the bare minimum, this may be an attempt. Or, if the person solicited progresses towards the commission of the crime, that person will be guilty of attempt and the solicitor will, because of his incitement, incur liability as a party to that attempt. [**State v. O'Neil,** 782 A.2d 209 (Conn. 2001) (mere solicitation by itself can never be an "attempt"; the inciting or urging, whether by letter or word of mouth, is a mere "solicitation")]

d. "Merger" of Solicitation

One who commits solicitation, and goes on to engage in further conduct constituting a conspiracy, attempt, or completed crime, probably cannot be convicted of both the solicitation and the conspiracy, attempt, or completed crime. This is because the solicitation most likely becomes a "lesser included offense." (This is not "merger" in additional common law sense, because the defendant may be charged and convicted of ***either*** the solicitation or the conspiracy, attempt, or completed crime; *see supra,* p. 22 *et seq.*)

EXAM TIP

Many professors draft exam questions that present facts that could support several crimes, and want you to figure out what crimes the particular defendant may be charged with or convicted of. Depending on the facts, you may find a defendant could be ***charged*** with solicitation, conspiracy, attempt, and as an accomplice to another crime. If so, you should discuss the elements of each crime in light of the facts. But if the question asks you about ***conviction,*** don't forget that solicitation most likely is a lesser included offense of conspiracy (and of attempt and the completed crime) and thus the defendant probably ***cannot be convicted*** of both solicitation and conspiracy (or solicitation and the attempt or the completed crime).

B. Conspiracy

1. In General

Like solicitation and attempt, conspiracy is a preliminary or inchoate crime. However, as will be seen, conspiracies are additionally significant because: (i) the parties to a conspiracy (unlike those who commit attempt) may be convicted of the ***object crime and the conspiracy*** if the conspiracy is carried out; and (ii) the parties may, on the basis of the conspiracy, incur liability for ***crimes committed by other members*** of the venture.

a. Common Law

At common law, it is a misdemeanor for two or more persons ***to agree*** to accomplish ***an unlawful purpose*** or ***a lawful act by unlawful means*** (*e.g.,* excessive force, extortion, etc.). [**Rex v. Jones,** 110 Eng. Rep. 485 (1832)]

b. Modern Statutes

Most American jurisdictions define conspiracy by statute and limit the scope of the crime. For instance, some states require an agreement to commit a ***crime,*** while others specify proscribed unlawful objectives somewhat more narrowly than the common law rule (*see infra,* p. 176).

2. Requirements for Liability for Conspiracy

The crime of conspiracy imposes several requirements for liability:

a. Mens Rea

The *mens rea* required for conspiracy has several aspects, each requiring separate consideration.

(1) Intent to Agree

The defendant must have actually ***intended to agree*** or combine with others. This requirement arises from the need for an agreement.

(2) Intent to Accomplish Objective

The defendant must also have a certain state of mind in regard to the objective of the agreement. Generally, this requirement is stated as one that the defendant must have ***intended to accomplish the objective*** of the conspiracy. [**United States v. United States Gypsum Co.,** 438 U.S. 422 (1978); *see* **People v. Ware,** 520 P.3d 601 (Cal.

2022) (insufficient evidence regarding defendant's intent to participate in conspiracy to commit murder; evidence must show that defendant intended to play some part in achieving the conspirator's unlawful ends; must be something more than knowledge, approval of or acquiescence in the object or the purpose of the conspiracy)] If this is applied literally, it is insufficient that the defendant merely knows he would further that objective; "supplier [is] culpable only if he has 'the purpose of promoting or facilitating' the crime." [**United States v. Blankenship,** 970 F.2d 283 (7th Cir. 1992)] However, there is some question about whether courts in fact enforce the requirement of intent to accomplish the objective. Some courts sometimes construe particular kinds of criminal conspiracies as requiring only proof that the defendant had knowledge that he would further the objective.

e.g. **Example:** The defendant agreed to let members of a drug ring use his trailer for one day to make drugs, in return for payment of $1,000, to be made after the use of the trailer. This was arguably sufficient to show that he desired the manufacture of the drugs to be made during that day, and thus that he was a member of a criminal conspiracy to manufacture those drugs. It was not, however, enough to show that he desired that the members of the drug ring succeed in their overall business; thus, he was not shown to be a member of a bigger conspiracy including other members of the ring who were not involved in this particular day of work. [**United States v. Blankenship,** *supra*]

e.g. **Example:** To satisfy the intent necessary in a prosecution, the defendants need not be shown to have acted with a conscious purpose of producing anticompetitive effects; rather, knowledge of the probable anticompetitive effects of their actions would suffice. A requirement of purpose would be burdensome to the government and would be unnecessary to establish that the conduct was blameworthy. [**United States v. United States Gypsum Co.,** *supra*]

(a) Proof of "Intent": A "Stake in the Venture"

A defendant's intent that the objective be achieved is often proved by showing that the defendant would benefit financially or otherwise from its successful completion. This is sometimes called showing a stake in the venture. In contrast, evidence that the accused would not gain any benefit should the venture succeed suggests that he lacked the requisite intent. [**Direct Sales Co. v. United States,** 319 U.S. 703 (1943) (sufficient evidence of the defendant's intent inferred from the fact that it actively stimulated repeated sales of unlimited quantities of a restricted commodity and thus received profits which it was known could only come from its encouragement of the illegal operation)]

(b) Providing Goods or Services

The major problem in this area arises when conviction is sought upon proof that the defendant merely provided goods or services to others, who then used them for an unlawful purpose. If the defendant had ***knowledge*** that the goods or services would be used for an unlawful purpose, is this enough for liability, or must the defendant have affirmatively ***desired*** that the unlawful objective be accomplished? The answer may turn on the nature of the crime that is the objective of the conspiracy:

1) Objective Is Not Serious Crime

If the crime is not a serious one, a mere showing that the defendant knew he was furthering an illegal purpose by providing the goods or services is probably ***not sufficient.*** [**United States v. Falcone,** 109 F.2d 579 (2d Cir.), *aff'd,* 311 U.S. 205 (1940) (suppliers of sugar, yeast, and cans were not conspirators to crime of operating illicit stills; "in prosecutions for conspiracy . . . his attitude towards the forbidden undertaking must be more positive. It is not enough that he does not forego a normally lawful activity, the fruits of which he knows that others will make an unlawful use; he must in some sense promote their venture himself, make it his own, have a stake in its outcome.")]

2) Objective Is Serious Crime

At least one court has suggested that ***the more serious the crime, the more likely the defendant-supplier will be found a conspirator*** simply upon proof that he had ***knowledge***, *i.e.,* that he was aware of the use to which his goods or services would be put. In such cases, a showing of an affirmative desire that the perpetrators achieve their unlawful objective is probably not crucial. [**People v. Lauria,** 251 Cal. App. 2d 471 (1967) ("a supplier who furnishes equipment which he *knows* will be used to commit a serious crime may be deemed from that knowledge alone to have intended to produce the result. . . . For instance, we think the operator of a telephone answering service with positive knowledge that his service was being used to facilitate the extortion of money, the distribution of heroin, or the passing of counterfeit money, and who continued to furnish the service with knowledge of its use, might be chargeable on knowledge alone with participation in a scheme to extort money, to distribute narcotics, or to pass counterfeit money.")]

(3) Requirement of "Corrupt Motive"

Some courts have suggested that, besides having the intent to agree and the intent to accomplish the objective, the parties must also have a "corrupt motive," *i.e.,* each of the purported conspirators must have known that the objective of their agreement was ***illegal.*** [**People v. Powell,** 63 N.Y. 88 (1875) (defendants prosecuted for conspiracy to violate a statute requiring public officials to advertise for bids before purchasing supplies; defendants asserted their unawareness of the statute; court held in their favor; a conspiracy "must have been entered into with an evil purpose, as distinguished from a purpose to do the act prohibited, in ignorance of the prohibition")] ***But note:*** Most recent decisions reject *Powell*, reasoning that there is no policy reason to require "awareness of the law" in this area of criminal liability. [**United States v. Cohen,** 260 F.3d 68 (2d Cir. 2001) (this court "has long expressed its discontent with the *Powell* doctrine;" court holds "that whatever remains of *Powell* does not apply to this case," where defendant charged with conspiracy to transmit bets in interstate commerce); **State v. Goggin,** 333 P.3d 112 (Idaho 2014) (irrelevant whether defendants were aware of illegality of their objective)]

b. Actus Reus

The *actus reus* of common law conspiracy is the ***entering into of the requisite agreement.*** [**United States v. Shabani,** 513 U.S. 10 (1994)] Modern versions of the crime, however, often imposed an additional requirement of an ***"overt act."***

(1) "Implied" Agreement Sufficient

The agreement need not be an express or formal one but can be ***implied*** from the cooperative actions of the parties. Thus, one who observes unlawful acts taking place and cooperates in their commission becomes a member of an agreement to carry out those acts, even if the participants never formally exchanged express commitments with each other. [**United States v. Henderson,** 107 F.4th 287 (4th Cir. 2024) (underlying agreement need not be formal and may instead be a tacit or mutual understanding); **Goldsberry v. State,** 957 A.2d 1110 (Md.App. 2008) ("essence of a criminal conspiracy is an unlawful agreement. The agreement need not be formal or spoken, provided there is a meeting of the minds reflecting a unity of purpose and design")]

Example: Officer approached X and asked X "for a joint." X turned to Defendant and commented that he did not "know" Officer. Defendant replied, "He looks okay to me." X then sold Officer some heroin. Defendant could be convicted of conspiring with X to sell heroin. A jury could infer from these facts that Defendant was acting pursuant to an earlier agreement or understanding under which he would later be compensated by X for evaluating Officer as a "safe" purchaser. [**United States v. Brown,** 776 F.2d 397 (2d Cir. 1985)]

(2) Connecting One to Existing Agreement

If the existence of a conspiracy is clearly shown, relatively slight evidence will be sufficient to connect a particular defendant with it. [**United States v. Knight,** 416 F.2d 1181 (9th Cir. 1969) (conspiracy to induce aliens to illegally enter the country, the evidence showed scheme by A and B to lure aliens into the country and charge them for transportation; D was found guilty as a co-conspirator simply upon proof that his car was used to transport some of the aliens and that he was present during portions of the unlawful activity)]

Compare: V barely squeezed by D's vehicle parked in an apartment complex driveway, after which "words were exchanged" and then "fists were flying"; women then existed D's vehicle and sprayed V with mace. D's conviction for conspiracy was reversed, because "the record contains no evidence that the actions undertaken by the women who exited the Jeep were pursuant to any form of agreement, spoken or otherwise, between them and D." [**Commonwealth v. Chambers,** 188 A.3d 400 (Pa. 2018)]

(3) Overt Act Requirement

At common law, the crime of conspiracy is complete when the agreement is made, and no act is required beyond the making of that agreement. Many jurisdictions still adhere to the common law rule. Some modern statutes, however, impose an additional requirement of an "overt act." [*See, e.g.,* Cal. Penal Code § 184; 18 U.S.C. § 371] The Model Penal Code requires an overt act except for conspiracies to commit more serious offenses. [Model Penal Code § 5.03(5)]

(a) Rationale for Overt Act Requirement

The crime of conspiracy is complete at the time of the agreement or (in some jurisdictions) at the time of the first overt act in pursuance of the conspiracy by any party. [**Yates v. United States,** 354 U.S. 298 (1957) ("The function of the overt act in a conspiracy prosecution is simply to manifest 'that the conspiracy is at work,' . . . and is neither a project still resting solely in the minds of the conspirators nor a fully completed operation no longer in existence.")] One purpose of the overt act requirement provides an opportunity for those who have agreed on a criminal venture to withdraw from the venture without incurring criminal liability. In jurisdictions with an overt act requirement, the defendant is not punishable if he withdraws before the overt act is committed. [**United States v. Herron,** 825 F.2d 50 (5th Cir. 1987)]

(b) Definition of "Overt Act"

If the agreement has been established but the object has not been attained, virtually any act will satisfy the overt act requirement. The overt act does not have to be a criminal or unlawful act in itself. [**Braverman v. United States,** 317 U.S. 49 (1942)] It may either ***affect the object of the conspiracy*** or have a ***tendency to further*** the objective. The United States Supreme Court regards the overt act as evidence of the conspiracy. [*Compare* **Yates v. United States,** *supra*, *with* **People v. Ramos,** 971 N.E.2d 369 (2012) (overt act is an element of conspiracy)] It need not be a "substantial step" towards the conspirators' objective as is required for attempt. [**State v. Dent,** 869 P.2d 392 (Wash. 1994)]

EXAM TIP

For your exam, remember that the extent of the act toward the commission of the target crime is different for attempt and conspiracy. ***Much less is needed for an "overt act"*** in conspiracy (when an act is even required by the jurisdiction) than for a "substantial step" (or similar concept, depending on the jurisdiction) in attempt (*see infra,* p. 187 *et seq.*).

(c) Discussions as Overt Acts

Conversations among the parties conducted while reaching an agreement probably not sufficient overt acts, because this is simply part of the agreement. [**People v. Olson**, *supra*] But *further* conversations among the conspirators after the agreement is reached may qualify as overt acts. [**United States v. Armone,** 363 F.2d 385 (2d Cir. 1966)]

(d) One Act of One Member Suffices

A single act in pursuit of the unlawful objective by ***any one*** of the members will suffice. When this act is performed, all parties to the agreement become liable for conspiracy. [**People ex rel. Conte v. Flood,** 53 Misc. 2d 109 (N.Y. Sup. 1966)]

(4) Number and Characteristics of Agreements

Traditionally, courts give considerable attention to the number and characteristics of the agreement alleged by the prosecution. This is sometimes difficult, given the complex situations leading to conspiracy prosecutions and the need for the prosecution to plead rather specifically describe the precise agreement it will prove at trial. Situations often fall into one of several basic patterns:

(a) One Agreement with Multiple Unlawful Purposes

If there is only a single agreement, there is only ***one*** criminal conspiracy, regardless of how many crimes the conspirators plan to commit. [**Doolin v. State,** 650 So. 2d 44 (Fla.App. 1995)]

e.g. **Example:** Defendants who plotted the illegal manufacture, transportation, and distribution of liquor in violation of a number of internal revenue laws could be punished for only one conspiracy. The plans to commit the various violations were all part of a ***single agreement,*** and it is the ***agreement*** that constitutes the conspiracy. [**Braverman v. United States,** *supra* ("[T]he precise nature and extent of the conspiracy must be determined by reference to the agreement which embraces and defines its objects. Whether the object of a single agreement is to commit one or many crimes, it is in either case that agreement which constitutes the conspiracy which the statute punishes. The one agreement cannot be taken to be several agreements and hence several conspiracies because it envisages the violation of several statutes rather than one.")]

e.g. **Example:** Defendants were convicted of conspiring to commit mail fraud. There was sufficient evidence that the coconspirators shared a common goal through participation in a telemarketing scheme. There also was sufficient evidence of aiding and abetting the mail fraud where D associated with, participated in and acted in aid of offense. It was not necessary to establish that the D was present when the ultimate crime was committed. [**United States v. Warren,** 986 F.3d 557 (5th Cir. 2021)]

(b) "Chain" Situation: Multiple "Links" Making up One Conspiracy

If a series of overlapping transactions is shown (such as sale and resale of narcotics), the situation will often be construed as involving ***only one*** overall agreement. Each transaction is regarded as a "link" in an overall single "chain" if the parties to each link transaction ***know that other links are involved and have a general interest in the success*** of the overall series of transactions.

e.g. **Example:** A smuggler agreed to import heroin and sell it to a "middleman," and the middleman agreed to resell the heroin to a retailer. While there was no express communication between the retailer and the smuggler, this was a single "chain" conspiracy to import, sell, and possess narcotics; each of the 88 members knew that "the success of [each] was dependent upon the success of the whole." [**United States v. Bruno,** 105 F.2d 921 (2d Cir.), ***rev'd on other grounds,*** 308 U.S. 287 (1939) ("[T]he conspirators at one end of the chain knew that the unlawful business would not, and could not, stop with their buyers; and those at the other end knew that it had not begun with their sellers."); *see* **United States v. Davis,** 826 F.3d 1078 (8th Cir. 2016) ("A buyer who acquires drugs intending to distribute some of them to other persons may be a co-conspirator with the seller in a drug distribution conspiracy")]

1) Distinguish: Independent Links

If those involved in each link transaction are unaware that the other transactions are taking place or know about other transactions but are indifferent as to whether they take place, the situation will be characterized as involving ***multiple*** and ***separate*** conspiracies. The participants in each link transaction are conspirators only with those involved in that particular link transaction. [**United States v. Peoni,** 100 F.2d 401 (2d Cir. 1938) (no conspiracy between D and Z where D sold counterfeit bills to X who resold to Z who passed them on to innocent purchasers because D was indifferent as to whether X passed the bills himself or sold them to a second passer)]

(c) "Wheel" and "Spoke" Situation

A "wheel" or "circle" arrangement is by its nature less likely to support the conclusion that the parties had a community of interest. Where one or more persons (the "hub of a wheel") enter into a number of different transactions with various other persons (the "spokes of the wheel") and the persons in each transaction are unconcerned with other transactions entered into by the "hub," the situation will be characterized as involving a number of ***different conspiracies.*** While the hub is a party to each conspiracy, the members of each spoke are regarded as conspiring only with the hub and the other members of that spoke transaction. [**Kotteakos v. United States,** 328 U.S. 750 (1946) (several companies involved where D made fraudulent loans at different times on behalf of several persons, and each loan was distinct because except for the common figure (D), no conspirator was interested in whether any other's loan went through)]

(d) Modern View: Situations Analyzed Flexibly

Some modern courts have abandoned the traditional concern with whether situations show "wheels and spokes" or "chains and links," and look instead to whether the prosecution has proven generally the sort of conspiracy it alleged in the indictment. [**Commonwealth v. Lynch,** 242 A.3d 339 (Pa. 2020)] The factors usually considered in this connection are: (1) the number of alleged overt acts in common; (2) the overlap in personnel; (3) the time period during which the alleged acts took place; (4) the similarity in the methods of operation; (5) the locations in which the alleged acts took place; (6) the extent to which purported conspiracies share a common objective; and (7) the degree of interdependence needed for the overall operation to succeed.

(5) Conspirator Agrees with "Unknown" Co-Conspirators

The parties to a conspiracy do not need to know the identity of every other member, or even be aware of the number of persons involved. Thus, a particular member will be regarded as having conspired with all those he ***must have known were involved*** in the transaction, whether or not he had specific information about them. [**Blumenthal v. United States,** 332 U.S. 539 (1947)]

(6) Husband-Wife Conspiracies

At common law, a conspiracy could not be formed between a husband and a wife because they were regarded as one person. Although this principle was accepted by early American courts, the current trend clearly rejects it as premised on an artificial concept of the spousal relationship. Thus, spouses can conspire with each other to commit a crime. [**United States v. Dege,** 364 U.S. 51 (1960)]

(7) Conspiracies Among Corporations

A corporation can be a party to a conspiracy, *i.e.*, a corporation can conspire with another corporation or with a natural person. [**United States v. General Motors Corp.,** 121 F.2d 376 (7th Cir. 1941)] But there is *no* criminal conspiracy when the alleged members are only a corporation and one of its agents, or two corporations and one person acting as agent for both. In such situations, only one human actor is involved and so the requisite agreement between two or more persons is lacking. [**United States v. Santa Rita Store Co.,** 113 P. 620 (N.M. 1911)]

c. Objective of the Agreement

The law's view on what objectives of agreements justify making those agreements criminal by means of conspiracy law has undergone considerable change from common law.

(1) Common Law

At common law, the objective of the parties' agreement did not have to be the commission of a crime. Common law conspiracies cover agreements to do things that would not be a crime if done by a single individual, including grossly immoral acts (*e.g.,* procuring a prostitute), acts injurious to the public welfare, and acts obstructing justice. The theory is that while such acts might not be injurious enough to criminalize when attempted by an individual, if committed by combinations they become sufficiently dangerous to warrant making them crimes. [**Rex v. Delaval,** 97 Eng. Rep. 913 (1763)]

(2) Modern Statutes

All modern statutes depart from the common law position. Some limit criminal conspiracies to agreements to commit ***crimes*** [*see, e.g.,* Model Penal Code § 5.03(1)], while others go beyond this, designating other unlawful purposes that will suffice. [*See* Cal. Penal Code § 182(a)(5) (criminalizing conspiracies to "commit any act injurious to the public health, to public morals, or to pervert or obstruct justice, or the due administration of the laws")]

(3) Vagueness Problems

Certain conspiracy statutes may be objectionable on constitutional grounds. The Supreme Court has recognized that some of the broader formulations of conspiracy law may be unconstitutionally ***vague*** because they do not indicate with the required specificity which agreements are criminal. [**Musser v. Utah,** 333 U.S. 95 (1948) (remanding for determination whether Utah statute criminalizing any conspiracy "to commit any act injurious to the public health, to public morals, or to trade or commerce, or for the perversion or obstruction of justice or due administration of the laws" is unconstitutionally vague); **State v. Musser,** 223 P.2d 193 (Utah 1950) (on remand from Supreme Court holding Utah conspiracy statute unconstitutional)]

3. Punishment

At common law, conspiracy is a misdemeanor. Modern statutes, however, vary in the manner punishments are provided. Some impose penalties related to, but less than, the penalties provided for the crime that is the conspiratorial objective. The Model Penal Code would impose the same punishment as is provided for the most serious offense that the parties conspired to commit. [Model Penal Code § 5.05(1)]

4. Conviction for Conspiracy and Completed Crime

At common law, a conspiracy followed by a completed crime merges into the completed crime. This approach no longer applies. Accordingly, defendants who conspire to commit a crime and who then commit it ***can be convicted of both*** conspiracy and the crime committed.

a. Rationale

Persons who commit crimes by joint action are more dangerous than those who commit them individually, because the group formed to commit the crime often continues to commit other offenses. Thus, sound policy dictates that such defendants suffer more severe punishment by conviction for the crime and the conspiracy. [**Pinkerton v. United States,** 328 U.S. 640 (1946)]

EXAM TIP

Recall that conspiracy differs from the other inchoate crimes discussed in this chapter in that the conspiracy defendant can be ***convicted of both*** the conspiracy and the crime committed. That is not the case for solicitation and the crime solicited or attempted and the completed crime; in those cases, the defendant can be convicted of either the inchoate crime ***or*** the crime committed, but not both.

5. Special Problems Applying Conspiracy Law

Application of criminal conspiracy law has given rise to a number of problems. Many of them are a result of taking quite seriously the requirement of an "agreement."

a. Acquittal of Co-Conspirators: No "Agreement"

In some situations, courts traditionally require the acquittal of a defendant charged with conspiracy based on the status of those the prosecution claims are co-conspirators.

(1) Traditional "Plurality" Requirement Approach

Traditionally, a criminal conspiracy requires a bilateral agreement, *i.e.*, an actual criminal ***agreement between at least two persons***. If the facts show that all other claimed co-conspirators except the defendant did not enter into an agreement, the defendant must be acquitted because conceptually there was ***no actual agreement.*** In fact, if one of the situations below is shown to exist after a defendant's conviction for conspiracy, some courts are willing to overturn that conviction. [**Eyman v. Deutsch,** 373 P.2d 716 (Ariz. 1962)]

(a) Acquittal of All Other Co-Conspirators

A defendant cannot be convicted of conspiracy under the plurality requirement approach if ***all other co-conspirators*** have been *acquitted* of conspiracy charges. Acquittal of the defendant is not required if some of the other co-conspirators, but not all, have been acquitted, because an agreement remains possible as long as there is at least one other possible guilty co-conspirator. [**State v. Ros,** 973 A.2d 1148 (R.I. 2009)]

1) Distinguish: Acquittals Regarded as Jury Leniency

Some courts reject this rule, reasoning that acquittal of the co-conspirators is not necessarily based on a conclusion that there was no agreement but may instead reflect the jurors' views that guilty co-conspirators simply deserve a "break." [*See, e.g.,* **United States v. Tyson,** 653 F.3d 192 (3d Cir. 2011)]

2) Note

The fact that the other co-conspirators are ***not apprehended*** does ***not*** prevent the defendant's conviction for conspiracy as long as the prosecution proves that there was an agreement between defendant and the absent parties.

(b) Dismissal of Charges Against Other Conspirators

Courts differ about whether ***dismissal of charges against all other members*** of the conspiracy requires dismissal as to the remaining defendant. Some equate dismissals with acquittals and require acquittal of the remaining defendant, but others reject the analogy and proceed with the prosecution against the remaining alleged conspiracy member. [**Regle v. State,** 264 A.2d 119 (Md. 1970)] The theory justifying this result is that the jury concluded that a conspiracy existed, but had doubts about the identity of one of its participants, or their participation therein, thus necessitating different verdicts.

(c) Showing That All Co-Conspirators Were "Feigning Accomplices"

A defendant cannot be held guilty of conspiracy where *all* the other co-conspirators are shown to have only feigned agreement, as for example where all others were actually police officers or government agents ***pretending a willingness to undertake the crime.*** Some courts even refuse to find a conspiracy where two or more persons enter into an agreement with a police officer who is feigning cooperation and the agreement contemplates that an essential ingredient of the offense is to be performed by the officer. These decisions appear to be based on the theory that because such conspiracies will clearly not be carried out, they do not pose the danger with which the law of conspiracy is concerned. [**People v. Liu,** 46 Cal.App.4th 1119 (Cal. 1996) (may be a conspiracy to murder even though the one person the others believe will carry out the deed is actually a government agent)]

(2) Distinguish: Model Penal Code "Unilateral" Analysis

The Model Penal Code would reach a different result in all the above situations by adopting a "unilateral" approach towards liability for conspiracy. Instead of defining liability as a bilateral agreement "between" the parties, the Penal Code simply requires a "unilateral" agreement ***"by" the defendant.*** Thus, a defendant ***can be convicted*** of conspiring with a person who has been acquitted or with a police officer feigning cooperation because the status of the co-conspirator is irrelevant and the only inquiry is whether the defendant "agreed." [Model Penal Code § 5.03(1); *see* **State v. Heitman,** 629 N.W.2d 542 (Neb. 2001) (per the unilateral approach; "only the defendant need agree with another person; the second party can feign agreement," even where "the party who feigns agreement is a government agent")]

b. Wharton's Rule: No Conspiracy to Commit Concerted Action Crimes

Usually, courts regard a conspiracy and the completed substantive offense that is the objective of the conspiracy as distinct crimes for which a defendant may be prosecuted and punished. However, many courts refuse to find a criminal conspiracy to commit a crime that ***by necessity involves two or more people*** (*e.g.,* sale of contraband). This rule was first articulated by the early treatise author Francis Wharton and is called "Wharton's Rule."

(1) Basic Prohibition

Wharton's Rule prohibits the prosecution of two persons for conspiracy to commit a particular offense when the offense in question can only be committed by at least two persons. In other words, where persons agree to commit an offense that by its definition ***necessarily requires a preliminary agreement*** between the participants, there can be no conviction for conspiracy. [**United States v. Parker,** 554 F.3d 230 (2d Cir. 2009) ("the objective to transfer the drugs from the seller to the buyer cannot serve as the basis for a charge of conspiracy to transfer drugs," as otherwise the legislative "policy to distinguish between transfer of an illegal drug and the acquisition or possession of the drug would be frustrated,")] The classic cases coming within Wharton's Rule are prosecutions for adultery, incest, bigamy, buying and selling contraband, giving and receiving bribes, dueling, and gambling. With those crimes, the parties to the agreement are the only ones who participate in the substantive offense and the immediate consequences of the crime rest primarily on the parties.

(a) Rationale

If the object crime always involves concerted preliminary action, an agreement to commit such crimes involves no socially dangerous behavior beyond what is already necessarily involved in the crime itself. Thus, the special danger of committing a crime by concerted action rather than by a single person's individual action is not presented. Further, the legislature must have taken into account that commission of the crime must have involved concerted action.

(2) Exceptions

Wharton's Rule is mitigated by several traditional exceptions to its general prohibition against conviction for conspiracy.

(a) Agreement Involving More than Essential Participants

The prevailing view is that the Wharton rule does not apply when the number of conspirators exceeds the essential participants in the contemplated crime. ***All the parties*** to the agreement may be convicted of conspiracy, because they have formed a group larger than necessary for the commission of the crime and thus the situation presents dangerous concerted action beyond what it necessarily involved in the crime itself. [**State v. Mendoza,** 889 A.2d 153 (R.I. 2005)]

e.g. **Example:** D conspires with A and B for the commission of adultery by A and B. Adultery necessarily involves an agreement by the two persons to the sexual activity. Because the agreement involves an additional person, it is beyond the scope of Wharton's Rule. Thus, D, A, and B may be convicted of conspiracy.

(b) Objective of Agreement Not Achieved

Some courts apply Wharton's Rule only where the parties have accomplished their objective; *i.e.,* the rule only bars conviction for ***both*** conspiracy and the completed crime. Thus, prosecution for conspiracy to commit adultery is permissible if the co-conspirators did not actually commit adultery or, some courts would say, if the prosecution chooses to ignore the completed adultery and prosecutes only for conspiracy. Other courts, however, criticize this limitation, and many decisions have not recognized it. [*See* **United States v. Morris,** 957 F.2d 1391 (7th Cir. 1992) ("Defendants convicted of crimes to which Wharton's Rule applies may not be punished for both the conspiracy and the completed substantive offense"); **State v. Clason,** 526 N.W.2d 673 (Neb. 1994) (refusal to apply Wharton's Rule where object of conspiracy is not achieved)]

(3) Wharton's Rule as Presumption of Legislative Intent

Wharton's Rule is merely a ***presumption*** that applies in the absence of any legislative intent to the contrary. Thus, if the rule would bar conviction in a given case, but there is also evidence of a legislative intent to impose liability, the legislative intent controls and criminal sanctions may be imposed, [**Iannelli v. United States,** 420 U.S. 770 (1975)]

c. Defenses to Conspiracy

(1) Impossibility of Success: Usually No Defense

Most courts take the view that proof that the parties to a conspiracy could not have accomplished their objective (*i.e.,* impossibility of any kind) is ***no defense***, at common law or under the Model Penal Code. [*see* **United States v. Jimenez Recio,** 537 U.S. 270 (2003) (impossibility does not terminate an existing conspiracy)] A few decisions disagree, however, and some, analogizing to the law of attempt, suggest that "legal," but not "factual," impossibility is a defense (*see infra,* pp. 191–193 for distinction between "legal" and "factual" impossibility). [*Compare* **United States v. Fornia-Castillo,** 408 F.3d 52 (1st Cir. 2005) (legal impossibility no defense) *with* **Ventimiglia v. United States,** 242 F.2d 620 (4th Cir. 1957) (legal impossibility a defense)]

(2) Withdrawal

Whether a defendant charged with conspiracy should have a defense of withdrawal or renunciation has given rise to some dispute in criminal law. In those jurisdictions which have added an overt act requirement by statute, the defendant is not punishable as a member of the conspiracy only if he withdraws before the overt act has been committed. As a practical matter, this is not significantly different from the common law rule.

(a) General Rule: Withdrawal No Defense

The general rule is that a defendant's withdrawal from a criminal conspiracy is ***no defense*** to the crime of conspiracy, no matter when the withdrawal took place or the defendant's motive for withdrawing. Defendants, however, ***are*** responsible for crimes flowing from the conspiracy prior to withdrawal. [**Smith v. United States,** 568 U.S. 106 (2013) (allocating to defendant the burden of proving withdrawal does not violate the Due Process Clause]

EXAM TIP

Remember that a conspiracy is complete upon the ***agreement with requisite intent and, when required, an overt act.*** Because the overt act can be a preparatory act, the conspiracy is usually complete very soon after the agreement. Thus, the defendant is ***guilty of conspiracy*** even if the facts show that she later had second thoughts, told her co-conspirators that she was backing out, warned the police, etc. In most jurisdictions, these actions come too late. (*But note:* Such actions may relieve the defendant of criminal liability for her co-conspirators' acts after this withdrawal (*see infra,* p. 184) but they have no effect on the crime of conspiracy.)

(b) Model Penal Code and Modern Position

The Model Penal Code and modern statutes extend a renunciation defense to a conspirator who proved that she "thwarted the success of the conspiracy under circumstances ***manifesting a complete and voluntary renunciation***" of the criminal purpose. [Model Penal Code § 5.03(6)] "[I]f an individual abandons the agreement, the conspiracy is terminated as to him only if and when he advises those with whom he conspired of his abandonment or he informs the law enforcement authorities of the existence of the conspiracy and of his participation. . . ." [Model Penal Code § 5.03(7)(c); *see* **State v. Wetter,** 35 A.3d 962 (Vt. 2011) (defendant's statements which "evidence a mere change in plans" but "do not tend to show that defendant no longer wanted her husband killed" or "that defendant no longer planned to participate in the crime" are insufficient for renunciation)]

EXAM TIP

Because the modern view allowing withdrawal as a defense to conspiracy requires the defendant to do more than just say, "Count me out," she must renounce the conspiracy by ***doing something that thwarts its success*** (*e.g.*, informing the police who arrive and prevent the crime).

(c) Distinguish: Defense to Crimes of Co-Conspirators

Although withdrawal is ordinarily no defense to the conspiracy itself, it may be a defense to charges against the defendant for crimes committed by other members of the conspiracy. (*See infra,* p. 184.)

6. Liability for Crimes of Co-Conspirators

The significance of conspiracy law is especially great because it not only creates a crime but also makes some persons guilty of crimes committed ***by other persons*** in situations that would not create liability as an accomplice.

a. General Rule of Co-Conspirator Liability

Membership in a conspiracy is sufficient for criminal liability not only as a co-conspirator but also for all specified offenses committed (i) as a reasonably foreseeable result of and (ii) in furtherance of the conspiracy. This rule is often called the *Pinkerton* Rule, after the leading Supreme Court case adopting it as a matter of federal conspiracy law. [**Pinkerton v. United States,** 328 U.S. 640 (1946); *see* **In re State ex rel. A.D.,** 52 A.3d 1024 (N.J. 2012)]

e.g. **Example:** D, an attorney, suggested to an underworld figure, X, that Dentist's house would be a good target for a burglary. D expected to share in the gains of any burglary. A year later, X and his companions robbed Dentist and his family at gunpoint, assaulted Dentist's wife, and when police arrived took Dentist's family hostage. Also, in an escape effort, X injured several police officers. Because D conspired with X to commit burglary, D could be convicted of the robbery and the assault on Dentist's wife, because these crimes were committed in furtherance of the conspiracy and were foreseeable. However, the kidnapping of Dentist's family and the assault on the police officers by X were not the necessary or natural results of the conspiracy and thus were not foreseeable; D could therefore not be convicted of those crimes. [**State v. Stein,** 360 A.2d 347 (N.J. 1976)]

e.g. **Example:** D was indicted both for conspiring with his brother to evade taxes **and** for specific tax evasions committed by his brother while D was in jail. The evidence tended to show that Pinkerton actually played a part in the planning, despite his incarceration. On appeal from the conviction, the Supreme Court affirmed, holding in effect that evidence of direct participation in the commission of the substantive offenses was not necessary, but the specific offenses needed to be reasonably foreseeable as a natural consequence of the unlawful agreement. [**Pinkerton v. United States,** *supra*]

EXAM TIP

A conspirator's liability for the crimes of the other co-conspirators, although broad, is not without limit. Remember that for liability to attach, the crimes committed must be a ***reasonably foreseeable result*** of the conspiracy ***and*** committed ***in furtherance*** of it.

(1) Distinguish: Accomplice Liability

The principle of co-conspirator liability often overlaps with the law of accomplice liability (*see supra,* p. 79 *et seq.*), but there are differences. Co-conspirator liability does not require the intent necessary for accomplice liability. Thus, persons may be liable for the crimes of others under the co-conspirator doctrine even though they would not be liable under the law of accomplice liability.

(2) Criticism of Pinkerton Rule

Opposition to the co-conspirator rule has grown in recent years, *e.g.*, the *Pinkerton* Rule was rejected by the drafters of the Model Penal Code. Critics argue that it extends liability beyond acceptable bounds and imposes liability for mere negligence (because the other crimes must be only "foreseeable"). In other words, the defendant can be convicted for crimes without proof that she had *any* role at all in their commission. [**People v. Torres,** 686 N.Y.S.2d 375 (1999) (rejecting *Pinkerton* Rule)]

(3) Limitations on Co-Conspirator Liability

(a) Just Basis for Liability

One court has limited co-conspirator liability by requiring that the crime not be too far removed or too remote from the objectives of the conspiracy to constitute a just basis for imposing criminal liability on co-conspirators for the crime. [**State v. Bridges,** 628 A.2d 270 (N.J. 1993)]

(b) Due Process Prohibition Against Co-Conspirator Liability Where Connection Is "Slight"

"Due Process constrains the application of *Pinkerton* where the relationship between the defendant and the substantive offense is slight." The defendant "played, at best, a small part in the overall conspiracy" and thus the use of a firearm was "unforeseeable." [**United States v. Castaneda,** 9 F.3d 761 (9th Cir. 1993)]

b. Liability for Crimes Committed Prior to Joining?

Language in some opinions suggests that one who joins an ***already existing conspiracy*** could be held liable for the crimes committed by other members prior to his joining. [*See, e.g.,* **United States v. Grovo,** 826 F.3d 1207 (9th Cir. 2016), quoting **United States v. Knight,** 416 F.2d 1181 (9th Cir. 1969) ("One may join a conspiracy already formed and in existence, and be bound by all that has gone on before in the conspiracy, even if unknown to him.")] But it appears that there have been no actual convictions for such crimes, and in view of the criticism of the rule creating liability for crimes of other conspirators committed ***after*** joining the group (*see* above), it seems very unlikely that any court would permit a conspirator to be convicted of crimes committed ***before*** he entered the scheme.

c. Withdrawal Preventing Liability

If a defendant ***effectively withdraws*** from a criminal conspiracy, he is not liable for crimes ***thereafter*** committed by his former co-conspirators. (He is still be liable for the crime of conspiracy.) There are, however, certain prerequisites to a legally effective withdrawal. [**Loser v. Superior Court,** 78 Cal. App. 2d 30 (1947) (notice is insufficient unless it is given to all other conspirators)]

(1) Communication to All Others

Traditionally, a withdrawal becomes effective ***only if and when it is communicated to all other members*** of the conspiracy. [**Loser v. Superior Court,** *supra*] However, a communicated withdrawal may fail if it does not prevent the other conspirators from carrying out the conspiratorial objective.

(a) Compare: Tendency to Relax Need for Actual Full Communication

Some courts may relax the standard. For example, the Supreme Court has noted that, in some situations, notifying all other members of the group would be an unmanageable task. The Court suggested that affirmative acts inconsistent with the object of the conspiracy and communicated in a manner reasonably calculated to reach co-conspirators would be sufficient. [**United States v. United States Gypsum Co.,** *supra*]

(2) Timeliness

Some courts require that a withdrawal be "timely," *i.e.*, ***in time for the remaining co-conspirators to follow the defendant's example*** and stop the activity. [**Commonwealth v. Chhim,** 851 N.E.2d 422 (Mass. 2006)]

(3) Prevention of Target Crime

At least one court has required that a defendant seeking to withdraw from a conspiracy must ***affirmatively and successfully*** persuade his co-conspirators not to pursue the conspiracy any further. [*See* **Eldredge v. United States,** 62 F.2d 449 (10th Cir. 1932)] Most decisions, however, have imposed no such limitation. Note that repudiating prior aid or attempting to do everything possible to repudiate could still fall short of reversing a chain of events that is unstoppable. [**Commonwealth v. Chhim**, *supra*]

EXAM TIP

Note the difference between an effective withdrawal as a defense to conspiracy and an effective withdrawal as a defense to later crimes of co-conspirators. As indicated *supra*, withdrawal generally ***is not a defense to the crime of conspiracy.*** However, an effective withdrawal may prevent liability for crimes committed ***by other co-conspirators after the defendant has withdrawn.*** Thus, in answering an exam question that raises the issue of withdrawal, be sure to distinguish between its use as a defense to the conspiracy itself and as a defense to later crimes. Also be sure that the withdrawal is effective, *i.e.*, it is ***communicated*** in some way to ***all conspirators*** (if feasible) ***in time*** for them to abandon the plan.

7. Duration of the Conspiracy

A conspirator is liable for the crimes of his co-conspirators that are committed during (in furtherance of) the conspiracy. Therefore, it is important to determine when the conspiracy ends. The determination of when a conspiracy ends frequently affects various procedural matters, such as a relevant statute of limitations and the admissibility of the acts and declarations of one co-conspirator against the others.

a. General Rule: Completion of Conspiratorial Purpose

Ordinarily, the conspiracy ends once ***all objectives*** of the agreement are accomplished successfully. However, the agreement might include objectives other than perpetration of the target crime, *e.g.,* division of the proceeds as part of a conspiracy to commit theft, burglary, or robbery. If so, the conspiracy terminates only on fulfillment (or abandonment) of the economic benefits. [*See, e.g.,* **United States v. LaSpina,** 299 F.3d 165 (2d Cir. 2002)]

e.g. **Example:** Because the conspiracy was to provide D's boyfriend with access to a gun that he otherwise was prohibited from possessing, the objective was not completed on the date that his access began. It continued as long as D allowed her boyfriend to possess her gun. [**Commonwealth v. Gross,** 101 A.3d 28 (Pa. 2014)]

b. Are Efforts to Conceal an Offense Within the Scope of the Conspiracy?

In defining the point at which a conspiracy terminates, a major issue may arise as to whether acts to conceal commission of the substantive offense are within the scope of the conspiratorial agreement. A conspiracy containing an agreement to conceal the offense might well last long beyond completion of the offense involved. However, because most offenders attempt to conceal the fact that they have committed a crime, courts have held that evidence of overt acts of concealment is ***not sufficient*** to make the act of concealment part of the conspiracy. In order to regard concealment of the crime as part of the conspiracy, there must be ***direct evidence*** that the parties ***specifically agreed,*** prior to commission of the crime, that they would act together to cover it up or otherwise conceal it. [**Grunewald v. United States,** 353 U.S. 391 (1957); **State v. Twiggs,** 187 A.3d 123 (N.J. 2018)]

8. Tactical Advantages for Prosecution

Conspiracy law may provide the prosecution with a number of tactical advantages. Whether these advantages are justified is subject to dispute.

a. Flexibility

The looseness and pliability of conspiracy doctrine provides the prosecutor with substantial flexibility concerning the sort of conduct by the defendant that needs to be proved. From defendants' perspective, effective preparation for trial becomes more difficult.

b. Increased Punishment

By charging a defendant with both a completed substantive crime and a conspiracy to commit that crime, as well as crimes committed by co-conspirators, the prosecution can greatly increase the penalty to which a defendant may be subjected upon conviction.

c. Choice of Venue

Because venue in a conspiracy prosecution lies anywhere an overt act was committed, the prosecution can often select from a broad range of places to try the case, thereby making a conviction more likely.

d. Hearsay Exception

Because statements by conspirators are admissible against their co-conspirators (*see* Evidence Summary), a showing of a conspiracy often increases the evidence that can be used against a defendant.

e. Complex Joint Trials

Alleged co-conspirators are often tried together, and the evidence used is often extensive and complex. From the prosecution's perspective, this may enable the prosecution to make a more effective case against all defendants. From the defendants' perspective, this creates the risk that juries may find "guilt by association" rather than objectively evaluating the sufficiency of the evidence against each defendant. [*See* **Krulewitch v. United States,** 336 U.S. 440 (1949) (Jackson, J., concurring)]

C. Attempt

1. In General

At common law, it is a crime to attempt the commission of ***any felony or misdemeanor.*** [**Rex v. Scofield,** Caldecott 397 (1784)] Most modern statutes continue this approach. [Model Penal Code § 5.01] Attempt, like most crimes, requires proof of certain conduct, *i.e.*, a ***sufficient step*** towards the attempted crime and the requisite ***intent.***

2. Policy Considerations in Formulating the Law of Attempt

The basic principle that the criminal law does not impose liability for bad thoughts alone (*see supra,* p. 29) applies no less to attempt than it does to all other crimes. The law on attempts is dangerously close to punishing for mere intent, and the requirements for an attempt should provide reasonable assurance that those convicted are persons who would commit the target crime if left alone. Such a result can be achieved by a strict intent requirement and an approach to the act requirement that focuses on whether the defendant's conduct confirms both moral culpability and dangerousness regarding an actual willingness to commit the crime.

3. Elements of Attempt

Attempt consists of a ***specific intent*** to commit a crime and an ***act in furtherance*** of that intent that goes far enough towards completion of the crime.

a. Mens Rea

The *mens rea* of attempt has two components: (i) the intent to commit the acts or cause the result constituting the target crime; and (ii) the intent necessary for the target crime. [**People v. Matthews,** 258 N.E.2d 378 (Ill.App. 1970)] If the charge is attempted theft and theft is defined as requiring an intent to permanently deprive the owner of his property, that same intent must be established to prove the attempt. It is not enough to show that the defendant intended to do some unspecified criminal act.

e.g. **Example:** D decided to borrow V's car without V's consent for a few hours, after which he would return it. D approached the car but was apprehended as he touched the door handle. D is not guilty of attempted larceny. Attempted larceny requires both the intent to commit the ***acts constituting larceny*** (*i.e.,* wrongful taking and carrying away of the personal property of another) and the intent necessary for larceny (*i.e.,* intent to ***permanently deprive*** the owner of the property). D had the first component of this mental state, because he did intend to take and move V's car. But because he intended to return the car, he did not have the second component, the intent to permanently deprive V of the property.

EXAM TIP

Don't forget that attempt requires a specific intent even if the crime attempted does not. Thus, in the example above, if V had died, D would have been guilty of murder because awareness of a high risk of death is sufficient to show the *mens rea* for murder. But that mental state is not enough for ***attempted murder; attempted murder always requires the intent to kill.***

(1) No Attempt to Commit Crimes Requiring Nonintentional Result

If a crime requires a result and a mental state less than "intent" regarding that result, most courts hold that there is no crime of attempted commission of that offense. For example, suppose the completed crime consists of recklessly or negligently causing a certain result. If there were an intent to cause such a result, the attempt would not be to commit that reckless or negligent crime, but rather the greater crime of intentionally causing such a result. [**State v. Louis,** 384 P.3d 1 (Kan. 2016) ("attempted involuntary manslaughter is not a recognized criminal offense.")]

e.g. **Example:** D drove recklessly and nearly struck a police officer. It is an offense to recklessly cause injury to a police officer. D could not be convicted for attempted reckless injury to a police officer because the object crime required proof of a result (injury to a peace officer) and a mental state less than intent (recklessness). [**State v. Hemmer,** 531 N.W.2d 559 (Neb. 1995)]

(2) Strict Liability Crimes

Because intent is required for an attempt, there is no such thing as a strict liability attempt. Even if a completed strict liability crime may be committed without intent, knowledge, recklessness or negligence, the same is not true of an attempt to commit that crime. An attempt to commit a strict liability offense is possible only if it is shown that the defendant acted with an intent to cause the prohibited result. [**Gardner v. Akeroyd,** [1952] 2 Q.B. 743]

b. Actus Reus

The *actus reus* of attempt is an act that ***progresses sufficiently towards the commission*** of the offense or at least sufficiently beyond the mere intent to commit it. Traditionally, courts have applied a number of approaches to determine whether a defendant has done enough in furtherance of his intent to have committed attempt. One approach, the Model Penal Code approach, is gaining increasing acceptance among legislatures and the courts.

e.g. **Example:** D plots to shoot up and blow up his high school, shown by drawings and diagrams and death note, recruiting friend to assist and sharing with him information on how to make pipe bombs. The crime is not to occur for several months on the anniversary of a well-known massacre at another school. [*Compare* **B.T.E. v. State,** 108 N.E.3d 322 (Ind. 2018) (qualifies as an attempted aggravated battery, because corroboration of D's intent, the severity of offense that justified drawing an "early line," D might have opted for earlier date); *with* **State v. Sawyer,** 187 A.3d 377 (Vt. 2018) (insufficient evidence to establish attempt under state law; an attempt "requires an intent to commit a crime, coupled with an act that, but for an interruption, would result in the completion of a crime;" "the defendant undertook no act that was the 'commencement of the consummation' of the crime" he was charged with.)] "Commencement of the consummation" typically is associated with the physical proximity test.

e.g. **Example:** D was 25 feet away from bank that he intended to rob; The only actions left for him "were to put on the beard and mustache [disguise], walk into the bank and up to the counter and demand money." Because armed robbery is a serious offense, the defendant possessed "all the necessary materials," and "defendant was armed with a pellet gun that could cause serious injury," he is guilty of attempted bank robbery. [**Commonwealth v. McWilliams,** 45 N.E.3d 94 (Mass. 2016)]

(1) Act of "Perpetration" Rather than "Preparation"

Traditionally, courts have said that the defendant must have gone ***beyond mere "preparation"*** into the area of "perpetration." However, because there is much confusion as to when preparation ends and perpetration begins, this formulation is not particularly useful. [**State v. Wilson,** 895 S.E.2d 355 (N.C. 2023) ("if an individual intends to commit a crime and performs an overt act beyond mere preparation for that purpose but falls short of completing the criminal offense, he is guilty of attempting the crime.")]

(2) Last Proximate Act

An early case intimated that, for completion of an attempt, the defendant must have committed the "last proximate act" before the completion of the crime. [**Regina v. Eagleton,** 6 Cox Crim. Cas. 559 (1855)] This strict approach has been ***universally rejected;*** all jurisdictions agree that the defendant need not have come so close to completion of the crime. [**People v. Mahboubian,** 543 N.E.2d 34 (N.Y. 1989) ("the fact that defendants had not yet taken the final step necessary to obtain [fruits of the theft] does not mean that the steps they had taken could not constitute an attempt to do so;" defendant hired the burglars, provided them with the tools, and induced them to break into warehouse)]

(3) Control over All Indispensable Elements

Some courts may require that the defendant have gone far enough to have obtained control over all factors that are indispensable to the commission of the crime. Thus, ***nothing must be left undone*** that would prevent the defendant from committing the crime; a simple example would be that a person cannot attempt an assault with a deadly weapon until he acquires the weapon. [*See, e.g.,* **State v. Fielder,** 109 S.W. 580 (Mo. 1908) (no attempt to vote illegally until D obtains ballot)]

(4) Physical Proximity Test

Some courts have suggested that the defendant's conduct must be physically proximate to the intended crime. The emphasis is not so much upon what the defendant has done as upon what remains to be done; the seriousness of the crime, the uncertainty of the result, and the time and place at which the intended crime is supposed to occur take on considerable importance. [**State v. Melton,** 821 S.E.2d 424 (N.C. 2018) (no attempted murder occurs when the defendant provided details about the victim to the hired killer and provided partial payment); **People v. Garton,** 412 P.3d 315 (Cal. 2018) (acts within state to commit out-of-state murder, including leading car with weapons and driving toward state line with intent to murder victim in Oregon next day, was insufficient to satisfy overt act element of attempt; defendant was in no "close proximity" to victim)]

(5) "Probable Desistance" Test

A few courts have found an attempt only where the act, in the ordinary course of events, would lead to completion of the crime in the absence of intervening outside factors. The emphasis is on the ***likelihood that the defendant would cease efforts to commit the crime,*** given the conduct he has already committed. [**Hernandez-Cruz v. Holder,** 651 F.3d 1094 (9th Cir. 2011)]

(6) "Equivocality" or "Res Ipsa Loquitur" Test

One variation of the attempt criteria provides that an act amounts to attempt only if the act, when ***considered alone***, firmly ***shows the actor's intent to commit the crime.*** Hence, the defendant's behavior is considered without reference to other evidence that may demonstrate criminal intent (such as a confession). The ***act constituting attempt must "speak for itself"*** in establishing intent. [*See*, *e.g.*, Wis.Stat.Ann. § 939.32(3) (defendant's acts must "demonstrate unequivocally under all the circumstances that the [defendant] formed that intent")]

(7) Model Penal Code: "Substantial Step Strongly Corroborative" of Intent

The Model Penal Code requires (i) "an act or omission constituting a ***substantial step*** in a course of conduct planned to culminate in the [defendant's] commission of the crime," and (ii) the act does not constitute a substantial step "unless it is ***strongly corroborative*** of the [defendant's] criminal purpose." [Model Penal Code § 5.01(2)] The MPC emphasis is upon what the defendant has already done instead of what remains to be done. *See*, *e.g.*, [**State v. Daniel B.,** 201 A.3d 989 (Conn. 2019) (while "consideration of what the actor has left to do is not completely irrelevant," the "main focus . . . will be on what the defendant 'has already done.' ")] The Model Penal Code's approach is gaining increasing acceptance in courts and legislatures.

e.g. **Example:** Given the MPC emphasis "on what the actor had already done," a substantial step toward intended for a "mass shooting" was established by defendant's "purchase of assault rifles and ammunition, together with extensive target practice." [**State v. Lammers,** 479 S.W.3d 624 (Mo. 2016)]

e.g. **Example:** D's attempted prison escape was supported by collecting the necessary items to create a dummy, fabricate the dummy, and then place the dummy in his bed. [**People v. Bell,** 145 N.E.3d 740 (Ill.App. 2020)]

(a) List of Potentially Sufficient Acts

The Model Penal Code lists several categories of conduct that are sufficient as a matter of law if they are strongly corroborative of the defendant's purpose. [*See*, *e.g.*, **United States v. Washington,** 653 F.3d 1251 (10th Cir. 2011) (defendant guilty of attempted murder; while traveling to city where planned murder was to occur had pair of latex gloves that are used to hide fingerprints)] The list shows how the MPC defines an attempt differently from the foregoing standards. If the prosecution proves such conduct, it is entitled to a jury instruction about whether the defendant progressed far enough toward commission of the crime. These acts include:

(i) ***Lying in wait, searching for, or following*** the contemplated victim of the crime,

(ii) ***Enticing or seeking to entice the contemplated victim of the crime to go to the place*** where the crime is to be committed,

(iii) ***Reconnoitering the place*** where the crime is to be committed,

(iv) ***Unlawfully entering a structure, vehicle, or enclosure*** in which the crime is to be committed,

(v) ***Possessing materials to be employed in the commission of the crime,*** if those materials are ***specially designed*** for the unlawful use or serve no lawful purpose of the defendant,

(vi) ***Possessing, collecting, or fabricating materials to be used in the commission of the crime at or near the place*** at which the crime is to be committed, where this serves no lawful purpose of the defendant, and

(vii) ***Soliciting an innocent agent*** to engage in conduct constituting the crime and a willingness to commit the crime.

[Model Penal Code § 5.01(2)]

EXAM TIP

As indicated in the discussion of conspiracy, *supra*, ***the act required for attempt is much more substantial*** than the overt act sometimes required for conspiracy. When an overt act for conspiracy is required by the jurisdiction, it need only be an act that in some general sense is in furtherance of the conspiracy. This act can be a fairly minor step towards the object of the conspiracy. Attempt, on the other hand, ***always requires an act that progresses significantly towards*** the intended crime. Thus, conspiracy can be completed by an act that would not be enough for attempt under any of the above tests for attempt.

(b) Failure to Identify Specific Victim or Target

Some courts hold that a defendant's failure to identify the specific victim or target of the intended crime means that the defendant has not gone far enough for attempt. [**People v. Oduwole,** 985 N.E.2d 316 (Ill.App. 2013) (no attempt of terrorist threat where paper contained alleged threats found hidden in defendant's car and there was no evidence defendant "had identified a particular audience for his communications")]

e.g. **Example:** Smith took a train to the city of the robbery and then took a taxi to a neighborhood and instructed the driver to drive around to look for a Mexican jewelry store Smith intended to rob. He failed find it. Smith is not guilty of attempted robbery, even under the Model Penal Code approach. Because Smith had not identified the store to be robbed, his actions could not be regarded as reconnoitering the place where the crime is to be committed. [**People v. Smith,** 593 N.E.2d 533 (Ill. 1992)]

4. Defenses to Attempt

a. Impossibility

Sometimes a defendant believes he can successfully commit a crime but, for reasons unknown to him, its commission is in fact impossible. In that case, conduct that would be sufficient for attempt may not constitute the offense of attempt because of the impossibility. Thus, a "defense" of impossibility may be applicable to attempt.

(1) Policy Considerations

Ideally, a defense of impossibility would apply in those situations where despite having done enough with the required *mens rea*, the defendant lacks either the blameworthiness or the dangerousness to justify criminal liability. Whether a defense can be formulated that provides for acquittal of such attempt defendants, and only those defendants, is at best doubtful.

(2) Traditional Rule: Only "Legal" Impossibility Is Defense

The traditional rule is that "legal" impossibility, but not factual impossibility, is a defense to attempt. [**People v. Dlugash,** 41 N.Y.2d 725 (1977) (whether shooting a corpse could be attempted murder; if the circumstances had been as D believed them to be (that V was alive when D shot V); legal impossibility was a defense to committing attempted murder of V; D is guilty of attempted murder)] The major difficulty in applying this rule is distinguishing legal from factual impossibility. Some courts have abolished legal impossibility as a defense to an attempt charge. [*See, e.g.*, **State v. Curtis,** 603 A.2d 356 (Vt. 1991)]

(a) "True" Legal Impossibility

Sometimes a defendant sets out to do things (or to cause a particular result) that he believes would, if completed, constitute a crime but which were not in fact made criminal by the law. The person's only ***misunderstanding*** concerns the ***"law":*** He mistakenly believes that the law makes it is a crime to do what he sets out to do. Such a person has not demonstrated a willingness to do things actually prohibited by the law, and thus has not shown actual dangerousness. This situation involves clear ***legal impossibility,*** and the defendant has a ***defense*** to a charge of attempt.

e.g. **Example:** D sets out on November 3 to shoot a deer that day and does kill one. D believes that killing a deer in November is a crime. In fact, it is a crime to hunt deer in December but not in November. D is obviously not guilty of killing a deer out of season. Nor is D guilty of an attempt to commit this crime. Under the law as D thought it to be, he was illegally killing a deer in November, but that is not a crime. D believes this would be a crime, but this mistake ***as to what the law provides*** does not create criminal liability.

e.g. **Example:** D cannot be convicted of Attempted Receipt of Stolen Property, because the coat he was charged with stealing had lost its status as "stolen" after police had recovered the coat. The justification for allowing legal impossibility as a defense is that D should not be punished just for having a criminal mind. A prosecutor would argue that D didn't merely have a thought, because he turned his thought into a substantial step toward committing a crime. If D believed that he was committing a crime but the law does not prohibit D's conduct, there is no attempt liability.

EXAM TIP

One way to keep "true" legal impossibility straight in your mind is to think of it as being the flip side of the "ignorance of the law is no defense" axiom. One who commits a statutorily prohibited act may be convicted of a crime despite the fact that he may have not realized his act was prohibited. Conversely, one who commits an act that is ***not*** statutorily prohibited (***assuming there isn't a factual mistake concerning attendant circumstances***) is not guilty of a crime, despite the fact that he may have believed his acts were prohibited.

(b) Factual Impossibility

Sometimes a defendant sets out to do things (or to cause a particular result) that would, if completed, constitute a crime, but because of factors of which he is unaware, there is ***no chance he will succeed*** in doing these things or causing the result. Because his actions demonstrate his dangerousness and culpability, this ***factual impossibility*** of committing the crime is universally ***rejected as a defense*** to a charge of attempt. [**People v. Fiegelman,** 33 Cal. App. 2d 100 (1939)]

Example: D reaches into V's purse intending to steal money that D believes is in the purse. D does not know that V has taken the money out of her purse. It is thus impossible for D to take the money. Under the facts as D thought them to be, he believed that he was about carry out his intent to steal V's money. D is guilty of attempted larceny of the empty purse, because this is only factual impossibility.

(c) "Mixed" Legal and Factual Impossibility: Mistake as to Surrounding Circumstances

In other situations, the defendant has set out to do things (or cause results) believing that this would be a crime. In fact, however, because he misunderstands the surrounding circumstances, his conduct, if completed, would ***not actually constitute a crime,*** but if the circumstances were as he believes them to be, his intended conduct ***would*** constitute a crime. Whether such a person had adequately demonstrated sufficient blameworthiness and dangerousness to justify convicting him of a crime is a difficult question. Courts have consequently divided on whether defendants in such "mixed" factual and legal impossibility situations are guilty of attempt.

1) Traditional Rule: Defense

The traditional rule, however, is that in a mixed situation the crime of attempt has not been committed, *i.e.,* that a defense of impossibility ***is available.*** [**People v. Jaffe,** 78 N.E. 169 (N.Y. 1906)]

Example: D receives some property from X. D believes that X stole this property. D thus thinks that he is committing the offense of receipt of stolen property. In fact, X had permission of the owner in an effort to apprehend D in possession of stolen property. Because the property is not actually stolen property, D has not, by taking possession of it, committed the crime of receipt of stolen property. Whether D is guilty of ***attempted*** receipt of stolen property is less clear. D was not mistaken with regard to a pure matter of "law," but rather with regard to the circumstances, *i.e.,* whether the property was still unrecovered by authorities and thus still "stolen." Under the traditional approach, D has a defense of impossibility.

2) Modern View: No Defense

Most courts today, often applying statutes based to some extent on the Model Penal Code (*see* below), hold that a defendant in this situation has no defense to attempt.

Example: D was shown to have shot a gun into V's dead body. The prosecution claimed that D thought V was still alive and intended to kill him; D maintained that he knew V was dead. If the prosecution proves that D thought V was still alive, D can be convicted of attempted murder even though it was impossible for D to commit murder by shooting at V's dead body. If the circumstances had been as he believed them to be, *i.e.*, if the object had been a live person, D's conduct in shooting would have been murder. Thus, D would have no defense to attempt under the prosecution's version. (*Note:* If D's version of the facts is believed, he cannot be convicted of attempt because he lacked the *mens rea* required, *i.e.*, the intent to kill.) [**People v. Dlugash,** *supra*]

e.g. **Example:** In an exchange of messages in a Web chat room, D arranged to meet V at a motel for sexual activity. D believed that V is 13 years old. When D went to the motel, he found out that V is a 38-year-old sex crimes detective. Charged with attempted child molestation, D has no defense of impossibility. V's actual age made commission of child molestation by sexual activity with V impossible for D. However, D's mistake here was as to a factual circumstance, *i.e.*, the age of V. Because the impossibility constitutes factual impossibility, it is not a defense to attempt.

(d) Model Penal Code Position: Only "True Legal Impossibility" Precludes Liability

The Model Penal Code and some modern statutes and decisions purport to reject any impossibility defense as defined above. They define the crime of attempt as consisting of behavior that would constitute a crime (or a substantial step towards commission of a crime) ***if the circumstances were as the defendant believed them to be.*** [Model Penal Code § 5.01(1)] What would be "true legal impossibility" under traditional legal analysis (*see* above) would probably still require acquittal, however, because in those situations even if all the factual circumstances were as the defendant believed them to be, his actions would not constitute a crime or be a substantial step towards a crime; this would be the case only if the criminal law were as the defendant believed it to be.

(e) "Inherent" or "Obvious" Impossibility

In a few very unusual situations, it has been held that an attempt is not criminal if it is ***blatantly obvious*** that the defendant's chosen method of committing the crime could not result in the completion of the crime. [**Attorney General v. Sillem,** 159 Eng. Rep. 178 (1863)]

e.g. **Example:** D sticks pins in a doll representing V, believing that D's voodoo powers will enable her to cause V's death in this manner. Because of her obvious inability to accomplish her intended result, D is not guilty of criminal attempt. [**Attorney General v. Sillem,** *supra*]

EXAM TIP

To summarize, ***only true legal impossibility*** is a sure-fire defense to attempt. Thus, when an exam question raises impossibility:

(i) Consider first whether the defendant *misunderstood the law* and mistakenly thought the law made what he intended to do a crime. If so, this is legal impossibility and he *has an impossibility defense*.

(ii) Next, consider whether the defendant mistakenly believed he could ***do the things or cause the result*** constituting the crime. If so, the situation involved factual impossibility and he has ***no impossibility defense***.

(iii) Finally, consider whether the defendant mistakenly believed the ***surrounding circumstances*** were such as to make his intended actions a crime. If so, the majority of (but not all) courts will say this is also factual impossibility, and that he has no impossibility defense.

b. "Withdrawal" or Abandonment

If the defendant has, with the requisite intent, proceeded far enough in a criminal plan to constitute attempt (*i.e.*, he has taken a substantial step), may he escape liability by abandoning his scheme?

(1) Policy Considerations

Those opposed to a defense of voluntary abandonment reason that the defendant has demonstrated his dangerousness and culpability by having completed an attempt. They also emphasize the ease with which a defense of abandonment could be falsified, and believe that the small chance of acquittal would not motivate many persons to abandon their efforts to commit crimes. [**United States v. Young,** 613 F.3d 735 (8th Cir. 2010) ("a defendant cannot abandon an attempt once it has been completed")]

On the other hand, those in favor of such a defense argue that a truly voluntary abandonment (*e.g.,* change of heart ***not*** motivated by changed circumstances that make the crime more difficult) would seldom be found. In those few cases where the defense would be successful, the evidence would show that the defendant is not presently culpable or dangerous. Moreover, the law should provide an incentive for abandonment, thereby encouraging the actor to desist from his criminal plan. [Model Penal Code § 5.01, comment (Tent. Draft No. 10, 1960)]

(2) Traditional Rule: Even "Voluntary" Abandonment Is No Defense

The traditional common law rule is that abandonment is ***never a defense,*** regardless of how voluntary it might be. However, the cases in point are usually ones in which there is little credible evidence that the abandonment was truly voluntary and not based on increased difficulty or risk. Courts may examine withdrawal for individuals differently from a withdrawal when a conspiracy includes corporations.

e.g. **Example:** D and accomplices intended to rob a gas station with masks and guns in hand, but after finding the station busy with customers at 2:00 a.m., they changed their plan instead to rob the station's back office; no abandonment of the robbery attempt occurred; abandonment must be voluntary due to outside causes. [**Jones v. State,** 87 N.E.3d 450 (Ind. 2017) (when D and accomplices "saw how busy the store was, . . . [they] altered their criminal plan from brash robbery to stealthy burglary;" no abandonment)]

e.g. **Example:** D's "mere withdrawal, particularly when faced with resistance by the victim. . . is insufficient evidence of abandonment." [**O'Shaughnessy v. People,** 269 P.3d 1233 (Colo. 2012)]

(3) Model Penal Code Position: Possible Abandonment Defense

The Model Penal Code recognizes the defense even after the last proximate act, if the criminal result can thereafter be avoided, but not where the actor "has put in motion forces which he is powerless to stop." Model Penal Code § 5.01, comment. Based on the idea that the defendant is no longer "dangerous," the MPC and modern statutes based on it permit a defendant to avoid liability by proving voluntary abandonment, subject to two conditions:

(i) The abandonment must have been *entirely voluntary,* which means it must not have been motivated in any way by circumstances not present or apparent earlier which increase the risk of detention or apprehension or which merely increase the difficulty of committing the crime.

(ii) The abandonment must have been ***complete,*** which means it must not have been simply a decision to postpone the crime until a better time or until a different victim or opportunity is found.

[Model Penal Code § 5.01(4)]

e.g. **Example:** D planned a mass shooting and purchased two assault rifles and engaged in target practice; his substantial step was not negated by his purported "abandonment" by storing the rifles at the home of his girlfriend's father, apparently done to prevent his mother's discovery of his plan. [**State v. Lammers,** *supra*]

e.g. **Example:** D entered an elevator with a woman intending to rob her at knifepoint, but when she screamed and resisted, he abandoned his efforts. The abandonment was no defense because D apparently concluded that such action would "increase the probability of [his] detection or apprehension." [**State v. Riley,** 123 A.3d 123 (Conn.App. 2015)]

EXAM TIP

If you encounter an exam question involving a defendant who decides to back out of his intended crime, first consider whether the ***elements of attempt are established***, *i.e.*, did he take the necessary substantial step towards completion of the crime with the required intent? If not, that ends the analysis. But if he did, you need to consider a ***possible defense of abandonment*** if the jurisdiction permits such a defense. If you reach this question, the key issues will be whether his abandonment was ***both complete and voluntary.*** If the facts indicate the defendant realized he was about to get caught, or that the crime was becoming more complicated than he envisioned, his decision to back out is not voluntary and perhaps not complete (because he may have intended to try again in a different situation). Remember that it will be a rare case where the defendant has the required spontaneous and complete change of heart.

---

(4) Distinguish: Abandonment as Showing Lack of Intent

If abandonment is not a defense, evidence of abandonment may nevertheless be introduced to show that the defendant had only a "half formed" or provisional intent and therefore ***lacked the mens rea*** required for attempt.

(5) Distinguish: Abandonment as Showing No Substantial Step

A voluntary withdrawal may arguably characterize defendant's prior acts as mere preparation. [**State v. Rollins,** 321 S.W.3d 353 (Mo.App. 2010) (abandonment may raise doubt about whether defendant satisfied statutory definition of a "substantial step")]

5. Punishment

a. Penalties for Attempt

While statutes vary widely in the penalties attached to a criminal attempt, many attempts are commonly punishable by a ***lesser penalty*** than the completed crime (*e.g.,* one-half the maximum for the completed crime). The Model Penal Code, however, would authorize the ***same penalty*** as that for the completed crime. [Model Penal Code § 5.05(1)]

b. Relationship of Attempt to Completed Crime

Although an attempt does not "merge" into the completed crime, it is clearly a lesser included offense of the completed crime. Therefore, the defendant ***cannot be convicted of both*** attempt and the completed crime (*see supra,* p. 24). While there is some early authority to the contrary, the better view is that a defendant can be convicted of attempt even if the proof at trial shows that he successfully completed the crime. [**People v. Pickett,** 175 N.W.2d 347 (Mich.App. 1970)]

c. Relationship to Other Crimes

(1) Attempt to Commit "Attempt-Like" Crimes

It has been suggested that an attempt to commit a crime that is itself an offense consisting of preparatory action (*e.g.,* burglary, which requires a breaking and entering with the intent to commit a felony inside the building, or assault as an attempted battery) should not be made a crime, *i.e.,* there can be no "attempted attempt." Some courts, however, have upheld convictions of this sort. [*See, e.g.,* **McQuirter v. State,** 63 So. 2d 388 (Ala.App. 1953) (upholding conviction of attempted assault with intent to rape)]

(2) Solicitation as Attempt

Although there is authority to the contrary, the better view is that a mere solicitation is not also an attempt. [*Compare* **United States v. Desposito,** 704 F.3d 221 (2d Cir. 2013) (defendant was guilty of attempting to obstruct official proceedings by sending repeated letters from jail trying to get others to produce false evidence for defendant's forthcoming trial, although none of the intended recipients agreed to the scheme or took any step to cooperate; court emphasized defendant's repeated efforts) *with* **State v. Molasky,** 765 S.W.2d 597 (Mo. 1989) (inmate's solicitation of fellow convict to commit murders, discussing payment, time and manner of killing, is not attempted murder, because the solicitation was not accompanied by concrete arrangements for payment or by providing pictures of locations of proposed victims)] However, if the solicitation is accompanied by additional acts beyond what is required for solicitation that also meet the attempt standard, the defendant may be punished for attempt. [**United States v. Desposito,** *supra*]

SUMMARY OF INCHOATE CRIMES	SOLICITATION	CONSPIRACY	ATTEMPT
MENTAL STATE	Intent to cause the person solicited to commit the crime	Specific intent to: (i) enter into agreement; and (ii) achieve the objective of the conspiracy	Specific intent: (i) to commit the acts or cause the result constituting the target crime; and (ii) intent necessary for target crime
ACTUS REUS	Counseling, inciting, or inducing another to commit an offense	Entering into agreement to commit a crime and an "overt act"	Performance of an act that progresses sufficiently towards the commission of the intended crime
"MERGER" INTO COMPLETED CRIME?	Yes	No	Yes
WITHDRAWAL A DEFENSE?	Generally no	No, except for further crimes of co-conspirators	Generally no

Chapter Eight

Homicide Crimes

CONTENTS	PAGE

Key Exam Issues

Because of the complex grading schemes relating to homicide offenses, examination questions concerning homicide are quite common. If you find a homicide question on your exam, decide first whether it should be answered under the ***common law rules or whether modern homicide statutes*** such as the Model Penal Code are applicable. In either case, unless you are asked to apply statutes that provide other distinctions, your analysis of the questions should proceed along the following lines:

1. Did the defendant act with a state of mind that is sufficient to establish ***malice aforethought. For example,***

   - Did the defendant act with ***intent to kill***?
   - Did the defendant act with ***intent to cause serious bodily injury***?
   - Did the defendant act with ***awareness of high risk*** that death or serious bodily injury would be caused?
   - Was death caused in the commission of a felony sufficient to invoke the ***felony murder*** rule?

   If the defendant had any of these states of mind at the time of the defendant's conduct that caused the victim's death, the killing might well be ***murder.***

2. Is there an applicable statute that separates ***degrees of murder***? If so:

   - Are there facts suggesting that the killing was ***premeditated***? Under many such statutes, this will make the killing ***first degree murder.***
   - Was the killing caused during the commission of ***specifically listed felonies***? Often this will be ***first degree murder.***

   Under such schemes, all killings that meet the general definition of murder that are not raised to first degree murder by these two methods will be ***second degree murder. But note:*** In the absence of a statute, do not worry about degrees of murder. Common law murder is not divided into degrees.

3. If the facts suggest that the killing was murder, do those facts also include all four elements of ***adequate provocation***?

   - A sufficient provocation;
   - A showing that the provocation did in fact motivate the defendant's killing of the victim;
   - A lack of a cooling period between the provocation and the killing; and
   - The failure of the defendant to have actually cooled off after the provocation.

   If so, the killing will most likely be reduced from murder to ***voluntary manslaughter.***

4. After covering the possibility that the killing might be murder or voluntary manslaughter, consider as an alternative whether the killing might be ***involuntary manslaughter*** under either of the following approaches:

   - Did the defendant act without malice aforethought but with ***criminal negligence***?
   - Was the death of the victim caused during the commission of an ***unlawful act*** that does not bring into play the felony murder rule?

Also watch for a statute in the question creating the crime of ***criminally negligent homicide.*** If such a statute is applicable, a negligent killing will constitute this crime rather than involuntary manslaughter.

5. If there is any chance that any of these offenses apply, consider whether there are problems of ***causation.*** Consider separately three different possibilities:
   - Is there any chance that the victim failed to die within a ***year and a day*** so as to invoke this special rule?
   - Was there ***factual causation;*** *i.e.,* did the defendant's acts cause the victim to die as and when the victim did die? (*See supra,* p. 66.)
   - Was there ***proximate causation***? Most importantly, was any factor interjected into the chain of causation between the defendant's conduct and the death of the victim that might be regarded as a ***superseding factor***? (*See supra,* p. 69.)

A. Definition and Classification

1. Definition

A homicide is the killing of one human being by another human being.

2. Common Law Classifications

At common law, homicides are classified as justifiable, excusable, or criminal. ***Justifiable*** homicides are those commanded or authorized by law; they are not punishable. ***Excusable*** homicides are those in which the killer is to some extent at fault but where circumstances do not support infliction of full punishment for criminal homicide; the killing remains criminal but the penalty is reduced. Any killing that is not justifiable or excusable is ***criminal*** homicide and is known as either murder or manslaughter.

3. Classification Under Modern Law

Modern statutes tend to abandon the common law scheme above. Excusable homicides are no longer punished, and so the justifiable-excusable distinction is of no significance. Modern statutes often add to homicide law the additional offense of ***negligent homicide.*** With regard to murder, a common pattern is to divide murder into two degrees (first degree and second degree). More recently, a number of states have distinguished murder from the separate offense of "capital murder," for which the death penalty may be imposed.

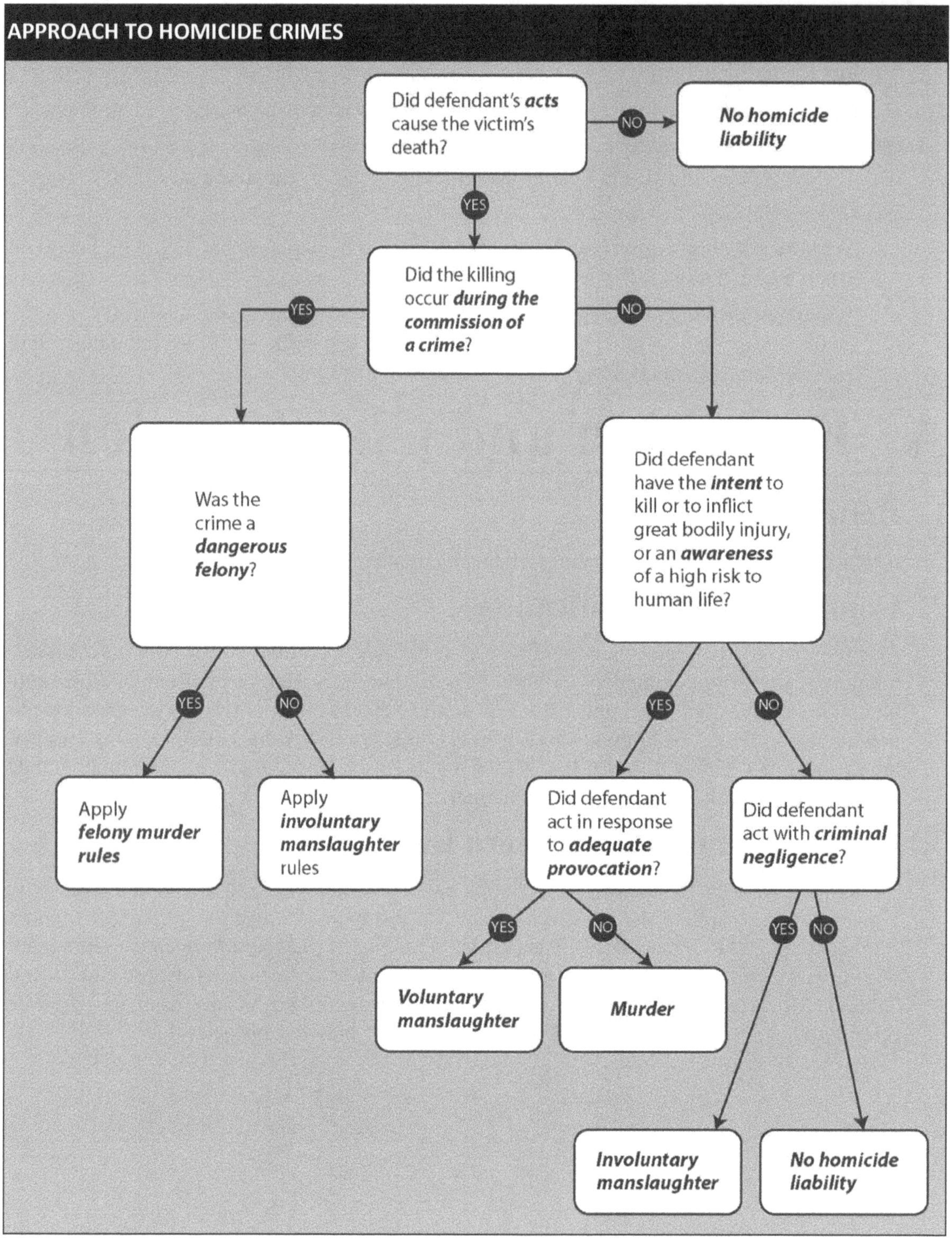

B. Murder

1. Murder Defined

At common law and under many present statutes, murder is the unlawful killing of another human being with ***malice aforethought.***

2. "Malice Aforethought"

"Malice aforethought" is sometimes defined as "the intention to kill, actual or implied, under circumstances which do not constitute excuse or justification or mitigate the offense to manslaughter." The intent to kill is "actual" where the defendant ***consciously desired to cause death.*** It is "implied" where the defendant ***intended to cause great bodily harm*** or where the ***natural tendency of her behavior*** was to cause death or great bodily harm. No ill will or hatred of the victim need be shown. [**People v. Morrin,** 187 N.W.2d 434 (Mich. 1971)]

a. Functional Definition

Malice aforethought is best regarded as a term of art encompassing several different mental states. Absent evidence of adequate provocation (which will reduce the killing to voluntary manslaughter, *see infra,* p. 215 *et seq.*), malice aforethought exists if, at the time of the killing, the defendant entertained ***any one*** of the following states of mind.

EXAM TIP

Homicides are emotionally charged crimes so you must be careful not to let your emotions lead you to an incorrect conclusion. Remember that "malice aforethought" does not mean ***ill will or hatred***; it simply means that the defendant had one of the following types of mental states:

(i) ***Intent to kill,***

(ii) ***Intent to inflict great bodily harm,***

(iii) ***Intent to commit a felony,*** or

(iv) ***Awareness of a high risk of death.***

If the defendant killed with one of these mental states, she is guilty of common law murder. If not, she is not guilty of murder (although she could be guilty of other crimes). Thus, even where the facts paint the defendant as a completely despicable human being (*e.g.*, a mass murderer), you cannot convict her of murder when she drives through a schoolyard, killing three children, ***if*** the incident was due to her fiddling with her cell phone. On the other hand, if a kind and caring defendant intends to kill her terminally ill mother to end her suffering, she is guilty of murder.

---

(1) Intent to Kill

If the defendant ***intended to cause the victim's death,*** the killing is with malice aforethought and thus murder.

e.g. **Example:** D shoots V with the intent to cause V's death. Unless there are mitigating circumstances that will reduce the killing to voluntary manslaughter, V's resulting death is clearly murder.

e.g. **Example:** Sufficient circumstantial evidence supported first-degree murder. The evidence showed a chronological and digital nexus between the online use of a forum for hitmen and the D's laptop. D was the only person with V around the time of death and the crime scene was inconsistent with suicide. D's hands tested positive for gunshot residue. [**State v. Allwine,** 963 N.W.2d 178 (Minn. 2021)]

(a) "Deadly Weapon" Doctrine

One who intentionally uses a deadly weapon (*i.e.*, a weapon calculated to or likely to produce death or great bodily injury) on another human being, and thereby kills him, is ***"presumed" to have intended the killing.*** Under the better (and probably constitutionally-required) view, this is not a mandatory presumption, but rather is a permissive inference, which means that the trier of fact may, but need not, infer from such use of a deadly weapon that the perpetrator did in fact have the intent to kill. [**Starks v. State,** 223 So.3d 1045 (Fla.App. 2017) ("[d]espite the fact that the victim was slumped unconscious in his chair and not defending himself, defendant continued to beat the victim's limp, unconscious body in a series of attacks")]

(2) Intent to Inflict Great Bodily Injury

If the defendant ***intended to inflict serious bodily injury*** upon the victim, even though she did not consciously desire to cause the victim's death, and did in fact cause the victim's death, the killing is with malice aforethought and thus murder. [**People v. Geiger,** 159 N.W.2d 383 (Mich. 1968)]

e.g. **Example:** H dealt W several blows, caused her to strike her head on the ground and, on discovering that she was unconscious, simply placed her in his car, where she died from the injuries. Although H lacked the intent to kill, he clearly intended to cause W serious bodily injury, and because with this *mens rea* he caused her death, he is guilty of murder. [**People v. Geiger,** *supra*]

(3) Intent to Commit a Felony

If the defendant was ***in the process of committing a felony*** when she did the act that caused death, and therefore had the intent to commit a felony, she acted with malice aforethought. This is the basis of the felony murder rule (*see infra,* p. 209 *et seq.*)

(4) Intent to Resist Lawful Arrest

Older authorities suggest that a killing caused in the resistance of a lawful arrest is murder even if it does not fall within one of the other categories. [**Donehy v. Commonwealth,** 186 S.W. 161 (Ky. 1916) ("where an officer is killed while attempting to make an arrest by one knowing him to be an officer, it is not necessary to constitute [the crime of murder] that the slayer should have had any particular malice")] But the modern and better view is that such a killing is murder only if it satisfies one of the other tests of malice aforethought (*i.e.,* intent to kill, felony murder, etc.). In other words, a killing with intent to resist a lawful arrest is ***not a separate type*** of murder. [**State v. Weisengoff,** 101 S.E. 450 (W. Va. 1919) (malice "cannot be inferred from the mere effort to escape arrest")]

(5) Awareness of a High Risk of Death: "Depraved Mind" or "Abandoned and Malignant Heart" Murder

Under certain exceptional circumstances, a defendant may be guilty of murder if she acts in the face of an ***unusually high risk that her conduct will cause death or serious bodily injury.*** Traditionally, the risk must have been so great that ignoring it demonstrates an "abandoned and malignant heart" or a "depraved mind." [**Commonwealth v. Malone,** 47 A.2d 445 (Pa. 1946); N.Y. Penal Law § 125.25(4) (statutory "depraved indifference" murder, requiring recklessly creating a grave risk of death to another under circumstances "evincing a depraved indifference to human life" and thereby in fact causing the death of another). *See* **People v. Bovio,** 168 N.Y.S.3d 632 (N.Y.App. 2022) (a person who is depravedly indifferent is not just willing to take a grossly unreasonable risk to human life—that person does not care how the risk turns out)]

Example: D killed V while playing a game of "Russian Roulette," which involved loading a revolver with one bullet and, after spinning the chamber, placing the gun to V's head and pulling the trigger. D was guilty of murder. Regardless of whether D intended to kill V or seriously injure him, D acted with the awareness that her conduct created an extremely high risk of V's death. [**Commonwealth v. Malone,** *supra*]

Example: Insufficient evidence of depraved heart murder; D led police on midday car chase through mixed commercial-residential neighborhood, resulting in death of pedestrian; although defendant swerved into opposing lanes of traffic and exceeded speed limit, he also actively attempted to avoid hitting other vehicles. [**People v. Maldonado,** 18 N.E.3d 391 (N.Y. 2014)]

(a) Awareness of Risk

There is dispute about whether the defendant must have been actually aware of the grave risk involved or whether it is enough that her conduct created that risk. While most of the cases are ambiguous on the matter, the ***better view*** would require a ***subjective realization of the risk***, on the theory that anything less is too far removed from intent-to-kill murder to justify treating the two situations alike.

(b) Creation of Risk to Many

Some jurisdictions limit this sort of murder to those situations in which the defendant has, by her conduct, created a high risk of death to several or many persons. Under this approach, it is not sufficient that the defendant created a high risk of death to only the victim. [**Ex parte McCormack,** 431 So. 2d 1340 (Ala. 1983)]

(c) Distinguish: Reckless and Negligent Killings

More than mere negligence, or even recklessness in modern terms, is required in "depraved mind" murder cases. The risk of death resulting from the defendant's conduct must be greater than that demanded by the criminal negligence required for traditional involuntary manslaughter. (*See infra,* p. 222.) Furthermore, actual awareness of the risk is more likely to be required for this type of murder than is required for involuntary manslaughter (*See infra,* p. 222.) In modern statutory schemes distinguishing reckless and negligent killings, depraved mind murder more closely resembles reckless killings (*see infra,* p. 225) than negligent ones (*see infra,* p. 225) because actual awareness of the risk is probably required. Of course, the risk of which the defendant must be aware has to be higher in depraved mind murder cases than is necessary in reckless killing cases.

b. Awareness of Obligation to Obey Laws

The California Supreme Court held that malice aforethought also requires an awareness of one's obligation to act within the general body of laws regulating society. [**People v. Conley,** 411 P.2d 911 (Cal. 1966) (mental disorder not amounting to legal insanity may preclude malice aforethought)] In 1981, however, the California statute defining malice was amended specifically to provide that an awareness of the obligation to act within the general body of laws regulating society is ***not required.*** [Cal. Penal Code § 188(b)]

c. Proof of Malice Aforethought

The various states of mind comprising malice aforethought may be proven by circumstantial evidence. Additionally, proof that the defendant killed the victim creates a presumption that she acted with malice aforethought. Under the better view, however, this means that the trier of fact may (but need not) infer from the fact of the killing that the defendant had one of the states of mind necessary for murder. If this "presumption" is interpreted as placing the burden of proving lack of malice on the defendant, it is inconsistent with the presumption of innocence and unconstitutional. [**State v. Cuevas,** 488 P.2d 322 (Hawaii 1971)]

3. Degrees of Murder

At common law, there are no degrees of murder. Statutes, however, often divide murder into first and second degree.

a. First Degree Murder

The offense of first degree murder has no common law equivalent; it is entirely a creature of statute. While generalization is somewhat difficult, statutes typically classify the following homicides as first degree murder:

(1) Premeditated Killings

Premeditated killings are those in which the intent to kill is formed ***with some reflection, deliberation, reasoning or weighing,*** rather than simply on a sudden impulse. Thus premeditation is, in a sense, the process by which intent to kill is formed or the defendant finally decides to act on the intent to kill. Although there is general agreement on the abstract definition of premeditation, courts disagree on the evidence necessary to show it. [**State v. Forrest,** 362 S.E.2d 252 (N.C. 1987) (substantial evidence that killing of the father by his son was premeditated and deliberate; D shot V four separate times with single-action gun that had to be cocked each time before it could be fired; V was lying helpless in hospital bed and did nothing to provoke D)]

(a) Proof of Opportunity

Some courts defer dramatically to juries' conclusions that defendants did premeditate and tend to uphold a verdict of guilty of premeditated murder if the evidence shows the defendant had ***sufficient time to premeditate*** and the jury found she in fact did. [**State v. Murray,** 773 S.E.2d 656 (W.Va. 2015) ("opportunity for some reflection" met, where defendant watched codefendant beat victim and then picked up wrench and struck victim on head several more times); **People v. Walker,** 948 N.W.2d 122 (Mich.App. 2019) ("premeditation may be established by circumstantial evidence tending to show that a defendant had an opportunity to think about, evaluate, or take a 'second look' at their actions. . . . opportunity must be adequate, but it need not be long.")]

1) No Appreciable Time Needed

e.g. **Example:** "Any interval of time between the forming of the intent to kill and the execution of that intent, which is of sufficient duration for the accused to be fully conscious of what he intended" is sufficient for deliberation and conviction of first-degree murder. [**State v. Guthrie,** 461 S.E.2d 163 (W.Va. 1995) (D stabbed co-worker in the neck after being taunted and hit in the nose with a dish towel; duration of premeditation and deliberation period cannot be arbitrarily fixed; the defendant's extent of reflection, not the time spent reflecting, is the primary concern for the jury's decision)] *Guthrie* suggests that the deliberation/premeditation standard should give juries guidance while allowing for "reasonable discretion."

e.g. **Example:** Evidence showed that D shot V four times and one witness testified he heard one shot, a brief pause, and then three more shots. Some courts hold that this is sufficient for a jury to find that D premeditated because under the "felled victim" rule, a showing of multiple wounds inflicted on the victim shows an adequate opportunity to premeditate between the infliction of the wounds. [**State v. Watson,** 449 S.E.2d 694 (N.C. 1994)]

2) Premeditation and Deliberation as Independent or Integrated Elements?

Deliberation focuses on the defendant's thought process (evaluating major facets of the choice or problem, "undisturbed by hot blood"), while premeditation relates to the quantity of time. [**People v. Morrin,** *supra*] Some courts treat deliberation and premeditation as "independent elements" while other courts treat them as "an integrated concept." [*Compare* **United States v. Begay,** 567 F.3d 540 (9th Cir. 2009) (independent elements) *with* **State v. Ros,** 973 A.2d 1148 (R.I. 2009) (integrated concept)]

(b) Proof of Actual Due Consideration

A few courts insist on somewhat direct proof that the defendant ***did in fact give the question whether to kill reasonably calm consideration.*** This evidence can consist of planning activity prior to the crime or some reasonable substitute, such as proof of a preexisting motive together with evidence that the killing was committed in such a way as to suggest a preconceived plan (*e.g.,* measuring a lethal dose of poison). [**People v. Oros,** 917 N.W.2d 559 (Mich. 2018) (sufficient that "defendant thought about killing the victim before proceeding to kill the victim, and defendant measured and evaluated his choices before proceeding to kill the victim")] The *Oros* dissent noted that "because the jury could reasonably infer that the defendant had enough time to subject his actions to a 'second look,' there was sufficient evidence to find beyond a reasonable doubt that he did premeditate and deliberate. That is, the possibility that he could have premeditated and deliberated is all that's required."

e.g. **Example:** Evidence showed that D armed himself with a handgun, practiced shooting with it, and wore a pistol grip glove to the place of the shooting. [**State v. Cox,** 884 N.W.2d 400 (Minn. 2016)]

(c) "Mature and Meaningful Reflection" Unnecessary in California

In 1981, the California homicide statutes were amended to provide that there is ***no need*** to prove that a defendant maturely and meaningfully reflected on the gravity of the killing to convict that defendant of first degree murder. [Cal. Penal Code § 189(d)]

(2) Killing During Enumerated Felonies

Killings committed during the perpetration (or attempted perpetration) of ***certain*** felonies are often made first degree murder. The relevant felonies are ***listed in the statute.*** The specified felonies typically include arson, rape, robbery, burglary, kidnapping, mayhem, and sexual molestation of a child. [Cal. Penal Code § 189] Killings committed during other felonies do not qualify for first degree murder.

EXAM TIP

Under statutes dividing murder into degrees, not all felony murders will be first degree murders. If a killing arises out of a felony, you must ***check the relevant statute*** to see if the felony is one that qualifies for ***first degree murder.*** If not, it is most likely second degree murder (*see* below).

---

(3) Killing by Poison, Lying in Wait, or Destructive Device or Explosive

State statutes rarely specifically list these types of killings. [*e.g.*, Cal. Penal Code § 189] A poison is not necessarily something administered internally; it may be inhaled or injected. [**State v. Jeffers,** 661 P.2d 1105 (Ariz. 1983) ("poison," is any substance introduced into the body by any means which by its chemical action is capable of causing death, includes heroin)] "Lying in wait" usually requires watching and waiting in a concealed position with an intent to kill or cause serious bodily injury. Killings committed by use "of a destructive device or explosive" are sometimes specifically deemed first degree murder. [Cal. Penal Code § 189] If not, these types of killings also may be regarded as highly probative of premeditation.

(4) Killing by Torture

Statutes sometimes make killings by torture first degree murder. This has been held to require proof of intent to inflict pain and suffering for purposes of revenge, humiliation, or some similar motive, and a causal relationship between the torture and the death of a victim. [**State v. Brock,** 416 P.2d 601 (Ariz. 1966)]

b. Second Degree Murder

Under statutes that divide murder into degrees, all killings committed ***with malice aforethought*** that are ***not specifically made first degree murder*** are second degree murder. Thus, the following constitute second degree murder: (1) intent-to-kill murder without premeditation and deliberation; (2) intent-to-do-serious-bodily-injury murder, whether or not premeditated and deliberated; (3) depraved-heart murder; and (4) felony-murder, where the felony in question is not a listed one, *e.g.*, abortion, larceny.

e.g. **Example:** D is charged with causing V's death in the course of committing the crime of obtaining property by false pretenses (felony murder). Under the governing statute, first degree murder consists of killings committed during the perpetration of certain enumerated felonies. If "false pretenses" is not on the list, then if D is to be convicted of murder, it must be second degree murder.

4. Capital Murder

Some modern statutes distinguish the offense of capital murder from murder. The offense of capital murder requires proof of at least one of several ***enumerated aggravated factors*** or ***"special circumstances"*** Under this approach, a defendant may be sentenced to death ***only if*** convicted of the separate offense of capital murder because the jury finds sufficient proof of a statutory aggravator.

e.g. **Example:** Under the Virginia statute, murder is "capital murder" if it was willful, deliberate, and premeditated, ***plus*** one of more than a dozen "aggravating factors," including: the murder was "for hire," more than one person was killed as part of the same transaction, the victim was a law enforcement officer, the killing was related to the commission of rape, abduction, or robbery, or it came within one of the other similar statutory provisions. [Va. Code § 18.2–31]

C. Felony Murder

1. Felony Murder Rule

A killing, even an accidental one, will be murder if it was caused ***with the intent to commit a felony.*** This is the "felony murder rule." Broadly speaking, the rule provides that any killing committed during the course of a felony is murder. No intent to kill or other mental state regarding the occurrence of death is required; thus, this is a form of limited strict liability. The felony on which a particular prosecution is based is often called the ***"predicate felony."***

a. Rationale

Two justifications have been advanced in support of the felony murder rule: First, the rule is believed to ***deter felonies*** by adding to the threat of conviction and punishment for the felony the additional threat of conviction and punishment for murder if death occurs. Second, the rule ***discourages the use of violence during the commission of felonies*** by imposing the threat of additional punishment if the felon causes death. Some have questioned whether the rule actually functions in either way.

b. All Co-Felons Liable for Felony Murder

Generally, when several participants commit the predicate felony, if one of those felons accidentally caused a death, the ***other felons*** as well as the one actually causing the death may be guilty of felony murder. This results from application to these cases of the co-conspirator rule making all conspirators guilty of foreseeable crimes of their co-conspirators committed in furtherance of the conspiracy. [**Collins v. State,** 610 S.W.3d 653 (Ark. 2020) (child victims killed during robbery of children's mother's apartment; predicate felony occurred even if the victims did not own the stolen property); *see supra,* p. 182]

c. Applies When Co-Felon Is Killed by Another Co-Felon

Felony murder liability may exist even if the person killed is ***one of the participants in the predicate felony.*** [**People v. Billa,** 79 P.3d 542 (Cal. 2003) (felony murder applied to unintended death of defendant's arson coconspirator, who caught fire and burned to death; defendant and all coconspirators were present at burning, all were active participants acting in furtherance of the conspiracy to commit arson, including the acts that resulted in death, and no third party contributed to death; *see infra,* p. 213)]

2. Limitations on Felony Murder

Several major limitations on felony murder have developed. These reflect misgivings regarding the wisdom of the rule itself, at least when it is applied without qualification or limitation. California in 2019 substantially repealed much of its felony-murder statute. A jury must find that the defendant was the "actual killer" and acted with malice. The prosecution is no longer able to rely on a legal attribution of malice to the defendant based solely on the defendant's participation in the triggering felony. [**People v. White,** 2022 WL 1284217 (Cal.App. 2022)]

a. Death of Another Must Be "Foreseeable"

Some, but not all, courts require that the death of another have been a ***foreseeable result of the felony*** as a condition of applying the felony murder rule. [*Compare* **State v. Noren,** 371 N.W.2d 381 (Wis. 1985) (foreseeability required), *with* **People v. Stamp,** 2 Cal. App. 3d 203 (1969) (foreseeability not required)] Courts are willing to find the required foreseeable risk of death on the facts of particular cases.

e.g. **Example:** D set a building on fire. Firefighters arrived to fight the fire. One firefighter using a breathing apparatus ignored the alarm that signaled his air was about out and remained in the burning building. His air ran out and the firefighter died of carbon dioxide poisoning. Even though the firefighter was considerably negligent, D is guilty of felony murder. A reasonable person would foresee dangerous firefighting as a result of setting fire to a building, and even some negligence on the part of the firefighters is a foreseeable result of arson. Thus, felony murder liability exists. [**State v. Leech,** 790 P.2d 160 (Wash. 1990) (human error in fighting a fire is not an extraordinary occurrence); *see* **State v. Frahm,** 444 P.3d 595 (Wash. 2019) (intoxicated motorist's hit-and-run, injuring motorist, was legal cause of death of passerby who stopped to help motorist)]

b. Felony Must Be "Dangerous"

A number of states limit the felony murder rule to underlying felonies of a specific nature. Usually, the predicate felony must be a ***"dangerous"*** one. [**People v. Washington,** 402 P.2d 130 (Cal. 1965) ("The felony-murder doctrine attributes malice aforethought to the felon who kills in the perpetration of an inherently dangerous felony")] There are two different approaches for determining whether a felony is dangerous:

(1) "Inherently" Dangerous

A few jurisdictions adopting the dangerous felony approach require that the felony be ***"inherently" dangerous***, *i.e.,* always dangerous to human life when evaluated in the abstract rather than on the facts of any particular case. [*Compare* **Ramirez v. State,** 235 P.3d 619 (Nev. 2010) (inherently dangerous felony is one where death is a foreseeable consequence of the felony) *with* **State v. Anderson,** 666 N.W.2d 696 (Minn. 2003) (possession of stolen firearm not inherently dangerous; nothing about the offense "in the abstract" that "involves a special danger to human life")]

e.g. **Example:** Angered over being ripped off in a drug deal, D went to the apartment of the man who ripped D off and fired several shots at the apartment. A young girl in the apartment was killed. D's actions constituted the felony of willful discharge of a firearm at an inhabited dwelling. D could be convicted of felony murder, because the predicate felony was an inherently dangerous one. Because people are generally in or around inhabited dwellings, the offense inherently involves a significant risk of death. [**People v. Hansen,** 885 P.2d 1022 (Cal. 1994)]

(2) Dangerous as Committed

Most courts examine the circumstances under which the felony was committed and apply the felony murder rule ***only if the felony as committed*** on the facts of the case involved a foreseeable danger to human life. [**State v. Stewart,** 663 A.2d 912 (R.I. 1995)] This approach appears to encourage a court to speculate about how the felony is "usually" committed before being able to guess how it was committed in the case at bar. [*See, e.g.*, **Commonwealth v. Wojcik,** 843 N.E.2d 716 (Mass.App. 2006) (while "larcenies typically do not involve placing others at physical risk," the defendants here "sought to defraud an insurance company by intentionally causing an automobile accident, and crashing a large truck into a oncoming vehicle," which resulted in death).

e.g. **Example:** D was a convicted felon and possessed a pistol. D went to a friend's house and while D was attempting to unload the pistol it accidentally discharged. V was killed when the bullet went through the floor and into V's basement apartment. D's possession of the pistol was the felony offense of possession of a firearm by a convicted felon. The court held that D could not be convicted of felony murder. Whether a felony suffices as a predicate felony turns on whether it is dangerous as committed. Here, D's commission of the felony of possession of a firearm by a convicted felon was not committed in a dangerous way. [**Ford v. State,** 423 S.E.2d 255 (Ga. 1992)]

c. Felony Must Be "Independent": Felony-Murder "Merger" Rule

Most courts hold that the felony murder rule can be applied only where the *predicate felony is somewhat independent of the killing.* If the predicate felony is the assault or battery by which the victim's death is caused, the felony "merges" into the killing and thus does not retain sufficient independence to be a predicate felony. [**State v. Jones,** 155 A.3d 492 (Md. 2017); **People v. Chun,** 203 P.3d 425 (Cal. 2009)] By contrast, because the "intent to steal does not cause a homicide, an armed robbery does not merge with the killing." [**Commonwealth v. Holley,** 87 N.E.3d 77 (Mass. 2017)]

(1) Rationale

Because most killings result from actions constituting assault or battery, permitting these crimes to be used as predicate felonies would expand felony murder to cover far more situations than intended by the legislature. [**People v. Hansen,** *supra*]

(2) Problem: Determining Whether Felonies Are "Independent"

Courts have had considerable difficulty determining whether felonies beyond assaults and batteries *are* sufficiently independent of the killing that they do not merge into the killing. Some courts apply a flexible test, asking whether permitting the felony to be used as a predicate felony would expand felony murder and frustrate the legislature's intent to provide for a meaningfully limited felony murder rule. Others apply a more focused test and say that a felony does not merge only if the felony involves an intention collateral to and independent of the physical attack on the victim. [**People v. Chun,** *supra* (all felonies that are "assaultive," that is, that involve a threat of immediate injury, merge with a homicide and cannot support conviction for felony murder)]

e.g. **Example:** In **People v. Chun,** *supra,* D was charged with felony murder based on the felony of shooting at an occupied vehicle. Shooting at an occupied vehicle involves a threat of immediate injury and is assaultive. Under this court's approach, such a felony merges with a resulting death and cannot be a predicate felony sufficient to support felony murder.

d. One of the Felons Must "Directly" Cause Death: Intervening Actors

When a death is caused by someone other than one of the felons, the killing can hardly be considered to be "in furtherance" of the commission or attempted commission of a felony. In these situations the death was caused directly by an "intervening actor," such as a resisting victim or a pursuing police officer. There are two approaches to determining whether the felons incur felony murder liability.

(1) Agency Analysis: No Felony Murder Liability

Many (probably most) courts reason that felony murder applies only when the death is caused by the defendant or someone acting as the defendant's "agent." Because neither the victim of the felony nor intervening police officer are in any sense agents of the felons, a death directly caused by them cannot give rise to felony murder. [**Commonwealth v. Tejeda,** 41 N.E.3d 721 (Mass. 2015)]

(a) Policy Analysis: Would Liability Serve Purposes of Rule?

Some courts have refused to find felony murder liability in these situations on the ground that the deterrent purposes of the felony murder rule (*supra,* p. 209) would not be served by applying it where the killing is not actually caused by one of the felons. Because such homicides are not within the direct control of the felons, imposing felony murder liability would discourage neither the commission of felonies nor killings during felonies. [**People v. Washington,** *supra* (unreasonable to premise a rule of law on so fortuitous a circumstance as the marksmanship of victims and police officers); **Commonwealth ex rel. Smith v. Myers,** 261 A.2d 550 (Pa. 1970)] Other courts, however, have reasoned that imposing felony murder liability even for these killings will add to the incentive the law provides to discourage persons from committing dangerous felonies. [**People v. Pugh,** 634 N.E.2d 34 (Ill. 1994)]

(2) Alternative "Proximate Cause" Approach: Felony Murder Liability Can Exist

Some courts reject the agency approach and find felony murder liability when a non-felon causes the death, reasoning that these situations present all that is necessary, a showing that the victim as a proximate result of the felon's commission of the felony. [**Commonwealth v. Almeida,** 68 A.2d 595 (Pa. 1949) *overruled by* **Commonwealth ex rel. Smith v. Myers,** *supra;* **People v. Hernandez,** 624 N.E.2d 661 (N.Y. 1993) (legislative changes in felony murder statute rejected earlier case law finding no liability)]

(a) Distinguish: When Co-Felon Is Killed

A leading line of cases finding felony murder liability when the killing was committed by the police, or a resisting victim suggested that felony murder liability would ***not*** be found where the deceased was ***one of the felons.*** [**Commonwealth v. Redline,** 137 A.2d 472 (Pa. 1958)] Other courts, however, rejected this distinction. [*See* **State v. Oimen,** 516 N.W.2d 399 (Wis. 1994) (felony murder statute rejected "majority rule" and imposes liability where resisting robbery victim killed one of robbers)] Furthermore, the above situation should be distinguished where the death is caused by the acts of another felon. (*See supra,* p. 209.)

(3) Distinguish: Murder Liability on Other Grounds

If the felony murder rule does not apply to these situations, the killings may still constitute murder if the defendant, in addition to committing the felony, has engaged in activity involving such a ***high risk to human life*** that malice aforethought can be established under the "awareness of a high risk" rule (*see supra,* p. 204). [**Taylor v.**

Superior Court, 477 P.2d 131 (Cal. 1970) ("the central inquiry in determining criminal liability for a killing committed by a resisting victim or police officer is whether the *conduct* of a defendant or his accomplices was sufficiently provocative of lethal resistance to support a finding of implied malice")]

e.g. **Example:** A and B set out to rob V. A waved a gun at V, threatening him. V grabbed the weapon in response and shot and killed A's co-felon, B. Although felony murder did not apply because V rather than one of the felons was the trigger person, a murder conviction could be obtained if A's actions in threatening V rose to the level of "awareness of high risk" conduct, *i.e.*, if murder could be established without reference to the felony murder rule. [**Taylor v. Superior Court,** *supra*]

e. Death Must Be Caused in Perpetration of Felony

All courts agree: the killing must be caused ***in the perpetration*** (or attempted perpetration) of the predicate felony. However, the death does not have to occur in the course of the predicate felony but only must be part of a continuous transaction. Even if a felony murder statute requires that the death be caused "in furtherance" of the felony, this means only that the act causing death was part of the felony. [**Commonwealth v. Witkowski,** 169 N.E.3d 496 (Mass. 2021); *compare* **Jones v. State**, 678 S.W.3d 778 (Ark. 2023) (in felony murder case, the deaths resulting from motor vehicle accident were in furtherance of defendant's felonious fleeing; court rejects defendant's argument that "in furtherance of" means to "advance" or "promote" the felony)]

e.g. **Example:** D was convicted of murder in the first degree based on felony murder with aggravated rape as the predicate felony. The proof showed that the homicide and aggravated rape were parts of one continuous event, *i.e.*, the evidence allowed the jury reasonably to infer that V had not moved from the position in which she was raped, and thus that the sexual intercourse did not occur long before her death. [**Commonwealth v. Witkowski**, *supra*]

(1) Duration of Felony

Some courts hold that application of the felony murder rule stops immediately after completion or abandonment of the felony while other courts apply the rule to killings further removed from the felony. [*See, e.g.,* **State v. Metalski,** 185 A. 351 (N.J. 1936) (killing of police officer who was pursuing defendants two hours after a robbery many miles away)] A middle and probably preferable position is that a killing is felony murder if it occurs during the commission of the felony ***or in immediate flight*** from the crime. Under this approach, "immediate flight" ends when **all the perpetrators** have reached the earlier of a position of temporary safety or complete custody. Deaths caused after reaching that position of safety or complete custody are not felony murder. [*See, e.g.*, **People v. Wilkins,** 295 P.3d 903 (Cal. 2013) (defendant had reached place of temporary safety after driving 62 miles from burglary at normal speed without being followed, and without indication that the burglary had been discovered); **Auman v. People,** 109 P.3d 647 (Colo. 2005) ("immediate flight terminates when a sole participant in the subject felony is subject to complete custody, or, alternatively, when all participants in a predicate felony involving more than one participant are subject to complete custody")]

EXAM TIP

When the facts of a question tell you that there was a killing during the commission of a felony, think about the felony murder rule. But before you "convict" the killer, pause to consider the ***limitations on the rule***:

- Was the death ***foreseeable***?
- Was the felony a ***"dangerous"*** felony?
- Was the felony sufficiently ***independent of the killing*** to avoid merger?
- Did one of the ***felons directly*** cause the death?
- Was the death caused ***in perpetration of the felony***?

If you answer no to any of these questions, it is likely that the felony murder rule does ***not*** apply to this defendant. But again, pause before you now "acquit" the killer of murder, and consider whether she can be convicted of murder under any of the other categories, such as ***awareness of a high risk of death.***

3. Future of Felony Murder

The felony murder rule is a well-established part of American criminal law. Some courts have expressed dissatisfaction with the rule, however, reasoning that it imposes essentially strict liability for a serious crime in violation of basic principles of criminal liability. Nevertheless, some legislatures have expanded felony murder liability, sometimes in response to judicial limitations on it. By contrast, other states like California have repealed much of its felony-murder statutory framework.

a. English Abolition

England abolished the felony murder rule in 1957. [Eng. Homicide Act, 1957, 5 & 6 Eliz. 2, c. 11, § 1]

b. Model Penal Code Position

The Model Penal Code does not make felony murder a separate category of murder. It does, however, raise a presumption of "extreme indifference to the value of human life" (sufficient for murder) if the defendant killed while committing or fleeing from a major felony (*e.g.*, robbery, forcible rape, arson, etc.). [Model Penal Code § 210.2(1)(b)] New Hampshire is the only state to have adopted the MPC presumption. [N.H.Rev.Stat. § 630:1–b]

c. Constitutional Considerations

A few courts have expressed concern that felony murder liability, or at least broad versions of it, may impose serious criminal liability without sufficient assurance of blameworthiness, *i.e.*, such strict liability may run afoul of Due Process. [**State v. Ortega,** 817 P.2d 1196 (N.M. 1991) (because of concern with strict liability and presumption issues, court construes felony-murder provision as requiring intent to kill)] The Supreme Court has clearly held that the Eighth Amendment prohibition against cruel and unusual punishment does not prohibit felony murder liability with only the intent required by the predicate felony, although before the ***death penalty*** can be imposed, the intent to kill or reckless indifference must be shown. [**Hopkins v. Reeves,** 524 U.S. 88 (1998)]

d. Judicial or Legislative Abandonment of Felony Murder in the United States

Several courts have wholly or in part abandoned the felony murder rule. As a result, the fact that a killing occurred in the course of a felony is simply one of the considerations to be considered in determining whether the defendant acted with actual malice aforethought. [**State v. Ortega,** *supra* (effectively abandoning felony murder by construing felony murder statute as requiring a *mens rea* otherwise necessary for murder); **Commonwealth v. Brown,** 81 N.E.3d 1173 (Mass. 2017) ("we should abandon the fiction of constructive malice—that where a killing occurs in the commission of a felony, the intent to commit the felony is sufficient alone to establish malice"); **People v. Holtschlag,** 684 N.W.2d 730 (Mich. 2004) ("while the commission of a felony is not dispositive in determining whether a 'murder' has been committed because. . . evidence of a felony is no longer sufficient proof in itself of malice, the fact that the defendant committed a felony still is *relevant*, even if not dispositive, evidence that the defendant acted with malice.")] As mentioned, California by statute in 2019 repealed much of its felony-murder doctrine, *e.g.*, a defendant must be the actual killer, and his malice is derived from his actions. [**People v. White**, *supra*]

D. Voluntary Manslaughter

1. Voluntary Manslaughter Defined

A killing that would ***otherwise be murder*** but that was committed ***in response to certain provocation*** has traditionally been regarded as being committed without malice aforethought and therefore voluntary manslaughter. The defendant must, of course, have acted with one of the states of mind necessary for malice aforethought (*see supra,* pp. 203–206), but the provocation ***reduces*** the killing from murder to manslaughter.

2. Roles of the Court and Jury

Courts have traditionally mistrusted juries in this area. Consequently, they are quite willing to find defendants' claims of adequate provocation insufficient "as a matter of law," on the ground that no reasonable jury could reduce the charge to voluntary manslaughter. This is especially true regarding whether particular kinds of proffered provocation are sufficient under the objective standard. Why juries should be particularly mistrusted on this issue is not clear.

The modern trend is opposite this view; courts are more likely to permit juries to decide whether the defendants' showings of provocation are adequate. Nevertheless, pay careful attention to two issues: (i) is a case for manslaughter sufficient to "go to the jury" and (ii) if so, is it sufficient to persuade the jury?

3. Elements of Provocation Reducing Murder to Manslaughter

At common law, a killing is reduced from murder to manslaughter only if the facts meet all of the following elements. Even under modern statutes, all or most of these requirements are often retained.

(i) There must have been *provocation* of the kind that would cause a *reasonable person to lose control* and act rashly and without reflection;

(ii) The defendant must have ***in fact been provoked,*** and the provocation must have caused the defendant to kill the victim;

(iii) The ***interval*** between the provocation and the killing must ***not have been long enough*** for the passions of a reasonable person to cool; and

(iv) The defendant must ***not have actually cooled*** off during the interval between the provocation and the killing.

ELEMENTS OF PROVOCATION		
THERE ARE OBJECTIVE AND SUBJECTIVE ELEMENTS FOR VOLUNTARY MANSLAUGHTER:		
	OBJECTIVE	SUBJECTIVE
PROVOCATION	A ***reasonable person*** would have been provoked by victim's conduct	The ***defendant*** was ***actually*** provoked by victim's conduct
COOLING OFF PERIOD	A ***reasonable person*** would not have cooled off	The ***defendant*** did not ***actually*** cool off

a. Reasonable Provocation

Whether provocation is reasonable under the circumstances is traditionally judged by an ***objective standard;*** *i.e.,* the situation must be one in which a ***reasonable person*** would have been provoked. Generally, the provocation must be such as might render ordinary persons of average disposition liable to act rashly, without deliberation, and from passion rather than judgment. [**State v. Yanz,** 50 A. 37 (Conn. 1901) (reasonable though erroneous belief on the part of the husband that his wife is committing adultery is a sufficiently reasonable provocation)]

(1) Characteristics of the "Reasonable Person"

Courts have struggled with the extent to which the reasonable person should be regarded as having the peculiar characteristics that may have made defendant unusually susceptible to provocation. Fairness seems to persuasively argue that some of the defendant's characteristics should be taken into account. At some point, however, giving the reasonable person the defendant's characteristics destroys the objective nature of the standard.

(a) Purely Objective Standard

Some courts take the position that the reasonable person should not be regarded as having ***any*** of the defendant's peculiar characteristics, because this would deprive the standard of its objective nature. [**Bedder v. Director of Public Prosecutions,** [1954] 2 All E.R. 801 (in deciding whether prostitute's jeering an impotent defendant constituted adequate provocation for his killing her, jeering should not be evaluated according to its impact on a reasonable but on an impotent person)]

(b) Compromise Standard

Other courts adopt a compromise position that permits consideration of ***some*** of the defendant's personal characteristics. Under this approach, though, the reasonable person is not regarded as having any unusual reduced capacity for self-control that the defendant may have had, because this would excessively deprive the standard of its objective nature. [**State v. Ott,** 686 P.2d 1001 (Ore. 1984)]

(c) Model Penal Code Position

The Model Penal Code provides that the reasonableness of the disturbance that reduces a killing to manslaughter (*see infra,* pp. 221–221) is to be determined from the viewpoint of a person in the defendant's position ***under the circumstances as the defendant believed them to be.*** This allows the court to take into account some of the defendant's special characteristics, but the statutory formulation fails to make clear where the line is to be drawn, *e.g.*, "personal handicaps and some external circumstances," such as "blindness, shock from traumatic injury, and extreme grief," but not his "idiosyncratic moral values." [Model Penal Code § 210.3(1)(b), Comment at 62–63 (1980)]

e.g. **Example:** Where the evidence showed that D was intoxicated, the trial judge should not instruct the jury that the adequacy of provocation should be determined by using the standard of a reasonable ***sober*** person. But given the modern view that some characteristics of the defendant should be given to the reasonable person, the trial judge should also not require the jury to give no effect to the defendant's intoxication. [**State v. Thunberg,** 492 N.W.2d 534 (Minn. 1992) (voluntary manslaughter statute, by referring to what "would provoke a person of ordinary self-control under like circumstances," is deemed to manifest adoption of "middle ground." so that it was improper to instruct jury to use a "sober person" test)]

(2) Particular Situations

Because of the traditional tendency of courts to treat some situations as insufficient "as a matter of law" to reduce a killing to voluntary manslaughter, the law has tended to categorize situations presented in these cases. The resulting rules are probably of less importance in modern analysis than they were traditionally, but courts still often invoke them.

(a) Words Alone

The traditional view is that mere words, no matter how insulting, are ***not adequate provocation.*** [**Lang v. State,** 250 A.2d 276 (Md. 1969)]

1) Trending View

Many jurisdictions have rejected such a rigid rule, particularly if the words are ***informational***, *i.e.,* conveying information of a fact that would constitute reasonable provocation if observed, rather than simply insulting or abusive. [**Paz v. State,** 777 So.2d 983 (Fla.App. 2000) (defendant killed victim when defendant's wife indicated that victim "has sexually assaulted" her; murder conviction reduced to voluntary manslaughter); *see infra,* p. 218]

e.g. **Example:** Would a combination of threatening words and a present ability to carry out the threats adequately provoke a defendant? [*See* **Anderson v. State,** 901 S.E.2d 543 (Ga. 2024) (defendant argued that he was provoked by victim pounding on the door, yelling, and cursing at him, and even threatening to get a gun; court held that threats and insults are insufficient to support an instruction for voluntary manslaughter)]

(b) Battery

A minor blow, even if technically a battery, does not constitute adequate provocation, because it would not provoke a reasonable person to a killing passion. [**State v. Bernhardt,** 372 P.3d 1161 (Kan. 2016)] But a ***violent and painful*** blow can be sufficient provocation, whether administered with the hand or a weapon. [**People v. Harris,** 134 N.E.2d 315 (Ill. 1956) (victim severely beat defendant with nightstick)]

1) Distinguish: Defendant Provoked Blow

Even where the defendant has killed in response to a vigorous blow, the homicide will ***not be reduced*** to voluntary manslaughter if the defendant was ***at fault*** in stimulating the blow (as where the defendant was the initial aggressor in the altercation). [**Commonwealth v. Rodriguez,** 958 N.E.2d 518 (Mass. 2011) (not sufficient provocation here, as victim merely "walked hastily" toward defendant before defendant "attempted to strike the victim," though "defendant was struck first")]

(c) Assault

The cases are split as to whether an unsuccessful attempt to commit a battery can constitute adequate provocation. The better view, however, is that it may, especially in aggravated cases. [**Stevenson v. United States,** 162 U.S. 313 (1896) (attacker fired gun at defendant)]

(d) Illegal Arrest

Courts have also differed as to whether the victim's unlawful arrest of the defendant can constitute adequate provocation. Probably the better view is that it can, particularly where the defendant was aware of the unlawful nature of the arrest. [**Bad Elk v. United States,** 177 U.S. 529 (1900)] A lawful arrest does not constitute sufficient provocation. [**State v. Wood,** 607 S.E.2d 57 (S.C. 2004)]

(e) Adultery

Discovery of one's spouse in the act of committing adultery is ***clearly sufficient*** for a jury to find as provocation. [**People v. McCarthy,** 547 N.E.2d 459 (Ill. 1989)] Moreover, the modern trend is to extend this rule beyond situations where one spouse actually catches the other in the act. Some courts find sufficient provocation where the defendant is told of the spouse's adultery [*See* **Raines v. State,** 277 S.E.2d 47 (Ga. 1981); **Haley v. State,** 85 So. 129 (Miss. 1920)] or even simply sees a person known to be having an affair with the spouse [**People v. Bridgehouse,** 47 Cal. 2d 406 (1956)].

(f) Mutual Quarrel or Combat

If two persons ***voluntarily engage*** in a fight (*e.g.,* "If we are going to fight, let's go outside"), in the course of which one is killed, the homicide is only manslaughter. [**State v. Rich,** 3 A.3d 1210 (Md. 2010)] Conceptually, the suddenness of the affray, rather than any specific action by the victim, is the provocation. It is not controlling which person struck the first blow because the intent to fight is mutual. However, the killing may not be reduced to manslaughter if ***at the beginning*** of the fight the defendant took an unfair advantage. [**Whitehead v. State,** 262 A.2d 316 (Md. 1970)]

(g) Fear of Victim

Evidence that the defendant was "very afraid" of the victim is not sufficient to establish heat of passion. [**Tarpely v. State,** 782 S.E.2d 642 (Ga. 2016)]

(3) Mistake Concerning Provocation

On principle, a killing should be reduced to manslaughter as long as the defendant ***reasonably believed*** that a situation constituting adequate provocation existed. In other words, if the defendant was mistaken as to the existence of the provocation but his mistaken belief was a reasonable one, the killing should still be mitigated. [**Howell v. State,** 917 P.2d 1202 (Alaska App. 1996) (legislature wanted to codify "traditional doctrine of heat of passion" and thus phrase "provocation by the victim" in statute includes where defendant mistakenly but reasonably believed the victim had engaged in serious provocation)]

(4) Provocation by Someone Other than Victim

The voluntary manslaughter rule is often stated as requiring that the provocation have been by the person killed, but this may not be entirely true. Situations in which the source of the provocation came from someone ***other than the person killed*** by the defendant should be divided into two categories:

(a) Defendant Intends to Kill Provoking Party

If the defendant intended to kill the provoking party but killed someone else, either by accident or because he was mistaken as to who had provoked him, the killing is still only voluntary manslaughter. [**State v. Griego,** 294 P.2d 282 (N.M. 1956)]

(b) Defendant Intends to Kill Nonprovoking Party

If the defendant intended to kill someone he knew was not the person who provoked him, the killing is ***not reduced*** to manslaughter. Thus, even if there is adequate provocation, a homicide is murder where the defendant is so enraged that he simply strikes out at some innocent third party. [**Commonwealth v. Camacho,** 36 N.E.3d 533 (Mass. 2015) (defendant not entitled to provocation/manslaughter instruction, stated as "evidence insufficient to conclude that the victim was one of the aggressors in the fray or did anything to reasonably provoke the actions that led to his death")]

(5) Injury to Persons Other than Defendant

Generally, the defendant must be the target or victim of the provoking conduct. If the subject of the provocation is a ***close relative*** of the defendant, however, at least some courts hold that the provocation may still be adequate. [**State v. Copling,** 741 A.2d 624 (N.J. 1999) (while "person can be provoked by conduct that causes injury to a relative," defendant's mother told him his younger brother had been attacked by person defendant thereafter killed, mother also said brother "was uninjured" and thus insufficient provocation here)] The case law suggests that this rule would not be applied if the subject of the provocation were a distant relative or a mere friend [**State v. Madden,** 294 A.2d 609 (N.J. 1972)], but modern courts, reluctant to hold offered provocation inadequate as a matter of law, might well permit such cases to go to the jury.

b. Actual Provocation

No matter how reasonable the provocation, a killing will not be reduced to manslaughter unless the defendant was ***actually provoked***. This is a purely ***subjective*** requirement. In other words, it must be shown that the provocation was such as would cause a reasonable person to lose control ***and*** that ***the defendant in fact*** became so enraged that his conduct was directed by passion rather than reason. [**State v. Robinson,** 185 S.W.2d 636 (Mo. 1945); *see* **State v. Ruffner,** 911 A.2d 680 (R.I. 2006) (while other party first slashed defendant on chest with knife, defendant's own testimony showed he merely responded with acts intended to be in the nature of self-defense and without the "uncontrollable rage, anger and resentment" needed for heat of passion)] If the defendant has a cooler temperament than the reasonable man, he is not actually provoked, he is guilty of murder and cannot have his intentional killing reduced to voluntary manslaughter.

c. Absence of Reasonable Cooling Period

Voluntary manslaughter law places special emphasis on the time between the provocation and the killing.

(1) Majority Rule: Objective Standard Applied

The general rule is that a homicide is not manslaughter if between the provocation and the killing there elapsed sufficient time to enable the ***passions of a reasonable person*** to cool. This is an ***objective*** test, and it is therefore irrelevant that despite the passage of such time the defendant did not in fact cool off. [*See, e.g.*, **Commonwealth v. Lopez,** 53 N.E.3d 659 (Mass. 2016) ("if a defendant leaves the scene of the provocation . . . and then returns to attack the victim, the defendant is considered to have had adequate opportunity for his anger to subside"); **Fulcher v. State,** 778 S.E.2d 159 (Ga. 2015) (voluntary manslaughter instruction unnecessary; prior "verbal altercation" was "the day before the shooting")]

(2) Minority View: Subjective Standard Applied

A minority of courts require only that the defendant's own passions not have subsided. Under this approach, it is immaterial that the passions of a reasonable person would have cooled during the lapse of time, as long as the defendant himself was still enraged at the time of the killing. [**State v. Hazlett,** 113 N.W. 374 (N.D. 1907)]

(3) Events Preceding a Final Culmination

Some courts consider earlier events as to which a considerable time has elapsed, if they are part of a development that culminates in a defendant's provocation to kill without delay. In such cases, a court considers whether the provocation is sufficient by looking at both the culminating event and the earlier preceding events in combination. [**Commonwealth v. Voytko,** 503 A.2d 20 (Pa. 1986)]

(4) "Reinflaming" Occurrences

Although an adequate cooling period may have passed, intervening events can remind the defendant of the provoking event and "reinflame" his passions. Courts have varied on whether the cooling period should begin anew with the reinflaming occurrence, although the better view is that it should. An event which, standing alone, would not suffice to act as such a trigger may nonetheless suffice to rekindle an earlier passion. [*See, e.g.*, **People v. Berry,** 556 P.2d 777 (Cal. 1976) (only event immediately before killing was wife's screaming, which was sufficient to rekindle passion regarding her earlier confession of adultery)]

d. No Actual Cooling Off

Regardless of the period of time between the provocation and the killing, it must be shown that the defendant's passion did ***not in fact*** subside. Thus, if the defendant is unusually controlled and regains composure in a short period of time before killing, the homicide is murder even though the passions of a reasonable person would not have cooled in that time. [**Commonwealth v. Lopez,** 53 N.E.3d 659 (Mass. 2016) ("if a defendant leaves the scene of the provocation and then returns to attack the victim, the defendant is considered to have had adequate opportunity for his anger to subside")]

EXAM TIP

Note the different standards for the various elements of manslaughter: You use the objective ***reasonable person standard*** to determine whether the ***provocation is sufficient*** (would a reasonable person be provoked) and whether there was a ***sufficient cooling off period*** (would the passions of a reasonable person have cooled). However, you use a ***subjective standard*** to determine whether there was ***actual provocation*** (was ***this particular defendant*** actually provoked) and whether there was an ***actual cooling off*** (has this particular defendant's passions cooled).

4. Model Penal Code Position: "Extreme Mental or Emotional Disturbance"

Under the Model Penal Code, a killing that would otherwise be murder is reduced to manslaughter if it was committed "under the influence of ***extreme mental or emotional disturbance*** (EMED) for which there is ***reasonable explanation or excuse***." This embodies much of the concept of adequate provocation, but it also encourages submission of cases to the jury where the matter is doubtful rather than having trial judges find the evidence offered in mitigation inadequate as a matter of law. [Model Penal Code § 210.3(1)(b); **State v. Paris,** 338 A.3d 1139 (Conn. 2025) (assessment of reasonableness is made with respect to the excuse for the extreme emotional disturbance itself, not the criminal act or the choice of victim)] "The burden is on the defendant to prove extreme emotional disturbance by a preponderance of the evidence." [**State v. Raguseo,** 622 A.2d 519 (Conn. 1993)]

e.g. **Example:** D returned to his apartment at midnight, to find someone's car parked in D's assigned slot. The police refused to tow the car away. About 2 a.m., V returned to the car and a confrontation between D and V occurred. D stabbed V to death. Some evidence indicated that D was extremely upset, but other testimony was that he was quite calm. Under a modern statute based on the Model Penal Code, the judge was required to submit to the jury whether the killing was under the influence of extreme disturbance. The issue was close enough, however, that a jury verdict rejecting D's contention and convicting D of murder was supported by the evidence. [**State v. Raguseo**, *supra*]

a. Note: Anger, Embarrassment Not Enough

Even under the liberal Model Penal Code approach, some courts require that the defendant have suffered an identifiable disturbance resulting in loss of self-control. A mere showing that the defendant was made angry or embarrassed by the victim's "provoking" conduct will *not* be sufficient. [**People v. Walker,** 64 N.Y.2d 741 (1984)]

5. "Imperfect" Defense Situations as Voluntary Manslaughter

Some courts have created an additional category of voluntary manslaughter consisting of the so-called imperfect defense cases, *i.e.,* cases in which the defendant has produced evidence tending to establish a defense, but which falls short of doing so, usually because his conduct was unreasonable. [**Sanchez v. People,** 470 P.2d 857 (Colo. 1970)]

e.g. **Example:** D killed V, acting under what D believed to be the need to defend himself, but the evidence showed that D used more force than was reasonably necessary to defend himself. D was held guilty only of manslaughter rather than murder. Because the force used was unreasonable, the case was one of "imperfect" self-defense, thereby mitigating the killing from murder to manslaughter. [**Sanchez v. People,** *supra*]

E. Involuntary Manslaughter

1. Involuntary Manslaughter Defined

An ***unintended*** killing is involuntary manslaughter if (i) it is the result of ***criminal negligence*** or (ii) it is caused during the commission of an ***unlawful act*** that is not a felony or that for some other reason is insufficient to trigger the felony murder rule.

2. Killing by Criminal Negligence

An unintentional killing caused by the commission of any act, even a lawful one, in a ***criminally negligent manner*** is involuntary manslaughter. [**Commonwealth v. Welansky,** 55 N.E.2d 902 (Mass. 1944) (defendant nightclub owner failed to provide proper fire escapes, causing deaths of 490 persons in a fire; manslaughter conviction proper because of the "grave danger" to others; "even if a particular defendant is so stupid [or] so heedless . . . that in fact he did not realize the grave danger, he cannot escape [criminal liability] if an ordinary normal man under the same circumstances would have realized the gravity of the danger")]

a. More than "Civil" Negligence Required

Although it is often unclear what precisely is required for criminal negligence, the courts agree that there must be more than is necessary to establish civil liability for damages. Thus the situation must have been one in which there was both a ***high and unreasonable risk*** of death of another. [**Gill v. State,** 474 S.W.3d 77 (Ark. 2015) (driver's failure to see vehicle that pulled out onto highway not sufficient for criminal-negligence homicide, which requires something more than "a failure to perceive a risk of death"); **Commonwealth v. Welansky,** *supra* (facts must show "wanton or reckless" conduct, which must go beyond even gross negligence)]

e.g. **Example:** D went hunting with friends. They became separated; all were in camouflage attire with no hunter's orange. Hiding in some thick brush, D saw what he thought was the head of a deer with antlers and shot his rifle. He went to the location and found V shot in the head, dead on the ground. These facts showed the extreme negligence required for criminally negligent homicide. [**People v. Smith,** 887 N.Y.S.2d 511 (N.Y. 2009)]

b. Awareness of Risk May Be Required

Under traditional homicide analyses, courts often did not draw the distinction between "recklessness" and "negligence" that is drawn under modern statutes (*see supra,* p. 56). As a result, it is sometimes unclear whether the "criminal negligence" required for involuntary manslaughter requires an awareness of the risk of death. If actual awareness is required, the mental state becomes what modern terminology would regard as recklessness rather than negligence.

EXAM TIP

For your exam, remember that the definition of a crime ***in a statute or case law*** is frequently more important than the label assigned to the crime. For example, under a traditional approach, "involuntary manslaughter" is defined, in part, as a killing committed as the result of criminal negligence and is unclear whether the defendant must be aware of the high risk of death by his conduct. However, if "involuntary manslaughter" is defined under modern terminology, it will probably require "***recklessness***" on the part of the defendant as opposed to negligence, which likely will require that the defendant be aware that his conduct carries with it a high risk of death. If the defendant's conduct is particularly egregious, do not forget to discuss the possibility that he might be subject to criminal liability for a ***second degree*** (malice-type) murder.

3. Killing by Commission of an Unlawful Act: "Misdemeanor Manslaughter"

An unintentional killing caused during the commission of an unlawful "predicate" act is involuntary manslaughter.

a. Nature of Unlawful Act

A misdemeanor will suffice for manslaughter. But the doctrine is broader than this. A felony that, for any reason, does not support felony murder (*see supra,* p. 210 *et seq.*) will be enough for involuntary manslaughter. Some acts, even though not criminal under the law, have been held "unlawful" for manslaughter purposes although it is unlikely that modern courts would follow this approach. [**Commonwealth v. Mink,** 123 Mass. 422 (1877)]

e.g. **Example:** D attempted to kill herself with a revolver. Her fiancé intervened, trying to disarm her, but the revolver accidentally discharged and he was killed. Although attempted suicide was not a crime, it was an "unlawful act" and D was therefore convicted of manslaughter. [**Commonwealth v. Mink,** *supra*]

b. Limitations upon Doctrine

Misdemeanor manslaughter, like felony murder, has sometimes been judicially disfavored because it imposes strict liability for a relatively serious offense. Because involuntary manslaughter is a much less serious crime than murder, however, these courts have generally not regarded misdemeanor manslaughter as suspect as felony murder. [*See, e.g.,* **People v. Datema,** 533 N.W.2d 272 (Mich. 1995) (although court had abandoned felony murder, misdemeanor manslaughter based on assault as predicate offense is not subject to same objections)] In part because of this judicial disfavor, limitations on misdemeanor manslaughter have developed. In the absence of statutory changes, courts may interpret the word "misdemeanor" in a statute to exclude minor misdemeanors punishable by fine only.

(1) Predicate Offense Must Be "Malum In Se" Rather than "Malum Prohibitum"

Some jurisdictions hold that the predicate act must be not only unlawful but also ***malum in se*** (*i.e.,* wrong in itself) rather than simply *malum prohibitum* (*i.e.,* prohibited for convenience). *Malum in se* is applied to the defendant's commission or attempted commission of conduct that unintentionally causes another's death. The defendant is guilty of involuntary manslaughter, without regard either to the foreseeability of the victim's death or to the existence of any causal connection between the "unlawful excess" portion of the defendant's conduct and the victim's death. [**State v. Davis,** 196 N.W.2d 885 (Iowa 1972) (defendant, driving car while intoxicated, caused a death; driving while intoxicated is *malum in se*, so that to cause death by drunken driving is manslaughter)]

e.g. **Example:** Traffic offenses are only *malum prohibitum* and hence are often held an insufficient predicate for misdemeanor manslaughter. [**State v. Collins,** 616 N.E.2d 224 (Ohio 1993) (legislature did not intend failure to stop at stop sign to be sufficient for misdemeanor manslaughter)]

(2) Negligence in Addition to Unlawful Act Required

Some courts impose the additional requirement that the defendant have acted with criminal negligence, especially where the predicate offense is only *malum prohibitum*. [**People v. Pavlic,** 199 N.W. 373 (Mich. 1924) (defendant sold liquor, a felony; buyer drank it, became drunk, died of exposure and acute alcoholism; not felony murder because sale of liquor, though a felony, "is an act not itself directly and naturally dangerous to life"]

Civil negligence at one time provided the unlawful act that could lead to involuntary manslaughter convictions. [*See, e.g.*, **State v. Williams,** 484 P.2d 1167 (Wash.App. 1971) (Native American parents, afraid that state welfare services would take their child, did not take him to the hospital; he died from an abscessed tooth; on appeal from the manslaughter conviction, the court found that a reasonable person, under similar circumstances, would have been sufficiently put on notice concerning the severity of the child's medical condition; failure to seek medical attention constitutes negligence; the state statute under which the criminal charges were brought was later repealed)]

(3) Unlawful Aspect of Activity Must Cause Death

A few courts require a showing that the ***unlawful aspect*** of the defendant's activity caused the victim's death; *i.e.,* it may not be enough that the course of conduct constituting the unlawful act caused death. [**People v. Penny,** 44 Cal. 2d 861 (1965)]

e.g. **Example:** An unlicensed cosmetologist who caused a patient's death by a poisoned face-lifting treatment was held not guilty of manslaughter. While the lack of a license was a misdemeanor, this was not the aspect of the cosmetologist's activity that caused the death. [**People v. Penny,** *supra*]

F. Modern Statutory Distinctions

1. Model Penal Code Scheme

Modern statutes, or at least those that are part of a comprehensive revision of a state's entire criminal code, tend to redefine the homicide offenses by grading them according to the different states of mind as defined by the Model Penal Code (*see supra,* p. 54 *et seq.*). Note the absence of common law terms such as premeditation and deliberation.

a. Murder

Under this approach, murder is defined as a killing committed (i) purposely, (ii) knowingly, or (iii) recklessly under circumstances manifesting extreme indifference to the value of human life. [Model Penal Code § 210.2(1)]

b. Manslaughter

The Model Penal Code abandons the distinction between the two traditional types of manslaughter (voluntary and involuntary), and instead creates a single manslaughter offense. Under this scheme, manslaughter is (i) a killing committed recklessly, or (ii) a killing that would otherwise be murder but is committed under the influence of extreme mental or emotional disturbance for which there is reasonable explanation or excuse. [Model Penal Code § 210.3(1)]

c. Negligent Homicide

In addition, the Model Penal Code creates the new homicide offense of "negligent homicide" consisting of killings committed negligently. [Model Penal Code § 210.4(1)]

2. Homicide Caused During Operation of a Motor Vehicle

Modern criminal codes often contain a separate offense for death caused in the negligent operation of a motor vehicle or by operating a motor vehicle in an unlawful manner. In some states, this offense is a "new" type of manslaughter, but the penalties that may be imposed are often less severe than those assigned to the more traditional kinds of manslaughter. [Cal. Penal Code §§ 192(c), 193]

G. General Problems Relating to Homicide Liability

1. Introduction

Several collateral problems (discussed below) are common to all the homicide crimes:

2. Causation

All homicide crimes require that the conduct of the defendant be proved to have caused the death of the victim. Consequently, problems of causation (*see supra,* p. 64 *et seq.*) often arise in homicide cases.

3. Victim Must Be a Living Human Being: Killing of Fetus

A killing cannot be a criminal homicide unless the victim is a ***living human being***. [**Keeler v. Superior Court,** 2 Cal. 3d 619 (1970)] What then is the result if the defendant causes the death of a fetus; is the victim in such cases a "living human being"?

a. General Rule: Fetus Not Living Human Being

The traditional common law rule is that a fetus is not a living human being until it has been ***"born alive,"*** *i.e.,* fully brought forth from the mother and having an independent circulation. [**People v. Ehlert,** 654 N.E.2d 705 (Ill. 1995)] At least one case has extended this to include a fetus ***in the process of being born*** if in the natural course of events the birth would have been completed. [**People v. Chavez,** 77 Cal. App. 2d 621 (1947)] Most courts have been reluctant to make any further inroads on the common law rule. [**Keeler**

v. Superior Court, (refusing to extend the rule to killing of unborn but viable fetus not in the process of birth)] However, some states that maintain the "born alive" rule have ruled that injury to a fetus before birth may be homicide if the fetus dies after being born alive. [*See, e.g.*, **State v. Cotton**, 5 P.3d 918 (Ariz.App. 2000)]

b. Minority View: Fetus Protected by Homicide Laws

One court has reasoned that the traditional rule was based on the difficulty of proving that a defendant in fact caused the "death" of a fetus that would otherwise have been born alive, and that modern medical knowledge has rendered this rationale invalid. Thus, that court held that homicide law permits prosecution on the basis that the defendant caused the death of a fetus that would otherwise have been born alive. [**Hughes v. State,** 868 P.2d 730 (Okla. 1994) (court rejects "obsolete, antiquated common law rule" and holds that the phrase "human being" in homicide statute covers a viable fetus)]

c. Statutory Changes Extending Homicide Protection to Fetus

Some states have amended their homicide statutes to include a fetus within the definition of a human being. [Cal. Penal Code § 187 (defining murder as the unlawful killing of a human being ***or fetus*** with malice aforethought)] Statutes of this sort have been upheld against contentions that women's constitutional right to abort a fetus bars criminalization of this conduct. [**People v. Davis,** 872 P.2d 591 (Cal. 1994) (women's constitutional right of privacy does not apply if fetus is aborted without woman's consent)] Most of these statutes specifically exempt legally performed abortions from their reach.

4. When Does Death Occur: Definition of Death

Any of the homicide crimes may also raise issues regarding the definition of death, especially if a defendant argues that the victim's death for legal purposes was actually caused by action taken by treating doctors. For example, suppose a physician removes a victim's organs for purposes of an organ transplant before the victim's legally defined death. If the physician is regarded as having legally caused the death, a defendant who had earlier shot the victim may be relieved of liability for criminal homicide and the physician may be guilty of a crime. It is, therefore, important to determine at what point life ends for purposes of homicide law.

a. General Rule: Death Is Cessation of Heartbeat and Respiration

The traditional rule is that death occurs when the victim's heartbeat and respiratory functions stop. [**Thomas v. Anderson,** 96 Cal. App. 2d 371 (1950)]

b. Alternative Standard: "Brain Death"

A more appropriate criterion would define death as the cessation of the functioning of the brain. Under this standard, death occurs when an electroencephalograph ("EEG") reads flat for a given period of time, even if the victim's heart and breathing remain active. The "brain death" standard for defining the death of a homicide victim has been accepted by all states. [**State v. Fierro,** 603 P.2d 74 (Ariz. 1979) (defendant shot the victim in head, and victim was taken to the hospital where preliminary determination was that he had suffered brain death; victim was maintained on life support systems for three days, during which time follow-up studies confirmed that conclusion; doctor then terminated the support measures, and defendant was thereafter charged with murder)]

5. Death Must Occur Within a Year and a Day

Traditionally, the victim's death must occur within a ***year and a day*** from the time the fatal blow was given or the cause of death (*e.g.*, poison) was administered. The limitation is independent of the ordinary causation requirements; even if the victim would not have died as and when he did "but for" the defendant's acts, there can be no homicide prosecution if the death transpired after the year-and-a-day time period. [**Ball v. United States,** 140 U.S. 118 (1891)]

a. Rationale

The rationale for this seemingly arbitrary rule is that otherwise, proof of causation might be so difficult that there is too great a danger of unjustified prosecutions and convictions. [**Rogers v. Tennessee**, 532 U.S. 451 (2001)]

b. Rule Modified or Abandoned

New advances in crime detection and medicine have arguably reduced the difficulties of proving the cause of a homicide victim's death despite the passage of time. Some legislature and courts have consequently abandoned the traditional time limit requirement. [*See* **Rogers v. Tennessee,** *supra*; **People v. Carrillo,** 646 N.E.2d 582 (Ill. 1995)] Some states have adopted a modified requirement. California first retained the rule, but then extended the time limit to three years and one day, only to subsequently provide that if death occurs beyond that three year and one day requirement, there is a rebuttable presumption that the killing was not criminal. [*See* Cal. Penal Code § 194]

6. Aiding or Causing Suicide

Special problems are caused when the victim has requested to be killed or has actually participated in taking her own life.

a. Common Law Position: Offense Is Murder

Suicide is murder at common law and therefore one who assists another, whether actively or passively, in taking her own life is a party to that offense. [**Burnett v. People,** 68 N.E. 505 (Ill. 1903)]

b. Modern Position: Separate Offense

Under modern statutory schemes, suicide itself is not an offense; thus, the aider cannot be guilty of such a crime as a party. However, some statutes create the separate crime of aiding suicide. [Cal. Penal Code § 401]

(1) Distinguish: Actively Killing Another

"[T]he difference between murder and aiding suicide generally hinges upon whether the defendant *actively* participates in the overt act directly causing death, or whether he merely provides the means of committing suicide. . . . This rule applies even where the victim has given his consent or requested the actual assistance provided." [**State v. Sexson,** 869 P.2d 301 (N.M.1994); **People v. Matlock,** 336 P.2d 505 (Cal. 1959) (one who actively takes the life of another, even at the other person's specific request, is guilty of murder)]

Chapter Nine

Other Crimes Against the Person

CONTENTS	PAGE

Key Exam Issues

In evaluating possible liability for crimes against the person (other than homicide), consider first the nature of the attack upon the victim:

1. Was the attack sexual in nature? (Consider ***rape*** and related offenses.)
2. Did the attack involve restriction of the victim's liberty? (Consider ***false imprisonment*** and ***kidnapping***.)
3. Was the attack some other type of physical attack? (Consider ***assault, battery***, and ***mayhem***.)

Especially look for these crimes in situations that at first suggest a homicide, but either (a) where the victim did not die and the defendant did not have the state of mind required for attempted murder, or (b) where there appears to be insufficient causation between the defendant's conduct and the death of the victim. In these cases, although the defendant cannot be convicted of murder or some other form of homicide, it may be possible to find the defendant liable for one of the assaultive crimes discussed in this chapter.

A. Assault and Battery

1. Terminology

Although the terms "assault and battery" are often used together, under traditional analysis they represent different and distinct crimes. While there are some similarities between these crimes and the ***torts*** of "assault" and "battery," there are also significant differences.

2. Battery

Battery is the unlawful application of force to the person of another. [**State v. Briggs**, 9 N.W.3d 632 (Neb. 2024) (common law battery requires "intentional physical contact that is not consented to and is unwarranted by the social usages prevalent at the time and place at which the contact is inflicted")]

a. Actus Reus

The *actus reus* of battery is simply the ***application of force*** to the person of another.

(1) No Injury Required

Traditionally, a battery does not require an injury to the victim; indeed, the touching need not have left any mark at all on the victim. [**People v. James,** 9 Cal. App. 2d 162 (1935)]

(2) Indirect Application of Force

Moreover, the force can be applied directly ***or indirectly***, as where the defendant sets in motion the force that causes the touching. [**State v. Monroe,** 28 S.E. 547 (N.C. 1897) (D administers poison in candy to V, causing V internal injury; D has committed battery)]

e.g. **Example:** D exposed his genitals and compelled a six-year-old girl to hold them. D is guilty of battery; it is immaterial that the girl did the actual touching. [*See* **Beausoliel v. United States,** 107 F.2d 292 (D.C. Cir. 1939)]

(3) Battery Under Modern Statutes

As criminalized under modern statutory provisions, battery is somewhat different than under traditional law.

(a) Injury or Offensive Touching Required

Modern statutes often abandon the position that any touching constitutes the offense. Instead, such statutes frequently require either that ***bodily injury*** be caused ***or*** that the touching is intended or likely to be regarded as ***offensive***. [*See, e.g.*, **State v. Struzyk,** 869 N.W.2d 280 (Minn. 2015) (throwing bodily fluid on another person not sufficient, "as mere *potential* to cause bodily harm through the transfer of bodily fluids or feces does not satisfy the legal standard for bodily harm")]

(b) Battery Made Form of Assault

Modern statutes frequently abandon the "battery" terminology and make the offense one type of assault. [*See* Model Penal Code § 211.1(1)(a) (injury required)]

EXAM TIP

As mentioned above, you will often hear the terms "assault and battery" used as if it is one crime and not two (or three; *see* exam tip, p. 232, *infra*). Sometimes exam questions will require you to analyze the ***common law*** crimes and so you should discuss the crimes separately. But if the question provides a statute, examine the statutory definition and be aware that many statutes use only the term "assault" but define it to include a battery.

---

b. Mens Rea

It is sometimes said that the application of force must have been intentional. This is not true, and such statements probably reflect confusion between the crime of battery and the intentional tort of battery.

(1) Negligence Sufficient

Traditionally, battery requires only that the defendant act with criminal negligence, as where he ***should have been aware*** that his conduct would cause the application of force to the person of another. These cases use a fiction, saying that intent is necessary but that criminal negligence supplies the intent. [**Fish v. Michigan,** 62 F.2d 659 (6th Cir. 1933) (if one recklessly injures another, it is a battery, for the law "holds him to have intended" the injury and "treats him as if he had done an intended wrong")]

(2) Unlawful Act Sufficient

Some, but not all, courts traditionally also find a battery simply on the basis that the defendant was engaged in the commission of an unlawful act at the time of the application of force to another. However, some of these courts may require that the unlawful act be *malum in se* rather than *malum prohibitum*. [**Commonwealth v. Adams,** 114 Mass. 323 (1873) (defendant, speeding in sleigh in violation of ordinance, struck pedestrian; conviction of battery reversed, because speeding is *malum prohibitum* and not *malum in se*)] Under modern statutes, an unlawful act is unlikely to be sufficient.

c. Effect of Consent

There is no battery if the victim ***effectively consented*** to the application of force. (*See supra,* p. 143, for discussion of the circumstances in which consent is legally effective.)

d. Punishment

At common law, battery is a misdemeanor, and "simple" battery is generally a misdemeanor under modern statutes. Most modern statutes also make certain ***"aggravated"*** batteries (batteries committed with intent to kill, rob, or rape, those resulting in serious bodily harm to the victim, and those committed with a dangerous or deadly weapon) felonies. [*See*, *e.g.*, **Blea v. State,** 483 S.W.3d 29 (Tex.App. 2016) (court should consider disfiguring and impairing quality of injury as inflicted and not amelioration or exacerbation of injury by actions not attributable to defendant, such as medical treatment)]

3. Assault

Two different kinds of activity may constitute a criminal assault: (i) an ***attempt to commit a battery***, and (ii) ***intentionally placing another in fear*** of a battery. Not all states punish both types.

EXAM TIP

Think of assault as two separate crimes. On an exam remember to check the facts for elements of ***both types of assault*** because one may apply even though the other does not. Many people, probably remembering their Torts class, discuss the intentional placing in fear type of assault, but forget about the attempted battery assault. Be sure to review the facts for *both* types of assault.

a. Attempted Battery as Assault

Common law criminal assault was apparently limited to attempts to commit a battery. Virtually all jurisdictions now recognize this form of assault.

(1) Mens Rea

Although there is some confusion concerning the *mens rea* required for an attempted battery type of assault, it is clear that an ***intent to frighten*** the victim will ***not suffice*** for this type of assault. [**Hayes v. State,** 781 S.E.2d 777 (Ga. 2016) (if the defendant is charged with the attempted battery variety of assault, there is no need to show that the victim was placed in reasonable apprehension of injury, as would be required for the intentional-scaring variety of the crime); **McGee v. United States,** 533 A.2d 1268 (D.C.App. 1987) (where only attempted-battery type charged, defendant's mere "brandishing" of gun did not prove intent to injure)]

(a) Intent to Commit a Battery

The general rule is that the defendant must have intended to commit a battery, which means she must have ***intended the application of force*** to the victim. Thus, there can be no conviction for assault where the evidence shows that the defendant was only reckless, *i.e.,* only aware of a substantial risk that her conduct would result in a battery.

EXAM TIP

Notice the difference in *mens rea* requirements for battery and attempted battery assault. While the ***intent to apply force is not necessary for battery*** (negligence is enough), for ***attempted battery*** the defendant ***must have that intent***. This, as you recall, is the requirement of specific intent for attempt.

(b) Intent to Commit Dangerous Act

At least one court has held that assault simply requires an intent to willfully commit an act, the direct, natural, and probable consequences of which (if successfully completed) would be injury to another. Under this approach, the defendant need not have intended the injury. [**People v. Rocha,** 479 P.2d 372 (Cal. 1971)]

(2) Actus Reus

Because this type of assault is attempted battery, the rules applicable to attempt apply (*see supra,* p. 187 *et seq.*). Thus, the defendant must have progressed sufficiently towards completing the battery. [**State v. Gordon,** 584 P.2d 1163 (1978) ("when a person holds a deadly weapon in a position so that it could immediately be used to physically injure another, he need go no further; it sufficient here that defendant held knife to victim's neck)]

(3) Present Ability to Succeed

Under statutes in ***some*** states (although not under the common law definition), assault requires proof that the defendant had the actual ***present ability to succeed*** in an attempt to commit a battery. [**People v. Sylva,** 76 P. 814 (Cal. 1904) (attempt to shoot V with unloaded gun that D believed to be loaded was not an assault; no present ability to commit a battery)]

(4) Conditional Assault

The fact that the defendant expressly or impliedly represented that she would not commit a battery if the victim complied with certain demands does not bar a conviction for assault.

e.g. **Example:** D points a gun at V, saying, "Put up your hands." D is guilty of assault. D's words and actions imply that she will shoot V, but ***only if*** V does not comply with the demand to raise his hands. The fact that the assault is conditional, because the victim could avoid the threatened harm by giving in to the demand, is immaterial, and D can be convicted of assault. [**People v. Thompson,** 93 Cal. App. 2d 780 (1949)]

b. Intentional Placing in Fear as Assault

Most states extend the crime of assault to include the intentional act of putting another in fear of immediate bodily harm. In these jurisdictions, an assault can be committed ***either*** by an attempted battery ***or*** by intentionally putting another in fear.

(1) Intent to Cause Apprehension of Harm

Under this form of assault, the defendant must have ***intended to put the victim in fear***, although a showing that the defendant intended to actually harm the victim will also suffice. [**United States v. Ford,** 613 F.3d 1263 (10th Cir. 2010) (even if defendant's "gunshots were diversionary, they were intended to cause apprehension" and thus "constituted an assault under any definition known to American law")]

(2) Victim Must Be Apprehensive

In addition, proof that the victim was ***aware*** of the assault is essential, as is a showing that the victim *in fact* experienced ***apprehension of immediate harm***. [**United States v. Acosta-Sierra,** 690 F.3d 1111 (9th Cir. 2012) (A, unknown to B, threw rock at B, who "did not become aware of the threat until after it had dissipated")]

(3) Conduct Sufficient to Create Reasonable Apprehension

The defendant's conduct must have been of the sort ***likely to induce a fear*** of immediate harm ***in a reasonable person***. [**United States v. Ford,** *supra*] Thus, ***mere words*** are usually ***not*** enough for this kind of assault, although words accompanied by some action may be sufficient. [**State v. Hazen,** 165 P.2d 234 (Kan. 1946) (defendant with fists clenched threatened to hit and stomp victim, frightening him; assault is committed by threatening injury, without actually doing injury)]

cf. **Compare:** D verbally threatens to strike V but *makes no physical move* to do so. This is not criminal assault, although it could be if D also raises her fist if to act on her threats. [**State v. Hazen**, *supra*]

c. Model Penal Code Position

The Model Penal Code defines an assault as including:

(i) An attempt to cause bodily injury to another; ***or***

(ii) An attempt by physical menace to put another in fear of imminent serious bodily harm.

[Model Penal Code § 211.1(1)(c)]

(1) Note

This latter type of assault (sometimes known as "menacing") differs from the traditional "putting in fear" form of assault in two ways: (i) ***no actual fear*** need exist in the victim, because an attempt to put in fear is enough; and (ii) the attempt must be to put the victim in fear of ***serious*** bodily harm.

d. Punishment

Assault is a misdemeanor at common law, and "simple" assault remains so today. However, modern statutes often make certain ***"aggravated" assaults*** felonies. The aggravated assaults generally include assaults with intent to kill, rob, or rape; assaults on a police officer; and assaults with a deadly weapon.

4. Stalking

Stalking did not exist at common law. In relation to the common law offenses of assault and battery, "[t]he stalking statute was intended to fill gaps in the law by criminalizing conduct that fell short of assault or battery . . . by ensuring that victims did not have to be injured or threatened with death before stopping a stalker's harassment." [**Curry v. State,** 811 So.2d 736 (Fla.App. 2002)]

a. Rationale for Stalking

The offense of stalking "serves significant and substantial state interests by providing law enforcement officials with a means of intervention in potentially dangerous situations before actual violence occurs, and it enables citizens to protect themselves from recurring intimidation, fear-provoking conduct and physical violence." [**State v. Ruesch,** 571 N.W.2d 898 (Wis. 1997)]

b. The Scope of Stalking Statutes

Stalking frequently is defined as the stalker's intentional engages in a course of conduct directed at a specific person or persons, that seriously alarms, annoys, intimidates or harasses the person or persons, and serves no legitimate purpose. A course of conduct would cause a reasonable person to suffer substantial mental distress.

(1) Course of Conduct

This constitutes a pattern of conduct composed of two (2) or more acts, evidencing a continuity of purpose. One (1) or more of these acts may include the use of any equipment, instrument, machine, or other device by which communication or information is transmitted, including computers, the Internet or other electronic network, cameras or other recording devices, telephones or other personal communications devices, scanners or other copying devices, and any device that enables the use of a transmitting device.

(2) Protected Activities

Constitutionally protected activity is not included within the meaning of "course of conduct." If the defendant claims that he was engaged in constitutionally protected activity, the court shall determine the validity of that claim as a matter of law and, if found valid, shall exclude that activity from evidence.

(3) Aggravated Stalking

More serious punishment is possible for a defendant who has either a prior stalking conviction when arrested, was subject to a protective order, or was on probation or other conditional release for the current offense when arrested.

COMPARISON OF BATTERY AND ASSAULT

		ASSAULT	
	BATTERY	ATTEMPTED BATTERY	INTENTIONAL PLACING IN FEAR
ACTUS REUS	Direct or indirect ***application of force*** to another's person	***Attempt to cause a battery***	Conduct that is ***likely to induce fear*** in a reasonable person and which does in fact induce fear in victim
MENS REA	***At least negligence*** (should have been aware the force would result)	***Intent*** to apply force to another's person	***Intent*** to put victim in fear of a battery

B. Mayhem

1. In General

At early common law, mayhem consisted of maliciously depriving another of the use of such of his members as might render him less able to fight. The crime was later extended by English statute to cover injuries that disfigured but did not disable the victim.

a. Modern Statutes

Modern statutes sometimes retain the crime of mayhem, generally defining it to require either that the defendant ***disable or disfigure*** another. [Cal. Penal Code § 203 (defining crime of mayhem as disabling, disfiguring, or rendering useless a member of another's body, depriving another of such a member of the body, or cutting or disabling the tongue, putting out an eye, or slitting the nose, ear, or lip)]

2. Actus Reus

The defendant must have caused the victim bodily injury that permanently disfigures or disables him.

a. Disablement

"Disablement" requires the ***loss of use*** of a major part of the body (*e.g.,* arm, hand, finger, leg, foot, eye, front-tooth, or testicle), although that part need not actually be removed. [**Bowers v. State,** 7 S.W. 247 (Tex. 1888)]

e.g. **Example:** D commits mayhem by biting off a portion of V's thumb only if the injury substantially deprived V of the use of the thumb. [**Bowers v. State,** *supra*]

b. Disfigurement

"Disfigurement" requires an ***alteration*** of the victim's face or body that changes his normal appearance, such as severing or slitting the nose, lip, ear, or tongue. [**State v. Raulie,** 59 P.2d 359 (N.M. 1936)]

c. Permanent Damage Required

For either disablement or disfigurement, the injury must be ***permanent.*** [**State v. Raulie,** *supra* (cutting of V's lip not mayhem where lip was stitched and healed, leaving no mark)]

3. Mens Rea

It is often said that the defendant must have acted "maliciously," and statutes sometimes require an "intent to disable or disfigure." Nevertheless, an ***intent to injure*** the victim will generally suffice. Moreover, some courts have even held it enough that the defendant intended to commit a minor battery on the victim, even though she had no intent to inflict serious injury at all. [**State v. Hatley,** 384 P.2d 252 (N.M. 1963) (defendant deliberately struck victim, unintentionally putting out his eye; conviction of mayhem under statute requiring intent to maim or disfigure affirmed; his intent to do wrong in causing the battery suffices)]

4. Punishment

Mayhem is a felony at common law, punishable by mutilation (*i.e.,* loss of the same member as suffered by the victim). Although the penalty is not as drastic today, the crime ordinarily remains a felony under modern statutes.

C. Rape and Related Offenses

1. In General

At common law, rape is unlawful sexual intercourse with a female person without her consent. For analytical purposes, it is useful to distinguish between cases in which the intercourse is accomplished by means of force, threats, or fraud ("forcible" rape) and those in which consent is given but is ineffective because of the victim's age ("statutory" rape). Modern statutes often redefine the offense and rename it as sexual assault, classifying it as a crime against the person rather than a sexual offense.

2. Forcible (or Common Law) Rape

Common law rape consists of unlawful carnal knowledge of a woman against her will. [**State in Interest of M.T.S.,** 609 A.2d 1266 (N.J. 1992) (the issue is whether the complaining witness gave "affirmative permission," not what the defendant did; her permission must be to the specific act of intercourse, as opposed to lesser form of sexual intimacy)] Several aspects of this definition have given rise to difficulty.

a. "Carnal Knowledge": Sexual Intercourse

The requirement of carnal knowledge means that the defendant must have completed an act of sexual intercourse. however, only the ***slightest penetration*** of the female sexual organ is required; emission is not necessary. [**Commonwealth v. Mazariego,** 47 N.E.3d 420 (Mass. 2016)]

b. Husband Cannot Rape Wife

Traditionally, the intercourse must be "unlawful." Thus, at common law, a husband cannot be convicted of raping his wife, even if he compels her to submit to intercourse.

(1) Rationale

The term "unlawful" was originally used to mean "not authorized by law," and intercourse between a husband and wife was authorized. A wife was regarded as "consenting" to intercourse with her husband during the marital relationship.

(2) Distinguish: Termination of Marriage

A man who engaged in intercourse with his ***former*** wife (*i.e.,* after a divorce) without her consent can be convicted of rape. [**State v. Parsons,** 285 S.W. 412 (Mo. 1926)]

(3) Distinguish: Liability as Accomplice to Rape

While a husband cannot commit common law rape by having sexual intercourse with his wife, he can be convicted as a ***party*** to a rape of his wife by some other man (*see supra,* p. 90).

EXAM TIP

Even though the common law rule is that a husband cannot rape his wife, keep in mind this exception: A husband ***who acts as an accomplice to the rape*** committed by another person is guilty of rape of his wife. Similarly, a woman can be guilty of rape if she acts as an accomplice.

(4) **Modern Statutes**

In about 75% of the states, modern statutes have abolished all forms of the marital rape exception. Even some of those states have retained the exception with respect to statutory rape. A few states have adopted a statutory provision explicitly excluding marriage as a defense to rape. [*See*, *e.g.*, Wis.Stat. § 940.225(6)]

c. Against the Will of the Woman: Without Consent

The requirement that the intercourse be against the will of the woman has proven difficult to apply. Several situations must be distinguished. All effectively involve situations in which the act is accomplished without the effective consent of the woman.

Recent revisions to Article 213 of the Model Penal Code address sexual assault. The definition of consent includes the idea that consent can be inferred from behavior, and that it can be revoked at any time. Revised Article 213 also explicitly recognizes psychological coercion as a factor negating consent, including situations where a victim feels pressured or intimidated into sexual activity without physical force. Consent also is ineffective if given by someone who is incompetent or if the circumstances prevent them from freely exercising consent.

e.g. **Example:** D was convicted of having sexual intercourse with V while the latter was asleep. [*See* **Travis v. State,** 98 A.3d 281 (Md.App. 2014) (physically helpless individual included the instant case of "sexual intercourse with a sleeping victim")]

(1) Intercourse Accomplished by Force

Intercourse accomplished by force is, of course, without consent. However, there is no rape if the victim resisted during the early portion of the encounter but consented before the actual act of intercourse. [**Wade v. State,** 138 S.E. 921 (Ga. 1927)]

(2) Intercourse Accomplished by Threats

Consent or submission obtained by placing the victim in fear of great and immediate bodily harm is legally ***ineffective***, and the intercourse is rape. [**State v. Schuster,** 282 S.W.2d 553 (Mo. 1955)]

(3) Incapacity to Give Effective Consent

If the victim was ***incapable*** of giving a legally effective consent, because of intoxication, mental deficiency, or insanity, intercourse with her is against the woman's will and is rape. [**Arroyo v. State,** 903 S.E.2d 712 (Ga.App. 2024) ("evidence constitutes more than 'mere intoxication' and was sufficient for the jury to find lack of consent and constructive force based on the victim's heavy intoxication."); *see* **State v. Ericson,** 566 P.3d 468 (Idaho App. 2025) (victim was legally incapable of consenting to massage therapist's digital penetration due to trauma of incident; sufficient expert testimony about phenomenon of "tonic immobility" during sexual assaults)]

(4) Consent Obtained by Fraud

Under certain limited circumstances, consent obtained by fraud renders the consent ineffective, and thus the intercourse is against the will of the woman and is rape. "Fraud in the factum" invalidates consent, while fraud in the inducement does not negate consent.

(a) Fraud as to Whether Act Is Intercourse

If the defendant deceives the victim into believing that the act involved is ***something other than intercourse***, her consent to that act will not bar a rape conviction. This is regarded as "fraud in the factum", *i.e.,* fraud as to the ***nature of the act***. [**State v. Ely,** 194 P. 988 (Wash. 1921)]

e.g. **Example:** D told V that in the course of medical treatment it would be necessary for him to insert a medical instrument as part of a vaginal examination. V consented to this. D in fact had sexual intercourse with her. D was guilty of rape, as there was no effective consent to the sexual act. [*See, e.g.,* **State v. Ely,** *supra*]

1) Distinguish: Fraud as to Medical Value of Intercourse

Fraud in the inducement occurred when the victims were touched in exactly the manner represented to them. The consents, therefore, were not vitiated. [**State v. Bolsinger,** 709 N.W.2d 560 (Iowa 2006)] Fraud also occurs when defendant misrepresents his HIV status. [**State v. Doe,** 249 A.3d 658 (Vt. 2020)]

EXAM TIP

In analyzing whether the fraud nullifies a woman's consent to sexual intercourse, remember the distinction between fraud as to the ***nature of the act*** and other types of fraud. Fraud that deceives the woman as to the ***fact that it was intercourse***, fraud in the factum, does nullify her consent. Other types of fraud including fraud as to reasons why she should consent, fraud in the inducement, do not affect the consent. If the woman consented to what she understood would be an act of intercourse, her consent is effective and there is ***no rape***.

(b) Fraud as to Whether Defendant Is Husband

There is a split of authority where the defendant has intercourse with the victim after fraudulently inducing her into believing that they are married, *e.g.,* by pretending to be her husband or by deceiving her into believing that a sham ceremony has caused them to be married. Some courts find that intercourse under these circumstances is not rape on the theory that the victim has not been deceived as to the nature of the act (*i.e.,* whether it is sexual intercourse). [**State v. Brooks,** 76 N.C. 1 (1877)] But other courts have found the fraud sufficiently related to the nature of the act to support a rape conviction. [**Crosswell v. People,** 13 Mich. 427 (1865)]

(c) Fraud as to Identity

Consent to sex with one person does not imply consent to sex with another. When D entered V's home, he knew that V intended to have sex with another man, but not with him. D knew V never consented to any physical contact with him, sexual or otherwise. Instead, D decided that fact gave him license to proceed. His intent to engage in conduct legally constituted a sexual offense. [**State v. Kelso-Christy,** 911 N.W.2d 663 (Iowa 2018)]

d. Mens Rea

The *mens rea* required for rape is not clearly defined. The major question is whether the defendant must be aware that the act is being performed against the will of the woman.

This is particularly important in those cases in which the defendant asserts a mistaken belief that the victim did consent. Mistake of fact applies only if rape requires awareness of non-consent and thus the defendant's mistake negates the required *mens rea*. [**Commonwealth v. Lopez,** 745 N.E.2d 961 (Mass. 2001) (taking the minority view, "mistake as to consent cannot . . . negate a mental state required for commission of the prohibited conduct," *i.e.,* no *mens rea* is required for the element of non-consent)]

(1) Awareness of Non-Consent Not Required

Some courts take the position that no awareness of non-consent is required by rape. [**Commonwealth v. Lopez**, *supra* (common law rape requires only intent to have sexual intercourse)]

(2) Alternative View: Reasonable Mistaken Belief That Victim Consented Will Preclude Liability

Several courts have held that a defendant's mistaken belief that the victim consented to the sexual activity will prevent conviction only if *both* (i) the defendant ***honestly and in good faith*** had such a belief; and (ii) the facts were such that mistake was ***objectively reasonable***. [**United States v. Short,** 4 C.M.A. 437 (1954)]

(a) Requirement of Equivocal Conduct by Victim

Several leading mistake cases hold that an issue of mistake of fact is raised for jury consideration when the facts tend to show equivocal conduct by the victim that could have led the defendant to reasonably believe the victim consented.

e.g. **Example:** D was entitled to a mistake of fact jury instruction regarding V's consent, if he "entertains a reasonable and bona fide belief that a prosecutrix voluntarily consented to" sexual intercourse) [**People v. Mayberry,** 15 Cal. 3d 143 (1975)]

e.g. **Example:** D was tried for raping V. D testified that V consented; V testified that she resisted D's efforts but D (the then heavyweight boxing champion) overcame her resistance. The jury did not have to be instructed on mistake as to consent, because D presented no evidence of equivocal conduct on V's part that could have led him to reasonably believe she consented. [**Tyson v. State,** 619 N.E.2d 276 (Ind.App. 1993)]

(3) Alternative View: Unreasonable Mistake Can Be Sufficient to Preclude Liability

In a leading decision, the House of Lords held that under English rape law then in effect, a rape defendant's even unreasonable mistaken belief that the victim was consenting would prevent conviction, because it showed the lack of the *mens rea* required by the crime. [**Regina v. Morgan,** A.C. 182 (1976) (a subjective test interpreted to mean "that recklessness regarding consent is the *mens rea* required to support a rape conviction"]

Note: If rape requires that the defendant have been aware that the act was performed against the will of the woman, *Morgan* is consistent with the position of the Model Penal Code that acquittal is required by any mistake of fact that negates the state of mind required, even if that mistake was unreasonable (*see supra,* p. 123). American courts, however, have been reluctant to adopt that view in this situation.

e. Special Problems

(1) Corroboration of Victim's Testimony

Several states used to require that the rape victim's testimony be corroborated, on the rationale that a charge of rape is easy to make and difficult to disprove. By the time the Model Penal Code adopted a general corroboration requirement for rape and other felony sex offenses [Model Penal Code § 213.6(5)], no state had retained such a requirement. Still, a few states retain a corroboration requirement in specific rape situations. [*See, e.g.*, Ga.Code § 16–6–3(a) (statutory rape); N.Y.Penal Law § 130.16 (lack of consent due to mental defect or incapacity)]

(2) Requirement of Resistance "to the Utmost"

At common law, resistance defined the force justifying a conviction for forcible rape. If the male used or threatened to use force likely to cause grave harm to the female, *i.e.*, force that would be "futile" to resist, she was not required to resist. [**People v. Taylor,** 268 N.E.2d 865 (Ill. 1971) (facts fall far short of proof that victim was paralyzed by fear, or overcome by the superior strength of her attacker, or that resistance would be futile, or that her life would be endangered by an assailant armed with a deadly weapon)] Without extreme force (or its threat), a rape conviction is impossible unless the victim resisted; when he overcame her resistance, that became the requisite force. Some courts traditionally applied a rigorous requirement that the V had a duty to resist D's efforts with all her powers. For other traditional crimes, the focus was on D's behavior, but here V's failure to adequately resist could result in D's acquittal.

e.g. **Example:** D was prosecuted under a rape statute that required "resistance." Although courts often do not distinguish between physical and verbal resistance, verbal resistance is sufficient, as when V repeatedly pled with D to stop his attack. [**State v. Jones,** 299 P.3d 219 (Idaho 2013)]

(a) Legislative Modification of the "Utmost Resistance" Standard

Once legislatures realized that victims who gave their utmost resistance could be killed, they modified the requirement in forcible rape cases to require only that resistance that is proportional to the circumstances of the attack (considering the size/strength of the parties as well as the futility of *any* resistance). Finally, once some states abolished resistance, defendants could not escape liability because the victim had ceased to resist in order to survive the attack. [*See, e.g.,* Mich.Comp.Laws § 750.520i (the victim "need not resist")] Even if resistance is removed as an element of rape, it may remain significant as a matter of evidence, *e.g.*, proving the rape beyond a reasonable doubt.

(3) Effect of Victim's Promiscuity

Rape imposes no formal requirement that the victim have been chaste, but evidence of the victim's prior sexual activity has traditionally been admissible on the question of whether she consented. The modern trend, however, is to ***limit the use of such evidence***, at least to those situations in which it is shown to have some direct and meaningful relationship to the consent issue. [*See, e.g.*, Mich. Stat. Ann. § 750.520j(1) (evidence of victim's prior sexual behavior not admissible unless and to the extent that trial judge finds the evidence material to a fact at issue and that its inflammatory or prejudicial nature does not outweigh its probative value)]

f. Special Age Defense

The common law rule is that a boy under the age of 14 is incapable of committing rape. This is a ***conclusive presumption***; it cannot be refuted by evidence showing the boy's ability to have sexual intercourse. [**King v. Groombridge,** 173 Eng. Rep. 256 (1836); **State v. Rogers,** 168 S.E.2d 345 (N.C. 1969)]

(1) Distinguish: Age Rule Completely Abolished

Many jurisdictions have explicitly abolished any specific age rule applicable to defendants charged with rape. [*See, e.g.*, N.C. Stat. § 14–27.35 (no presumption that person under age 14 is physically incapable of committing rape)]

(2) Distinguish: Age Rule Modified

Some states have modified the rule to a rebuttable presumption. Accordingly, a boy under age 14 can be convicted of rape where the evidence proves beyond a reasonable doubt his ability to have intercourse. [*See, e.g.*, Va. Code § 18.2–61(B)2. (rebuttable presumption that juvenile over the age of 10 but less than 12 does not have physical capacity to commit rape)]

3. "Statutory" Rape

In most jurisdictions, intercourse with a female ***under the age of consent*** is rape, regardless of whether she consented.

a. Age of Consent

The age of consent varies by statute among the states. [*See, e.g.*, Cal. Penal Code § 261.5 (age 18)]

b. Awareness of Victim's Age Not Necessary

Under most statutory schemes, this form of rape is a ***strict liability crime*** (*see supra,* p. 42) in that the defendant need not be aware of the victim's underage status. Consequently, even a ***reasonable mistaken belief*** that the victim was old enough to consent does *not* prevent a conviction. [**State v. Holmes,** 920 A.2d 632 (N.H. 2007) (absent legislative action, reasonable mistake of age is no defense)]

(1) Distinguish: "Defense" of Reasonable Mistake

A small number of jurisdictions have provided for the acquittal of a defendant accused of statutory rape upon an affirmative defensive showing that he reasonably believed that the victim was over the age of consent. [**People v. Hernandez,** 393 P.2d 673 (Cal. 1964)]

c. Defense: Minor Age Discrepancy Between Defendant and Victim

Some states permit a defendant to avoid conviction or reduce the seriousness of the offense by showing that there was only a small difference between his age and that of the victim. The purpose is to limit this crime to situations in which it is most likely that the defendant exercised undue influence or persuasion over the victim (*e.g.*, when the defendant is significantly older than the victim). [*See, e.g.*, Cal. Penal Code § 261.5(b) (distinguishing for penalty purposes between perpetrators not more than three years older or younger than victims and others); Tex. Penal Code § 22.011(e) (affirmative defense to sexual assault on "child" that D was not more than three years older than victim, and victim was age 14 or older)]

d. Defense: Perpetrator's and Victim's Ages Both Under the Age of Consent

To make the statutory rape statute consistent with the child abuse reporting statute and with statutory family planning services, and to avoid discriminatory enforcement and interference with the privacy interests of defendant and the asserted victim, Vermont's statutory rape statute is "inapplicable in cases where the alleged perpetrator is also a victim under the age of consent." [**In re G.T.,** 758 A.2d 301 (Vt. 2000)] *Compare* **Matter of T.V.T.,** 675 S.W.3d 303 (Tex. 2023) (aggravated sexual assault prosecution upheld; the accused and the complainant both were under the statutory age of fourteen; the accused was the "neighborhood bully" as well as a recidivist; "the possibility that a child could be 'both a victim and an offender' does not authorize us to read an exception into the statute that does not exist.")]

4. Equal Protection Issues Regarding Sex Offenses

Insofar as rape and related offenses apply only to, or fall most heavily on, male persons, it can be argued that Equal Protection has been denied such male offenders. However, statutes creating such sex crimes will be upheld if the distinction realistically reflects a difference in the actual situation of the sexes. [**Michael M. v. Superior Court,** 450 U.S. 464 (1981)]

e.g. **Example:** Statutory rape statutes typically impose a penalty on the male participant in consensual intercourse. But the statutes are aimed at the important problem of teenage sexual activity and resulting pregnancies. Because the male participants in the sexual activity incur far fewer risks relating to such pregnancies, it is not unreasonable for states to address the problem by imposing penalties only on the male participants. [**Michael M. v. Superior Court,** *supra* (upholding statutory rape provision defining the offense as unlawful sexual intercourse with a female under 18; one interest underlying the statute is prevention of illegitimate teenage pregnancies, justifying the legislative punishment for the participant who suffers fewer of the harmful consequences of such a pregnancy; a gender neutral statute would frustrate state's interest in enforcement because female is less likely to report a violation if she was also subject to prosecution)]

5. Modern Trend: Offense of Sexual Assault

Most states have replaced rape with a new offense, ***sexual assault*** or criminal sexual conduct, that is designed to be sexually neutral. The Michigan statute is a widely followed model. [Mich.Comp. Laws §§ 750.520b *et seq.*]

e.g. D was convicted of assault using an object to penetrate the genitalia or anus of another. State proved that the assault was committed by penetrating V's vagina with his finger while she was unconscious. The statute defined "object as anything viable or tangible and stable in form. [**State v. Zacarias,** 958 N.W.2d 573 (Iowa 2021)]

e.g. D was convicted of murder and third-degree sexual penetration of V after she died. Where D rendered V helpless through killing her, prior to penetration, she remained a legal person for the limited purpose of applying the statute. The state does not criminalize necrophilia or abuse of a corpse. [**State v. Martinez,** 483 P.3d 590 (N.M. 2021)]

a. Victim Can Be of Either Sex

Under these statutes, the offense need not involve a female victim but rather covers nonconsensual sexual behavior on victims of ***either sex***. Fewer than ten states have gender-specific provisions.

b. Offense Expanded to Cover More than Vaginal Penetration

Under these statutes, the offense is expanded to cover conduct other than the vaginal penetration of the victim necessary for the traditional crime of rape. Thus, these statutes cover nonconsensual cunnilingus, fellatio, anal intercourse, any other intrusion of a part of the perpetrator's body or of any object into the genital or anal openings of the victim's body, and the intentional touching of the intimate parts of the victim's body for purposes of sexual arousal or gratification. [Mich.Comp. Laws § 750.520a(r) (defining sexual penetration)]

6. Defining Offense as Sexual Attack "by Forcible Compulsion"

Some modern statutes defining rape or sexual assault omit any element like the traditional requirement of lack of consent. These statutes often substitute a requirement that the intercourse or other prohibited sexual activity be accomplished "by forcible compulsion." [18 Pa. Stat. Ann. § 3121(a)(1) (rape consists of engaging in sexual intercourse with another "by forcible compulsion"); N.J. Stat. Ann. § 2C:14–2a(6) (sexual assault defined as sexual penetration of another where the actor was using coercion)]

a. Rationale: Shifting Attention from the Victim to the Defendant

Critics of traditional rape law deemed rape's requirement that the intercourse be "against the will" of the victim, and thus without her consent, as inherently and undesirably focusing rape prosecution on the victim rather than on the conduct of the defendant. As a result, they contended, trials of rape charges tended to put the victim rather than the defendant on trial. Substituting the forcible compulsion requirement for non-consent is intended to focus attention on what the defendant did rather than whether the victim did not consent.

b. Problem: Defining "by Forcible Compulsion" Without Reference to Lack of Consent

Under these statutes, courts face a difficult task in defining what kind and degree of force or effort an accused used to be guilty of the offense. By requiring forcible compulsion and not simply lack of consent, the crimes seem to impose a proof requirement of some sort of aggressive action. Often courts cannot define the required force without resort to the concept of consent, which the legislature seems to have eliminated as a part of the offense, *i.e.*, non-consent and force are separate elements that both must be proved. Force is shown by the victim's physical resistance that exceeds the victim's verbal resistance. Consider the following examples.

e.g. **Example:** D and V were in a consensual relationship, but V ended it. During their relationship, V had sometimes passively consented to sexual relations with D "to accommodate" his violent demands. Soon after their breakup, he took her to a friend's house where they had sexual intercourse even after she refused. D was charged and convicted of forcible rape, but the appellate court reversed. Although there was evidence that she had refused to consent, the court concluded that there was no proof that D had used force to overpower her. The appellate opinion focused on V's behavior; it ignored V's general fear of D and his prior use of violence during their prior relationship. V's fear must be specific to the time of the act, not a general fear of the person; the opinion discounted his threat to "fix her face" if she resisted. [**State v. Alston,** 312 S.E.2d 470 (N.C. 1984) (non-consent and force are separate elements/issues; non-consent is not enough)]

Example: D met V at a bar, V gave him a ride to his place; on arrival he proceeded to take her keys to induce her to have sex with him. In an unfamiliar part of town, she feared for her safety. She asked, "If I do what you want, will you let me go?" After he said yes, V let him do what he wanted. He was convicted of forcible rape; the appellate court affirmed. The "reasonableness of her apprehension of fear" and her justification for not physically resisting, "was plainly a question of fact for the jury to determine." [**State v. Rusk,** 424 A.2d 720 (Md. 1981) (how resistance can serve the evidentiary purpose of proving nonconsent; threat of great and immediate bodily harm is not consent)]

Example: Under the Pennsylvania statute (above), proof that the defendant used only the force or effort necessary to complete the act of intercourse was not sufficient to show "forcible compulsion," although the victim said, "No," during the activity. Rape as defined in the statute requires force establishing lack of consent and inducement of the victim to submit without additional resistance. Thus, despite the efforts of the statute's reformers, the court reintroduced lack of consent as part of the definition of "forcible compulsion" which the defendant must be shown to have used. [**Commonwealth v. Berkowitz,** 641 A.2d 1161 (Pa. 1994) ("the complainant's testimony is devoid of any statement which clearly or adequately describes the use of force or the threat of force against her")]

7. Threats to Do Things Other than Cause Physical Harm

The traditional law of rape forcible rape did not occur when the defendant's threats were non-physical. [*See*, *e.g.*, **State v. Thompson,** 792 P.2d 1103 (Mont. 1990) (no rape when high school principal threatened not to permit a senior to graduate unless she had sex with him)] A victim's submission obtained by threats to do something other than cause physical harm presents a problem under some modern statutes, *i.e.*, if the crime is construed as committed after such threats, how can one adequately define or limit the persuasive techniques that can create liability for this serious offense?

Example: D threatened V that D would reveal V's affair with a coworker unless V engaged in sex with D. V submitted. Rape is defined in the jurisdiction as sexual intercourse with a person whose consent is the result of being overcome with force or fear. Did D commit rape? Yes, a jury could find that V, because of D's threats, was overcome by fear. The fear did not have to be the result of a threat to use force. [**State v. Brooks,** 317 P.3d 54 (Kan. 2014) ("force or fear" language in rape statute covered instant case, where defendant threatened to expose victim's extramarital affair with co-worker by sending e-mails to victim's employer and to co-worker's wife)]

D. False Imprisonment

1. Definition

Both at common law and under modern statutes, false imprisonment is the ***intentional unlawful confinement or restraint*** of another person. [Model Penal Code § 212.3 (restraining another so as to substantially interfere with his liberty)]

2. Actus Reus: Confinement

The defendant must have compelled the victim to remain where he did not want to remain or to go where he did not want to go. [**People v. Agnew,** 107 P.2d 601 (Cal. 1940)]

a. Means Used

The confinement may, of course, be accomplished by actual physical restraint. But the application of force is ***not*** essential; the confinement may also be accomplished by ***threats***. In such cases, however, the victim must have been aware of the threats and have submitted to them. [**People v. Scalisi,** 154 N.E. 715 (Ill. 1926)]

b. Distinguish: Preventing Person from Proceeding

It is not confinement simply to prevent a person from going in one direction, as long as the person may proceed in another direction and is aware of this opportunity.

3. Mens Rea

Almost a dozen states require that the defendant have ***intended to confine*** the victim. However, the Model Penal Code departs from this position, requiring only that the restraints be ***"knowingly"*** accomplished. [*See* **State v. Warfield**, 5 P.3d 1280 (Wash. 2000) ("knowingly" requirement modifies all the elements of the false imprisonment offense, including that the restraint is unlawful)] Thus, it would be sufficient if the defendant was aware that her conduct was practically certain to restrain another unlawfully. [Model Penal Code § 212.3]

4. Unlawful Confinement

The confinement must have been "unlawful," meaning that there must have been ***no legal authority*** for the detention. Thus, for example, if a person has a right to make an arrest (*see supra,* p. 158 *et seq.*), he is not guilty of false imprisonment. Another way to express this element is that the defendant knows about the unlawful nature of the restraint. [Model Penal Code § 212.3]

5. Punishment

False imprisonment is a common law misdemeanor and generally remains such under modern statutes.

a. Model Penal Code Position

The Model Penal Code makes false imprisonment a misdemeanor. However, if the restraint was effectuated under circumstances exposing the victim to a risk of serious bodily injury or involved holding the victim in a condition of involuntary servitude, the offense would be "felonious restraint," a felony. [Model Penal Code §§ 212.3 (false imprisonment), 212.2 (felonious restraint)] "Felonious restraint" may be classified as a more serious degree of false imprisonment.

E. Kidnapping

1. Common Law

Common law kidnapping consists of the forcible abduction or stealing away of a person from his own country and sending him into another country.

2. Modern Statutes

In virtually all jurisdictions, kidnapping has been substantially expanded beyond the common law definition. Thus, movement of the victim into another country is no longer required. Instead, modern kidnapping is generally regarded as a form of ***aggravated false***

imprisonment, requiring the same unlawful restraint as does false imprisonment but also ***some aggravating characteristic***.

a. Confinement and Movement (or Asportation)

Kidnapping is frequently defined as including ***forcible movement of a person*** from a safe area to another place. [*See, e.g.*, Cal. Penal Code § 207] Under such statutes, the major issue concerns the amount and nature of movement required.

e.g. **Example:** Although residence was near other homes, it was a "place of isolation," because the V's hands were tied and when the defendant fled, V was left bound in the house. [**Commonwealth v. Green,** 149 A.3d 43 (Pa. 2016)]

(1) Any Movement Sufficient

A number of courts have concluded that ***any movement*** is sufficient, reasoning that it is the fact and not the distance of forcible removal that controls.

e.g. **Example:** D moved V nine feet; that distance was sufficient for kidnapping, especially because it increased the risk of harm to V by secluding or confining her, making it less likely that others would find her. [**People v. Shadden,** 112 Cal.Rptr.2d 826 (Cal.App. 2001); *cf.* **Mercer v. Johnson,** 818 S.E.2d 246 (Ga. 2018) (moving one V from standing position to floor not sufficient for kidnapping, and movement of other V to the floor and later to safety in a different room also insufficient, because robbery was then ongoing and movement did not place V in more danger)]

(2) Substantial Movement Necessary

Other courts and statutes tend to require that the movement be ***substantial***, on the theory that otherwise, the defendant's behavior has not become sufficiently reprehensible to justify the heavy penalty attached to kidnapping. [**People v. Hall,** 325 Cal.Rptr.3d 344 (Cal. App. 2024) (victim was initially assaulted at front door, then was moved by defendant to living room area, then upstairs to open the safe, and then downstairs to kitchen, where he was tied up; jury must decide whether the movement was substantial in character by considering the totality of the circumstances); Model Penal Code § 212.1 (requiring movement of victim a substantial distance to vicinity where he was found)]

(3) Relationship to Other Crimes

The question of what movement or confinement is necessary for kidnapping is also raised by contentions that kidnapping must be defined so as to meaningfully distinguish it from what are often closely related crimes (*see infra,* pp. 249–249). State statutes express that kidnapping should not be recognized as a separate offense whenever the asportation relied upon to establish the kidnapping is "merely incidental" to another offense, such as rape or robbery. Many states use jury instructions "to criminalize only those instances in which the removal or confinement of a victim is independently significant from an accompanying felony, such as rape or robbery." [**State v. White,** 362 S.W.3d 559 (Tenn. 2012)]

b. Confinement in Secret Place

Kidnapping is often defined as including restraint of the victim in a secret place, *i.e.*, a place where he is unlikely to be found. [*See* N.Y. Penal Law §§ 135.00; 135.25]

c. Confinement Accomplished by Deadly Force

In addition, some states punish a confinement of the victim that is accomplished by the use or threat of deadly force as kidnapping. [Tex. Penal Code § 20.03]

d. Confinement for Extortion or Ransom

Abducting another for purposes of holding him for ransom, reward, or extortion is sometimes a kind of kidnapping. [Cal. Penal Code § 209]

e. Confinement for Sexual Abuse

Sometimes kidnapping includes confinement of the victim for purposes of sexually abusing him. [N.Y. Penal Law § 135.25(2)(a)]

3. Confinement: How Accomplished

Kidnapping statutes and court decisions differ as to how the detention or confinement may be accomplished:

a. Force or Threats

Generally, a confinement or movement accomplished by force ***or threats of force*** is sufficient. [**Burton v. State,** 426 A.2d 829 (Del. 1980) (movement must be more than incidental to the underlying crime, and the movement must substantially increase the victim's risk)]

b. Deception

Under some statutes, it is enough that the confinement or movement was accomplished by deception. [N.Y. Penal Law § 135.00(1); ***but*** *see* **People v. Stephenson,** 517 P.2d 820 (Cal. 1974) (deception not enough under statute defining crime as "forcibly" carrying away another)]

c. Minors and Incompetents

Some statutes provide that the mere ***persuading*** of a minor or incompetent to remain in one place or to move will suffice, despite the acquiescence of the victim, ***if*** the victim's parents have not acquiesced. [Tex. Penal Code § 20.01(1)(B)]

d. Subsequent Restraint of Initially Willing Victim

If movement of the victim is required for kidnapping and the victim willingly accompanies the defendant, the crime is still committed if the defendant later uses force or threats and compels the victim to accompany the defendant further. But there ***must be some movement*** of the victim ***after*** the defendant has found it necessary to use force or threats. [**People v. Camden,** 548 P.2d 1110 (Cal. 1976)]

4. Confinement: Duration

Modern statutes often "require that the victim's confinement be for a "substantial period." Inclusion of that requirement in the statutory definition of "confinement" is to "avoid having kidnapping include conduct that was merely incidental to the commission of some other crime against the victim." [**State v. Hofland,** 58 A.3d 1023 (Maine 2012)] An allegation of kidnapping in a home invasion robbery fails when the restraint is brief, its purpose is to prevent interference with the robberies, and does not involve removal from the home. [**State v. Korum,** 86 P.3d 166 (Wash.App. 2004), *rev'd on other grounds*, 141 P.3d 13 (Wash. 2006)] e.g. **Example:** D entered an elementary school with a gun and held a group of students in a classroom as protection. The students' confinement lasted less than thirty minutes. A jury rationally could have found that D restrained the students for a substantial period of time in violation of the state statute. [**State v. Hofland**, *supra*]

5. Mens Rea

Case law does not clearly define the *mens rea* required for kidnapping. If compelled to address the issue, however, the courts are likely to require an ***actual intent to confine or move*** the victim.

a. Distinguish: Specific Intents Required by Statute

Those statutes that define kidnapping as abduction for some specified purposes clearly require proof of a specific intent. [*See, e.g.*, Tex. Penal Code § 20.04(a)(1) (abduction with the intent to hold victim for ransom or reward)]

6. Relationship of Kidnapping to Other Crimes

Commission of other crimes, such as robbery or rape, often shows confinement or movement of the victim that comes within the definition of kidnapping. Courts are sometimes reluctant in these situations to permit conviction for both the robbery or rape and kidnapping. Some courts find that conviction for both offenses is unconstitutional, violating Due Process of Law or Double Jeopardy. [**State v. Anthony,** 817 S.W.2d 299 (Tenn. 1991)]

a. Modern Trend: Confinement or Movement Must Not Be Merely "Incidental"

Most courts hold that, as applied to these situations, conviction for kidnapping (in addition to conviction for robbery or rape) requires that the confinement or movement of the victim ***must not be merely incidental*** to the robbery or rape. A kidnapping is not merely incidental if it can be established by proof that the confinement or movement went beyond what was necessary to accomplish the robbery or rape, that it increased the risk of harm to the victim, or that it facilitated the defendant in avoiding detection during the crime or in escaping. [**Stinnett v. Commonwealth,** 364 S.W.3d 70 (Ky. 2011) (restraint of victim exceeded that which is ordinarily incident to commission of murder; defendant could have killed victim without taking extended time to terrorize her)]

b. Incidental Nature of Confinement or Movement as a Jury Issue

A few courts hold that in these situations, whether an alleged kidnapping was merely incidental to the commission of another offense such as robbery or rape is a question for the jury. An elaborate instruction explaining when confinement or movement is merely incidental may be appropriate or even necessary. [**State v. White,** *supra*]

c. Broader View: Conviction Permitted Where Kidnapping Technically Proved

Some courts conclude that neither constitutional considerations nor the definition of kidnapping bar conviction for both robbery or rape and kidnapping, as long as the evidence technically shows the confinement or movement required for kidnapping. Under this approach, whether the kidnapping was merely incidental to the commission of another serious crime is irrelevant. [**State v. Jacobs,** 380 P.2d 998 (Ariz. 1963)]

7. Punishment

Kidnapping is generally a felony and was traditionally a capital crime. However, it is likely that courts today would find the death penalty disproportionately severe for the offense.

a. "Simple" vs. "Aggravated" Kidnapping

Many states recognize a distinct crime of ***aggravated kidnapping*** and provide for a more severe penalty than would otherwise follow under the general kidnapping statute. [Cal. Penal Code § 209 (kidnapping for ransom, reward, extortion, or robbery)]

b. Mitigating Circumstances

Some statutes authorize a ***reduced*** penalty if the defendant has released the victim in a safe condition. [Model Penal Code § 212.1]

Chapter Ten

Crimes Against the Habitation

CONTENTS	PAGE

Key Exam Issues

The traditional crimes of *burglary* and *arson* protect a citizen's security in her dwelling or building. The common law crimes are rather limited in scope (*e.g.,* burglary could take place only in the nighttime), but modern statutes have expanded these crimes.

In answering questions involving possible habitation offenses, consider the following general issues. If your question has provided you with a statute, be sure to consider these issues in light of any ***statutory modification*** of the common law.

1. Was the structure or place one protected by the statutory or common law definition of the crimes? (Traditionally, it must be the ***dwelling of another***.)
2. Was there sufficient intrusion upon protected interests? (Traditionally, there must be an ***entry by breaking*** for burglary or a ***burning*** for arson.)
3. Was the intrusion made with the requisite intent? (Traditionally, this requires intent to ***commit a felony*** for burglary or ***malice*** for arson.)

A. Burglary

1. Common Law

At common law, burglary is the breaking and entering of the dwelling house of another in the nighttime, with the intent to commit a felony there.

EXAM TIP

The common law crime of burglary has very technical requirements, many of which have been changed by statute. If a question calls for analysis of ***common law burglary***, look for ***all of the technical requirements*** (*e.g.,* the building must be a dwelling, the acts must take place at night, etc.). If any one of those requirements is not met, there has been no burglary (although it is quite likely that another crime has been committed). If the question includes a ***burglary statute***, read it carefully to determine whether it changes the common law requirements. Look to see, for example, whether it includes a requirement that the place entered be a dwelling or that the entry be at night. If ***no statute*** is given and the question doesn't indicate that the common law applies, then discuss the common law elements and note where most modern statutes (*see infra,* p. 258 *et seq.*) have changed the common law.

a. Entry

For burglary, there must be an ***actual*** or ***constructive entry*** into the structure.

(1) Entry of Person

The slightest intrusion into the structure by the defendant or some ***part of the defendant's body*** is sufficient. This is true whether the intrusion of a part of the defendant's body was for the purpose of actually committing the intended offense (*e.g.,* to steal an object inside) or only to gain entry (*e.g.,* reaching in to open a window). [**State v. Bryant,** 101 So.3d 429 (La. 2012) (while kicking in a door, defendant's foot necessarily crossed the threshold, even if only minimally)]

(2) Entry of an Instrument

An "entry" is also accomplished by the defendant's insertion of a tool or other instrument into the structure, ***but only if*** the purpose of the intrusion is ***to commit the intended felony***.

e.g. **Example:** D uses a straightened clothes hanger to reach through a gate and pull out a vacuum cleaner. This is an entry of the building for purposes of burglary, because D inserted an instrument into the structure for the purpose of committing the intended felony. [**Sears v. State,** 713 P.2d 1218 (Alaska 1986) (using an instrument to reach some property therein constituted an entry)]

(a) Distinguish: Instrument Used to Gain Entry

If, on the other hand, the tool or instrument is inserted simply to enable the defendant himself to gain entry, this is ***not sufficient***. [**State v. Watkins,** 720 S.E.2d 844 (N.C.App. 2012)] *Note:* A few jurisdictions, however, make any entry by an instrument for any purpose sufficient. [**People v. Moore,** 31 Cal. App. 4th 489 (1994) (entry into the space between a storm or screen door and the wooden door is sufficient)]

A defendant can break the plane of protected space in other ways. [*See, e.g.,* **Tindall v. State,** 997 So. 2d 1260 (Fla.App. 2009) (where defendant crawled under wood frame house supported by cinder block foundation in order to steal copper wire, entry occurred because defendant "penetrated the invisible, vertical plane into the airspace of the house")]

EXAM TIP

Note the difference between entry of the defendant's body and entry by an instrument. The defendant's insertion of an instrument is sufficient for burglary ***only if the instrument is inserted for the purpose of committing the intended felony***, not for some other reason such as to gain entry. Intent is the key. Thus, if the tool is used to grab an item and bring it out, there has been an entry as soon as the tool is inserted into the structure. If that same tool is used only to open a window to gain entry, the insertion of the tool into the structure does not constitute an entry for purposes of burglary. (But note that "entry" will occur once the defendant himself enters, and that making an opening with a tool would probably be sufficient for ***attempted*** burglary.)

---

(3) "Constructive" Entry by Innocent Agent

A "constructive" entry occurs (and is sufficient for burglary) where the defendant causes a person incapable of committing a criminal offense (*e.g.*, an insane person) or who is under his control (*e.g.*, a child) to enter the structure to commit the defendant's felonious purpose.

(4) Entry of Part of Dwelling

Although burglary is most often committed by entering the dwelling structure as a whole, the entry can also be made of a part of the dwelling, as long as all the requirements for the offense are established. [*See*, *e.g.*, **People v. Sparks,** 47 P.3d 289 (Cal. 2002) (defendant's entry into bedroom of single-family home from inside home's living quarters, with intent to commit rape, constitutes burglary under statute defining burglary as entry into any house or "room" with intent to commit felony)]

b. Breaking

The entry must have been accomplished by a "breaking." This requires the use of ***actual or constructive force*** to create an ***opening*** of the structure ***by trespass*** (without consent). The creation of an opening of ***any closed part*** of the structure will suffice. Entry through a pre-existing opening, such as an open door or window, did not constitute a breaking at common law.

(1) Use of Force to Create Opening

It is sufficient for a breaking that the defendant used force, albeit only a small amount of force, to create an opening where none previously existed. Thus, it is a "breaking" when the defendant pushes open a closed but unlatched door. [**State v. Boon,** 35 N.C. (13 Ired.) 244 (1852)]

EXAM TIP

Remember that "breaking" as used in the burglary context requires ***much less force*** than is suggested by the ordinary use of that term. Thus, for example, the defendant need not have broken down a door in the manner we usually think of for "breaking"; it is enough that he pushes open the door.

(2) Distinguish: Use of Force to Enlarge Existing Opening

Traditionally, the application of force to ***enlarge*** an already existing opening, as by further pushing open a door that is already open, would ***not*** suffice. *But note:* A number of courts now hold to the contrary. [**Davis v. State,** 770 N.E.2d 319 (Ind. 2002)]

(3) "Constructive" Force

Several situations involve "constructive" force and therefore constitute a "breaking." *See, e.g.*,

- Obtaining entry ***by fraud***,
- Obtaining entry ***by threatening the use of force***,
- Entering ***through a chimney***, and
- Obtaining entry by ***having a servant or some other co-conspirator within the structure open the door***. [**Alexander v. State,** 89 S.W. 642 (Tex.Crim. 1905)]

e.g. **Example:** D's entry of home under the pretense of being a potential home buyer was "without authority"; "consent to enter that is given based on a fraud or deceit perpetrated by the defendant is an unauthorized entry." [**State v. Newton,** 755 S.E.2d 786 (Ga. 2014)]

e.g. **Example:** D used keys and a garage door opener to enter; D obtained those items without the owner's authorization; such entry constitutes a "constructive breaking." [**Hobby v. State,** 83 A.3d 794 (Md. 2014)]

(4) Distinguish: Breaking to Leave

There is dispute as to whether burglary is committed if the defendant does not use force ***to enter*** the structure but commits a breaking ***in order to leave***. Most courts hold that this is ***not burglary***. [**Rolland v. Commonwealth,** 82 Pa. 306 (1876)]

(5) Requirement of Trespass: Effect of Consent to Enter

The breaking for purposes of burglary must be *trespassory* (*i.e.*, without the occupant's consent). If the defendant has permission to enter, he cannot be guilty of burglary until he began assaulting those inside the residence. [**State v. Clinton,** 108 N.E.3d 1 (Ohio 2017)]

e.g. **Example:** D opens the door of a store and enters during regular business hours with the intent to rob the storekeeper. There is no breaking and hence no burglary; as a member of the public, D has entered with consent. [**State v. Stephens,** 91 So. 349 (La. 1922)]

(a) Limitation: Scope of Consent

The scope of any purported consent to enter must be examined. The defendant must have had authority to be on the premises ***at the time and in the particular part*** of the premises in question. [**State v. Corcoran,** 143 P. 453 (Wash. 1914)]

e.g. **Example:** Homeowner provides D with a key to Homeowner's house and gives D the ***unrestricted*** right to enter. D is not guilty of burglary even if he uses the key to gain entry for purposes of stealing Homeowner's jewels. [**State v. Corcoran,** *supra*]

cf. **Compare:** D would be guilty of burglary if Storeowner had authorized D to enter only one room of a commercial establishment but D then is caught in an area off-limits to him and the public, with intent to steal there.

(6) Causal Relationship Between Breaking and Entry

To be sufficient for burglary, the breaking must be the means by which the entry is accomplished. [**Regina v. Davis,** 6 Cox Crim. Cas. 369 (1854)]

e.g. **Example:** D opened a window to X's house, intending to crawl through, but D then noticed an open door and entered through the door. D is not guilty of burglary, because the breaking (*i.e.,* the opening of the window) was not the means by which the entry was ultimately accomplished. [**Regina v. Davis,** *supra*]

c. Dwelling House

The structure entered must be a dwelling, which means a place ***used regularly for sleep***. [**Foreman v. State,** 546 So.2d 977 (Ala.App. 1986)]

(1) Use for Other Purposes

As long as the building is used to sleep in on a regular basis, the fact that it is also used for business or other purposes will not prevent it from being a dwelling. [**Smith v. State,** 355 A.2d 527 (Md. 1976) (barn, store, or similar building qualifies where portion of it functions as someone's dwelling)]

(2) Yet Unoccupied Structures

A structure intended to be used as a residence, but which is not yet occupied as such, is *not* a dwelling. [**Ex parte Vincent,** 26 Ala. 145 (1855)]

(3) Temporary Absence of Resident

On the other hand, a structure used as a dwelling remains such despite the ***temporary absence*** of those living in it, *e.g.,* summer cottage burglarized in winter. However, it ceases to be a dwelling if the residents ***permanently leave***. [**P.P.M. v. State,** 447

So.2d 445 (Fla.App. 1984) (once a person moves in with requisite intention, the building constitutes a dwelling until that person permanently abandons the premises, such a when a dweller vacated the premises with the intent to cease using that place as a home), *cf.* **State v. Fazenbaker**, *supra* (burglary of a recreational vehicle occurred even if it was unoccupied and had been winterized, covered and stored for the season)]

(4) Other Buildings Within "Curtilage"

The "curtilage" is the area surrounding a dwelling, usually enclosed by a fence. Buildings not used as living quarters but which are within that fenced-in area are considered to be part of the dwelling. Thus, barns, stables, garages, and similar structures can be the subject of a burglary. Merely breaking and entering the fenced-in area is not burglary; there must be a breaking into a *structure* within the curtilage.

(5) Entry of Rooms and Other Closed Parts of a Dwelling

Burglary can be committed by entering **a closed part of a dwelling**, such as a specific room or even a closet or wall safe. All of the requirements or burglary must be met, so the entry must be by breaking and done in the nighttime. [**People v. Sparks**, *supra*] However, the place entered must be a ***part of the structure***. Consequently, entry into a trunk within the dwelling is not enough. [**Allen v. State,** 231 P. 96 (Okla. 1924)]

e.g. **Example:** D enters X's house without any intent to commit a crime inside. Once inside, however, D remembers that X keeps money in the refrigerator, and D decides to steal it. D opens the refrigerator to commit the larceny and inserts his hand. D probably has not committed burglary, because the refrigerator he entered with intent to commit larceny was not a part of the dwelling structure. If the refrigerator were constructed as a part of the structure (*i.e.*, a built-in), D would be guilty of burglary. [**Allen v. State,** *supra*]

d. Of Another

The structure must be the dwelling of another person. [**Clarke v. Commonwealth,** 66 Va. 908 (1874)]

(1) Right of Habitation Determinative

To determine whose dwelling it is, the ***right of habitation***—not ownership or title—controls. A home is still a dwelling of another after the owner "left it vacant and listed it for sale." [**State v. Gilley,** 124 A.3d 683 (N.H. 2015)] Likewise, a home is a "dwelling" where the owner had previously occupied it, where it had been unoccupied for eight months but it was "intact and suitable for occupancy." [**Hobby v. State,** *supra*] Similarly, a landlord can commit burglary in a house or apartment that she owns but has leased to another to use as a residence, because the house or apartment is the dwelling of the tenant and not of the landlord. [**State v. Harold,** 325 S.E.2d 219 (N.C. 1985)]

(2) Premises Occupied by Defendant and Another

If the defendant ***jointly occupies*** the premises with others, the defendant cannot commit burglary by entering the jointly occupied premises because the premises are ***his own dwelling***. [**People v. Gauze,** 542 P.2d 1365 (Cal. 1975)] An argument can be made, however, that this position ignores the legitimate interests of others who occupy the premises.

e.g. **Example:** D and V share a dwelling. If D enters the structure by force to steal V's money, there is no burglary. Nor would a third person be guilty of burglary if he entered by force for the same purpose, if he was authorized by D to enter. [**McCreary v. State,** 212 P. 336 (Ariz. 1923); **People v. Gauze,** *supra*]

cf. **Compare:** If a court order gave V ***exclusive possession*** of the joint dwelling of D and V, and D enters by breaking with the requisite intent, D has committed burglary. The premises are the dwelling of V even if title to those premises is in D's name. [**Ex parte Davis,** 542 S.W.2d 192 (Tex. 1976)]

(3) Part of Premises May Constitute Dwelling of Another

Premises that are jointly occupied ***may be separated*** so that some parts are the dwelling of one occupant and other parts are the dwelling of the other. In such cases, one occupant can commit burglary by entering the parts of the structure that constitute the dwelling of the other. [**State v. Rio,** 230 P.2d 308 (Wash. 1951)]

e.g. **Example:** V hired D to work on V's farm and permitted D to live in V's house. D did not, however, have access to V's bedroom. D entered V's bedroom intending to commit felony assault on V. D committed burglary by entering a part of the house that was the dwelling of another and not his own dwelling. [**State v. Rio,** *supra*]

e. In the Nighttime

The breaking and entry must occur in the nighttime.

(1) "Nighttime" Defined

"Nighttime" is the period when the countenance of a person cannot be discerned by natural sunlight.

(2) Breaking and Entering on Different Nights

Although the acts constituting the crime must take place at night, and there must be a causal relationship between the breaking and entering (*see supra,* p. 255), the acts do not have to occur on the same night. Thus, the breaking can be made on one night and the entry (made possible by the breaking) the next. [1 Hale, Pleas of the Crown 551 (1778)]

f. With the Intent to Commit a Felony

At the *time of the entry,* the defendant must *intend to commit a felony* **within** the structure. There is no burglary if the felonious intent is formed ***after*** the entry is completed. [**Austin v. United States,** 315 A.3d 580 (D.C. 2024) (older requirement of contemporaneousness states that intent to commit felony must exist at time of the entry, rather than after entry is effectuated); *cf.* **McCarthy v. Commonwealth,** 867 S.W.2d 469 (Ky. 1993) (under "enters or remains" statute, a defendant may form intent after entry)]

(1) Intent to Commit Misdemeanor Not Sufficient

The intent must be to commit a crime that is presently a felony under the governing law. An intent to commit a misdemeanor will not support a burglary conviction. [**Commonwealth v. Newell,** 7 Mass. 245 (1810)]

(2) Actual Commission of Felony Not Required

All that is required is the felonious ***intent***. For burglary, the defendant need not complete his plan to commit a felony. In this sense, then, burglary is a "preparatory crime" similar to attempt.

(3) Abandonment of Intent Irrelevant

Abandonment of the plan once entry is obtained will not prevent conviction for burglary. The crime is ***complete at the moment entry is made with the requisite intent***.

EXAM TIP

A common issue in burglary questions involves the concurrence of the intent and the entry. Remember that the defendant must have the ***intent to commit a felony when he enters the building***. Don't be fooled by situations where the defendant enters the building without any intention of committing a felony (as when he enters to get out of the rain), but ***once inside*** decides to steal something or commit some other felony. In such a case, the defendant has not committed burglary because he did not have the intent to commit a felony when he entered. On the other hand, if the defendant ***did have the requisite intent when he entered***, the burglary was complete ***upon entering***. A change of heart after entry is irrelevant; the defendant is guilty of burglary even though he did not commit a felony inside the dwelling.

(4) "Within" the Structure

The traditional definition of burglary requires an intent to commit a felony "in" the structure entered. It would not be a burglary to pass through a dwelling as a matter of choice on the way to an offense elsewhere, although it would be if the route was necessary to reach the object or situs of the intended crime. [*See* **People v. Wright,** 206 Cal. App. 2d 184 (1962); *compare* **State v. Russell,** 922 A.2d 191 (Conn.App. 2007) (defendant charged with burglary for entering victim's home "with the intent to criminally violate a protective order," but the only order violated was "one disallowing defendant from entering," no showing of "intent to commit a crime therein")]

e.g. **Example:** D entered a dwelling of another with the intent to take a child to the roof and there commit the felony of child molesting. D was guilty of burglary, although he did not literally intend to commit a felony "in" the dwelling. His plan required him to pass through the dwelling to reach the place of the intended crime; therefore, the place of entry and place of felonious intent were sufficiently connected to support a burglary conviction. [**People v. Shields,** 70 Cal. App. 2d 628 (1945)]

2. Modern Statutes

Modern statutes have ***significantly modified*** common law burglary. [Model Penal Code § 221.1; Cal. Penal Code § 459] The following changes are typical:

a. Structure Need Not Be a Dwelling

Many structures ***other than dwellings*** often can be the subject of a burglary. Some statutes also extend the crime to entry of motor vehicles and sometimes to other things. *See, e.g.*, **State v. Joseph,** 405 P.3d 993 (Wash. 2017) ("premises" in trespass statute defined as "any building" and statutory definition of "building" includes any vehicle)]

Example: Under the Model Penal Code, entry of any building would be burglary if the other requirements are met. [Model Penal Code § 221.1(1)] The California Penal Code covers entry of a house, room, apartment, tenement, shop, warehouse, store, mill, barn, stable, outhouse or other building, tent, vessel, floating home, railroad car, cargo container, trailer coach, house car, inhabited camper, vehicle (if doors are locked), aircraft, or mine. [Cal. Penal Code § 459]

(1) More Severe Punishment for Burglary of Dwelling

Burglary of a dwelling or its equivalent is often made punishable by a more severe penalty than other burglaries. [*See, e.g.*, 460(a) (burglary of inhabited dwelling or portion of building is burglary of first degree)]

b. Breaking Not Required

Often the requirement that the entry be accomplished by a breaking is eliminated. As a result, ***any entry*** (however accomplished (even without a breaking) is sufficient.) [Model Penal Code § 221.1(1); Cal. Penal Code § 459]

(1) Entry Must Be Unlawful or Without Consent

Modern statutes dispensing with a breaking requirement usually explicitly or implicitly require that the entry be "unlawful" or at least without consent. [*See, e.g.*, **State v. Clinton**, *supra* (even if defendant's initial entry was by consent of victim, and thus lawful, jury was justified in concluding that defendant's privilege to remain "terminated the moment he began assaulting her and her children")]

(2) Premises Open to the Public

Under modern statutes, the requirement that entry be without consent often means that burglary is not committed by entry of premises, such as a store, that are at the time open to the public. [Model Penal Code § 221.1(1)] Some courts, however, reason that one who enters such premises concealing his criminal purpose engages in deception that nullifies the consent. Thus, entry of a store open to the public can constitute burglary. [**State v. Baker,** 161 N.W.2d 864 (Neb. 1968) (though defendant had consent to enter store to do custodial work, his entry still unlawful because of his intent to steal existing at the time of entry)]

c. Time of Entry Irrelevant

Modern statutes typically dispense with the requirement that the breaking and entry be in the nighttime. Thus, a burglary can occur at any time of day. [Model Penal Code § 221.1(1); Cal. Penal Code § 459]

(1) More Severe Punishment for Burglary at Nighttime

Burglary in the nighttime is sometimes punished more severely than other burglary. [Conn. Penal Code § 53a–101(a)]

(2) Redefinition of Nighttime

Modern codes that distinguish between burglary in the daytime and burglary in the nighttime often define "nighttime" in relationship to sunrise and sunset. [Conn. Penal Code § 53a–100(a)(3) (night is period between 30 minutes after sunset and 30 minutes before sunrise)]

d. Spousal Burglary

As mentioned, the right of habitation and not the ownership of property controls the question of whether a dwelling was another's, *e.g.*, an estranged husband can commit burglary of the former family home in which he no longer lives. [*Compare* **People v. Gill,** 159 Cal.App. 4th 149 (2008) (wife had asked husband to leave and neighbor collected house key from husband and gave it to wife) *with* **State v. White,** 330 P.3d 482 (Nev.App. 2014) (defendant had separated from spouse and moved out, but he did not commit burglary in entering the residence, because he retained his keys and entered home on weekly basis to stay with children on weekends)]

e. Intent to Commit Misdemeanor Sufficient

The intent element of burglary is frequently broadened to include offenses that are not felonies. Thus, statutory schemes often require an intent to commit a felony ***or any theft*** (whether felony theft or not). [*See, e.g.*, Cal. Penal Code § 459 ("with intent to commit grand or petit larceny or any felony")] The Model Penal Code would go further and require only an intent to commit ***any crime***. [Model Penal Code § 221.1] More than half the states apply the Model Penal Code standard. [*See* **State v. Hatchett,** 844 N.W.2d 610 (S.D. 2014) ("any crime is sufficient," including so-called "reactive crimes" such as avoiding apprehension by police officer)]

ELEMENTS OF BURGLARY—A COMPARISON

COMMON LAW BURGLARY	STATUTORY BURGLARY
Breaking	Breaking Not Required
Entry	Entry
Of the Dwelling House of Another	Expanded to Include Other Structures (and Even Motor Vehicles)
At Nighttime	Nighttime Not Required
With the Intent to Commit Felony Therein	Intent to Commit a Felony, or Any Theft Often Will Suffice

e. Punishment

Burglary is a common law felony and remains such in most (if not all) jurisdictions. However, statutes commonly divide burglary into ***degrees,*** and authorize more severe penalties for one degree than the other. [Cal. Penal Code § 460]

(1) "Aggravated" or "First Degree" Burglary

Burglaries that are more severely punished and often include:

(a) Burglary of an ***inhabited dwelling*** [Cal. Penal Code § 460];

(b) Burglary while ***armed with a deadly weapon*** [Model Penal Code § 221.1(2)(b)]; or

(c) Burglaries involving ***assault*** upon a person [Model Penal Code § 221.1(2)].

(2) Conviction for Both Burglary and Intended Crime

Under generally applicable rules, if the defendant successfully completes the crime that he intended to commit at the time of entry, he can be convicted and punished for ***both*** the burglary and the target crime (*see supra,* p. 22 *et seq.*). The Model Penal Code, however, would bar conviction for both crimes unless the target offense was an extremely serious one. [Model Penal Code § 221.1(3)]

3. Compare: New Crime of Home Invasion

Some jurisdictions have created new crimes, sometimes titled "home invasion," covering particularly egregious entries of dwellings. These differ significantly. Sometimes they require forcible entry of a dwelling and/or the use of force or threats while inside. [Fla. Stat. § 812.135 (home-invasion robbery consists of entry of dwelling with intent to commit robbery and commission of robbery of occupants)]

B. Arson

1. Common Law

At common law, arson is the malicious burning of the dwelling house of another.

a. Dwelling House

The structure burned must be a dwelling. "Dwelling" as used in arson is the same as in the context of burglary. (*See supra,* p. 255.)

b. Of Another

As in burglary, the dwelling must be that of another person. It is ***not*** arson to burn one's own home. Again, it is the ***right to possession*** rather than ownership that controls. Thus, a landlord's burning of her own structure is arson ***if*** the tenant was entitled to use it as a residence. [**State v. Toole,** 29 Conn. 342 (1860)]

(1) Distinguish: Misdemeanor of "House Burning"

One who intentionally burns her own dwelling commits the common law misdemeanor of "house burning" if the house is located in a city or town or sufficiently close to other houses to create a risk of their burning. [**Rex v. Holmes,** 2 East P.C. 1022 (1634)]

c. Burning

There must be an actual "burning" of some part of the structure.

(1) Definition of Burning

"Burning" requires some combustion of a part of the material out of which the dwelling was constructed, but it is ***unnecessary that the structure be destroyed*** or even seriously damaged. [**State v. Spiegel,** 83 N.W. 722 (Iowa 1900) ("actual ignition" needed)]

EXAM TIP

Note that "burning" for arson requires ***much less*** than what we tend to think of when we use that term. The dwelling need ***not*** be burned down, nor need there be any significant damage; there just must be some consuming by the fire.

(2) Dwelling Must Be Burned

The burning must involve some ***part of the dwelling structure.*** Arson is not committed by burning some item, such as personal property, inside the dwelling. [**State v. Spiegel**, *supra*]

(3) Scorching vs. Charring

Some combustible part of the structure must have been at least damaged ***(charred).*** [**Hinkley v. State,** 389 S.W.2d 667 (Tex.App. 1965)] Thus, there need not be an open flame or "blaze." However, mere discoloration by heat (a "scorching") or blackening by smoke is ***not*** sufficient. [**Honey v. State,** 17 S.W.2d 50 (Tex. 1929)]

e.g. **Example:** D sets fire to a chest of drawers in V's house, but the only damage to the house itself is a blackening of the ceiling from smoke. D is not guilty of arson. There has been no "burning" of a part of the structure. The burning of the chest, which is not a part of the dwelling, is not arson, and the ceiling, which is a part of the dwelling, was not burned.

(4) Damage by Explosion Not Sufficient

Common law arson is not committed if the only damage to the dwelling is that done by an explosion. However, if the explosion ***causes a fire,*** which ***in turn "burns"*** a part of the structure, arson is committed. [**Landers v. State,** 47 S.W. 1008 (Tex. 1898) (burning of severed parts will not suffice if the fire does not spread to the structure)]

EXAM TIP

Like burglary, common law arson has some technical requirements. Most notable is the burning requirement. For you to find that there has been a "burning," you must see facts that show: (i) a ***fire*** (not just an explosion), (ii) that ***at least charred*** (burned, not just discolored), (iii) part of the ***structure*** (not just the contents of the house). If the facts don't show ***all*** of the above, there has been no arson. (As with burglary, if the question doesn't specify whether the common law or a statute applies, discuss the common law elements and then mention the major statutory departures therefrom.)

d. Mens Rea: Malice

The *mens rea* required for arson is "malice." However, this does not require ill will towards the occupant or the structure itself. Malice exists if the defendant (i) ***intended to burn*** the structure; (ii) ***knew*** that it would burn; or (iii) intentionally and without justification or excuse created an ***obvious fire hazard*** to the structure. [*See, e.g.*, **In re V.V.,** 252 P.3d 979 (Cal. 2011) (minors who set off firecrackers on hillside committed arson, as where they "did not intend to set the hillside on fire, [but] knew that their intentional acts created a fire hazard," is sufficient to show malice)]

(1) Negligence Not Sufficient

A burning caused by mere negligence is not common law arson. [**Morris v. State,** 27 So. 336 (Ala. 1900)]

EXAM TIP

Like malice for murder, malice for arson ***does not require ill will*** but rather indicates certain mental states. For arson, the mental states are:

(i) ***Intent to burn,***

(ii) ***Knowledge*** that the ***structure would burn,*** or

(iii) ***Intent to create an obvious fire hazard.***

If the defendant did not have one of these mental states, she is not guilty of arson. Thus, an accidental fire or one caused by the defendant's negligence would not be arson.

---

(2) Commission of Crime Not Sufficient

No arson is committed where a building is accidentally burned during the commission of a crime; *i.e.,* there is ***no "felony arson"*** rule analogous to the felony murder rule. [**Regina v. Faulkner,** 13 Cox Crim. Cas. 550 (1877)]

(3) High Risk Created by Burning Own Dwelling

If a person sets fire to her own dwelling and this creates a high risk that ***other residences*** will catch fire, she is guilty of arson if one of them does. This person has acted with the intentional-creation-of-a-fire-hazard type of malice (*see supra,* p. 262). [**Isaac's Case,** 2 East P.C. 1031 (1799)]

2. Modern Statutes

Modern statutes vary, but they often somewhat change the nature of arson. Generally, they expand the crime to cover situations that might not be covered by traditional arson. Often they create a number of arson offenses that vary in seriousness depending on such factors as the nature of the property affected or targeted and whether persons were placed at risk by the crime.

a. Act and Result Required

Modern statutes take several different approaches to defining the act and any result required by arson:

(1) Model Penal Code Approach

The Model Penal Code proposes that arson be defined basically as starting a fire with the purpose of destroying a covered structure. [Model Penal Code § 220.1] Some modern statutes take this approach, although some expand the crime to cover starting a fire with intent to either destroy or merely damage a covered structure. [Penn Stat. Ann. § 3301(a)(1)(ii) (starting a fire with the purpose of destroying or damaging an inhabited or occupied building)]

The Model Penal Code also proposes a less serious offense, "reckless burning or exploding," consisting of starting a fire or causing an explosion and thereby recklessly placing a building or occupied structure of another in danger of destruction or damage. [Model Penal Code § 220.1(b)]

(2) Approach Requiring Damage

Some modern statutes follow a more traditional approach and thus require some actual damage to the structure. [N.Y. Penal Law § 150.20(1) (first degree arson includes intentionally damaging a building or motor vehicle by causing a fire)]

b. Culpable Mental State

Most modern statutes do not require traditional "malice." Those modern statutes defining the offense as starting a fire, of course, require a purpose to damage or destroy protected property, and the starting of the fire itself must be at least reckless. Those statutes defining the offense as requiring actual damage to the protected property often require that the defendant have had the purpose of causing such damage or the knowledge that such damage would occur.

c. "Burning" Not Required

Modern statutes based on the Model Penal Code require no impact on the structure and thus do not require a "burning" in the technical sense of common law arson. Even modern statutes requiring damage to a structure do not require that this damage meet the common law definition of a burning.

d. Explosion Sufficient

Modern statutes often explicitly provide that arson can be committed by fire or by explosion. [N.Y. Penal Law § 150.20(1) (arson is damaging covered property "by causing an explosion or fire")]

e. Structures Other than Dwellings Protected

Arson is often expanded so that the building damaged or targeted need not be a dwelling. Some modern arson statutes even expand the crime to include damaging ***motor vehicles*** and ***even other personal property.*** [Cal. Penal Code § 451 (arson is willful and malicious setting fire to or burning of any structure or property)]

f. Ownership and Occupancy

Some modern arson statutes prohibit even the burning of covered property regardless of ownership or occupancy, so a person could commit the offense by burning a structure she owned and occupied. Courts may limit these statutes by interpretation; for example, courts sometimes exempt situations in which the defendant was unaware of any risk to others created by her action. [**Brown v. State,** 403 A.2d 788 (Md. 1979)]

g. Arson with Intent to Defraud Insurer

Modern statutes often include within arson or related crimes certain conduct only when this conduct is accompanied by an intent to defraud an insurer. The Model Penal Code generally limits arson to starting a fire or causing an explosion with the purpose of destroying a covered structure, but "arson" under the Model Penal Code also includes starting a fire or causing an explosion with the purpose of destroying or damaging any property, if this is done with the purpose of collecting insurance for the loss. [Model Penal Code § 220.1(1)(b); *see* **State v. Burroff,** 598 N.E.2d 1081 (Ind.App. 1992) (sufficient that the defendant was shown to have acted to collect on a policy he believed existed)]

3. Punishment

Arson is a common law felony and remains a felony by statute in virtually all jurisdictions.

ELEMENTS OF ARSON—A COMPARISON	
COMMON LAW ARSON	**STATUTORY ARSON**
Malicious	Two-Part Culpable Mental State: (i) At Least *Recklessness* in Starting the Fire; and (ii) *Purpose* of Destroying or Damaging Property Often Required
Burning	Starting a Fire
Of the Dwelling House	Expanded to Include *Other Structures* and Sometimes *Personal Property*
Of Another	*Property* of Another
Emphasis Placed on *Result*—the Burning of the Dwelling of Another	Emphasis Placed on *Conduct*—Starting a Fire with the Objective of Damaging or Destroying the Structure

Chapter Eleven

Crimes Against Property—Acquisition Offenses

CONTENTS	PAGE

Key Exam Issues

An examination question involving a possible wrongful appropriation of property by a defendant will be governed either by a modern theft statute or by the traditional property offenses. If the question does not include an applicable theft statute or otherwise refer you to the modern crime of theft, you should consider the following questions to determine whether the appropriation constitutes one of the traditional property offenses:

1. Begin by asking whether the defendant has committed ***larceny*** (*i.e.,* the trespassory taking and asportation of the personal property of another with the intent to permanently deprive the owner of possession).
2. At the time of the wrongful acquisition of the property, was it arguable that the defendant was already in possession of the property? (Consider ***embezzlement.***)
3. Is it arguable that the property was obtained with permission of the victim but that this permission was obtained by misrepresentations? (Consider ***false pretenses*** as well as ***larceny by trick.***)
4. Is it arguable that the defendant obtained the property by means of force or threats? (Consider ***robbery*** and perhaps ***extortion.***)

Note that if the question includes reference to a statutorily defined offense of ***theft,*** it is likely that many of these traditionally different offenses will be lumped together in the definition of that offense.

A. Introduction

1. Distinctions Among Offenses

The basic crimes against property are those involving a ***wrongful acquisition*** of property. At common law, the "acquisition offenses" have detailed technical requirements which reflect a begrudging expansion of the crimes by the early courts to cover more and more situations. The important distinctions between the offenses can be summarized as follows:

a. Larceny

The wrongful ***taking*** of property ***from the possession of another*** person who has a superior right to its possession, with the ***intent to permanently deprive.***

b. Embezzlement

A ***misappropriation*** of property by a person who ***already has it*** in his possession, with intent to defraud.

c. False Pretenses

Distinguishable from larceny in that the perpetrator obtains ***title and possession*** from another by means of ***deception.*** (But note: the taking for purposes of larceny can also be rendered wrongful if accomplished by deception.)

d. Robbery

Larceny from the victim's person or presence where the taking is accomplished by force or threats.

e. **Extortion**

Obtaining or attempting to obtain property from the victim by ***threats not sufficient to constitute robbery.***

f. **Receipt of Stolen Property**

The ***acceptance*** of property after the larceny by which it was acquired has been completed.

2. Modern Statutes: Theft

In modern criminal codes, a single offense is often created that includes what previously was larceny, embezzlement, false pretenses, receipt of stolen property, and sometimes other offenses such as extortion. This offense is generally labeled ***theft.*** [Model Penal Code § 223.1]

B. Larceny

1. Elements

Larceny is primarily an infringement of another's ***possessory*** interest in property. The elements of the offense are:

a. ***A trespassory***

b. ***Taking*** (or "caption") and

c. ***Asportation*** (carrying away) of

d. The ***personal property*** of

e. ***Another***

f. With the ***intent to permanently deprive*** the owner of possession of the property.

2. Subject Matter of Larceny: Personal Property

Only ***tangible personal property*** (*i.e.,* goods and chattels) can be the subject of larceny.

a. **Realty and Fixtures**

As a general rule, realty or fixtures (*i.e.,* items permanently affixed to the land) are not within the scope of larceny. [**State v. Jackson,** 11 S.E.2d 149 (N.C. 1940) (cemetery tombstone regarded as fixture)]

e.g. **Example:** The use of a landfill without paying dumping fee, the use of property without paying the fees therefore, and the money owed as a fee does not constitute "property" within the law of larceny. [**Commonwealth v. Rivers,** 583 N.E.2d 867 (Mass. 1991)]

(1) **Distinguish: Severed Fixtures, Crops, or Minerals**

Once fixtures, crops, or minerals are ***severed*** from the realty, they become personal property and can be the subject of larceny, ***provided*** they come into the possession of the landowner and are then ***taken from his possession.*** Severed items come into the possession of the landowner if the defendant relinquishes possession of them after they are severed and while they are still on the land. [**State v. Jackson,** *supra*]

e.g. **Example:** D dug up five pounds of potatoes from V's garden and placed them in a pile. D then dug up another five pounds but placed them in a sack as he removed them from the ground and carried the sack away as soon as it was full. Later, D returned and took the first five pounds of potatoes. D is guilty of larceny only of the ***first five pounds.*** Although these potatoes were initially part of the realty, D severed them, making them personal property, and left them on the property long enough that they came into the possession of the owner prior to D's taking and asportation of them. But with regard to the second five pounds, D's severance and asportation of the potatoes were part of the ***same act,*** and those potatoes were never in the possession of the owner, and their removal, therefore, could not be larceny. [**Bell v. State,** 63 Tenn. 426 (1874)]

b. Animals

Whether animals can be the subject of larceny requires that several distinctions be drawn.

(1) Domestic Animals

Livestock and animals of domestic value (horse, pig, chicken, and the like) can be the subject of larceny. At common law even some domesticated animals, *e.g.*, dogs, were not capable of being stolen. Today dogs may be the subject of larceny, either by statutes which mention dogs in particular or animals in general or under statutes which refer broadly to personal property of all kinds. [**People v. Hutchinson**, 9 N.Y.S.2d 656 (1938) (the honey of wild bees, located on another's land, cannot be the subject matter of larceny)]

(2) Wild Animals

Wild animals are not considered to be the property of anyone and thus cannot be the subject of larceny. If, however, a wild animal is ***killed or captured,*** it is treated in the same fashion as a severed fixture; the animal becomes personal property. If it remains on the property long enough to come into the possession of the landowner, taking it can be larceny; if it is killed (or captured) and removed in the same continuous transaction, however, there is no larceny, as the landowner never came into possession. [**Regina v. Townly,** 12 Cox Crim. Cas. 59 (1871)]

c. Intangible Property

Intangible personal property cannot be the subject of larceny. Documents, records, and choses in action are regarded as being merged into the thing they represent, and therefore are ***not "property"*** themselves. [**People v. Caridis,** 29 Cal. App. 166 (1915) (misappropriation of winning lottery ticket in an illegal game is not larceny)]

d. Services

Services are clearly ***not property.*** Thus, the wrongful acquisition of the benefits of someone's services (*e.g.*, a train ride, a night's lodging, or theater admission) is not larceny. [**Chappell v. United States,** 270 F.2d 274 (9th Cir. 1959) (Air Force sergeant used airmen under his command during duty hours to paint three houses owned by him; conviction reversed; to convert there must be property, not services)]

e. Electricity

Under the common law definition, it is questionable whether electricity is sufficiently tangible to be "taken," and therefore it might not be the subject of larceny. Nevertheless, courts tend to hold that larceny is committed when electrical power is "taken," as when it is diverted by improperly hooking up to a transmission line. [**People v. Menagas,** 11 N.E.2d 403 (Ill. 1937)]

f. Stolen Property and Contraband

Because larceny is a crime against possession (rather than title), stolen property and contraband can be the subject of larceny. [**People ex rel. Koons v. Elling,** 190 Misc. 998 (N.Y. Sup. 1948)]

g. Distinguish: Modern Statutes

Statutes often broaden the scope of property that can be the subject of larceny or theft.

(1) Real Property

It may be theft to unlawfully transfer real property (or an interest in real property) with the requisite intent, and it is now commonly theft to take fixtures, crops, or similar items. [Model Penal Code § 223.2(2) (theft of "immovable property"); Cal. Penal Code § 495 (specifically incorporating into theft offenses the removal of fixtures and things attached to realty)]

e.g. **Example:** Because the consolidated theft statute includes realty, the defendant was guilty of theft by physically occupying and attempting to obtain record ownership of a foreclosed house. [**State v. Gentry,** 538 S.W.3d 413 (Tenn. 2017)]

(2) Intangible Property

Likewise, intangible property (such as documents or records) is frequently brought within the purview of modern theft or larceny statutes. [Tex. Penal Code §§ 31.01(5)(B) (property includes intangible personal property), 31.01(5)(C) (property includes a document presenting or embodying anything of value)]

(a) Contents of Documents

It is arguably theft under some statutes to take the contents of documents, as by copying them. [**State v. Telek,** 216 A.2d 242 (N.J. 1966)]

(3) Theft of Labor or Services

Additionally, it may also be theft to wrongfully acquire the advantages of another's services. [Model Penal Code § 223.7; Tex. Penal Code § 31.04 (separate offense of theft of service); **Cruz-Reyes v. State,** 74 P.3d 219 (Alaska App. 2003) (when defendant obtained access to premium cable TV channels by installing machine that decoded them and enabled his TV to play them, he had "obtained" such service even if he never watched the premium channels, as the fee others paid for what he acquired is merely "for access—the *opportunity* to watch")]

(4) Gas

Whether natural gas can be the subject of common law larceny is uncertain. But it has been held to constitute "property" under a modern larceny statute. [**People v. Neiss,** 73 App. Div. 2d 938 (1980)]

(5) Images and Sound

Images and sounds of movies captured on video cassette tapes, are not "property" within a state statute defining what may be the subject of larceny. *See, e.g.,* **Commonwealth v. Yourawski,** 425 N.E.2d 298 (Mass. 1981) (images and sounds of "Star Wars," movie, captured on cassette tapes, is not "property" within statute defining what constitutes larceny).

(6) Modern Statutes

Model Penal Code § 223.0(7) specifically includes contraband in the definition of property which can be stolen.

h. Computer-Related Issues

Misappropriation of new types of "property" created by computers gives rise to special problems.

(1) Not Covered by Larceny or Theft

A computer program may be the subject of larceny or theft. [**Hancock v. State,** 402 S.W.2d 906 (Tex. 1966)] Unauthorized use of a computer may not be larceny under a statute that defines the crime as taking any "thing of value." [**Lund v. Commonwealth,** 232 S.E.2d 745 (Va. 1977)]

(2) Modern Trend: Property Crimes Cover Computer-Related "Property"

In some jurisdictions the protection of larceny or theft has been expanded to such property. [*See* Mass. Gen. Laws Ann. ch. 266, § 30(2) (property that can be the subject of larceny includes "electronically processed or stored data, either tangible or intangible" and "data while in transit")]

3. Asportation

Larceny requires that the property be *"carried away."* This is the requirement of asportation.

a. Slightest Movement Sufficient if Part of "Carrying Away"

All that is required for asportation is the ***slightest movement.*** However, this movement must be ***part of the process of carrying away*** the property; movement as part of preparation to begin carrying away will not suffice. [*See, e.g.,* **Ali v. Commonwealth,** 701 S.E.2d 64 (Va. 2010) ("asportation was complete only when the defendant yanked money from the victim's hands); **State v. Spears**, 196 P.3d 1037 (Ore.App. 2008) (the removal of boxes from a trailer and placing them on the ground satisfied the asportation element for theft)] By contrast, it is not enough for theft to shoot an animal for purpose of stealing it, even though it moves from a standing to a prone position when shot. [**Molton v. State,** 16 So. 795 (Ala. 1895)]

b. Modern Statutes

Modern statutes that make larceny one type of theft (*see infra,* p. 304 *et seq.*) often dispense with the requirement of asportation entirely. [*See* Model Penal Code § 223.2(1) (requiring only a "taking" or "exercise of control" over property); Tex. Penal Code § 31.03(a) ("unlawfully appropriates")]

4. Taking

The defendant must have completed a taking, or "caption," of the property. This means that the defendant must have acquired ***dominion and control*** over (*i.e.,* possession of) the property. [**Thompson v. State,** 10 So. 520 (Ala. 1892)]

a. Distinguish: Asportation

Usually, the movement that suffices for asportation will also show sufficient dominion and control to establish the taking necessary. But this is not always the case.

EXAM TIP

Asportation and taking are two separate elements of common law larceny. "Asportation" is a fancy way of saying ***"carrying away."*** "Taking" means ***"asserting dominion and control"*** over the property. Even though they are separate elements, and you should consider them separately, often one action is ***enough for both*** an asportation and a taking. For example, if a defendant picks up the victim's watch from the victim's desk and puts it in his pocket with the intent to steal it, the defendant has both carried and taken it (he moved the watch in the process of carrying it away and he exercised dominion and control over it by putting it in his pocket). On the other hand, if the defendant placed the watch on a nearby windowsill where his accomplice, hiding outside, could grab it, he has carried the watch but not taken it.

b. Means of Caption

The caption can be affected by the defendant directly or by an innocent agent. A defendant may therefore commit larceny by causing possession to be taken by another. [**United States v. Morgan,** 805 F.2d 1372 (9th Cir. 1986) (asportation satisfied where thief, by deception, directed investment company employee to transfer funds by wire from a federally insured savings and loan to a fraudulent account elsewhere)]

c. Modern Statutes

Modern statutes often define larceny-type crimes in terms of a "taking," an "appropriation," or an "exercise of control" over the property. Thus, it is likely that the traditional common law analysis regarding a "caption" will still apply. [Model Penal Code § 223.2(1); Tex. Penal Code §§ 31.01(4), 31.03(a) (theft consists of appropriation, defined as a defendant's exercise of control over property)] *See, e.g.,* [**Jones v. State,** 256 P.3d 527 (Wyo. 2011) (when a purchaser loaded a car onto a trailer and towed it away, asportation element was satisfied)]

5. Requirement of a "Trespass"

Larceny requires that the taking be ***trespassory,*** *i.e.,* wrongful. [**State v. Lewis,** 433 P.2d 617 (Ore. 1967)] Courts have limited the significance of trespass by declaring "constructive possession" to exist in several situations, as where an employer delivers property to his employee; the owner delivers property to another for a transaction to be completed in his presence; a bailee breaks bulk; a wrongdoer obtains possession of (but not title to) the property by lies; a wrongdoer finds lost or mislaid property; or property is delivered to a wrongdoer by mistake.

a. Taking Without Consent

The taking is trespassory if it is ***without the consent*** of the victim. Thus, if the victim acquiesces in the taking, there is ordinarily no larceny.

b. "Larceny by Trick": Taking with Consent Induced by Deception

A taking with the victim's permission can be sufficient for larceny if the ***permission is obtained by deception.*** The courts reason that, in light of the fraud or deception, the victim retains constructive possession of the property, and the defendant therefore misappropriates it from that possession. Larceny committed in this fashion is traditionally called "larceny by trick" [**Dobberke v. State,** 40 P.3d 1244 (Alaska App. 2002) (although defendant obtained possession of rental vehicle by consent of franchise owner, evidence indicated defendant "fraudulently obtained" that consent)]

(1) Fraud Required as to a Past or Present Fact

It is often said that larceny by trick (as well as false pretenses) requires a misrepresentation concerning a ***past or present fact.*** Under this view, a false ***promise*** (which is a misrepresentation of a "future fact") will not suffice. *But note:* There is some authority for the proposition that a false promise can give rise to larceny by trick, if the prosecution shows that in making the promise the defendant misrepresented his present intent to carry out the promise which would be a matter of "present fact." [**People v. Miller,** 62 N.E. 418 (N.Y. 1902) (defendant obtained money from victim by falsely stating his intention to invest it on the stock market, to pay weekly interest, and to return the money on demand; conviction of larceny by trick affirmed because (a) title to the money did not pass to the defendant and (b) false promises will not do for false pretenses)]

e.g. **Example:** In a leading English case, D asked V for his horse, saying that he wanted to borrow it for the day and promising to return it that evening. Actually, D intended to keep the horse. V consented to D's taking the horse. The mere fact that D obtained the horse by means of a promise he did not keep would ***not*** be enough to establish the fraud required to make the taking larceny. But the court found larceny was proved on a very narrow ground: It held that D obtained the horse by ***misrepresenting his intentions*** for use of the horse, a present fact. [**Rex v. Pear,** 168 Eng. Rep. 208 (1779) (the opinion indulged in the fiction that the owner of the horse retained possession until the time of its sale by D; it was not until several years after the *Pear* decision that spoken words were held to constitute "false pretenses")]

(a) Note

Some courts are inclined to define larceny more broadly, finding it on a different and broader ground, *i.e.*, that D obtained the property by means of a promise that he misrepresented he intended to keep. This would be a sufficient misrepresentation of present fact for larceny.

EXAM TIP

Note that obtaining an item by a promise to return it and then breaking that promise is not larceny (luckily so for most of us!). Some courts say this is larceny by trick if, ***when the defendant promised*** to return the item, he did ***not intend to keep that promise.*** He then obtained the item by deception as to his intent. However, if he did intend to keep his promise when he made it, but ***later changed his mind,*** there has been ***no larceny.***

(2) Consent to Taking for Purposes of a Trap

In some situations, the owner of the property anticipates the defendant's actions and is aware of the defendant's taking of the property but allows the defendant to act so that he may be caught committing the crime. It is generally held that this awareness and passive acquiescence in the defendant's action does *not* constitute consent; the defendant's conduct is still larceny. [**Smith v. United States,** 291 F.2d 220 (9th Cir. 1961) (bank robbery conviction upheld; defendant spoke to bank teller about plan to rob bank; teller pretended to agree but told bank manager, who told teller to hand defendant a bag when defendant "held him up"; defendant was arrested in possession of money; the bank did not consent to a taking in a trespass sense, but merely smoothed the way for the crime's commission)] However, some cases hold that there is no larceny if the owner or an employee acting on his order goes so far as to actually hand the property over to the defendant. [**Topolewski v. State,** 109 N.W. 1037 (Wis. 1906)]

(3) Limitation: Defendant Must Obtain Possession Only

Larceny by trick is committed only if the defendant uses deception to obtain ***possession.*** If title is also obtained, the crime may be false pretenses (*see infra,* p. 287), but it is not larceny. [**People v. Ashley,** 267 P.2d 271 (Cal. 1954) (defendant was agent for a corporation near insolvency, he obtained $25,000 loan by representing that he would build a theatre; he used the borrowed money to pay the corporation's operating expenses; conviction of false pretenses affirmed; a promise made without intent to perform is a false representation of present fact and so a false pretense)]

c. "Shoplifting"

Determining whether the taking, asportation, and trespass required for larceny occur in a shoplifting context presents special problems. Some handling of the items by customers is with the owner's consent, but a shoplifter can complete larceny without actually leaving the store with the merchandise, *i.e.*, if the shoplifter conceals the item and perhaps moves towards an exit, so as to move the property (thus ***carrying*** it) and exercises control over it that is inconsistent with the owner's rights (thus ***taking*** it) and clearly beyond what the owner has authorized customers to do (thus acting in a ***trespassory*** manner). The intent to steal (*see infra,* p. 277 *et seq.*) must, of course, exist as well. [**Carter v. Commonwealth,** 694 S.E.2d 590 (Va. 2010) (sufficient taking by shoplifter who has not left store, if he has exercised control wholly inconsistent with the owner's rights, which may be demonstrated by, *e.g.*, concealing the goods under clothing or in a container)]

d. Modern Statutes

Modern statutes typically define theft as requiring that the defendant exercise ***unlawful*** control over the property and define "unlawful" as including without effective consent. Deception renders consent ineffective. [Tex. Penal Code §§ 31.01(3), 31.03]

(1) False Promises Sufficient

If a defendant obtained property by making a promise that ***at the time*** he did ***not intend to keep,*** his exercise of control over the property will generally be considered unlawful and will constitute theft.

(2) Distinguish: Unkept Promise

If a defendant obtained property by making a promise that ***at the time he intended to keep,*** his exercise of control over the property does not become theft simply because he ***later*** failed to keep the promise. Moreover, the mere fact that the defendant failed to keep a promise will not by itself permit the inference that the defendant intended at the time the promise was made not to keep it. [Model Penal Code § 223.3(1)]

(3) "Possession/Title" Distinction Irrelevant

Under modern statutes, the false pretenses-larceny by trick distinction is ***abolished;*** therefore, whether the defendant obtained possession or title is irrelevant.

6. "Of Another"

The property involved must be that of another person. However, because larceny is basically a ***crime against possession,*** this means only that the defendant must have taken the property from the possession of another person who had a ***right to possession that was superior to that of the defendant.*** [*See, e.g.*, **State v. Marsala,** 755 A.2d 965 (Conn. 2000) (larceny where bailor took his car from lawful possession of bailee, who had filed a lien on the vehicle for unpaid repairs)]

a. Larceny by Owner's Taking from Another

Thus, a person can commit larceny by taking her ***own property*** from the possession of someone else who has a superior right to possession. [**State v. Cohen,** 263 N.W. 922 (Minn. 1935)]

e.g. **Example:** D takes her coat to Tailor for alterations. Tailor does the work and thereby acquires a possessory lien on the coat to secure his right to payment. D then takes the coat from Tailor, without paying, *i.e.,* with the intent to deprive Tailor of his interest. D is guilty of larceny. She took property "of another" (Tailor as a lienholder) even though title to it was in D. [**State v. Cohen,** *supra*]

b. "Possession" vs. "Custody"

There is ***no larceny*** where the defendant had ***possession*** of the property at the time she misappropriated it (although she may be guilty of embezzlement; *see infra,* p. 284). On the other hand, there may well be a larceny if the defendant simply had custody rather than possession. Thus, the distinction between custody and possession is crucial.[*See, e.g.*, **Hildebrand v. People,** 56 N.Y. 394 (1874) (A handed B a $50 bill to pay for 10-cent soda; B threw A out of the saloon and kept the money; B is guilty of larceny)]

(1) Possession Requires Significant Authority

Ordinarily, whether a defendant has possession or only custody is a factual one and turns on the amount of control vested in the defendant. If the defendant was given ***significant authority over the property,*** she has ***possession;*** but if she was given ***only limited authority*** over it, she has only ***custody.*** [**Morgan v. Commonwealth,** 47 S.W.2d 543 (Ky. 1932)]

e.g. **Example:** D was in charge of the local telegraph office and was the only person with the combination to the office safe. According to routine practice, money was placed in the safe until it was forwarded to the company's main office. D broke into the safe and took the money inside. **D** was ***not guilty*** of larceny. *Rationale:* D had sufficient authority over the money at the time of the misappropriation to give D possession, and so D did not take it from the possession of another; crime was embezzlement, not larceny. [**Morgan v. Commonwealth,** *supra*]

(2) Employee Misappropriation Cases

The possession/custody issue becomes particularly important where property has been entrusted to and then misappropriated by an employee. An employer who hands his property to his employee retains possession of it, and the employee has mere custody. Thus, the employee who misappropriates the property is guilty of larceny. [*See, e.g.*, **Fitch v. State,** 185 So. 435 (Fla. 1938) (night watchman of a bar took money from cash register; upholding larceny conviction, because the night watchman had custody of the property while the proprietor had possession)]

However, if a third person gives the property to the employee for his employer, the employee acquires possession until he puts the property into a receptacle like a cash drawer designated by the employer; the employee's misappropriation before he transfers possession to the employer is not larceny. (The crime of embezzlement was created to plug the loophole left by this gap in larceny.) Special rules apply depending on whether the property was delivered to the employee by a third party or by the employer. (*See infra,* p. 283 *et seq.* for a detailed discussion.)

c. Joint Owners

The common law view of larceny is that one co-owner (*e.g.*, a partner, tenant in common, joint tenant) cannot steal from the other co-owner. Thus, if two or more persons jointly own property, most courts hold that a misappropriation by one is *not larceny. Rationale:* Both owners have the right to possession, and thus the property is not that "of another."

e.g. **Example:** The terms of agreement between D and her father regarding a joint bank account were that she added only to be able to access the account on his behalf if he unable to do so. Evidence supported her conviction for theft when, without father's consent or knowledge, she withdrew those funds. [**Wagner v. State,** 128 A.3d 1 (Md. 2015)]

d. Larceny from Spouse

At common law, one spouse cannot commit larceny of the other spouse's property because of the identity of the husband and wife, *i.e.*, spouses are considered as "one." Some courts, however, have upheld convictions where the guilty spouse had separated from the other or was in the process of doing so at the time of the theft.

e. Model Penal Code

The Model Penal Code excludes from its theft provisions efforts by debtors "to dispose of personal or movable property subject to a security interest in ways that prejudice the secured creditor." That approach was relied on in a case where the victim held only a security interest in restaurant equipment in the defendant's possession. Based on the MPC, the court held the equipment was not the "property of another," thereby exempting the defendant from a theft conviction. [**State v. Collyns,** 99 A.3d 300 (N.H. 2014)]

7. Mens Rea: "Intent To Permanently Deprive"

Larceny requires an ***intent to permanently deprive*** the victim of his interest in the property. It is not necessary that the victim actually be permanently deprived; rather, what matters is what the defendant intends at the time of taking.

a. Intent to Keep

Intent to permanently deprive exists, of course, if the defendant intends to personally and permanently keep the property.

(1) Distinguish: Intent to Borrow and Return, or Intent to Pay

If the defendant takes the property with the intention of returning it or paying for it, the taking does not amount to larceny. [**People v. Brown,** 105 Cal. 66 (1894) (where defendant took bicycle to "get even" with victim but intended to return it, no larceny; instruction that temporary taking will satisfy larceny was reversible error; one must "intend to permanently deprive the owner of his property"); **Lee v. Commonwealth,** 105 S.E.2d 152 (Va. 1958) (no intent to steal if the defendant takes goods offered for sale and intended to and did pay the full price for them)]

EXAM TIP

A fairly common exam issue involves a defendant who with permission borrows someone's property but later decides to keep it. This is ***not*** larceny because ***when the defendant took the property,*** she did not intend to permanently deprive the victim. Her later decision to do so is not enough. Note, however, that if she "borrowed" the property ***without permission*** and later decided to keep it, she would be considered to have the necessary intent to permanently deprive the victim under the continuing trespass doctrine (*see infra,* p. 281).

b. Intent to Create Substantial Risk of Permanent Loss

If the defendant takes the property with the intent of doing something with the property that would create a ***substantial risk*** of its ***permanent loss*** to the owner, this is sufficient for larceny. [**Johnson v. Commonwealth,** 694 S.W.3d 232 (Ky. 2023) (taking victim's cell phone and subsequently breaking it constituted deprivation of property; "taking of property and its subsequent destruction so that it can no longer function as normal constitutes an act of withholding property of another permanently. The act of destruction is the means by which the withholding is accomplished"); **State v. Langis,** 444 P.2d 959 (Ore. 1968) (despite defendant's protest that he intended to leave car in "perfect condition," his intent to permanently deprive could be inferred from abandonment of the car because of "considerable risk that the owner would suffer a permanent deprivation of property")]

e.g. **Example:** D takes V's car, intending to drive it some distance and abandon it there. D may be convicted of larceny, but only if the jury determines that the circumstances of the intended abandonment would involve a substantial risk that the car would never be returned to V. [**State v. Langis,** *supra*]

EXAM TIP

Another possible exam question involves the defendant's taking property with the intent to return it, but before she does so it is permanently lost to the owner. The analysis here must concern ***how risky the defendant's intended actions were.*** If, for example, she borrowed her friend's car without permission to go to the grocery store, and someone stole the car while she was shopping, most likely she did not take the car with the necessary intent to deprive. If, however, the store was in a very high crime area, she parked it on a side street near the store, and someone stole it while she was shopping, she probably would be found to have taken the car with the intent of putting it ***at so high a risk of permanent loss*** that a court would find sufficient intent for larceny.

(1) Indifference as to Owner's Interest

A few courts have held that ***indifference*** as to whether the owner ever gets the property back is sufficient for larceny. [**State v. Little,** 868 A.2d 686 (Vt. 2004) (defendant guilty of theft of gun notwithstanding his claim he took it to attempt suicide, thereby making the gun again available to owners; at best "defendant was indifferent about the disposition of the gun and did not act in a way that assured its return to the victims")] Under this approach, the prosecution apparently does not need to establish that the intended disposition of the property involved a high or even substantial risk of loss to the owner.

c. Intent to Sell to Owner or to Pledge

It is also sufficient for larceny that the defendant intended to return the property to the owner but only upon payment or that the defendant intended to pledge the property as security or to pawn it. This is on the theory that the owner may refuse or be unable to pay the price or to redeem it, and thus the defendant's intended disposition of the property involves a ***sufficient risk of permanent loss.*** [**People v. Davis,** 965 P.2d 1165 (Cal. 1998) (defendant's intent to claim ownership of certain merchandise taken from shelf of store and to return it to the store on condition that the store pay refund constitutes intent to permanently deprive within meaning of larceny)]

d. Intent to Pay for Property

If property is for sale and the defendant takes it with the intent to pay and the present ability to pay, no larceny has occurred. However, taking property with only a ***vague intent*** to pay for it sometime in the future ***is*** generally held to be larceny. Courts vary on situations in between. A sound approach is to find larceny despite an intent to pay unless the defendant reasonably believes the owner would be willing to sell the property for the amount the defendant intends to tender to the owner. [**Mason v. State,** 32 Ark. 238 (1877) (evidence showed that defendants took 30 cents worth of beer after owner, who had sold beer, had gone to bed and refused to get up and serve them; next day defendants offered to pay $3 for the beer; owner demanded $30, which defendants refused to pay; evidence insufficient for larceny of the beer)]

e. Intent to Return Equivalent Property

The cases are not clear as to whether it is larceny to take property with the intent to return the ***equivalent but not the identical item.*** Under the better view, there is no larceny if the property is of a type that it is unlikely to make any difference to the owner whether she gets the original back or an equivalent substitute. [**State v. Savage,** 186 A. 738 (Del. 1916) (not larceny to take gasoline if intending to return an identical amount)]

f. Intent to Collect Debt or Taking Under Claim of Right

It is not larceny for the defendant to take specific money that she reasonably believed due her as a debt or to take property as security for payment of a debt honestly believed to exist [**Guzell v. Hiller,** 223 F.3d 518 (7th Cir. 2000) (travel agent's holding of customer's passport not theft if customer "pledged the passport to him as security for his advancing her the money for the airline ticket")] Such takings under "claim of right" show the defendant's belief that she had a legal right to the property taken (*i.e.,* she thought it was "hers") and therefore that she did not intend, by taking it, ***to deprive anyone else of his interest*** in the property.

(1) Distinguish: Taking to Satisfy a General Claim

The cases are split where the defendant takes property with no claim that she has a right to ***that property*** but only pursuant to a claim that the defendant is owed an amount equal to the value of the property taken (*e.g.,* jewelry taken in satisfaction of $500 debt). Probably the best approach is to find that larceny was committed ***unless*** the defendant took the property honestly believing that she had a legal right to engage in this sort of "self-help" and thus believed she had an interest in the property that entitled her to take it. Only in such cases does the defendant lack the intent to deprive another of property she knows belongs to the other person.

g. Modern Statutes

Modern theft statutes tend to retain the essence of the common law requirement of intent to permanently deprive. [People v. Jaso, 4 Cal.App. 3d 767 (1970) (Cal. Penal Code theft requires specific intent to deprive owner of his property)]

(1) Model Penal Code: Intent to Deprive

"Theft" under the Model Penal Code requires that the defendant act with the purpose of depriving another person of the property involved. "Deprive" is defined as including any of the following:

(i) ***Withholding property of another permanently or for so extended a period*** as to appropriate a major portion of its economic value,

(ii) ***Withholding property with intent to restore it only upon payment*** of a reward or other compensation, or

(iii) ***Disposing of property in such a way as to make it unlikely that the owner will recover it.***

[Model Penal Code §§ 223.2, 223.0(1)]

(2) Model Penal Code Defenses: Claim of Right and Similar Matters

The Model Penal Code accommodates a defendant's claim that she believed she had a right to take the property by recognizing three defenses applicable to theft. These must be raised by the defendant, but once raised the burden of proof is on the prosecution. It is a defense to theft that:

(i) The defendant was ***unaware that the property was that of another,***

(ii) The defendant acted under an ***honest claim of right*** to the property or a claim that she had a right to acquire or dispose of it as she did, or

(iii) The defendant took property exposed for sale ***intending to promptly purchase and pay*** for it or reasonably believing that the owners, if present, would have consented to her taking of it.

[Model Penal Code § 223.1(3)]

e.g. **Example:** D was entitled to jury instruction on affirmative defense of claim of right where her claim regarding removal of documents from her employer's premises was in order to use them to prosecute a civil claim of employment discrimination. [**State v. Saavedra,** 117 A.3d 1169 (N.J. 2015)]

e.g. **Example:** D's claim of right defense applies to defendant's "good faith belief that he was the owner of the cell phone that was the object taken during the robbery." [**T.D.W. v. State,** 42 So.3d 959 (Fla.App. 2010)]

(3) Special Problem: Vehicles and "Joyriding"

Although generally it is not a crime to take property of another without the intent to deprive, many jurisdictions make special provision for such takings of vehicles. It is an offense frequently called joyriding to take or operate the vehicle of another without the consent of the owner. ***No intent to deprive*** is required. [Model Penal Code § 223.9 ("unauthorized use of automobile and other vehicle"); Cal. Vehicle Code § 10851 (taking vehicle for the purpose of temporarily depriving owner)]

8. Taking and Intent Must Coincide

As a general rule, the *mens rea* and *actus reus* must concur in a point of time (*see supra,* p. 50). Thus, for larceny the intent to permanently deprive must exist ***at the very moment of the taking.*** [**Ennis v. State,** 167 P. 229 (Okla. 1917)]

e.g. **Example:** D had V's corn in his possession and, pursuant to V's direction, D sold the corn and received payment. After receiving the money, D decided to steal the money. D did not commit larceny, because his intent to steal did not exist at the time he took possession of the money. [**Ennis v. State,** *supra*]

a. Exception: "Continuing Trespass" Situations

Under certain circumstances, the wrongful intent need not exist at the time the property is first taken. If the defendant's act of taking the property is ***wrongful*** (although not necessarily criminal) and later, while in possession of the property, the defendant forms the requisite intent, the initial trespass is said ***to "continue"*** until the formulation of the intent, at which point the necessary concurrence is established and the actions constitute larceny. [**State v. Coombs,** 55 Me. 477 (1868)]

e.g. **Example:** D obtained a horse and sleigh, lying as to his intended destination and length of absence but intending to return them. Later, D decided to steal the property and sold it. Because of D's concealed intent, the initial taking was trespassory. Hence, D became guilty of larceny when he subsequently converted the property to his own use. [**State v. Coombs,** *supra*]

(1) Distinguish: Possession Rightfully Obtained

The "continuing trespass" doctrine will ***not*** apply if the defendant's initial possession was ***rightfully*** obtained. Thus, if D in the above example had not misrepresented his intended use, his later misappropriation would not be larceny.

b. Modern Statutes

Modern theft statutes eliminate this problem by defining the crime as committed by any exercise of control of the property. In the example above, suppose D could not be convicted of traditional larceny because his original taking of the sleigh was not wrongful. If the jurisdiction had a modern theft statute, D could be prosecuted on the basis of him exercising control over the sleigh after he decided to steal the sleigh, rather than on the basis of his initial acquisition of the sleigh.

9. Special Problem Areas

Special problems are raised by several situations that should be considered individually.

a. Property Acquired by Finding

Whether a person commits larceny of property he found depends on whether the property was ***abandoned or only lost or mislaid.***

(1) Abandoned Property

Abandoned property is property that has been ***intentionally cast away*** by its owner with the intent of relinquishing all rights in that property. Abandoned property has no owner and therefore is not the "property of another." Accordingly, it ***cannot be the subject of larceny.*** [**United States v. Smiley,** 27 F. Cas. 1132 (1864) (treasure aboard a sunken steamer, abandoned by owners, is "abandoned property, which could be acquired by anyone who might have the energy and enterprise to seek its recovery"; therefore, larceny charge properly dismissed)]

(2) Lost or Mislaid Goods

Lost or mislaid goods, on the other hand, ***can*** be the subject of larceny, subject to the application of special rules.

(a) Definitions

Property is ***"lost"*** when the owner ***accidentally gives up possession*** not knowing where it is. Property is ***"mislaid"*** when the owner has ***intentionally placed*** the property somewhere but later ***forgot where.*** Conversely, property is not lost or mislaid simply because the owner does not know exactly where it is at the moment. [**People v. Stay,** 19 Cal. App. 3d 166 (1971)]

(b) Special Requirements for Larceny of Lost or Mislaid Goods

Property that is lost or mislaid is regarded as being in the ***constructive possession of the owner.*** Therefore, if the finder takes possession of the property, he does so from the possession of the owner. [**Foulke v. New York Consolidated Railroad,** 127 N.E. 237 (N.Y. 1920) (mislaid property left on seat in subway car; "the owner was still constructively in possession of it")] Nonetheless, the taking is larceny ***only if the*** following two requirements are met:

1) Clue to Ownership

The defendant must have a "clue to ownership" of the property. This means that the defendant must either ***know who the owner is*** or have reason to believe that the owner ***can he located*** at the time he finds the property. A clue to ownership requires only that ***reasonable efforts*** by the defendant would have disclosed the owner's identity. If the defendant would have had to use extraordinary diligence to discover the owner, he does not have an adequate clue to ownership. [**Brooks v. State,** 35 Ohio St. 46 (1878) (lost property; it is "larceny by the finder when, at the time he finds it, he has reasonable ground to believe, from the nature of the property or the circumstances under which it is found, that if he does not conceal it but deals honestly with it, the owner will appear or be ascertained")]

2) Intent Must Exist at Time of Finding

In addition, the defendant must have the intent to steal ***at the time he finds the property*** and takes it into his possession. If he takes it innocently and thereafter forms the intent to steal, he is not guilty of larceny. [**Regina v. Thurborn,** 169 Eng. Rep. 293 (1848) (lost property; it is not larceny if the finder, with intent to take the entire dominion over the property, really believes, when he takes the property, that the owner cannot be found; it is larceny if, with like intent, he reasonably believes the owner can be found)]

b. Misappropriations by Employee

Employee misappropriations of property belonging to the employer present special problems. The issues differ depending on whether the property was delivered to the employee ***by a third party*** or ***by the employer.***

(1) Delivery by Third Party

If ***a third party*** delivers property to a servant or employee on behalf of the employer, the servant or employee receives ***possession.*** Therefore, if the servant or employee subsequently misappropriates the property, larceny is not committed, because the property has not been taken from the possession of another.

e.g. **Example:** Owner delivered two jewels to Employer's store and handed them to the clerk, D. D placed one in his pocket, intending to steal it, and the other in the safe, which was where Employer had told him to deposit all delivered jewels. D is not guilty of larceny of the jewel that he pocketed because that jewel was never in Employer's possession, and so D did not take it from the possession of another.

(a) Duration of Possession

The servant or employee keeps possession until he delivers the property to his employer or places it in a receptacle provided by the employer for the employer's purpose. If he ***thereafter*** misappropriates the property, he commits larceny. [**Bazeley's Case,** 2 East P.C. 571 (Cr. Cas. Res. 1799)] The principle applies beyond household servants, *i.e.*, to store clerks, bank tellers, and caretakers. [**Guerrero v. State,** 277 P.3d 735 (Wyo. 2012) (waiter's theft conviction overturned; lack of proof of "taking" from employer, because funds were converted during waiter's shift, and practice was for each waiter to serve as own cashier and then turn the money over at the end of the shift)]

(b) Distinguish: Liability for Embezzlement

An employee who misappropriates such property before it goes into the possession of the employer may commit embezzlement. Thus, in the example above, D may be guilty of embezzlement of the first jewel. (*See* below.)

(2) Delivery by Employer

When property is entrusted to a servant or employee ***by the master or employer,*** a different set of rules apply. The result turns on the amount of trust placed in the servant or employee.

(a) Ordinary Servant or Employee

Ordinarily, a servant or employee merely has ***custody*** of the employer's property. Thus, any misappropriation by the servant or employee ***is from the possession of the employer*** and therefore larceny. [**Warren v. State,** 62 N.E.2d 624 (Ind. 1945) (maintenance crew member working under a foreman had key to a storage building belonging to his employer; the crew member misappropriated property from the building; conviction of larceny affirmed)]

(b) "Trusted" Employee

However, if the employer has delegated significant authority to the employee, the employee obtains ***possession*** of the property. He therefore does ***not commit larceny*** by subsequently misappropriating the property. [**United States v.**

Whitlock, 663 F.2d 1094 (D.C.Cir. 1980) (defendant who took money from bank vault committed embezzlement, defendant "in a high position of trust . . . as an assistant cashier and assistant manager with the special trust powers that gave her access to the keys, the combination and the money")]

EXAM TIP

In an employee misappropriation question the issue is who has possession of the property. If the employee has possession, there can be no larceny if the employee decides to steal the property because there is no taking ***from the possession of another.*** When, then, does an employee have possession? ***"Trusted" employees,*** meaning those given significant authority (not necessarily those who wouldn't steal), always have possession, and ***any employee who receives the property from a third person*** has possession. Thus, trusted employees and recipients of property from third parties cannot commit larceny. (They may, however, be guilty of embezzlement.)

C. Embezzlement

1. Statutory Crime

Embezzlement is a ***statutory crime,*** and thus, its definition varies among jurisdictions. Generally, however, it involves the *fraudulent conversion of the property of another by one who is already in lawful possession* of it. Unlike larceny, which is a crime against possession, embezzlement is a crime against ***ownership.***

2. Historical Background

The first statute making embezzlement a crime was enacted in England in 1799 and was clearly designed to close the "loopholes" created by courts' definition of larceny as requiring a taking ***from the possession of another.***

3. Elements of the Crime

Embezzlement requires proof that the defendant:

(i) ***Converted;***

(ii) ***Property;***

(iii) ***Of another;***

(iv) In his ***lawful possession;***

(v) With intent ***to defraud.***

a. Conversion

"Conversion," as used in embezzlement, requires a ***serious act of interference*** with the owner's rights in the property, *e.g.*, using it up, selling it, pledging it, giving it away, delivering it to someone not entitled to it, inflicting serious damage to it, claiming it against the owner, or unreasonably withholding possession of it. Mere movement of the property is not sufficient. [**State v. Archie,** 943 P.2d 537 (N.M.App. 1997) (defendant removed electronic monitoring device from his ankle, damaged it and threw it into field, court found conversion because "person having possession of another's property treat[ed] the property as his own")] e.g. **Example:** D, a deputy sheriff, was in possession of a departmental patrol car. In the early morning, D drove it to a lawn mower repair shop, placed someone else's mower in it, and sped away from and eluded another police officer. D is guilty of embezzlement, because the use of the patrol car was clearly inconsistent with the owner's rights and the trust reposed in D. [**People v. Redondo,** 19 Cal. App. 4th 1428 (1993)]

b. Property

The property that can be the subject of embezzlement is often ***defined more broadly*** than it is in larceny. It may, for example, include real property. Thus, it would be embezzlement to claim ownership in land held for another. [**People v. Roland,** 134 Cal. App. 675 (1933) (a real estate agent refused to convey property to his principal on demand, falsely claiming to be the owner; real property, under state statute, could be embezzled; agent's conviction affirmed)]

c. Of Another

Clearly, one who converts her own property cannot be guilty of embezzlement. Cases sometimes raise a difficult question as to whether the property at issue was given to the defendant and thus is not the property "of another," or rather was simply entrusted to the defendant and thus remains property of another which can be the subject of embezzlement. [**State v. Kalinowski,** 460 P.3d 79 (N.M. 2019) (defendant not guilty of embezzlement absent "the essential element of entrustment")]

e.g. **Example:** V hires D, a contractor, to build a swimming pool. V gives D an advance payment of $5,000, believing that D will use this to buy materials for construction of the pool. In fact, D uses the money to pay for materials used on her last job. Is D guilty of embezzlement? Most likely there was no agreement between V and D that D would receive the money for the limited purpose of conveying it to a seller of materials for V's pool; if there had been such an agreement, the money would have remained V's, and D's actions would most likely have been a fraudulent conversion. However, because V simply gave D the money, the money became D's, and although D did not live up to V's expectations she did not "convert" property "of another."

(1) Distinguish: Co-Owners and Agents

Generally, a co-owner of property does not commit embezzlement by misappropriating jointly owned property in her possession because it is not property of another. Similarly, an agent authorized to collect money for her principal and to keep a certain portion as a commission is often regarded as a co-owner of the money collected and thus does not commit embezzlement if she misappropriates it. *But note:* Embezzlement statutes sometimes address this specifically and make such agents guilty of embezzlement if they misappropriate the collected money. [**People v. Riggins,** 132 N.E.2d 519 (Ill. 1956) (independent collection agent committed embezzlement by misappropriating money collected for principal)]

d. Lawful Possession

The defendant must have ***lawful possession*** of the property at the time of the conversion. Some statutes specifically set forth those persons who can come within the scope of the crime (*e.g.,* employees, bailees, bankers). Others are worded broadly enough to cover any persons entrusted with property. [*See, e.g.,* Cal. Penal Code § 503 ("Embezzlement is the fraudulent appropriation of property by a person to whom it has been entrusted")]

EXAM TIP

This requirement that the defendant have ***lawful possession*** at the time of conversion is the primary distinguishing characteristic of embezzlement. Thus, on an exam, if the defendant is an employee, bailee, or other person with lawful possession of the property, look for the elements of ***embezzlement*** rather than larceny.

e. Fraudulent Intent

At the time of the conversion, the defendant must have a fraudulent intent. Precisely what is sufficient to constitute the required fraudulent intent is not entirely clear.

(1) Intent to Permanently Deprive Not Required

While the intent and ability to restore equivalent property may be a defense to larceny, in embezzlement cases, the property commonly involved is money spent for his own purposes, perhaps with the intent to put back other money at a later date. The wrongdoer sometimes has enough resources to return the money before the discovery of his misconduct. The intent to restore the equivalent property even under these conditions is no defense to embezzlement. Perhaps the reason why such an intent is not defense is that there is no substantial ability to restore. The defendant often has used the money to gamble or in the stock market. [**State v. Joy,** 549 A.2d 1033 (Vt. 1988) (defendant not entitled to instruction that intent to repay is a defense)]

(a) But Note: Mitigation of Punishment

Evidence that the accused intended to or actually did restore the property may be used to mitigate punishment. [Cal. Penal Code §§ 512–513 (intent to restore or actual restoration of property before accused is charged is no defense but may mitigate punishment)]

(2) Claim of Right

If the defendant honestly believed that she was entitled to the property (*see supra,* p. 279), her conversion is not embezzlement. [**People v. LaPique,** 120 Cal. 25 (1898) (real estate agent was authorized to sell homeowner's house for $1,150 and sold it for $1,450; honestly though mistakenly believing he was entitled to a commission of all funds over $1,150, he converted $300; his bona fide claim of title negates the mental requirement; embezzlement conviction reversed)]

(3) Suggestion: Intentional Deception That Conversion Is Occurring

Arguably, all that embezzlement requires as a practical matter is that the defendant have deceived the victim by implicitly misrepresenting that the defendant was not converting the property. It seems to be sufficient that the defendant simply took advantage of the circumstances, rendering the owner unaware that the defendant was converting the property.

(a) Embezzlement by Public Officials

In states with special embezzlement statutes for public officials, the possible punishment increases because the public does not watch public officials as closely as employees or agents of businesses in the private sector. [**State v. Brown,** 422 S.E.2d 489 (W.Va. 1992) (while "proof of intent to steal or misappropriate is not required, proof that the public official intended to do the act or acts that resulted in the embezzlement is necessary")]

(4) Modern View: Statutory Schemes Requiring Intent to Permanently Deprive

Under some modern theft statutes, what was previously the separate crime of embezzlement is one way of committing theft. This means that the defendant must have acted with the ***intent required for theft,*** which is usually the intent to permanently deprive the owner of the property.

(a) Distinguish: Related Offense of Misapplication of Property

The Model Penal Code takes the above approach, but also contains a somewhat overlapping offense: misapplication of entrusted property, which requires that the accused misapply property entrusted to her and do so with ***knowledge that this misapplication creates a substantial risk of loss or detriment*** to the owner. [Model Penal Code § 224.13]

4. Demand for Return

A demand for the return of the property is ***not a formal requirement*** of embezzlement. However, in some situations, proof of a conversion is facilitated by evidence that the victim demanded the property and the defendant refused. Indeed, in a few cases it is likely that a conversion could not be shown without evidence of demand and refusal. [*Cf.* **State v. Britt,** 213 S.W. 425 (Mo. 1919) (mere failure for a long time to return the property to the owner, without a demand by the owner, may not be a conversion that is required for embezzlement)]

a. Demand Not Substitute for Proof of Conversion

While "demand and refusal" may be relevant evidence, it is ***not a substitute*** for showing a conversion of the property by the defendant. The prosecution must prove that the defendant did something with the property constituting a conversion. [**State v. Williams,** 179 N.W.2d 756 (Iowa 1970)]

D. False Pretenses

1. Statutory Crime

False pretenses (sometimes identified as "larceny by false pretenses"), like embezzlement, is a ***statutory crime*** and its definition therefore varies among jurisdictions. But in general, the offense consists of ***obtaining title*** to property ***by means of a material false representation*** and ***with intent to defraud*** the victim.

2. Historical Background

Under technicalities of the law of larceny (and specifically larceny by trick), one who obtained ***title*** (rather than mere possession) by means of deception could not be guilty of larceny (*see supra,* p. 273). In 1757, the English Parliament closed this "loophole" by creating the statutory crime of obtaining property by false pretenses. Most American jurisdictions have enacted statutes covering the situations addressed by the English enactment. [**State v. McMahon,** 140 A. 359 (R.I. 1928) (the English statute was part of the common law of the state)]

3. Policy Considerations

Courts are often concerned that false pretenses and similar crimes will apply to make what are really mere breaches of contract into criminal offenses. This concern may discourage aggressive but desirable commercial bargaining. These crimes are consequently often interpreted narrowly to minimize this risk. [**People v. Norman,** 650 N.E.2d 1303 (N.Y. 1995) (defendant's actions in selling car amounted to a representation that he had a sufficient interest in the vehicle to be able to sell it; prosecution may rely on that misrepresentation and does not have to prove present intention not to deliver the vehicle to convict of false pretenses)]

4. Elements of the Crime

False pretenses requires proof that the defendant:

(i) ***Obtained title,***

(ii) ***To property,***

(iii) By a ***false representation,*** **and**

(iv) With ***both knowledge*** of the misrepresentation's ***falsity and the intent to defraud.***

a. Obtaining Title

For a conviction of false pretenses, the defendant by his lies must acquire ***title*** to the property; it is not enough that the victim parts only with possession. [**Blackledge v. United States,** 447 A.2d 46 (D.C.App. 1982) (when defendant presented a stolen credit card to pay for the gas just put into the tank of his car, he was attempting false pretenses, as he only had possession of and was trying to obtain title to the gas by using the card)]

Usually, the victim's intention determines what the defendant receives: If the victim intends to transfer title to the defendant, the defendant gets title; if the victim intends to transfer only possession, the defendant gets no more than possession and is guilty of larceny (also known as larceny by trick, if the state separately defines that offense. *See supra*, p. 273).

(1) Absolute Title Not Required

"Title is synonymous with ownership, [and] the type of title that is obtained by the accused through his use of false pretenses is at most voidable title. The requirement . . . that title be obtained does not mean absolute title because such a requirement would make it impossible for the crime to be consummated." [**Bohling v. State,** 388 P.3d 502 (Wyo. 2017)]

Example: When D purchased a new car from V, he gave his old car in trade and represented to V that the old car was completely paid for. The new car was purchased on a conditional sales contract, in which *V retained title to the car as security* for the loan to D. D's representations as to having paid for the old car were untrue, and D was held guilty of false pretenses. The court acknowledged that any title obtained by fraud is arguably *voidable* but held that nevertheless D had obtained a sufficient property interest to support conviction of the crime. [**Franklin v. State,** 214 So.2d 924 (Ala. 1968)]

(2) Asportation Not Relevant

False pretenses, unlike larceny, has no requirement of asportation, meaning that the crime of theft by false pretenses ends at the moment that the defendant acquires title to the property. [**People v. Williams,** 305 P.3d 1241 (Cal. 2013) (false pretenses cannot become robbery by defendant's use of force)]

EXAM TIP

The fact that the defendant ***obtains title*** and not just possession is the clearest way to distinguish between false pretenses and larceny by trick. Therefore, when you see a defendant gain property by misrepresentation, first check to see if she obtained title or merely possession.

b. Property

As with embezzlement, the property that can be the subject of false pretenses is often broader in scope than that which can be the subject of larceny. Thus, the crime may be committed by obtaining title to real property, instruments or securities, and in some states by statute regarding theft of services, credit, and board and lodging. [**Stokes v. State,** 366 P.2d 425 (Okla. 1961) (telephone service is a "valuable thing" within meaning of false pretenses statute)]

c. False Representation

The defendant must have obtained the property by means of a false representation. There are, however, several traditional limits on the situations that will qualify.

(1) Nature of False Representation

The courts' concern that false pretenses not be applied so as to criminalize what is essentially a breach of contract or unpaid debt is reflected in the somewhat limited definition of the misrepresentations that will suffice for this offense.

(a) Past or Existing Fact

Clearly, a misrepresentation of a ***past or existing fact*** will suffice. [**Ross v. State,** 424 S.W.2d 168 (Ark. 1968)]

(b) Future Facts or False Promises

Most courts hold that the crime of false pretenses ***cannot*** be premised on misrepresentations of ***"future facts" or false promises,*** even if the defendant did not intend to keep the promise at the time it was made. [**Chaplin v. United States,** 157 F.2d 697 (D.C. Cir. 1946) (defendant told the victim that he was a liquor dealer (true) and owned liquor which he could not sell without first affixing tax stamps (true) and that if the victim would advance $1075 to him, he would buy stamps, sell the liquor and repay the money advanced (false); defendant's intent not to carry out these promises was evidenced by the fact that, after he got the money, he never used it to buy the stamps and never repaid the $1075; held, not guilty of false pretenses)]

1) Rationale

This position has been defended on the ground that it is not the purpose of the criminal law to provide redress for every victim of a bad bargain. Civil remedies suffice for such situations. [**Chaplin v. United States,** *supra*]

2) Modern Trend

There is an apparent trend among modern cases and statutes to hold that false promises ***will*** suffice ***if*** the prosecution proves that the defendant intended not to perform when he made the promise. [**State v. Letts,** 986 A.2d 1006 (R.I. 2010) (while statute requires "misrepresentation of a past or existing fact," it is deemed to cover "present state of mind" regarding "a future obligation;" here, defendant promised to complete paving job within a specified time notwithstanding "the fifty plus job backlog and the poor weather conditions")]

(c) Passive Nondisclosure

Ordinarily, a defendant does ***not*** commit false pretenses simply by the failure to correct a false impression that she knew was harbored by the victim. [**Stumpff v. People,** 117 P. 134 (Colo. 1911)] Courts may be persuaded to find that silence is enough, however, if the defendant was ***responsible*** (even innocently) ***for creating the false impression.*** [**People v. Tepper,** 64 N.E.3d 98 (Ill. 2016) (defendant failed to disclose his interest in vendor's business; court concluded that the requisite "deception was carried out in large part by his silence, as opposed to speech, concerning his supplemental employment, but in the context of fraud, that is a distinction without a difference")]

(2) Materiality

The misrepresentation must concern a material fact; *i.e.,* it must have been a ***"controlling inducement*** for the victim's parting with the property. However, it need not be the sole inducing reason; it is enough that the misrepresentation was one of several factors relied on by the victim in deciding to transfer the property to the defendant. [**Whitmore v. State,** 298 N.W. 194 (Wis. 1941)]

(3) Causal Factor (Reliance)

In addition, the victim must have relied on the misrepresentation; *i.e.,* it must have ***caused*** the victim ***to transfer the property*** to the defendant. Thus, if the victim was not in fact deceived by the misrepresentation, the crime of false pretenses has not been committed. [**State v. Finch,** 573 P.2d 1048 (Kan. 1978) (no false pretenses where defendant bought dress at lower price by switching sale tag from another garment; security guard alerted cashier this had occurred)]

e.g. **Example:** D misrepresented certain facts to V, hoping to persuade V to give D money. Although V did not believe D's lies, V wanted to catch D in the commission of a crime and therefore gave D the money. Because V was not deceived by the misrepresentations, D is not guilty of false pretenses. [**Commonwealth v. Johnson,** 167 A. 344 (Pa. 1933)]

(a) Distinguish: Liability for Attempt

However, even though the victim was not deceived, the defendant can be convicted of ***attempted*** false pretenses. [**Commonwealth v. Johnson,** *supra*]

d. Mens Rea

The *mens rea* for false pretenses is twofold:

(1) Knowledge of Falsity

The defendant must have ***"knowledge" that the representations were false.*** If she believes them to be true, even though her belief is unreasonable, she has not committed false pretenses. It is not enough that she tells what she knows or believes to be false or what she knows she does not know to be true; in addition she must have an intent to defraud. [**State v. Agosta,** 787 A.2d 1252 (Vt. 2001)]

(2) **Intent to Defraud**

In addition to knowledge about the false representations, it must also be shown that the defendant had the ***intent to defraud*** the victim. In order for a defendant to have an intent to defraud, she must intend the victim to rely upon her misrepresentation, an intention which generally can be inferred from the fact that the defendant actually obtained the victim's property or money by telling lies. [**Commonwealth v. Green,** 94 N.E.2d 260 (Mass. 1950) ("it must appear that there was a false statement of fact known or believed by the [defendant] to be false made with the intent that the person to whom it was made should rely upon its truth")] Precisely what this requires is not entirely clear.

(a) **Situations Precluding Intent to Defraud**

Generally, there is no intent to defraud if (i) the defendant believed the property to be her own; (ii) she intended to restore the property; or (iii) she believed that she was entitled to the property because of a debt owed her by the victim.

(b) **Less Required than for Larceny**

The intent to defraud required for false pretenses demands less than the intent to permanently deprive required by larceny. However, the precise difference between the two "specific intents" has not been developed by the courts. [*See, e.g.,* **State v. Mills,** 396 P.2d 5 (Ariz. 1964) (intent to repay loan will not prevent conviction for false pretenses based on obtaining loan by misrepresentations, even though intent to repay would preclude conviction for larceny)]

5. Special Evidentiary Requirement

Some jurisdictions impose special evidentiary requirements (*e.g.,* corroboration) in false pretenses cases. These rules are apparently designed to prevent convictions based solely on the victim's testimony. For instance, in California certain false pretenses cases require a handwritten misrepresentation, two witnesses to the misrepresentation, or one witness to the misrepresentation and corroborating circumstances. [Cal. Penal Code § 532(b)]

6. Related Offense: Identity Theft

Identity theft refers to a crime in which someone wrongfully obtains and uses another person's personal data. [*See, e.g.*, Cal. Penal Code § 530.5(a) ("Every person who willfully obtains personal identifying information of another person and uses that information for any unlawful purpose, including to obtain or attempt to obtain credit, goods, services, real property, or medical information without the consent of that person is guilty of a crime.")] The identity thief may use the victim's name, Social Security number, or credit card number or other financial information to gain money or other economic or private benefit realized by the identity thief and any coconspirators.

a. Elements

Identity theft requires proof that the defendant:

(i) ***stole personal identification information belonging to another***; and

(ii) ***fraudulently misused such information*** to economically enrich or benefit the identity thief and others.

b. Examples

(i) The defendant intentionally misleads law enforcement to believe that the person cited or arrested is someone else. If the impostor ignores a request to appear in court, authorities may issue an arrest warrant in the name of the identity theft victim, who is arrested later for failure to appear in court.

(ii) Defendant fraudulently billed Medicaid for services not rendered, by presenting a patient's actual Medicaid reimbursement number Defendant's conduct constituted illegal use of means of identification of another person, in violation of federal identity theft statute (18 U.S.C. § 1028A(a)(1)). [**United States v. Dubin,** 27 F.4th 1021 (5th Cir. 2022)]

(iii) Stolen information may be used to open new accounts in the victim-consumer's name. The harm to the victim usually consists of out-of-pocket expenses and the time necessary to repair the damage. [*See, e.g.,* **People v. Lee,** 217 Cal.Rptr.3d 392 (Cal.App. 2017)]

c. Punishment

Every state statutorily criminalizes identity theft as a felony, with incarceration as the penalty. [*See, e.g.,* **Flores-Figueroa v. United States,** 556 U.S. 646 (2009) (federal criminal statute prohibits "aggravated identity theft" imposes a mandatory two-year prison term)] In addition, half the states have specific ***restitution*** provisions for identity theft. Several states have ***forfeiture*** provisions for identity theft crimes, and a few states have created ***identity theft passport programs*** to help victims avoid continuing identity theft.

E. Robbery

1. Elements

Robbery is basically aggravated larceny. It requires proof of all of the elements for larceny (*see supra,* p. 269 *et seq.*) ***plus*** two other things:

(i) The property must be taken ***from the victim's person or presence,*** and

(ii) The taking of the property must be accomplished ***by means of violence or intimidation.***

[*See, e.g.,* Cal. Penal Code § 211 (robbery is "taking of personal property in the possession of another, from his person or immediate presence. . . . accomplished by means of force or fear")]

EXAM TIP

When you analyze and discuss the crime of robbery on an exam, you must first find and discuss the ***elements of larceny*** (*i.e.*, an unlawful taking and carrying away of the property of another with intent to permanently deprive), because robbery is aggravated larceny. If you find those elements, then discuss the additional ones for robbery, *i.e.*, a taking from the victim's ***person or presence, by violence (force) or intimidation.***

2. Taking from Victim's Person, Proximity, or Control

Robbery requires a taking from the ***presence*** of the victim. The crime is sometimes described as requiring that the property be taken from the person of another, but this is too narrow. Some case law and statutory definitions of robbery speak of the requirement that the taking must be "from the person of another" without adding "or in his presence." Yet even under the narrower wording, a taking in the presence of the victim is still sufficient for robbery. [**Commonwealth v. Cruzado,** 901 N.E.2d 1245 (Mass. 2009) (sufficient that the taking of a vehicle was from the victim's presence where the victim had a "protective concern" for the car, stolen from outside his place of employment); **State v. Green,** 220 So.3d 103 (La.App. 2017) (sufficed that defendant took victim's phone from porch while the victim was inside the house, but then threatened the victim when she stepped outside)]

a. "Presence"

Property is within the victim's "presence" for purposes of robbery if it is in proximity to the victim and ***within his control*** in the sense that he could have prevented its taking had it not been for the defendant's use of violence or threats. [**United States v. Soler,** 759 F.3d 226 (2d Cir. 2014) (presence, per federal carjacking statute, exists if vehicle "is so within [victim's] reach, inspection, observation, or control" that victim could retain possession if he had not been overcome by fear)]

e.g. **Example:** Hotel clerk was lured from motel lobby to defendant's apartment on second floor, where the defendant tied her up and took $500 from cash register in the lobby. The taking was deemed from the "presence" of the clerk. **People v. Clemons,** 89 P.3d 479 (Colo.App. 2003)]

b. Distinguish: Model Penal Code

Departing from traditional formulations of robbery, the Model Penal Code would not require that the taking be from the person or the presence of the victim. [*See, e.g.*, **Burton v. State,** 510 S.W.3d 232 (Tex.App. 2017) (completed theft not required to establish a robbery; "the gravamen of robbery is the assaultive conduct and not theft;" defendant's return of purse and cell phone not relevant)] Instead, it is only necessary under the Code that ***violence or threats*** be used in the course of committing theft. [Model Penal Code § 222.1] "For example, an offender might threaten to shoot the victim in order to compel him to telephone directions for the disposition of property located elsewhere or the threat may be to one person in order to secure property from another who is not then present." [Model Penal Code § 222.1, Comment at 112 (1980)] Many modern criminal codes follow this approach, although some states require that the defendant made the threats or engaged in the violence with the intent of obtaining the property being stolen. [*See, e.g.,* Tex. Penal Code § 29.02]

e.g. **Example:** D entered tattoo shop where co-owners B and A were present with friend C. D shot B. and took money from his pocket and fled. D was convicted of three counts of armed robbery for taking from "presence" of B, A and C, respectively. There was no robbery of C, because there was no evidence that C "had control over the money." There was a robbery of A, who as co-owner had sufficient ownership or control over the money in B's pockets. [**People v. Williams,** 297 P.3d 1011 (Colo.App. 2012)]

3. Taking by Violence or Intimidation

The taking of the property must be accomplished by violence or intimidation. The victim need not be aware that the violence or intimidation had such consequences. Thus, it is robbery even if the violence or intimidation was used for the purpose of making the victim unaware of the taking. [**People v. Bartowsheski,** 661 P.2d 235 (Colo. 1983)] On the other hand, absent evidence of a close pursuit, as well as intervening time, distance, and events may break the link between a theft and the subsequent use of force. [*See, e.g.*, **State v. Tolbert,** 433 P.3d 501 (Ore.App. 2018) (defendant's later struggle with police officers' attempt to arrest him did not occur immediately before or after the theft; robbery conviction reversed)]

a. Violence

The taking is accomplished by violence within the meaning of robbery if ***any force*** is used to obtain the property.

(1) "Pickpocket" Situations

It is ***not*** robbery to stealthily take property from the pocket of the victim because ***no use of force*** is involved; the crime is simply larceny, although the fact that it is "larceny from the person" often means that it is punishable by a more severe penalty than ordinary larceny. Such pickpocket situations can ***escalate into robbery***, however, if the defendant pushes or jostles the victim, or if the victim becomes aware of what is happening and the defendant struggles with the victim to keep possession of the property. [**Robinson v. State,** 692 So.2d 883 (Fla. 1997) ("the perpetrator must employ more than the force necessary to remove the property from the person")]

(2) "Snatching" Situations

The defendant also does not commit robbery by simply snatching property from the victim's grasp so suddenly that the victim offers no resistance, because such a taking of the property involves ***no use of force*** within the meaning of robbery. [**Stokeling v. United States,** 586 U.S. 73 (2019) (robbery as defined by Congress as requiring use of "force or violence" refers to common law requirement of sufficient force "to overcome resistance")] But there is a robbery if the items are attached to the victim's person (as by a chain) so that force is required to remove them. [**United States v. Rodriguez,** 925 F.2d 1049 (7th Cir. 1991) (robbery committed; victim's "key chain was attached to his clothing, and [defendant] had to pull the chain once or perhaps twice to snatch the keys")] Robbery may even be committed if the victim becomes aware that the object is being taken and resists by grabbing the item so the defendant must ***wrest*** it from the victim's grasp over resistance. [**United States v. Gattis,** 877 F.3d 150 (4th Cir. 2017)]

EXAM TIP

When checking the facts of an exam question for "violence," recall that there does ***not have to be a lot of force used.*** A light shove or a snapping of a purse strap will do for robbery.

(3) Victim Rendered Helpless

It is robbery to render the victim helpless by use of force and then take the property. This is true even if the victim is rendered helpless by the administration of a drug or an intoxicating substance, because this amounts to a battery (unlawful application of force; *see supra,* p. 230). [**Chaney v. State,** 739 So.2d 416 (Miss.App. 1999) (defendant reached in pocket of 87-year-old man, who was aware that defendant took his wallet; on finding only $2, defendant then turned man's pants pockets inside out and took the change inside, causing man to fall to floor)]

(4) Distinguish: Model Penal Code Requirement of Serious Injury

The Model Penal Code would limit this type of robbery (*i.e.,* a taking by violence) to situations in which the defendant inflicts ***serious bodily injury.*** [Model Penal Code § 222.1(1)(a); *cf.* Model Penal Code § 222.1, Comment at 108 (1980) ("Any taking from the person will involve some use of 'force' and perhaps 'fear' in some general sense of being startled. But it is force or threat of force directed at placing the victim in serious fear for his safety that justifies the escalated penalties of the robbery offense.")]

b. Intimidation

Even where actual violence is not employed, a taking of property is nonetheless robbery if accomplished by means of intimidation (*i.e., threats*).

(1) Victim Must Be Placed in Fear

Robbery by intimidation requires that the victim have ***actually been placed in fear.*** Sometimes this requirement is expressed as requiring that the taking was accomplished by threats, which means that the threats must have instilled fear in the victim and caused that victim to give up the property. Intimidation requires that the victim's fear be ***attributable to the defendant's actions;*** simply showing that the victim was placed in fear is not sufficient by itself. [**S.W. v. State,** 513 So. 2d 1088 (Fla.App. 1987) (robbery conviction improper where evidence showed victim was not in fear)]

(a) Distinguish: Threats Sufficient

The Model Penal Code and some modern statutes based on it do not require that the victim be placed in fear ***as long as*** the defendant threatened serious bodily injury. [Model Penal Code § 222.1(1)(b)]

(2) Objectively Sufficient Threatening Conduct Necessary

The victim's fear must be ***reasonable,*** which means that the defendant's actions must have been such that a reasonable person would have felt the necessary fear. [**State v. Garcia,** 923 N.W.2d 725 (Neb. 2019) ("finder of fact must determine . . .whether the defendant's conduct would have placed a reasonable person in fear"; defendant handed bank teller a note stating "This is a robbery put the money on the counter")] The threat need not, however, be explicit and an implied threat is sufficient. [**People v. Hollingsworth,** 457 N.E.2d 1062 (Ill. 1983)]

e.g. **Example:** D approached V, a convenience store cashier, and then placed his hand in the cash drawer. When V grabbed D's wrist and demanded, "What are you doing?" D clenched his fist and glared at V. V released D's wrist and D left with money from the drawer. V testified that she feared that V would hurt her if she did not let him go. D is guilty of robbery. V's fear alone is not enough. Here, D's clenching his fist and glaring was an implied threat that would place a reasonable person in fear. V's testimony showed V was placed in fear and this caused her to give up the property. [**Wilmeth v. State,** 808 S.W.2d 703 (Tex. 1991)]

(a) Distinguish: Purposely Putting in Fear Sufficient

The Model Penal Code and modern statutes based on it do not require that the defendant's conduct meet any objective standard, but instead require that the defendant have ***purposely*** put the victim in fear. This reflects the view that robbery should be found even if the victim was unusually susceptible to threats and the defendant both knew and intentionally exploited this to place the victim in fear, although by conduct that would not have had this effect on others. [Model Penal Code § 222.1(1)(b)]

(3) Nature of Threat

Traditionally, the injury threatened must be of ***death, bodily injury,*** or ***destruction of the victim's dwelling house.*** Threats to ***accuse the victim of sodomy*** have also been held sufficient, but threats to accuse the victim of other crimes are not enough. [**Montsdoca v. State,** 93 So. 157 (Fla. 1922)]

(a) Distinguish: Model Penal Code

The Model Penal Code would require that the threat be of ***serious bodily injury.*** [Model Penal Code § 222.1(1)(b)]

(4) Target of Threat

The threat need not be directed at the owner of the property; one can commit robbery by threatening harm to a ***member of the owner's family or other relative,*** or to ***anyone in the owner's presence.*** [**Lear v. State,** 6 P.2d 426 (Ariz. 1931) ("The fear may be either of an unlawful injury to the person or property of the person robbed, or of a relative or member of his family; or of an immediate and unlawful injury to the person or property of any one in the company of the person robbed at the time of the robbery")]

(5) Immediacy Required

The threat must be of ***immediate injury.*** A general threat to harm the subject at some time in the future will not suffice. [**People v. Rudelt,** 6 App. Div. 2d 640 (1958) (statement, "I must have that money; I could kill you but I won't," could be construed as creating necessary fear of immediate injury)]

EXAM TIP

If you don't find force in the facts of a robbery question, check for ***a threat.*** The threat must be enough to ***instill fear*** in the victim. To be a threat sufficient for robbery, check that:

(i) The defendant's actions have ***placed the victim in fear*** of harm,

(ii) The fear is of ***imminent harm,*** and

(iii) The action is such as would cause a ***reasonable person*** to be placed in fear.

Thus, a threat that unless the victim hands over her wallet, the defendant will cause bodily harm to the victim or her family, or even to the stranger standing next to her, is enough. But a threat to cause such harm to her husband when he returns from overseas is not imminent harm and thus is insufficient.

---

c. Violence or Intimidation Used to Take Property

The force or intimidation must be used to take the property. Thus, it is necessary that the violence or threats occur ***before or during the taking*** of the property. If the taking is complete before the force or intimidation is used, this requirement is not met. [**State v. Long,** 675 P.2d 832 (Kan. 1984) (just as the defendant took money from box inside building and stuffed it into his shirt, the victim appeared and tried to block the doorway; defendant pushed her aside; taking, obtaining dominion and control, is not complete where it is "immediately resisted by the owner before the thief can remove it from the premises or from the owner's presence")]

(1) Taking May Be Broadly Construed

In applying this requirement, courts sometimes construe the "taking" concept broadly so that robbery covers the use of violence or intimidation after the defendant has done enough with the property so that under larceny law the taking and asportation of the property would have been complete before that violence or intimidation occurred.

e.g. **Example:** D entered a small building; he then took money from a cash box and put it in his pocket. When D was surprised by V, the owner, he pushed V out of the way and rushed out. D is guilty of robbery, because he had not completed his taking of the property when he used the force against V because he had not yet removed the money from V's immediate presence. It is likely, however, that this court would have said that for purposes of larceny, D had completed the necessary taking when he put the money in his pocket. [**State v. Long,** *supra*]

(2) Situations Created for Other Purposes

According to the weight of authority, the violent or intimidating acts do not always have to be committed for the purpose of taking the victim's property. Thus, a defendant who uses violence or intimidation for some other purpose commits robbery if he takes advantage of that situation to obtain property from the person or presence of another. [**Carey v. United States,** 296 F.2d 422 (D.C. Cir. 1961)]

e.g. **Example:** During an argument with V, D stabbed V to death, and then for the first time decided to steal the money that V had on her person. Even though the intent to steal did not arise until after the violence was used, D was guilty of robbery. [**Carey v. United States,** *supra*]

d. Modern Statutes and Model Penal Code positions

Modern statutes address this aspect of robbery in a number of different ways.

(1) Model Penal Code: Force During Theft or Escape from Theft

The Model Penal Code and modern statutes based on it dispense with the need for the use of force or intimidation to obtain the property. Under this approach, it is only necessary that the defendant seriously wound another, threaten another with serious bodily injury, or commit or threaten to commit a serious felony "in the course of committing" theft. "In the course of committing theft" is defined as including escape from committing or attempting to commit theft. [Model Penal Code § 222.1]

(2) Force Used to Take or Retain Property

Some statutory formulations cover force or intimidation used during theft or immediate flight from such a crime with intent to obtain the property or to retain it. [Conn. Gen. Stat. § 53a–133]

(3) Special Problem: Forced Used to Escape an Unsuccessful Attempted Theft

Modern robbery statutes differ as applied to situations in which the defendant is proved to have used force or intimidation to escape after discarding the property or otherwise terminating an attempted larceny or theft. This would be robbery under the Model Penal Code approach, but not be under the Connecticut statute because the defendant would no longer have the intent to obtain or retain the property. [**State v. Preston,** 728 A.2d 1087 (Conn. 1999)]

4. Possible Defense: Taking Under Claim of Right

Because robbery requires that the defendant committed larceny by violence or intimidation, the elements of larceny must also be proved, including the intent ***to permanently deprive.*** If the facts show that a defendant lacked the intent to rob because he ***honestly believes he is entitled*** to the property taken, should he be acquitted and allowed to take the property from the person or presence of another by violence or intimidation? [**People v. Tefunga,** 987 P.2d 168 (Cal. 1999) (claim-of-right defense to robbery does not extend to forcible taking purported to satisfy, settle or otherwise collect a debt, liquidated or unliquidated; nevertheless, claim-of-right instruction should have been given here, where defendant claimed he brought $200 to give to victim to pay bills and thereafter took back the very same $200 upon concluding she was not going to use it for that purpose but would instead give it to her mother); *and see supra,* p. 279]

a. Note: Refusal to Apply Claim of Right

Because self-help involving violence or threats poses risks of escalating dangerous conduct, courts have sometimes strained to avoid applying claim of right law to robbery, even if they would apply it to simple larceny situations. For example, some courts have held that claim of right does not apply to robberies where the behavior involved would be illegal even if it was with the full consent of the victim. [**Jupiter v. State,** 616 A.2d 412 (Md. 1992) (claim of right not established where intoxicated defendant paid full value for beer taken at gunpoint after seller refused to make sale because law prohibits sale to intoxicated person); **Burton v. State,** 510 S.W.3d 232 (Tex.App. 2017) ("completed theft. . . not required to establish a robbery," as "the gravamen of robbery is the assaultive conduct and not the theft"; defendant's return of victim's purse and cell phone not relevant)]

5. Punishment

Robbery is a common law felony and remains a felony in most if not all modern jurisdictions, ***regardless of the value of the property taken.*** [Cal. Penal Code § 213; Tex. Penal Code § 29.02(b)] However, for purposes of punishment, statutes often distinguish between simple robbery and aggravated robbery, imposing a heavier penalty for the latter. [*See* Tex. Penal Code § 29.03 (robbery raised to aggravated robbery if perpetrator causes serious bodily injury to another or uses or exhibits a deadly weapon); *see* **State v. Williams,** 95 A.3d 721 (N.J. 2014) (use of simulated deadly weapon suffices for aggravated robbery; defendant claimed to be armed with a bomb and he was wearing baggy clothes that could have concealed such a weapon; defendant's hands not visible to victim)]

6. Compare: Carjacking

A new robbery-like crime often called "carjacking," is a crime in several states. Carjacking often consists of taking a motor vehicle from the possession of another by force or threats. The need for this new crime arose in part because robbery often requires an intent to permanently deprive the owner of the property and thus does not cover some dangerous taking of vehicles. [*See, e.g.*, Cal. Penal Code § 215; **United States v. Soler,** 759 F.3d 226 (3d Cir. 2014) presence, under federal carjacking statute, exists if the vehicle "is so within [victim's] reach, inspection, observation, or control that he or she could, if not overcome by violence or prevented by fear, retain possession of it")]

F. Extortion (or Blackmail)

1. Common Law

Common law extortion is the corrupt collection of an unlawful fee by a public officer under color of office. It is a misdemeanor.

2. Modern Statutes

Modern statutes have expanded the crime of extortion to include what is generally regarded as ***blackmail,*** although they may denominate the crime by various names. [Cal. Penal Code § 518 ("extortion"); Ky.Rev.Stat. § 509.080 ("criminal coercion")]

a. Statutory Schemes

Modern extortion statutes typically fall into two distinct patterns:

(1) Property Obtained by Threats

Some statutory schemes require that the defendant actually ***obtain property*** by means of threats or coercion. [Cal. Penal Code § 518(a) (obtaining property with subject's consent where the consent is induced by wrongful use of force or fear or under color of office); Model Penal Code § 223.4 (obtaining property by certain enumerated threats)]

(a) Distinguish: Liability for Attempt

Under these statutes, a defendant who has only threatened the victim but not yet received the property he wants cannot be convicted of the completed offense, but he may be liable for attempted extortion. [**People v. Franquelin,** 109 Cal. App. 2d 777 (1952)]

(2) Threats Alone Sufficient

Most statutes, on the other hand, require only the making of certain prohibited ***threats with the intent to thereby obtain property*** or something of value. [Ky.Rev.Stat. § 509.080 (defining criminal coercion as threats made with intent to compel person to engage in conduct or refrain from conduct)]

b. Type of Threats Required, Generally

Jurisdictions vary as to the type of threats that suffice for the crime. Typically, however, the threats covered are insufficient for robbery because they do not involve the harm necessary for robbery or because the harm is not threatened immediately. Often, extortion or blackmail is committed by threats to do things that themselves could be done without violating the law; thus, it is a crime to threaten to do certain things ***as a means of seeking property*** even though the things threatened could be ***lawfully done.***

EXAM TIP

When you review a question looking for the elements of robbery, if the threatened harm is ***not bodily injury or not very immediate bodily injury,*** consider whether ***extortion*** is the more appropriate crime to analyze under the facts.

(1) Typically Sufficient Threats

Extortion statutes commonly define the following threats as sufficient:

(a) Threats to unlawfully ***injure the person or property*** of another [Cal. Penal Code § 519(1)],

(b) Threats to ***accuse*** the individual threatened or a relative or family member ***of a crime*** [Cal. Penal Code § 519(2)],

(c) Threats to ***expose or impute*** to the individual threatened or any of these persons ***"a deformity, disgrace, or crime"*** [Cal. Penal Code § 519(3)],

(d) Threats to ***expose any secret*** affecting these persons. [Cal. Penal Code § 519(4)], and

(e) Threats to report the person's immigration status [Cal. Penal Code § 519(5)].

e.g. **Example:** D, a lawyer, represented W in a divorce proceeding. D obtained photographs of her spouse, H, in a criminal sexual act. D showed the photos to H and told him that, unless he agreed to a property settlement in the divorce proceedings, D would use the photos in court and thus reveal H's commission of the criminal sexual act. D was guilty of extortion under a statute defining the offense as maliciously threatening to accuse another of an offense with intent to extort money. [**State v. Harrington,** 260 A.2d 692 (Vt. 1969)]

c. Causation Required

Under statutes requiring that property actually be acquired by the prohibited threats, it is necessary to show a ***causal connection*** between the threats and the victim's surrender of the property. With extortion, the *victim* of the threats or misrepresentation, rather than the *defendant*, acts with two intentions, *e.g.*, after the lady threatened to accuse her male victim of adultery with her, the man paid her money, partly from love for her and partly from fear of her threats. [**People v. Williams,** 127 Cal. 212 (1899) (the fear induced by the threat must have been the ***"operating or controlling cause"*** of the payment; a showing that the threat was merely a factor in the victim's decision is insufficient)]

d. Claim of Right Defense

Some, but not all, jurisdictions recognize a defense consisting of a good faith belief by the defendant that he was entitled as a matter of legal right to the money or property he sought to obtain by the threat. The defense may be limited to some types of extortion. [**State v. Privette,** 721 S.E.2d 299 (N.C.App. 2012) (refusing to read claim of right defense into extortion statute providing no such defense)]

e.g. **Example:** Under New York law, a defendant charged with larceny by extortion committed by instilling fear in the victim that he would be charged with a crime may assert an affirmative defense consisting of proof that (i) the defendant reasonably believed the threatened charge to be true; and (ii) the defendant's sole purpose was to induce the victim to make good the wrong that was the subject of the threatened charge. [N.Y. Penal Law § 155.15(2)]

(1) Defense Inapplicable When Damage Uncertain

Jurisdictions recognizing the claim of right defense are unlikely to apply it to situations in which the defendant claims to be entitled to the property because of wrong done by the victim that caused damage or harm of an ***uncertain value.*** [**State v. Greenspan,** 374 S.E.2d 884 (N.C. 1989)]

e. Punishment

Extortion is generally punished as a felony. [Cal. Penal Code § 520]

G. Receiving Stolen Property

1. Historical Background

At early common law, one who simply received stolen property incurred no criminal liability, not even as an accessory after the fact, because he did not harbor the thief himself. While later English statutes provided for accomplice liability in such situations (even if the thief himself had not been convicted), it was not until 1827 that a separate statutory crime of receiving stolen property knowing it to be stolen was promulgated.

2. Elements Under Modern Statutes

Although modern statutes differ to some extent in their definitions of the crime, generally four elements are included:

(i) ***Receiving,***

(ii) ***Stolen*** property,

(iii) ***Knowing*** it to be stolen, and

(iv) With the ***intent to deprive*** the owner of the property.

a. Stolen Property

It is essential that the property have been "stolen" within the meaning of the statutory language. Two problems arise in applying this requirement:

(1) Property Acquired by Crimes Other than Larceny

Although the statutes are usually interpreted to include property obtained by robbery or burglary, some courts have construed the language narrowly, finding it not to cover property obtained by embezzlement or false pretenses. [**State v. George,** 173 S.W. 1077 (Mo. 1915)] Some statutes avoid such interpretative problems by specifically including property obtained by any of the acquisition offenses.

(2) Property Recovered

If the owner (or law enforcement authorities acting on the owner's behalf) recovers the property, it is ***no longer "stolen."*** Therefore, a person who subsequently receives it has not "received stolen property," even though she may erroneously believe she has done so. [**People v. Rojas,** 358 P.2d 921 (Cal. 1961)]

(a) Distinguish: Liability for Attempt

While such a defendant cannot be convicted of the completed offense, she may be guilty of attempted receipt of stolen property. (But recall that some courts find this involves legal impossibility, thereby precluding liability for attempt; *see supra,* p. 192.)

b. Receiving

The property must be received by the defendant. But this does not mean that she must take actual personal possession of the property. It is sufficient if she ***indirectly exercises control*** over it, as where she has the thief deposit the property in a designated place.

[**LeFanti v. United States,** 259 F. 460 (3d Cir. 1919) (thieves brought their stolen goods to defendant at his saloon; because the business was under surveillance, he instructed them to take the goods to the "dumps" where later on a signal from him they left the goods in the bushes; defendant without stopping to pick up the goods returned to his saloon and was later arrested at his home; conviction of receiving stolen property affirmed; though he never actually possessed the goods, he had "constructive" possession); **People v. Candiotto,** 183 Cal. App. 2d 348 (1960) (D guilty of receipt of stolen goods if someone else with D's knowledge or consent concealed stolen goods on D's premises)]

c. Knowing Goods to Be Stolen

Most statutes require that the defendant ***know*** the goods were stolen at the time she received them. [Cal. Penal Code § 496(a)] This knowledge may occur from personal observation of the crime by which the goods were acquired or may be inferred from circumstantial evidence, *e.g.*, proof the goods were acquired from a person of dubious character or that the defendant paid a disproportionately low price for them. [**Commonwealth v. Hunt,** 739 N.E.2d 284 (Mass. 2000) (circumstantial evidence may be relied upon to establish knowledge); **State v. Chester,** 707 So.2d 973 (La. 2000) (knowledge properly inferred here, given "the disproportionately small sale price" as compared with "the value of the tools")]

(1) Reasonable Grounds to Believe Goods Stolen

In some jurisdictions, it is enough that there existed reasonable grounds to believe the goods were stolen. As long as such grounds were present, the defendant is guilty whether or not she actually knew the goods were stolen. This imposes liability for negligence regarding this element. [Ala. Crim. Code § 13A–8–16]

(2) Abolition of Knowledge Requirement: Constitutionality

A few statutes have imposed liability without regard to whether the recipient knew or should have known that the goods were stolen (*i.e.,* imposed strict liability). However, some such statutes have been struck down as violating Due Process (*see supra,* p. 52). [**People v. Estreich,** 272 App. Div. 698 (1947), *aff'd,* 79 N.E.2d 742 (N.Y. 1948) (statute punished junk dealers who receive stolen machinery equipment; statutory knowledge or lack of diligence is required with other receivers and other property; statute unconstitutional under Fourteenth Amendment Due Process clause)]

d. Intent to Deprive Owner

Some courts hold that the defendant must have a "bad" intent in addition to knowledge of the stolen nature of the goods, even if the statute defining the crime does not explicitly require this. [**Hensel v. State,** 604 P.2d 222 (Alaska 1979) (intent-to-deprive-owner element read into statute)] Otherwise, for example, a police officer who takes stolen property from an apprehended thief would be guilty of the crime. These courts often require a showing that the defendant ***intended to deprive the owner*** of the property. [**People v. Block,** 540 N.E.2d 512 (Ill. 1989)]

(1) No Intent to Restore

Occasionally, statutes approach this subject negatively, defining the crime as committed by the knowing receipt of stolen property in the absence of an intent to restore it to the owner. [Model Penal Code § 223.6(1) (receipt of stolen property criminal "unless the property is received . . . with intent to restore it to the owner");

Ala. Crim. Code § 13A–8–16(a) (offense committed by receipt of stolen property unless this is done "with intent to restore it to the owner")]

SUMMARY OF CRIMES AGAINST PROPERTY		
PROPERTY OFFENSE	**ACT**	**INTENT**
LARCENY	Wrongful ***taking*** of property ***from the possession of another***	Intent to ***permanently deprive*** owner of possession
EMBEZZLEMENT	***Conversion*** of property by a person ***already in possession*** of the property	Intent ***to defraud***
FALSE PRETENSES	Wrongful taking of ***title*** to property ***by misrepresentation*** to the owner	***Knowledge of falsity*** of the misrepresentation ***and*** intent ***to defraud*** owner
ROBBERY	Wrongful taking of property ***from victim's person or presence by violence or intimidation***	Intent to ***permanently deprive*** owner of possession
EXTORTION	Obtaining or attempting to obtain property ***by threats*** not sufficient to constitute robbery	Intent to ***obtain property*** through wrongful threats
RECEIPT OF STOLEN PROPERTY	***Acceptance*** of property after it has wrongfully been taken from another	Intent ***to deprive*** owner of property ***known to be stolen***

(2) "Bad" Intent Not Uniformly Required

Some statutes are silent as to the requirement of a "bad" intent, and the case law under some of them contains no suggestion that such an intent is essential. [**People v. Wielograf,** 101 Cal. App. 3d 488 (1980) (receiving stolen property requires only "general criminal intent" to aid thief, render recovery of property by owner more difficult, or to deprive owner of property)]

3. Conviction of Thief for Receiving Stolen Property

Several situations raise an issue as to whether ***a participant in the larceny*** by which the property was acquired can be convicted of receiving it.

a. Where Defendant Was the Actual Thief

At one time, courts would not uphold the conviction for receiving stolen property of the person who ***actually stole*** the property, *i.e.*, the thief cannot receive from himself. However, because the traditional rule became a tactical weapon to escape conviction altogether, courts take a contrary position. [**Commonwealth v. McArthur,** 773 N.E.2d 448 (Mass. 2002) (not inconsistent to charge and convict the actual thief of the crime of possession of the stolen property, "for it facilitates the prosecution of individuals for the theft of property where proof of the actual taking of the property, an element of the offense of stealing the property, may be difficult to establish")]

b. Other Participants in Crime

Whether participants in the theft other than the actual thief, the person who took the property, can be convicted of receiving stolen property is less clear. Most courts hold that if the defendant was a party to the crime but was ***not an active participant*** in its commission (*i.e.,* an accessory before the fact), she can be convicted of receiving property from the participant who actually stole it. But the courts are about evenly divided on whether a participant who was ***actually present*** (*i.e.,* a principal in the second degree) can be convicted of receiving the property.

c. Conviction of Both Offenses

The better rule is that one who could be convicted of either the crime by which the property was acquired or receiving it (as in p. 304, above) ***cannot*** be convicted of ***both*** and given consecutive sentences, although there is some authority to the contrary. [**Milanovich v. United States,** 365 U.S. 551 (1961) (defendant wife transported thieves to building where they entered and stole money and later handed money to defendant; convictions of both larceny and receiving were improper, but Court stated that evidence supported defendant's conviction of either larceny or receiving)] *Compare* **Metcalf v. State,** 124 So. 427 (Fla. 1929) (confederate of thief may not be guilty of both receiving and concealing the property which the thief has stolen)]

H. Consolidation of Acquisition Offenses: Theft

1. In General

As indicated, modern criminal codes often consolidate some or nearly all of the property acquisition offenses into a single offense called "theft." This crime, purely a creature of modern statutes and unknown to the common law, requires proof that the defendant:

a. Exercised ***control*** (*see supra,* pp. 272, 273),

b. Over ***property*** (*see supra*, p. 271) ***of another,***

c. ***Unlawfully*** (*see supra*, p. 275 *et seq.*), and

d. With intent to ***permanently deprive*** that person of the property (*see supra,* p. 280).

2. Statutory Patterns

Modern codes reflect several approaches towards the consolidation of the property acquisition crimes:

a. Single Crime of Theft

Some codes create a single crime of theft designed to encompass many of the same situations covered by the traditional offenses. However, robbery is seldom included in this consolidation; it is usually preserved as a separate crime. [*See, e.g.,* Tex. Penal Code §§ 31.03 (defining theft); 31.02 (expressing legislative intent to create single crime superseding prior separate offenses of theft, theft by false pretext, acquisition of property by threat, embezzlement, extortion, and receiving stolen property)]

b. Multiple Theft Crimes

An alternative approach creates multiple theft crimes that correspond to the traditional common law crimes. [*See, e.g.,* Cal. Penal Code §§ 484 (theft defined as including larceny, false pretenses, and embezzlement); 485 (theft by appropriating lost property); 496 (receiving stolen goods as separate crime)]

c. Model Penal Code Approach

The Model Penal Code adopts a single crime of theft but contains numerous sections setting forth the different methods by which it may be committed. The Code's intention is to permit a prosecutor simply to charge a defendant with theft and then at trial prove that it was committed in any of the enumerated ways, unless failure to specify the appropriate subsection in advance would deprive the defendant of fair notice. [Model Penal Code §§ 223.1(1) (providing for single theft offense); 223.2 (theft by unlawful taking or disposition); 223.3 (theft by deception); 223.4 (theft by extortion); 223.6 (theft by receipt of stolen property)]

3. Punishment

Theft is often divided into degrees, typically ***grand theft*** (a felony) and *petty theft* (a misdemeanor). Some statutes, however, simply provide different penalties for the crime without formally designating two degrees. Among those thefts commonly designated as felonies are:

(i) Theft of ***property or services of a value above a given level*** (*e.g.*, $1,000),

(ii) Theft of ***items regarded as especially important*** without regard to value (*e.g.*, automobiles, firearms, or farm animals), and

(iii) Thefts ***from the person*** of another, without regard to the value of the property taken.

[Cal. Penal Code § 487]

a. Property or Service of Value

The trend of modern criminal codes is to include any property of value which can be moved. [**State v. Waterhouse,** 373 P.3d 131 (Or. 2016) (prosecution is not required to establish a specific value of scrap metal taken, only that it had "some value," and evidence here justified inference that a market exists for scrap metal based on weight and type)] Even property which cannot be moved may be the subject of theft. [*See* **State v. Gentry,** 538 S.W.3d 413 (Tenn. 2017) (state's consolidated theft statute encompasses *real* property; therefore, defendant is guilty of theft by physical occupation and attempt to obtain record ownership of a foreclosed house)] To establish the value of the stolen property, the owner usually testifies as to its value. [**State v. Shedrick,** 518 P.3d 559 (Or. 2022)]

ELEMENTS OF LARCENY—A COMPARISON	
COMMON LAW LARCENY	**"STATUTORY" LARCENY**
A Trespassory	Replaced by ***"Unlawful,"*** Which Includes Taking Property Without Effective Consent
Taking (or "Caption") and	Replaced by ***"Exercised Control"***
Asportation (Carrying Away) of	Frequently ***Eliminated*** Altogether

The Personal Property of	Expanded to Include ***Real and Intangible Property***
Another	Typically ***Retained***
With the Intent to Permanently Deprive the Owner of Possession of the Property	Typically ***Retained***

Chapter Twelve

Offenses Against Government

CONTENTS	PAGE

Key Exam Issues

Treason and related offenses are of limited applicability on criminal law exams, but where they may apply, watch especially for two considerations:

1. The defendant must have had ***allegiance to the government.***
2. There may be ***special proof requirements,*** *e.g.*, proof often requires testimony of two witnesses to the defendant's conduct.

A. Treason

1. Ancient Definition

Under ancient English law, it was "high treason" to kill the king, promote revolt in the kingdom or armed forces, or counterfeit the great seal. "Petit treason" consisted of a killing of a husband by his wife, a master or mistress by a servant, or a prelate by a clergyman. Treason was neither a felony nor a misdemeanor but a crime in a separate class by itself.

2. Modern Formulations of the Crime

Treason is now a ***statutory*** crime, and its definition is fixed both by the United States Constitution and state criminal codes.

a. Federal Crime

Treason is the only crime provided for in the United States Constitution. It is there defined as levying war against the United States, adhering to their enemies, or giving their enemies aid and comfort. [U.S. Constitution, Article III, Section 3, clause 1]

b. State Crimes

Where treason is made a crime under state statutes, the definitions often emphasize action directed against state government. [Cal. Penal Code § 37 (treason consists of levying war against the state, adhering to its enemies, or giving its enemies aid and comfort)]

3. Requirements

a. Allegiance

Because treason is essentially a breach of allegiance, the defendant can be convicted ***only if he owed allegiance*** to the prosecuting government. Thus, one who has lost or renounced his American citizenship cannot thereafter commit treason against the United States. [**Kawakita v. United States,** 343 U.S. 717 (1952)]

b. Overt Act

Disloyal thoughts alone are not enough for treason. Some *overt act of aid*, such as affirmative encouragement of the enemy, is required. [**Cramer v. United States,** 325 U.S. 1 (1945)]

c. Intent to Betray

The defendant must have had the *intent to betray* the government, but a showing that *he was aware* that his actions would assist an enemy of the government will suffice.

[**D'Aquino v. United States,** 192 F.2d 338 (9th Cir. 1951) (in treason trial of "Tokyo Rose," an American who broadcast from Japan to U.S. troops to lower their morale, the court's instruction covering duress limited its scope to apprehension of immediate death or serious bodily harm; instruction was correct; conviction of treason affirmed)]

d. Special Evidentiary Requirement

Under federal law and the law of many states, conviction for treason requires either (i) the testimony of *two witnesses to the overt act* or (ii) the defendant's *confession in open court.* [U.S. Constitution, Article III, Section 3, clause 1; Cal. Const. art. 1, § 20]

4. Misprision of Treason

Misprision of treason is *concealment* of the known treason of another. It is punishable under federal law and the law of some states. [18 U.S.C. § 2382; Cal. Penal Code § 38]

B. Treason-Like Crimes

1. In General

There are a number of offenses resembling treason that proscribe certain activities thought to constitute a threat to the government.

2. Rebellion

It is a federal crime to incite or engage in any rebellion against the United States. [18 U.S.C. § 2383]

3. Advocating Overthrow of Government

It is also a violation of federal criminal law to knowingly or willfully advocate the overthrow or destruction of the government of the United States or any state. [18 U.S.C. § 2385]

Chapter Thirteen

Offenses Against the Administration of Justice

CONTENTS	PAGE

Key Exam Issues

If an examination question involves action by a participant that frustrates efforts to ***capture, prosecute, or convict another suspect,*** consider possible liability for one or more of the following offenses, specifically the nature of the participant's action:

1. Did the participant conceal the suspect or otherwise attempt to assist the suspect in avoiding conviction? (Consider ***misprision of felony*** or ***hindering apprehension or prosecution.***)
2. Did the participant enter into an agreement that involved his nonparticipation in the prosecution? (Consider ***compounding.***)
3. Did the participant misrepresent facts during in-court testimony? (Consider ***perjury.***)

A. Hindering Apprehension or Prosecution of Felon

1. Liability as Accessory After the Fact

Under common law "party" rules, one who assists a known felon in escaping arrest, prosecution, or conviction can incur liability for the felony committed as an accessory after the fact (*see supra,* pp. 76, 77). This approach, however, has been universally ***abandoned.***

2. Modern Statutes

a. Accessory After the Fact

If the terminology of "accessory after the fact" is retained in modern criminal statutes, it is used to identify a *specific offense* punishable by its *own penalty* rather than a basis for making a person guilty of a crime previously committed by another. [*See, e.g.,* Cal. Penal Code §§ 32, 33 (one who "harbors, conceals, or aids" another who has committed a felony with knowledge that the person had committed a felony and with intent that the person escape from arrest, trial, conviction, or punishment is an accessory after the fact to the felony, and is punishable by one year imprisonment and/or a fine of not more than $5,000)]. Other examples include:

- concealing, destroying or altering evidence [**United States v. Lepanto,** 817 F.2d 1463 (10th Cir. 1987)],
- inducing a witness to absent himself or to remain silent [**Jones v. United States,** 716 A.2d 160 (D.C.App. 1998)], and
- giving false information to the police in order to divert suspicion away from the felon [**People v. Duty,** 74 Cal.Rptr. 606 (1969)]

b. Hindering Apprehension or Prosecution

Modern statutes sometimes create a *new crime* for former liability as an accessory after the fact, punishing much the same behavior (*i.e.,* aiding or warning another with the intent to hinder that person's apprehension, conviction, or punishment). [*See, e.g.,* Tex. Penal Code § 38.05; **Maddox v. Commonwealth,** 349 S.W.2d 686 (Ky. 1960)]

B. Misprision of Felony

1. Common Law

At common law, one who ***fails to report or prosecute*** a person known to have committed a ***felony*** is guilty of the misdemeanor of misprision of felony. However, persons who merely had knowledge of the commission of a felony and failed to report it were rarely (if ever) actually prosecuted for this offense.

2. Modern Statutes

Federal statutes and those in some states retain misprision of felony as a crime. Federal law defines the offense as: (i) having ***knowledge of the actual commission of a felony*** cognizable by federal courts; and (ii) ***concealing*** and failing as soon as possible to make this known to a judge or other person of authority under the United States. [18 U.S.C. § 4]

a. Limitation: Active Assistance Required

The federal crime is not a true misprision statute in that it requires affirmative steps to conceal the felony, in addition to failure to disclose. Thus, one who simply has knowledge of the commission of a felony and fails to report it is not punishable. [**United States v. White Eagle,** 721 F.3d 1108 (9th Cir. 2013)]

C. Compounding a Crime

1. Common Law

It is the common law misdemeanor of compounding a crime to ***agree for consideration not to prosecute*** another for a felony.

2. Modern Statutes

Compounding often remains an offense under modern statutes. The crime is often defined as agreeing to forgo prosecution of ***any*** offense, felony or misdemeanor. [Model Penal Code § 242.5; Cal. Penal Code § 153 (defining crime as accepting or agreeing to accept a benefit in consideration of refraining from reporting an offense or information relating to an offense)]

3. Elements

Compounding consists of

(i) an agreement,

(ii) for valuable consideration, and

(iii) to fail to report or cooperate in the prosecution of a crime.

a. Agreement

An ***agreement*** is an essential element of the crime. Thus, compounding is not committed if the defendant simply provides aid or fails to assist in the prosecution of another, hoping for a reward from that person. [**Fidelity & Deposit Co. v. Grand National Bank,** 69 F.2d 177 (8th Cir. 1934)]

b. Valuable Consideration

It must be shown that pursuant to the agreement the defendant was entitled to valuable consideration (*i.e.,* money or anything of value or advantage) in return for her failure to prosecute. [**State v. Davis,** 26 P.3d 681 (Kan. 2001) (plea bargain with defendant's accomplice not to initiate criminal prosecution if accomplice testified truthfully against defendant does not constitute compounding a crime, because state did not receive anything of value as consideration)]

4. "Settlement" of Crimes

It is unclear under many compounding crimes to what extent the victim of a crime will be exposed to liability for compounding if she accepts restitution from the offender and in return agrees not to press charges. Some states permit certain compromises. [Cal. Penal Code § 153 (offense of compounding does not apply to certain statutorily permitted compromises of misdemeanors)] The Model Penal Code would provide for an affirmative defense to the crime of compounding consisting of a showing that the amount received under an agreement not to prosecute does not exceed an amount which the defendant believed to be due her as restitution or indemnification for the harm done by the crime. [Model Penal Code § 242.5]

D. Perjury

1. Common Law

At common law, the misdemeanor of perjury is the willful giving of a false statement under oath in a judicial proceeding.

2. Modern Statutes

Perjury is still a crime under modern law. However, modern statutes have sometimes modified the common law definition:

a. Any False Testimony Where Oath May Be Administered

Generally, perjury is no longer limited to the context of a judicial proceeding. It is also perjury to give false testimony under oath ***in any proceeding wherein*** the law authorizes the administration of an oath. Thus, perjury can be committed before a legislative or administrative committee or board, if that body has authority by law to administer an oath to witnesses who appear before it. [Cal. Penal Code § 118]

b. Limitation: "Material" Matter

There is no perjury unless the false statement is shown to have been ***"material,"*** meaning that the statement could probably have *influenced the outcome* of the proceeding in which it was given. Thus, a false statement under oath concerning a matter that has no bearing on the proceeding is not perjury. [**United States v. Wells,** 519 U.S. 482 (1997) (term "false statement" does not mean statement must be material, as this is so only as to some common law crimes involving false statements, such as perjury; statute in case ta bar was distinct from perjury statute)]

c. Misleading but Not False Statements

When a federal statute prohibits knowingly making false statements to a federal agency, it does not criminalize statements that are misleading but not false. [**Thompson v. United States,** 604 U.S. 408 (2025)]

3. Special Evidentiary Requirements

At common law, perjury must be proved by the testimony of at least two witnesses. Some jurisdictions have now relaxed this requirement, but many still impose a higher than ordinary requirement of proof. [*See, e.g.,* Cal. Penal Code § 118(b) (conviction for perjury cannot rest on testimony by a single person, although falsity of the testimony can be proved by "indirect" evidence)]

4. Effect of Retraction

Courts have divided on the significance of a witness's retraction of perjured testimony. Some hold there can be no conviction if the witness retracts her testimony in the same proceeding and before its falsity has been established. [**People v. Ezaugi,** 141 N.E.2d 580 (N.Y. 1957)] Others, however, find no defense in such a showing. [**United States v. Norris,** 300 U.S. 564 (1937)]

5. Subornation of Perjury

The different offense of subornation of perjury is closely related to perjury.

a. Definition

One who intentionally causes another to commit perjury is guilty of the common law misdemeanor of subornation of perjury. This often remains an offense under modern statutes. [*See, e.g.,* Cal. Penal Code § 127]

b. Requirements

Two requirements are often imposed for conviction: (i) the defendant must have *known* that the testimony to be given by the witness would be false, and (ii) the defendant must have *actually caused* the witness to actually give the false testimony. [**Niehoff v. Sahagian,** 103 A.2d 211 (Me. 1954)]

Exam Questions and Answers

Question I

Marvin Rutledge approaches Vera Parks and suggests that the two join in a scheme to defraud Jim Kelp of a large amount of money. The scheme involves selling to Kelp a complicated-appearing machine that the two will represent to Kelp as having the ability to change glass into a substance indistinguishable from diamonds. Parks wants to learn more about the matter. The two approach Mike Mechanic, a handyman, to tell him of the plan and ask him if he can construct a device that will meet their needs. Mechanic is about to leave the country but says he will delay his departure to prepare such a device if Rutledge and Parks will pay him the full $10,000 fee in advance. Rutledge pays Mechanic $10,000. Rutledge and Parks then proceed to a restaurant where Rutledge believes that Kelp is eating lunch. While Parks waits in the bar, Rutledge makes contact with Kelp. After about an hour, Rutledge returns to Parks, informing her that Kelp is suspicious and talking about going to the local bunco squad. "I can't let him do that," Rutledge says, to which Parks responds, "Now that I can see what you're getting into, I want no part of it." Parks then leaves the bar. Rutledge joins Kelp. They leave the restaurant and, as they pass an alley, Rutledge pulls a knife and stabs Kelp. Kelp dies immediately.

Discuss the possible criminal liability of Mechanic and Parks.

Question II

Dinah Mite parks her Ford pickup truck near the tightly guarded warehouse of Acme Chemicals, intending to gain entry and steal a quantity of "Bango," a new and highly efficient explosive. Dinah has wire cutters, a flashlight, and a .45 pistol. She uses the wire cutters to enter the building and immediately spots the cabinet with the explosives. She fills her knapsack with Bango and leaves the building. As she is reentering her truck, a guard sees her and orders her to halt. Instead, Mite slams the car door shut and speeds away. About five miles from the warehouse, a police officer who has been alerted by radio to the break-in and given a description of Mite's truck observes Mite pass. The officer begins pursuit. As Mite's car careens around a corner, it leaves the road and strikes a tree. The knapsack with the Bango is thrown clear of the car but lands in a campfire built by two Boy Scouts and their Scoutmaster. In the resulting explosion, the Scoutmaster suffers a severe stomach wound. He is rushed to a nearby hospital where surgery begins. After successfully administering to the wound, the surgeon notices that the Scoutmaster has a small hernia and decides to repair it, because he has opened the body cavity anyway. While the surgeon is doing so, the Scoutmaster suddenly dies. Later, conflicting evidence on the immediate cause of death is produced. One physician testifies that the anesthesiologist must have not been carefully observing the patient, because, had he done so, he could have prevented the death. Another testifies that the death was sudden, unforeseeable, and unpreventable. The state statute defines murder as "the killing of another human being with malice aforethought, either express or implied." What issues are presented by a charge of murder against Mite, based on the death of the Scoutmaster? Discuss.

Question III

Dant is the foreperson of a loading dock crew. During a noonday break, Dant enters a partially loaded boxcar where Vic Tern, one of the crew members, is eating his bag lunch. Dant and Tern begin talking, and Dant complains bitterly about the company's failure to pay him the overtime that he believes the company owes him. Dant sees an apparently expensive wrench lying on a box. He picks it up and comments that the company owes him 10 times what the wrench is worth. Tern then asserts that whatever an employee's "beef" against the company, there is no excuse for stealing company property. The discussion becomes more heated and the two come to blows. Dant strikes Tern and Tern falls to the floor, unconscious. Dant then picks up the wrench and jumps out of the boxcar. He is immediately confronted by company security personnel who take him into custody, retrieve the wrench, and call the police. The wrench in fact belongs to the company.

What is Dant's possible criminal liability? Discuss.

Question IV

Martin Roke is charged with burglary, rape, and murder. The rape and murder victim was Bess Franks; the burglary charge is based on Roke's entry into Franks's residence with intent to rape her. At trial, the prosecution introduces evidence establishing that on the date in question, Roke broke into Franks's apartment, compelled her to have intercourse with him against her wishes, and then shot her six times, causing her death. The defense produces a psychiatrist who testifies that Roke has a long history of mental illness and is a paranoid schizophrenic. He has been undergoing treatment for this disorder for years and has been taking powerful medication for the illness. The psychiatrist further testifies that in his opinion Roke's condition caused him to believe that Franks was a witch with supernatural powers and that she was using these powers against him. It was because of these beliefs that Roke entered Franks's residence and attacked her. In response to a question from defense counsel, the psychiatrist testifies that if Roke consumed intoxicating beverages while taking his medication, the intoxicants would have a far more serious effect upon him than they would have on a person not taking such drugs. Another defense witness testifies that he observed Roke and a companion, "Smokey," drinking in a bar on the night of the crime. Both appeared to be intoxicated. According to the witness, Roke told Smokey of his belief in Franks's supernatural powers and Smokey encouraged this belief. The witness further adds that Smokey helped Roke leave the bar and by following them he, the witness, was able to observe Smokey confirming Roke's conclusion regarding Franks and telling Roke that he, Roke, had to do something about the situation. The witness then says that he saw the two stop in front of an apartment building, later identified as that of Franks, and that Smokey appeared to be cajoling and almost pushing Roke into the building. After this testimony, the defense rests.

Discuss the various theories, if any, upon which Roke might rely in attempting to avoid conviction for any of the offenses charged.

Question V

Peter Linin has been charged with a violation of the following criminal statute:

> **§ 567.89. Criminal Nonsupport.**
>
> An individual commits an offense, punishable by a fine of no more than $500 and/or by a jail term of no more than 30 days, if he fails to provide for the lawfully required support of his children.

The prosecution's evidence will show that Linin was approached by Elizabeth Holden and told by her that her soon-to-be-born child had been fathered by him. Holden further demanded that Linin make arrangements for reasonable support of the child.

It is undisputed and the prosecution will show that Holden's child was born and that for a year Linin provided no support for the child. The prosecution will also introduce evidence tending to show that Linin is the father of the child and was financially able to provide support.

The defense will produce evidence tending to show that Linin is not in fact the father of the child. In addition, defense evidence will tend to show that after Holden initially approached Linin, Linin called Lawyer's Referral Service (run by the State Bar) and was referred to I. M. Shyster, a local attorney. Shyster, after listening to Linin's story (including a denial of paternity based upon what Linin understood to be Holden's reputation for sexual promiscuity), informed Linin that in light of the dispute about paternity he was not liable for support of the child. Moreover, he advised Linin that he had nothing to lose by refusing to provide support, because the worst that could happen would be that Holden would bring a civil action on behalf of the child and, if Linin lost, he would simply have to pay the support. Shyster was unaware of the statute under which Linin is now being prosecuted.

Identify and briefly discuss the issues presented by Linin's prosecution.

Question VI

Lois Kane is the owner of Lois's Pawn Shop in State X. Because her various business ventures require much of her time, she hired a manager, Clark Lent, to assume general operating responsibility for the shop. Under the law of State X, it is a misdemeanor to sell a handgun to any person with an unexpunged felony conviction. On June 14, while Kane is in another state tending to her earthworm farm there, Lent is in charge of the shop. Mary Parks enters the store and tells Lent that she would like to purchase a small revolver, but that she has been unsuccessful in other stores because everybody knows about her five-year-old conviction for armed robbery. Lent indicates that he cannot sell her a gun either and informs her of the statutory prohibition. Parks then tells Lent that she and her three-year-old son are forced by financial considerations to live in an undesirable area of the city, that on two occasions persons have attempted to break into their apartment, and that her son's safety depends upon her being able to secure a weapon for use in self-defense. Lent, with tears running down his cheeks, removes a small revolver from the display case and hands it to Parks, saying, "Well, look this over and see if it will do." At this point, another person who has entered the store during this discussion identifies himself as a police officer and arrests Lent. Evidence is available to establish that Parks was acting as a paid agent of the police in an effort to identify pawn shops illegally selling guns and that she in fact had no felony convictions. Kane is ultimately charged with attempted violation of the statute prohibiting sale of handguns to convicted felons.

Discuss the issues presented by this charge.

Question VII

Jim Ambler was walking down a street at 9:30 p.m., when he was approached by a uniformed police officer, Kim Belligerent. Belligerent informed Ambler that he was under arrest for the robbery of a nearby convenience store. When Ambler protested that he knew nothing about it, Belligerent struck him repeatedly with her nightstick. Ambler noticed that he was near the apartment of a friend, Martin Doubt, and ran towards the apartment. The door was open and Ambler, with Belligerent in pursuit, rushed in. Seeing Doubt sitting at his kitchen table eating, Ambler shouted, "Help me get rid of this killer cop!" But Doubt, seeing Belligerent at the door, responded, "You handle your own problems." Belligerent then took custody of Ambler. Later, it was determined that Belligerent had no basis for believing Ambler to be the perpetrator of the robbery and the arrest was therefore clearly invalid. Ambler, however, is charged with burglary. He is prepared to testify that he cannot recall any of the events of that evening that occurred after the first blow struck by Belligerent with her nightstick.

Among the criminal statutes in the jurisdiction are the following:

> § 23. **Burglary.** It is a felony offense to enter the habitation of another with the intent to commit a felony or any theft.
>
> § 36. **Solicitation.** It is an offense to solicit another to commit any offense. Solicitation is a felony if the offense solicited is a felony.
>
> § 76. **Battery.**
>
> a. The offense of battery consists of causing the application of force upon the person of another.
>
> b. Battery is a felony under the following circumstances: . . . (5) It is committed upon the person of one known to be a police officer.

Identify and discuss the issues raised by the burglary charge against Ambler.

Question VIII

Marvin Tubb is charged with the rape of Myna Winters, who is 26 years of age and is mentally retarded. Tests show that her I.Q. is approximately 45. Police interviews with Winters resulted in eliciting the following version of the relevant events: Tubb and Winters had been neighbors and friends for several months. On August 14, Tubb suggested to Winters that the two of them enter into a common law marriage after eloping. Winters agreed, with reservations. That night, the two left their homes about 8:00 p.m. and went to a nearby park where they exchanged rings. Tubb assured Winters that they were then married. They then went to Tubb's apartment where he began making sexual advances to Winters. She tells the officers that they ultimately had intercourse and that "I didn't want to, and I told him so. But he made me do it." When asked if she fought him, she responds, "I was afraid. He just said we had to do it because we were married." Tubb, on the other hand, tells the officers that he never specifically represented to Winters that the exchange of rings was a legal marriage. He also denies compelling her to engage in intercourse. "I had to urge her on," he says, "but you always have to guide her. She's not too smart, you know." The jurisdiction has no common law marriage doctrine, and the state courts have specifically rejected arguments that the doctrine should be accepted.

Identify and discuss the issues presented by the pending charge against Tubb.

Answers to Question I

Mechanic's Liability

Conspiracy: It is unclear whether Mechanic would be criminally liable for the criminal conspiracy to defraud Kelp. The issue is whether Mechanic had sufficient intent to be guilty of conspiracy. Conspiracy requires two or more persons *to agree* to commit an unlawful act or to commit a lawful act by unlawful means. "To agree" requires that the defendant ***actually intended to agree*** with others to commit the act. Additionally, the defendant must ***intend to accomplish the objective of the conspiracy.*** Some courts will apply this requirement literally, requiring that the prosecution prove that the defendant intended to accomplish the objective, which can sometimes be proved by showing that the defendant would benefit if the conspiracy succeeds. Other courts, however, will require only that the defendant knew that his aid would further the objectives of the conspiracy. In terms of the situation when the defendant provides goods or services to the conspiracy, providing goods or services is probably not sufficient to show that a person was a member of the conspiracy; however, if the crime is not serious, it is less crucial to show that the defendant intended to accomplish the objective of the conspiracy.

In this case, if knowledge that his participation would aid in the accomplishment of the object crime is sufficient, Mechanic is probably guilty; he knew what the device would be used for. However, if intent to accomplish the objective is required, he is probably not guilty. He was fully paid for the device and therefore had no financial interest in the crime's success. (In fact, he would not even be in the country.) Consequently, the most likely inference is that Mechanic was indifferent about the scheme's success. It can also be argued that because Mechanic merely provided goods, the object crime is not very serious (*i.e.,* a nonviolent fraud crime). Thus, intent or purpose should be required. Both arguments are persuasive, and the issue ultimately turns on which view the court adopts.

Murder: Mechanic will not be criminally liable for the murder of Kelp. The issue is whether Mechanic is guilty of murder even though he is not the one who stabbed Kelp. Because he did not perpetrate the homicide himself, Mechanic is liable only under the rule of co-conspirator liability. To be criminally liable for the crimes of co-conspirators, the proof must establish that the crime was a foreseeable result of the conspiracy and committed in furtherance of it. "Committed in furtherance of the conspiracy" requires that the conspiracy existed at the time of the other crime (*i.e.,* if the conspiracy has ended, so does potential criminal liability for the acts of any co-conspirators). Here, Marvin killed Kelp, not pursuant to the conspiracy's objectives, but as part of an independent effort to avoid being reported to officials. Moreover, it is doubtful, given the nondangerous nature of the scheme and the lack of any indication that violence was to be used or even threatened, that the act of killing was foreseeable, at least from Mechanic's perspective. Further, most courts hold that acts of concealment are not a part of the conspiratorial objective absent direct evidence that the parties agreed, prior to the commission of the crime, that they would act together to cover up or conceal the crime. In this case, Marvin killed Kelp to conceal the offense. Thus, the killing occurred after the conspiracy ended. For these reasons, Mechanic should not be held criminally liable for the killing.

Parks' Liability

Conspiracy: Parks probably is criminally liable for the conspiracy. The general rules for conspiracy are discussed in the first paragraph, above. The initial question is whether she actually joined Marvin's scheme. She at no point expressly indicated a willingness to participate actively, and at no point did she accept a specific role. In fact, neither of them identified such a role. However, the requisite agreement is implied from their actions; Parks' actions suggest a more than tentative willingness to be part of the criminal design.

Assuming that Parks entered into an agreement with Marvin (and perhaps Mechanic), the intent issue is more easily satisfied than in Mechanic's case, above. The likely inference is that she acted with the intent of participating in and benefiting from the scheme, and she thus joined with the purpose of furthering the object crime.

It is unlikely that Parks' abandonment of the scheme has any effect on her liability for the conspiracy itself. Most courts find that abandonment after the agreement is no defense. Even if the court follows the minority view, Parks' "abandonment" was insufficient because it was not voluntary, *i.e.,* arguably she abandoned the scheme due to her fear of apprehension. Kelp was "suspicious" and was considering going to the police. She lacked an honest and sincere desire to avoid involvement in a venture that she did not understand fully until Marvin revealed his willingness to use violence. Withdrawal as a defense to conspiracy usually requires the defendant to "thwart the success of the conspiracy." Mere words expressing a withdrawal are insufficient. Parks only told Marvin that she wanted nothing more to do with the plan; she did nothing else to thwart the success of the conspiracy. For these reasons, her withdrawal is not a valid defense to the conspiracy for Parks.

Murder: Although the same issues are raised about Mechanic's liability, the prosecution's case is stronger against Parks for murder but it is still unlikely that Parks is criminally liable for murder. Parks' liability turns on the co-conspirator theory. Liability for subsequent crimes committed by co-conspirators requires that the subsequent crime is the reasonably foreseeable result of the conspiracy and committed in furtherance of the conspiracy. Because Parks was more involved in the scheme than Mechanic and knew more details, the killing was foreseeable from her perspective. However, the acts of concealment likely did not occur outside of the conspiracy and thus not in furtherance of it.

If Parks is liable for the killing on a co-conspirator theory, the remaining question is whether her abandonment before the killing prevents her liability. Although she clearly communicated her abandonment to Marvin, she did not communicate it to Mechanic. If he is a member of the conspiracy, her efforts to abandon the scheme were insufficient until he was notified. On the other hand, perhaps a more just rule would require that notice is necessary only to the members of the conspiracy who are currently active in the scheme at issue; otherwise the burden is impossible and could destroy the incentive to withdraw from a complex criminal design. For the reasons above, it is unlikely that Parks will be criminally liable for the killing.

Answers to Question II

Two theories may support the murder charge against Mite, felony murder and murder based on her awareness of a high risk of death.

Felony Murder: The issue is whether a felony murder conviction is likely because the death occurred during commission of statutory burglary (trespassory breaking and entering of the warehouse with intent to steal Bango) and theft (or larceny) (trespassory taking and carrying away of Bango with intent to steal). Many jurisdictions require that death be a *foreseeable result* of the felony. Here, arguably the death was not foreseeable to Mite. This crime was a simple burglary of a non-dwelling and theft, rather than a life-threatening robbery. On the other hand, Mite not only had a pistol with her (and may have contemplated a killing), but also knew the dangerous nature of the substance she was stealing. Thus, possibly the accidental explosion and resulting death were foreseeable.

In addition, a number of states limit the felony murder rule to "dangerous" felonies. Some courts require that the felony be "inherently" dangerous, but some courts require that the felony be dangerous as committed. The burglary of a non-dwelling and theft here are not inherently dangerous to human life. Given the questionable nature of the felony murder rule, the defense can argue that the inherently dangerous felony requirement limits the rule to situations where it is most necessary. On the other hand, the prosecution may argue that the crimes here were sufficiently dangerous ***as they were committed***, and that this should suffice for felony murder. Assuming that the purpose of the felony murder rule is to encourage felons to avoid dangerous situations, the rule is applicable to any situation where the felony was committed in a dangerous way (*i.e.,* where the felons did what the rule seeks to deter).

A final problem under the felony murder theory is that the death took place after completion of both the burglary and the larceny. Does the felony murder rule still apply? Under the better view, probably so, because the homicide occurred during "immediate flight" and thus was part of the felony.

Awareness of a High Risk of Death: If the felony murder theory fails, Mite is still liable for murder on the theory that she acted with awareness of a sufficient risk of death that brings into play the "abandoned and malignant heart" doctrine. The major question then is whether the risk Mite took (and of which she seems to have been aware) was serious enough to bring her within the doctrine. The prosecution can emphasize the increased risk related to the illicit obtaining of a dangerous material as well as Mite's manner of attempting to evade escape. The defense, on the other hand, should emphasize the absence of specific evidence that Mite was aware of how his handling the explosive would cause it to detonate, thus rebutting her awareness of a risk. Even if she was aware, the defense would argue that the risk was not high enough to be legally equivalent to an intent to cause death.

Causation: Assuming that either of the above theories is successful, a problem of "proximate causation" still exists. The scoutmaster's death was directly caused by a means outside the scope of the risks involved under both murder theories. The issue is whether the manner in which death actually occurred "broke the chain of causation." Under one version of the facts, death was caused by such gross negligence on the part of the anesthesiologist (not observing the patient carefully) that the immediate cause of death was not foreseeable and thus broke the chain. On the other hand, the scoutmaster's hernia was a preexisting condition; even if it played a role in directly causing death, it did not break the chain of causation. A strong argument is that no unforeseeable intervening factor entered into the causal chain at all, *i.e.,* the primary factor in causing death was the surgery made necessary by Mite's action, and extending that surgery to correct minor problems and errors by the medical staff is arguably foreseeable.

Answers to Question III

Larceny: Dant is probably guilty of larceny. His guilt turns on the resolution of three subissues. First, did he "take" or "capture" the wrench? Although moving the wrench constitutes asportation, the capture element requires Dant's exercise of dominion and control over the property. Dant never removed the property from the premises; in fact, he was only out of the boxcar for a matter of seconds before he was apprehended. A capture is not necessarily measured in units of time. Dant did disable the person who apparently had prior control of the wrench and did have it within his own control after knocking Tern unconscious. Thus, a persuasive argument can be made that there was a sufficient capture.

Second, assuming there was a capture, did Dant take the wrench from the "possession" of another? Dant was the foreperson of the crew and exercised some control over the area in which the activity took place. It is reasonable to assume that he had certain control over company property in that area, including the wrench he is charged with stealing. If his control over the wrench amounted to possession, he could not have taken it from the possession of another and therefore could not be guilty of larceny. But here, it is likely (although more facts would be helpful) that as a "mere" employee without special rights, his authority over company property at most showed that he had only "custody" of it. As a result, he most likely did take it from the possession of the company.

Finally, did Dant have the requisite intent, given the evidence that he may have taken the wrench because of his belief that the company was indebted to him? Larceny requires the intent to permanently deprive another of *its* property. However, if Dant honestly (although perhaps unreasonably) believed that the wrench was rightfully his because of the company's failure to pay him overtime, he did not have the intent to deprive the company of *its* wrench. The facts are unclear as to what Dant actually was thinking. Arguably, he was not acting out a belief that the wrench was his, but thought that he was morally justified in engaging in conduct he knew constituted larceny. Under this theory, he had the requisite intent. Thus, given that Dant, with the required intent, "captured" the property of another, it appears that Dant is criminally liable for larceny of the wrench.

Attempted Larceny: If Dant did not "take" the wrench he cannot be convicted of larceny, but he may be guilty of attempted larceny. The issue is whether he had clearly progressed far enough towards commission of the crime to satisfy any of the tests for attempt. However, as with the completed crime, the major issue concerns Dant's intent, *i.e.*, if he lacked the intent necessary for larceny, he also lacked it for attempted larceny.

Embezzlement: If Dant did not take the wrench from the "possession of another," he may be guilty of embezzlement because he had possession of the wrench pursuant to a trust agreement and converted it. Again, however, the problem is one of intent; if he believed the wrench was his, he probably lacked the requisite intent to defraud.

Robbery: Dant is likely guilty of robbery. Can Dant be convicted for robbery, assuming he is guilty of larceny? First, did Dant take the wrench from the presence of his victim that is required for robbery? The wrench was not on Tern's person. Moreover, it also was arguably not within Tern's presence, absent evidence that he had used it and temporarily set it down or otherwise had some special relationship to the wrench. On the other hand, the wrench was clearly within Tern's reach and had it not been for the fight he probably could have retained control. That strongly suggests that the wrench was in his presence.

Second, was the taking accomplished by force? Dant will contend that he and Tern simply had an argument over the ethical propriety of stealing from the company in general, and that Tern's participation in the fight was not resistance to Dant's removal of the wrench. In fact, the evidence arguably reveals no effort to remove the wrench, or even a solidified intent to do so, until after the use of force on Tern. Thus, the facts show a battery upon Tern (*see* below) followed by larceny of the wrench. The prosecution, on the other hand, can make a strong argument that Dant formed the intent to take the wrench and communicated this to Tern before the brawl. Tern then physically attempted to thwart Dant's efforts and only by his use of force did Dant accomplish the taking. Under this interpretation, the taking was accomplished by force and constituted robbery. As a result, the prosecution has a strong argument that Dant took the wrench from Tern's presence, making him guilty of robbery.

Battery: Dant is guilty of battery, *i.e.*, the unlawful application of force to the person of another, resulting in bodily injury or an offensive touching. Both elements are present, *i.e.*, Dant struck Tern in the course of a fight, and Tern suffered an injury resulting in loss of consciousness. Specific intent is not required for battery, although the intent to strike Tern is apparent in this case. Thus, Dant is guilty of battery.

Answers to Question IV

Insanity: Roke is entitled to an acquittal if he was legally insane at the time of the crimes. If the defense psychiatrist is believed, Roke was clearly mentally ill. But whether this should result in acquittal depends upon which "insanity test" the jurisdiction follows. If this is a *M'Naghten* jurisdiction, the prosecution can argue that the evidence falls short of establishing insanity. Even if the beliefs induced by Roke's mental illness were accurate (*i.e.,* if Franks had been a witch and had been using her powers against Roke), Roke was not legally entitled to enter Franks's apartment, rape her, and kill her. Even so, the defense might prevail on the theory that because of his mental illness and the beliefs it caused, Roke did not understand the nature and quality of raping and killing Franks or the acts (such as the burglary) that were incident thereto. This latter theory will satisfy the *M'Naghten* test.

If the jurisdiction applies one of the control tests (*i.e.,* the irresistible impulse test or the Model Penal Code test), the issue is still difficult. The defense can argue that one who believes that another has such supernatural powers and intends to use them against him lacks the capacity to avoid responding violently towards the victim; it is unreasonable to expect that normal influences will prevent such action. The prosecution can argue that this does not explain why Roke raped Franks, and thus the crimes were not the result of such delusions. The prosecution could also argue that even if Roke believed Franks was a witch with supernatural powers, Roke still could seek less violent solutions to the situation.

Diminished Capacity: If the insanity defense fails, Roke might rely upon the psychiatric testimony as showing lack of capacity to form the intent required for at least some of the crimes charged. However, not all courts recognize the diminished capacity doctrine. It may therefore be necessary for defense counsel to argue that evidence of mental illness relates to intent. Arguably, the requirement of intent provides a desirable vehicle for mitigating punishment and, at the same time, not excusing a defendant. If the court agrees, at most Roke should be convicted of less serious offenses, such as trespass rather than burglary and manslaughter rather than murder. The prosecution's counter argument is that evidence of mental illness should be restricted to the insanity defense, and the doctrine of diminished responsibility should be rejected. Regarding burglary and murder, the defense evidence does not tend to demonstrate an inability to form the requisite intents. If it does not tend to do so, no issue of diminished capacity is raised, and thus whether the doctrine is accepted is irrelevant.

Intoxication: Roke does not appear to have an intoxication defense. The primary issue is whether the intoxication is voluntary or involuntary. Roke has a complete defense only if he was *involuntarily* intoxicated at the time of the crimes and, because of that intoxication, met either the *M'Naghten* test or any of the control tests (described above). Roke's intoxication may be involuntary if he was unaware of the reaction that would result from his mixing the medication and liquor. However, the prosecution can argue that, because Roke voluntarily consumed the beverages knowing of their intoxicating nature, his intoxication should be regarded as *voluntary* only. Even if it is involuntary, there is no basis in the facts for concluding that because of his intoxication Roke lacked the ability to understand the wrongfulness of his actions, to understand their nature and quality, or to avoid committing them.

If Roke's intoxication is characterized as voluntary, the defense might argue that it demonstrates a lack of intent required for the crimes charged. The prosecution can stress that voluntary intoxication is irrelevant to guilt for rape, because it is available only to disprove specific intents and rape is not a specific intent crime. Moreover, for burglary and murder, the facts provide no basis for concluding that because of his intoxication, Roke lacked the intent to commit rape (and therefore was not guilty of burglary) or lacked the intent to kill (and therefore was not guilty of murder). Without specific evidence showing the effect of his voluntary intoxication on his ability to form an intent, no apparent bar to conviction exists.

Duress; Absence of "Voluntary" Act: Smokey's actions in reinforcing Roke's beliefs and in encouraging Roke to act on those beliefs constitutes a defense based either on duress or the lack of a "voluntary" act. (Entrapment is unavailable because there is no evidence that Smokey was a government agent or was acting under the direction and control of such an agent.) Duress is raised only by evidence tending to show that the defendant was acting in response to threats of serious bodily harm to himself or another. Smokey may have encouraged Roke, but he did not threaten him. There is little possibility of the duress defense succeeding. Arguably, Smokey's conduct when considered in light of the other factors (including Roke's mental illness and intoxication) rendered Roke's behavior involuntary, and was not an "act" upon which liability is based. This argument is weak at best; from the facts, it does not appear that Smokey's actions were compelling enough to override Roke's ability to exercise volitional control as to characterize his subsequent behavior as involuntary within the meaning of the "act" requirement. As a result, duress and the absence of a voluntary act are not good defenses for Roke.

Answers to Question V

Application of Statute to Linin: Prosecution of Linin will not succeed if the statute does not apply to him. The issue is whether Linin is, in fact, the father of the child. If it is established that he is not, he is not liable because one element of the crime is that the unsupported person is the child of the defendant. If, however, the evidence in fact shows paternity, several more complex issues are present.

Mistake of Fact: Does Linin's belief that he is not the parent of the child prevent liability? This "mistake of fact" issue becomes whether the state of mind required by the crime is such that the mistake establishes the lack of intent. Because the statute does not expressly address the question of state of mind, the issue is a matter of interpretation and legislative intent. There are four possibilities:

(1) The statute requires ***knowledge,*** *i.e.,* that the defendant be aware to a practical certainty that the person is his child;

(2) The statute requires ***recklessness,*** *i.e.,* that the defendant is aware but disregards a substantial and unjustified risk that the person is his child;

(3) The statute requires ***negligence,*** *i.e.,* that the defendant fails to perceive a substantial and unjustified risk that the person is the defendant's child and that a reasonable person would have been aware of this risk; and

(4) The statute imposes ***"strict liability,"*** *i.e.,* that it does not require any intent or negligence in regard to the fact of paternity.

Arguments that this is a strict liability crime stress that the crime is not a traditional one, it involves only a relatively minor penalty, and it is part of a broad scheme to regulate support of children; therefore, the legislative intent was to dispense with any requirement of intent and Linin's mistake is irrelevant.

However, an argument can be made that conviction for nonsupport involves a moral condemnation and the legislature could not have intended to impose such condemnation upon a person who was unaware that he even had a child to support; thus, strict liability could not have been intended. To impose liability absent a showing of some intent might violate Due Process. The statute states that, to be criminally liable, one must fail to provide support for *"bis children"* that is *"lawfully required."* A plain reading of the statute indicates that paternity must be established and that some sort of knowledge is required. Support is "lawfully required" when paternity is established. (The statute does not say "presumed children" or "putative children," for example.) "Lawfully required" also implies some knowledge by the defendant, *i.e*., a person is not "lawfully required" to support a child who is not his. Thus, the statute here most likely does not impose strict liability.

If the statute is held not to impose strict liability, the prosecution might argue that it requires no more than negligence or recklessness, on the ground that this would assure blameworthiness but would not impose so great a hurdle to enforcement as to make the statute worthless. In light of Holden's claim about paternity, and the only evidence contradicting that being Linin's perception of Holden's general reputation for promiscuity, the facts show awareness of a risk of paternity (if recklessness is required) or at least a risk of which Linin should have been aware (if negligence will suffice). Linin, on the other hand, would argue for a requirement of knowledge, *i.e*., limiting the statute to those who know the person not supported is their child is the only way to assure blameworthiness. Because such knowledge is not difficult to show, the requirement does not impair the statute's general effectiveness. Applying this standard, the facts show a good faith dispute concerning paternity and therefore establish the absence of the knowledge that should be required for liability.

Assuming the facts show a mistake of fact that is logically inconsistent with Linin having the requisite state of mind, it is still arguable that the mistake should be given no legal effect unless it was reasonable. Reliance on the traditional rule that if a mistake of fact is offered to "disprove" a "general intent," would show that the mistake is reasonable. Any mistake that Linin made about paternity, the prosecution would assert, was unreasonable, especially because it was based only upon what Linin believed to be Holden's reputation. The defense might argue that whatever the traditional rule, even an unreasonable mistake should be given legal significance if it negates the essential state of mind. Any other rule nullifies the "intent" requirement of the crime and is arbitrary. An argument that Linin's error was reasonable: a person's general reputation is something that is widely relied upon in many contexts, and Linin was therefore justified in relying upon Holden's reputation in formulating a doubt as to whether he was the father.

Mistake of Law: Will the advice Linin received from Shyster and the state of mind that advice created prevent liability? When a person has done all he reasonably can do to ascertain the law (*i.e.,* consult an apparently reputable attorney), there is no reason to hold him liable if the advice given is wrong. Linin contends that courts should recognize this defense of "mistake of law." However, no court has recognized this defense; the general rule is that ignorance of the law is no excuse. Although reasonable reliance upon an official interpretation of the law or a court decision is recognized as a defense, similar treatment is not given to advice from a privately retained attorney. Hence, it is almost certain that the defense will lose on this argument.

But Shyster's advice has some effect. The statute requires proof that the support was "lawfully required." Applying state of mind analysis, the prosecution must show that Linin was ***at least*** reckless in regard to each element of the offense, *i.e.*, Linin was aware of a substantial and unjustifiable risk that the support he was not paying was required by law. If Linin believed Shyster's advice, a judge or jury could reasonably conclude that Linin was unaware of a risk that the support was legally required. On the other hand, the facts do not necessarily preclude a finding of recklessness. Linin did not believe Shyster fully and, in light of Holden's claims, was aware of a high enough risk that Shyster was wrong and that the support was legally required. Given the difficulty of proving that defendants charged under the statute were aware of the legal situation, the legislature might have intended to impose strict liability for the element of "lawfully required support" (in which case even a complete and honest mistake by Linin about his duty to pay the support is irrelevant). Or, if negligence suffices, the prosecution can rely on Holden's claim and Shyster's off-the-cuff and cavalier opinion to establish that a reasonable person would have been aware of a substantial risk that the support at issue was legally required. The question of whether strict liability or liability for negligence is intended can be argued similarly to the question of the intent required regarding paternity (discussed above).

Answers to Question VI

Kane: Because Kane did not directly participate in the offense and did not know of its commission, she is not liable as a party to the offense committed directly by Lent. The issue is whether vicarious liability and strict liability may be imposed and whether a defendant who is vicariously liable may assert entrapment and impossibility defenses.

Vicarious Liability: Kane can be convicted only if the statute was intended to impose vicarious liability, *i.e.,* only if she is liable for crimes committed by her employees. Here, a strong argument exists that the apparent legislative intent is to impose such liability. The underlying conduct (sale of handguns) is of the sort likely to be engaged in by employees of stores. The legislative purpose of preventing handguns from getting into the hands of felons would be frustrated if sales by employees are excluded. The crime is only a misdemeanor, and there is no indication of an intent to require personal fault on the part of the defendant.

Kane may be able to escape liability by showing that she instructed Lent to abide by the statute and that he disregarded this instruction, or that she took all reasonable steps to prevent any sales in violation of the statute. The facts, however, do not suggest that these arguments have any basis.

Strict Liability: Kane did not have any awareness that the attempted sale was made; if the crime requires proof of *mens rea* she almost certainly lacked it. While the fact that the statute is intended to impose vicarious liability may suggest that it was also intended to impose strict liability, the strict liability issue is separate and must be addressed independently. This offense is a "public welfare" offense and thus is likely to impose strict liability; it is part of a general scheme regulating the availability of handguns. It is not a traditional crime for which *mens rea* is required, and it is only a misdemeanor. On the other hand, imposing liability without regard to the actor's awareness of the facts, especially the buyer's felony record, would result in convictions of persons who are not culpable and whose conduct is not directly contrary to the legislative scheme. On balance, it appears likely that the statutory intent imposes strict liability and therefore Kane's lack of awareness about the sale and its circumstances does not prevent liability.

Lent's Guilt: Kane is vicariously liable for Lent's crime only if Lent himself is guilty of attempted violation of the statute. Thus, Kane may assert any defenses that Lent may have. There are two possible barriers to a conclusion that Lent is guilty.

(1) **Entrapment:** Here, a police agent arguably entrapped Lent into the actions relied upon to constitute the offense. Lent initially resisted Parks' urging that he sell the gun in violation of the statute. There is no showing of predisposition to sell in contravention of the bar. Further, she secured his willingness only by making pleas of an essentially personal nature that invoked his sympathy for the plight of her alleged son. Arguably, the facts show that Lent's intention to commit the crime was stimulated or created by Parks' entreaties and thus constituted entrapment. (Because there was no evidence of predisposition, it is irrelevant whether the objective or subjective standard is used to resolve the issue.)

(2) **Impossibility:** Parks did not in fact have a felony conviction. Therefore, if Lent had actually sold her the gun, the sale would not have violated the statute even though Lent mistakenly believed that it would have. This case presents a classic example of "legal impossibility": Lent could not have committed the crime by completing the course of conduct which he began. The question is whether this prevents his having committed attempt. Under traditional rules, this does prevent liability, and this is an appropriate position because Lent and others like him have not demonstrated a willingness to engage in conduct that in fact creates a social danger. On the other hand, a number of courts have abandoned the traditional rule and have held that even legal impossibility does not prevent conviction for attempt. Arguably, Lent and others like him have shown their willingness to break the law and thus are both dangerous and culpable; the fact that fortuitously their conduct would not have constituted a violation if completed does not negate this. Whether or not Lent's conduct constituted attempt will depend upon the court's willingness to adopt the traditional approach or the more modern one.

Answers to Question VII

The burglary charge rests on the proposition that Ambler entered Doubt's apartment with the intent of committing the felony offense of soliciting a battery upon Belligerent. There are three problems here: whether the conduct constituted burglary; whether the conduct in which Ambler intended to engage was a felony, given the potential availability of the right of self-defense; and whether given his possible unconsciousness he has committed an "act" upon which liability can be based.

Burglary: The statute is a modern burglary statute that dispenses with the traditional requirement of breaking. The apartment was the habitation of another or Ambler entered it. Apart from the question of whether his intent was "to commit a felony" (discussed in the next section), the only issue presented is whether he had the intent at the time of entry. If he did not form the intent to solicit the battery upon Belligerent until after he entered the apartment, he is not guilty of burglary. Here, arguably Ambler probably did not decide to ask Doubt for help until he found that Doubt was actually in the apartment; his entry into the apartment was with the intent only of avoiding apprehension, and is not shown to be a felony. It is important to note that he did not cry out and thus show his intent to solicit the battery until after he was in the apartment. On the other hand, arguably the inference from the circumstances is that he expected to find Doubt there, that he ran into the apartment with the intent of soliciting Doubt's help, and thus that the entry was made with the requisite intent.

Was the Solicitation a Felony? If an application of force by Doubt upon Belligerent is not subject to some defense, it would be a felony under section 76; therefore, soliciting Doubt to engage in this conduct would be a felony solicitation under section 36. The solicitation is complete when the request is made; the instant rejection of it by Doubt does not prevent it from constituting the offense of solicitation. If, however, Ambler had the right to strike Belligerent in self-defense, and if Doubt had the right to assist Ambler in self-defense, the conduct would not be an offense and its solicitation would not be an offense under section 36.

Ambler's Right of Self-Defense: Under the traditional rule, a person has the right to use force to defend against an unlawful arrest, and that use of force is not itself a crime. If this rule applies, Ambler had the right to use force against Belligerent; the arrest was unlawful and it appears that he intended to use no more force than reasonably necessary to avoid the arrest. Given the trend towards abandonment of this rule, Ambler may have no right of self-defense. The prosecution might urge the court to adopt the modern view that force used to resist arrest, especially an arrest being made by a person known to be a police officer, is not privileged; the prosecution would argue the strong policy of discouraging resolution of disputes concerning arrests by fights in the streets, and would urge that persons like Ambler be encouraged to save their objections until a legal forum is provided.

Even under the modern position, an arrestee is entitled to resist excessive force used to make an arrest. Ambler may argue that, even if he had no right to resist the arrest being attempted by Belligerent, he nevertheless had the right to resist her excessive force (by hitting him with the nightstick) despite his nonresistance. Ambler could urge that, because any legal remedy he might have for the detention resulting from the arrest would not undo the effect of the excessive force, he should be entitled to use self-help in response. While the prosecution may argue that Belligerent's use of force was not excessive given Ambler's "protests," the facts suggest he merely verbally objected to the arrest, and therefore Belligerent's actions in striking him were unreasonable in response.

Commission of "Act": Ambler's loss of memory concerning the events suggests that he was, as the result of the blow struck by Belligerent, unconscious at the time of the entry into the apartment. If true, his movements did not constitute a voluntary "act" upon which liability can be based; therefore, he cannot be convicted. The prosecution may argue that loss of memory is not sufficient proof of unconsciousness at the time of the entry, and it may argue that if Ambler was rendered unconscious by the blow, this blow was caused by his improper resistance to the arrest. Thus, it cannot be given any immunizing significance. Ambler, of course, may respond by urging that his protests were not resistance and do not make him responsible for Belligerent's violent response.

Answers to Question VIII

Tubb's conduct may constitute rape under any of three theories: (a) Winters's consent was invalid because of her incapacity; (b) Winters's consent was invalid because of Tubb's deception; and (c) the intercourse was accompanied by force without Winters's consent. Under each theory, there are possible *mens rea* problems. The facts also possibly raise a problem of corroboration of Winters's testimony.

Mens Rea: The *mens rea* required for rape unfortunately is unclear. Specifically, it is uncertain whether the defendant must be aware that the circumstances making the intercourse unlawful actually exist, or at least aware of a substantial risk that they exist. Tubb, of course, would urge that he is culpable only if the proof shows actual awareness of the circumstances. The state could argue that this presents an unrealistic burden on it, and at most that a showing of awareness of a risk is required.

Incapacity Theory: Intercourse amounts to rape regardless of the woman's articulated consent, if she was by reason of mental impairment incapable of giving effective consent. The prosecution's argument: Winters's I.Q. demonstrates that she is unable to comprehend what is involved in consenting to intercourse and thus, that her consent is not effective. Tubb's argument: Winters still retained at least the capacity to understand the nature of intercourse and thus may consent. If Winters is in fact incapable of giving consent, Tubb most likely had the required *mens rea*. His admission to the officers shows that he was actually aware of her impairment; even under that standard most favorable to him, he had the awareness required under this theory.

Deception Theory: Under limited circumstances, intercourse accomplished pursuant to the woman's consent is rape when the consent was induced by fraud. The issue is whether the fraud that is proved is the kind of fraud that invalidates the woman's consent. Courts are split about whether deceiving a woman into believing that a marital relationship exists invalidates consent. The prosecution argues that this deception relates to a matter so important to the conduct as to be equivalent to deception concerning whether the conduct constitutes intercourse. Tubb, on the other hand, argues that only a deception about whether the act was intercourse can invalidate consent, because otherwise there is no reasonable way to limit the type of deception that will invalidate consent. If the jury accepts Tubb's version of the facts, no deception invalidating the consent took place.

There may also be an issue under this theory as to whether Tubb had the requisite *mens rea*. If Winters understood the events in the park to be a purportedly valid marriage, but Tubb did not intend them, Tubbs may argue that even if Winters was deceived he was unaware of that and therefore lacked the required *mens rea*. Tubb would argue that rape requires actual awareness of the fact that the woman was deceived about a marital relationship. The prosecution would respond that it should be sufficient that Tubb was or should have been aware of a risk about how Winters would construe the events, and in light of his awareness of her mental disability, he was conscious of a high risk that she was misled.

Rape by Force Theory: Winters's statement suggests that she submitted to intercourse because she believed Tubb would use force to compel her to do so if she did not submit. Whether this proves rape by force is problematic. Winters did not resist at all, and certainly did not resist to the "utmost," but the prosecution's argument is that resistance should not be required when it is prevented by the victim's perception that resistance will be met by force and harm. Tubb, however, may respond that, while threats as well as actual force can give rise to rape, evidence of specific threats is required and none occurred here. The prosecution, on the other hand, may rely upon Winters's perception of the coercive nature of the situation in Tubb's apartment as effectively communicating to her that resistance is useless and potentially harmful.

Important *mens rea* issue under this theory: If Winters was coerced into submission by the nature of the circumstances, did Tubb possess adequate awareness of this? Again, he can argue that the prosecution must prove that he was aware that Winters felt coerced and that such awareness cannot be shown. The prosecution can argue that the circumstances, including Winters's reluctance, either did or should have alerted Tubb to a risk that she felt coerced and that this is sufficient.

Corroboration: The only testimony relevant to the events is from Winters. Some courts require corroboration of the victim's testimony. Tubb argues that corroboration is required because a charge of rape is easy to make and difficult to challenge, especially when relatively subtle matters are at issue. The prosecution, on the other hand, may argue that rape cases are no different from those in other prosecutions, and there is no justification for a special corroboration requirement in rape cases.

Review Questions and Answers

Review Questions

FILL IN ANSWER

CLASSIFICATION OF CRIMES

1. Carol is charged with a statutory crime that is punishable by up to two years in the state prison. Upon conviction, however, the judge sentences Carol to only a period of probation. Has Carol been convicted of a felony? __________

BURDEN OF PROOF

2. Debussy is prosecuted for intentionally causing damage to Rimsky-Korsakov's piano. The jury will be instructed that the prosecution must prove beyond a reasonable doubt that Debussy intended to cause the damage. May the judge also instruct the jury that the law presumes a person intends the ordinary consequences of his voluntary acts? __________

BASIC LEGAL LIMITS UPON CRIMINAL LAW

3. Police officers executing a search warrant for Dirty's apartment find pornographic literature in a dresser drawer. May Dirty's be convicted of possession of pornographic items? __________
4. Don is charged with violating a statute that prohibits "any conduct infringing upon the public welfare." Is the statute constitutionally valid? __________
5. In the following situations, can Darren be sentenced to death without violating the Eighth Amendment's prohibition against cruel and unusual punishment?
   a. Darren is convicted of raping Vicki at a time when Darren was 23 years old, and Vicki was 21. __________
   b. Darren is convicted of murdering Vicki at a time when Darren was 15 years of age. __________
   c. Darren is convicted of murdering Vicki at a time when Darren was 17 years old. __________
6. Pete throws a match under Vic's porch, intending to burn the house and to kill Vic, who is sleeping inside. The house burns and Vic is killed. May Pete be convicted of both arson and murder if he is tried for both crimes at the same time? __________
7. Ernie and Bert agree to kill Kermit. Pursuant to the plan, Ernie obtains a gun and the two of them break into Kermit's house at night. Bert then shoots Kermit to death.
   a. At common law, can Ernie and Bert be convicted of conspiracy, burglary, and murder? __________
   b. Would the result be different under modern law? __________
8. Defendant was arrested while cruising the streets. Criminal charges are brought against her pursuant to an ordinance that prohibits "being a common prostitute." May she be convicted? __________

9. Suppose the same arrest as in question 8, but the charge is for "loitering for purposes of prostitution." Now may Defendant be convicted? __________

ELEMENTS OF CRIMES

10. Denise slips while walking on the sidewalk. She instinctively reaches out to grasp some support. Instead, her finger pokes out the eye of Vern, who was also walking on the sidewalk. Has Denise committed an "act" upon which a criminal battery charge can be based? __________

11. Drew is a sleepwalker. One night, while sleepwalking, she pushes over and destroys a valuable vase belonging to a neighbor. Has Drew committed an "act" upon which a prosecution for malicious mischief can be based? __________

12. Dell is walking down a street when he hears a person scream. He turns around and sees a woman being dragged into a dark alley by a man with a knife in his hand. Dell decides to do nothing and walks away.

    a. Has Dell "acted" so as to be guilty of a crime against the woman? __________

    b. Assume Dell recognized the woman as a neighbor whom he despised. He was glad to witness her peril and intentionally decided not to intervene. If the woman is killed, can Dell be convicted of any form of criminal homicide? __________

    c. Assume instead that Dell recognized the woman as his wife but still chose not to intervene. Has Dell "acted" so as to be guilty of a crime against his wife? __________

13. Dinah is having a clandestine love affair with Vinny, who is married to another woman. While in Dinah's apartment, Vinny becomes violently ill and begs Dinah to call a doctor for him. However, Dinah refuses, fearing that Vinny's wife will find out about the affair. If Vinny dies because of lack of medical attention, is Dinah guilty of some form of criminal homicide? __________

14. Dan is employed as a lifeguard on a public beach. During a period when he is supposed to be working, he leaves his guard station to visit a friend. While Dan is gone, a swimmer drowns. If the swimmer was a stranger to Dan, can Dan be convicted of some form of criminal homicide? __________

15. Dom is speeding down a highway at night when his car strikes and injures Monroe. Because of the darkness, Dom is unaware of the accident and does not stop. Has Dom "acted" so as to be guilty of violating a hit-and-run statute? __________

16. Dad's child is ill and doctors report that surgery is essential. Dad does not have money to pay for further medical care and therefore does nothing. If the child dies because the surgery is not performed, is Dad guilty of some homicide offense? __________

17. Jack is charged with selling alcoholic beverages in a "dry" county. At trial, he testifies that he did not know the beverages in question were alcoholic. Must the jury be instructed that Jack should be acquitted unless the proof shows he was aware that the beverages were alcoholic? __________

18. During the course of an argument, Dennis shoved Vic, causing Vic serious injury when he fell and struck his head on the ground. Dennis is charged

with aggravated battery under a statute defining the crime as "purposefully or knowingly causing serious bodily injury to another." Should Dennis be convicted? ____________

19. Donna threw a rock intending to break the window at Vikki's house. However, Donna missed her target and the rock struck and broke a window at Floyd's house. Can Donna be convicted of malicious mischief based upon the accidental damage to Floyd's home? ____________

20. Dillon intends to kill Villain and buys a rifle for this purpose. While Dillon is engaged in target practice in his own backyard, Villain unexpectedly walks by and is killed by a bullet that ricochets from the target. Is Dillon guilty of murder? ____________

21. Intending to kill Missy, Danny takes a shot at her while she is standing in a street. Although Danny is a champion shooter, he surprisingly misses his target. However, seconds later a truck hits Missy and kills her.

    a. Is Danny guilty of murder? ____________

    b. Assume instead that the truck strikes Missy first. While she is lying near death in the middle of the street, Danny lives up to his champion reputation and shoots Missy, killing her instantly. It is clear that Missy would have died shortly from the truck wound alone. Is Danny guilty of murder? ____________

22. While Ursula is standing on the side of a busy highway, Dennis approaches her from behind and stabs her. Ursula pulls away from him, falling onto the highway. Shortly thereafter, a passing car strikes Ursula and she dies from the combined effects of the knife wound and the injuries inflicted by the car. Is Dennis guilty of any form of criminal homicide? ____________

23. Dudley, an aging, soon-to-retire pitcher for the Lost Angels Bums, decides to kill T.T. Terrific, predicted by sportswriters to be the only one standing in the way of Dudley's last chance to receive the Cy Young Award. Pursuant to his plan, Dudley substitutes a knife for the baseball when T.T. comes to bat. The knife strikes T.T. in the chest and he collapses, whereupon he is immediately rushed to the hospital. Is Dudley guilty of any form of criminal homicide in the following situations?

    a. At the hospital, Nurse mistakenly gives T.T. a lethal gas instead of oxygen and T.T. dies. ____________

    b. Surgery is successfully performed on T.T., and he is slowly recovering. However, because of his prolonged absence from the team he is eliminated from Cy Young contention. T.T. becomes despondent over this development and kills himself at the hospital. ____________

    c. T.T.'s wound turned out to be only a superficial laceration; he is treated immediately and released. As he walks out of the hospital, however, he is struck by an arriving ambulance and dies instantly. ____________

SCOPE OF CRIMINAL LIABILITY

24. Al, who harbored a grudge against Vivian, encouraged Boyce and Colin to rob Vivian's hot dog stand. Upon their arrival at the stand, Boyce stood guard outside while Colin went in and robbed it of its cash (and several hot dogs with everything). Following the robbery, Vivian called the police who responded in immediate pursuit of the perpetrators. Fearful of their

probable apprehension, Boyce and Colin approached Dorian for help; Dorian permitted them to live in his basement until police concern with them subsided.

a. Identify the principal(s) in the first degree to the robbery of Vivian. ______________

b. Identify the principal(s) in the second degree. ______________

c. Identify the accessory(ies) before the fact. ______________

d. Identify the accessory(ies) after the fact. ______________

25. Assume the same facts as in question 24., above. At common law, could Al be convicted if Boyce and Colin had been tried and acquitted? ______________

26. Dee leases an apartment to Natalie, knowing that Natalie intends to use the apartment as her headquarters for a bookmaking operation. Is Dee an accomplice to Natalie's offense of bookmaking? ______________

27. Clerk Dent is approached by Harry Habit and asked to help Habit take drugs from the store in which Dent works. Pursuant to the scheme, Dent leaves the door unlocked for Habit who enters later that night and takes the drugs. Both are soon apprehended and Dent is charged as an accessory before the fact to Habit's larceny.

a. Suppose Dent can establish that Habit was entrapped into committing the crime. Is Dent guilty? ______________

b. Suppose instead that before Habit left to enter the store, Dent telephoned him and reported that he, Dent, was withdrawing from the scheme. Dent, however, had already unlocked the door and Habit proceeded with the larceny. Ignoring any entrapment question, is Dent guilty as an accessory before the fact? ______________

28. Virginia, age 15, convinces her younger sister, Missy, who is age 13, to have intercourse with her boyfriend, Adam. Virginia invites Adam to her house, telling him he can have intercourse with her and Missy. Assuming that Adam responds affirmatively to the invitation and that there is a statute making 16 years the age of consent—

a. Is Virginia an accomplice to Adam's "statutory rape" of her? ______________

b. Is Virginia an accomplice to Adam's "statutory rape" of Missy? ______________

29. Sam, a tavern owner, employs Woody as bartender. Woody sells liquor to minors in violation of a state statute.

a. Can Sam be convicted of selling liquor to minors? ______________

b. Can Sam be convicted even if he was unaware that Woody was selling liquor to minors? ______________

c. Would Sam be guilty if Woody had deliberately violated Sam's previous instructions not to sell to minors? ______________

30. Acme Tavern is owned by Acme Corporation. The corporation employs a bartender who sells liquor to minors in violation of a local ordinance making this a misdemeanor and, on one occasion, commits a felony assault on a patron whom he dislikes.

a. Can Acme be convicted of a misdemeanor? ______________

b. Can Acme be convicted of felony assault? ______________

DEFENSES

31. Don suffers from a severe mental illness, most recently manifested by his erroneous belief that Lana has maliciously slandered him to all his friends. Upset over this, Don purchases a gun and kills Lana. A defense psychiatrist testifies at the murder trial that Don knew killing was wrong but was compelled by his illness to take Lana's life.

    a. Would Don be entitled to acquittal by reason of insanity under the *M'Naghten* rule? ______________

    b. Would he be entitled to acquittal under the irresistible impulse test? ______________

    c. Would he be entitled to acquittal under the *Durham* rule? ______________

32. Lenny is severely developmentally disabled. He shoots George, killing him. Later he asks when George will come to visit him and cannot understand why George does not show up. In a prosecution for murder, would Lenny be entitled to acquittal under the *M'Naghten* rule? ______________

33. Ben goes into a bar for a couple of drinks. He has more than a few and comes out hours later quite intoxicated. On his way home, he gets into an altercation with Victor, who had inadvertently bumped into Ben while crossing the street. Ben strikes Victor; Victor falls down. Ben takes Victor's wallet and leaves.

    a. Can Ben be convicted of larceny of the wallet? ______________

    b. Can Ben be convicted of assault and battery on Victor? ______________

    c. Suppose instead that Ben orders a nonintoxicating drink, but as a practical joke, the bartender spikes it with a substantial amount of an intoxicating substance. Does Ben now have a defense to an assault and battery charge? ______________

34. Dudley drives away in Vanessa's car, honestly but unreasonably believing that it is his own car. Is Dudley guilty of larceny? ______________

35. Dirk has intercourse with Zelda, honestly believing that she has consented. In fact, Zelda was objecting and resisting with sufficient seriousness that a reasonable person would have perceived that she was not consenting to the intercourse. Is Dirk guilty of rape? ______________

36. Following the death of his father, Toby, Dick takes all of Toby's money and spends it on frivolous items for himself. Charges are later brought against Dick for larceny.

    a. At trial Dick testifies that when he took the money he thought the laws of intestate succession made him Toby's sole heir; in fact, the law was otherwise. Assuming his testimony is believed, should Dick be convicted of larceny? ______________

    b. Would the result be different if Dick testified that he knew the money was not his but that he talked with a lawyer and, on the basis of that conversation, concluded that there was no criminal penalty involved in taking the money from family members? ______________

37. Martin is charged with willful failure to pay federal income tax due on the wages he received from his employer, Acme Refrigerator Company. Would he be entitled to acquittal in either of the following situations?

a. Martin convinces the jury that he actually believed that under the federal income tax law "wages" are not included within the "income" subject to tax, and the prosecution responds with convincing testimony that no reasonable person could entertain such an erroneous view of federal tax law. __________

b. Martin convinces the jury that he actually believed that because of technical irregularities in adoption of the Sixteenth Amendment authorizing a federal income tax, the amendment is not effective and thus the federal income tax system is unconstitutional and hence unenforceable. __________

38. Doug sees a forest fire burning towards a town. Believing that the only way to stop the fire and save the town is to set a backfire that would destroy Nel's home, Doug sets the backfire. Does Doug have a defense to an arson charge? __________

39. Badman forces Hapless at gunpoint to drive him away from the scene of a robbery. Badman then compels Hapless to drive into an officer trying to flag the car down to kill the officer so he cannot pursue the duo.

 a. Should Hapless be convicted as an accessory after the fact to Badman's robbery? __________

 b. Does Hapless have a defense to the charge of intentionally murdering a police officer? __________

40. Narcotics agents operating undercover approach D and, representing that one of them is suffering from withdrawal, ask D to get them some heroin. D first refuses but after several pleas, she complies, procuring the heroin and selling it to the agents. D is promptly arrested.

 a. In a prosecution for illegal sale of narcotics, can D successfully claim entrapment? __________

 b. Would the result in a. be different if it were proven that D regularly sold narcotics? __________

 c. Can D claim entrapment after testifying at her trial that she had not provided the agents with the heroin? __________

41. Fred Fanatic decides to mutilate himself to protest the government's increase in taxes and asks Mark Mayhem to assist him. Mayhem complies by amputating Fanatic's arms. Mayhem is charged with battery.

 a. Does evidence of Fanatic's request establish a defense? __________

 b. If Fanatic testifies that he forgives Mayhem, does Mayhem have a defense? __________

42. Stu Suspicious accuses Slick Vic of making advances to Stu's spouse. Vic raises his arm as if to strike Stu who, fearing the blow, strikes first. Vic sustains minor injuries.

 a. Does Stu have a defense to a battery charge? __________

 b. Would Stu have a defense to a battery charge if it were proven that Vic only raised his hand to scratch his head? __________

 c. Assume that instead of striking Vic, Stu shot and killed him. Would Stu have a defense to a murder charge? __________

43. A plainclothes police officer is attempting validly to arrest Winnie on a public drunkenness charge. Darren comes by and, reasonably believing that Winnie is the victim of an unlawful assault, intervenes and injures the officer. If charged with battery, does Darren have a defense? ______________

44. Diego's automobile was stolen. Three days later, he sees it parked on the street with Vance sitting inside. Diego tries to take possession, but Vance resists. In overcoming the resistance, Diego strikes and injures Vance.

    a. If charges are brought against Diego for battery, does he have a defense? ______________

    b. Suppose Diego announced he was arresting Vance for larceny and then used force to overcome Vance's resistance. When charged with battery, would Diego then have a defense? ______________

PRELIMINARY OR INCHOATE CRIMES

45. Dumbo approaches Mickey and says, "I'll give you $500 if you'll beat up Goofy." Mickey is an undercover police officer and arrests Dumbo. Has Dumbo committed a criminal offense? ______________

46. Arnie knows where a large amount of counterfeit money can be purchased and decides to ask Benny to help him pass the bills if he obtains them. Upon disclosure of the scheme to Benny, Benny responds, "What a break for you. You'll make a fortune." On the basis of these facts alone, are Arnie and Benny guilty of criminal conspiracy? ______________

47. Hillary, Bill, and Chelsea agree to rob a bank. Pursuant to the plan, Bill, who is to provide a getaway vehicle, steals a car and parks it in Chelsea's garage. The next day, Hillary tells Chelsea that she has changed her mind and will not join in the crime. Chelsea informs Bill of Hillary's change of heart at their meeting just before the robbery. Chelsea and Bill nevertheless carry out the robbery themselves.

    a. Are Hillary, Bill, and Chelsea all guilty of criminal conspiracy? ______________

    b. Are Hillary, Bill, and Chelsea all guilty of the larceny of the car? ______________

    c. Are Hillary, Bill, and Chelsea all guilty of robbery? ______________

48. Connie is charged with conspiring with Spiro and Sy to kill Verna. Spiro and Sy are acquitted. Can Connie be convicted? ______________

49. Madame X, a married woman, is having an affair with her administrative assistant, Gil. The two agree to spend the night together at the Bijou Hotel, although adultery is a crime. Can they be convicted of criminal conspiracy? ______________

50. Lou has amassed a huge gambling debt at the local casino and has no resources to pay it back. He decides to kill his father and use the inheritance to satisfy the debt. Pursuant to this plan, he buys a gun.

    a. Is Lou guilty of attempted murder? ______________

    b. Suppose that after buying the gun Lou goes to his father's house and conceals himself in the bushes waiting to take his father by surprise. Is Lou guilty of attempted murder? ______________

51. Christopher plans to buy stolen property from A.J., whom he knows will be at a given location at midnight. Christopher arrives at the location as scheduled, but A.J. has since been arrested and will not show up.

   a. Is Christopher guilty of attempted receipt of stolen property? _______________

   b. Suppose a plainclothes police officer arrives at the location and offers to sell Christopher a purportedly stolen radio. The radio in fact belongs to the police officer. If Christopher buys the radio thinking it is stolen, is he guilty of receipt of stolen property or attempted receipt of stolen property? _______________

HOMICIDE CRIMES

52. Can Deadly be convicted of common law murder in the following situations?

   a. Deadly intentionally stabs Vicky in the leg. The wound proves fatal and Vicky dies. _______________

   b. Deadly throws a bottle in Vicky's direction, intending to frighten her. The bottle shatters against the wall; a piece of glass strikes Vicky, and she bleeds to death. _______________

   c. Deadly, showing off to friends, pilots his new speedboat through a crowd of swimmers. Going at full speed, he intends only to scatter the swimmers, but one of them is hit by the boat and dies. _______________

53. Dan is charged with first degree murder for the premeditated killing of Vic Tim. The prosecution establishes that Dan killed Vic with a pistol. If Dan shows that he formed the intent to kill Vic only seconds before the homicide actually took place, may he be convicted of first-degree murder? _______________

54. Starkmad and Disgusting rob a bank. During the robbery, Disgusting becomes attracted to Teller and forces his attentions upon her, despite Starkmad's urging to avoid this. Finally, Starkmad strikes Disgusting with the butt of his gun to discourage the attack on Teller; the gun discharges accidentally and kills Disgusting. Is Starkmad guilty of felony murder? _______________

55. Sipowitz and Simone are in the process of burglarizing Fancy's gas station at night when Kelly, a police officer, comes upon the scene. Sipowitz and Simone run into nearby woods with Kelly in pursuit. Simone accidentally drops a gun he is carrying; the gun discharges and Kelly is killed.

   a. Is Simone guilty of felony murder? _______________

   b. Assuming Simone is guilty of felony murder, is Sipowitz also guilty? _______________

56. Domino is in the process of holding up a liquor store with a toy pistol which appears to be real. The police arrive and order Domino to throw down his weapon; Domino runs instead. The police open fire, but they miss Domino and kill Vega, an innocent bystander. Would all courts find Domino guilty of felony murder? _______________

57. Would the killings in the following situations more likely be voluntary manslaughter than murder?

   a. Vince calls Debbie several names that reflect on her ethical standards and her mother's sexual practices. Debbie becomes irate and kills Vince. _______________

b. Dean and Jimmy are arguing over a place in a theater line. They agree to settle the matter by fighting it out. During the fight, Jimmy is killed. ______________

c. While Dennis, Russell, and Randy are sitting around a table, Randy tells Dennis that Russell has committed adultery with Dennis's wife. Dennis immediately kills Russell. ______________

d. Vondra throws a rock at Denise and runs away. The next day, Denise sees Vondra and kills her. ______________

e. Vondra throws a rock at Denise and runs away. Denise, frustrated at her inability to obtain revenge against Vondra, sees Xaviera, an innocent bystander, and kills Xaviera. ______________

58. Should the following killings be charged as involuntary manslaughter?

a. Beaver intentionally drops a large rock from a highway overpass. Distracted by the approaching rock, Wally loses control of his car on the highway and is killed in the ensuing crash. ______________

b. Andy is cleaning his gun when the telephone rings. He leaves the gun on the table while he goes to the adjoining room to answer the phone. Meanwhile, Opie, Andy's four-year-old son, wanders into the room and takes the gun to play with it; it discharges, killing Opie instantly. ______________

c. Barney is carefully carrying a concealed weapon which accidentally discharges, killing Bea. ______________

d. Mary is attempting to commit suicide. Rob intervenes to prevent this, and in the struggle the gun that Mary was using discharges, killing Rob. ______________

OTHER CRIMES AGAINST THE PERSON

59. Can Dastardly be convicted of battery in the following situations?

a. Dastardly puts poison in Hapless's drink, and she drinks it. ______________

b. Dastardly intentionally spits on Hapless's shoe. ______________

c. Dastardly, driving a car in a highly negligent manner, strikes Pedestrian. Dastardly did not intend to injure anyone. ______________

60. Donna points a gun at Vivian and pulls the trigger. Unknown to Donna, the gun is defective and will not fire. Is Donna guilty of assault? ______________

61. Danielle attacks Violet as a result of which Violet's face is severely disfigured. Danielle is charged with mayhem, but at the time of the trial, two years later, Violet's face has returned to normal. Can Danielle be convicted? ______________

62. Dance and Vance are at a party. Both have consumed large amounts of liquor. Vance passes out, and Dance engages in an act of intercourse with her while she is unconscious. Is Dance guilty of rape? ______________

63. Diego tells Vanna that unless she submits to intercourse with him, he will report her to the police as a prostitute. Vanna submits. Is Diego guilty of rape? ______________

64. Dunbar tells Veronica that if she will engage in intercourse with him, he will pay her $150. He does not intend to pay her, and after the act is complete he refuses to pay her. Is Dunbar guilty of rape? ______________

65. Deitrich and Val have been living together for two years but Val refuses to have intercourse with Deitrich until they are married. Deitrich arranges a sham marriage ceremony and convinces Val that they are married. Val then consents to intercourse. Is Deitrich guilty of rape? ______________

66. In Deft's prosecution for rape of Vicky, Deft testifies that Vicky consented to the intercourse. Vicky testifies for the prosecution that she did not consent but rather physically resisted as much as she could. Deft asks that the jury be instructed that he should be acquitted if the jury determines that he reasonably believed Vicky consented, whether or not she actually did. Does the prosecution have a viable argument that this instruction should not be given? ______________

67. While Slim is walking down a hall in a public building, Bull moves in front of him and refuses to permit him to proceed. Is Bull guilty of false imprisonment? ______________

68. Doug Delude, as part of an extortion scheme, tells Dupe that his wife is in the hospital calling for him. Dupe willingly accompanies Delude to his car and drives away with him. Is Delude guilty of kidnapping? ______________

69. D breaks into V's house and finds her in the kitchen. He compels her to go into the adjoining room and rapes her there. Is D guilty of kidnapping as well as rape? ______________

CRIMES AGAINST THE HABITATION

70. Delilah, intending to kill Samson, throws a bomb through a closed window in Samson's house at night. Has Delilah committed burglary? ______________

71. Digby, intending to steal Villareal's family jewels, pushes open a partially opened window in Villareal's house and crawls in. Has Digby committed burglary? ______________

72. Jay persuades Oprah's cook to let him into Oprah's house late one night to steal her valuable Picasso. The cook does so. Is Jay guilty of burglary? ______________

73. Darlene owns a house that she rents to Vi. One night while Vi is away, Darlene decides to steal Vi's money and enters the house with her passkey. Has Darlene committed burglary? ______________

74. To escape a rampaging storm, Desperate breaks and enters Handy's home. Once inside, Desperate sees Handy's wallet lying on the floor and decides to steal it. Has Desperate committed burglary? ______________

75. Ditsy breaks and enters David's house during the nighttime. Will the following facts preclude Ditsy's conviction for common law burglary?

    a. David and all other occupants were on vacation, and so no one was present in the house. ______________

    b. Once inside, Ditsy abandoned her intent to steal. ______________

    c. Ditsy was voluntarily intoxicated at the time of entry. ______________

    d. Ditsy's intent on entering was to find a place to sleep for the night. ______________

76. Delinquent throws a firebomb into Violet's house. It lands on a sofa, burns the fabric, and then goes out. Is Delinquent guilty of arson? ______________

77. Klutz, while burglarizing a house, accidentally leaves a cigarette burning. The cigarette sets fire to the house, and before help arrives the house burns down. Is Klutz guilty of arson? ________________

78. Tenant sets fire to his cottage in protest of Landlord's failure to repair the premises. The fire accidentally spreads to other cottages in the area, causing them severe damage. Is Tenant guilty of arson? ________________

CRIMES AGAINST PROPERTY

79. Can the following items be the subject of common law larceny?

    a. A purebred Siamese cat of champion stock. ________________

    b. An Angus bull. ________________

    c. Stock certificates in a corporation. ________________

    d. Corn growing in a field. ________________

    e. A stolen car. ________________

    f. A wallet lost by its owner. ________________

80. Lucy leaves her TV with Desi for repairs. Desi repairs it but refuses to return it to Lucy until she pays for the work. When Desi is not looking, Lucy takes the TV and runs, intending never to pay the repair bill. Is Lucy guilty of larceny? ________________

81. Scully and Mulder own a taxi business together. Scully takes Cab 804 (which belongs to the business) and refuses to return it. Is Scully guilty of larceny? ________________

82. Husband takes Wife's jewelry and gives it to Beggar as a gift. Is Husband guilty of common law larceny? ________________

83. Looking for some fuel to feed his furnace, Cheapskate takes some old posts lying in Neighbor's backyard. He intends to pay Neighbor for them should Neighbor complain about the taking. Is Cheapskate guilty of larceny? ________________

84. Smart picks up a briefcase in a public restroom at an airport believing it to be his own. When he opens it later that day, however, he finds it belongs to Chaos, whose name is on the papers inside. The briefcase also contains over $100,000 in cash. After giving the matter a few days thought, Smart decides to keep the briefcase and its contents. Is Smart guilty of larceny? ________________

85. Aldo goes to Betty's office to give Betty $500. Betty's receptionist, Cassandra, accepts the money and, as Aldo leaves, places it in her purse and walks out, intending to keep it. Is Cassandra guilty of larceny? ________________

86. Busy gives her errand clerk, Delivery, $500 to deposit for her in the bank. On the way to the bank, Delivery decides he has better uses for the money and absconds with it. Is Delivery guilty of larceny? ________________

87. Abdul loans Bathsheba $5,000 and agrees to hold Bathsheba's diamond ring as security. Abdul immediately sells the ring for $7,500. Is Abdul guilty of embezzlement? ________________

88. Botticelli promises to deliver a rare painting to DaVinci for $5,000. DaVinci gives Botticelli the $5,000.

    a. Botticelli then absconds. Is Botticelli guilty of false pretenses? ________________

b. Suppose instead that Botticelli does deliver the painting, but that it has damage to the back of it which substantially reduces its value. Botticelli knew of the defect all along but did not call the matter to DaVinci's attention. Is Botticelli guilty of false pretenses? ______________

89. Gemstone enters Tiffany's jewelry store and misrepresents that Peacock has sent him to pick up certain emeralds for Peacock's inspection and possible purchase. Tiffany gives the jewels to Gemstone and he agrees to return with the jewels or the cash for their purchase later that day. Immediately thereafter, Gemstone converts the emeralds to his own use as he had intended to do all along. Is Gemstone guilty of false pretenses? ______________

90. Slight O'Hand, a professional pickpocket, lifts Bozo's wallet at a circus. Bozo was busy watching the elephants perform at the time and did not feel a thing. Is O'Hand guilty of robbery? ______________

91. After an illegal gambling game, Loser, one of the participants, pulls a gun and demands his losses back. The money is quickly handed over, and Loser runs off. Is Loser guilty of robbery? ______________

92. Doorong attempts to rape Virginia, but Virginia escapes, leaving her purse behind. Doorong finds the purse and keeps it. Is Doorong guilty of robbery? ______________

93. Brutus enters Tashi's home, ties him up, and forces him to tell where his money is hidden. Brutus then goes into another room to get the money from the hiding place. Is Brutus guilty of robbery? ______________

94. Mei's child is away at boarding school. Silvio threatens to harm the child when the child returns from school in a week, unless Mei gives Silvio all the money in her home. Fearful for her child's life, Mei complies.

    a. Is Silvio guilty of robbery? ______________

    b. Is Silvio guilty of extortion? ______________

95. Mel and Vera are having an adulterous affair. Mel threatens to tell Vera's spouse about the affair unless Vera pays Mel $10,000. Assuming Vera has not yet paid Mel the money, is Mel guilty of extortion? ______________

96. Maria purchased a dog from Harold for $1,500, with the understanding that the dog was well trained. The first time Maria took the dog outside, it ran away despite her commands to "come." Maria told Harold that unless he gave her $1,500, she would contact the district attorney and press criminal charges for criminal fraud. As a result, Maria is charged with extortion. Does she have a defense? ______________

97. Delbert encourages Xena to steal certain items from Vic. Delbert is not present when Xena commits the crime. Xena sells the items to Delbert. Delbert is convicted of the larceny as an accessory before the fact. Can Delbert also be convicted of receiving stolen property? ______________

OFFENSES AGAINST GOVERNMENT AND THE ADMINISTRATION OF JUSTICE

98. Claudine, a Canadian citizen, is visiting the United States. She obtains certain U.S. military secrets and passes them to Country X, which is at war with the United States. Is Claudine guilty of treason? ______________

99. Loyal knows that her dear friend Zip has committed robbery but neither reports this information to authorities nor tells the authorities where Zip can be found. As a result, Zip avoids capture and conviction.

   a. Is Loyal guilty of misprision of felony under federal law? ______________

   b. Assume instead that Loyal knows Zip is hiding in the apartment next door. Police come by and ask Loyal if she has seen Zip, and Loyal tells them that she believes he is hiding in another neighborhood. The police leave to check this out, and Zip escapes. Is Loyal now guilty of misprision of felony? ______________

100. Whitney observed Julius kill Ron. When the police question Whitney about the incident, he falsely tells them that Ron attacked Julius and that Julius killed in self-defense. Whitney hopes that Julius will reward him for this help. Is Whitney guilty of compounding a crime? ______________

Answers to Review Questions

1.	**YES**	Whether or not a crime is a felony depends upon the punishment that *may be* imposed upon conviction—not the punishment actually imposed. Accordingly, under any of the tests used to distinguish felonies from misdemeanors, this crime would be a felony. [p. 3]
2.	**NO**	The jury might understand the instruction as requiring that Debussy prove he did not intend to cause the damage. Thus, the instruction would violate Debussy's Due Process right to have all elements of the crime proved beyond a reasonable doubt. [p. 5]
3	**NO**	The right of privacy embodied in the First Amendment prohibits punishing a person for possession of obscene materials in the privacy of his home. [p. 17]
4	**NO**	The statute is clearly "void for vagueness" under the Due Process Clauses of the Fifth and Fourteenth Amendments because it is lacking in certainty as to the conduct made criminal. [p. 17 *et seq.*]
5.a.	**NO**	The death penalty is constitutionally excessive for the crime of rape of an adult woman. [p. 21]
b.	**NO**	The death penalty is constitutionally excessive if the defendant was younger than age 18 at the time of the crime. [p. 21]
c.	**NO**	The Eighth Amendment prohibits the death penalty if the defendant was younger than age 18 at the time of the crime. [p. 21]
6.	**PROBABLY YES**	The federal constitutional prohibition against double jeopardy is not violated by conviction for several overlapping offenses if this occurs in a single trial. [p. 23] However, legislative intent may have been to have the arson "merge" into the murder and thus to bar conviction for both. [p. 24] If the intent is to bar conviction for both, the constitutional provision would be violated by multiple convictions. The *Blockburger* test suggests that the legislative intent was to permit conviction for both because each crime requires proof of something that the other does not (arson requires the burning of a dwelling while murder does not, and murder requires the death of the victim while arson does not). [p. 24] *But note:* There may be a more stringent state statutory or constitutional law prohibiting multiple convictions for what is essentially the same conduct. [p. 25 *et seq.*]
7.a.	**NO**	At common law, conspiracy (a misdemeanor) merges into the object crimes (which are felonies). But there is no merger of crimes of the same degree, and thus Ernie and Bert can be convicted of burglary and murder. [p. 22]
b.	**YES**	Merger is not recognized under modern law. [p. 22]
8.	**NO**	A crime punishing a given status offends the Eighth Amendment prohibition against cruel and unusual punishment. [p. 30]
9.	**YES**	There is no prohibition against making specific acts criminal, even if those acts are closely related to a status which cannot itself be made a crime. [p. 30]

10.	**NO**	This was not volitional action and so does not meet the legal requirements for an "act." [p. 31]
11.	**NO**	Where criminal liability is predicated on an affirmative act, there must be a showing of some *conscious* and *volitional* movement. [p. 31]
12.a.	**NO**	From the facts given, Dell had no legal duty to assist the woman (a moral obligation alone is not enough). Therefore, his failure to help her does not constitute an "act." [p. 34 *et seq.*]
b.	**NO**	He still has not "acted" within the meaning of the criminal law. The fact that Dell and the woman were neighbors does not create a legal duty to act, and his bad or "criminal" intent alone cannot render him liable. [p. 34]
c.	**YES**	The marriage relationship obligated Dell to do whatever he was capable of doing to avert the peril (whether by intervening personally or seeking others to help). Having failed to perform a legal duty where it was possible to do so, Dell has "acted" for purposes of criminal liability. [p. 35]
13.	**POSSIBLY**	The modern trend is to expand on the common law legal duties. Thus, a court might find that the relationship between Dinah and Vinny obliged her to act to save Vinny's life. If such a duty is found, Dinah's omission will support a criminal homicide conviction. [p. 39]
14.	**YES**	Dan breached a contractual duty (to maintain his post and aid swimmers in distress), and that omission was an "act" that caused death. [p. 38]
15.	**NO**	Although the statute may have imposed a duty to act, there is no "act" for criminal law purpose unless Dom was *aware* of the facts creating that duty. Here, he was not. [p. 39 *et seq.*]
16.	**POSSIBLY**	An omission is an "act" only if the defendant could have *performed* the duty violated. Thus, if Dad could not have obtained medical assistance, his failure to do so will not support a homicide conviction. However, Dad's own financial straits are not conclusive; he can be held criminally liable if other sources of help (such as welfare agencies) were available. [p. 40]
17.	**NO**	This crime is a "regulatory offense" and thus will most probably be interpreted as imposing strict liability. Accordingly, no intent is necessary as to the critical element of the nature of the beverages sold. [p. 51 *et seq.*]
18.	**PROBABLY NOT**	The apparent inference to be drawn from the facts is that Dennis did not consciously desire, nor contemplate to a practical certainty, the *serious* injury to Vic that actually occurred; had he intended to cause such severe harm he no doubt would have dealt Vic a blow (or the like) rather than simply giving Vic a shove. Therefore, in regard to the nature of the result, Dennis did not act with "purpose" or "knowledge" as these terms are defined in modern codes. [p. 54 *et seq.*]
19.	**YES**	Although Donna did not intend the harm actually caused (damage to Floyd's home), there was considerable similarity between the contemplated harm and the resulting harm (broken window). Therefore, the doctrine of "transferred intent" applies and Donna will be treated as if she intended to break Floyd's window. [p. 61 *et seq.*]
20.	**NO**	While Dillon had the intent required and performed an act causing death, there was not the requisite *concurrence* between the intent and the act; *i.e.,*

because the act was not attributable to Dillon's culpable state of mind, he cannot be convicted of murder. [p. 63]

21.a.	**NO**	There was no factual causation between the death and Danny's action. (Missy would have been hit by the truck whether or not Danny fired at her.) [p. 66]
b.	**YES**	The facts now show "but for" causation. It is immaterial that Danny merely hastened the inevitable—"but for" his act Missy would not have died when and as she did. [p. 68]
22.	**YES**	Although death was caused in an uncontemplated manner, there is nothing here to break the chain of causation; it was clearly foreseeable that a struggling victim along the side of a highway might accidentally fall into traffic. [p. 71 *et seq.*]
23.a.	**PROBABLY**	In the absence of evidence that the medical mistreatment was grossly negligent, it will not break the chain of proximate causation (*i.e.,* Nurse's mistake is not a superseding factor). [p. 72]
b.	**PROBABLY**	T.T.'s depression was directly related to the injury inflicted by Dudley. Hence, a court will most likely find that T.T.'s conduct in taking his own life was a foreseeable intervening factor that does not break the chain of proximate causation. [p. 73]
c.	**NO**	Here T.T.'s death was caused by an *unforeseeable* accident that broke the chain of proximate causation. [p. 71 *et seq.*]
24.a.	**COLIN**	The actual perpetrator of the crime is the principal in the first degree. [p. 76]
b.	**BOYCE**	Boyce facilitated Colin's perpetration of the robbery and by acting as a lookout was constructively (if not actually) present at its commission. [p. 77]
c.	**AL**	Al encouraged Colin to commit the robbery but was not present at its commission. [p. 77]
d.	**DORIAN**	Dorian assisted Boyce and Colin in their efforts to avoid apprehension by police, knowing that they had committed a felony. [p. 77]
25.	**NO**	At common law, conviction of the principal was essential to conviction of an accessory. (However, the rule is otherwise in most jurisdictions today. [p. 77])
26.	**SPLIT**	Some jurisdictions require that an accessory act with the purpose of aiding the principal; and under these facts, it does not appear that Dee had such intent. (Knowledge of Natalie's illegal activity alone would not be enough.) But other jurisdictions require only that the accessory be aware that her actions will assist the commission of a crime, in which case, Dee would be guilty. [p. 83 *et seq.*]
27.a.	**UNCLEAR**	Whether an accessory can assert defenses available to the actual perpetrator is subject to a split of authority (although at least one circuit court has held that an accessory could not rely on the perpetrator's entrapment defense). [p. 85] If the defense does not extend to Dent, he can be convicted for abetting Habit's commission of the crime.
b.	**YES**	Dent was an *abettor* (not simply an inciter), because he physically assisted commission of the crime. An abettor cannot withdraw by a renunciation alone, but must deprive his earlier action of its effectiveness. This Dent did

not do (door remained unlocked), and his attempted withdrawal is therefore ineffective. [p. 88]

28.a. **NO** She is within the class of persons protected by the statutory rape statute and therefore is not liable despite her participation. [p. 89]

b. **YES** Virginia was not the "victim" of this crime. Moreover, the fact that she could not commit rape upon Missy directly does not preclude her conviction as an accessory to Adam's rape of Missy. [p. 90]

29.a. **PROBABLY** Statutes of this sort are often read as imposing vicarious liability on an employer for the acts of employees, but the matter is ultimately one of legislative intent. [p. 92 *et seq.*]

b. **PROBABLY** But note that this is an issue of *strict* rather than *vicarious* liability. This statute is likely to be interpreted as imposing both strict and vicarious liability, but the questions are separate. [p. 92]

c. **SPLIT** Some courts hold employers liable despite such instructions, while others find that such instructions relieve employers of vicarious liability. Even in these latter jurisdictions, however, it may be necessary for Sam to show that the instructions were vigorously given and unambiguous. [p. 93]

30.a. **YES** This is a minor offense (misdemeanor) committed by an employee in the course of his employment. [p. 97]

b. **SPLIT** Some courts would invoke the standard governing minor crimes, in which case Acme would be liable. But in other jurisdictions, a corporation is liable for a serious crime only if the offense was authorized or tolerated by a management official. Because the felony was perpetrated because of the bartender's personal grudge, it is unlikely that Acme would be found liable under the latter approach. [p. 97]

31.a. **NO** Any compulsion that Don experienced is irrelevant under *M'Naghten.* Here, Don had not lost the capacity to know his act was legally wrong, because his symptoms did not cause him to believe he was legally justified in killing. Moreover, the fact that he purchased a gun to accomplish the killing demonstrates that he did know the nature and quality of his act. [p. 109 *et seq.*]

b. **PERHAPS** A jury might find that because of his illness, Don could not control the urge to act as he did. He would then be entitled to acquittal. [p. 111 *et seq.*]

c. **YES** The evidence establishes that "but for" his mental illness, Don would not have killed Lana [p. 112]

32. **YES** Developmental disability can give rise to insanity, and here Lenny clearly did not understand the nature and quality of the act of killing (otherwise, he would not have been awaiting George's visit). [p. 108]

33.a. **DEPENDS** Larceny requires proof of the specific intent to steal. If because of his voluntary intoxication Ben lacked that intent, he cannot be convicted of larceny. [p. 119]

b. **YES** Assault and battery are not specific intent crimes. Therefore, Ben's voluntary intoxication is no defense. [p. 119]

c. **DEPENDS** Under these facts, Ben's intoxication would be involuntary, because he was unaware of the intoxicating nature of the drink. However, involuntary intoxication is only a complete defense if it renders the defendant insane within the meaning of the jurisdiction's insanity test. [p. 118]

34. **NO** He has a mistake of fact defense. Because Dudley thought he was driving his own car, he clearly lacked the intent to deprive Vanessa of *her* car. Moreover, it is irrelevant that the mistake was unreasonable, Because it disproves a *specific* intent required for larceny. [p. 123]

35. **YES** Rape is not a specific intent crime. Therefore, an unreasonable mistake of fact cannot be used to prove lack of intent. [p. 123]

36.a. **NO** He has a "mistake of law" defense. His mistake concerning intestate succession law shows he lacked the intent to steal required by larceny and therefore prevents liability. [p. 126]

b. **YES** A belief that the criminal law is such that it does not cover one's acts is generally not a defense. This situation does not come within any of the exceptions; none of the exceptions covers a belief based on advice of counsel. [p. 127]

37.a. **YES** "Willfulness" as used in this crime requires that the accused be shown to have failed to pay tax that he knew was due. Martin's testimony establishes that he did not know the tax was due and thus the prosecution's evidence fails. Because his testimony actually establishes his lack of the required *mens rea*, it is irrelevant that his belief was objectively unreasonable. [p. 126]

b. **NO** "Willfulness" as required by this crime does not require knowledge that the statutes imposing the tax are constitutionally valid. Hence his testimony does not show that he lacked the *mens rea* required by the crime and he can be convicted. [p. 126]

38. **YES** This is a classic necessity defense situation—Doug reasonably believed that burning Nel's home was the only way to prevent the occurrence of a greater harm (destruction of the town). [p. 131 *et seq.*]

39.a. **NO** Hapless can successfully assert the defense of duress because he was compelled to act under threat of immediate serious bodily harm. [p. 134 *et seq.*]

b. **NO** Duress is not a defense to the intentional killing of another, and no other defenses are apparent from the facts. (Duress may be offered to negate premeditation, however, and thus it may preclude conviction for first degree murder.) [p. 135 *et seq.*]

40.a. **PROBABLY** The facts set forth a persuasive case for entrapment. Applying the traditional standard, the agents' repeated requests and their appeals to D's sympathy indicate D was not predisposed to commit the crime. And, under the modern standard, it is likely that the agents' perseverance would have induced a reasonable person to commit the crime. [p. 138 *et seq.*]

b. **YES** Now it appears that D was predisposed to commit the crime and that the agents merely provided her with the opportunity to do so. Hence, there would be no entrapment under the traditional approach. [p. 138] However, D would probably still have a defense if the jurisdiction adopts the minority ("objective") standard, under which her own predisposition would be immaterial. [pp. 140–141]

c. **PROBABLY NOT** In many and perhaps most jurisdictions, the accused cannot both claim entrapment and deny commission of the crime. [p. 138]

41.a.	**NO**	Consent is not a defense to crimes involving serious bodily injury. [p. 142]
b.	**NO**	The victim's forgiveness is never a defense. [p. 144]
42.a.	**YES**	Stu reasonably believed he was about to suffer imminent harm and so was entitled to act in self-defense. [p. 145 *et seq.*]
b.	**YES**	The defense of self-defense is available as long as it *reasonably appeared* to the defendant that force was necessary to prevent imminent harm. [p. 145]
c.	**NO**	Deadly force can be used in self-defense only if the defendant reasonably believed he was threatened with death or serious bodily injury; Vic's raising his arm did not pose such a threat. [p. 147]
43.	**SPLIT**	Courts disagree on whether force can be used in defense of others where the person defended would not have had the right to act in self-defense. [p. 153 *et seq.*]
44.a.	**NO**	Not even nondeadly force can be used to retake property wrongfully in the possession of another. The actor must resort to legal process. [p. 156]
b.	**PROBABLY**	A private citizen can use nondeadly force to make a felony arrest if the felony was in fact committed and the citizen reasonably believes the arrested person committed it. [p. 160 *et seq.*]
45.	**YES**	This is a completed solicitation; the person incited need not respond affirmatively. [p. 167]
46.	**NO**	An ***agreement*** to combine is essential to the crime of conspiracy. Here, however, Benny did not agree to anything; he simply expressed approval of Arnie's participation. [p. 172 *et seq.*]
47.a.	**YES**	All entered into the agreement, and Hillary's later withdrawal is no defense. [p. 181]
b.	**YES**	The theft was foreseeable and committed in furtherance of the conspiratorial objective. [p. 192] Moreover, there is no question of withdrawal as a defense to Hillary's liability because she did not renounce the scheme until after the larceny was committed. [p. 184]
c.	**NO (most courts)**	Hillary is not liable for the robbery, because she effectively withdrew from the conspiracy before the robbery took place. (While at least one court has required the withdrawing member to prevent her co-conspirators from completing the object crime, most courts hold that a timely communication is enough.) [p. 184 *et seq.*]
48.	**NO**	Because there must be an agreement between at least two persons, acquittal of all other members of the alleged conspiracy generally means that the remaining member cannot be guilty. [p. 178]
49.	**NO**	Under "Wharton's Rule," there can be no conviction for conspiracy to commit an offense which by its definition requires a preliminary agreement between the parties (here, adultery). [p. 181 *et seq.*]
50.a.	**NO**	Although there are various tests for determining whether or not a person has gone far enough to constitute attempt, it is unlikely that merely purchasing the gun is enough under any of these tests. [p. 187 *et seq.*]
b.	**PROBABLY**	Under most tests, Lou has now gone far enough toward commission of the crime. He may not, however, have met the "last proximate act" test or the "control over all indispensable elements" test. [p. 187 *et seq.*]

51.a. **YES** This is a case of "factual impossibility"—Christopher has done everything he could do to consummate the crime and failed only because of A.J.'s intervening arrest. Factual impossibility will not prevent liability. [p. 191]

b. **PROBABLY NOT** He is not guilty of receipt of stolen property, because the property was not in fact "stolen." Moreover, because it is "legally impossible" to commit the crime by receiving this item, some courts, applying the traditional rule, would find no liability for attempt. (Other courts, however, reject this rule and would permit Christopher's conviction.) [p. 192 *et seq.*]

52.a. **YES** Deadly acted with intent to inflict serious bodily injury and this is enough. [p. 204]

b. **NO** Deadly's intent to frighten Vicky and the fortuitous events that followed do not demonstrate malice aforethought. [p. 203 *et seq.*]

c. **YES** Deadly's conduct evidences an awareness of a high risk of death or serious bodily injury to the swimmers and this is sufficient. [p. 204 *et seq.*]

53. **DEPENDS** Courts disagree on whether premeditation requires proof of an opportunity for extended reflection. Some jurisdictions require proof of an appreciable period of time during which deliberation could have occurred; others do not. [p. 206 *et seq.*]

54. **DEPENDS** Some courts require the death to have been a foreseeable consequence of the felony. In these jurisdictions it is unlikely that the felony murder rule would be applied because Disgusting was on an independent venture of his own—the incident that prompted the killing was not a foreseeable result of commission of the robbery. [p. 210]

55.a. **PROBABLY** Although the felony itself had terminated, many courts apply the felony murder rule to deaths caused after technical completion of the felony—particularly if the death is caused before the felons reach a place of temporary safety. [p. 213 *et seq.*]

b. **YES** Each felon is liable for those killings by his co-felons that are the natural and probable result of the felony. [p. 209]

56. **NO** The modern trend limits application of the felony murder rule to situations in which one of the felons directly causes death. (Here death was caused by the act of a police officer.) However, the modern view is not universally accepted; some courts might convict Domino for felony murder on the theory that "but for" his attempted perpetration of the robbery, Vega would not have been killed. [p. 211 *et seq.*]

57.a. **PROBABLY NOT** Traditionally, mere words are not adequate provocation. [p. 217 *et seq.*]

b. **YES** A killing during mutual combat is voluntary manslaughter. [p. 218]

c. **DEPENDS** Some courts find adequate provocation only where one spouse actually observes the other spouse committing adultery; others also find it where the defendant-spouse is told of the adultery. [p. 218]

d.	**NO**	While a battery is adequate provocation if it is a serious one [p. 218], here the time that elapsed between the provocation and the killing was most probably sufficient for the passions of a reasonable person to cool. [p. 220 *et seq.*]
e.	**NO**	A killing is not reduced to voluntary manslaughter where the provocation causes the defendant intentionally to strike out at innocent third persons. (Note that the result would be different if Denise intended to kill Vondra but accidentally killed Xaviera. [p. 219])
58.a.	**NO**	This involves such a high risk to human life that it would properly be charged as murder. [p. 204 *et seq.*]
b.	**YES**	Inadvertently leaving the gun within the reach of a four-year-old child most likely involves criminal negligence. [p. 222 *et seq.*]
c.	**DEPENDS**	While the killing was caused during the commission of a prohibited act, some jurisdictions also require that the act be *malum in se*. Here the unlawful act was only *malum prohibitum* and so is not necessarily sufficient to make the killing manslaughter. [p. 223 *et seq.*]
d.	**PROBABLY**	This is an unintentional killing caused during the commission of an unlawful act. [p. 223 *et seq.*] However, a few courts might find no liability, and if suicide is still murder in the jurisdiction (as it is at common law), there may be liability for felony murder. [p. 209 *et seq.*]
59.a.	**YES**	Indirect application of force is still a battery. [p. 230]
b.	**YES**	No injury is necessary. [p. 230]
c.	**YES**	Battery need not be intentional; criminal negligence will suffice. [p. 231]
60.	**DEPENDS**	Some jurisdictions in which assault is defined as an attempted battery also require a showing that the defendant had the present ability to succeed. Here, however, the gun was defective and therefore Donna could not be convicted. [p. 241] Other jurisdictions extend the crime of assault to include intentionally putting another in fear of immediate bodily harm; arguably, Donna has done just that here. [p. 233 *et seq.*]
61.	**NO**	Violet's normal appearance was only temporarily impaired; mayhem requires a ***permanent*** disfigurement. [p. 236]
62.	**YES**	If the victim is unable to give consent, intercourse with her is rape. [p. 238]
63.	**NO**	Consent obtained by use of threats is vitiated only where the threats are of bodily harm. [p. 238]
64.	**NO**	This is not one of the types of fraud that will invalidate consent. [p. 238 *et seq.*]
65.	**SPLIT**	Courts disagree as to whether fraud concerning the existence of a marital relationship invalidates consent. [p. 239]
66.	**YES**	Some courts hold that such an instruction is appropriate *only* if there is some evidence of equivocal conduct on the victim's part that might have supported a belief by the defendant that the victim consented. [p. 240]
67.	**NO**	Simply preventing the victim from proceeding is not a "confinement" for purposes of false imprisonment. [p. 246]

68.	**DEPENDS**	Statutes differ on whether causing the movement of the victim by deception is sufficient. [p. 248]
69.	**DEPENDS**	D might be guilty under statutes defining kidnapping as detention and movement of the victim, although there may be a question as to whether the forced movement was substantial enough. [p. 247] But here the detention and movement of the victim were incidental to the commission of another serious crime, rape. In this situation, many courts would require that the risk to the victim have been increased beyond what is involved in rape. [pp. 249]
70.	**YES**	Entry by an instrument with which Delilah intended to commit the underlying crime is enough. [p. 253]
71.	**DEPENDS**	The issue here is whether there was a "breaking." Some courts require that force be used to *create* an opening. But others hold it sufficient that force is used to enlarge an existing opening. [p. 254]
72.	**YES**	Obtaining entry with the aid of a co-conspirator already in the dwelling is "constructive force" and will suffice for a breaking. [p. 254]
73.	**YES**	Because Vi had the right to use the house to live in, it was Vi's dwelling. [p. 256]
74.	**NO**	The felonious intent must exist at the time of entry. [p. 257]
75.a.	**NO**	Temporary absence of the residents does not mean the structure is not a dwelling. [p. 256]
b.	**NO**	The crime is complete on entry. The intent need not be carried out. [p. 258]
c.	**DEPENDS**	Only if the intoxication proves the lack of intent to commit a felony in the structure will the conviction be barred. [p. 257]
d.	**YES**	Ditsy did not intend to commit a felony at the time of entry. [p. 257]
76.	**NO**	For arson, some part of the structure itself must be "burned." [p. 262]
77.	**NO**	Neither negligence nor the commission of another crime (here, burglary) will supply the malice required for arson. [p. 262 *et seq.*]
78.	**YES**	Creating a high risk of damage to other dwellings by setting one's own dwelling on fire establishes the malice necessary for arson. [p. 263]
79.a.	**NO**	Household pets cannot be the subject of larceny. [p. 270]
b.	**YES**	Domestic animals of value can be the subject of larceny. [p. 270]
c.	**NO**	Intangible personal property cannot be the subject of larceny. [p. 270]
d.	**NO**	Crops are part of the realty and thus not the subject of larceny. [p. 269]
e.	**YES**	Even stolen property or contraband can be the subject of larceny. [p. 271]
f.	**YES**	Lost property can be the subject of larceny (although a defendant can be convicted only if there was a "clue to ownership" and the defendant intended to steal the item when he found it). [p. 282 *et seq.*]
80.	**YES**	Because Desi had a right to possession superior to that of Lucy, Lucy's taking is larceny. [p. 276]
81.	**NO**	Most courts hold that one joint owner cannot commit larceny from the other joint owner. [p. 277]

82.	**NO**	At common law, spouses are regarded as "one." Hence, one spouse cannot commit larceny by taking the property of the other. [p. 277]
83.	**PROBABLY**	Cheapskate's vague and conditional intent to pay for the property (which was apparently not for sale) is probably insufficient to prevent his actions from being larceny. [p. 279]
84.	**NO**	The misappropriation of lost property is not larceny unless the intent to steal exists at the time of the finding. [p. 282]
85.	**NO**	Because Cassandra received possession of the money when it was delivered to her, her placing of it in her purse did not involve a taking from the possession of another. Betty never got possession of it, so the money was not taken from the possession of Betty. [p. 283]
86.	**PROBABLY**	As an errand clerk, it is doubtful that Delivery was a "trusted employee." Thus, Delivery most probably received only custody from Busy, and when Delivery misappropriated the money he did so from the possession of another (Busy). [p. 283]
87.	**YES**	A had lawful possession of the ring pursuant to the security agreement and converted it with fraudulent intent. [p. 284 *et seq.*]
88.a.	**NO (most courts)**	Botticelli has not made a misrepresentation of past or present *fact.* The crime of false pretenses traditionally cannot be premised on a false promise. [p. 289]
b.	**NO**	Ordinarily, passive nondisclosure of facts is not enough for false pretenses. [p. 290]
89.	**NO**	Gemstone did not obtain *title* to the jewelry by means of the false representation; he only obtained possession and so cannot be guilty of false pretenses. [p. 288 *et seq.*] He is, however, guilty of larceny by trick. [p. 273 *et seq.*]
90.	**NO**	The property was not taken by means of violence or intimidation. [p. 293]
91.	**DEPENDS**	The issue is whether Loser had the requisite intent to permanently deprive another of his property. If Loser believed he was legally entitled to reclaim his money because the game was illegal, he was taking it under a claim of right and has not committed robbery. However, the facts are unclear as to what Loser's belief was. [p. 298]
92.	**NO**	The property was not taken from Virginia's person or presence. [p. 293]
93.	**YES**	Although the property was not taken from Tashi's person, it was taken from his "presence"—*i.e.,* from a place close enough to him that he could have prevented the taking had Brutus not tied him up. [p. 293]
94.a.	**NO**	The threats for purposes of robbery must be to do *immediate* harm. [p. 296]
b.	**PROBABLY**	The threats are of the sort likely to suffice for extortion; immediacy is not essential. [p. 300]
95.	**SPLIT**	Although the threats are of the sort likely to constitute extortion [p. 300], some statutes require that the defendant actually obtain the property; others punish the mere making of the threats with the intent to obtain property. [p. 299]
96.	**PERHAPS**	Some jurisdictions recognize a defense of "claim of right" to extortion. If this jurisdiction does, Maria has a defense based on her belief that she was

entitled to the money she demanded from Harold. The fact that her claim was of a specific amount tends to support the defense, if the jurisdiction recognizes it. [p. 300]

97.	**PROBABLY NOT**	One who was a party to, but not an active participant in, the larceny can probably be convicted of receipt of the stolen property. But under the better view, such a person cannot be convicted of both the larceny and receipt of the property. [p. 303 *et seq.*]
98.	**NO**	Treason cannot be committed by a person who does not owe allegiance to the government. Therefore, Claudine, as a Canadian citizen, cannot be convicted. [p. 308]
99.a.	**NO**	The federal statute has been interpreted to require the rendering of some affirmative assistance to the felon. Thus, Loyal's nondisclosure alone will not support a federal conviction. [p. 313]
b.	**YES**	Loyal has taken affirmative steps to conceal Zip, knowing he committed a felony. [p. 313]
100.	**NO**	Compounding a crime requires an agreement between the defendant and the person assisted. Here, no such agreement exists. [p. 313]

Table of Cases

Index